*C*apture the essence of healthy living as we guide you through *Essential Concepts for Healthy Living,* Second Edition and the integrated technology package featuring *The Human Condition TeleWebCourse.*

Essential Concepts *for* Healthy Living

SECOND EDITION

Sandra Alters
Wendy Schiff

Jones and Bartlett Publishers and INTELECOM Intelligent Telecommuni-cations have partnered to create a new health package for educators. *Essential Concepts for Healthy Living,* Second Edition, will serve as the basis of a college credit course when combined with *The Human Condition TeleWebCourse.*

The Human Condition

The Human Condition, produced by INTELECOM Intelligent Telecommunications, takes a visionary look at the state of health and health care today. In 26 television episodes this compelling new TeleWebCourse offers teachers and learners an up-to-the-minute look at health and health care issues–from weight management to cardiovascular disease, and from the latest in HIV/AIDS treatment to changes in health-care delivery systems. *The Human Condition* combines interviews with leading health professionals, dynamic location footage, and illustrative case studies, to bring each lesson to life.

The Human Condition takes a comprehensive view of health care, focusing on ten areas:

- What is Health?
- Who Is at Risk?
- The Life Cycle
- Emotional and Mental Health
- Sexual Health

- Health and Chemical Substances
- Promoting Well-Being through Fitness and Nutrition
- Health Risks: The Role of Heredity and Lifestyle

- Infectious and Non-Infectious Diseases
- The Individual in the Medical Marketplace

Supplements for the Instructor and Student

CyberClass—the online component of *The Human Condition*—will enable teachers to customize this distance learning course, while offering students easy access to a world of information on health and health care.

The Human Condition Faculty Guide, available in electronic or print form to instructors who license the course, provides additional learning objectives linked to each lesson as well as an examination bank and answer key.

The Human Condition Study Guide (ISBN 0-7637-1591-3) combines information from both the *Essential Concepts for Healthy Living,* Second Edition, textbook and *The Human Condition TeleWebCourse.* For each episode, the *TeleWebCourse* study guide provides learning objectives, an overview of the lesson, assignments, key terms, video viewing questions, self-test, expanded analysis questions, and the answer key for the self-test.

The Human Condition TeleWebCourse Packages

The Human Condition Study Guide with *Essential Concepts for Healthy Living,* Second Edition.
Use ISBN 0-7637-1626-X.

The Human Condition CyberClass, The Human Condition Study Guide, with *Essential Concepts for Healthy Living,* Second Edition.
Use ISBN 0-7637-1582-4.

INTELECOM Intelligent Telecommunications is a leading producer of educational media for distance learning. To learn more about *The Human Condition* contact INTELECOM at 150 East Colorado Boulevard, Suite 300, Pasadena, CA 91105-1937. (626) 796-7300. www.intelecom.org

the human condition

telewebcourse packages

Jones and Bartlett continues to stay on the cutting-edge of textbook development and the associated Internet technology that is so important in today's classrooms. In addition to *The Human Condition TeleWebCourse,* we also provide online resources and technology tools that are available for you and your students!

Healthy Living Online

www.jbpub.com/healthyliving

Special icons throughout each chapter point out Web connections to relevant and reliable health-related information that can be accessed through content links on the www.jbpub.com/healthyliving home page.

Instructor's ToolKit
(0-7637-1507-7)

The Instructor's ToolKit CD-ROM contains a variety of programs and files to help you teach your course. All of the materials are cross-platform for Windows and Macintosh systems. The ToolKit CD-ROM includes:

The Lecture Success Image Bank program offers full-color art files of more than 100 of the text's illustrations in formats appropriate for computer projection and for printing overhead transparencies.

The Computerized TestBank helps you choose an appropriate variety of questions organized by chapter, create multiple versions of a test, and even administer and grade tests online.

PowerPoint Lecture Outline Slides provides a template for each chapter, that includes the chapter outline, for building your lecture presentation.

The Instructor's ToolKit also contains *Annotated Lecture Outlines* and *Warm-up Exercises,* which can be used as creative discussion starters.

This interactive and informative web site offers students and educators an unprecedented degree of integration of their text and the online world through the following features:

eLearning for students

- Content Links
- Web Exercises
- Additional Resources
- Key Term Review
- Student Reviews
- Healthy People 2010

eTools for educators

- Transparencies
- WebBoard

healthy living online

Essential Concepts for Healthy Living, CyberClass Edition
(0-7637-1581-6)

Welcome to the fastest and easiest way to add an online component to your course. *CyberClass* is a customizable Web-based teaching and learning environment. It allows instructors to quickly and easily post material specific to their course, such as a syllabus, assignments, and favorite hot links. Instructors can also administer tests online, receive and respond to email from students in the course, and maintain a secure online grade book. Students can use *CyberClass* to access course materials, use online practice exams and study tools, contact classmates, and post messages to a class bulletin board.

key student outcomes

Essential Concepts for Healthy Living, Second Edition is the perfect text for use with *The Human Condition TeleWebCourse* or as the core text for a traditional personal health course.

This new text provides personal strategies developed with concepts grounded in scientific research to achieve a balance between science and practical application. It includes a look at alternative medicine and new information about noninfectious conditions. Timely topics informed by current research provide a comprehensive overview of today's health issues.

Essential Concepts for Healthy Living has been revised with key student outcomes in mind. At the end of this personal health course, students will leave the classroom able to:

1. understand the most recent scientifically based personal health information.

2. master textual material through the use of effective pedagogy.

3. think critically about health information published and distributed by various sources.

4. apply personal health information to their lives.

5. analyze their own health-related behaviors and attitudes and change them to improve health and maintain well-being.

Key Outcome 1: Students will understand the most recent scientifically based personal health information.

Essential Concepts for Healthy Living, Second Edition, has been developed from the latest scientific and medical research, relying heavily on primary sources, which are cited in the text. Because understanding health involves understanding science, especially the biological sciences, this text includes basic biological information that relates to health, presenting it in an easy-to-understand manner. Additionally, Chapter 1 briefly discusses scientific methods so students can understand how health-related research is conducted, thereby becoming more critical consumers of health information. To accommodate various learning styles, photographs have been chosen that are meaningful visual aids and boxes are used judiciously to avoid overwhelming and distracting students.

ISBN 0-7637-1432-1
To order call 800-832-0034

Healthy People 2010 Updates

Students and instructors will be able to access Healthy People 2010 Updates that are pertinent to *Essential Concepts for Healthy Living,* Second Edition at **www.jbpub.com/healthyliving**

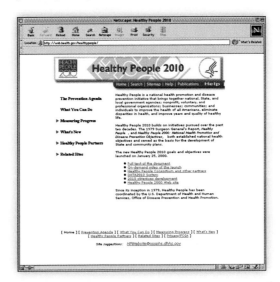

key outcome 1

2

Key Outcome 2: Students will master textual material through the use of effective pedagogy.

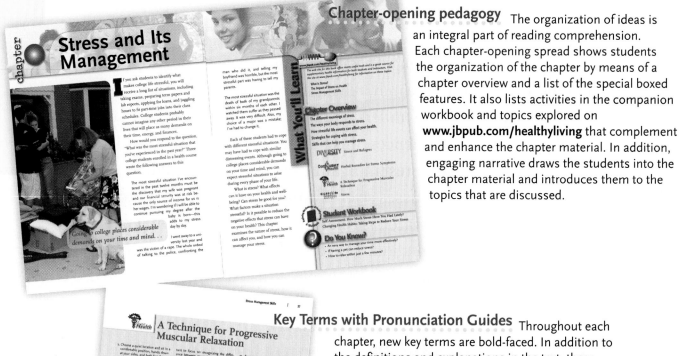

Chapter-opening pedagogy

The organization of ideas is an integral part of reading comprehension. Each chapter-opening spread shows students the organization of the chapter by means of a chapter overview and a list of the special boxed features. It also lists activities in the companion workbook and topics explored on **www.jbpub.com/healthyliving** that complement and enhance the chapter material. In addition, engaging narrative draws the students into the chapter material and introduces them to the topics that are discussed.

Key Terms with Pronunciation Guides

Throughout each chapter, new key terms are bold-faced. In addition to the definitions and explanations in the text, these terms are defined in the margin of each two-page spread, with pronunciation guides for words that might be difficult—reinforcing students' confidence and familiarity with health-related terminology.

Diversity in Health Essays

This feature fosters an interest in and appreciation for the health status and practices of various ethnic, cultural, and racial groups in the United States, as well as people in other countries. Although the diversity essays focus on multiculturalism, multicultural information is weaved through-out the book as well.

DIVERSITY in Health | Stress and Refugees

During the last decade, ethnically diverse former Yugoslavia was torn apart by civil wars in Bosnia/ Herzegovina and Kosovo. Thousands of people were wounded or killed. At least 2 million individuals were forced to flee their homes, cross into un-familiar neighboring countries, and live under deplorable conditions in refugee camps (Figure 3-A). Before leaving, some of them watched as their houses were destroyed and their loved ones were taken away. Some were tortured, and many witnessed the torture and/or mur-der of family members or friends. The stress of living under such uncertainty, terror, and violence resulted in high rates of severe psychological disturbances among the refugees. Recent studies indi-cate that as many as 40% of refugees from the former Yugoslavia suffer from depression, up to 50% experience post-traumatic stress disorder (PTSD), and about 20% have both psychological dis-turbances (Mollica et al., 1999; Favaro et al., 1999). Post-traumatic stress disorder is a chronic condition characterized by distressing psychological symptoms such as recurrent nightmares, emotional numbness, and unwanted recollections and flashbacks of the terrible events. PTSD can affect people who survive any life-threatening situation, including nat-

▲Figure 3-A **Refugee Camp Survivors from Former Yugoslavia.** According to recent stud-ies, significant percentages of the refugee camp survivors experienced depression, post-traumatic stress disorder, or a combination of both conditions.

ural disasters, plane crashes, and hostage situations. For the refugees, the negative effects of enduring such extremely stress-ful conditions were more pronounced among those who were widowed or never married, had low levels of education, and had little association with family mem-bers. Depression and PTSD are associ-ated with long-term consequences includ-ing physical disability, social impairment, and loss of productivity. Therefore, mental health workers in nations providing havens for refugees from the former Yugo-slavia need to identify persons who are at risk and offer treatment.

reduce stress.

Interest in tai chi and yoga is increasing in the United States; if you would like to learn the exercises, check with the physical education department on your campus or the local YMCA/YWCA to determine if they offer classes in these activities. Before beginning any new physical activity program, especially the martial arts and yoga, it is advisable to receive approval from a qualified health-care practitioner.

Healthy LIVING PRACTICES

- If dwelling on negative self-thoughts creates stress for you, think about your strengths and develop a list of affirmative self-statements to repeat regularly.
- Consider setting aside some time to relax every day, perhaps by using the techniques discussed in this chapter.
- Try breathing slowly and deeply before or during a stressful situation as a simple but effective way to relax.
- Engaging in tai chi, yoga, and moderate exercise and physical activity on a regular basis can reduce your stress.

across the Lifespan

Stress

Distressed adults may recall images of a carefree childhood, but children also experience stress. Common stressors for children include separation from a parent through divorce or death, moving to a new neighborhood and changing schools, or illness of a close family member (Grey, 1993).

When children are distressed, they often exhibit regressive behaviors, like clinging to and acting more dependent on their parents. In addition to acting immature, distressed youngsters may become depressed and withdrawn, suffer sleep disturbances, or experience problems at school. Parents can help their children learn healthy ways to cope with stressful situations by teaching them problem-solving skills and relaxation exercises.

As mentioned in Chapter 2, the adolescent years are stressful because individuals undergo numerous physical and social changes during this time. Distressed youth who do not have effective and healthy coping mechanisms are likely to suffer from depression, abuse drugs, have serious

they must raise their grandchildren are unable, unwilling, or unavailable (e.g., deceased) to do so. Older adults frequently experience distress when they must care for spouses with debilitating mental or physical illnesses.

Coping with loneliness and the deaths of friends or close family members is especially difficult for aging individuals as they face the reality of their own mortality. Suffering from disabling illnesses creates additional distress for many elderly people. The inability to cope with stress can have serious results; rates of emotional depression and suicide are high among the isolated elderly. To enhance the well-being of elderly people, communities often have programs that encourage social interaction among aged members of the population. Additionally, elderly residents of most nursing homes can participate in social and physical activities that combat the stress of isolation (■ Figure 3-7).

▲ Figure 3-7 **Social Interaction among the Elderly.** To enhance the well being of elderly people and combat the stress of isolation, communities often offer programs that encourage social interaction among aged members of the population.

Across the Lifespan This unique section relates the main topics of the chapter to the various stages of life— infancy, childhood, adolescence, young adulthood, middle age, and the elderly years.

Chapter Summaries Research tells us that students learn how to identify the key ideas of stories in elementary school, but that they often have difficulty identifying key ideas in textbooks in their later years. Therefore, we provide chapter summaries to help students with this task. The chapter summaries follow the organization of the chapter. Additional features from the chapter-ending pedagogy that focus on critical thinking are described on the next two pages.

60 | Chapter 3: Stress and Its Management

Chapter Review

Summary

Stress can refer to a threatening or demanding situation, a person's responses to a situation, or the interactions that take place between a person and a situation. Various situations or conditions, referred to as stressors, create stress. Situations with unwanted or negative outcomes produce distress, those with positive outcomes produce eustress. Stress can make life more challenging and interesting, but too much can make life miserable.

In a combined response, the nervous and endocrine systems prepare the body to confront or leave dangerous situations. Hans Selye proposed the general adaptation syndrome to describe the three stages of the body's adaptive physical responses to stressors. The stress response produces physical changes that may reduce the activity of certain white blood cells and the effectiveness of the immune system. As a result, enduring too many stressful life events can negatively affect one's susceptibility to disease. Interest in the role of stress in psychological health has led to a new area of research called psychoneuroimmunology.

People use either problem-focused, emotion-focused, or social-support coping strategies to deal actively with stressful situations. Although these strategies can be effective methods of helping people take control over their stressors, some coping methods can be harmful to health. For example, avoiding and denying stressors are coping mechanisms that usually do not eliminate the sources of stress.

Many stress management activities involve learning skills that enable one to relax. Relaxation can reverse many of the normal but damaging physical responses to stress. Relaxation techniques include deep breathing exercises, progressive muscular relaxation, meditation, and mental imagery. Journal writing, positive self-talk, and moderate physical activity can also reduce stress.

Common childhood stressors include separation from a parent through divorce or death, moving to a new neighborhood and changing schools, and the illness of a close family member. Older distressed youths are often depressed, abuse drugs, and experience problems with parents and school authorities. Aging people often find that coping with loneliness, disability, and the deaths of friends or close family members is especially stressful.

Applying What You Have Learned

1. Using the techniques described in this chapter, develop a personal stress-reduction program that you can incorporate into your daily schedule. (Application)

4. Evaluate your present situation. Determine and list the sources of distress in your life. (Evaluation)

Key Outcome 3: Students will think critically about health information published and distributed by various sources.

The focus of education today is not just to give students information, but to teach them how to acquire and evaluate information. Unlike other personal health textbooks, the critical thinking features discussed below teach students higher-order thinking skills and give them practice in using these skills in every chapter.

Applying What You Have Learned This unique end-of-chapter feature is a series of questions and activities that require critical thinking–application, analysis, synthesis, and evaluation. Each question is labeled as to what type of critical thinking is required, and a key provides a brief explanation of the process students need to follow to answer the question or conduct the activity.

Applying What You Have Learned

1. Using the techniques described in this chapter, develop a personal stress-reduction program that you can incorporate into your daily schedule. (*Application*)

2. You have two final exams scheduled for the same day. Describe how you could use a negative coping strategy to reduce your stress. Describe how you could use a positive coping method to deal with the same situation. (*Application*)

3. Plan a program that uses social support as a coping strategy to help distressed elderly people who live in your community. (*Synthesis*)

4. Evaluate your present situation. Determine and list the sources of distress in your life. (*Evaluation*)

KEY
Application: Using information in a new situation.
Synthesis: Putting together information from different sources.
Evaluation: Making informed decisions.

Reflecting On Your Health

The questions in this journal-writing activity, at the end of each chapter, stimulate students to consider what they have learned and understand how their thoughts and feelings about health might have changed as a result of their new knowledge. Compiling these activities and reviewing them from time to time, especially at the end of the semester, will offer tangible evidence of changes and growth.

Reflecting On Your Health

1. Review the physical adaptations to stress that are listed in Table 3-1. The last time you were faced with a stressful situation, did you experience these changes? How did you feel?

2. Recall that stress can have positive outcomes. Reflect on a stressful experience that made you feel happy, challenged, or successful. Why did the experience make you feel this way?

3. Each person can appraise a situation differently; what is distressing to one can be thrilling to another. Choose a situation that distresses you. Why do you think it affects you in this manner? Do you think other people would find this situation distressing? Why or why not?

4. Chronic stress can have negative effects on health. What was the most stressful situation that you had to endure in the past year? How did this experience affect your health and well-being?

5. How do you usually react when faced with stressful situations? Are your responses positive or negative? How do you think you could reduce the impact of stress on your health?

● key outcome 3

Analyzing Health-Related Information This innovative feature teaches students the critical thinking skill of analysis. Students use this skill and the model provided to analyze the reliability of health-related information in articles, advertisements, Web sites, and other sources. Learning such a skill and practicing it helps students become knowledgeable consumers of health-related information and products.

ANALYZING *Health-Related Information*

The following article appeared in FDA Consumer, the July/August 1998 issue. Read the article and explain why you think it is a reliable or an unreliable source of information. Use the model for analyzing health information to guide your thinking; the main points of the model are noted below. A full explanation of the model can be found on p. 12 to 13.

1. Which statements are verifiable facts; which are unverified statements or value claims?
2. What are the credentials of the person writing the article? If this information is available, does the author's background and education qualify him or her as an expert in the topic area?
3. What might be the motives and biases of the person writing the article? State reasons for your answer.
4. Which information is relevant to the issue or main point of the article; which information is irrelevant?
5. Is the source reliable? Does it have a reputation for publishing misinformation?
6. Does the article attack the credibility of conventional scientists or medical authorities?

Based on the above analysis, do you think that this article is a reliable source of health-related information? Summarize your reasons for coming to this conclusion.

Sleepless Society

Tamar Nordenberg, staff writer for FDA Consumer

Millions of Americans undersleep by choice, burning the candle at both ends because of hectic work and family schedules. Recent surveys show that Americans sleep seven hours each night on average, down from 9 hours in 1910 when, without electricity, people generally went to sleep as darkness fell.

"People don't respect sleep enough," says Daniel O'-Hearn, a sleep disorders specialist at Johns Hopkins University. "They feel they can do more—have more time for work and family—by allowing themselves less time for sleep. But they do sleep; they sleep at work, or driving to work."

Nodding off at work isn't just unproductive; in the worst cases, it causes serious industrial accidents. The 1989 Exxon Valdez Alaskan oil spill, for example, was reportedly due at least in part to the severe fatigue of the tanker's sleep-deprived third mate.

Also, like drunk driving, drowsy driving can kill. The National Highway Traffic Safety Administration estimates that more than 200,000 crashes each year involve drivers falling asleep at the wheel, and that thousands of Americans die in such accidents annually.

"Besides being an unpleasant sensation, when we're tired, we're less alert and less able to respond," says FDA drug reviewer Bob Rappaport, M.D.

Lack of sleep can cause memory and mood problems, too, Rappaport says, and may affect immune function, which could lead to an increased incidence of infection and other illnesses. In studies performed on rats, prolonged sleep deprivation resulted in death.

Beyond the observable consequences of sleep deprivation, why humans—or any animal, for that matter—need sleep remains largely a mystery. "What happens in the brain while we're sleeping is what we're trying to untangle," says James Kiley, director of the National Center for Sleep Disorders Research of the National Institutes of Health. "We're just beginning to understand why a third of our life is spent sleeping. What we do know is that sleep is an important biological need, like food and drink, and that the brain is very active while we're sleeping."

The leading sleep theories focus on "rest and resuscitation for the body and psyche," says Rappaport. During sleep, the brain may recharge its energy stores and shift the day's information that has been stored in temporary memory to regions of the brain associated with long-term memory.

So just how much nightly R and R does a person need? That can change throughout one's life based on age and other factors. For most people, though, seven and a half to eight and a half hours of sleep each night fulfills the basic physical need, Rappaport says, adding that this is "very individual" and can range from as few as four or five hours to as many as nine or ten.

The Mayo Clinic of Rochester, Minnesota, defines an adequate amount of sleep as whatever produces daytime alertness and a feeling of well-being. People should not need an alarm clock to wake them if they are getting enough sleep.

Source: Nordenberg, T. (1998). Sleepless society. FDA Consumer, 32(4):11.

Key Outcome 4: Students will apply personal health information to their lives.

Essential Concepts for Healthy Living, Second Edition, encourages students to adopt healthier lifestyles and recommends practical ways to do so.

Healthy
LIVING PRACTICES

- If dwelling on negative self-thoughts creates stress for you, think about your strengths and develop a list of affirmative self-statements to repeat regularly.
- Consider setting aside some time to relax every day, perhaps by using the techniques discussed in this chapter.
- Try breathing slowly and deeply before or during a stressful situation as a simple but effective way to relax.
- Engaging in tai chi, yoga, and moderate exercise and physical activity on a regular basis can reduce your stress.

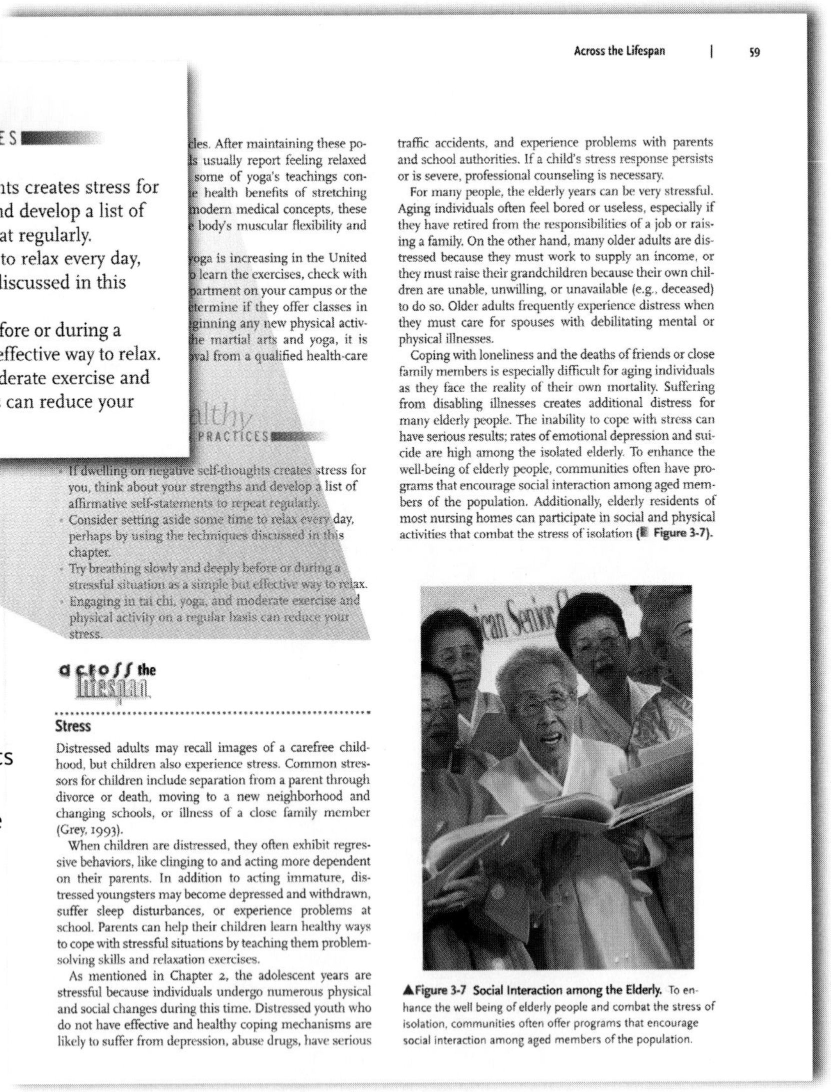

cles. After maintaining these po-
... usually report feeling relaxed
... some of yoga's teachings con-
... health benefits of stretching
... modern medical concepts, these
... body's muscular flexibility and

... yoga is increasing in the United
... learn the exercises, check with
... partment on your campus or the
... determine if they offer classes in
... ginning any new physical activ-
... the martial arts and yoga, it is
... val from a qualified health-care

traffic accidents, and experience problems with parents and school authorities. If a child's stress response persists or is severe, professional counseling is necessary.

For many people, the elderly years can be very stressful. Aging individuals often feel bored or useless, especially if they have retired from the responsibilities of a job or raising a family. On the other hand, many older adults are distressed because they must work to supply an income, or they must raise their grandchildren because their own children are unable, unwilling, or unavailable (e.g., deceased) to do so. Older adults frequently experience distress when they must care for spouses with debilitating mental or physical illnesses.

Coping with loneliness and the deaths of friends or close family members is especially difficult for aging individuals as they face the reality of their own mortality. Suffering from disabling illnesses creates additional distress for many elderly people. The inability to cope with stress can have serious results; rates of emotional depression and suicide are high among the isolated elderly. To enhance the well-being of elderly people, communities often have programs that encourage social interaction among aged members of the population. Additionally, elderly residents of most nursing homes can participate in social and physical activities that combat the stress of isolation (■ Figure 3-7).

Healthy
LIVING PRACTICES

- If dwelling on negative self-thoughts creates stress for you, think about your strengths and develop a list of affirmative self-statements to repeat regularly.
- Consider setting aside some time to relax every day, perhaps by using the techniques discussed in this chapter.
- Try breathing slowly and deeply before or during a stressful situation as a simple but effective way to relax.
- Engaging in tai chi, yoga, and moderate exercise and physical activity on a regular basis can reduce your stress.

across the lifespan

Stress

Distressed adults may recall images of a carefree childhood, but children also experience stress. Common stressors for children include separation from a parent through divorce or death, moving to a new neighborhood and changing schools, or illness of a close family member (Grey, 1993).

When children are distressed, they often exhibit regressive behaviors, like clinging to and acting more dependent on their parents. In addition to acting immature, distressed youngsters may become depressed and withdrawn, suffer sleep disturbances, or experience problems at school. Parents can help their children learn healthy ways to cope with stressful situations by teaching them problem-solving skills and relaxation exercises.

As mentioned in Chapter 2, the adolescent years are stressful because individuals undergo numerous physical and social changes during this time. Distressed youth who do not have effective and healthy coping mechanisms are likely to suffer from depression, abuse drugs, have serious

▲ **Figure 3-7 Social Interaction among the Elderly.** To enhance the well being of elderly people and combat the stress of isolation, communities often offer programs that encourage social interaction among aged members of the population.

Healthy Living Practices Unique to this text, these short lists of bulleted statements throughout the chapter summarize key points and concisely state concrete yet simple actions students can take to improve their health.

Managing Your Health These features contain lists of tips or short essays that focus on ways to live a healthier life.

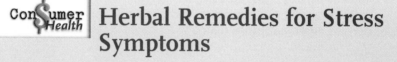

A Technique for Progressive Muscular Relaxation

1. Choose a quiet location and sit in a comfortable position, hands down at your sides, and both feet flat on the floor.
2. Close your eyes and take a few deep breaths; concentrate on becoming as relaxed as possible.
3. With your arms at your sides, make a fist with one of your hands. Hold your clenched fist for about 5 seconds, release your hand from this position, and concentrate on the feeling as the muscular tension "drains" out of your hand.

This basic exercise is repeated as you tense muscles, hold the tensed position for 5 seconds, and then relax the major muscle groups in your body. It is impor-

tant to focus on recognizing the difference between muscular tension and relaxation sensations. Continue breathing normally as the activity progresses. Begin with your head.

4. Tense your forehead and scalp muscles; feel the tight muscular sensations as you hold this position for 5 seconds; relax these muscles.
5. Tense your facial muscles; hold this position for 5 seconds; relax.
6. Tense the muscles of your neck and jaw; hold this position; relax.
7. Tense your back muscles—but not too tight; hold this position; relax.
8. Tense your right arm; hold; relax.
9. Tense your left arm; hold; relax.
10. Tense your chest muscles; hold; then relax.

11. Tense your stomach muscles; hold; relax.
12. Tense your buttocks; hold; relax.
13. Tense your right leg—but not too tight; hold; relax.
14. Tense your left leg—but not too tight; hold; relax.

Now, imagine traveling back through your body searching for muscles that are not relaxed. As you find tense muscles, relax them. Maintain this position for several minutes, concentrating on your breathing. In this relaxed state, you may practice tranquil imagery and positive self-talk. To regain your normal physical activity, open your eyes, stand, and stretch your muscles.

Consumer Health These commentaries and tips provide practical information and suggestions to help students become more careful consumers of health-related goods and services. In addition to being highlighted in this feature, consumer topics are woven throughout the book and are the subject of scrutiny in the "Analyzing Health-Related Information" activities.

Herbal Remedies for Stress Symptoms

Since ancient times, people have treated their stress symptoms with herbs and other plants. As mentioned in Chapter 1, many plants contain chemicals that have medicinal properties. Recently, many Americans have tried kava, valerian, and feverfew to relax or treat their stress-related symptoms. Does kava induce relaxation? Is valerian effective for treating insomnia? Can feverfew prevent migraines? Are these alternative therapies safe?

For hundreds of years, a ceremonial beverage made from the roots of the kava plant has been used by South Pacific Islanders to reduce anxiety, relax muscles, and induce sleep. Conventional medical experts, however, are concerned about the herb's growing popularity among Americans because the long-term safety

of kava, including its potential for addiction, is unclear. It is known that kava produces serious side effects when consumed in very large doses (Pepping, 1999). Furthermore, the herb can intensify the effects of depressant drugs including alcohol. Therefore, check with your physician before consuming products made from this herb.

Ancient Romans were aware of the medicinal value of heliotrope plant, commonly known as valerian. Roots of the plant are dried, then brewed into a tea that is used to induce sleep. Valerian is available in pills or mixed with alcohol to make a tincture. Valerian may have usefulness as a mild tranquilizer (Fugh-Berman & Cott, 1999). In a few studies, however, the herb had toxic side effects

(Wong et al., 1998). You should consult your physician before taking valerian.

Feverfew has been used for centuries to treat headaches, menstrual problems, and fever. Before supplements were available, people would chew the leaves of the plant, but this practice caused sores to form in the mouth. Feverfew may reduce the risk of migraines. The herb does not seem to be toxic when consumed in recommended amounts, but it may cause allergic responses and even headaches in some people ("Herbal Rx," 1999). As in the case of all herbal treatments, check with your physician before trying feverfew. Be aware that feverfew can upset the stomach, and stop taking it (or any herbal product) if you have adverse reactions.

Key Outcome 5: Students will analyze their own health-related behaviors and attitudes and change them to improve health and maintain well-being.

Applying Concepts for Healthy Living: A Workbook contains two features that address self-assessment and changing health habits. Together, these two activities help students assess their behaviors and attitudes, and provide a mechanism that will help students change health-related behaviors if they choose. We do not tell students which decisions are most valuable; instead we provide background information and guidance through the use of thought-provoking techniques to make responsible decisions.

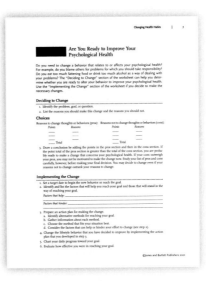

Self-Assessments These evaluation tools help students assess their health status, attitudes, and beliefs. Most assessments are research-based rather than derived from the popular press. Each chapter contains one or two assessments, and all relate directly to chapter topics.

Changing Health Habits These activities have two parts. The first helps students determine if they desire change or are ready for change; the second guides students to facilitate change if they choose. The student workbook contains one activity per chapter. This allows students to practice decision-making and the implementation model, making the transfer of these skills to their daily lives more likely.

key outcome 5

Special value packages save students money!

Applying Concepts for Healthy Living: A Workbook is **FREE** with every purchase of the text! Use ISBN 0-7637-1583-2 to order.

Students also get access into the *CyberClass* online course management system.

Use ISBN 0-7637-1581-6 to order.

Read all about the power of CyberClass on page M3.

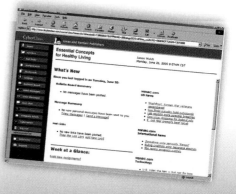

special value packages

Jones and Bartlett and INTELECOM— Leading the way to a new personal health experience!

Join Us!

Bundle any of these great health resources with
Essential Concepts for Healthy Living, Second Edition!

Healthy People 2010

U.S. Department of Health and Human Services
©2001, 704 pp., Paper,
ISBN 0-7637-1432-1
The latest addition to the *Healthy People* series, *Healthy People 2010* sets broad public health goals for the next decade. Organized under three broad approaches—health promotion, health protection, and preventive services— the objectives in this critical text chart a 10-year course for individual, collective, and environmental change.

Physical Activity and Health: A Report of the Surgeon General

U.S. Department of Health and Human Services
©1999, 300 pp., Paper,
ISBN 0-7637-0636-1
With this report, the U.S. Department of Health and Human Services sends the message that Americans can improve their health and quality of life substantially by including moderate amounts of physical activity in their daily lives. This report goes a step farther and studies how to promote more active lifestyles and implement appropriate programs—critical to improving the health of the nation.

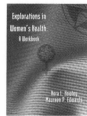

Explorations in Women's Health: A Workbook

Nora Howley and Maureen Edwards, both of Montgomery College
© 1999, 250 pp., Paper,
ISBN 0-7637-0868-2
Explorations in Women's Health: A Workbook gives students the opportunity to apply what they have learned about important issues in women's health to their lives and to the community. Activities include all aspects of personal and community health including women in the health-care system, social and mental health, nutrition, fitness, sexual and reproductive health, addiction, chronic illness, and aging.

Health and Wellness Journal Workbook

Brian Luke Seaward, Ph.D., Center for Human Caring, University of Colorado, Denver
© 1996, 128 pp., Paper,
ISBN 0-7637-0179-3
The journal covers an assortment of topics, and contains several self-exploration exercises that challenge or support attitudes, values, and beliefs about students' health behaviors.

Managing Stress: A Creative Journal, Second Edition

Brian Luke Seaward, Ph.D., Center for Human Caring, University of Colorado, Denver
© 1996, 174 pp., Paper,
ISBN 0-7637-0281-1
Journal writing has proved to be an effective coping technique to deal with stress. Writing in a journal for a period of weeks or months, and then reading over the passages, allows students to identify stressors in their lives. Dr. Seaward's creative exercises increase awareness of stress and help students develop skills and strategies to cope with it.

Managing Your Health: Assessment and Action

David A. Birch, Ph.D., Indiana University
Michael J. Cleary, Slippery Rock University
©1996, 320 pp., Paper,
ISBN 0-7637-0139-4
This book reviews specific information relevant in making healthy choices and then, through a series of structured activities, puts the emphasis on participation.

Brief Contents

Essential Concepts *for* Healthy Living

SECOND EDITION

Sandra Alters

Wendy Schiff

JONES AND BARTLETT PUBLISHERS

Sudbury, Massachusetts

BOSTON   TORONTO   LONDON   SINGAPORE

World Headquarters
Jones and Bartlett Publishers
40 Tall Pine Drive
Sudbury, MA 01776
978-443-5000
info@jbpub.com
www.jbpub.com

Jones and Bartlett Publishers Canada
2406 Nikanna Road
Mississauga, ON L5C 2W6
CANADA

Jones and Bartlett Publishers International
Barb House, Barb Mews
London W6 7PA
UK

Production Credits
Chief Executive Officer: Clayton Jones
Chief Operating Officer: Don W. Jones, Jr
Executive V.P., and Publisher: Tom Manning
V.P., National Sales Manager: Paul Shepardson
V.P., Managing Director: Judith H. Hauck
V.P., College Editorial Director: Brian L. McKean
V.P., Director of Design and Production: Anne Spencer
Director of Manufacturing and Inventory: Therese Bräuer
Sponsoring Editor: Suzanne Jeans
Associate Editor: Amy Austin
Senior Production Editor: Lianne Ames
Text Design: Anne Spencer
Editorial Production Service: Joan Flaherty
Photo Research: Sharon Donahue

Typesetting: Graphic World
Cover Design: Anne Spencer
Printing and Binding: Courier Companies
Cover Printing: John Pow Company

Unless otherwise acknowledged, all photographs are the property of Jones and Bartlett Publishers.

Cover Photo Credits
Cover Photo © Anne Spencer
Back Cover Photo Banner © PhotoDisc

Text photo credits follow the index which constitutes a continuation of the copyright page.

Library of Congress Cataloging-in-Publication Data

Alters, Sandra
   Essential concepts for healthy living / Sandra Alters, Wendy Schiff.--2nd ed.
       p. cm
   Includes bibliographical references and index.
   ISBN 0-7637-1354-6
   1. Health.   I. Schiff, Wendy.   II. Title.
   RA776.5 .A596 2000
   613--dc21

                                                          00-055824

Printed in the United States of America

04 03 02 01 00   10 9 8 7 6 5 4 3 2 1

Contents

Contents

Contents

Contents

Contents

Contents

Features

ANALYZING *Health-Related Information*

The authors' writing is only one small portion of the work that goes into the development and production of a textbook. Many people work long hours with a shared goal: to produce a visually appealing, error-free, up-to-date, high-quality textbook for students. We would like to acknowledge the dedication and hard work of these individuals, for without them this project never would have been realized.

Paul Shepardson welcomed our book to Jones and Bartlett and Sally Beaty to INTELECOM, both working to forge a partnership for distance learning. We are thrilled that *Essential Concepts for Healthy Living,* Second Edition, is an integral part of the TeleWebCourse *The Human Condition,* and thank both Sally and Paul for making this marriage of text and video a reality.

Many thanks to Suzanne Jeans, Acquisitions Editor, for her contributions to the project. Suzanne came to Jones and Bartlett after this project had begun, but she stepped right in without missing a beat to help us create a vision for this text. Also, *Essential Concepts for Healthy Living* would not be a reality without the hard work of Developmental Editor Amy Austin, who managed the book and its supplements on a day-to-day basis. Amy wore many hats on this project, and wore them all extremely well. Thank you, Amy.

Anne Spencer is responsible for the outstanding design of this textbook. Anne is a true professional who created a dynamic look for the second edition. Mark Rodrigues assisted Anne in this endeavor, helping turn her ideas into reality. Thanks for a wonderful job, Mark.

Lianne Ames, along with Marcia Craig of Graphic World Publishing Services, managed the production, doing an amazing job to keep an incredibly complex process running smoothly. Lianne Ames also helped Sharon Donahue locate the photographs throughout the book, helping choose visually interesting teaching tools.

Joan Flaherty did a marvelous job of copyediting and helping tie up a myriad of loose ends. A heartfelt thanks to you all.

Jones and Bartlett is a company on the cutting edge of integrating technology with print materials for learning. The superb Web-based materials that are a part of the *Essential Concepts for Healthy Living* program could not have been developed without W. Scott Smith, Adam Alboyadjian, Nicole Healey, and Kristin Ohlin.

Other key members of the Jones and Bartlett team are Tom Manning, Jennifer Jacobson, and Lynn Protasowicki. These members of the Sales and Marketing group have helped everyone involved in the book's development to remain focused on the needs of students and instructors. A special thanks to Lynn, with whom we had our day-to-day contact.

A heartfelt thanks to Judy Hauck for her instant focus on our project whenever we needed her input.

Two of our opening narratives introduced individuals who allowed us to explore their healthy lifestyles. Our thanks to Matt Schicker, the formerly obese college student who discussed his experiences in achieving a healthy body weight, and to Catherine Wanslow, a centenarian who embodies healthy living.

Many health teachers and researchers have made significant contributions to the development of this book. A special thank you to Linda J. Tiedt, St. Louis Community College–Meramec, for her insightful and thorough review of Chapter 11. Although the authors alone have written the test bank, annotated lecture outlines, and warm-up activities, others helped prepare additional supplement materials. Special thanks to Kathryn Hilgenkamp of Coastal Carolina University, Michael Maina and Julie Maina of Valdosta University, and Caile Spear of Boise State University for their help.

Acknowledgments

Reviewers

Our gratitude goes to the following reviewers whose expertise gave invaluable direction to the development of *Essential Concepts for Healthy Living,* Second Edition:

Martin Ayim, *Grambling University*
Charles Baffi, *Virginia Technical Institute*
Cathy Kennedy, *Colorado State University*
Jennifer McLean, *Corning Community College*
Mark Oliver, *University of Central Arkansas*
Jeff Schulz, *Mississippi State University*
Andrew Shim, *Southwestern College*
Carol Weideman, *Grand Valley State University*

We would also like to acknowledge the reviewers of the first edition of *Essential Concepts for Healthy Living,* whose advice helped us move on to the second edition:

Donna Jean Allis, *Seattle Pacific University*
Judy B. Baker, *East Carolina University*
Gene Barnes, *University of South Alabama*
Rick Barnes, *East Carolina University*
Lois Beach, *SUNY–Plattsburgh*
Luana J. Beeson, *Oregon State University*
Robert J. Bensley, *Western Michigan University*
David R. Black, *Purdue University*
Jill M. Black, *Cleveland State University*
David L. Blievernicht, *Wayne State University*
Mary Ann Borysowicz, *Purdue University*
Bob Bowers, *Tallahassee Community College*
Ruth C. Bragg, *University of Tampa*
James Brik, *Willamette University*
Gary W. Brinkman, *Oxnard College*
Susan Burge, *Cuyahoga Community College*
Lorraine D. Campbell, *California State University, Bakersfield*
Marion T. Carr, *University of South Carolina*
James Lester Carter, *Montana State University*
John S. Carter, *Health and Physical Education*
Dan Connaughton, *University of Florida*

Lori L. Dewald, *Shippensburg University*
Lawrence G. Doty, *Linfield College*
Marvin Druger, *Syracuse University*
Jack Ellison, *University of Tennessee*
Jule Gast, *Utah State University*
Stephen C. Goodwin, *University of Delaware*
John Gratton, *Bee County College*
Jack E. Hansma, *Baylor University*
Joanna Hayden, *The William Paterson College of New Jersey*
David Hines, *Ball State University*
Chester Jones, *University of Arkansas*
Arnold W. Joyce, *Virginia Military Institute*
Walt Justice, *El Camino College*
Greg Kandt, *Fort Hays State University*
Catherine A. Kennedy, *Colorado State University*
Jean Levitan, *William Paterson College of New Jersey*
Loretta M. Liptak, *Youngstown State University*
J. Lisk, *University of South Carolina–Aiken*
Beverly Saxton Mahoney, *Pennsylvania State University*
Terry M. Manning, *University of North Carolina–Charlotte*
Larry K. Olsen, *Pennsylvania State University*
Christopher S. Ousley, *North Carolina State University*
John Paxman, *Portland Community College*
Sally A. Radmacher, *Missouri Western State College*
Linda L. Rankin, *Idaho State University*
Richard S. Riggs, *University of Kentucky*
Jim Sartoris, *Glendale Community College*
Mary Schutten, *Calvin College*
John Sciacca, *Northern Arizona University*
Melinda J. Seid, *California State University, Sacramento*
John C. Smith, *Springfield College*
Harry Specht, *Pennsylvania College of Technology*
Sue Viscomi, *SUNY–Oswego*
J. Dale Wagoner, *Chabot College*
David M. White, *East Carolina University*
Susan Yeager, *Mesa State College*

Sandra Alters
Wendy Schiff

Essential Concepts for Healthy Living, Second Edition, was written by an author team with extensive credentials and background in biology, health, and education. Sandra Alters holds a Ph.D. degree in Science Education and a Master's degree in biology. Formerly of the University of Missouri–St. Louis and Salem State College (Massachusetts), Dr. Alters has authored several textbooks in addition to *Essential Concepts for Healthy Living,* a laboratory manual, a children's science book, many articles in professional literature, and over sixty chapters and features in books. Additionally, she has written the instructional design for a variety of science-related software products for students. With twenty-five years of teaching experience, Dr. Alters brings her educational expertise, background in biology and human biology, and extensive writing experience to the author team.

Wendy Schiff holds a Master's degree in Human Nutrition. She is an Adjunct Instructor in the departments of physical education and biology at the St. Louis Community College–Meramec Campus. Ms. Schiff has authored a college health textbook, many educational manuals, and published articles in professional journals. She has served as a consulting nutritionist, reviewer of health education materials, and a freelance health essayist. With her educational background in health and her experience teaching college health, health education, nutrition, and sexuality courses, Ms. Schiff complements Dr. Alters' expertise in biological sciences and science education.

About the Authors

Health: The Foundation for Life

What is the status of our health in the United States? *Healthy People 2000 Review, 1998–1999* (U.S. Department of Health and Human Services [USDHHS], 1999), a report issued by the Centers for Disease Control and Prevention (CDC) in Atlanta, indicates that since 1985 many Americans have altered their lives to improve their health. Between 1985 and 1997 more adults exercised regularly and ate the recommended amounts of fruits and vegetables. During this period, fewer adults smoked cigarettes and drank alcohol, and fewer people died as a result of alcohol-related motor-vehicle accidents than before 1985. The number of deaths from AIDS, heart disease, cancer, and homicides dropped dramatically.

According to this same report, however, the findings concerning other aspects of our current health are less encouraging. Although more people are exercising than prior to 1985, nearly one-fourth of adults seldom exercise. Since 1960 the percentage of overweight adults has increased. Today, more than 50% of adults are too fat. Binge drinking is common among high school students. The percentage of college students who engage in this risky behavior has

> *"Between 1985 and 1997, more adults exercised regularly . . . "*

remained about the same (40%) since 1989. Clearly, people living in the United States have more lifestyle changes to make if they are to live longer and healthier lives.

Lifestyle is a way of living. As a college student, your lifestyle includes a variety of behaviors that promote or impair good health and longevity. Although you may be unable to prevent severe birth defects or inherited disorders from affecting your health, you can modify many health risk factors, reducing the likelihood that you will develop serious medical problems, especially as you grow older. A **risk factor** is a characteristic that increases an individual's chances of developing a condition. For example, physical inactivity, tobacco use, emotional stress, and a high-fat diet are risk factors for heart disease, hypertension, and certain types of cancer. You can dramatically lower your risks of developing these conditions by incorporating exercise into your daily schedule, choosing not to use tobacco products, practicing relaxation techniques, and eating a low-fat diet. Of course, the decision to adopt a healthier lifestyle is up to you.

What You'll Learn

www.jbpub.com/healthyliving

The web site for this book offers many useful tools and is a great source for supplementary health information for both students and instructors. Visit the site at www.jbpub.com/healthyliving for information on these topics:

The Nation's Health
Analyzing Health Information
Conventional versus Alternative Medicine
Consumer Health: Consumer Protection

Chapter Overview

How the dimensions of health influence your well-being.
The major health concerns of our nation.
How your decisions affect your health.
How to analyze health-related information.
The differences between conventional and alternative treatment methods.

DIVERSITY *in Health*   Minority Health Status in the U.S.

Con$umer *Health*   Consumer Protection

Managing Your Health   Routine Health Screening

across the Lifespan   Health

Applying Concepts for Healthy Living
A Workbook

Student Workbook

Self Assessment: Healthstyle
Changing Health Habits: Altering your behavior for better health

Do You Know?

- How your lifestyle affects your health?
- How to make responsible health-related decisions?
- How to analyze health-related information?

To evaluate the impact of your lifestyle on your health, answer the questions in the Healthstyle Assessment in the Student Workbook.

Are you concerned about your health? What are you doing to protect it? What steps can you take to enhance your state of health so you can enjoy life more fully? Where can you find reliable information concerning health? The information and recommendations in this textbook can help you make choices that will improve your health.

The Dimensions of Health

What Is Health?

Most people can describe how it feels to be healthy or ill, but trying to define *health* is not an easy task. In 1948 the World Health Organization (WHO) constitution defined health as "a state of complete physical, mental, and social well-being and not merely the absence of disease or infirmity" (p. 2). This definition, however, is too limited. Consider the person in ▌**Figure 1-1.** Although he is in a wheelchair he is able to compete as an athlete. If you judged his state of health using WHO's 1948 definition, you might conclude that he is unhealthy. Many physically disabled people are able to function adequately in society and do not consider themselves ill or infirm.

The Ottawa Charter for Health Promotion (WHO, 1986) defined health as "a resource for everyday life . . . a positive concept emphasizing social as well as personal resources, as well as physical capabilities." According to this charter, health requires "peace, shelter, education, food, income, a stable ecosystem, sustainable resources, social justice and equity." In addition to these conditions, most healthy adults want to function independently; enjoy eating, sexual, and physical activities; feel good about themselves; and be with family and friends.

Behavioral scientist Godfrey Hochbaum (1979) proposed a simple definition for health: "Health is what helps me be what I want to be . . . do what I want to do . . . [and] live the way I would like to live." Using Hochbaum's definition, you might conclude that the wheelchair-bound athlete in Figure 1-1 is as healthy as a person who is capable of running.

Health and Wellness

Health and wellness are related concepts. Good **health** enables one to function independently within a constantly changing environment; **wellness** is a sense that one is functioning at his or her best level. ▌**Figure 1-2** illustrates the concept of health as a continuum; there are degrees of health. The absence of functioning (premature death) is at one end of this continuum, and the highest level of functioning (optimal well-being) is at the other end. Many people accept responsibility for the quality of their health and well-being. These people are willing to take various steps to improve their health, achieving a higher degree of wellness in the process.

Most health educators agree that health and wellness are **holistic**, that is, they involve all aspects of the individual. Thus, the holistic concept of health encompasses not only the physical, psychological, and social aspects, but also the intellectual, spiritual, and environmental dimensions of a person. Each dimension is an integral part of a person's health, and any change in the quality of one component of health affects the others. For example, individuals who exercise with others to increase their level of physical health often report a sense of improved psychological and social health.

The Components of Health

Physical Health Physical health refers to the overall condition of the organ systems, such as the cardiovascular system (heart and blood vessels), respiratory system (lungs), reproductive system, and nervous system. When certain organs do not function adequately, a person has various signs and symptoms of illness. **Signs** are the observable and measurable features of an illness such as fever, rash, or abnormal behavior. **Symptoms** are the subjective

lifestyle
a way of living, including behaviors that promote or impair good health and longevity.

risk factor a characteristic that increases an individual's chances of developing a health condition.

health good health is the ability to function adequately within a constantly changing environment.

▲Figure 1-1 **Wheelchair Athlete.** Many physically disabled people do not consider themselves ill or infirm because they can function well in society. According to Hochbaum's definition of health, individuals with physical disabilities can still be healthy and enjoy life.

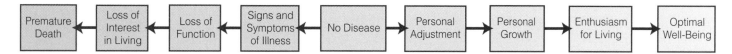

| Premature Death | Loss of Interest in Living | Loss of Function | Signs and Symptoms of Illness | No Disease | Personal Adjustment | Personal Growth | Enthusiasm for Living | Optimal Well-Being |

▲**Figure 1-2 A Health Continuum.** Some people view health as a continuum; that is, there are degrees of health. Premature death is at one end of this continuum, and optimal well-being is at the other end. (Source: Adapted from Ebersole, P., & Hess, P. (1994). *Toward healthy aging.* St. Louis: Mosby-Year Book, Inc.)

complaints of an illness, such as reports of fatigue, headaches, or numbness. A healthy person's systems function properly; the individual feels well and is free of disease.

Psychological Health Psychological (mental) health involves the ability to deal effectively with the psychological challenges of life. Psychologically healthy people accept responsibility for their behavior, feel good about themselves and others, are comfortable with their emotions (feelings), and have positive, realistic outlooks on life. Although experiences such as losing a job or a family member may cause stress or grief, psychologically healthy people are able to limit the extent to which crises affect their lives.

Social Health Social health is the sense of well-being that one achieves by forming emotionally supportive and intellectually stimulating relationships with family members, friends, and associates. Living in communities rather than in isolation, identifying with social groups, and belonging to organizations strengthen the social dimen-

sion of health. When social networks break down, health declines.

Intellectual Health Intellectual health is the ability to use problem-solving and other higher-order thinking skills to deal effectively with life's challenges. Healthy people analyze situations, determine alternative courses of action, and make decisions. After making decisions, intellectually healthy individuals are able to judge the effectiveness of their choices and learn from their experiences. Effective intellectual skills enable people to feel in control of their lives.

Spiritual Health Spiritual health is the belief that one is a part of a larger scheme of life and that one's life has purpose. For many individuals, identifying with a religion and having religious beliefs influence their spiritual health. However, spirituality is not confined to those who belong to organized religious groups or have religious beliefs. People can develop spirituality without practicing a particular religion or believing in the power of a supreme being. Whatever the nature of their spirituality, many individuals achieve a sense of inner peace and harmony as well as emotional fulfillment by believing that their lives have a purpose. As in the other wellness dimensions, a breakdown in spiritual health can have a negative impact on one's well-being.

Environmental Health Nothing affects the quality of wellness components as much as the state of the environment—the conditions where people live, work, and play. Environmental concerns that influence wellness include the provision of clean water and air, the management of wastes, and the control of distressing social problems such as crime and family violence. Humans cannot achieve a high degree of wellness if their environment is polluted or unsafe (**Figure 1-3**). Chapter 16 discusses environmental health concerns.

Figure 1-4 is a model that illustrates how these six components of wellness are interrelated and integrated into a holistic approach to

wellness a sense that one is functioning at his or her best level.

holistic (hole-IS-tic) a characteristic involving all aspects of the person.

signs observable and measurable features of an illness.

symptoms subjective complaints of illness.

▲**Figure 1-3 Environmental Health.** The state of the environment in which people live, work, and play affects the quality of their health. People cannot achieve a high degree of wellness if their environment is polluted or unsafe.

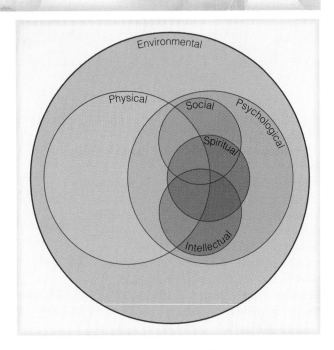

▲Figure 1-4 **The Components of Health.** The components of health are interrelated. According to this wellness model, the social, intellectual, and spiritual components of health are in the large spheres of physical and psychological health, which are in the larger sphere of environmental health.

understanding health. This model has the physical and psychological health components at the core of the larger environmental component. The social, intellectual, and spiritual components involve thought processes; therefore, they are found in the psychological health dimension. When the components of health integrate and function well, the individual has a sense of well-being.

The Nation's Health

www.jbpub.com/healthyliving

Many people fail to recognize that health involves more than just personal health—health is a national concern, too. Many of the crucial social, political, and economic issues facing this country are health-related, such as violence in schools and workplaces, health-care reform, and care of the aged.

Tracking the Nation's Health

The United States government, particularly the Public Health Service of the Department of Health and Human Services, monitors the nation's health in a variety of ways. One way is by recording cases of certain diseases and causes of death. ▌ **Table 1-1** shows the ten leading causes

of death for all Americans. In the United States, heart disease is the leading cause of death, followed by cancer and strokes.

The major causes of death differ for members of various age groups. ▌ **Table 1-2** shows the leading causes of death in two age categories: 15 to 24 years and 25 to 44 years. Unintentional injuries (accidents), homicide and legal intervention (imposing the death penalty, for example), and suicide are the leading causes of death of people between 15 and 24 years of age. Note that unintentional injuries, cancer, and heart disease are the leading causes of death of people between 25 and 44 years of age.

Over the past 100 years, Americans made great progress toward improving their health, well-being, and longevity. In 1900 the life expectancy of a newborn baby was less than 50 years. **Life expectancy** is the average number of years that an individual of a particular age can look forward to living. Compared to people living in the first half of the twentieth century, many Americans can now expect to live longer and healthier lives. In 1998 the average life ex-

| Table 1-1 | The Ten Major Causes of Death in the United States |

Rank	Cause	Approximate Percentage of Total Deaths
1	Heart disease	31.0
2	Cancers	23.1
3	Stroke	6.8
4	Chronic lung diseases	4.9
5	Pneumonia/influenza	4.1
6	Unintentional injuries	4.0
7	Diabetes mellitus	2.8
8	Suicide	1.3
9	Kidney disease	1.1
10	Chronic liver disease	1.1
—	Other causes	19.8

Martin, J. A., Smith, B. L., Mathews, M. S., & Ventura, S. J. (1999). Births and deaths: Preliminary data for 1998. *National Vital Statistics Reports,* 47(25):1-25.

Table 1-2 — Causes of Death: Selected Age Groups of Americans (all races)

Ages 15-24

Rank	Cause
1	Unintentional Injuries
2	Homicide/legal intervention
3	Suicide
4	Cancer
5	Heart disease

Ages 25-44

Rank	Cause
1	Unintentional Injuries
2	Cancer
3	Heart disease
4	Suicide
5	AIDS/HIV

Martin, J. A., Smith, B. L., Mathews, M. S., & Ventura, S. J. (1999). Births and deaths: Preliminary data for 1998. *National Vital Statistics Reports, 47(25):1-25.*

pectancy of a newborn American was 76.7 years ("Mortality Patterns," 1999). This progress occurred largely because various government agencies provided greater access to health care, conducted health education and research programs, and regulated the safety of the environment. For example, childhood vaccination programs have removed the threat of smallpox and polio, and controlled other infectious diseases such as measles, diphtheria, rubella, and tetanus. Food fortification programs almost have eliminated nutritional deficiency diseases such as goiter, rickets, and pellagra. Efforts to educate the public concerning the hazards of tobacco use and drinking and driving have reduced the prevalence of smoking among adults and made motor-vehicle travel safer.

Federal, state, and local governments can help individuals develop healthy lifestyles by providing educational and professional services. How does the federal government monitor the health of its citizens? What is being done to improve the nation's health?

Health Promotion: *Healthy People* 2000 and *Healthy People* 2010

In their efforts to improve the life expectancy and health of Americans, government officials use national studies to identify areas to emphasize for health promotion. Health promotion is the practice of helping individuals become healthier by encouraging them to change their lifestyles. In the late 1980s, a team of concerned health experts, health educators, and U.S. government officials collected and analyzed the results of recent studies, reports, and recommendations that summarized the health status of Americans. In 1991 these experts published their findings in a report called *Healthy People* 2000 (USDHHS, 1991).

Healthy People 2000 has three general goals: increase the healthy life span of Americans, improve the health status of American minorities, and extend the accessibility of preventive health services to all Americans. The overall goal was for Americans to achieve the health objectives by the year 2000; as more *Healthy People* 2000 objectives were met, the overall health status of Americans would improve.

Staff of various federal, state, and local agencies develop and implement health educational efforts that support *Healthy People* 2000 goals. Additionally, they collect data to monitor Americans' progress in meeting these health objectives. The U.S. Public Health Service publishes reports at regular intervals to show national trends

life expectancy

the average number of years that an individual can expect to live.

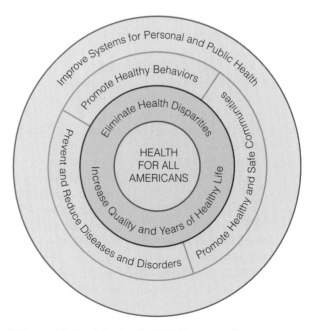

▲ **Figure 1-5** *Healthy People 2010* **Strategy.** The Surgeon General's *Healthy People 2010* strategy is to increase the years and quality of healthy life by eliminating health disparities among population groups.

in achieving the goals. The information concerning the state of Americans' health that was given in the beginning of this chapter is from the latest *Healthy People 2000* progress report. Several chapters of this textbook highlight findings from this report.

By 1997 members of the original *Healthy People 2000* team were focusing their attention on preparing a national health promotion and disease prevention agenda that would be relevant for the year 2010. Differences in death and illness rates between the nation's rich and poor as well as among its diverse ethnic and racial groups are major public health concerns. For example, more African Americans die of cancers and diseases of the heart and blood vessels than members of other ethnic and racial groups. The reasons for this difference are unclear, but lifestyle choices, environmental conditions, and socioeconomic situations are major contributing factors. ▮ **Figure 1-5** illustrates the Surgeon General of the United States' *Healthy People 2010* strategy to increase the years and quality of healthy life by eliminating the disparities in health among population groups (Richmond, 1999).

Minority Health Status

For hundreds of years, immigrants from around the world have been changing the face of the United States as they settle in this country. Each new group of immigrants brings different cultural traditions and various ethnic identities with them (▮ **Figure 1-6**). Culture consists of the unique social characteristics of a population, such as its customs, rit-

---

DIVERSITY in Health | Minority Health Status in the U.S.

Did you know that Hispanic people living in the United States have a lower death rate than white or black Americans? Were you aware that Black women are three times more likely to die from complications during and after pregnancy than White women? Did you know that 35% of Native Americans 18 years of age and older smoke cigarettes, whereas only 18% of Hispanics smoke cigarettes? The differences in death and illness rates for various population subgroups reflect numerous factors such as socioeconomic status and access to medical care. By investigating reasons for these differences, health scientists have learned a great deal about the health of American minorities. A major goal of the U.S. Department of Health and Human Services is improving the health of *all* Americans through research, education, and better access to health care.

African Americans

In the United States, African Americans are the largest minority group, and despite recent improvements, the health status of black Americans is generally poorer than that of other minorities. The life expectancies of Whites and Blacks reflect differences in each group's health status. In 1998 the life expectancy of African American females was 74.7 years; the life expectancy of White American females was 79.9 years ("Mortality Patterns", 1999). At the same time, the life expectancy for African American males was 67.2 years, and that of White males was 74.6 years. Although the major causes of death for Black Americans are similar to those of Whites and Hispanics, Black death rates (usually reported in deaths per 1000, 10,000, or 100,000 people) for seven of the fifteen leading causes of death are higher. Compared to members of other racial or ethnic groups, Blacks are 7 times more likely to be the victim of a homicide than Whites (Fox and Zawitz, 1999). AIDS is the leading cause of death for Black Americans ages 25 to 44 ("Mortality Patterns," 1999).

Childbearing is more risky for an African American woman: She is more likely to die during pregnancy or childbirth and give birth to a low-birth-weight infant than a White woman (Hoyert et al., 1999). Low-birth-weight infants weigh less than about 5 1/2 pounds and are more likely to die in the first few weeks after birth or suffer long-term health problems than newborns who weigh between 5 1/2 and 9 1/3 pounds. Additionally, the infant death rate of Black infants is twice that of White babies.

Hypertension (chronic high blood pressure) is twice as common in Blacks as in Whites. The reason for this high prevalence is unclear, but the consensus is that diet, genetics, stress, and smoking play roles. Smoking cigarettes increases the risk of hypertension. Twenty-six percent of Blacks 18 years of age and older smoke cigarettes. Overall, about 25% of Americans smoke.

Black Americans are less likely to die from chronic lung diseases, Alzheimer's disease, and suicide than Whites ("Mortality Patterns," 1999). Furthermore, cancer deaths of Blacks have declined since 1990. Cervical cancer rates, however, are higher among Black females than White females.

Latinos

Hispanic, or Latin, people have immigrated to the United States or have ancestors from Spanish-speaking countries, especially Mexico, Puerto Rico, Central and South America, and Cuba. Currently, Hispanics make up the second largest minority group in the United States; by the year 2010, population experts project that Hispanics will be the largest minority group in this country.

Hispanic persons have a lower overall death rate than Whites or Blacks

◄**Figure 1-6 An American Family.** Culture consists of the unique social characteristics of a population, such as its customs, rituals, beliefs, and practices. Immigrants who settle in the United States from regions such as Southeast Asia contribute much to the racial, ethnic, and cultural diversity of the population.

("Mortality Patterns," 1999). The leading causes of death for Hispanics are heart disease, cancer, and unintentional injuries. Latinos are less likely to commit suicide and smoke cigarettes than their White counterparts. Their homicide rate, however, is considerably higher than that of Whites.

Poverty and poor education are barriers to good health for many Hispanics. One out of four Hispanics live in poverty, and about one of every two has not completed high school (Reed & Ramirez, 1998). Medical experts believe that the health disorders associated with poverty, such as tuberculosis and malnutrition, are more common in certain Spanish-speaking subgroups. Almost one-third of Hispanic people younger than 65 years do not have health insurance, compared to about 18% of the total population.

Asian and Pacific Islanders

As the fastest growing minority group, Asian Americans and Pacific Islanders (API) are a diverse group of people who immigrated to the United States from China, Japan, Vietnam, Korea, India, the Philippines, and other Pacific Islands. In the past, the health status of this group has not received much attention outside of California and Hawaii, where many members of this minority group have settled. Reports indicate that individuals with Chinese and Japanese ancestry generally enjoy a higher standard of living and better health than most Whites. Recently, the National Center for Health Statistics conducted the first study to compare the health status of Asian minority groups (Kuo & Porter, 1998). The results of this study indicated that people with Vietnamese ancestry are not as healthy as persons with ancestors from other Asian countries. People of Indian descent had the lowest rate of smoking; persons with Korean ancestry were three times more likely to be smokers than people of Indian origin.

American Indians and Alaskan Natives

Smaller and more diverse than other U.S. minority groups, Native Americans and Alaskans generally have more health problems than Whites. About one-third of this population live in designated areas such as reservations, and about one-half live in cities. Low incomes, lack of education, and difficulty accessing health care translate into poor health status for many Native Americans. It is difficult to determine the status of this population's health because death certificates often contain inaccurate information concerning the causes of death. As a result, current rates for the leading causes of death may be higher than reported in earlier studies.

The rate of diabetes among Native Americans is more than twice that of the rest of the population. In addition to diabetes, alcohol-related deaths such as accidents, homicides, and suicides are major health concerns. Although rates of *fetal alcohol syndrome* (FAS) have increased for all Americans, the rate for Native Americans is about ten times that of the total population (USDHHS, 1999). FAS is a condition that seriously affects newborns and is caused by drinking alcohol during pregnancy.

The Impact of Social Conditions on Health Status

Although genetic factors may cause many health problems, socioeconomic status, including income level, health insurance coverage, educational attainment, and years living in the United States, play a major role in determining a particular group's state of health. Many diseases, such as tuberculosis and malnutrition, are associated with poor standards of living. Other health threats often associated with poverty include substance abuse, homicide, and lead poisoning. Poverty, however, is not limited to any population group in the United States. Regardless of their racial or ethnic background, individuals who achieve a higher level of education usually have higher incomes and better health than those with less education.

uals and health beliefs and practices, which are passed down from generation to generation. An ethnic group is one that shares a common national, religious, racial, or ancestral identity. According to the U.S. Department of Health and Human Services, the major American racial/ethnic subpopulations are Caucasians (Whites), African Americans (Blacks), Latinos (Hispanics), Native Americans (American Indians), and Asian and Pacific Islanders. The same terms, however, are not used by all agencies. Throughout this textbook, terms such as *Caucasian* may be used in one context and *Whites* in another; we reflect the language of the agency or researcher when reporting statistics or results of research studies.

Today in the United States, the majority of Americans have European ancestry, particularly Northern European. The National Center for Health Statistics refers to this population as "white, non-Hispanic." Traditionally regarded as ethnic or racial minorities, 28 percent of the U.S. population identifies itself as African American, Hispanic, or Asian American.

Collecting accurate information concerning the health status of minorities is a challenging task. Self-reported data regarding race and ethnicity may be unreliable because individuals of mixed heritage often have difficulty classifying their racial or ethnic identity on standardized forms. However, researchers have collected information concerning the health status of people who identify with a particular minority group, such as Native American or Asian American. Throughout this textbook, the "Diversity in Health" essays feature topics that concern a variety of populations in the United States as well as around the world. The "Diversity in Health" essay in this chapter, "Minority Health Status in the United States," discusses differences in the overall health of certain minority groups in the United States.

motivation the force or drive that leads people to take action.

efficacy (EF-fih-ka-see) regarding health education, the belief that one is capable of changing his or her behavior.

Understanding Health-Related Behavior

Regardless of their cultural and ethnic background, not all Americans share the same level of concern for their health. How many times have you heard a smoker say, "I can stop smoking whenever I want to; now is just not a good time" or "You've got to die of something; it might as well be lung cancer." You may know people who eat too many fatty foods, do not exercise regularly, and smoke cigarettes. You may know other people who follow a low-fat diet, walk at a brisk pace for 45 minutes nearly every day, and avoid drugs such as alcohol and tobacco. Why do some people adopt more positive health-related behaviors than others?

Changing Health-Related Behavior

"I wish I had the willpower to stop smoking." "I just can't seem to find the motivation to exercise more often." Do these statements sound familiar? Is having a lot of willpower the key to becoming healthier?

Health educators often refer to willpower as **motivation**, the force or drive that leads people to take action. Past experiences, perceived needs, and personal values influence one's motivation level. For example, a person who has tried unsuccessfully to stop smoking several times and claims to enjoy smoking may have little motivation to make another attempt to quit.

Efficacy enhances motivation. **Efficacy** is the belief that one is capable of changing behavior. Various barriers such as poor education or lack of support from family members can interfere with someone's motivation to change behaviors.

Having knowledge about risky behaviors and the seriousness of a health-related condition does not necessarily motivate individuals to take appropriate actions. For example, most people know that seat belts reduce the possibility of a serious injury in an automobile accident and that most states require them to wear seat belts in a car. Nevertheless, individuals often make a variety of excuses to explain why they fail to buckle up. Additionally, many students enrolled in health education classes can correctly identify behaviors that promote optimal health, yet they do not practice what they know. Acquiring knowledge about health is important, but becoming motivated to adopt a healthier lifestyle is essential if individuals are to make long-term changes that can benefit their health.

Taking an active role in achieving and maintaining good health depends on certain personal factors: degree of vulnerability, level of motivation *(willpower)*, sense of control, and perceived value of the behavior. People are motivated to take action if they feel that a sufficient threat to their health exists and that the consequences of changing the behavior are worthwhile.

Assume, for example, that diabetes affects several members of your family. You have heard that diabetes may be inherited, therefore, you are aware that you have a good chance of developing this condition *(vulnerability)*. You know that family members who have diabetes suffer from kidney damage, blindness, and premature heart disease. Since you want to avoid these consequences, you are motivated to change certain behaviors *(motivation)*. Additionally, you believe that your actions influence the quality of your health *(sense of control)*. Concerned, you decide to learn more about diabetes and determine what actions can reduce your risk of developing the disease. You now have a reason to take action because you believe it is important *(value)* to prevent this disease, even if it means making lifestyle changes now while you are still healthy.

Making Positive Health-Related Decisions

How I Quit Smoking

About a month ago I was a smoker—about 10 cigarettes a day during the week and up to a pack a day on weekends. After thinking about quitting for about a year, it happened. Without even giving it any consideration, I was able to not buy a pack for 2 days. On day 3, I realized my success and told myself I would never buy a pack again. I miss it, especially after a drink or a meal, but I'm glad I've gone this far. There have been times when I've really wanted one, but that's when you realize how powerful of a drug it is. At least that's how I talk myself out of having one. Before, I never thought of myself as being addicted—too harsh of a word—but I was just like all of the other smokers out there. It's a filthy habit—I'm glad I stopped.

Although this college student smoked less than a pack of cigarettes a day, he took about a year to quit smoking. He made the final decision to stop smoking while listening to other students' habit-breaking experiences in his health class. Some people take less time to make health-related decisions than others, and some people have less difficulty making lifestyle changes than others. ▌**Figure 1-7** illustrates the complex process of decision making.

To enjoy a long, healthy, and productive life, it is important for you to make numerous health-related decisions every day. If you act impulsively and base these decisions simply on cues, attitudes, and emotions, you may make poor choices. However, you are likely to make responsible choices if you follow a systematic method of decision making. The "Changing Health Habits" feature in the student workbook describes a useful decision-making process. The first part of the process involves deciding to change a health-related behavior; the second part describes implementing the behavioral change. To practice making responsible health-related choices, complete the decision-making activities in *Applying Concepts for Healthy Living: A Workbook.*

Routine Health Screening for Disease Prevention

Managing Your Health

The following recommendations concerning routine screening applies to people who have low risks of disease. People who have higher risks may need more frequent testing and to begin testing at earlier ages.

Medical Test/ Measurement	Recommended Frequency
Blood pressure	Every medical visit; at least once every 2 years
Height/weight (by health-care practitioner)	Every 1 to 3 years
Cholesterol	Every 5 years after 18 years of age
Glucose (diabetes screening)	Annually after 50 years of age
Dental	Every 6 to 12 months
Glaucoma	Annually after age 65 years
Prostate (PSA)	Annually after 50 years of age
Testicular examination (cancer)	Monthly after puberty

Medical Test/ Measurement	Recommended Frequency
Breast examination (cancer)	
By health-care practitioner	Annually after 40 years of age
By woman	Monthly after 20 years of age
Mammograms*	Baseline by age 40; every 1 to 2 years between 40 and 49; annually after 50 years of age
Pap test for cervical cancer*	Every 1 to 3 years after first sexual intercourse
Colon/rectal examination (cancer)	
Fecal occult blood test	Annually for people ages 50 and over
Sigmoidoscopic exam	Every 3 to 5 years for people ages 50 and over

*Recommendations vary somewhat among medical organizations such as the American Cancer Society and the American College of Physicians. Persons should discuss the frequency and appropriateness of various medical tests with their physicians.

Source: Adapted from Sox, H. C. (1994). Preventive health services in adults. *Journal of the American Medical Association, 330:* 1589-1595.

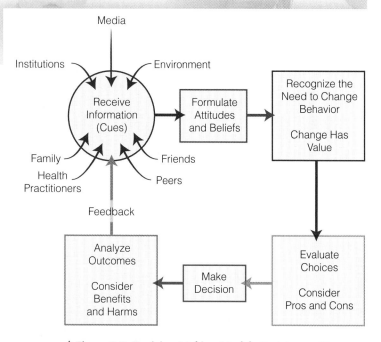

▲ **Figure 1-7 Decision-Making Model.** Decision making can be a complex process. Information, personal attitudes, and experiences influence your decision-making process. To change health-related behaviors, you must recognize a need to change, that the change has personal value, and that it is consistent with your beliefs.

Can Good Health Be Prescribed?

No one has a crystal ball that predicts future health, nor can anyone guarantee good health. Numerous factors contribute to one's chances of enjoying a long and productive lifetime of good health. Several of these factors are the result of lifestyle choices that people can make, while they are still young, to prevent or delay disease. You may know someone or have heard about individuals who avoided exercise, smoked a pack of cigarettes, and consumed a six-pack of beer each day, yet lived to a ripe old age. Such behavior defies nearly every reasonable prescription for good health. Perhaps these people inherited the hardiness to withstand the effects of their risky lifestyles. You might wonder if these people enjoyed good health throughout their lives, or if they spent their last years in poor health. Would their lives have been even longer if they had followed more health-conscious behaviors?

Health experts generally base their recommendations for healthier lifestyles on scientific information collected from numerous studies that involved large numbers of people and not on reports of individual cases. This textbook presents findings from current research for you to use in your own health decision-making process.

- To change your health-related behaviors, you must determine that you need to change and that you value the change.
- Use a decision-making plan as a tool to help you make responsible decisions.

www.jbpub.com/healthyliving

Analyzing Health Information

"Take natural antioxidants to live longer." "Drink red wine to prevent heart attacks." "Improve your memory with ginkgo biloba." Every day, Americans are barraged with a confusing array of health-related information in newspapers; magazines; and television and radio talk shows, commercials, and infomercials. In addition to the media, family members, friends, teachers, health-care professionals, and the Internet supply information about health and health-related products. Are these sources reliable? Not necessarily. There are no laws that prevent anyone from making statements or writing books about health, even if their information is false. The First Amendment to the U.S. Constitution protects freedom of speech and freedom of the press. This protection extends to talk-show guests, authors, and salespeople in health food stores who might provide health misinformation.

Companies and individuals make considerable amounts of money by selling untested remedies, worthless cures, toxic herbal preparations, unnecessary nutrient supplements, and books filled with misinformation. Health frauds include the promotion or sale of substances or devices that are touted as being effective to diagnose, prevent, cure, or treat diseases or other conditions, but that lack scientific evidence of their safety and effectiveness. Despite the regulatory activities of the Food and Drug Administration (FDA) and the Federal Trade Commission (FTC), the sale of fraudulent products and services and the circulation of misleading or false health information continue to be concerns of medical experts and public health officials.

Keep in mind that if the claim sounds too good to be true, it probably is not true. Some other tell-tale signs that information about a health-related product or service is questionable include:

- claims that a secret formula or ingredient gives the product its beneficial effects on health
- uses promotional techniques that rely heavily on mail-order outlets, newspaper ads, or infomercials

- claims that the product or service is the result of a miraculous scientific discovery
- claims that the product or service provides "quick," "painless," "effortless," or "guaranteed" cure or other desirable result
- provides details of the product's or service's benefits, but does not mention its risks
- relies on testimonials and anecdotes as supporting evidence
- cites few references to indicate that the product has been scientifically tested
- discredits scientific studies or conventional medical practices

Becoming a Wary Consumer of Health Information

As shown in Figure 1-7, information is a crucial element of decision making. Although health information from some sources is based on scientific evidence and can be extremely useful, that from other sources is unreliable. Relying on flawed information can waste time and money and can be dangerous. To be a wary consumer of health information, you need to know how to analyze it.

Analyzing information is easier to do if you follow a particular model of analysis. A model is a plan or pattern that can be used as a guide. Analyzing something simply means breaking it down into its component parts for study. In analyzing health-related information, there are certain questions you need to ask, the answers to which will help you determine if the information is reliable and applicable to your everyday life.

The "Analyzing Health-Related Information" feature in this chapter provides questions to help you determine the value of health-related information. Similar analysis activities appear throughout this textbook. To sharpen your critical thinking skills, analyze the information in these features using the model that is described on pages 12 and 13. The model may be modified slightly to fit each example.

If you need additional help to determine the validity of information that concerns health, pose your questions to people trained in specific health-related fields. If you have a question about a psychological condition, for example, contact a mental health professional. You can usually obtain reliable answers to your health-related questions from experts at state and local health departments, universities and colleges, local hospitals, and federal health agencies. You can access reliable health information from various government, university, and not-for-profit agencies through www.healthfinder.gov. The Jones and Bartlett Web site includes links to many associations and agencies where you can find reliable health information. Additionally, the "Consumer Health" features in this and other chapters provide tips to help you become a better consumer of health information. The "Consumer Health" feature below describes various agencies that protect consumers and their interests.

Consumer Protection

The U.S. government has some laws and agencies to protect consumers against health fraud. As a result of the Federal Food, Drug, and Cosmetics Act passed in 1938, manufacturers may not place false or misleading claims on the labels of food, medicinal, or cosmetic products. Later legislation protects consumers by requiring that manufacturers of medications and medical devices prove the safety and effectiveness of their products before they can be marketed.

The federal agencies that enforce consumer protection laws include the Food and Drug Administration (FDA) and the Federal Trade Commission (FTC). The FDA protects consumers by regulating the information that manufacturers can place on food or drug product labels. In addition, FDA personnel alert consumers about fraudulent health practices and can seize untested or unsafe medical devices and drugs. The manufacturers of such products can be punished (usually fined) for their illegal practices. The FTC regulates claims made in advertisements for products and services. Both agencies only regulate products and services involved in interstate commerce.

Besides government agencies, various voluntary organizations such as the American Council on Science and Health and the American Association for Retired Persons (AARP) provide consumers with reliable health information. The National Council Against Health Fraud investigates and evaluates health claims, supports laws that protect consumers against quackery, and provides educational materials to help people combat deceptive health practices.

To avoid being victims of health frauds, people must take the initiative and be very critical when judging the reliability of health-related information. If you suspect fraudulent activity, you can file a complaint with the local office of the FDA or your state's attorney general. You can also file a lawsuit if you have been injured as a result of following the advice or using the services or products of unscrupulous practitioners and manufacturers.

ANALYZING Health-Related Information

Maybe you've seen an ad for a food supplement that you might buy. How do you know if the information in the advertisement is true? Will the product do what the manufacturer claims? Or will you merely be wasting your money?

The example applies a model of analysis to an advertisement for a product, but this model is designed to be used with a variety of health information. The model is a series of questions that will help you evaluate the information. Read the advertisement first. Would you buy this product? Why or why not? Then analyze the information in the ad using the model. Are your answers to those two questions still the same?

Analysis Model

1. **Which statements are verifiable facts, and which are unverified statements or value claims?** In the context of this model, *verifiable facts* are conclusions drawn from scientific research or statements that are supported with other types of evidence. *Unverified statements* are conclusions that have no such support. *Value claims* are statements suggesting that something is useful, effective, or has other worthwhile characteristics. Unverified statements and value claims may or may not be true.

2. **What are the credentials of the person who wrote the article or advertisement? Does the author appear to have appropriate background and education in the topic area? If it is difficult to tell if the author has specific health expertise, what can you do to check his/her credentials?** People with marketing backgrounds usually write advertisements, but people with appropriate credentials may have supplied the information. Articles usually state the name and credentials of the author. Does the author have appropriate background and education in the topic area? It may be hard to tell if someone has specific health expertise. The author's credentials may not be well defined. Also, in certain cases the author's credentials may be fraudulent; for example, this person may have purchased a diploma through the mail. If the information you are reading is extremely important to your health care, you can check the author's credentials by contacting the institution to which he or she claims to be affiliated.

3. **What might be the motives and biases of the author?** *Motive* is the incentive, purpose, or reason why someone writes an article or advertisement. Advertisements are always written with the motivation to have the consumer buy the product. Even if a person with bona fide health credentials supplies information for an advertisement, that person may have also developed the product and may profit from its sale. Therefore, this researcher may be biased.

A *bias* is the tendency to have a particular point of view. Newspaper reporters, for example, may be biased with respect to their political and other personal views. A researcher may be biased toward a particular outcome of his or her work. In analyzing health-related information, it is important to try to determine the biases of the persons or companies writing the information so that you can take their inclinations into account as you draw conclusions from the information.

4. **What is the main point of the article? Which information is relevant to the issue, main point, or product? Which information is irrelevant?** Look for *red-flag* terms, which are expressions that indicate the possibility of misinformation, such as "patented formula," "all natural," "chemical-free," "scientifically proven," "guaranteed to cure," or "everyone is using." Ignore information and terms that are not pertinent to the point; they will only confuse or muddle your analysis.

5. **Is the source reliable? Does it have a reputation for publishing misinformation? Does the article present both the pros and cons of the topic discussed?** Articles that appear in scientific journals generally are reliable because they have been *peer reviewed*, meaning their content was critiqued by experts in that field before it was accepted for publication. If peer reviewers think a study was designed poorly or provides questionable conclusions, the article describing the study is likely to be rejected by the journal's editor.

Many types of literature have purposes other than providing accurate, up-to-date information. The purpose of some publications is to sell health products. These publications, however, are often designed to look like bona fide health-related literature. One sign of such publications is the inclusion of articles with accompanying advertisements for products described in the article. For example, such a publication may include an article describing the benefits of bee pollen supplements; at the bottom of the next page may be an advertisement for bee pollen.

Publications containing articles that do not present both sides of an issue may not be reputable. For example, a reliable article about taking bee pollen should present scientific evidence to support or refute health claims. Reliable articles often caution people about the hazards of using treatments, and they may include recommendations to seek more information from experts.

6. Does the ad or article attack the credibility of conventional scientists or medical authorities? In some instances, writers of advertisements or articles try to confuse readers by implying that the Western scientific establishment is unreliable. For example, the ad may state, "unknown to Western medicine" or "used for centuries in China" to suggest that U.S. scientists lag behind in finding a cure or treatment. Statements that attack the reliability of conventional medical practitioners are usually indications that the information in the ad or article is unreliable.

Based on the above analysis, do you think that this advertisement is a reliable source of health-related information? Summarize your reasons for coming to this conclusion.

This statement is a value claim that is not supported with evidence. Additionally, such wide-ranging properties are unrealistic and vague.

No treatment contains everything each person needs to improve his or her health.

"Clinical proof" is a red flag. The medical experts, the medical schools, or journals where their research has been published are not identified. Objective testing could show the product is neither safe nor effective. The ad should cite the specific effects of the product. This, again, is an unsubstantiated value claim.

"Chemical-free" is a red flag; herbs, other plants, all matter is chemical. Furthermore, scientific studies should be cited to provide evidence for these value claims. These statements are not verifiable facts.

A testimonial from an individual is not scientific evidence. This student's G.P.A. may have risen for a variety of reasons. Studies conducted to show that a treatment is useful in particular ways should contain at least 30 subjects, and hundreds or thousands if possible.

"Potency" is a vague and undefined red-flag term. Again, this testimonial is a value claim that is unsupported by scientific evidence.

This is irrelevant information. Where the product is sold has nothing to do with its quality or characteristics. The authors of the ad are simply trying to make their product look superior to other similar products because it is sold only in health food stores where "discriminating" people shop.

This statement gives people the impression that there is no time to investigate the product thoroughly. It is intended to make consumers think that the product will sell out if they wait, and they will miss out on a good thing. Again, this information is irrelevant.

This suggests that American scientists do not understand that medicines can be derived from plant sources, when, in fact, American researchers often rely on plants as sources of chemicals that have medicinal uses. No scientific evidence is cited to show that the herbs in Panacea have the touted properties. These two sentences, then, contain only value claims; thus the information may be unreliable.

No scientific evidence is cited that a daily Panacea pill prevents illness, or keeps away doctors. Additionally, this statement attacks conventional medical practitioners by implying that they are interested only in making money, which suggests that physicians can't be trusted.

For centuries, doctors in the Orient have known about the wonders of herbal medicines—nature's botanical cures for human ailments.

SwayCon Pharmaceuticals has developed a capsule that contains everything you need to reduce suffering, enhance health, and regain youthful vigor.

A team of medical experts from three major medical schools in the United States have clinical proof that the ingredients of Panacea are effective! Panacea contains a mixture of natural enzymes and exotic herbs that

- relieve up to 80% more arthritis pain than aspirin;
- lower blood pressure by up to 20%;
- lower cholesterol by up to 45%;
- reduce lung cancer risk by as much as 50%, even in smokers;
- and reduce the risk of heart attack by 75%.

Other remarkable findings

Taking Panacea for a few months can improve intelligence. R.P., a college student at a large East Coast university reports, "At the beginning of the fall semester, I started taking three capsules of Panacea a day. My G.P.A. went from a 1.8 to a 3.4! Panacea has helped me get all A's!"

Reports are coming into our offices that Panacea acts as a sexual stimulant, increasing potency. S.D., a computer programmer in St. Louis, writes, "Thanks for saving my marriage. Before taking Panacea, my husband complained about my lack of interest in sex. One of my friends told me that Panacea can help. Just a few days after taking the capsules, our marriage turned into a perpetual honeymoon."

Panacea is only available in fine health food stores. Order a three-month supply now, while supplies last.

Finally, American scientists are recognizing the healthful benefits of these herbs.

A PANACEA PILL A DAY KEEPS THE EXPENSIVE DOCTORS AWAY!

Conclusion: This ad is merely a compilation of value claims that are unsubstantiated by scientific research. The ad further attempts to encourage the reader to purchase the product by suggesting that it is better (and less expensive) than conventional therapies. It claims to relieve a wide range of ills and to provide a wide range of attributes to people who take the product. The red-flag phrases and testimonials rather than scientific evidence, the lack of details concerning the scientists' credentials, and the lack of caution about the hazards of using the product all suggest an unreliable source of health-related information.

Assessing Information on the Internet The Internet is a valuable source of health-related information, but anyone with a computer and the appropriate software can produce and post a Web page. Therefore, you must analyze health-related information on the Web as you do information from other sources. One way is to use the model for analyzing health-related information provided in this chapter. Note the source of the information. Is the Web site sponsored by a single individual? Is the Web site a commercial site (".com") that is selling products? Identifying the site's sponsor will help you determine its bias and reliability.

At www.jbpub.com/healthyliving we provide Web sites that are pertinent to content in each chapter. Many of these sites are developed and maintained by governmental organizations (note ".gov" in their Web addresses) or educational institutions (".edu"). Such sources are widely regarded as providing reliable information. Nonprofit organizations (".org") are usually reliable.

anecdotes personal stories that describe the effects of using a health product or service.

testimonials claims about the effectiveness of a product or service that people are usually paid to make.

placebo a sham treatment that has no known physical effects; an inactive substance.

Healthy LIVING PRACTICES

- Use the model for analyzing health-related information to evaluate information from the media and other sources.
- To obtain reliable answers for your health-related questions, consult experts at clinics or hospitals, state and local health departments, universities and colleges, federal health agencies, and nationally recognized health associations and foundations.

www.jbpub.com/healthyliving

Conventional Versus Alternative Medicine

Conventional medicine (scientific or Western medicine) relies on modern scientific principles, modern technologies, and scientifically proved methods to prevent, diagnose, and treat health conditions. The notion that certain agents of infection such as bacteria and viruses cause many health disorders is accepted by conventional medical practitioners. To practice in their professions, *conventional health-care practitioners,* such as physicians, nurses, and dentists, must meet established national and/or state standards concerning their education and pass licensing examinations. To maintain their professional certification or licensing, certain types of conventional health-care practi-

tioners must update their medical backgrounds regularly by participating in continuing education programs. Most Americans use the services of conventional medical practitioners.

Alternative medicine (traditional medicine) is a diverse system of preventing, diagnosing, and treating diseases that emphasizes spirituality, self-healing, and harmonious interaction with the environment (Eskinazi, 1998). Herbal supplements, acupuncture, chiropractics, homeopathy, and massage therapy are popular forms of alternative medicine. Scientific studies to determine the effectiveness of most alternative therapies have not been conducted (Fontanarosa & Lundberg, 1998). Promoters of alternative medical practices often use anecdotal reports and testimonials to support claims of their method's effectiveness. **Anecdotes** are personal reports. A young woman, for example, may tell friends that she feels more relaxed after drinking an herbal tea. **Testimonials** are claims individuals make concerning the value of a product. Advertisers often rely on celebrities such as sports figures to provide testimonials. The celebrities usually receive money or other types of compensation from promoters of the products. Anecdotes may be interesting and testimonials may be persuasive, but these sources of information are not scientific evidence.

In 1997 David Eisenberg, a physician, and his colleagues (1998) conducted a national survey to estimate the extent to which Americans use unconventional medical therapies. According to their results, 42% of adults used an alternative medical therapy in 1997. Eisenberg and colleagues estimate that Americans spent almost $27 billion on alternative medical practices in that year. Much of this cost was not covered by insurance plans.

The natural or exotic nature of many alternative therapies, such as herbal pills and teas, coffee enemas, shark cartilage, or acupuncture may appeal to people who distrust modern technology or have lost faith in conventional medical care (▌ **Figure 1-8).** Others use alternative therapies to prevent or treat ailments because they want more control over their health. Conventional medical practitioners are concerned when people with serious conditions forgo or delay conventional treatments and rely instead on questionable alternative therapies. These could be life-threatening decisions. Many forms of cancer, for example, respond well to conventional treatments, particularly if the disease is in an early stage. A recent study by Druss and Rosenheck (1999), however, indicates that the majority of people who use alternative medical therapies choose them to complement rather than replace conventional treatments.

Alternative Treatments: Possible Placebos

Regardless of treatment, many acutely ill people recover with time (Turner et al., 1994). Persons with chronic health problems such as osteoarthritis or multiple sclerosis often report remissions, times when their conditions improve. If individuals use alternative treatments when they are recov-

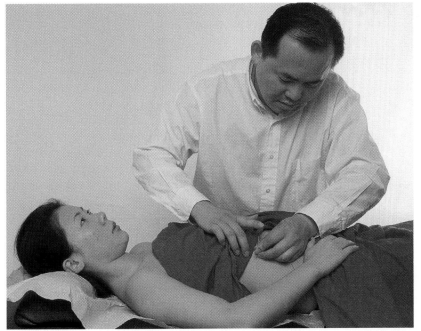

◀**Figure 1-8 Acupuncture.** Many physicians consider acupuncture an alternative form of medical care.

improve certain symptoms in men with a common condition that affects their prostate glands (Wilt et al., 1998), and green tea contains compounds that may protect against cancer (Ahmad & Mukhtar, 1999). Furthermore, numerous studies indicate that St. John's wort can provide relief for mild to moderate cases of depression (Fugh-Berman & Cott, 1999; Wong et al., 1999).

Before marketing their products, the manufacturers of herbal and dietary supplements are not required to submit proof of safety and effectiveness to the FDA. Thus, many of these products have not been scientifically tested to determine if they are effective or have side effects and react with others drugs. Certain plant products, including sassafras, comfrey, chaparral, and germander, are known to be unsafe. Recently, the use of certain Chinese herbs to treat skin disorders and lose weight was associated with more than 100 cases of serious kidney disorders (Lord et al., 1999). A "natural" treatment is not necessarily a safe or effective one.

Conventional practitioners are likely to be skeptical of alternative medical techniques if they have not been shown scientifically in large-scale studies to be safe or more helpful than placebos. The National Center for Complementary and Alternative Medicine (formerly the Office of Alternative Medicine) within the National Institutes of Health funds research to determine the safety and effectiveness of alternative medical practices. In 1998 this center supported 50 scientific studies concerning the value of specific alternative medical therapies at 13 research facilities in the United States (Marwick, 1998). Until supportive data are available from these and other controlled studies, consumers should be wary of many alternative medical practices.

Alternative Therapies in Perspective

Before using alternative therapies, discuss your options with your physician and consider taking the following steps to protect yourself:

- Contact a variety of reliable sources of information to determine the risks and benefits of the treatment. For example, ask persons who have used the treatment to describe its effectiveness and side effects. Conduct a review of literature, but recognize that popular

ering or their illnesses are in remission, they are likely to think the treatment cured or helped them. Additionally, people who combine alternative therapies and conventional medical care may attribute any improvement in their health only to the alternative treatments.

Before adopting a method of treatment, conventional medical practitioners want to know if it is safe and effective. To find the answer, scientists usually conduct controlled studies on human subjects. Controlled studies to determine the effects of various medical treatments on humans usually include placebos. A **placebo** can be a sham treatment, or an inactive substance, often referred to as a "sugar pill." Since a person's positive expectations can result in positive findings, placebos help rule out the effects of such wishful thinking. Researchers give subjects placebos to compare their responses to subjects receiving the actual treatment. In double-blind studies, subjects and researchers are unaware of the identity of those taking placebos. Placebos can temporarily relieve subjective complaints, such as pain, lack of energy, and poor mood. Thus, subjects who are given placebos often report feeling better even though the treatment has no known physical effects. Scientists refer to these reports as the *placebo effect*. The placebo effect may be responsible for many reports of the beneficial results of alternative therapies.

Certain alternative therapies have positive effects on the mind and body. Aromatherapy and therapeutic massage can be soothing and relaxing. Yoga can relieve some symptoms of carpal tunnel syndrome, a condition that causes pain and numbness in the wrist and hand (Garfinkel et al., 1998). Specific herbs can provide measurable physical benefits such as reducing inflammation or inhibiting bacterial growth. For example, saw palmetto plant extracts can

sources of information such as health magazines and the Internet are often unreliable. Be suspicious of sources that provide information about the benefits of alternative treatments without describing their harmful aspects. Instead, look for articles in medical journals or news magazines that have information concerning the usefulness of conventional as well as alternative medical approaches to care.

- Ask persons who are administering the treatment to provide proof of their medical training. Investigate the validity of their educational credentials. People who promote certain alternative medical practices often have little or no medical and scientific training. Anyone can call himself or herself a "nutritionist," "doctor," or "health expert." A Ph.D. or the title "Certified . . ." after someone's name is no guarantee that this person has had extensive training in a health or science field from an accredited educational program. Additionally, membership in a professional organization may not be evidence of medical expertise or training. Individuals can buy certain doctorate degrees through the mail from unaccredited colleges called "diploma mills." Frequently, graduates from such colleges are not required to attend classes. In many instances, diploma mills do not even offer classes. To determine whether an educational institution is accredited, you can contact the Council on Postsecondary Education, One Dupont Circle, Suite 305, Washington, DC 20036.

- Determine the cost of treatment and whether your health insurance covers the particular alternative therapy. If it does not, find out why. You may find that your health insurer considers the treatment risky or ineffective.

- Ask your primary care physician for his or her opinion of the treatment.
- If you decide to use an alternative therapy, keep your physician apprised of your actions.
- Investigate the possibility that the alternative medicine can interact with conventional medications that you take and produce serious side effects.
- If you are pregnant, do not use alternative therapies without consulting your physician.
- Do not give alternative therapies to children. Do not use them along with conventional treatments or abandon conventional treatments for any medical problem without consulting your physician.

Healthy LIVING PRACTICES

- Before using an alternative therapy, obtain reliable information concerning the pros and cons of the treatment and discuss your options with your physician.

across the Lifespan

Health

Although the focus of this text is adult health, the "Across the Lifespan" feature in each chapter briefly describes health concerns that are specific to other stages of life, such as infancy, childhood, adolescence, and the elderly years. ▌ Table 1-3 indicates the approximate age groupings for these life stages. Why should college students learn about health conditions that can affect very young or very old members of the population? This information is relevant because some college students have children, and those who are not parents may have children in the future. Additionally, many college students are middle-aged or have elderly parents and grandparents. The following information highlights some major life cycle health concerns of Americans.

In the United States, about 7 babies in 1000 die during the first year after birth. Most of these deaths are due to birth defects, low birth weights, and breathing difficulties that arise from prematurity, being born too early (▌ Figure 1-9). Public health efforts aimed at educating and providing medical care for pregnant women can reduce the number of infant deaths.

Unintentional injuries (accidents) are the major health threat to children over one year of age. Most deaths from unintentional injuries are preventable, such as deaths due to motor-vehicle crashes, drownings, and house fires. Today, children between the ages of 1 and 14 are less likely to die as a result of these causes than in 1990 (USDHHS,

Table 1-3	Life Stages
Stage	**Approximate Age**
Prenatal period	Conception to birth
Infancy	Birth to 1 year
Childhood	1 to 12 years of age
Adolescence	13 to 20 years of age
Adulthood	21 to 65 years of age
Older adult	Older than 65 years of age

Source: Based on Smith, R. E. (1993). *Psychology*. West Publishing Company, p. 120.

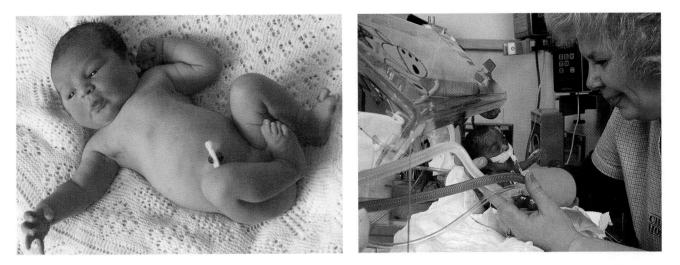

▲Figure 1-9 **Healthy and Premature Newborns.** The baby on the left is a healthy, full-term infant. The baby on the right is premature. Infants born prematurely have a greater risk of serious health problems than healthy full-term infants.

1999). Appendix A, "Injury Prevention and Emergency Care," provides information concerning safety.

Adolescence is a time when youngsters establish behaviors that may last a lifetime and when experimentation with risky behaviors usually begins. Unintentional injuries, homicide, and suicide are major causes of death for people of ages 15 to 24 (Martin et al., 1999). Three-fourths of the preventable deaths in this age group involve motor-vehicle crashes. Young people are less likely to commit suicide, carry weapons, and engage in fighting than in 1990, but heavy drinking among high school students is increasing (USDHHS, 1999).

Although teenage birth rates have been declining since 1991, unplanned pregnancies and sexually transmitted infections (STIs) continue to be major health problems for adolescents. As many as 2.5 million adolescents become infected with sexually transmitted infections each year. AIDS is primarily a sexually transmitted infection; sexually active adolescents are at risk of becoming infected with HIV. HIV infection is the ninth leading cause of death for people between 15 and 24 years of age (Martin et al., 1999; Trends in HIV-Related Sexual Risk, 1999).

Elderly people now make up about 13% of the population; this percentage is expected to increase rapidly. Americans are living longer, but a growing number of people over 70 years of age report having difficulty performing daily activities such as bathing and dressing (USDHHS, 1999). Furthermore, the number of deaths attributed to falls and motor-vehicle crashes is increasing among members of this age group. Chapter 15 discusses the health-related concerns of elderly Americans.

Chapter Review

Summary

Lifestyle includes behaviors that promote or deter good health and longevity. Wellness is an optimal degree of health. The holistic approach to health integrates physical, psychological, social, intellectual, spiritual, and environmental dimensions. Contemporary definitions of *health* reflect not only how one functions, but also what one can achieve, given his or her circumstances.

Heart disease and cancer are the major killers of Americans. Lifestyle choices contribute to the development of these and many other life-threatening diseases. *Healthy People 2000* established key objectives for improving the overall health of Americans by the year 2000. *Healthy People 2010* sets additional goals for the future. The distribution of health problems differs among the various ethnic and racial groups in the United States.

Experiences, knowledge, needs, and values affect one's motivation to change health-related behaviors. People are motivated to take action if they feel that a sufficient threat to their health exists and that the consequences of changing their behavior are worthwhile.

Although no one can guarantee good health, many factors contribute to one's chances of enjoying a long and productive lifetime of good health. Several of these factors are the result of lifestyle choices that people can make, while they are still young, to prevent or delay disease. Responsible health-related lifestyle choices involve a systematic approach to decision making.

People can become more careful consumers of health-related information, products, and services by learning to recognize misinformation. To obtain reliable health-related information, check with experts in federal, state, and local agencies and organizations.

Throughout the life span, health concerns vary. The most common causes of infant deaths are birth defects, low birth weights, and prematurity. Preventable injuries are the major causes of death for children and youth. Additional serious public health concerns for adolescents are suicide, homicide, drug abuse, pregnancy, and sexually transmitted infections (including AIDS). Americans are living longer, but a growing number of persons over 70 years of age report having difficulty performing daily activities such as bathing and dressing.

Applying What You Have Learned

1. Develop a plan to improve your health. *(Application)*
2. Analyze a health-related advertisement or article to determine the validity of its information. *(Analysis)*
3. Identify sources of health information that you have used in the past year. Explain why you think each source is reliable or unreliable. *(Synthethis)*
4. Think of a health-related decision that you made recently. For example, did you decide to turn down an offer to use a mind-altering drug, wear a helmet while riding a motorcycle, lose a few pounds, or use an herbal product to treat a condition? When you made this decision, did you use the decision-making process described in this chapter or did you act impulsively? Explain why you would or would not make the same decision today. *(Evaluation)*

KEY

Application: Using information in a new situation.
Analysis: Breaking down information into component parts.
Synthesis: Putting together information from different sources.
Evaluation: Making informed decisions.

Reflecting On Your Health

A reflective journal is a personal record of your thoughts and expressions of your feelings. The purposes of keeping this journal are to stimulate your thinking about what you have learned about health, and to help you understand how your thoughts and feelings about your health might have changed over the semester. Thinking about new information can help you determine its usefulness, which can influence your attitudes and behaviors.

The "Reflecting on Your Health" questions at the end of each chapter are designed to guide your thinking. If you want to write about something else that is related to the contents of the chapter, feel free to do so, but make sure to identify the topic in your opening sentence. Write your journal entries in the first person, using "I" statements to express your thoughts, as though you were talking to a close friend. Don't worry about your spelling, punctuation, or grammar—just let your thoughts flow.

Some instructors make journal writing an optional activity; others require that you respond to all of the questions, and they grade journals. Still other instructors simply check to see if students are doing the assignment. Refer to the course syllabus or ask your instructor about his or her grading practices and other instructions concerning the journal.

Journal Questions

1. What does the term *health* mean to you?
2. What do you think of the idea that people should strive to achieve optimal health?
3. What impact does spiritual health have on your sense of well-being? If spiritual health is important to you, describe the role it plays in your life.
4. Do you agree with the idea presented in the chapter that social health influences your physical health? Why or why not?
5. Under what circumstances would you consider using alternative therapies?

References

Ahmad, N., & Mukhtar, H. (1999). Green tea polyphenols and cancer: Biologic mechanisms and practical implications. *Nutrition Review* 57(3):78-83.

Druss, B. G., & Rosenheck, R. A. (1999). Association between use of unconventional therapies and conventional medical services. *Journal of the American Medical Association, 282:*651-656.

Eisenberg, D. M., Davis, R. B., Ettner, S. L., Appel, S., Wilkey, S., Rompay, S. V., & Kessler, R. C. (1998). Trends in alternative medicine use in the United States, 1990–1997. *Journal of the American Medical Association, 280:*1569-1575.

Eskinazi, D. P. (1998). Factors that shape alternative medicine. *Journal of the American Medical Association. 280*(18):1621-1623.

Fontanarosa, P. B., & Lundberg, G. D. (1998). Alternative medicine meets science. *Journal of the American Medical Association. 280*(18):1618-1619.

Fox, J. A., & Zawitz, M. W. (1999). *Homicide trends in the United States.* Bureau of Justice Statistics, Washington, DC: United States Department of Justice. http://www.ojp.usdoj.gov/bjs/homicide/homtrnd.htm

Fugh-Berman, A., & Cott, J. M. (1999). Dietary supplements and natural products as psychotherapeutic agents. *Psychosomatic Medicine, 61:*712-728.

Garfinkel, M. S., Singhal, A., Katz, W. A., et al. (1998). Yoga-based intervention for carpal tunnel syndrome: A randomized trial. *Journal of the American Medical Association, 280:*1601-1604.

Hochbaum, G. M. (1979). An alternative approach to health education. *Health Values, 3:*197-201.

Hoyert, D. L., Kochanek, K. D., & Murphy, S. L. (1999). Deaths: Final data for 1997. *National Vital Statistics Reports, 47*(19):27-51.

Kuo, J., & K. Porter. (1998). *Health status of Asian Americans: United States, 1992–1994.* Advance Data No. 298. Hyattsville, MD: National Center for Health Statistics (U.S.).

Lord, G. M., Tagore, R., Cook, T., Gower, P., & Pusey, C. D. (1999). Nephropathy caused by Chinese herbs in the U.K. *The Lancet.* 354(9177):481-482.

Martin, J. A., Smith, B. L., Matthews, M. S., & Ventura, S. J. (1999). Births and deaths: Preliminary data for 1998. *National Vital Statistics Reports, 47*(25):1-25.

Marwick, C. (1998). Alterations are ahead at the OAM. *Journal of the American Medical Association. 280*(18):1553-1554.

Mortality patterns—United States, 1997. (1999). *Morbidity and Mortality Weekly Report, 48:*664-668.

Reed, J., & Ramirez R. R. (1998). The Hispanic population in the United States: March, 1998 (Update). *Current Population Reports.* Washington, DC: U.S. Bureau of the Census. http://www.census.gov.80/prod/3/98pubs/p20-51/.pdf

Richmond, J. B. (1999). Building the next generation of healthy people. *Public Health Reports, 114:*212-217.

Trends in HIV-related sexual risk behaviors among high school students: selected U.S. cities, 1991–1997. (1999). *Morbidity and Mortality Weekly Report, 48:*440-443.

Turner, J. A., Deyo, R. A., Loeser, J. D., Korff, M. V., & Fordyce, W. E. (1994). The importance of placebo effects in pain treatment and research. *Journal of the American Medical Association, 271:*1609-1614.

U.S. Bureau of the Census. (1999). *Blacks: Selected social characteristics of the population by sex, region, and race: March 1998.* Washington, DC: Government Printing Office.

U.S. Department of Health and Human Services (USDHHS), Office of Disease Prevention and Health Promotion. (1999). *Fact sheet: Healthy people in healthy communities.* Washington, DC: Government Printing Office. http://www.health.gov.healthypeople/

U.S. Department of Health and Human Services (USDHHS), Public Health Service. (1991). *Healthy people 2000: National health promotion and disease prevention objectives.* Washington, DC: Government Printing Office.

U.S. Department of Health and Human Services (USDHHS), Public Health Service. (1999). *Healthy people 2000 review, 1998–1999* (Publication 99-1256). Washington, DC: Government Printing Office. http://odphp.osophs.dhhs.gov/pubs/hp2000/prog_rvw.htm

Wilt, T. J., Ishani, A., Stark, G., MacDonald, R., Lau, J., & Mulrow, C. (1998). Saw palmetto extracts for treatment of benign prostatic hyperplasia: A systematic review. *Journal of the American Medical Association, 280:*1604-1609.

Wong, A. H. C., Smith, M., & Boon, H. S. (1998). Herbal remedies in psychiatric practice. *Archives of General Psychiatry, 55:*1033-1044.

World Health Organization (1948). *Official records of the World Health Organization, No. 2. Proceedings and final acts of the international health conference held in New York from 19 June to 22 July 1946.* New York: United Nations, WHO Interim Commission.

World Health Organization (WHO) (1986). *Ottawa Charter for Health Promotion.* Ottawa, Canada: World Health Organization. Retrieved December 16, 1999, from the World Wide Web: http://www.who.dk/policy/ottawa.htm

chapter 2

Psychological Health

Observing newborn infants in a hospital nursery is a fascinating experience. While some of the babies sleep peacefully, others are awake, calmly gazing around at their surroundings while sucking their thumbs or knuckles. A few of the newborns are restless; one tries to stretch her hand into the air as though she is reaching for something hanging above the bassinet. Another fussy baby frowns and closes his eyes tightly, before kicking his feet and howling in pain. Moments later, several of the other babies begin to grow fussy. Soon a chorus of crying babies shatters the calmness of the nursery. The infants' caretakers scurry around to each bassinet, trying to determine which infants are crying and the reasons why. Why do some newborns respond differently when all of them are in the same situation?

Each newborn is a unique person. All infants, however, have basic physical needs that must be met if they are to survive. Additionally, children have psychological needs that must be met if they are to mature into healthy adults. What if there were a crystal ball in the nursery that would enable you to predict each baby's future? Which of these

"Why do some newborns respond differently. . . ?"

infants will be psychologically healthy, achieving personal fulfillment and being satisfied with themselves and their lives? Which ones will be emotionally distressed and lead troubled lives?

Psychological (mental) health is dynamic, becoming more positive or negative as one responds to a constantly changing environment. Many individuals, however, manage to maintain high degrees of positive psychological functioning throughout their lives. People with positive mental health are able to deal effectively with the psychological challenges of life. Such people accept themselves, have realistic and optimistic outlooks on life, function independently, form satisfying interpersonal relationships, and cope effectively with change (see ▮ Table 2-1). In addition to these traits, psychologically healthy individuals resolve their problems without resorting to violence, and they assert themselves in social situations.

The quality of one's psychological health often affects the other components of health, such as social, spiritual, and physical health. This chapter discusses factors that

What You'll Learn

www.jbpub.com/healthyliving

The web site for this book offers many useful tools and is a great source for supplementary health information for both students and instructors. Visit the site at www.jbpub.com/healthyliving for information on these topics:

Adjustment and Growth
Understanding Mental Illness
Common Psychological Disorders
Suicide

Chapter Overview

How your nervous system affects your psychological health.

How biological, social, and cultural forces interact to mold your personality.

How psychological adjustment leads to psychological growth.

How to identify common psychological disorders.

How to recognize suicidal behavior and prevent suicide.

DIVERSITY *Health* Culture and Psychological Health

Con$umer *Health* Locating and Selecting Mental Health Therapists

Managing Your Health Resolving Interpersonal Conflicts Constructively

across the lifespan Psychological Health

Applying Concepts for Healthy Living
4 Workbook

Student Workbook

Self Assessment: The Self-Esteem Inventory
Changing Health Related Behaviors: Are You Ready to Improve Your Psychological Health?

Do You Know?

- If you are psychologically healthy?
- Why emotions are useful?
- How to resolve conflicts in a healthy manner?

Table 2-1 Characteristics of Psychologically Healthy People

Psychologically healthy people

- accept themselves and others.
- respond to changing situations with spontaneity.
- desire privacy.
- function independently.
- enjoy interpersonal relationships.
- display creative abilities.
- show appropriate emotional responses.
- are aware of reality.
- are concerned about the needs of others.
- have goals in life.

Source: Based on Maslow, A. H. (1970). *Motivation and personality* (2nd ed.). New York: Harper & Row.

influence positive psychological health as well as those that contribute to the development of psychological disorders. Chapter 3 examines the impact of psychological stress on health; Chapter 4 focuses on the effects of violence on health.

The Basics of Psychological Health

Understanding psychological health involves learning about **physiology**, the study of body functions, and **psychology**, the study of the mental processes that influence human behavior. Cognitive processes such as thinking, perceiving, remembering, and responding rely on the functioning of the nervous system. The nervous system is an elaborate biological communications network that contains billions of nerve cells, or neurons, which are designed to receive, send, and interpret messages in your body by means of electrical and chemical signals. As you can see in ▌ **Figure 2-1,** this network consists of two interrelated parts: the **central nervous system (CNS)**, the brain and spinal cord;

central nervous system (CNS) of the two primary divisions of the nervous system, the one that consists of brain and spinal cord.

peripheral nervous system (PNS) of the two primary divisions of the nervous system, the one that consists of nerves, which relay information to and from the CNS.

neurotransmitters chemicals produced and released by nerves that convey information between most nerve cells.

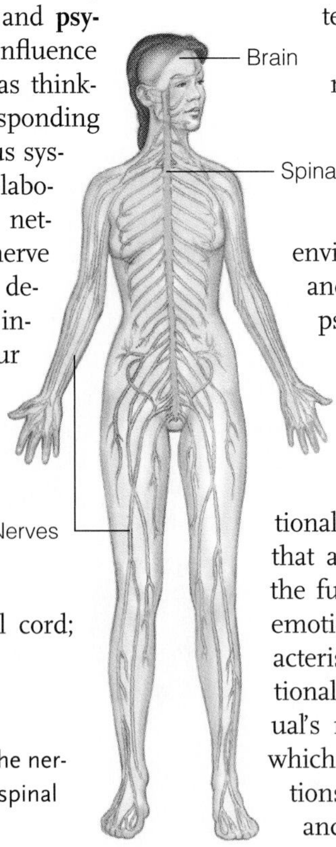

and the **peripheral nervous system (PNS)**, nerves that relay information to and from the CNS.

Most nerves produce and release **neurotransmitters**, chemicals such as acetylcholine, dopamine, and serotonin that convey information between nerve cells. By altering the levels of various neurotransmitters, the nervous system transmits information and produces physical responses, thoughts, and emotions. People use emotions to communicate their feelings to others. Furthermore, emotions often influence one's thoughts and actions.

The mind thinks about what takes place, finds meaning in events, considers actions, makes decisions, and plans for the future. Conditions that alter the normal chemistry of the brain can disrupt the mind, producing negative moods or abnormal behaviors. Today, many individuals with these conditions can feel and function well by taking medications that correct their abnormal brain chemistries.

Personality Development

Personality is a set of distinct thoughts and behaviors, including emotional responses, that characterizes the way a person responds to situations. Many factors, including biological, cultural, social, and psychological forces, interact to mold personality.

Biological Influences Heredity is the transmission of biological information, coded within genes, from parents to offspring. This information determines, in part, an individual's physical, emotional, and intellectual characteristics. Much of a person's **temperament**, the predictable way an individual responds to the environment, is inherited. Soon after birth, parents can usually describe their children's temperamental styles, such as irritable, fearful, or pleasant. As children mature, social and cultural influences modify their temperaments.

Social and Cultural Influences From the moment of birth, the social environment, such as interactions with parents and other family members, influences the psychological development of an individual. Most people learn how to respond to situations in socially and culturally acceptable ways when they are children. The circumstances surrounding a situation influence the kind and extent of an emotional display. Consider, for example, emotions that are appropriate to express while attending the funeral of a child. Showing the appropriate emotion in a particular social situation is a characteristic of an emotionally healthy adult. Additionally, cultural differences influence an individual's responses to situations and the extent to which one is comfortable showing certain emotions. The "Diversity in Health" essay "Culture and Psychological Health" examines how cul-

— Brain

— Spinal cord

Nerves

▶ **Figure 2-1 The Nervous System.** The nervous system consists of the brain, the spinal cord, and peripheral nerves.

DIVERSITY in Health | Culture and Psychological Health

Although symptoms may differ, mental illnesses affect individuals from every culture. Conventional mental-health practitioners have been taught to identify normal and abnormal behaviors and diagnose mental illness by using an established set of standards. Often, these experts do not consider the importance of culture when dealing with members of minority groups. For example, a Hopi child living in the Southwestern United States tells his parents that he has seen ancestral spirits. To this child's family and Hopi acquaintances, his ability to experience these visions is a wonderful gift, but to a physician who is unfamiliar with the Hopi culture, the child is having hallucinations and is mentally disturbed.

Native Americans recognize that some people behave abnormally and suffer from psychological disorders. According to some traditional Native American beliefs, the symptoms of mental illnesses result from supernatural forces exerting control over the person. In other

Native American traditions, the emotionally disturbed individual is in a state of disharmony with the rest of Nature or in a hopeless state of health. Spiritual health is linked closely to psychological health; therefore, prayers and religious ceremonies are often used as therapy. Elderly relatives, particularly caring grandmothers, play a psychotherapeutic role as traditional healers. In addition to relying on traditional healing methods, many Native Americans will accept conventional forms of treatment for mental-health problems.

Medical practitioners need to recognize the importance of cultural traditions before labeling the behavior of a Native American, or any individual, as abnormal. Furthermore, mental-health care providers often gain the trust and respect of clients from various cultural backgrounds by learning about traditional healing methods and accepting them as adjuncts to conventional psychotherapies.

▲ **Figure 2-A** Many Native Americans believe that spiritual health is linked to psychological health.

---

tural background can influence a person's perceptions of mental health.

Theories of Personality Development

Freud's Framework of Personality More than one hundred years ago, physician Sigmund Freud pioneered modern approaches to the diagnosis and treatment of psychological disturbances. Freud observed that people have an element of the mind that lacks awareness of certain thoughts, feelings, and impulses. He proposed that this "unconscious" component of the mind influences much of one's behavior. The unconscious mind, for example, engages various defense mechanisms such as repression and avoidance to cope with anxiety and guilt.

Defense mechanisms are ways of thinking and behaving that reduce or eliminate anxiety and guilty feelings by altering the individual's perception of reality. Nearly everyone uses defense mechanisms to protect their minds against psychological conflicts and threats. A basic defense mechanism is *repression,* the unconscious forgetting of anxiety-producing feelings, thoughts, or impulses. For example, adults who were sexually or physically abused as children may repress the memories of the abuse. Students who blame teachers for their lack of academic success, instead of themselves for skipping classes or not studying, may be using *projection* as a defense mechanism. ▌ **Table 2-2** lists repression, projection, and some other common defense mechanisms and describes instances in which the uncon-

scious mind employs them. Although these strategies may protect the mind and reduce anxiety in the short run, defense mechanisms usually do not provide long-term solutions to problems.

Freud believed that unconscious desires or drives, particularly the *libido,* or sex drive, control human behavior by creating psychological tension. Relieving this tension produces pleasurable sensations. However, members of society establish *moral values,* rules for good and bad behavior that often prevent individuals from satisfying all of their desires. If a person who accepts the moral values of society acts or thinks in ways that conflict with these rules, he or she usually feels anxious and guilty. Many people use moral values as guidelines to judge their behavior, themselves, and others.

Erikson's Psychosocial Stages of Development Erik Erikson (1964a, b) modified Freud's ideas by proposing that social influences play a greater role in shaping personalities than do sexual drives. According to Erikson, individuals progress

physiology the study of bodily functions.

psychology the study of the mental processes that influence human behavior.

personality a set of distinct thoughts and behaviors that characterizes a person's response to situations.

heredity the transmission of biological information, coded within genes, from parents to offspring.

temperament the predictable way an individual responds to situations and others, such as being pleasant, outgoing, or shy.

defense mechanisms ways of thinking and behaving that reduce or eliminate anxious and guilty feelings.

Table 2-2 Common Defense Mechanisms

Defense Mechanism	Behavior	Example
Repression	Blocking unpleasant thoughts, or feelings	A woman suppresses the memory of being sexually abused as a child.
Rationalization	Making up excuses for unpleasant behavior or situations that are false and self-serving	A man makes excuses for not being hired for a job.
Denial	Refusing to acknowledge unpleasant situations or feelings	A young man does not accept the fact he has been diagnosed with a terminal illness.
Projection	Attributing unacceptable thoughts, feelings, or urges to someone else	A woman accuses her boyfriend of being unfaithful while repressing her desire to have an affair.
Displacement	Redirecting a feeling or response toward a target that usually is less of a threat	An abused wife does not fight back, but mistreats her child instead.
Avoidance	Taking action to prevent situations that produce powerful feelings	A woman will not date because she is afraid of falling in love.
Regression	Reducing anxiety by acting immature to feel more secure	A 6-year-old child begins to suck its thumb after the birth of his baby brother.

Table 2-3 Erikson's Psychosocial Stages of Personality Development

Conflicts	Approximate Age Ranges
Trust vs. mistrust	Birth to 1 year
Autonomy vs. doubt and shame	1 to 3 years
Initiative vs. guilt	3 to 6 years
Industry vs. inferiority	6 to 12 years
Identity vs. identity confusion	12 to 18 years
Intimacy vs. isolation	Young adulthood
Generativity vs. stagnation	Middle age
Integrity vs. despair	Old age

through eight psychosocial stages during their lifetimes (Table 2-3). Each stage has major social crises or conflicts that people must manage or resolve to achieve a sense of emotional well-being.

Infants require a considerable amount of care and nurturing from adults to survive and to develop normally. Erikson thought that babies learn to *trust* other individuals if their parents or other caretakers meet their basic physical and emotional needs. Establishing trusting relationships with caring and loving adults enables infants to begin the process of developing high degrees of psychological well-being later in life.

Erikson viewed adolescence as a critical period in which youth develop a sense of *identity*. During this stage, adolescents become increasingly responsible for making their own decisions. They begin to function separately from their families and define who they are as well as what their future roles will be. According to Erikson, the three major areas of concern that adolescents must clarify relate to their future occupation, sexuality, and social conduct. Adolescents begin to establish their identities when they begin to clarify their feelings and positions about their roles in life. Identity confusion results when youth are unable to develop sound self-concepts and function independently of their families.

As adolescents mature into young adulthood, they face the challenge of *intimacy*, forming close and loving relationships with others. Adults who did not develop a sense of trust earlier in their lives or have not clarified their identities may be unable to establish intimate relationships and thus feel isolated. During middle age, individuals who have mastered previous developmental tasks focus on meeting the needs of others through activities such as raising families and performing community service. Erikson coined the term *generativity* to refer to these psychosocial tasks. In the final stage of life, people seek *integrity*, a feeling that their lives have been fulfilling and complete.

Maslow's Hierarchy of Human Needs According to Abraham Maslow (1962), individuals behave in response to their values rather than to their unconscious drives. Maslow thought that healthy people value the freedom to achieve personal fulfillment by developing their talents and competencies. This freedom becomes a psychological need that drives personality development. Maslow created a hierarchy of five human needs, from the most basic biological requirements that contribute to human survival to the one that is most essential for psychological fulfillment, *self-actualization* (█ Figure 2-2). To achieve self-actualization, each level of needs from the base to the top of the hierarchy must be met, in order.

▶ **Figure 2-2 Maslow's Hierarchy of Human Needs.** Maslow created a hierarchy of five human needs, from the basic biological survival requirements to psychological fulfillment; or self-actualization. Before achieving self-actualization, a person must satisfy each of the preceding needs.

Self-Actualization
A need for achievement and mastery

Esteem Needs
A need to have a high self-image

Love Needs
A need to give love and receive love

Safety Needs
The need for a secure environment in which one can live, work, and play

Physiological Needs
The most basic human needs are air, water, food, housing, sleep, and sexual activity

Self-actualized persons are psychologically healthy and mature. They feel free to pursue their creative and intellectual capabilities. The possibility of self-actualization exists in all people, but unless the prerequisite needs are met, individuals can never fully realize their potentials. According to Maslow and others, only about one person in a hundred will reach the top of the human needs hierarchy. Nevertheless, Maslow admitted that many people are satisfied with their lives even if they have not achieved self-actualization.

Healthy
▬▬▬ LIVING PRACTICES ▬▬▬

- Seek practical solutions to your problems rather than avoid them by using defense mechanisms.

Adjustment and Growth

Each day, individuals respond to the demands of other people, their physical environment, and themselves. Throughout life, these demands are changing constantly. Being in college is especially demanding, but consider how your life will change after you graduate. What do you think your life will be like 10, 20, or 30 years after graduation? What kinds of adaptations do you expect to make over your lifetime?

Adapting to change, which is called adjustment, involves the responses people make to cope with the demands of life. **Psychological adjustment** occurs when an individual learns that certain responses meet these demands more effectively than others. For example, one way a new student might psychologically adjust to college life is by scheduling time each week for various tasks, such as studying, attending classes, and going to work. Maintaining the new schedule may be challenging, particularly if the student followed a less structured lifestyle in the past.

Psychological growth occurs when a person discovers that certain adjustment strategies, such as studying more or planning for the future, enhances one's sense of freedom and control over oneself and the environment. To adjust in beneficial ways and to experience psychological growth, an individual needs to obtain reliable information, set realistic goals, plan effective ways to achieve those goals, take actions that are based on reasonable judgments and decisions, and evaluate the consequences of his or her choices.

If not managed effectively, interpersonal conflicts can hinder psychological adjustment and growth. Such conflicts often arise when people do not share the same opinions, values, needs, or beliefs. In these situations, many individuals respond by expressing anger or aggression. *Aggressive* reactions often injure other people physically or psychologically, therefore, these responses do not facilitate social interactions.

Assertiveness is a way of reacting to social situations by maintaining one's rights without interfering with the rights of other people and without harming them. Consider how students respond to an instructor who failed to consider certain possible answers to an essay question. An

psychological adjustment
changing one's thoughts, attitudes, and behaviors to cope effectively with the demands of the environment.

psychological growth
the process of learning from one's experiences.

Resolving Interpersonal Conflicts Constructively

In addition to compromise, consider using the following tips to resolve conflicts constructively:

1. Focus on one issue; state your perception of the problem as clearly as possible.
2. Consider the feelings of others; avoid criticizing, name-calling, threats, or sarcasm.
3. Use "I feel" statements. "You" statements make others defensive. For example, say "I feel angry when you . . ." instead of "You make me angry."
4. Do not assume how other people feel, what they believe, or how they will react.
5. Discuss the current concern; avoid dredging up past arguments.
6. Think before you speak; choose your words carefully to avoid confusion.
7. Listen carefully to others; avoid interrupting them while they talk.
8. Offer reasonable solutions.
9. Give others time to consider, accept, or reject your ideas.
10. Be patient; keep the door open for future communication.

aggressive student might take class time to argue a point, verbally lashing out at the teacher. An assertive student might arrange to meet with the instructor after class, using the time to discuss his or her case in a more thoughtful and rational manner.

Another way healthy people constructively resolve interpersonal conflicts is by using compromise. An individual who disagrees with a friend over an issue, for example, may decide that preserving the friendship is more valuable in the long run than "winning" the argument. This person is willing to compromise by modifying his or her attitudes. The "Managing Your Health" feature in this chapter provides additional suggestions for resolving conflicts constructively.

Psychological growth fosters the development of **autonomy,** or self-control. People with a high degree of autonomy function independently. Autonomy is associated with **self-esteem,** the extent to which a person feels worthy and useful.

Self-Esteem

Self-esteem is a key component of personality that influences one's thoughts, actions, and feelings. Positive self-esteem is a characteristic of psychologically healthy people. Individuals who have positive or high self-esteem have a high degree of autonomy, are self-confident, have self-respect, and are satisfied with themselves. These people work well with others, accept challenging tasks and responsibilities, seek supportive and loving relationships, and adjust easily to change. When they make mistakes, they accept responsibility for their actions without blaming others or making excuses. People with low self-esteem have difficulty making decisions, resist changing their behavior, and resent any form of criticism, even if it is constructive. These individuals tend to put down others to make themselves look or feel better. The Self-Esteem Inventory found in the workbook, can help you assess your present level of self-esteem.

People begin developing self-esteem early in childhood. Parents play a crucial role in determining their children's level of self-esteem. By interacting with parents and other family members, for example, young children learn that certain behaviors are good or bad. Children use this information to begin forming an impression of their *self-image,* the way they view themselves. Positive relationships between children and their caretakers are essential for the youngsters to become psychologically well-adjusted adults. Children with positive self-images have high self-esteem because they see themselves as being good, lovable, and possessing many worthwhile and valuable characteristics such as honesty and sensitivity.

When children enter school, their social environment enlarges to include more children, teachers, and other members of the community. These individuals provide new learning experiences that can have positive or negative impacts on the personality, self-image, and self-esteem of children. If a child who has a negative self-image enters school and has experiences that reinforce this perception, emotional disturbances can develop that persist into adulthood. With the help of others, children can develop positive self-concepts that establish the foundation for a lifetime of wellness. Parents and other adults help children feel good about themselves by spending time with them, listening to their concerns, and treating them with respect.

During adulthood, a variety of social factors including relationships and experiences at school, work, and home influence self-esteem. Relationships and experiences that are rewarding, enriching, and satisfying support positive self-esteem. In addition to having self-respect, people with a high degree of self-esteem gain the respect and approval of colleagues and others.

Self-esteem is a deep-rooted aspect of an individual. Although self-esteem may rise or fall over the course of a day, its basic nature remains fairly stable over longer periods. Individuals with persistent low self-esteem can improve their negative thoughts and feelings about themselves. By analyzing their situations, these people can determine factors that contribute to their poor self-concepts. For example, working in a dull job or remaining in an abusive relationship can affect self-esteem negatively. In these instances, people may improve their situations and feelings of self-worth by finding new jobs or ending the self-destructive relationships.

To feel better about themselves, persons with low self-esteem can learn to identify and appreciate their positive traits and abilities, instead of focusing on their negative characteristics and shortcomings. It can also help if the individual recognizes that not all criticism is destructive and insensitive. Accepting constructive criticism can support personal growth. Making a few lifestyle changes such as developing new interests, changing some bad habits, or taking an assertiveness training class can improve one's psychological outlook. To overcome low self-esteem, psychological counseling may be necessary to help individuals develop the ability to evaluate themselves realistically and form accurate self-perceptions.

Improving Your Psychological Health

What can you do to improve your psychological health? You can enhance the quality of your mental health primarily by improving the other dimensions of your health. Exercising regularly can boost your mood (Artal, 1998). Getting enough sleep, eating a nutritious diet, and maintaining a healthy weight for your height also enhance psychological health by improving physical health. In addition to taking good care of your physical needs, fostering positive social contacts, whether with family, friends, or colleagues, is very important. Everyone needs to communicate with other persons on a regular basis. For example, one goal to improve your psychological health could be to make and maintain at least one new social contact each year. You can improve your intellectual health by reading challenging books, playing stimulating games such as crossword puzzles or chess, or serving as a tutor. Some people find that keeping a journal or diary in which they record their most private feelings helps them cope with daily life. Attending to your spiritual needs can provide personal fulfillment also. For example, you can volunteer to serve as a mentor for troubled children or become involved in your religious organization. Finally, taking an active role in ensuring and protecting the quality of your environment will support all dimensions of your health.

Healthy
LIVING PRACTICES

- To experience psychological adjustment and growth, set realistic goals, plan effective ways to achieve those goals, take actions that are based on reasonable judgments and decisions, and evaluate the consequences of your choices.
- To facilitate your psychological adjustment, learn ways to manage interpersonal conflicts constructively, without being aggressive. When such conflicts arise, decide when it is best to compromise or assert your position.
- To improve your self-esteem, avoid making negative statements about yourself. Identify and be realistic about your strengths and weaknesses; focus on your accomplishments and positive characteristics.
- To improve your psychological health, take steps to improve the quality of the other dimensions of health.

www.jbpub.com/healthyliving

Understanding Mental Illness

Having "the blues," feeling "scared to death," or being "worried sick"—perhaps you can recall situations in which you experienced these strong emotions or uncomfortable sensations. Occasionally, healthy people have disturbing thoughts, experience unpleasant feelings, or display inappropriate behaviors. In most instances, these are normal responses and adaptive reactions to unpleasant or threatening situations. For example, it is normal to be sad after learning about the death of a friend or to be afraid when a snake crosses your path.

The observable physical and behavioral changes that signal an emotional state are referred to as **affect**, or mood. Expressing emotions appropriately is a characteristic of a psychologically healthy individual; extreme or improper emotional responses can indicate a serious psychological disturbance. The key features that distinguish any normal emotional response from an abnormal one are the *intensity* and *duration* of the feelings. Mentally ill individuals experience abnormal feelings, thoughts, and behaviors that persist, interfere with daily life, and hinder psychological adjustment and growth.

A *psychotic* individual has disorganized thoughts and unreal perceptions that result in strange behavior, social isolation, delusions, and hallucinations. **Delusions** are inaccurate and unreasonable beliefs that often result in

autonomy sense of independence and self-control.

self-esteem the extent to which a person feels worthy and useful.

affect observable expressions of mood.

delusions inaccurate and unreasonable beliefs that often result in decision-making errors.

decision-making errors. For example, a person suffering from a delusion might think that he or she can fly, so this individual jumps off a tall building. **Hallucinations** are false sensory perceptions that have no apparent external cause, but they are real to the psychotic individual. Examples of hallucinations include hearing instructions from pictures, seeing ghostly images, or feeling insects crawling underneath skin. Psychotic conditions can be acute or chronic; they result from brain damage, chemical imbalances in the brain, or substance abuse.

Situations and cultures provide the context in which behaviors are judged as normal or abnormal. If a person who is living in a country torn apart by civil war bombs a crowded marketplace, people may view this individual as a terrorist or a hero, but not necessarily mentally ill. However, if this bombing occurs in an American shopping mall, and the bomber says that a dog gave the order to perform the deed, you might suspect that this person is psychotic. Only a small percentage of psychotic persons become violent, and they are most likely to attack family members or other individuals who set limits on their behavior (Binder, 1999).

hallucinations
false sensory perceptions that have no apparent external cause.

The Impact of Mental Illness

Why is it important to learn about mental illness? Mental illness affects members of most American families. About 1 in 5 Americans experience some form of mental illness during their lifetime (USDHHS, 1999). According to data from the National Comorbidity Survey (Kessler et al., 1994), depression and alcohol dependence are the most common psychological disturbances that affect Americans (Table 2-4). Depression is becoming recognized as a major cause of poor health throughout the world (Doris et al., 1999).

The emotional and economic costs of mental illness are high not only for affected individuals and their families but also for society. People may drop out of college or abuse alcohol and other drugs because of unresolved emotional problems or underlying mental illnesses. Mental illness frequently has a negative impact on the quality of life and the productivity of workers.

In the past, mentally ill individuals were often misunderstood and mistreated. Having a mental illness was considered disgraceful by people who associated the condition with bizarre behaviors, violent acts, and long stays in mental-health care facilities. Today, being diagnosed with a mental illness is no longer a hopeless situation, because scientists are understanding more about the various biological and social factors that influence behaviors. Nevertheless, these disorders do not receive the kind of interest and concern from public health officials that conditions such as heart disease, cancer, and stroke generate. Why? Richard Neugebauer (1999), thinks mental illnesses do not get much attention because of the stigma associated with them and the lack of major risk factors that can be modified to prevent them.

Although mental health disorders are common and can be quite disabling, many of these conditions can be managed effectively with medications and other forms of therapy. According to the *Healthy People 2000* progress report (USDHHS, 1999), in 1993 about 14% of Americans 18 years of age and older sought help for their emotional problems; in 1995, that number increased to almost 19%. The target for the year 2000 was to increase to at least 20% the proportion of American adults who seek such help. Because negative attitudes toward mental illness persist, many psychologically disturbed people are reluctant to seek beneficial therapy; they live in misery, hiding their illness from others. Seeking professional help for psychological problems is a sign of personal strength, not weakness.

What Causes Psychological Disorders?

There are numerous psychological disorders, and in each case, it may be impossible to determine a single cause. Alterations in the normal chemical and physical environment of the brain often produce mental illness. In many instances, these alterations are the result of genetic defects that adversely affect neurotransmitter levels. Additionally, people whose brains have been physically damaged by injuries, tumors, or infections often display abnormal behavior. When introduced into the body, drugs such as cocaine can interfere with the brain's ability to produce, use, or

Table 2-4	Lifetime Prevalence of Mental Health Disorders	
Disorder		**Percentage of Americans Affected***
Any mood disorder		19.3
Major depressive episode		17.1
Any anxiety disorder		24.9
Panic disorder		3.5
Simple phobia		11.3
Social phobia		13.3
Generalized anxiety disorder		5.1
Any substance abuse/dependence		26.6
Alcohol dependence		14.1
Drug dependence other than alcohol		7.5
Any mental health disorder		48.0

*Many individuals reported suffering from more than one disorder.
Source: Based on Kessler, R. C., et al. (1994). Lifetime and 12-month prevalence of *DSM-III-R* psychiatric disorders in the United States: Results from the National Comorbidity Survey. *Archives of General Psychiatry*, 51:8-19.

eliminate neurotransmitters. Furthermore, pollutants such as pesticides and toxic minerals such as lead, mercury, and arsenic can damage the brain.

Scientists note that certain mental illnesses such as schizophrenia and most major mood disorders tend to occur within the same family. These observations support the role of inheritance in their development. Genetic factors alone, however, do not explain the development of every psychological disorder. Several members of a family could develop similar forms of mental illness because they are more likely to experience the same physical, economic, and social environments than unrelated individuals.

Environmental conditions influence the expression of many inborn traits, including psychological responses. Children, for example, often learn ways of reacting to situations by observing their parents. Think about how you respond when angered or frustrated. Are your responses like those of your mother or father?

Personal experiences can trigger the onset and influence the severity of some psychological disturbances. Some experts think that a child's brain can be altered by exposure to extremely stressful situations, increasing the youngster's risk of developing depression later in life. Even psychologically healthy individuals can develop *post-traumatic stress disorder,* a severe anxiety disorder, after surviving life-threatening experiences (■ **Figure 2-3**). Researchers have yet to understand completely the extent to which biological and environmental factors interact to influence psychological health.

Treating Mental Illness

Many people with mental illness respond well to treatment. Treating psychological disorders involves the cooperation of the affected individuals and their families and the assistance of mental health therapists who have had

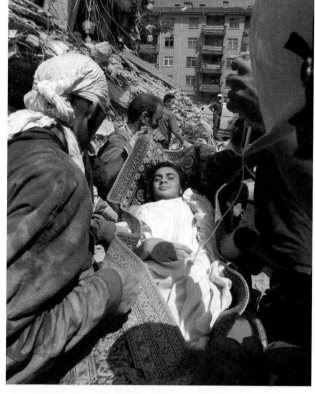

▲**Figure 2-3 Surviving a Disaster.** After surviving life-threatening situations, such as an earthquake, individuals can develop post-traumatic stress disorder.

specialized training. ■ **Table 2-5** lists the major types of mental health therapists and some information concerning their qualifications. These individuals often use medications, behavior therapy, group therapy, and psychother-

Locating and Selecting Mental Health Therapists

The following tips can help you find and select qualified mental health specialists:

- Discuss psychological health concerns with your general medical practitioner or with medical staff at your student health center. These individuals can assess your health and refer you to qualified mental health specialists if necessary.

- Contact local mental health associations or agencies for information about psychological health. Members of these associations can give you information about local support groups and mental health services.
- Contact your state's social welfare department or the social services de-

partment of a local hospital to identify qualified therapists.
- Interview therapists before making any agreements for services.
- Ask therapists about treatment philosophies, methods, insurance coverage, and payment expectations before agreeing to use their services.

apy in the treatment of emotional disturbances. ▌ **Table 2-6** lists some medications that are commonly prescribed to treat various psychological disorders. More than one form of treatment may be necessary to alleviate or control the disorder. In severe cases, psychologically disturbed people require hospitalization.

Many people learn to cope with various problems such as drug addictions or the loss of loved ones by joining *support groups*. The support group is an informal approach to treatment. Support group participants have regular meetings in which they discuss personal adjustment problems. Group members, rather than mental health therapists, usually conduct these meetings. In addition to attending regular meetings, some group members need professional mental health counseling.

Mental health therapists have a variety of effective treatments that enable many psychologically ill people to remain in their communities and lead normal lives. If you or someone you know needs mental health care, the Consumer Health feature "Locating and Selecting Mental Health Therapists" provides suggestions for finding and choosing qualified help.

Healthy ▌LIVING PRACTICES▌

- Many mental illnesses respond well to treatment. If you think you may have a psychological problem, ask your personal health care practitioner or the medical staff at your campus health center for help.

www.jbpub.com/healthyliving

Common Psychological Disorders

Anxiety Disorders

Do you feel uneasy when you ride in an elevator, enter a classroom to take a test, or give a speech? Nearly everyone experiences anxiety, the uncomfortable feelings of appre-

Table 2-5	Major Types of Mental Health Therapists
Therapist	**Training and Degrees**
Counseling and Clinical Psychologists	M.A., Ph.D., or Psy.D. in psychology; 5 or more years in psychotherapy methods, research, and assessment
Psychiatrists	Medical (M.D. or O.D.) degree and at least 3 years of specialized training in psychiatry
Psychoanalysts	Have undergone personal psychoanalysis and completed 7 to 10 years of part-time psychoanalytic training (most are psychiatrists)
Psychiatric Social Workers	MSW; most states require certification by the Academy of Certified Social Workers
Clinical Mental Health Counselors	Master's degree (or equivalent) and 2 years of counseling experience; certified by National Academy of Certified Clinical Mental Health Counselors
Psychiatric Nurse Practitioners	Registered nurses with additional education and experience working in psychiatric settings
Marital and Family Therapists	Master's degree. Licensed or certified in about one-half of the states; member of the American Association for Marriage and Family Therapy
Sexual Therapists	Minimum of a master's degree, a license in related field, specialized sex education and sex-therapist training, extensive supervised individual and group therapy experience; the American Association of Sex Educators, Counselors and Therapists provides certification
Abuse Counselors	Substance abuse training; often counselors are recovering substance abusers
Clergy	Religious training; may have spiritual and family counseling training

Source: Cornacchia, H. J., & Barrett, S. (1993). *Consumer health.* St. Louis: Mosby.

Table 2-6 Medications Frequently Prescribed for Psychological Disorders

Type of Medication	Medications (brand names)	Disorders
Antianxiety	Xanax, Librium, Paxil, Buspar, Ativan, Serax, Valium	Anxiety, obsessive-compulsive, psychosomatic disorder
Antidepressants	Elavil, Prozac, Zoloft, Luvox, Wellbutrin, Effexor, Serzone	Depression, eating disorders, obsessive-compulsive disorder (Prozac & Luvox)
Lithium	Eskalith, Lithane	Certain types of depression, especially bipolar disorder
Antipsychotics	Thorazine, Haldol, Prolixin, Zyprexa, Seroquel	Schizophrenia
Non-amphetamine stimulants	Ritalin	Attention deficit disorders

hension or uneasiness that result while expecting a vague threat. The physical changes associated with anxiety states include increased heart rate, rapid breathing, and elevated blood pressure. Anxious people may report feeling tense, distressed, or worried; and they may be emotionally upset, sweating, and trembling. Anxiety disorders are common; according to the results of the National Comorbidity Survey, nearly one in four Americans suffers from these conditions at some time in their lives (Kessler et al., 1994).

Generalized Anxiety Disorder When you perceive a threat, it is normal to feel mildly anxious as your body physically prepares to deal with the danger. However, if the anxiety interferes with your ability to perform daily activities, the condition is abnormal. During their lifetimes, as much as 5% of the population suffers from **generalized anxiety disorder**, a condition characterized by uncontrollable chronic worrying, anxiousness, and nervousness. People with this disorder have unrealistic and excessive concerns about their jobs, children, health, or minor situations such as making home repairs. They are tense, irritable, and restless, and they often experience sleeping problems. Treatment usually includes antianxiety and antidepressant medications as well as psychotherapy.

Phobias A **phobia** is an intense and irrational fear of a situation or object. *Agoraphobia* is the fear of open places or public areas. *Social phobias* are fears of performing in situations that involve people, such as giving speeches or taking tests (Leaman, 1999). *Specific phobias* (formerly called simple phobias) are fears of certain animals or situations such as snakes or flying. According to the results of the National Comorbidity Survey, phobias are among the most common psychological disturbances in the United States (Kessler et al., 1994). About 13% of Americans report having social phobias, and about 11% of Americans report experiencing specific phobias. It is not uncommon for a person to be affected by more than one phobia. Although people who suffer from phobias know that their behavior is irrational, they still become anxious in the situations that arouse their fears (**Figure 2-4**).

Most cases of phobia are mild; affected individuals often learn to live with their phobias by avoiding situations that arouse the anxiety. Severe phobias can interfere with normal social functioning. For example, people with agoraphobia may refuse to leave their homes. Individuals who are severely affected by phobias can seek professional treatment that includes behavioral therapy and medications to control irrational feelings and reduce anxiety.

Panic Disorders An estimated 3 million Americans suffer from **panic disorders** that feature *panic attacks,* unpredictable episodes of extreme anxiety and loss of emotional control. During a panic attack, people usually experience shortness of breath, shakiness, faintness, nausea, and a rapid, pounding heartbeat. Affected individuals often feel terrified because they think they are becoming insane or having a heart attack. Severe phobias, certain drugs, or frightening experiences may trigger panic attacks, but they can occur spontaneously.

Therapists combine behavioral therapy, psychotherapy, and medications to treat panic disorders. People who have frequent panic attacks should seek medical help because studies indicate that they are at risk of committing suicide.

generalized anxiety disorder a condition characterized by uncontrollable chronic worrying and nervousness.

phobia an intense and irrational fear of an object or a situation.

panic disorder psychological condition that features panic attacks, unpredictable episodes of extreme anxiety, and loss of emotional control.

▲**Figure 2-4 Phobias.** Phobias are intense and irrational fears of certain situations or objects that can interfere with everyday functioning. This woman has a fear of heights.

Post-Traumatic Stress Disorder Individuals who survive extraordinary life events such as a sexual assault, natural disaster, or combat, may develop *post-traumatic stress disorder (PTSD)*. People can suffer from PTSD even after automobile accidents. Symptoms of PTSD may take months to develop fully and include being unable to feel emotions or having disturbing recollections or nightmares of the event. Affected persons often avoid thinking about or discussing the traumatic experiences, and they may abuse drugs as a way of coping. Treatment of PTSD usually includes medications to relieve anxiety.

Obsessive-Compulsive Disorder Although the experts disagree, *obsessive-compulsive disorder (OCD)* is generally classified as an anxiety disorder. An **obsession** is a persistent, inappropriate, and repetitive thought or impulse that produces anxious feelings. Obsessions are often related to self-doubt or fears of becoming contaminated. A **compulsion** is the behavior that usually follows the obsessive thoughts or impulses. Compulsive behaviors reduce the obsessed individual's anxiety. A young person, for example, might have recurring thoughts of injuring a family member. This individual may wash his or her hands hundreds of times a day and take numerous long showers to reduce anxious feelings. Other typical compulsive behaviors include hoarding useless items like plastic containers or making repetitive actions such as checking the oven frequently to see if it is turned off. Affected individuals often think that their obsessions

obsession a repetitive thought that produces anxious feelings.

compulsion the behavior that follows obsessive thoughts and reduces anxiety.

anorexia nervosa a severe psychological disturbance in which an individual refuses to eat enough food to maintain normal weight.

and compulsions are repulsive or troublesome, but efforts to stop create more anxiety. Treatment includes medication and psychotherapy. In most cases, the longer the obsessive-compulsive behavior pattern has been in place, the more difficult the disorder is to treat.

Unclassified Impulse Control Disorders

Some psychologists consider problem gambling, promiscuous sexual activity, and certain eating disorders to be subtypes of obsessive-compulsive disorder. These activities, however, are distinguished from true compulsions because the affected person enjoys the activity, at least until the persistent behavior interferes with his or her well-being, relationships, or job (Hollander et al., 1999).

Nearly every state now permits some form of gambling. As opportunities for adults to gamble legally became more widespread during the past 10 years, the prevalence of "problem" or *impulsive gambling* increased. Gambling among young people, especially high school and college student males, is increasing (Langewisch & Frisch, 1998). An estimated 2 million Americans are problem gamblers (National Academy of Sciences, 1999). Impulsive gambling often accompanies other risky behaviors, such as substance abuse. Gamblers Anonymous is a self-help group that can help problem gamblers control their behavior, but many affected individuals do not remain in treatment (Wise & Tierney, 1999). ▌ **Table 2-7** lists typical features of problem gamblers.

Table 2-7	Typical Features of Problem Gambling

The problem gambler
- seems to think only about gambling or how to get money to gamble.
- loses friends, family members, and jobs because of his or her behavior.
- gambles more often over time.
- has no control over the impulse to gamble.
- becomes restless, angry, or agitated when he or she tries to gamble less often (withdrawal).
- gambles to escape problems or cope with depression, guilt, or anxiety.
- gambles again, trying to recover losses.
- lies to cover up the behavior.
- has others financially bail him or her out.
- resorts to illegal acts, such as forging checks and stealing money, to obtain money for gambling.
- abuses mind-altering drugs.

Eating Disorders

Bulimia nervosa, anorexia nervosa, and binge eating disorder affect an estimated 5 million Americans each year (Becket et al., 1999). These conditions are more common among females than males; an estimated 3% of young women have an eating disorder. Although usually considered nutritional problems, eating disorders are often symptoms of low self-esteem and psychological disturbances including mood and obsessive-compulsive disorders (Fairburn et al., 1999). Treating the underlying psychological problems may reduce the frequency of the abnormal eating behavior, but many people with severe eating disorders do not respond to treatment.

Hormonal, genetic, sociocultural, and psychological factors influence the development of eating disorders. While it is true that excess body fat is not healthy, a society that emphasizes thinness makes many young women overly concerned about their body shape and dissatisfied with their body size, even when it is normal. As a result of societal influences, many American girls admire the bodies of fashion models, actresses, and ballet dancers who look as though they are starving. Female athletes are especially at risk for developing these conditions (▮ Figure 2-5). The results of several studies indicate that 15% to 62% of female athletes suffer from eating disorders (Tofler et al., 1996).

In the United States, many men experience social pressure to attain muscular rather than thin body builds. This may explain why eating disorders are more prevalent among American women than among men. It is interesting to note that eating disorders are uncommon in regions of the world where the food supply is limited and starvation is an everyday occurrence.

Anorexia Nervosa Occasionally nearly everyone has *anorexia,* appetite loss that can occur under various circumstances such as excitement or fever. **Anorexia nervosa,** however, is a severe psychological disturbance in which an individual refuses to eat enough food to maintain a normal body weight. People with anorexia nervosa *(anorexics)* have an irrational fear of becoming fat, maintain strict control over food intake, and are preoccupied with calorie counting and food preparation. About 90% of the cases involve women, particularly teenage girls.

People with anorexia nervosa have a distorted image of their bodies. They deny that they are severely underweight even though they weigh 15% or more below normal for their height. Typically, women with the condition lose their normal menstrual cycles and feminine body contours. Without an adequate supply of fat to insulate their bodies against heat loss, people with anorexia feel cold easily and often wear layers of clothing to provide extra warmth.

Many people who suffer from anorexia nervosa occasionally lose control over their food intake, eating excessive

▲ **Figure 2-5 Gymnast Christy Henrich: A Fatal Case of Eating Disorders.** Female athletes, particularly gymnasts, are at risk for developing eating disorders such as anorexia nervosa. In 1994, World Class gymnast, Christy Henrich, was only 22 years old when she died as a result of anorexia and bulimia nervosa.

amounts of food *(bingeing)*. To avoid gaining weight, these individuals induce vomiting or abuse laxatives *(purging)*. Additionally, people with this condition often exercise excessively to "burn up" calories. ▮ **Table 2-8** lists these and other typical signs of anorexia nervosa.

About one in a hundred adolescent females develops anorexia nervosa, usually while in high school; only about half of the people with this condition will recover completely (Becker et al., 1999). Treatment for anorexia nervosa includes individual and family counseling; patients must reach about 85% of their normal body weight before antidepressant therapy is useful. In severe cases, people with anorexia nervosa die unless they are given special feedings and monitored closely in hospitals. Death from suicide or the self-imposed starvation occurs in as many as 15% to 20% of cases. The people with anorexia nervosa who survive often continue to maintain their low body weights, practicing their unusual eating and physical activity habits into adulthood.

Table 2-8 Typical Signs of Anorexia Nervosa

In addition to refusing to gain weight despite weighing 15% or more below that which is healthy, a person who has anorexia nervosa typically

- has an intense drive to achieve a thin body.
- seems unaware that body size has changed.
- denies malnourished appearance.
- derives little satisfaction from his or her body shape.
- fears losing control over appetite.
- becomes full after eating small amounts of food.
- is a "picky" eater; avoids foods that contain fat, starch, or sugar.
- exercises excessively.
- lacks menstrual periods (females).
- is depressed.
- has low self-esteem.
- has perfectionist tendencies.

Source: Based on Garfinkel, P. (1992). *Classification and diagnosis.* In K. A. Halmi (Ed.), *Psychobiology and treatment of anorexia nervosa and bulimia nervosa.* Washington, DC: American Psychiatric Press.

Bulimia Nervosa While people with anorexia nervosa are so thin they are easy to identify, those with bulimia nervosa may be more difficult to recognize because their weights are often normal. **Bulimia** is a craving for food that is difficult to satisfy; bulimic people typically eat excessive amounts of food at one time because they are depressed or anxious rather than hungry. Some bulimic persons are able to maintain normal body weights because after bingeing, they purge by fasting, practicing self-induced vomiting, taking laxatives and diuretics, or exercising. Vomiting prevents the body from absorbing and using the nutrients in food and beverages. Laxatives speed up the movement of the intestinal tract and can lead to watery diarrhea; diuretics increase urine production and elimination. Vomiting and abusing laxatives and diuretics can seriously disrupt the body's normal fluid and chemical balance, which can be life threatening.

Occasional episodes of bulimic behavior are common among young women who are trying to control their weight. It is estimated that about 2% of adolescent and young adult women suffer from bulimia nervosa. In a survey of college students in the United States, 4.2% of females and less than 1% of males reported to have either vomited or taken laxatives to avoid gaining weight during the 30 days preceding the survey ("Youth Risk," 1997).

Many young women, especially on college campuses, accept and openly practice bingeing and purging. Other bulimic individuals are disgusted with their disordered eating behavior, hiding it from roommates, friends, and family members. Some people practice bingeing and purging twice a week; in severe cases, affected individuals engage in these behaviors several times a day. Severely bulimic people can become so preoccupied with eating that they shoplift food to supply their binges and experience legal problems as a consequence. College students with bulimia frequently encounter academic problems after they neglect to attend their classes.

An estimated 40% of binge eaters are boys or men (Becker et al., 1999). Men, for example, may be affected by bulimia nervosa if they regularly consume too much food or excessive amounts of alcohol and then vomit afterwards. Furthermore, some young men who participate in sports that require maintaining low weight such as wrestling and gymnastics practice the behaviors associated with bulimia nervosa to remain competitive.

Typically bulimic individuals are more socially outgoing than girls with anorexia nervosa, but they experience low self-esteem, anxiety, and depression; eating temporarily relieves their anxiety. Although antidepressant medications and psychotherapy are useful treatments, people with bulimia nervosa often do not seek help for their behavior. Affected women tend to improve over time, but 10 years following diagnosis, about 30% still suffer from the condition (Keel et al., 1999). Childhood sexual abuse is a risk factor for bulimia nervosa (Wonderlich et al., 1996).

Binge Eating Disorder About one-third of overweight people engage in regular episodes of binge eating that are rarely followed up with purging or heavy exercise. This behavior is called **binge eating disorder.** Some binge eaters report *blackouts,* periods of time that they cannot recall when they had overeating episodes, but empty food containers provide them with evidence of the incidents. Like persons with bulimia nervosa, binge eaters have poor self-esteem, and they often feel disgusted, depressed, and guilty about their eating behavior and physical appearance. These feelings may trigger additional episodes of overeating. *Night eating syndrome,* which is more common among obese than normal weight persons, may be a variation of binge eating disorder. People with night eating syndrome are not hungry during the day, but have difficulty staying asleep at night; they awake often and frequently get out of bed to eat large amounts of food (Birketvedt et al., 1999).

If you or someone you know suffers from an eating disorder such as bulimia nervosa or binge eating, ask the staff at your campus health center or your personal physician to recommend mental health practitioners who specialize in treating these conditions. Additionally, check hospitals in your area because many have self-help groups for people with eating disorders.

Mood Disorders

Until a few years ago, the two words that best described my life were fear *and* loneliness. *As a child, I experienced physical, emotional, and verbal abuse from my parents. There were some instances when the beatings were so severe, I just forgot about them. I married a man who also physically abused me. Having no savings or college degree, I lacked the self-confidence to walk out of the marriage. I felt trapped. Deep depression set in; I cried a lot of the time and felt guilty because I was unable to carry out the normal daily responsibilities of cooking and cleaning the house. I began to think suicidal thoughts.*

Finally, I entered a hospital that had a stress unit. Between the group sessions and private therapy, I learned a lot about those who abuse others and how to handle stress. However, spending three weeks in the hospital did not cure my depression. I realized that the only thing that would do that would be to remove myself from its cause. I separated from my husband and started college.

It has been a struggle financially, but I am determined to make it. I am preparing to graduate this semester with a Bachelor of Arts degree, and I plan to continue on to get a Master of Arts degree. The best change is my new self-confidence gained from overcoming the obstacles and becoming independent.

This middle-aged college student's case not only illustrates the harsh origins of her depression, but also how an emotionally resilient person can recover from depression, resolve problems, and regain self-esteem. How can you distinguish a normal period of sadness from one that signals a major depressive disorder?

It is normal for people to feel "down" after a loss or disappointment. After a significant loss, such as the death of a close friend or relative, one normally feels *grief,* an intense sadness that may persist up to a year after the loss. Most grieving individuals soon recover their emotional balance and resume their usual activities. Grieving people are probably severely depressed if they become so profoundly sad that they withdraw and isolate themselves for several months and harbor feelings of guilt, low self-worth, and suicide. Enduring other stressful experiences can trigger the first episode of depression in susceptible persons.

Major depressive disorder is a mood disorder characterized by persistent and profound sadness, hopelessness, helplessness, and feelings of worthlessness. Depressed people often report a lack of energy, the loss of interest in usual activities, the inability to concentrate on tasks, and appetite disturbances. Insomnia is a common complaint of depressed individuals; the most reliable sign of early depression is waking up too early in the morning (Rakel, 1999). Depressed people may be anxious and irritable, and they often use alcohol or illegal drugs to alter their emotional state. An estimated 15% of severely depressed people commit suicide (American Psychiatric Association, 1994).

Nearly one in five Americans experiences a major depressive disorder during his or her lifetime (Kessler et al., 1994). Physicians, however, often fail to diagnose the condition in their patients. As a result, about half of the individuals who suffer from depression do not obtain treatment (Gelenberg, 1999). Although a small percentage of these untreated persons recover spontaneously and never experience another bout with the disorder, the remaining untreated individuals suffer from chronic depression or recurrent episodes of depression (Citrome, 1994; Glass, 1999).

Depression is a treatable disorder. Currently, many severely and chronically depressed people can obtain dramatic relief from their disabling symptoms by receiving psychotherapies that include prescribed antidepressant medications (Gelenberg, 1999). Alternative remedies for depression are becoming popular in the United States. The herb St. John's wort may be helpful as a treatment for mild to moderate depression (Walter & Rey, 1999). SAMe, a compound that is made in the body and sold as a dietary supplement, has antidepressant properties also (Fugh-Berman & Cott, 1999). St. John's wort and SAMe have been reported to cause side effects, so one should not take these substances without consulting his or her physician.

Some severely depressed people feel better by engaging in regular physical activity. According to the Surgeon General's report on physical activity and health (Centers for Disease Control and Prevention [CDC], 1996), a moderate amount of physical activity each day may reduce symptoms of anxiety and depression and improve mood and sense of well being.

bulimia an eating disorder characterized by a craving for food that is difficult to satisfy.

binge eating disorder a pattern of eating excessive amounts of food in response to distress such as anxiety or depression.

major depressive disorder a mood disorder characterized by persistent and profound sadness, hopelessness, helplessness, and feelings of worthlessness; lack of energy; loss of interest in usual activities; loss of the ability to concentrate; suicidal thoughts; and appetite and sleep disturbances.

Healthy LIVING PRACTICES

If you or someone you know has an eating or other psychological disorder, seek help from the medical staff at the campus health center or from your personal health-care provider.

ANALYZING *Health-Related Information*

The following ad promotes a series of compact discs designed to improve the functioning of the mind. Read the advertisement and evaluate it using the model for analyzing health-related information. The main points of the model are noted below; the model is fully explained on pages 12 to 13.

1. Which statements are verifiable facts, which are unverified statements or value claims?
2. What are the credentials of the person who wrote the ad? Does the author appear to have appropriate background and education in the topic area? If it is difficult to tell if the author has specific health expertise, what can you do to check his/her credentials?
3. What might be the motives and biases of the author?
4. What is the main point of the ad? Which information in the ad is relevant to the product? Which information is irrelevant?
5. Is the source reliable? Does it have a reputation for publishing misinformation? Does the ad present both the pros and cons of this product?
6. Does the ad attack the credibility of conventional scientists or medical authorities?

Based on the above analysis, do you think that this ad is a reliable source of health-related information? Explain why you would or would not buy the audiocassettes. Summarize your reasons for coming to this conclusion.

ADVERTISEMENT ADVERTISEMENT ADVERTISEMENT ADVERTISEMENT ADVERTISEMENT

Can't seem to learn new tricks? Getting forgetful? Having memory lapses?

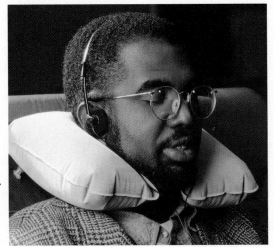

As you age, mental functioning declines. Before you know it, you can't seem to follow even the simplest instructions, you can't remember your children's names, and you can't keep your mind from wandering when you should be paying attention.

"How can I ever thank you? I've tried three other neurotechnology products, but BRAINFIT was the only one that worked."

B. J., London, England

"Please send another copy of the miraculous BRAINFIT CD— my sister took mine and won't return it!"

S. A., New Delhi, India

Fortunately, you can learn how to prevent your mind from slipping away from you. Now you can benefit from the latest discovery in subliminal microtechnology that produces phenomenal advances in brain functioning. Scientists from around the world are predicting that this incredible breakthrough will be the greatest medical discovery of the 21st century!

Our amazing new **BRAINFIT CD** can increase your mental capacity without the need for potentially harmful drugs. Listening to the CD has been scientifically proven to improve learning by up to 35%, enhance memory by up to 28%, and boost awareness by up to 55%. Millions of people in 60 countries report that **BRAINFIT** really works!

For the first time, **BRAINFIT** is available in the United States. Order your copy now. We guarantee that BRAINFIT will improve your mental functioning. **BRAINFIT** is easy to use at home, work, or even as you drive your car!

FOR YOUR PERSONALIZED COPY OF BRAINFIT, SEND A MONEY ORDER FOR $39.95 TO: ▬▬▬▬

Bipolar depression, formerly called manic-depression, is an uncommon mood disorder in which the person experiences periods of depression followed by episodes of extremely elevated mood called *mania.* Individuals with mania typically brag about themselves and their accomplishments, engage in excessive physical activity and rapid talking, and sleep very little. Another characteristic of mania is excessive participation in pleasurable activities that can lead to unwelcome consequences, such as careless sexual encounters or costly shopping sprees. During each phase of the bipolar illness, the mood of the affected person gradually reaches an extreme level, which is maintained sometimes for weeks before it swings gradually to the opposite mood. These cyclic mood shifts may recur several times during one's life. Medications, such as lithium carbonate, and hospitalization are often used to treat persons with mania.

Besides bipolar depression, other mood disorders occur in cycles. Seasonal changes, for example, influence the onset of *seasonal affective disorder (SAD).* Affected individuals become depressed around mid-to-late fall, and their depression ends in late winter or early spring. Besides feeling depressed and tired, people with SAD also report craving sweets and gaining weight. Since these symptoms resolve when the daylight period lengthens or when people with the condition spend time in sunnier climates, medical experts think SAD may be related to a lack of exposure to bright light. Light therapy is an effective form of treatment for this disorder (Lamberg, 1998).

Psychosomatic Disorders

What affects the mind can affect the body. For many people, psychological conflicts result in distressing physical signs and symptoms such as pain, tiredness, tremors, numbness, intestinal upsets, or breathing problems (Kellner, 1994). When medical examination and testing fail to confirm that serious physical problems are the source of the complaints, these conditions may be referred to as **psychosomatic disorders.** Psychosomatic disorders can coexist with physical problems, which often complicates diagnoses.

People who visit medical practitioners seeking diagnosis and treatment for their physical complaints frequently have psychosomatic disorders. For example, patients who report feeling tired all of the time often have underlying psychological disorders such as depression as the primary reason for their fatigue (Kellner, 1994). Some individuals who seek medical care for various psychosomatic symptoms suffer from *hypochondriasis,* an unrealistic preoccupation with their physical health. Although the reasons are unclear, women are more likely than men to have hypochondriasis.

Dementia

People who suffer from **dementia** experience impaired cognitive functioning, particularly memory loss, confusion, disorientation, and delusions. Dementia can be a tempo-rary or progressive condition, and it occurs in young as well as aged persons. Brain injuries or tumors, Parkinson's disease, exposure to certain drugs, and infection with human immunodeficiency virus (HIV) can produce dementia. Insufficient blood flow to the brain and *strokes,* bleeding within the brain that results in tissue destruction, frequently produce senile dementia in the elderly. However, about 50% of senile dementia cases involve Alzheimer's disease (see Chapter 15). The following information provides some insights into schizophrenia, a form of dementia that appears to have a genetic basis.

Schizophrenia An estimated 2 million Americans suffer from **schizophrenia.** Lay people often believe schizophrenia means split or multiple personalities, but actually, people with schizophrenia experience extremely disorganized thought processes, including hallucinations and delusions. These individuals often display strange behavior and inappropriate emotions. Communicating with affected individuals is difficult because their speech often consists of words strung together into meaningless sentences. The causes of schizophrenia are unknown, but the brains of people with the disorder tend to have biochemical or structural defects that many medical experts think are inherited.

psychosomatic disorder physical signs and symptoms of illness that are the result of psychological conflicts.

dementia impaired cognitive functioning, particularly memory loss, confusion, disorientation, and delusions.

schizophrenia a form of dementia.

Schizophrenia often develops during childhood, adolescence, and young adulthood; the disorder affects about 1% of the population (Kessler et al., 1994). Some affected persons have one schizophrenic episode and recover, but others experience recurrent episodes and require long-term treatment. By taking special medications, many people with this form of dementia experience relief from their symptoms and live as productive members of society. Some people with severe forms of schizophrenia must live in mental health care facilities because their behavior is unmanageable or dangerous to themselves or others.

www.jbpub.com/healthyliving

Suicide

Suicide, the deliberate ending of one's own life, is not a mental illness. However, such extreme violence against oneself is often the behavioral consequence of a severe psychological disorder. Most people who choose to end their lives feel overwhelmed by the demands of life; they are unable to solve their problems or adapt to their situations.

Overall, suicide accounts for only a small percentage of deaths in the United States. In 1998 about 1% of deaths was attributed to suicide; more than 54% of deaths were the result of heart disease and cancer (see Table 1-1: The Ten Major Causes of Death in the United States). In 1997 suicide was the second leading cause of death for white persons between 15 and 24 years of age and the third leading cause of death for their black or Hispanic counterparts (Hoyert et al., 1999).

Alcohol consumption is associated with suicide. An estimated one-third to two-thirds of teenagers consumed alcohol prior to taking their lives. According to Birckmayer and Hemenway (1999), efforts to lower the minimum legal drinking age to 18 in the United States could increase the number of suicides in the 18-to-20-year-old population by nearly 10%.

A goal of *Healthy People 2000* was to reduce the overall suicide rate to 10.5 per 100,000 Americans by the year 2000. According to the latest *Healthy People 2000* progress review (USDHHS, 1999), the suicide rate is down slightly from the 1987 rate. Elderly persons have a high risk of committing suicide. Although the suicide rate for white males 65 years of age and older has declined since 1987, the rate is almost four times that of youth who are 15 to 19 years of age.

In spite of what many people believe, the Christmas holiday season is not the time that suicide rates peak; intentional deaths are generally low in winter, and high in late spring (Dubovsky & Buzan, 1999). Although women are more likely to attempt suicide, men are more likely to complete the act of killing themselves. Most people use a firearm to end their lives; however, taking drug overdoses and crashing motor vehicles are also frequent suicide methods. Thus, it is difficult to determine the actual number of suicides that occur each year. Taking one's own life places a social stigma on surviving family members, and some medical practitioners may want to protect them by ruling that the death was unintentional rather than a suicide.

Preventing Suicide

Most suicide victims suffered from a psychological disturbance, particularly a major depressive condition that included alcohol abuse (Statham et al., 1998). Other characteristics associated with a high risk of committing suicide are past suicide attempts; a family history of suicide; excessive grieving over the death of a loved one; marital or financial problems; and schizophrenia, an eating disorder, or a terminal illness. Some persons with severe or terminal health problems seek the help of others, particularly family members or physicians, to commit suicide. (Chapter 15 discusses the "right to die" and physician-assisted suicide.) People who know or treat individuals with these characteristics or conditions should be aware of their suicide risk and initiate intervention methods to prevent them from ending their lives.

Suicidal persons usually feel intense emotional strain, are preoccupied with thoughts of death, and often communicate their intentions to others. These individuals might say "everyone would be better off if I were dead" or "I am going to kill myself," discuss the pros and cons of various suicide methods, and make unsuccessful suicide attempts. After deciding to kill themselves, suicidal individuals often seem cheerful and relaxed. When survivors recall the positive emotional state of the victims, they may report that these persons showed no signs of distress prior to dying. ▌ Table 2-9 lists these and other behavioral warning signs of suicidal persons.

It is always important to take suicidal conversations or gestures seriously and obtain suicide prevention counseling for these individuals immediately. Most major metropolitan areas have mental health centers with trained counselors who provide 24-hour crisis intervention services. The Yellow Pages of local telephone books usually list these facilities under "suicide prevention centers."

Table 2-9	Behavioral Warning Signs of Suicide

Behavior and examples

- Discussing, joking, or writing about suicide or death
- Giving away prized possessions
- Making final arrangements: planning a will or making funeral plans
- Displaying severe depressive symptoms
- Reporting feelings of hopelessness and helplessness
- Performing risky behaviors: playing with guns, driving while drunk, or performing daredevil stunts
- Injuring oneself by cutting, burning, or hitting
- Behaving in a manner that is different from usual: showing no interest in usual activities or becoming socially withdrawn
- Planning the suicide: buying a gun or hoarding a supply of barbiturates
- Expressing anxiety over an impending action: worrying about a divorce, dropping out of school, or losing a job
- Showing physical signs of a previous suicide attempt: cut or scarred wrists, neck bruises

Healthy LIVING PRACTICES

- If you are or someone you know is suicidal, immediately contact a suicide prevention center to obtain specific instructions concerning ways to prevent yourself or another from committing this act.

across the lifespan

Psychological Health

Children and adolescents establish the foundation for a lifetime of good mental health by developing positive self-concepts. Parents can help their children feel good about themselves by spending time with them, listening to their concerns, and helping them learn to adjust to a changing world.

School-age children who live in dysfunctional families are vulnerable to develop emotional disorders such as depression and school anxiety. However, childhood depression can occur in any child who experiences a traumatic event such as the loss of a parent through death or divorce (▋ Figure 2-6). Children who are anxious about going to school often complain of morning headaches and stomach upsets before leaving for school, and they return home in a distressed state. Parents and teachers need to recognize the symptoms of childhood depression and anxiety. By receiving individual and family counseling, many distressed children and their families can learn positive ways of handling crisis situations.

Attention-deficit hyperactivity disorder (ADHD) is the most common childhood behavioral disorder; an estimated 3% to 6% of American school-age children, mostly boys, have ADHD (Goldman et al., 1998; LeFever et al., 1999). This condition is characterized by an inability to focus and maintain attention on tasks, such as doing homework or following simple instructions. Children with ADHD also display excessive levels of physical activity and restlessness. They cannot sit still; they rush through meals, dash away from their caretakers, and resist efforts to relax or fall asleep. Their attention spans are so short, they are often unable to follow instructions or complete tasks. Additionally, children with this condition demonstrate impulsive behaviors such as interrupting conversations, talking when inappropriate, and acting before thinking. Some children with ADHD are aggressive, argumentative, and defiant. These behaviors often persist through adolescence and adulthood. Not surprisingly, children with ADHD frequently have conflicts with their family members, peers, and teachers. In addition to prescribing stimulant medications (usually Ritalin), many physicians recommend behavioral and family counseling to treat the condition. Recently, some mental health practitioners expressed concern that ADHD is overdiagnosed and overtreated in the United States. Nevertheless, there is little scientific evidence to support these concerns (Goldman et al., 1998)

During the maturation process, an adolescent undergoes numerous hormonal, physical, social, and other changes necessary to become an independent adult. Many youth make this transition smoothly with a minimum of prob-

▲Figure 2-6 Childhood Depression. Parents and teachers need to recognize the signs and symptoms of childhood depression and anxiety.

lems; but for some, the teenage years are filled with emotional turmoil and family conflict. Certain forms of mental illness, including major depression and eating disorders, are likely to develop during this period. As mentioned earlier, suicide is a major cause of death for adolescents.

By the time people reach late adulthood, they may have raised a family, retired from working outside of the home, and maintained a network of friends and family. Elderly persons who approach the end of their lives with a sense of satisfaction with their accomplishments are more likely to feel emotionally fulfilled. Many elderly people, however, suffer from sleep disturbances and depression after the death of a spouse and friends, family separation or disintegration, financial instability, or a disabling physical illness. As noted earlier, Americans over 75 years of age are more likely to commit suicide than younger persons. It is important for elderly persons and their families to recognize the symptoms of depression and obtain professional help. Chapter 15 discusses the health concerns of elderly individuals in detail.

Chapter Review

Summary

A person's psychological health often affects or is affected by other wellness components such as one's physical and social health. Psychological health is dynamic, becoming more healthy or unhealthy as one responds to a constantly changing environment. Psychologically healthy people accept themselves, are assertive, have realistic and optimistic outlooks on life, function independently, form satisfying interpersonal relationships, cope with change, and find effective solutions to their problems.

Understanding mental health involves the study of physiology and psychology. Biochemical changes in the brain elicit myriad human responses, including thoughts, emotions, and behaviors. Conditions that alter normal brain chemistry can disrupt the mind, producing negative moods or abnormal behaviors. A variety of medications are available that correct abnormal brain chemistry, making affected individuals feel and function better.

Personality is a set of distinct thoughts and behaviors, including emotional responses that characterize the way one responds to situations. Biological, cultural, social, and psychological forces interact to mold one's personality.

Over the past 100 years, numerous psychologists, including Freud, Erikson, and Maslow, provided valuable insights into human behavior, laying the foundation for our present understanding of personality development. Freud thought unconscious drives control human behavior. Erikson identified eight stages of the life span in which different social forces influence personality. Maslow believed that the freedom to achieve personal fulfillment is a psychological need that motivates human behavior.

Psychological adjustment and growth occur when one adapts effectively to the demands of life by altering one's thoughts, attitudes, and responses. Self-esteem, a feeling of self-worth, is a key component of personality. Positive self-esteem is a characteristic of psychologically healthy people.

Intensity and duration are the key features that distinguish a normal emotional response from an abnormal one. Mentally ill individuals experience abnormal feelings, thoughts, and behaviors that persist, interfere with daily life, and hinder psychological adjustment and growth.

There are numerous psychological disorders; each may have multiple causes. Alterations in the normal chemical and physical environment of the brain often produce mental illness. These alterations may be the result of genetic defects, injuries, tumors, infections, or exposure to certain drugs or pollutants. Additionally, social interac-

tions, including those with one's family, contribute to the quality of an individual's psychological health.

In many cases, medications and/or behavioral treatments such as psychotherapy are effective treatments for mental health problems. People can learn to cope with various problems by seeking the help of mental health therapists or by joining self-help groups.

It is common for individuals to experience phobias, anxiety, panic attacks, or mood disorders at some time in their lives. In many cases, these disorders are mild and do not interfere with the affected person's ability to function in society. In other instances, mental illnesses such as schizophrenia, generalized anxiety, or major depression impair functioning to the extent that affected individuals require professional treatment.

Eating disorders are often symptoms of underlying mental illnesses, particularly depression and obsessive-compulsive disorders. Self-imposed starvation and denial of thinness characterize anorexia nervosa. Bulimic individuals and some people with anorexia nervosa engage in food bingeing and purging practices. Binge eaters overeat but rarely follow up with purging.

When it is progressive, dementia is a devastating mental illness. Impaired thought processes, particularly memory loss, disorientation, confusion, and delusions, characterize dementia. Schizophrenia is a serious form of dementia that often begins during adolescence or young adulthood.

Suicide is not a mental illness, but in many instances, suicide is the behavioral consequence of a major depressive illness that included substance abuse. Individuals who are contemplating suicide often discuss their feelings and intentions with others. Thus, people should take someone's suicidal conversations or gestures seriously and assist the individual by obtaining immediate intervention.

Parents can help their children feel good about themselves by spending time with them, listening to their concerns, and helping them learn to adjust to a changing world. Some children develop psychological disturbances, particularly anxiety and depression. Attention-deficit hyperactivity disorder is the most common childhood behavioral disorder. Most adolescents experience relatively few emotional problems as they mature into adults, but for some, the teenage years are filled with turmoil. Certain forms of mental illness, including major depression and eating disorders, are likely to develop during this period of life. Elderly persons who approach the end of their lives with a sense of satisfaction with their accomplishments are likely to feel emotionally fulfilled.

Applying What You Have Learned

1. Develop at least three recommendations for parents to follow that would build their children's self-esteem. *(Application)*
2. Analyze your present situation to determine your position on Maslow's human needs hierarchy. Explain how you determined your position. *(Analysis)*
3. Many persons have negative feelings about people with mental illness. Explain how the media contribute to these feelings. *(Synthesis)*

4. Consider your current state of mental health. Rate your mental health as excellent, good, fair, or poor. Explain how you determined this rating. *(Evaluation)*

KEY
Application: Using information in a new situation.
Analysis: Breaking down information into component parts.
Synthesis: Putting together information from different sources.
Evaluation: Making informed decisions.

Reflecting On Your Health

1. As described in this chapter, self-esteem develops during childhood. When you were a child, how did your interaction with family members influence the development of your self-esteem?
2. Using Table 2-1, the characteristics of psychologically healthy individuals, identify the characteristics that describe you best. Why did you choose those traits?
3. What have you done to improve your psychological health by improving your physical, social, intellectual, spiritual, and environmental health? How did your actions help?

4. As mentioned in this chapter, people often have negative feelings toward psychologically disturbed persons. How would you feel if you, a close friend, or a family member were diagnosed with a mental illness? If you, a close friend, or a family member has a mental illness, how does it affect you?
5. People over 65 years of age have a high risk of depression. What could you do or have you done to enhance the mental health of an elderly person whom you know, such as a grandparent?

References

American Psychiatric Association. (1994). *Diagnostic and statistical manual of mental disorders* (4th. ed.). Washington, DC: American Psychiatric Press.

Artal, M. (1998). Exercise against depression. *The Physician and Sportsmedicine, 26*(10):55-60, 70.

Becker, A. E., Grinspoon, S. K., Klibanski, A., & Herzog, D. B. (1999). Eating disorders. *New England Journal of Medicine, 340*(14): 1092-1098.

Binder, R. L. (1999). Are the mentally ill dangerous? *Journal of the American Academy of Psychiatric Law, 27*(3):189-201.

Birckmayer, J., & Hemenway, D. (1999). Minimum-age drinking laws and youth suicide, 1970–1990. *American Journal of Public Health, 89*(9): 1365-1368.

Birketvedt, G. S., Florholmen, J., Sundsfjord, J., Osterud, B., Dinges, D., Bilker, W., & Stunkard, A. (1999). Behavioral and neuroendocrine characteristics of the night-eating syndrome. *Journal of the American Medical Association, 282*(7):657-663.

Centers for Disease Control and Prevention (CDC) (1996). *Physical activity and health: A report of the Surgeon General.* Atlanta, GA: Author.

Citrome, L. (1994). Management of depression: Current options for this highly treatable disorder. *Postgraduate Medicine, 95*(1):137-145.

Doris, A., Ebmeier, K., & Shajahan, P. (1999). Depressive illness. *The Lancet, 354*:1369-1375.

Dubovsky, S. L., & Buzan, R. (1999). Mood disorders. In R. E. Hales, S. C. Yudofsky, & J. A. Talbott (Eds.), *Textbook of Psychiatry* (pp. 479–565). Washington, DC: American Psychiatric Press.

Erikson, E. H. (1982). *The life cycle completed.* New York: Norton.

Fairburn, C. G., Cooper Z., Doll, H. A., & Welch, S. L. (1999). Risk factors for anorexia nervosa. *Archives of General Psychiatry, 56*:468-476.

Fugh-Berman, A., & Cott, J. M. (1999). Dietary supplements and natural products as psychotherapeutic agents. *Psychosomatic Medicine, 61*:712-728.

Gelenberg, A. (1999). Depression is still underrecognized and untreated. *Archives of Internal Medicine, 159*:1657.

Glass, R. M. (1999). Treating depression as a recurrent or chronic disease. *Journal of the American Medical Association, 281*(1):83-84.

Goldman, L. S., Genel, M., Bezman, R. J., & Slanetz, P. J. (1998). Diagnosis and treatment of attention-deficit/hyperactivity disorder in children and adolescents. *Journal of the American Medical Association, 279*(14):1100-1107.

Hollander, E., Simeon, D., & Gorman, J. M. (1999). Anxiety disorders. In R. E. Hales, S. C. Yudofsky, & J. A. Talbott (Eds.), *Textbook of Psychiatry* (pp. 567–633). Washington, DC: American Psychiatric Press.

Hoyert, D. L., Kochanek, K. D., & Murphy, S. L. (1999). Deaths: Final data for 1997. *National Vital Statistics Reports, 47*(19):27-51.

Keel, P. K., Mitchell, J. E., Miller, K. B., Davis, T. L., & Crow, S. J. (1999). Long-term outcome of bulimia nervosa. *Archives of General Psychiatry, 56*:63-69.

Kellner, R. (1994). Psychosomatic syndromes: Somatization and somatoform disorders. *Psychotherapy and Psychosomatics, 61*:4-24.

Kessler, R. C., McGonagle, K. A., Zhao, S., Nelson, C. B., Hughes, M., Eshleman, S., Wittchen, H. U., & Kendler, K. S. (1994). Lifetime and 12-month prevalence of *DSM-III-R* psychiatric disorders in the United States: Results from the National Comorbidity Survey. *Archives of General Psychiatry, 51*:8-19.

Lamberg, L. (1998). Dawn's early light to twilight's last gleaming. . . . *Journal of the American Medical Association, 280*(18):1556-1558.

Langewisch, M. W. J., & Frisch, G. R. (1998). Gambling behavior and pathology in relation to impulsivity, sensation seeking, and risky behavior in male college students. *Journal of Gambling Studies, 14*(3):245-262.

Leaman, T. L. (1999). Anxiety disorders. *Primary Care, 26*(2):197-210.

LeFever, G. B., Dawson, K. V., & Morrow, A. L. (1999). The extent of drug therapy for attention deficit-hyperactivity disorder among children in public schools. *American Journal of Public Health, 89*(9):1359-1364.

Maslow, A. H. (1968). *Toward a psychology of being* (2nd ed.). New York: Van Nostrand Reinhold.

National Academy of Sciences. (1999). *Pathological gambling: A critical review.* Washington, DC: National Academy Press.

Neugebauer, R. (1999). Mind matters: The importance of mental disorders in public health's 21st century mission. *American Journal of Public Health, 89*(9):1309-1311.

Rakel, E. (1999). Depression. *Primary Care, 26*(2):211-224.

Statham, D. J., Heath, A. C., Madden, P. A. F., Bucholz, K. K., Bierut, L., Slutske, W. S., Dunne, M. P., and Martin, N. G. (1998). Suicidal behaviour: An epidemiological and genetic study. *Psychological Medicine 28*:839-855.

Tofler, I. R., Stryer, B. K., Micheli, L. J., & Herman, L. R. (1996). Physical and emotional problems of elite female athletes. *New England Journal of Medicine, 335*(4):281-283.

U.S. Department of Health and Human Services (USDHHS), Public Health Service. (1999). *Healthy people 2000 review, 1998–1999* (Publication 99-1256). Washington, DC: Government Printing Office. http://odphp.osophs.dhhs.gov/pubs/hp2000/prog_rvw.htm

Walter, G., & Rey, J. M. (1999). The relevance of herbal treatments for psychiatric practice. *Australian and New Zealand Journal of Psychiatry, 33*:482-489.

Wise, M. C., & Tierney, J. G. (1999). Impulse control disorders not elsewhere classified. In R. E. Hales, S. C. Yudofsky, & J. A. Talbott (Eds.), *Textbook of Psychiatry* (pp. 783–786). Washington, DC: American Psychiatric Press.

Wonderlich, S. A., Wilsnack, R. W., Wilsnack, S. C., & Harris, T. R. (1996). Childhood sexual abuse and bulimia behavior in a nationally representative sample. *American Journal of Public Health, 86*:1082-1086.

chapter 3

Stress and Its Management

If you ask students to identify what makes college life stressful, you will receive a long list of situations, including taking exams, preparing term papers and lab reports, applying for loans, and juggling hours to fit part-time jobs into their class schedules. College students probably cannot imagine any other period in their lives that will place as many demands on their time, energy, and finances.

How would you respond to the question, "What was the most stressful situation that you've experienced in the past year?" Three college students enrolled in a health course wrote the following answers to this question.

The most stressful situation I've encountered in the past twelve months must be the discovery that my wife was pregnant and our financial security was at risk because the only source of income for us is her wages. I'm wondering if I will be able to continue pursuing my degree after the baby is born—this adds to my stress day by day.

I went away to a university last year and was the victim of a rape. The whole ordeal of talking to the police, confronting

"Going to college places considerable demands on your time and mind. . ."

the man who did it, and telling my boyfriend was horrible, but the most stressful part was having to tell my parents.

The most stressful situation was the death of both of my grandparents within six months of each other. I watched them suffer as they passed away. It was very difficult. Also, my choice of a major was a mistake; I've had to change it.

Each of these students had to cope with different stressful situations. You may have had to cope with similar distressing events. Although going to college places considerable demands on your time and mind, you can expect stressful situations to arise during every phase of your life.

What is stress? What effects can it have on your health and well-being? Can stress be good for you? What factors make a situation stressful? Is it possible to reduce the negative effects that stress can have on your health? This chapter examines the nature of stress, how it can affect you, and how you can manage your stress.

What You'll Learn

www.jbpub.com/healthyliving

The web site for this book offers many useful tools and is a great source for supplementary health information for both students and instructors. Visit the site at www.jbpub.com/healthyliving for information on these topics:

What is Stress?
The Impact of Stress on Health
Stress Management Skills

Chapter Overview

The different meanings of *stress.*
The ways your body responds to stress.
How stressful life events can affect your health.
Strategies for coping with stress.
Skills that can help you manage stress.

DIVERSITY *in Health*   Stress and Refugees

Con$umer *Health*   Herbal Remedies for Stress Symptoms

Managing *Your* **Health**   A Technique for Progressive Muscular Relaxation

across the lifespan   Stress

Student Workbook

Self Assessment: How Much Stress Have You Had Lately?
Changing Health Habits: Taking Steps to Reduce Your Stress

Do You Know?

- An easy way to manage your time more effectively?
- If having a pet can reduce stress?
- How to relax within just a few minutes?

www.jbpub.com/healthyliving

What Is Stress?

Stress can have different meanings. *Stress* can refer to the situations that threaten or place demands on your mind and body. These stressful situations can be real, such as being confronted by an angry dog, or imaginary, such as worrying over your future employment possibilities. *Stress* can also describe your responses to a threatening situation; you feel stress. Imagine that a vicious dog attacks you. How would you feel?

Many experts define **stress** as a complex series of psychological and physical reactions that occur as a person responds to a situation. Each person views and appraises a situation to determine whether it will have positive, negative, or neutral consequences. Additionally, an individual appraises the situation according to his or her previous experiences and personality characteristics. Thus, it is possible that several individuals form different appraisals of the same event and that each person can, as a result, have a different response.

Stressors

Stressors are situations that create stress by placing physical or psychological demands on an individual. *Physiological* (physical) *stressors* include engaging in exercise; experiencing illness, pain, or injury; and being exposed to dangerous pollutants or extreme temperature changes. *Psychological stressors* include managing extreme emotions, handling difficult social situations, and dealing with troublesome thoughts and relationships. Psychologically demanding situations can add just enough stress to make life more challenging and interesting, but enduring too much stress, physical or psychological, can make life miserable.

The nature of a stressor has a major role in determining its impact on health. When people think of stress, they usually think of **distress**, that is, events that are difficult to control and that have unwanted or negative outcomes. Distressing experiences include having problems with one's education, job, family, and relationships. Other situations create *positive* stress or **eustress.** Becoming a new parent, competing in an athletic event, and accepting a desired job are examples of events that can have positive outcomes by making people feel happy, challenged, or suc-

stress a complex series of psychological and physical reactions that occur as one responds to a situation.

stressors events that produce physical or psychological demands on an individual.

distress events or conditions that produce unwanted or negative outcomes.

eustress (YOU-stress) events or conditions that create positive demands on a person, such as feeling happy, challenged, or successful.

hormones chemical messengers that convey information from a gland to other cells in the body.

endocrine system a group of glands that produce hormones.

general adaptation syndrome (GAS) the three-stage manner in which the human body responds to stress: alarm, resistance, and exhaustion.

cessful. Experiencing stressors with positive physical or psychological consequences may reduce the unhealthy effects of negative stressors.

Some stress experts point out that eustress still has negative effects on the body and mind, because any event that creates stress requires specific physical and psychological adjustments. These changes can damage the body and disturb the mind. Burnout is a common result of too much stress. In this chapter, the terms *stress* and *distress* are used interchangeably when referring to negative psychological stressors.

Stress Responses

Physical Responses

The environment constantly exposes organisms to stressful situations; to survive, they must deal physically with these stressors. In emergencies a person's nervous system instantly activates the adrenal glands to release certain hormones: cortisol, epinephrine (adrenaline), and norepinephrine (noradrenaline). **Hormones** are chemical messengers that convey information from a gland to other cells in the body. The glands of the **endocrine system** produce several different hormones and secrete them directly into the bloodstream (**Figure 3-1).** Some endocrine hormones

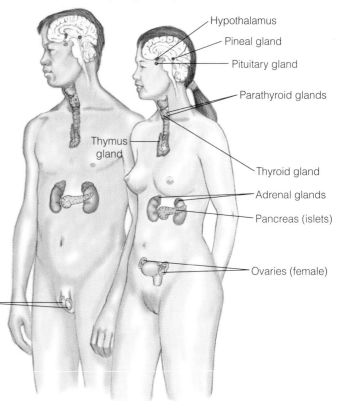

Hypothalamus
Pineal gland
Pituitary gland
Parathyroid glands
Thymus gland
Thyroid gland
Adrenal glands
Pancreas (islets)
Ovaries (female)
Testes (male)

▲**Figure 3-1 The Endocrine System.** The glands of the endocrine system produce chemical messengers called hormones, which enter the bloodstream via small ducts.

regulate body processes, growth, and development. Cortisol, epinephrine, and norepinephrine are often called the "stress hormones" because they prepare the body to respond when danger threatens.

The stress hormones increase heart rate, central nervous system activity, and blood flow to the heart and skeletal muscles, the muscles that move the body. At the same time, the blood flow to the skin, kidneys, and intestinal organs decreases. Certain cells in the body release a supply of fuels (fats and blood sugar) into the bloodstream, which transports these fuels to the active muscle or nerve cells. These and other adaptations enable the person's body to confront or leave a dangerous situation (the *fight-or-flight* response). ▌ **Table 3-1** lists the major physical adaptations to stress and their possible survival value.

Selye's General Adaptation Syndrome The classic research of Hans Selye (1907–1982) paved the way for our understanding of the relationship between the mind and body. Selye first used the term *stress* to describe the nonspecific response that allows a person to adapt physically or psychologically to any demand. The stress response is nonspecific because anything, from a kiss to a tornado, can create the effects on the mind and body. As a result of his classic observations, Selye developed a three-stage description of the physical responses to stressors, the **general adaptation syndrome (GAS)**. Selye identified the three GAS stages as alarm, resistance, and exhaustion and described the physical status of the body in each stage (▌ **Figure 3-2**).

Table 3-1	Physical Adaptations to Stress
Physical Change	**Effect**
Pupils enlarge	Improves vision
Energy stores released	Supplies fuels for muscular activity
Heart rate increases	Pumps more blood and faster
Blood pressure increases	Provides more pressure to circulate blood
Blood forms clots easier	Prevents bleeding
Skeletal muscles become tense and can work longer	Allows for fighting or escaping threats
Circulation increases to cells	Supplies more nutrients and oxygen to active heart, lungs, arms, and legs
Sweating increases	Removes extra heat created by muscular activity involved in fighting and escaping
Saliva flow decreases	Avoids wasting valuable body fluids
Respiratory tract (the smaller airways) dilates	Allows more air to move into and out of lungs, supplying more oxygen for energy and removing more carbon dioxide waste
Gastrointestinal tract movements decrease	Shifts blood to skeletal muscles for their more critical needs
Endorphin levels increase	Reduces sensations of pain

(a)

(b)

(c)

Figure 3-2 The Three Stages of General Adaptation Syndrome. ▲(a) In the alarm stage, the adrenal glands release stress hormones, preparing the body to deal physically with the stressful event. ▶(b) In the resistance/recovery stage, the body maintains its protective reactions to the stressor, and as the threatening situation eases, the body recovers its normal physical state. ▶(c) The exhaustion stage occurs if the level of stress persists and the body's defense mechanisms weaken.

When you think of or see a stressor, your brain sends an alarm through your nerves to your adrenal glands. Almost immediately, the adrenal glands release their stress hormones, preparing your body to deal with the stressful event. This activity is called the *alarm* stage. In the alarm stage, your entire body undergoes the dramatic physical changes listed in Table 3-1. Consider, for example, how quickly you respond to an unexpected loud noise.

If you manage to survive the initial encounter but the stressor persists, your body enters the *resistance phase* of the response. During this stage, your body maintains its protective physical reactions to the stressor. As the threatening situation eases, *recovery* of your body's normal physical state occurs. Generally, by resting and avoiding additional exposure to stressors, your body can repair any damage that has occurred. However, if the stressful situation persists, your body will not be able to maintain its resistance, and it will enter the *exhaustion* stage. In this stage, your physical stress defenses are weakened, and you become more susceptible to infections. Prolonged exposure to stress can even lead to death if the body depletes its response mechanisms. The "Diversity in Health" essay "Stress and Refugees" discusses the effects of severe stress on the physical and psychological health of refugees from the former Yugoslavia.

The stress response evolved to enable humans to react immediately to physical threats to their well-being. Indeed, when people are in life-threatening situations, these dramatic physical changes may be essential for their survival. The same dramatic adaptations, however, take place when

DIVERSITY *in* Health | Stress and Refugees

During the last decade, ethnically diverse former Yugoslavia was torn apart by civil wars in Bosnia/ Herzegovina and Kosovo. Thousands of people were wounded or killed. At least 2 million individuals were forced to flee their homes, cross into unfamiliar neighboring countries, and live under deplorable conditions in refugee camps (■ Figure 3-A). Before leaving, some of them watched as their houses were destroyed and their loved ones were taken away. Some were tortured, and many witnessed the torture and/or murder of family members or friends. The stress of living under such uncertainty, terror, and violence resulted in high rates of severe psychological disturbances among the refugees. Recent studies indicate that as many as 40% of refugees from the former Yugoslavia suffer from depression, up to 50% experience post-traumatic stress disorder (PTSD), and about 20% have both psychological disturbances (Mollica et al., 1999; Favaro et al., 1999). Post-traumatic stress disorder is a chronic condition characterized by distressing psychological symptoms such as recurrent nightmares, emotional numbness, and unwanted recollections and flashbacks of the terrible events. PTSD can affect people who survive any life-threatening situation, including nat-

▲Figure 3-A Refugee Camp Survivors from Former Yugoslavia. According to recent studies, significant percentages of the refugee camp survivors experienced depression, post-traumatic stress disorder, or a combination of both conditions.

ural disasters, plane crashes, and hostage situations. For the refugees, the negative effects of enduring such extremely stressful conditions were more pronounced among those who were widowed or never married, had low levels of education, and had little association with family members. Depression and PTSD are associ-

ated with long-term consequences including physical disability, social impairment, and loss of productivity. Therefore, mental health workers in nations providing havens for refugees from the former Yugoslavia need to identify persons who are at risk and offer treatment.

ANALYZING *Health-Related Information*

The following article appeared in FDA Consumer, the July/August 1998 issue. Read the article and explain why you think it is a reliable or an unreliable source of information. Use the model for analyzing health information to guide your thinking; the main points of the model are noted below. A full explanation of the model can be found on pages 12 to 13.

1. Which statements are verifiable facts; which are unverified statements or value claims?
2. What are the credentials of the person writing the article? If this information is available, does the author's background and education qualify him or her as an expert in the topic area?
3. What might be the motives and biases of the person writing the article? State reasons for your answer.
4. Which information is relevant to the issue or main point of the article; which information is irrelevant?
5. Is the source reliable? Does it have a reputation for publishing misinformation?
6. Does the article attack the credibility of conventional scientists or medical authorities?

Based on the above analysis, do you think that this article is a reliable source of health-related information? Summarize your reasons for coming to this conclusion.

Sleepless Society

Tamar Nordenberg, staff writer for FDA Consumer

Millions of Americans undersleep by choice, burning the candle at both ends because of hectic work and family schedules. Recent surveys show that Americans sleep seven hours each night on average, down from 9 hours in 1910 when, without electricity, people generally went to sleep as darkness fell.

"People don't respect sleep enough," says Daniel O'Hearn, a sleep disorders specialist at Johns Hopkins University. "They feel they can do more—have more time for work and family—by allowing themselves less time for sleep. But they do sleep; they sleep at work, or driving to work."

Nodding off at work isn't just unproductive; in the worst cases, it causes serious industrial accidents. The 1989 Exxon Valdez Alaskan oil spill, for example, was reportedly due at least in part to the severe fatigue of the tanker's sleep-deprived third mate.

Also, like drunk driving, drowsy driving can kill. The National Highway Traffic Safety Administration estimates that more than 200,000 crashes each year involve drivers falling asleep at the wheel, and that thousands of Americans die in such accidents annually.

"Besides being an unpleasant sensation, when we're tired, we're less alert and less able to respond," says FDA drug reviewer Bob Rappaport, M.D.

Lack of sleep can cause memory and mood problems, too, Rappaport says, and may affect immune function, which could lead to an increased incidence of infection and other illnesses. In studies performed on rats, prolonged sleep deprivation resulted in death.

Beyond the observable consequences of sleep deprivation, why humans—or any animal, for that matter—need sleep remains largely a mystery. "What happens in the brain while we're sleeping is what we're trying to untangle," says James Kiley, director of the National Center for Sleep Disorders Research of the National Institutes of Health. "We're just beginning to understand why a third of our life is spent sleeping. What we do know is that sleep is an important biological need, like food and drink, and that the brain is very active while we're sleeping."

The leading sleep theories focus on "rest and resuscitation for the body and psyche," says Rappaport. During sleep, the brain may recharge its energy stores and shift the day's information that has been stored in temporary memory to regions of the brain associated with long-term memory.

So just how much nightly R and R does a person need? That can change throughout one's life based on age and other factors. For most people, though, seven and a half to eight and a half hours of sleep each night fulfills the basic physical need, Rappaport says, adding that this is "very individual" and can range from as few as four or five hours to as many as nine or ten.

The Mayo Clinic of Rochester, Minnesota, defines an adequate amount of sleep as whatever produces daytime alertness and a feeling of well-being. People should not need an alarm clock to wake them if they are getting enough sleep.

Source: Nordenberg, T. (1998). Sleepless society. FDA Consumer, 32(4):11.

people deal with everyday hassles and worries. Although these situations usually do not represent direct or serious threats to people's physical well-being, they elicit the release of stress hormones into the bloodstream. People with higher than normal levels of the stress hormones and energy-supplying compounds in their blood are likely to develop diseases of the heart and blood vessels. Genetic factors, however, can modify the way one's body responds to stress. For example, men who have a family history of hypertension experienced higher blood pressure readings when stressed than men with no such history who also were stressed (Light et al., 1999).

Psychological Responses Stressful situations affect the mind as well as the body, but the psychological impacts are not easy to test, observe, or measure. Chapter 2 describes several mental health conditions, including depression and anxiety disorders, that have direct links to stressful life events. Distressed individuals are more likely to report psychological symptoms such as frustration, anxiety, and anger. They may be irritable most of the time, eat too much food, or abuse drugs. "Stressed-out" people often have difficulty focusing their attention, making decisions, and sleeping.

Stress can have positive effects on the mind. Low levels of psychological stress can enhance performance by increasing one's effort and attention to the task. As the degree of stress increases, however, the individual may respond by worrying too much about performance, which creates even more psychological stress. This response can reduce the ability of actors, athletes, and college students to concentrate on and perform tasks. Stage fright affects the best veteran actors, and many superb athletes "choke" under competitive pressure. Taking tests is stressful for many college students, but students with test anxiety overreact emotionally to the testing situation and have difficulty concentrating on test questions. In a recent study, Newcomer and colleagues (1999) treated healthy subjects with an amount of the hormone cortisol that simulates the level of the hormone in the body when one is under extreme stress. Subjects who received cortisol had more problems recalling certain information than subjects receiving a lower dose or a placebo. This finding may have implications for people with test anxiety. To avoid becoming overwhelmed by task-related anxiety, people can learn to use the stress management skills presented later in this chapter.

www.jbpub.com/healthyliving

The Impact of Stress on Health

Stressful Life Events

In 1967 Thomas Holmes and Richard Rahe introduced the Social Readjustment Rating Scale (SRRS), maintaining that people who experience numerous major life events within a short time span are likely to develop illnesses (Holmes & Rahe, 1967). Holmes and Rahe developed this scale by asking nearly 400 people to rate life events according to the average amount of social change the individuals thought would be needed to deal with the situation. Death of a spouse, for example, received the maximum score of 100 points (see ▊ **Table 3-2**). In studies using the SRRS, Rahe found that subjects who accumulated higher scores, because they had experienced more major life events in a year, were more likely to become ill at some time in the following year.

Although a few items on the original SRRS are outdated, such as "mortgage over $10,000," this scale has been a popular measurement of stress levels. Many stress experts, however, question the scale's ability to predict the onset of illness.

Using the SRRS as a model, Martin Marx and his colleagues (1975) developed the College Schedule of Recent Experience to assess the level of stress experienced by college freshmen (see the assessment activity "How Much Stress Have You Had Lately?" in the workbook). First-year college students often have difficulty coping with the unfamiliarity and demands of college life. Not surprisingly, these individuals have a high dropout rate. Concerned with the negative impact of change on first-year students, college administrators establish academic and social programs to ease the stress that new students feel during their first year in school.

Medical experts generally agree with the idea that stressful life events are related to illness. However, observing an association between stressful events and the onset of illnesses does not mean that stress *causes* poor health. Psychological, environmental, and biological forces can influence health in complex ways. Scientists need to collect more information before they can understand fully how psychological stress affects the body.

The Mind-Body Relationship

Certain health problems are associated with psychological stress (▊ **Table 3-3**). For example, persons with chronic conditions such as asthma, rheumatoid arthritis, migraines, and genital herpes report that the signs and symptoms of their illness tend to worsen or recur during stressful periods (Levenson et al., 1999). Anxiety and stress also worsen the signs and symptoms of irritable bowel syndrome (IBS). People with IBS have recurrent bouts of intestinal cramps, constipation, and diarrhea. Physicians estimate that as many as half of their patients who complain of intestinal disorders suffer from IBS (Kellner, 1994).

Psychoneuroimmunology, the study of the relationships between the nervous and immune systems, has emerged as a new and exciting field of medical research that explores the connection between mind and body. Scientists have discovered links between the nervous and immune systems that explain how some emotional responses affect physical health.

Table 3-2	Social Readjustment Rating Scale	
Rank	Life event	Value
1	Death of spouse	100
2	Divorce	73
3	Marital separation	65
4	Jail term	63
5	Death of close family member	63
6	Personal injury or illness	53
7	Marriage	50
8	Fired at work	47
9	Marital reconciliation	45
10	Retirement	45
11	Change in health of family member	44
12	Pregnancy	40
13	Sexual difficulties	39
14	Gain a new family member	39
15	Business readjustment	39
16	Change in financial state	38
17	Death of close friend	37
18	Change to different line of work	36
19	Change in the number of arguments with spouse	35
20	Mortgage over $10,000	31
21	Foreclosure of mortgage or loan	30
22	Change in responsibilities at work	29
23	Son or daughter leaving home	29
24	Trouble with in-laws	29
25	Outstanding personal achievement	28
26	Wife begins or stops work	26
27	Begin or end school	26
28	Change in living conditions	25
29	Revision of personal habits	24
30	Trouble with boss	23
31	Change in work hours or conditions	20
32	Change in residence	20
33	Change in schools	20
34	Change in recreation	19
35	Change in religious activities	19
36	Change in social activities	18
37	Mortgage or loan less than $10,000	17
38	Change in sleeping habits	16
39	Change in number of family get-togethers	15
40	Change in eating habits	15
41	Vacation	13
42	Christmas	12
43	Minor violations of the law	11

Source: Holmes, T. H., & Rahe, R. H. (1967). The social readjustment rating scale. *Journal of Psychosomatic Research, 11*:213–218. Reprinted by permission.

Table 3-3	Common Disorders Linked to Psychological State	
Eating disorders		Itchy skin
Tension headaches		Rapid or irregular heart rate
Migraines		Intestinal ulcers
Muscle spasms		Nausea and vomiting
Chest pains		Frequent urination
Excessive menstrual cramps		Irritable bowel syndrome
Acne		Rheumatoid arthritis flare-ups
Recurring herpes simplex		Asthma attacks
PMS		

The **immune system**, which includes the red bone marrow, spleen, lymph nodes, white blood cells, and thymus gland, defends body against disease-causing agents (**Figure 3-3).** The white blood cells are the key soldiers of the immune system, serving as the body's internal scouts and commandos. These special cells find, identify, and destroy many agents that may endanger one's health.

Recently, scientists discovered that the immune system does not function independently of the other body systems. Using nerves and neurotransmitters, the brain relays information about the person's emotional state to the places where white blood cells are made and located in the body. These specialized cells produce their own chemical messengers that enable them to communicate information about the state of the body back to the brain and the endocrine system.

Under stressful conditions, the nervous system also produces and releases chemical messengers called endorphins. Endorphins interfere with the ability of the brain to sense pain. Being less able to feel pain when injured may be a valuable adaptation, especially if the individual has to react quickly. Endorphins, however, may reduce the defensive activities of the white blood cells, which might explain why many people are more likely to develop illnesses during or after stressful experiences (Glaser et al., 1999).

According to the latest *Healthy People 2000* progress review (1999), 39% of adults experienced negative health effects of stress in 1993; in 1986, about 44% of the population reported experiencing such disorders. The goal of *Healthy People 2000* was to have no more than 35% of adult Americans reporting stress-related problems to their health-care providers.

Ulcers You probably know someone who has a stomach or intestinal ulcer—about 10% of the population will have

psychoneuro-immunology
(SIGH-ko-NEW-ro-im-mu-NOL-lo-gee) the study of the relationships between the nervous and immune systems.

immune system the specific defenses of the body that combat invading infectious agents.

an ulcer at some time in their lives. An **ulcer** is a sore in the lining of the esophagus (the food tube), stomach, or duodenum, which is the first part of the small intestine that leads from the stomach (see Figure 9-1). Ulcers may form in the stomach when its protective lining and overlying mucous layers do not resist the normal amount of certain chemicals, including hydrochloric acid, secreted by the stomach. Ulcers can form in the esophagus when the acidic contents of the stomach chronically splash back into the food tube. This "splash-back" *(reflux)* is often due to a relaxed muscle that serves as the "doorway" to the stomach from the esophagus. Cigarette smoking, alcohol, chocolate, fats, and peppermints relax this muscle. In addition, lying down immediately after eating or overeating promotes reflux. People with ulcers experience burning or aching sensations in the middle of their abdomens from 30 minutes to 2 hours after eating, or they feel bloated and nauseated after meals.

ulcer

a sore in the lining of the esophagus, stomach, or duodenum.

In some persons, the protective lining of the stomach may be chronically infected with the bacterium *Helicobacter pylori (H. pylori)*. This organism is thought to weaken the stomach lining and make the person more susceptible to ulcers. However, not all infected individuals have ulcers. Cigarette smoking, alcohol, and certain medications may also make the stomach lining susceptible to developing an ulcer (Levenson et al., 1999).

The avoidable risks associated with ulcers are cigarette smoking, chronic alcohol use, and chronic use of anti-inflammatory drugs such as aspirin and ibuprofen. These drugs may damage the stomach lining. Unavoidable risk factors are age and family history. As you age, your risk for ulcers increases; most ulcers are diagnosed in persons over 40 years of age. Infection with *H. pylori* is an additional risk factor, although most people do not know if they are infected.

Many people think that the "typical" individual who develops an ulcer has a hard-driving personality and endures a great deal of stress. Although stress contributes to the occurrence of ulcers, an ulcer-prone personality may not exist (Levenson et al., 1999). A distressed person, however, may smoke, drink too much alcohol, and not get enough rest; such behaviors alter the immune system, making ulcers more likely.

Ulcers can be serious, especially if they bleed. Signs and symptoms of a bleeding ulcer include dark, tarry stools; a bloating sensation, and weakness. If you suspect you have a bleeding ulcer, seek medical attention immediately.

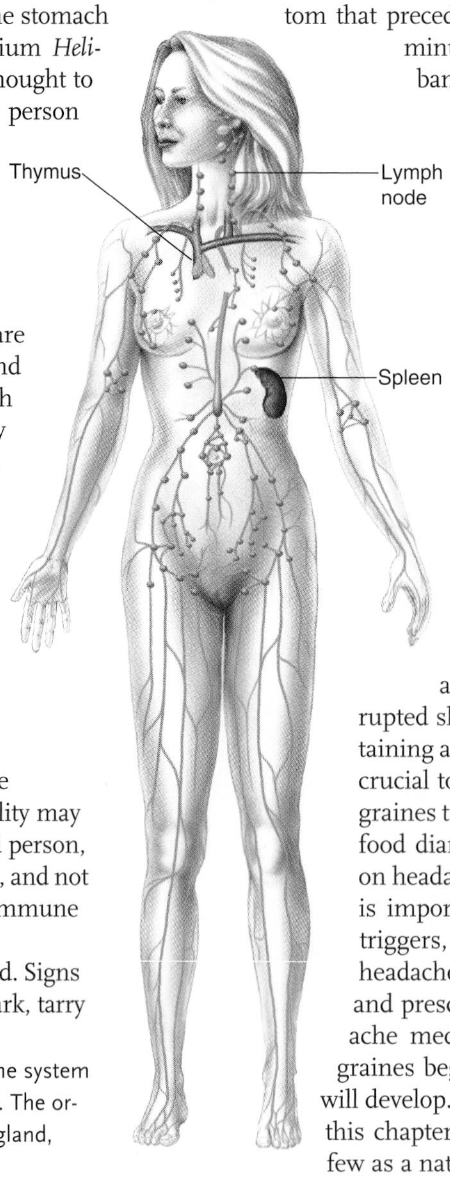

Headaches Nearly everyone has had a headache at one time or another. People who drink caffeinated beverages regularly may get headaches when they do not consume them, and physical problems such as sinus infections often cause headaches. Many people think muscle tension causes the most common type of headache, the stress headache (tension-type headache). Current evidence, however, indicates that nervous system disturbances, such as inflammation of nerves attached to the brain, are responsible for most headaches, especially migraine headaches (Saper, 1999).

The nervous system disturbances that contribute to migraine headaches can be triggered by environmental factors such as stress, fatigue, weather changes, excessive noise, and certain drugs or foods (Nordenberg, 1998). Many migraine sufferers experience an *aura,* a nerve-related symptom that precedes the headache by about 5 to 60 minutes. Aura includes visual disturbances such as flashing lights or zigzag lines or a "pins-and-needles" feeling on one side of the body.

The pain of migraine headaches is of moderate to severe intensity. The aching may occur only on one side of the head and may result in nausea and/or vomiting. Because their headaches are often aggravated by routine physical activity, light, and sound, migraine suffers usually retreat to a darkened, quiet room to rest. Migraine headaches usually persist for 4 to 72 hours.

The first line of defense against migraines is identifying and avoiding their triggers. Some people develop migraines, for example, from insufficient sleep or disrupted sleep patterns. In these cases, maintaining a regular, sufficient sleep schedule is crucial to avoiding attacks. Others have migraines triggered by certain foods. Keeping a food diary to determine which foods bring on headaches and then avoiding those foods is important. In addition to avoiding their triggers, people who suffer from migraine headaches can take various over-the-counter and prescription medications. Certain headache medications can be taken before migraines begin to lessen the chances that they will develop. The "Consumer Health" feature in this chapter discusses the usefulness of feverfew as a natural means to prevent migraines.

Thymus — Lymph node — Spleen

▶ **Figure 3-3 The Immune System.** The immune system defends the body against disease-causing agents. The organs of the immune system include the thymus gland, spleen, and lymph nodes.

Over-the-counter pain relievers get rid of most headaches. With some, simply applying hot packs to the head or neck and relaxing will have the same effect. Headaches rarely signal life-threatening conditions. ▌ **Table 3-4** describes circumstances under which you should seek immediate medical attention for a headache.

Personality, Disease, and Stress

Although exposure to any stress can increase one's susceptibility to illnesses, the same stressful situation can have a different impact on different individuals. Why do people often respond differently to a stressor? Each person's unique combination of personality traits and background experiences contributes to his or her stress response.

People who see only the negative aspects of a stressor may view a difficult situation as impossible to overcome and be more vulnerable to stress than those who make positive appraisals of the situation. As a result, vulnerable people are more likely to become anxious and depressed and to make poor decisions. By making poor decisions, people often create more stress for themselves. Additionally, distressed individuals may adopt lifestyles that undermine their health, such as obtaining insufficient sleep, making poor dietary choices, or abusing drugs.

People who are less vulnerable to the negative effects of stress may have personalities that act as buffers. These individuals generally have more positive outlooks on life, and they are more likely to appraise stressors as having positive

Table 3-4	Serious Headache Symptoms

Consult a physician if a headache

- is accompanied by confusion, unconsciousness, or convulsions.
- involves pain in the eye or ear.
- is accompanied by fever.
- is accompanied by nausea.
- occurs after a blow to the head.
- is persistent in someone previously free of headaches.
- is recurrent, especially in children.
- interferes with normal life.

Source: Farley, D. (1992, September). Headache misery may yield to proper treatment. *FDA Consumer*, p. 31.

outcomes. Stress-resistant people view the need to change as a challenge, but they recognize that it is a part of life. Although some aspects of the stress-resistant personality may be inherited, children learn various ways of handling stressful situations by observing and copying the behaviors of relatives in challenging situations. These youngsters often continue to employ the same positive behaviors to deal with stressors as they mature.

Are there specific personality types that increase one's risk of heart disease? For years, it has been popularly believed that people who have a type A personality (ambi-

---

ConSumer Health | Herbal Remedies for Stress Symptoms

Since ancient times, people have treated their stress symptoms with herbs and other plants. As mentioned in Chapter 1, many plants contain chemicals that have medicinal properties. Recently, many Americans have tried kava, valerian, and feverfew to relax or treat their stress-related symptoms. Does kava induce relaxation? Is valerian effective for treating insomnia? Can feverfew prevent migraines? Are these alternative therapies safe?

For hundreds of years, a ceremonial beverage made from the roots of the kava plant has been used by South Pacific Islanders to reduce anxiety, relax muscles, and induce sleep. Conventional medical experts, however, are concerned about the herb's growing popularity among Americans because the long-term safety

of kava, including its potential for addiction, is unclear. It is known that kava produces serious side effects when consumed in very large doses (Pepping, 1999). Furthermore, the herb can intensify the effects of depressant drugs including alcohol. Therefore, check with your physician before consuming products made from this herb.

Ancient Romans were aware of the medicinal value of heliotrope plant, commonly known as valerian. Roots of the plant are dried, then brewed into a tea that is used to induce sleep. Valerian is available in pills or mixed with alcohol to make a tincture. Valerian may have usefulness as a mild tranquilizer (Fugh-Berman & Cott, 1999). In a few studies, however, the herb had toxic side effects

(Wong et al., 1998). You should consult your physician before taking valerian.

Feverfew has been used for centuries to treat headaches, menstrual problems, and fever. Before supplements were available, people would chew the leaves of the plant, but this practice caused sores to form in the mouth. Feverfew may reduce the risk of migraines. The herb does not seem to be toxic when consumed in recommended amounts, but it may cause allergic responses and even headaches in some people ("Herbal Rx," 1999). As in the case of all herbal treatments, check with your physician before trying feverfew. Be aware that feverfew can upset the stomach, and stop taking it (or any herbal product) if you have adverse reactions.

tious, restless, competitive, impatient, and hostile) are more likely to develop heart disease than people who did not have these characteristics. During the 1980s, medical researchers recognized that many people with type A personalities did not develop heart disease. More recently, scientists have associated certain personality traits with the development of heart and blood vessel diseases (cardiovascular disease). People who harbor negative feelings toward others, such as anger, hostility, resentment, suspicion, and mistrust, are more likely to develop cardiovascular disease than people who do not (Williams, 1999).

The minds of some people overreact to stressors, and their bodies respond by releasing excessive amounts of stress hormones into the bloodstream. This response may lead to high blood pressure and other physical changes that damage the inside walls of certain blood vessels. Additionally, scientists have found that *platelets,* cell fragments that participate in the blood clotting process, become stickier when a person is distressed (Patterson et al., 1994). When a blood vessel is damaged and bleeding occurs, platelets clump together and form a plug that may stop blood loss. If a person is injured during a fight for survival, the ease with which the platelets form blood clots can be lifesaving. Many stressful encounters, however, do not include the risk of bleeding, yet the enhanced ability for blood clotting still occurs. In these instances, blood clots can be life threatening, particularly when a clot forms and blocks the blood flow to the heart muscle or the brain.

The stress response reduces the effectiveness of the immune system, possibly interfering with its ability to detect and destroy viruses or cells that become cancerous. According to Johan Denollet (1998), individuals who suppress their emotions, are depressed, have pessimistic outlooks on life, and have few social contacts may be at risk of developing cancer. Denollet refers to these distressed individuals as having Type D personalities. Most scientific studies, however, do not show an association between personality and cancer onset ("Cancer and the Mind," 1998). *After* being diagnosed with cancer, people who have optimistic outlooks and fighting spirits survive longer than those who do not have these characteristics (Faller et al., 1999). Chapter 12 presents more information concerning the development of cardiovascular disease; Chapter 13 discusses the development of cancer.

coping strategies
behavioral responses and thought processes that people use to deal with stressors.

Healthy
LIVING PRACTICES

- To reduce the risk of ulcers, avoid cigarette smoking, chronic alcohol use, lying down after eating, overeating, and chronic use of anti-inflammatory drugs.
- If you experience a burning or aching sensation in the middle of your abdomen after eating, or feel bloated and nauseated after meals, you may have an ulcer. See your health-care provider for diagnosis and treatment.
- To reduce the risk of tension headaches, learn to relax. Consult a physician if you have a severe headache.
- To become more stress-resistant, accept stress as a part of life and find some positive aspects of stressful situations.

Coping with Stress

Stress is a consequence of living. In today's world, many people cannot fight or escape some of their stressors because the sources of this stress are difficult to pinpoint and control. In other instances, distressed individuals are aware that their living conditions are violent, polluted, or impoverished, but they lack the resources to improve their situations. By learning ways to lessen the overall impact of everyday stressors on their health, many persons can live with their stress. To become more stress-resistant, for example, one can adopt a lifestyle that may reduce the negative effects of stress on the immune system, such as getting enough rest or becoming involved with spiritually uplifting activities (Glaser et al., 1999).

Coping strategies are behavioral responses and thought processes that individuals use to deal actively with sources of stress. Psychologists classify coping strategies as problem-focused, emotion-focused, or social-support methods of managing stressful situations. Although many coping strategies are useful, some can be harmful to health.

Problem-Focused Strategies

Problem-focused strategies, such as planning, confronting, and problem-solving activities, are behaviors that can directly reduce or eliminate the negative effects of stressors. For example, setting priorities, managing time, planning for retirement, or retraining for a career change are strategies that can make people feel more in control of stressful situations. When individuals identify the sources of their stress and think that they have some control over their stressors, they feel less distress and experience fewer health problems. The "Changing Health Habits" activity in the workbook can help you identify and change a distressing health-related habit.

Managing Your Time One of the most useful stress-reduction skills that you can learn is effective time management. Begin by making a list of all work, school, family, and leisure activities that you perform in a day. Then analyze the list so you can rank the activities according to level of priority. High-priority activities are those which you really want to perform and those which must be accomplished if you are to meet your goals. Are some activities relatively unimportant or "time wasters?" These activities have low priority. In order to allocate and use time well, you may decide to eliminate some activities from your schedule.

After analyzing and ranking the activities, determine the amount of time that is needed to carry them out. Allow more time to complete the high-priority tasks than for those of lesser importance. Perform the high-priority tasks first. Additionally, consider when is your "best time" of the day; plan to do the most challenging tasks during that period. To be successful in college, for example, you should allow time to attend all classes and prepare for each class, which includes setting some time aside for studying daily. Allow some time for unexpected situations; it is not necessary to lock yourself into a rigid schedule. Of course, you also need time to relax, sleep, eat, exercise, and socialize. If you work or have family responsibilities while you are in school, planning your time carefully is even more crucial.

To manage time, keeping a calendar to record when papers are due or exams are given can be helpful. Many people also make daily lists of "things to do," especially on very busy days. Individuals who balance the time that they spend performing task-centered responsibilities with the time spent engaging in pleasurable activities are able to improve their performance and feel a sense of accomplishment.

Journal Writing Coping with daily stressors may be easier if you keep a written record of personal events, thoughts, and feelings (Spiegel, 1999). Entering your thoughts in a journal regularly can help you focus on your emotional responses to situations. There are no rules to writing effective therapeutic journals. You do not have to write the passages in prose; some people express their feelings in poetry or as letters that are not to be mailed. First identify the problems or situations that are stressful and then write your thoughts concerning them, including ways you might be able to resolve these problems (see the "Reflecting on Your Health" activity in this chapter).

Emotion-Focused Strategies

Instead of directly dealing with stressors, many individuals use *emotion-focused* strategies to alter their appraisal of stressful situations. Such alterations can make the events less threatening. Chapter 2 described various defense mechanisms, such as denial and projection, that serve as coping strategies to defend one's mind against threats. In addition to using defense mechanisms, some distressed individuals overeat or make poor food choices (Oliver & Wardle, 1999). Others abuse alcohol. These unhealthy lifestyles often create even more stress. Emotion-focused strategies can have harmful consequences for individuals and those who must live or work with them. People need to recognize that stress is a part of life; trying to avoid stressors and denying the need to manage stress usually do not reduce its long-term impact on health.

Not all emotion-focused strategies are counterproductive; some are helpful, especially if the strategy aids in mental relaxation or encourages more positive thinking. Humor can serve as a "stress buffer," lessening the impact of both daily hassles and major life events (Seward, 1999; Williams, 1999). For example, the homeowners who post a "For Sale"

sign in front of their hurricane-damaged house are using humor to relieve some of their distress. Additionally, forming constructive rather than destructive appraisals of stressful situations is a useful emotion-focused strategy. Many successful athletes cope with the stress of competition by appraising each competitive event as an opportunity to challenge themselves and achieve excellence in their sport. By viewing the competition as a challenge rather than a threat, athletes are less likely to experience the emotionally and physically destructive effects of stress on their performance.

Social-Support Strategies

Besides these strategies, many individuals use *social-support strategies* to cope with stressful situations. Social-support strategies include seeking the advice, assistance, or consolation of close friends and relatives; participating in support groups; and obtaining spiritual help from members of the clergy or religious congregations.

When a major disaster occurs in a community, relief organizations like the Red Cross provide valuable social and financial support services that reduce the impact of the catastrophe on peoples' lives. The knowledge that other people, even strangers, are willing to provide assistance is comforting and reassuring for many distressed individuals. Humans are not the sole providers of social support; lonely people who love animals often find comfort in the companionship of their pets (▌ Figure 3-4).

People can use rest and relaxation to redirect their attention away from stressors. By learning how to relax, most

▲**Figure 3-4 Pets as Friends.** People who love animals often find comfort in the companionship of their pets.

people can manage the stress in their lives more effectively. The following section examines ways to cope with stress through relaxation.

Healthy LIVING PRACTICES

- Accepting stress as a part of life and finding some positive aspects of stressful situations can reduce the negative or harmful impact of stress on your health.
- Planning for the future, setting priorities, and managing time can help you feel more in control of your life.
- Recording your thoughts and feelings in a journal can help you manage stress.
- Viewing challenging situations as opportunities to experience psychological growth can help you manage your stress.
- Seeking the companionship and social support of others can reduce your stress.

Stress Management Skills

www.jbpub.com/healthyliving

Although no one can eliminate stress, you can use a variety of relaxation techniques to reduce its impact on your health. As you relax, your intestinal functioning becomes normal, your breathing and heart rate slow, and your blood pressure declines. Practicing relaxation techniques can restore many body processes to normal, and reverse the potentially damaging responses to stress that may have occurred in your body. The major objective of many relaxation activities is learning how to relax your skeletal muscles while remaining mentally alert.

Deep Breathing

While having panic attacks, people often *hyperventilate* (pant for air) and feel as though they are suffocating. Hyperventilation alters the chemistry of the blood, which increases the heart rate and causes dizziness. By deliberately breathing slower and deeper, distressed people can feel more relaxed as their blood chemistry values return to normal. Concentrating on breathing more deeply allows people to shift their attention away from stressors and toward the breathing activity.

Under normal conditions, you breathe an average of 12 to 18 times per minute, but to relax, you need to breathe

only 8 to 10 times per minute. The key is to take several deep breaths, using your abdominal muscles, and recognize how deep breathing feels different from your usual breathing pattern. Results from studies show that deep breathing is a quick and simple method to reduce the impact of stress on your health. You can use this breathing technique whenever you begin to feel excited or stressed; so before your next exam, speech, or job interview, relax by simply breathing deeply.

Progressive Muscular Relaxation

Although some degree of skeletal muscular tension is necessary to maintain a comfortable body posture, excess tension in forehead, scalp, jaw, and neck muscles may contribute to the development of some headaches. Distressed individuals often look tense because of their tightened facial muscles or clenched fists. Even when they are resting, stressed people still report feeling excess muscle tension. Teeth grinding is a common sign of stress that often occurs during sleep and may lead to pain in the **temporomandibular joint**, the joint where the lower jaw attaches to the skull in front of the ear (Figure 3-5).

The *progressive muscular relaxation* technique teaches people how to recognize the differences between a tensed muscle and a relaxed one. Individuals learn how to voluntarily release muscle tension, becoming aware of the relaxed sensations. When a person's skeletal muscles are completely relaxed, the individual is limp and feels calm. People often use the technique to fall asleep. The "Managing Your Health" tip entitled "A Technique for Progressive Muscular Relaxation" highlights the steps of this particular relaxation method.

Meditation and the Relaxation Response

For some people, praying or meditating reduces stress. **Meditation** is an activity in which one relaxes by mentally

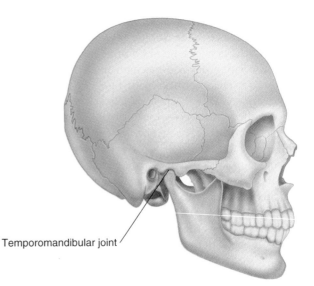

Temporomandibular joint

▶ **Figure 3-5 The Temporomandibular Joint.** The temporomandibular joint is the point at which the lower jaw attaches to the skull in front of the ear. Pain in the temporomandibular joint may result from grinding teeth during sleep, a common sign of stress.

A Technique for Progressive Muscular Relaxation

1. Choose a quiet location and sit in a comfortable position, hands down at your sides, and both feet flat on the floor.
2. Close your eyes and take a few deep breaths; concentrate on becoming as relaxed as possible.
3. With your arms at your sides, make a fist with one of your hands. Hold your clenched fist for about 5 seconds, release your hand from this position, and concentrate on the feeling as the muscular tension "drains" out of your hand.

This basic exercise is repeated as you tense muscles, hold the tensed position for 5 seconds, and then relax the major muscle groups in your body. It is impor-tant to focus on recognizing the difference between muscular tension and re-laxation sensations. Continue breathing normally as the activity progresses. Begin with your head.

4. Tense your forehead and scalp mus-cles; feel the tight muscular sensa-tions as you hold this position for 5 seconds; relax these muscles.
5. Tense your facial muscles; hold this position for 5 seconds; relax.
6. Tense the muscles of your neck and jaw; hold this position; relax.
7. Tense your back muscles—but not too tight; hold this position; relax.
8. Tense your right arm; hold; relax.
9. Tense your left arm; hold; relax.
10. Tense your chest muscles; hold; then relax.
11. Tense your stomach muscles; hold; relax.
12. Tense your buttocks; hold; relax.
13. Tense your right leg—but not too tight; hold; relax.
14. Tense your left leg—but not too tight; hold; relax.

Now, imagine traveling back through your body searching for muscles that are not relaxed. As you find tense muscles, relax them. Maintain this position for several minutes, concentrating on your breath-ing. In this relaxed state, you may practice tranquil imagery and positive self-talk. To regain your normal physical activity, open your eyes, stand, and stretch your muscles.

---

focusing on a single word, object, or thought. Current medical interest in the value of meditation as a stress management technique began with the transcendental meditation (TM) movement of the 1960s. Herbert Ben-son (1975) incorporated features of TM into his *relaxation response,* claiming that this method is effective for reduc-ing blood pressure and drug abuse. To practice Benson's method, find a quiet place where you can sit comfortably for 10 to 20 minutes. Close your eyes, breathe normally, and concentrate on repeating a simple word or main-taining a pleasant thought. Progressively relax groups of muscles, starting at your feet and moving up your body to your face. After relaxing your muscles, maintain this pose for at least 10 minutes. When you are ready to regain your usual degree of alertness, open your eyes, stand up, and stretch.

Imagery

Imagery is a mental activity that is often combined with progressive muscular relaxation exercises to enhance phys-ical relaxation. The technique is simple. After relaxing their muscles, individuals think of peaceful, pleasurable scenes, using their imaginations or past experiences to guide them. As these persons "see" the scenes in their minds, they imagine other sensations as well. For example, a per-son who enjoys outdoor activities might recall floating down a small stream in a canoe. This individual would imagine the peaceful feeling of floating gently on the water as well as the sound of birds singing and water flowing. Imagery, or visualization, can be a creative and en-joyable way to relax as it disengages the mind from thinking about problems.

Athletes, actors, and other performers often use imagery to reduce their stress and en-hance their performance. Before an event, for example, a pole vaulter often visualizes the entire sequence of events that takes place when approaching and vaulting over the pole. Although imagery is not a sub-stitute for actually practicing the required skills, the technique is a useful training ac-tivity for many competitive athletes.

You do not have to be an athlete or an actor to use imagery to reduce your stress levels. Be-fore facing a stressful situation, like giving a speech or interviewing for a job, imagine the set-ting. Then imagine the other people's responses and your own behavior. Mentally rehearsing the situation can reduce some of your anxiety by making you feel better prepared.

temporo-mandibular joint (TEM-pe-row-man-DIB-you-ler) the place where the lower jaw bone (mandible) attaches to the temporal bone of the skull.

meditation an activity in which one relaxes by mentally focus-ing on a single word, object, or thought.

Self-Talk

At times, people may have irrational or negative thoughts concerning their abilities to deal effectively with their stressors. Individuals can reduce their stress levels by identifying these self-defeating thoughts and replacing them with positive self-talk statements. Positive self-talk reflect a person's attributes and boosts self-confidence. However, thinking about oneself in a positive manner may be difficult for individuals who have low self-esteem. People with poor self-esteem often have self-degrading or self-critical thoughts, and they are unaccustomed to acknowledging their positive characteristics.

To practice positive self-talk, think of at least three affirmative statements to say about yourself, including your feelings, accomplishments, skills, and characteristics. Self-talk can be personal compliments ("I look great today"), statements of encouragement ("I can handle this problem"), or statements that reflect personal strengths ("I know I can ace that test"). Write these positive statements on a small card and place the card where you will see it daily. Repeat these statements to yourself every day and when you are feeling "stressed out." You can begin your daily relaxation sessions with progressive muscular relaxation followed by imagery, and then complete the stress management activity by repeating your positive self-statements.

Most relaxation methods are relatively easy to learn, but to be effective, the individual needs a high degree of motivation, self-control, and willingness to practice the skills. You can learn each technique and determine which one is the most effective. Regardless of the relaxation technique chosen, you will need to reserve about 10 to 20 minutes each day to practice the activity. At first, learning to relax may be difficult, but by practicing at least one of these techniques every day, you should be able to master the activity within a couple of weeks.

Physical Exercise

Whether it is square dancing or gardening, physical activity can reduce stress by shifting one's attention away from stressors and toward the enjoyable aspects of the activity. Besides this psychological benefit, physical activity can metabolize the extra energy released during the stress response, lessening the impact of stress on the body. Additionally, engaging in physical activity with others can enhance social and spiritual well-being. Nearly everyone can think of at least one physical activity that they can enjoy on a regular basis.

According to a position statement issued by the International Society for Sport Psychology (1992), regular exercise improves mood and self-image, while reducing anxiety and stress. Scientists have found that moderate physical activity or exercise enhances the functioning of the immune system, and this degree of activity can often reduce symptoms of depression and anxiety. Too much physical activity,

▲ **Figure 3-6 Managing Stress with Yoga.** Yoga includes specific physical exercises, breathing techniques, meditation activities, and dietary restrictions to promote a healthier body. After practicing yoga, trained individuals usually report feeling relaxed and refreshed.

however, can cause muscle exhaustion or damage, creating emotional stress. Thus, athletes who engage in endurance activities and extensive physical training may have less effective immune systems. During strenuous physical activity, like running, the nervous system releases *endorphins* that may be responsible for creating the "runner's high," the heightened sense of well-being that long-distance runners often experience. As mentioned earlier in this chapter, endorphins can reduce the activity of certain components of the immune system. Chapter 11 describes how most people can gain far more health benefits than harmful effects from regular, moderate exercise.

Tai Chi and Yoga Tai chi, a form of martial art that originated in China, emphasizes relaxation of the mind while the body is in motion. As people perform the gentle, gliding movements of tai chi, they focus their attention on this physical activity and disregard all other thoughts. In addition to tai chi, the other martial arts can be effective in reducing stress, increasing the body's flexibility, and boosting self-confidence. Tai chi, however, may be preferred by less physically active older adults because the exercises are less strenuous.

Yoga, a philosophy of living that originated in India thousands of years ago, includes specific physical exercises, breathing techniques, meditation activities, and dietary restrictions to promote a healthier body and manage stress (▌ **Figure 3-6).** As individuals practice the yoga exercises, they slowly move their bodies into positions that stretch their skeletal muscles. After maintaining these positions, trained individuals usually report feeling relaxed and refreshed. Although some of yoga's teachings concerning nutrition and the health benefits of stretching organs are not based on modern medical concepts, these exercises can enhance the body's muscular flexibility and reduce stress.

Interest in tai chi and yoga is increasing in the United States; if you would like to learn the exercises, check with the physical education department on your campus or the local YMCA/YWCA to determine if they offer classes in these activities. Before beginning any new physical activity program, especially the martial arts and yoga, it is advisable to receive approval from a qualified health-care practitioner.

Healthy ■LIVING PRACTICES■

- If dwelling on negative self-thoughts creates stress for you, think about your strengths and develop a list of affirmative self-statements to repeat regularly.
- Consider setting aside some time to relax every day, perhaps by using the techniques discussed in this chapter.
- Try breathing slowly and deeply before or during a stressful situation as a simple but effective way to relax.
- Engaging in tai chi, yoga, and moderate exercise and physical activity on a regular basis can reduce your stress.

across the Lifespan

Stress

Distressed adults may recall images of a carefree childhood, but children also experience stress. Common stressors for children include separation from a parent through divorce or death, moving to a new neighborhood and changing schools, or illness of a close family member (Grey, 1993).

When children are distressed, they often exhibit regressive behaviors, like clinging to and acting more dependent on their parents. In addition to acting immature, distressed youngsters may become depressed and withdrawn, suffer sleep disturbances, or experience problems at school. Parents can help their children learn healthy ways to cope with stressful situations by teaching them problem-solving skills and relaxation exercises.

As mentioned in Chapter 2, the adolescent years are stressful because individuals undergo numerous physical and social changes during this time. Distressed youth who do not have effective and healthy coping mechanisms are likely to suffer from depression, abuse drugs, have serious

traffic accidents, and experience problems with parents and school authorities. If a child's stress response persists or is severe, professional counseling is necessary.

For many people, the elderly years can be very stressful. Aging individuals often feel bored or useless, especially if they have retired from the responsibilities of a job or raising a family. On the other hand, many older adults are distressed because they must work to supply an income, or they must raise their grandchildren because their own children are unable, unwilling, or unavailable (e.g., deceased) to do so. Older adults frequently experience distress when they must care for spouses with debilitating mental or physical illnesses.

Coping with loneliness and the deaths of friends or close family members is especially difficult for aging individuals as they face the reality of their own mortality. Suffering from disabling illnesses creates additional distress for many elderly people. The inability to cope with stress can have serious results; rates of emotional depression and suicide are high among the isolated elderly. To enhance the well-being of elderly people, communities often have programs that encourage social interaction among aged members of the population. Additionally, elderly residents of most nursing homes can participate in social and physical activities that combat the stress of isolation (▌ **Figure 3-7**).

▲**Figure 3-7 Social Interaction among the Elderly.** To enhance the well being of elderly people and combat the stress of isolation, communities often offer programs that encourage social interaction among aged members of the population.

Chapter Review

Summary

Stress can refer to a threatening or demanding situation, a person's responses to a situation, or the interactions that take place between a person and a situation. Various situations or conditions, referred to as stressors, create stress. Situations with unwanted or negative outcomes produce distress, those with positive outcomes produce eustress. Stress can make life more challenging and interesting, but too much can make life miserable.

In a combined response, the nervous and endocrine systems prepare the body to confront or leave dangerous situations. Hans Selye proposed the general adaptation syndrome to describe the three stages of the body's adaptive physical responses to stressors. The stress response produces physical changes that may reduce the activity of certain white blood cells and the effectiveness of the immune system. As a result, enduring too many stressful life events can negatively affect one's susceptibility to disease. Interest in the role of stress in psychological health has led to a new area of research called psychoneuroimmunology.

People use either problem-focused, emotion-focused, or social-support coping strategies to deal actively with stressful situations. Although these strategies can be effective methods of helping people take control over their stressors, some coping methods can be harmful to health. For example, avoiding and denying stressors are coping mechanisms that usually do not eliminate the sources of stress.

Many stress management activities involve learning skills that enable one to relax. Relaxation can reverse many of the normal but damaging physical responses to stress. Relaxation techniques include deep breathing exercises, progressive muscular relaxation, meditation, and mental imagery. Journal writing, positive self-talk, and moderate physical activity can also reduce stress.

Common childhood stressors include separation from a parent through divorce or death, moving to a new neighborhood and changing schools, and the illness of a close family member. Older distressed youths are often depressed, abuse drugs, and experience problems with parents and school authorities. Aging people often find that coping with loneliness, disability, and the deaths of friends or close family members is especially stressful.

Applying What You Have Learned

1. Using the techniques described in this chapter, develop a personal stress-reduction program that you can incorporate into your daily schedule. *(Application)*
2. You have two final exams scheduled for the same day. Describe how you could use a negative coping strategy to reduce your stress. Describe how you could use a positive coping method to deal with the same situation. *(Application)*
3. Plan a program that uses social support as a coping strategy to help distressed elderly people who live in your community. *(Synthesis)*
4. Evaluate your present situation. Determine and list the sources of distress in your life. *(Evaluation)*

KEY

Application: Using information in a new situation.
Synthesis: Putting together information from different sources.
Evaluation: Making informed decisions.

Reflecting On Your Health

1. Review the physical adaptations to stress that are listed in Table 3-1. The last time you were faced with a stressful situation, did you experience these changes? How did you feel?
2. Recall that stress can have positive outcomes. Reflect on a stressful experience that made you feel happy, challenged, or successful. Why did the experience make you feel this way?
3. Each person can appraise a situation differently; what is distressing to one can be thrilling to another. Choose a situation that distresses you. Why do you think it affects you in this manner? Do you think other people would find this situation distressing? Why or why not?
4. Chronic stress can have negative effects on health. What was the most stressful situation that you had to endure in the past year? How did this experience affect your health and well-being?
5. How do you usually react when faced with stressful situations? Are your responses positive or negative? How do you think you could reduce the impact of stress on your health?

References

Benson, H. (1975). *The relaxation response.* New York: William Morrow and Company.

Cancer and the mind. (1998). *The Harvard Mental Health Letter, 14*(9):1-5.

Denollet, J. (1998). Personality and risk of cancer in men with coronary heart disease. *Psychological Medicine, 28*:991-995.

Faller, H., Bülzebruck, H., Drings, P., & Lang, H. (1999). Coping, distress, and survival among patients with lung cancer. *Archives of General Psychiatry, 56*:756-762.

Favaro, A., Maiorani, M. A., Colombo, G., & Santonastaso, P. (1999). Traumatic experiences, posttraumatic stress disorder, and dissociative symptoms in a group of refugees from Former Yugoslavia. *Journal of Nervous and Mental Disease, 187*(5):306-308.

Fugh-Berman, A., & Cott, J. M. (1999). Dietary supplements and natural products as psychotherapeutic agents. *Psychosomatic Medicine, 61*:712-728.

Glaser, R., Rabin, B., Chesney, M., Cohen, S., & Natelson, B. (1999). Stress-induced immunomodulation: Implications for infectious diseases? *Journal of the American Medical Association, 281*(24): 2268-2270.

Grey, M. (1993). Stressors and children's health. *Journal of Pediatric Nursing, 8*:85-91.

Herbal Rx: The promise and pitfalls. (1999). *Consumer Reports, 64*(4): 44-49.

Holmes, T. H., & Rahe, R. H. (1967). The social readjustment rating scale. *Journal of Psychosomatic Research, 11*:213-218.

International Society of Sport Psychology. (1992). Physical activity and psychological benefits: A position statement. *Sport Psychologist, 6*:199-203.

Kellner, R. (1994). Psychosomatic syndromes: Somatization and somatoform disorders. *Psychotherapy and Psychosomatics, 61*:4-24.

Levenson, J. L., McDaniel, J. S., Moran, M. G., & Stoudmire, A. (1999). Psychological factors affecting medical conditions. In R. E. Hales, S. C. Yudofsky, & J. A. Talbott (Eds.), *Textbook of Psychiatry* (3rd ed.). (pp. 635-661). Washington, DC: American Psychiatric Press.

Levenstein, S., Ackerman, S., Kiecolt-Glaser, J. K., & Dubois, A. (1999). Stress and peptic ulcer disease. *Journal of the American Medical Association, 281*(1):10-11.

Light, K. C., Girdler, S. S., Sherwood, A., Bragdon, E. E., Brownley, K. A., West, S. G., & Hinderliter, A. L. (1999). High stress responsivity predicts later blood pressure only in combination with positive family history and high life stress. *Hypertension, 33*:1458-1464.

Marx, M. B., Garrity, T. F., & Bowers, F. R. (1975). The influence of recent life experiences on the health of college students. *Journal of Psychosomatic Research, 19*:87-98.

Mollica, R. F., McInnes, K., Sarajlić, N., Lavelle, J., Sarajlić, I., & Massagli, M. P. (1999). Disability associated with psychiatric comorbidity and health status in Bosnian refugees living in Croatia. *Journal of the American Medical Association, 282*(5):433-439.

Newcomer, J. W., Selke, G., Melson, A. K., Hershey, T., Craft, S., Richards, K., & Alderson, A. L. (1999). Decreased memory performance in healthy humans induced by stress-level cortisol treatment. *Archives of General Psychiatry, 56*:527-533.

Nordenberg, T. (1998). Heading off migraine pain. *FDA Consumer, 32*(3):19-25.

Oliver, G., & Wardle, J. (1999). Perceived effects of stress on food choice. *Physiological Behavior, 66*:511-515.

Patterson, S. M., Zakowski, S. G., Hall, M. H., Cohen, R., Wollman, K., & Baum, A. (1994). Psychological stress and platelet activation: Differences in platelet reactivity in healthy men during active and passive stressors. *Health Psychology, 13*(1): 34-38.

Pepping, J. (1999). Kava: Piper methysticum. *American Journal of Health-System Pharmacy, 56*:957-958, 960.

Saper, J. R. (1999). Headache disorders. *Medical Clinics of North America, 83*(3): 663-690.

Selye, H. (1976). *The stress of life* (2nd ed.). New York: McGraw-Hill.

Seward, B. L. (1999). *Managing stress.* Boston: Jones & Bartlett.

Spiegel, D. (1999), Healing words: Emotional expression and disease outcome. *Journal of the American Medical Association, 281*(14):1328-1329.

U.S. Department of Health and Human Services (USDHHS), Public Health Service. 1999. *Healthy people 2000 review: 1998-1999* (Publication 99-1256). Washington, DC: Government Printing Office. http://odphp.osophs.dhhs.gov/pubs/hp2000/prog_rvw.htm

Williams, R. B. (1999). A 69-year-old man with anger and angina. *Journal of the American Medical Association, 282*(8):763-770.

Wong, A. H. C., Smith, M., & Boon, H. S. (1998). Herbal remedies in psychiatric practice. *Archives of General Psychiatry, 55*:1033-1044.

Violence and Abuse

Most of the campus security notices seemed to be for women, and I had a high school letter in wrestling, so I wasn't worried. Late one night, I was walking across campus, hardly watching where I was going, when a guy with a gun jumped out of some bushes and demanded my money. I gave him my watch and wallet, but he still hit me in the face with the gun barrel. I needed several stitches to close the wound.

According to the Federal Bureau of Investigation (FBI), one aggravated assault occurred every 32 seconds in the United States during 1998. One forcible rape took place every 6 minutes. One murder happened every 31 minutes (U.S. Department of Justice, 1998).

In 1997 child protective agencies in the United States confirmed more than 1 million reports of child mistreatment; about one-third were cases of physical, sexual, and emotional abuse (Leventhal, 1999). Partner-against-partner violence is common in the United States. During her lifetime,

". . . one aggravated assault occurred every 32 seconds in the United States during 1998."

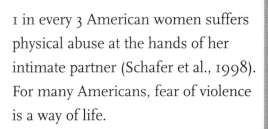

1 in every 3 American women suffers physical abuse at the hands of her intimate partner (Schafer et al., 1998). For many Americans, fear of violence is a way of life.

Every society tolerates certain controlled uses of force, for example, spanking unruly children or playing contact sports. In this chapter, **violence** refers to interpersonal uses of force that are not socially sanctioned. Such violence occurs when at least one person intentionally applies or threatens physical force on other(s). These incidents are usually one-sided—for example, a perpetrator attacking a victim—but they are sometimes mutual, such as in a barroom brawl, a schoolyard scuffle, or a fight between a husband and wife. No gender or life stage is exempt from violence: It may be directed against the elderly, adults, adolescents, children, and even infants. Certain groups of people, such as homosexuals, African Americans, or Jews, are often targets of violence *(hate crimes)*.

What You'll Learn

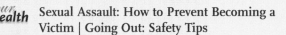

www.jbpub.com/healthyliving

The web site for this book offers many useful tools and is a great source for supplementary health information for both students and instructors. Visit the site at www.jbpub.com/healthyliving for information on these topics:

Violence in the United States
Major Types of Violence and Abuse
Preventing and Avoiding Violence

Chapter Overview

How violence affects your health.
Rates of violence in the United States.
Factors that contribute to violence.
Major types of violence and abuse.
How to assess your risk of becoming a victim of violence.
What you can do to prevent and avoid violence.

DIVERSITY in Health   Spouse Abuse: An International Problem

Con$umer Health   Natural Defense: Pepper Spray

Managing Your Health   Sexual Assault: How to Prevent Becoming a Victim | Going Out: Safety Tips

across the lifespan   Violence

Applying Concepts for Healthy Living
A Workbook

Student Workbook

Self Assessment: Assessing Your Anger
Changing Health Habits: Can You Reduce Your Risk of Violence?

Do You Know?

- If watching violent television shows can make the viewer violent?
- How to tell if your partner is likely to become physically abusive?
- What to do if you are sexually harassed?

Most physical violence in America could be regarded as nonsexual crimes against persons—mainly assault, robbery, and homicide. **Assault** is the intentional use of force to injure another person physically. **Abuse** occurs when one takes advantage of a relationship to mistreat a person, often by use of serious or frequent threats or force. Examples of abuse include spouse abuse, child abuse, elder abuse, and sexual harassment.

You have probably been affected by not merely the fear of violent crime but also by direct involvement in physical violence. As a child or youth, you may have been involved in incidents of shoving, slapping, punching, or kicking. Even during your adult years, you may have shoved or slapped someone or have been shoved or slapped. Moreover, you are likely to become involved in further violent episodes in the years to come. This chapter examines the impact of interpersonal violence on health and its causes, and it provides practical actions you can take to reduce your risk of being a victim.

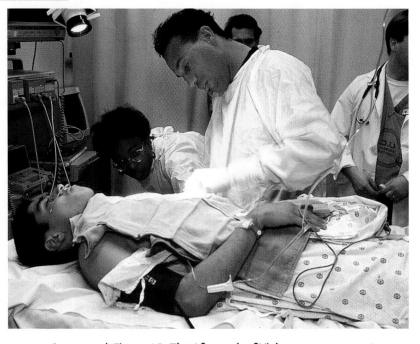

▲ **Figure 4-1 The Aftermath of Violence.** Injuries resulting from violence often require medical treatment.

How Violence Affects Health

Physical injuries resulting from violence now represent a large proportion of the patients in many hospital emergency rooms (■ **Figure 4-1**). Minor physical injuries from violence include bruises, cuts, and other injuries that require no hospitalization or less than 2 days' hospitalization. Serious injuries include broken bones, loss of teeth, penetrating wounds, loss of consciousness, rape or attempted rape injuries, and other injuries that require at least 2 days' hospitalization. Less direct physical effects of violence include the aggravation of preexisting conditions, such as heart problems, as well as infections with sexually transmitted infections (STIs) acquired through rape.

Long-term physical effects of violence include disabling conditions such as loss of vision, maiming, as well as pregnancy and HIV infection resulting from rape. The stress of fighting has been shown to compromise or suppress the immune system, which lowers bodily defenses against a variety of illnesses. Thus, a decline in overall health may be a long-term effect of violence. Death is, of course, the most serious consequence of violence. For Americans who are 15 to 24 years of age, homicide is the second leading cause of death (Hoyert et al., 1999).

Violent victimization is always injurious to psychological functioning, regardless of whether physical injury was sustained. The psychological effects of violence include anxiety and depression, which can result in substance abuse, eating disorders, and suicidal thoughts. Furthermore, external violence against a person often adversely affects the well-being of his or her family. Various family relationships may become strained, suspended, or even terminated, resulting in family disruption. Violence in a family nearly always produces disruption. Cases of marital separation or divorce often involve family violence. Another serious social effect is the *intergenerational* transmission of violence, in which abused children mature and become abusive parents, perpetuating family violence (Holtzworth-Munroe et al., 1997). This particular effect, however, occurs with only some abused children; a number of personality factors buffer some individuals from the long-term effects of child abuse. Overall, the financial costs of the impact of violence on physical, psychological, and social health are staggering; the cost in human misery is immeasurable.

www.jbpub.com/healthyliving

Violence in the United States

Exact figures on rates of violence are difficult to determine because so many of these incidents, especially rapes and domestic violence, are never reported. The FBI's annual *Uniform Crime Reports* and the Census Bureau's annual *National Crime Victimization Survey (NCVS)* provide data regarding rates of violence in the United States. The *Uniform Crime Reports* include violent incidents that are reported to the police and that violate a criminal statute. As a result, these official crime statistics omit an unknown number of violent incidents that are not reported to the police. The *National Crime Victimization Surveys* yield much more information about violent incidents than do the official tallies because they rely on self-reports.

Public perceptions of violence rates and risks do not always match the facts. Our lives are more dangerous than they used to be, but not nearly as dangerous as some media stories suggest. Although many Americans believe that violence is at an all-time high and that rates of violent crime are escalating, some of these rates have either leveled off or declined since 1990 (U.S. Department of Justice, 1998).

Violent Behavior: Contributing Factors

Violence is complex; there is no single cause of violence, nor is violent behavior limited to a particular group of people. Factors that contribute to violence include poverty, substance abuse, certain psychological disorders, and poor self-esteem. In many instances, however, violence is learned behavior. Each year, more than 3 million American children witness acts of abuse or violence between their parents (Eisenstat & Bancroft, 1999). Children who are exposed to violence in their homes are more likely to be abusive or violent as adults than children who do not witness or experience violence.

Many Americans are concerned that exposure to violence in the media is associated with subsequent violent behavior, as well as the development of values and attitudes that tolerate or accept violence. The average American child watches 23 to 27 hours of television per week (Willis & Strasberger, 1998). Numerous studies have found an association between viewing television violence and aggressive behavior that continues over time. How do the media contribute to violence in America?

The visual media, including television programs, computer games, and movies, offer opportunities for individuals to learn violent behavior. Although indirect, the media provide ways for one to participate in the violence, experience emotional states associated with being violent, and observe the consequences of violence. Violence is often glamorized, and the perpetrators usually are not punished. If the use of violence is portrayed as an effective means of getting what one wants, a young impressionable observer may consider violence as an option when similar circumstances arise, and may even generalize to other situations.

Recently, the television industry introduced a rating system to help parents select nonviolent programs for their children. Some children, however, use the ratings to find violent programs to watch. Thus, parents should exercise good judgment concerning appropriate visual media for their children and monitor their offsprings' viewing habits.

Major Types of Violence and Abuse

Community Violence

Community violence refers to violence that occurs in public settings such as street corners, bars, and public places. Among youths, community violence increasingly takes the form of gang violence. Although many people think gangs are a recent development, gangs have been a feature of urban life in American cities for more than a century. In the late 1800s, cities such as St. Louis had groups of adolescents who wore differently colored clothing to identify their particular gang membership (Decker, 1997). Today, typical members of a gang are males between 8 and 24 years of age who share similar racial or ethnic backgrounds. Such gangs are prevalent in certain neighborhoods of American cities and are becoming more common in many suburbs.

The use of violence is a characteristic of gang activities—gang members often resort to violence to defend their territory. The most common kinds of gang violence include homicides, attempted homicides, assaults, shootings, and robberies. Violent gang activities are more likely to occur on weekends, in the evenings, and on the streets. The late-night drive-by shooting, for example, has come to be associated with gang violence.

Why are some youths attracted to gangs, placing themselves at high risk for serious injury and even death? Adolescents, especially those who have few options for socializing with other young people in their communities, may join gangs for social reasons. Additionally, gang membership provides an opportunity for some youths to belong to a group and find self-identity, that is, to "be someone." Involvement with gangs, however, dramatically increases one's risk of being murdered. In 1997 homicide was the second leading cause of death for persons between 15 and 24 years of age and the number one cause of death for African American men and women in this age group (Hoyert et al., 1999).

Institutional Violence

School Violence Most acts of institutional violence occur in schools, where students attack their peers or even their teachers. Earlier generations of students engaged in shoving and punching to settle arguments; today's students

violence an incident that is not socially sanctioned in which at least one person intentionally applies or threatens physical force on other(s).

assault the intentional use of force to injure another person physically.

abuse mistreatment of a person, as by serious or frequent threats or applications of force, that takes advantage of a relationship.

community violence violence between strangers or acquaintances that occurs in public settings.

use guns and knives. In 1998 and 1999, several incidents in which students used guns to kill their classmates and teachers made headline news (Figure 4-2). Such terrible events, however, are rare. Less than 1% of murders and suicides involving youth take place on school property. Youth are less likely to carry weapons to school and engage in fighting than in 1990 (Brener et al., 1999). To determine the extent to which children have been victimized at school, Kevin Fitzpatrick (1999) surveyed nearly 1200 children attending third through twelfth grades. Eighteen percent of the high school students reported being victimized, compared to 14% of the youngsters in elementary school.

What can be done to reduce the risk of violence at school? Many urban schools now resort to using metal detectors and hiring uniformed police in an attempt to curb school violence. In some instances, elementary teachers and school administrators can identify potential troublemakers in their classrooms. Young children who are at risk of displaying violent behavior tend to poke, shove, or annoy other persons; act impulsively; bully other children; and defy authorities, such as parents or teachers. Many high-risk children model the aggressive and impulsive behaviors of their parents. To reduce the likelihood of violence, elementary and secondary schools in many communities offer conflict resolution classes for children that emphasize socially acceptable ways of resolving conflicts.

Violence on College Campuses Young adults may experience institutional violence as campus violence. Compared to 1997, the percentage of violent crimes on college and university campuses increased slightly in 1998 (U.S. Department of Justice, 1998). As in the general population, violence on American campuses is associated with the widespread use of drugs, especially alcohol, and the pro-

liferation of guns. According to the National College Health Risk Behavior Survey, one in ten American college students had been in a physical fight during the 12 months preceding the survey ("Youth Risk," 1997). Almost 3% of college students carried a gun during the month preceding the survey.

In 1990 Congress enacted the Student Right to Know and Campus Security Act. This legislation requires administrators of colleges and universities that receive federal funds to report statistics concerning the number of murders, assaults, rapes, and other specific crimes that take place on their campuses. Additionally, the administrators must develop programs that are designed to educate students about personal safety and campus security. To reduce the violence on their campuses, many college administrators have adopted security measures such as restricting access to campus buildings, limiting visitation hours in residence halls, and initiating escort services for female students.

Workplace Violence The majority of American adults will never experience the most dangerous types of workplaces, such as psychiatric hospitals and prisons. Many adults, however, work outside their homes, where they may encounter violent persons. Workplace violence is any act of violence or abuse directed toward an individual who is performing his or her job. Any workplace can be a setting for violence.

The media stereotype equating workplace homicides with vengeful reprisals by disgruntled workers is misleading. According to statistics compiled by the U.S. Department of Labor in 1999, work-related homicides are most likely to occur during robberies of grocery stores, restaurants, bars, and gas stations. Cab drivers, convenience store attendants, police, and security guards are especially

▶Figure 4-2 Columbine, Colorado high school students seek comfort from each other after two of their classmates shot and killed 12 students and a teacher before taking their own lives. Despite incidents such as this, youth are less likely to carry weapons to school than in 1990.

at risk of being murdered while working. The number of homicides that took place in retail establishments declined by nearly 50% in 1998, reaching its lowest point since 1992 (U.S. Department of Labor, 1999).

Some employees become violent when they are laid off, fired, or not promoted. Individuals most likely to become violent in the workplace are men between the ages of 25 and 40 who are loners, have marital and other family problems, appear angry and paranoid, abuse alcohol and/or other drugs, and blame others for their problems. Women are less likely to be perpetrators of workplace violence, but they are more likely to be victims.

Sexual Violence

Sexual Assault Sexual violence involves some type of sexual activity gained through force, threat of force, or coercion. **Rape** is sexual intercourse by force or with a person who is incapable of legal consent. Both men and women can be the perpetrators and targets of rape and sexual assault. Nevertheless, females are the targets of most attempted or completed rapes. According to a recent survey, 1 out of 6 American women and 1 out of 33 American men have been victims of an attempted or completed rape at some time in their lives (Tjaden & Thoennes, 1998).

In most cases, a woman is raped by someone she knows, particularly a current or former husband, cohabiting partner, date, or boyfriend. Although men are not as likely to be raped as women, they are usually raped by male strangers and acquaintances (Tjaden & Thoennes, 1998). According to the most recent survey of college students, about 1 in 5 female students reported that they had been forced to have sexual intercourse at some time in their lives ("Youth Risk," 1997).

> My first sexual experience was very unpleasant. It happened on San Padre Island over Spring Break when I was a freshman. I was 18, and he was 25 years old. He took me to an area where no one could see him or hear me. I was naive and thought I could stop him, but I couldn't. I had wanted to wait until I was married, or at least, in love with the person.

Acquaintance rape is forced sexual activity that occurs between adults who know each other. If the couple is involved in a dating relationship, it is called date rape. In acquaintance rape, the rapist has a need to demonstrate his dominance over women, but he is sexually motivated as well. He does not plan to sexually assault women; instead he plans to have vaginal intercourse. When a woman resists, he rapes to carry out his original plan. A man may expect sex as repayment for money spent on dinner or entertainment. He may think it is acceptable to insist on having sex, even if his date says "no" and physically resists. Survey data suggest that many men who rape do not think of themselves as rapists, especially if the victim is someone they know.

Table 4-1	Attitudes Toward Rape: Men and Women	
Attitude	**Percentage of Men Who Agree**	**Percentage of Women Who Agree**
Stranger rape is a serious act.	90	98
Acquaintance rape is a serious act.	70	88
Women are partially to blame in cases of acquaintance rape.	46	36
Women ask to be raped by the way they act, dress, or talk.	38	14

Source: Stacy, R. D., Prisbell, M., & Tollefsrud, K. (1992). A comparison of attitudes among college students toward sexual violence committed by strangers and by acquaintances: A research report. *Journal of Sex Education and Therapy, 18:*257–263.

Health educator Richard Stacy and his colleagues (1992) compared the attitudes of 170 college students concerning stranger and acquaintance rape. The results of their investigation show wide differences between the sexes in attitudes toward rape (**Table 4-1**). The majority of those responding thought that sexual activity initiated by a stranger was a serious offense, but women were more likely than men to hold this opinion. Women were also more likely than men to think that acquaintance rape was a serious offense. Additionally, more men than women agreed with the idea that women "ask" to be raped.

The use of alcohol or other drugs may weaken a person's inhibitions and alter his or her usual behavior. An intoxicated man may act more aggressively, and an intoxicated woman may be less able to prevent forced sex. A recent and frightening development is the deliberate use of *rohypnol* and other so-called date-rape drugs, to sexually assault unsuspecting persons. Rohypnol causes not only loss of consciousness but also loss of memory concerning events that occurred when the drug was taken. Chapter 7 includes information concerning date rape drugs.

Marital rape is the use or threat of force against one's spouse to coerce any form of sexual activity. Marital rape can encompass couples who are only living together, same-sex partners, and former partners. However, the focus of most marital rape research has been on heterosexual couples.

Reporting Sexual Assault Data from the Crime Victimization surveys suggest that sexual crimes occur more often than previously suspected because official rates include only rapes that have been reported to the authorities (Rennison, 1999). Rape victims do not report their experiences to the authorities for many reasons. Victims often feel

rape
sexual intercourse by force or with a person who is incapable of legal consent.

shame and embarrassment. They may fear further victimization by the assailant or negative reactions from family, friends, and coworkers. Some victims do not want to become involved in the criminal justice system. Victims of acquaintance rape are often very reluctant to report the incidents to authorities because they feel partially to blame. For example, a female college student may feel that if she had consumed less alcohol, she would have been able to resist the advances of her date. Sexual assault victims should obtain immediate medical attention for their injuries, preferably from hospital emergency room staff who are trained to manage rape cases. Additionally, victims should consider taking legal action against their attackers.

If the victim chooses to prosecute the rapist, she should preserve all physical evidence because it might assist the police. For example, she should not wash any part of her body or change clothes. Semen and pubic hair from the attacker can be used to identify this individual. Victims who are unsure if they want to take legal action against their assailant can contact a rape crisis center for free advice from trained

Sexual Assault: How to Prevent Becoming a Victim

To avoid stranger rape:

- Avoid high-risk situations such as being alone in isolated areas or using drugs that affect your physical responses to a threat or your decision-making abilities.
- Walk with your head up, looking alert and confident.
- Consider carrying a concealed device that propels pepper spray. (See the "Consumer Health" feature on the next page.)
- Have your keys or remote carlock device in your hand as you approach your parked vehicle so you do not have to stand outside your car looking for them. Check the area around your parked car and in the back seat before you enter it.
- If your car becomes disabled, do not accept a stranger's help. Place a "Help. Call police." sign in the window. Stay inside the car until police arrive. Do not hitchhike. If you travel alone frequently, consider investing in a cellular phone.
- Keep the doors and windows of your car and home locked. Install deadbolt locks and peepholes on all outside doors of your home.
- Be wary of strangers who want you to open your door to them; they may intend to harm you. If they ask to use

your phone or bathroom, tell them you will make the call for them or they should go elsewhere. Even if they appear to be from a business, do not open the door.

If you are attacked:

- Yell or scream "Fire" instead of "Help" to get people's attention. Do not stop screaming; making a loud commotion may scare your attacker away.
- Do not allow yourself to be moved to another location. Resist being forced to get into a car. If you leave the original scene of the assault, it becomes more likely that you will be seriously injured or murdered.
- Avoid kicking the man's groin area; men are wary of this maneuver and guard their genitals. Instead, making a swift, hard kick across the attacker's kneecap can disable the person, allowing you to escape.
- If your attacker has a weapon, he may intend to kill you regardless of whether you comply with his demands. In this instance, rape prevention experts often recommend that you use extreme actions to confuse or intimidate the criminal such as throwing up, acting mentally ill, or pretending to have a heart attack or other life-threatening condition. In other instances, you may

pretend to cooperate with your attacker, waiting until his guard is down to make a surprise move in your defense.

To avoid date-rape:

- Agree to meet a "blind date" at a crowded location, or agree only to a group dating situation until you feel comfortable going out with the individual.
- Be wary of men who spend excessive amounts of money during a date, for example, taking you out to dinner at an exclusive restaurant. Such men may expect sex as a form of repayment.
- Be wary of dates who show unreasonable or inappropriate behaviors such as aggressiveness, rudeness, dominance, or hostility in social situations that do not involve sex. These individuals may display the same behaviors when alone with you.
- Avoid wearing provocative clothing, such as low-cut dresses, very short skirts, see-through blouses, or tight pants.
- Do not send mixed sexual messages that confuse your date. Say "no" to unwanted sexual advances, and if this person persists, tell him clearly that his behavior is rape.

Consumer Health

Natural Defense: Pepper Spray

One way to protect yourself against an aggressor is to use pepper spray. Pepper spray contains capsaicin, a compound that is found in hot chili peppers. When sprayed in an assailant's eyes, pepper spray produces a painful burning sensation. Almost immediately, the person's eyelids swell shut and tears begin to flow. The spray also causes the attacker to experience difficulty breathing and lose control over body movements. These effects last for about 20 to 30 minutes, which gives you time to escape the situation and call police. Pepper spray is an effective and safe way to subdue an attacker, but it may take a few seconds to work on certain enraged or drugged individuals.

Hardware or variety stores often sell pepper spray in small canisters that can be carried in a coat pocket or purse. People under the age of 18, however, are not permitted to possess pepper spray. Some states may impose other restrictions concerning the use of pepper spray. Therefore, before buying the product, check with local law-enforcement agencies to determine if it is legal to use pepper spray. Always follow the package directions when using it as a defense, for example, do not spray into the wind because it probably will not hit your attacker and will get on you! Also, keep the canister out of the reach of children and irresponsible persons.

Source: Busker, R. W., & van Helden, H. P. M. (1998). Toxicological evaluation of pepper spray as a possible weapon for the Dutch police force. *American Journal of Forensic Medicine and Pathology*, 19(4):309–316.

counselors. Most major metropolitan areas have rape crisis centers; their phone numbers may be listed under "Rape Hotline" or "Women Self-Help" in phone books. The "Managing Your Health" feature on page 68 provides some suggestions to lower your risk of becoming a sexual assault victim.

Sexual Harassment

Sexual harassment is the intentional use of annoying and offensive sexually related comments or behaviors to intimidate people or coerce them into unwanted sexual activity. Under certain conditions, unwelcome sexually offensive jokes, lewd comments, or touching and fondling can constitute such abusive behavior. It is difficult to determine the scope of the problem because surveys often use different definitions of *sexual harassment*. Sexual harassment is not always easy to recognize. For example, if someone tells a sexually offensive joke, under what circumstances would you consider this sexual harassment?

Sexual harassment can happen anywhere. College instructors, for example, engage in sexual harassment if they provide special treatment, such as awarding a passing grade, to students who submit to their sexual advances. In addition to schools, sexual harassment frequently occurs in the workplace.

Sexual harassment creates stress and reduces people's job satisfaction, performance, and loyalty. It is especially devastating for individuals who feel that their position, career, or grade depends on enduring the harassing behavior or submitting to the intimidating person. Individuals often deal with the situation by avoiding or ignoring harassing persons. Other harassed people choose to confront their tormentors by telling them, verbally or in writing, to discontinue the annoying and unprofessional comments or behaviors. If the harassment persists, victims can initiate more aggressive legal actions.

Many educational institutions and businesses have policies concerning sexual harassment that follow guidelines established by the federal government's Equal Employment Opportunity Commission (EEOC). These policies usually identify steps that people can take to file harassment-related complaints. Before initiating such action, individuals should document episodes of sexual intimidation, recording the date and nature of the unwanted comments or behaviors. Other people may be willing to serve as witnesses, supporting the victim's story, especially if the same person has harassed them.

Domestic Violence

Domestic violence is a pattern of behavior characterized by physical assaults, psychological injury, or threats between family members, persons who are involved in intimate relationships, or unrelated individuals who live together. Such violence includes spouse, child, and elder abuse. Nearly 30% of violence occurs in family settings, and females are overwhelmingly the victims of such offenses (U.S. Department of Justice, 1998). Child neglect and child sexual abuse are often classified as forms of domestic abuse. The "Across the Life Span" section of this chapter provides information concerning child abuse and elder abuse.

Domestic violence exists within every racial, ethnic, socioeconomic, and religious group. The rates of such

sexual harassment the intentional use of annoying and offensive sexually related comments or behaviors to intimidate people or coerce them into unwanted sexual activity.

domestic violence violence or abuse between family members, people who are involved in intimate relationships, or unrelated individuals who live together.

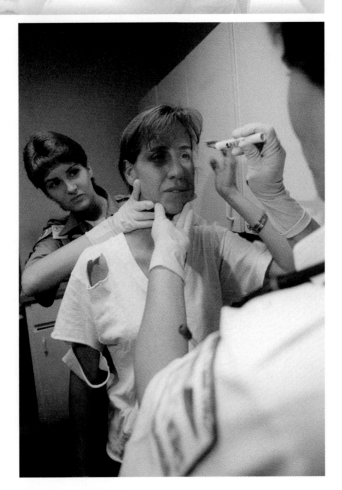

▲ **Figure 4-3 A Case of Domestic Violence.** One-third of all women experience violence in their marriages at some point. A woman is far more likely than a man to be seriously injured as the result of domestic violence.

violence, however, are higher among the poor, the unemployed, and those with low-status occupations. A husband who abuses alcohol heavily or thinks hitting his wife is acceptable behavior has a high risk of marital violence (Holtzworth-Monroe et al., 1997).

Dating and Marital Violence According to a recent survey, nearly 1 in 6 intimate couples experienced at least one episode of partner-against-partner violence during the previous year (Schafer et al., 1998). Violent acts may range from slapping, shoving, and punching to beating and murder. Dating violence, the use of force or the threat of force against one's partner during courtship, is quite common. Studies suggest that 25% to 36% of college students have experienced some form of violence in at least one dating relationship. Although both sexes perpetrate violent acts against their dates, men tend to use more severe forms of violence (Hamberger & Ambuel, 1998). Certain behaviors often characterize abusive individuals (Table 4-2). To avoid becoming a victim of dating violence, one should terminate a relationship if his or her partner displays any of these characteristics. Dating violence often is a precursor of marital violence.

The rates of intimate partner violence are similar for men and women, but women are far more likely to engage in violence against their partners as acts of self-defense than as perpetrators. Additionally, men are far more likely to injure seriously or murder the women with whom they live (Figure 4-3). According to the 1998 *Uniform Crime Reports,* 32% of female murder victims were killed by their spouses or boyfriends; only 4% of male murder victims were killed by their spouses or girlfriends (U.S. Department of Justice, 1998).

What causes violence between intimate partners? Certain individual or couple characteristics increase the risk of violence. Exposure to violence as a child, either as a direct

Table 4-2	Signs of Danger in a Relationship

A potentially abusive partner

- insists that you do things that you do not want to do and prevents you from doing things that you would like to do.
- argues with you over any issue.
- does not accept responsibility for his or her mistakes and blames you or other persons for his or her problems.
- prevents you from associating with your family and friends and threatens to end the relationship if you do not stop interacting with others.
- displays excessive jealousy or is too possessive.
- attempts to control your behavior, for example, tells you how to dress or wear your hair.
- is verbally abusive, for example, criticizes you or says degrading things to you either in private or in public.
- expects you to do everything perfectly and according to his or her wishes, and expects you to know what they are even without being told.
- reacts violently when things go wrong, he or she loses control, or he or she is embarrassed.
- exhibits cruelty to other persons or animals, usually without remorse.

Source: Mariani, C. (1996). *Domestic violence survival guide.* Flushing, NY: Looseleaf Law Publications.

Spouse Abuse: An International Problem

Throughout the world, women of all cultural, religious, ethnic, and socioeconomic groups are abused by their intimate partners. According to a recent report of the World Health Organization, 20% to 50% of women in 24 countries on four continents were physically abused by their husbands at one time in their relationships (Afkhami, 1999). Severe psychological and verbal abuse usually accompanies the physical violence, and the victim is often blamed for her mistreatment.

Why does spouse abuse persist? Certain non–Western cultures ascribe low status to women. Men living in these societies do not consider wife battering and other forms of mistreatment of their spouses as violence or abuse. Additionally, certain practices in such cultures increase the dependence of women on their spouses, which makes it difficult for women to leave their abusers. For example, women living in some countries lose their inheritance or the opportunity to earn an income outside of the home

when they marry. The power in these countries is unequally distributed in favor of men, and as a result, husbands feel entitled to control their wives and families. Male domination continues at community and state levels as women are often denied access to education and government positions. Thus, they lack the knowledge and political power necessary to change public policy. To eliminate the violence, people from around the world must work together to change the attitudes, behaviors, and laws

---

victim or as an observer of violent incidents between parents, may be a cause of spousal violence. Both perpetrators and victims tend to have low self-esteem and be highly dependent on their partners. Violent husbands often have problems asserting themselves and resort to the use of aggression to control and intimidate their partners. Often, one or both partners have ingested alcohol and/or other drugs when the violence between them erupts.

Why do wives stay in abusive marriages, sometimes for decades? Women often remain in these situations because of their emotional attachment to and economic dependency on the abuser. They feel trapped and isolated (Frank & Rodowski, 1999). Furthermore, the abusive spouse may be apologetic and loving after episodes of violence, raising the woman's hopes that the violence has ended. Spouse abuse is not just an American phenomenon; the Diversity in Health feature, "Spouse Abuse: An International Problem," discusses the nature of this behavior in non–Western societies.

Stalking

Sensational stories about celebrities who are pursued relentlessly by overly aggressive fans have led to interest and research into *stalking* behavior. Anyone can be the victim of a stalker. A stalker willfully and repeatedly follows and harasses another individual. The victim usually experiences extreme distress and often seeks legal means to make the stalker stop such unwanted behavior. In a national survey, 8% of American women and 2% of American men reported that they had been stalked at some point

in their lives (Tjaden & Thoennes, 1998). According to Paul Mullen and colleagues (1999), clinging, lonely ex-partners make up the largest group of stalkers. Relatively few stalkers are predatory strangers prone to become physically violent.

Assessing Your Risk of Violence

What are the chances that you, or some of the people you care about deeply, are at risk for violence? Are some more likely to suffer serious or fatal injury? The likelihood of a particular person experiencing such harm depends on specific risk factors. Peoples' risks of violence are either greater or less than average depending on who they are, where they are, and what their activities are.

Family disruption is a major risk factor for domestic and community violence. Family disruption may be the result of parental conflict that leads to separation, divorce, or desertion; or the presence of criminal, alcoholic, or drug-addicted parents. Neighborhood conditions, such as high rates of unemployment, can lead to high rates of family disruption. Other risk factors for domestic violence are social isolation, the presence of children with special needs, and a large number of children in the family. Risk factors for school violence are poor discipline in the classroom, weak administration, arbitrary enforcement of rules, and low levels of student interest in academic achievement.

Availability of drugs and guns enormously escalates the likelihood of serious injury or death in violent situations. A significant percentage of people who commit serious crimes test positive for alcohol, marijuana, cocaine, or combinations of mind-altering drugs at the time of their arrest (U.S. Department of Justice, 1999). Guns, especially handguns, are now involved in about 25% of violent incidents (Rennison, 1999). Most homicides are committed with guns (Fox & Zawitz, 1999).

Certain individuals are more likely than others to find themselves in places and situations in which violence is likely to occur. Age is one very important risk factor. Americans younger than 25 years old have a higher risk of involvement in violence than older persons. Youth who are 12 to 17 years of age commit 1 out of 4 serious violent offenses (Fox & Zawitz, 1999). Another key risk factor is gender. While in domestic settings women are as likely as men to use force, in community settings they are far less likely to do so. Men are more likely to be arrested for perpetrating crimes of violence; they are also more likely than women to be the victims of such crimes. Women, however, are more likely to be killed by their spouses than men.

Race and ethnicity are two other characteristics strongly related to involvement in violent incidents. A striking feature of American violence is the volume and concentration of violence within minority populations, particularly among young African American males living in urban areas. Blacks are 8 times more likely to commit murder than whites (Rennison, 1999). The overwhelming majority of murders are committed by persons who are members of the same racial group as their victims. An objective of *Healthy People 2000* (USDHHS, 1999) was to reduce the homicide rate from 8.5 per 100,000 (1987) to 7.2 per 100,000 Americans. The homicide rate declined to 6.8 per 100,000 Americans in 1997 (Fox & Zawitz, 1999).

Preventing and Avoiding Violence

Although many Americans doubt that violence can be prevented, they do think it can be contained. To reduce violent crime, communities are turning increasingly to environmental measures such as improved street lighting, neighborhood watch organizations, and surveillance by closed-circuit cameras,

There always will be violence, yet you can reduce your personal risk of victimization. Many avoidance measures are simple and inexpensive, and they work. To be effective, however, avoidance measures must become part of your routine. The most effective personal actions remove or distance an individual from high-risk situations and people. For example, a woman who does not attend a binge drinking party cannot be date-raped by another participant; a man who stays out of a high-crime district is unlikely to be a victim of a drive-by shooting. Simply put, people should avoid high-risk places and dangerous persons.

Home security is another avoidance measure, which aims to discourage and prevent intruders. In many break-ins, the intruder simply came through an unlocked door or window. The most important home or dorm safety measure is to have and always use good deadbolt locks on doors. Also, keep windows securely locked, especially when you are not home. Contact your police department or the campus security center to see if they will perform a free safety inspection of your residence.

If you live in a dangerous neighborhood, consider moving to a safer one if you can. This action is the most effective measure you can take to avoid violence. If you cannot leave the neighborhood, try to relocate farther away from known hot spots. If the new area looks safer, ask a few residents, and even local police, if they would prefer to live elsewhere. The police may have local crime statistics so you can compare the crime rates of various neighborhoods.

Daily life is filled with persons and situations that cannot be avoided, but you can use certain tactics to reduce your risks of victimization. If your usual routine requires traveling through dangerous neighborhoods, remove yourself from these high-risk areas by taking safer routes, even if they are out of your way. Avoid isolated places, such as deserted laundry rooms, infrequently used sections of libraries, or desolate parking lots.

A considerable percentage of violent crimes occur between 6 P.M. and midnight. Thus, if you must go out at night, do not go alone. If you are driving and someone in another car threatens you, do not stop, but drive to a well-lit public place; obviously, police stations or fire stations are the best choices. Stay in places where you can see other people. Being in the presence of others greatly reduces the risk of violence. If you are alone at night and on campus, use the college's escort service or use the "buddy system" when walking to and from buildings.

Regardless of the time of day, as soon as you enter your car, lock the doors. Keep your car doors locked even when you leave the car for a minute. Do not give rides to strangers or stop to help others. If you spend a lot of time in your car, obtain a cellular phone to call for assistance in any emergency. If you are involved in a minor accident, stay in your car and keep the doors locked until the police arrive. If someone demands that you surrender your car, do not argue with the person: Get out of the car and move away quickly. The "Managing Your Health" feature on page 73 lists some other important personal safety tips.

Avoid contact with dangerous people and risky activities. Family and workplace ties are difficult to end, but you can excuse yourself from situations that have the potential to become dangerous. In the workplace, learn your company's security measures, for example, the locations of fire alarms so you can activate one in case of any trouble. Perhaps most important, strive to get along with coworkers

Managing Your Health

Going Out: Safety Tips

To reduce your risk of being victimized, practice the following security rules:

- Before you leave, check to see if your home or dorm is secure. Make sure windows are locked. Leave some lights and a radio on to give the impression that someone is there.
- When riding in a car, keep doors locked at all times, and windows rolled down no more than one inch.

- If using public transportation, sit near the driver or conductor.
- If violence erupts anywhere near you, run away if you can.
- Look alert.
- Park in a well-lit area. Check inside and underneath the car before entering. If you need to use public transportation, choose well-populated stops.

- As you approach your home or dorm room, do not enter if you see signs of a break-in or suspicious persons in the area. Go to a neighbor or public phone and call the police. If surprised, burglars often become assailants.
- Lock the door immediately after entering your home or dorm room.

and the public. Many workplace incidents result from acts of vengeance; therefore, help create positive situations and relationships by displaying a friendly attitude, good manners, tact, and diplomacy. The "Changing Health Habits" activity for this chapter in the workbook can help you identify and change habits that may increase your risk of becoming a victim of violence.

If you become involved in a disruptive episode or heated dispute, keeping calm may prevent the situation from escalating into a violent one. For example, breathe deeply, count to ten, "bite your tongue," or make some excuse and quickly leave the scene. The relaxation techniques described in Chapter 3 can help you maintain your composure in such situations.

Relying on destructive responses such as anger to manage interpersonal conflicts can lead to physical violence. The FBI reports that 40% of homicides arise out of interpersonal arguments. The student workbook activity "Assessing Your Anger" can help you identify situations that make you angry. Learning conflict management skills such as impulse control, anger management, and negotiation techniques can help you defuse tense situations safely.

Self-Protection

When faced with the threat of force, your actions can influence the outcome of the situation. For example, you may obtain help from others by calling the police, pressing an alarm button, blowing a whistle, or screaming to attract attention. When cornered and facing a threatening person alone, a person might try to defuse the situation verbally by reasoning with his or her assailant.

If you become overwhelmed by fear or conclude that you cannot escape, your response may be to offer no resistance. However, the gut responses to danger are the "flight-or-fight" reactions described in Chapter 3. Sometimes flight—simply running away—is the best means of escaping threatening situations. The opposite response is to fight by

making counterthreats or by physically attacking another person. Many Americans carry with them, or keep handy in their homes, a weapon for self-defense such as a gun, knife, or chemical spray (see the "Consumer Health" feature). When danger threatens, other people may rely on improvised weapons, such as car keys, scissors, or a flashlight. Some people seek training in personal defense or in firearm use to enhance their ability to defend themselves (Figure 4-4).

▲**Figure 4-4 In Self Defense.** Fighting back is one way of responding to violent situations.

Should victims always resist their attackers? No uniform answer can be given. Each potential victim must assess each situation to decide how to respond under the circumstances.

Treating the Effects of Violence

If you are attacked, you must decide whether to report the incident. You should report any attempted or completed crime of violence by strangers or acquaintances to the police. Most large police departments include specially trained domestic violence and sexual assault units that provide sympathetic and appropriate responses.

You may feel reluctant to inform police of domestic or sexual violence in certain cases. In such instances, consider reporting the incident to a socially sensitive agency, such as a rape crisis center or a women's self-help service, that can assist you in dealing with the legal or medical establishments. Nationwide, a 24-hour, toll-free domestic violence hotline can be reached at 1-800-799-SAFE. Seeking help is beneficial to one's recovery from violence.

Hospitals, physicians, and physical therapists play the leading roles in treating physical injuries resulting from violence. A 911 call usually gains access to the appropriate emergency services. Psychologists, psychiatrists, and counselors provide treatment for the psychological injuries of violence. The social support and crisis counseling offered through specialized victim assistance services and rape crisis centers are useful for treating the immediate effects of violence, such as emotional distress. Early treatment of emotional distress may avert some of the longer-term psychological impact of violent victimization. If you have been a victim of violence while attending college, you can often obtain referrals to appropriate psychological services through your campus student health center.

Managing the short- and long-term effects of the violent incident on the victim's family and friends also is important. Useful services include marital counseling, couple therapy, financial and legal aid, and family therapy. Access to such services and information concerning local self-help groups can usually be arranged through your campus student health center or through social service agencies in your community.

child physical abuse overt physical violence against a child who is under 18 years of age.

child sexual abuse sexual activity with a child that takes place as a result of force or threat, or by taking advantage of an age difference or caretaking relationship.

pedophile (PEE-doe-file) an individual who is sexually aroused by fantasizing about or by having physical contact with vulnerable children.

- To reduce your risk of violence, avoid high-risk places and dangerous persons.
- When faced with disruptive episodes or heated disputes, try to keep calm to prevent the threatening situation from escalating into a violent one.
- Conflict management skills can help defuse tense, angry situations. Some college campuses offer courses in conflict management; consider taking a class to learn these techniques.
- Recognize that there is no single way to react whenever someone threatens your safety. You must assess each situation to decide how to respond under the circumstances.
- If you are a victim of violence, report the attack to police. In addition, obtain prompt treatment of your physical injuries and emotional distress.

across the lifespan

Violence

Child physical abuse includes beating, squeezing, burning, cutting, suffocating, binding, or poisoning a child who is under 18 years of age. Most physical violence against children is committed not by strangers or casual acquaintances but by parents and other adults known to the victims, such as neighbors, baby-sitters, and family friends. A substantial percentage of child physical abuse takes place in institutional settings, such as day care centers and schools, but homes are by far the most common setting. Abused children under 2 years of age are at greatest risk of fatalities, primarily from head injuries. Many children receive less severe injuries on a regular basis. Such violence is not confined to impoverished families or to any particular racial or ethnic group. In the United States, the actual prevalence of child abuse is not known; many fatal cases are not identified as child mistreatment (Herman-Giddens et al., 1999).

Why do some parents abuse their children? An important factor is the lack of effective parenting skills. Parents who abuse their children frequently have unrealistic expectations concerning their offspring and distorted notions about the causes of their children's behavior. Additionally, abusive parents tend to be under tremendous stress, and they tend to be isolated from other persons who could provide helpful social support.

Child sexual abuse refers to sexual activity with a child that takes place as a result of force or threat, or by taking advantage of an age difference or caretaking relationship. A **pedophile**, or "child molester," is an individual who is sexually aroused by fantasizing about or by having physical contact with vulnerable children. The abuse usually involves fondling a child's body, but it may include completed or attempted vaginal, anal, or oral sex. In general, girls are more likely to be targets than boys, especially girls between 8 and 10 years old. Most abusers are heterosexual males with female targets.

Many people think that pedophiles are strangers who are mentally ill, looking for children to kidnap, molest, and murder. In fact, most cases involve adults whom the children know and trust, such as baby-sitters, family friends, relatives, teachers, camp counselors, coaches, and even clergy. Only 3% of murdered children were killed by strangers (Fox & Zawitz, 1999). However, the increasing number of children who have access to personal computers provides a new method for sophisticated child abusers to communicate with vulnerable children through the Internet or electronic bulletin boards.

Data from various studies indicate that many adults were victims of sexual abuse during childhood. As many as 15% of children, primarily girls, are sexually abused (Weiss et al., 1999). In 1998 more than one-third of the victims of family rape were under 12 years of age (U.S. Department of Justice, 1998). **Incest**, sexual experiences between family members who are not spouses, is the most serious form of sexual abuse. Victims may be boys, although girls are at much greater risk. Incest is often nonviolent, but coerced, and it typically escalates over time. The risk factors for incest are similar to those of nonsexual abuse: childhood victimization of the perpetrator and high levels of stress within the family.

To prevent child sexual abuse, parents should teach their young children how to recognize and report sexual abuse. Since most cases involve persons the youngsters know, simply telling children "Don't talk to strangers" is not sufficient advice. Very young children need to learn which parts of their bodies are private. Additionally, these children need to learn that if anyone touches them in ways that make them feel uncomfortable, they should report the incidents to parents.

Studies show that abused children behave more aggressively at every stage of the life span. As adults, they are more likely to be violent against dates, spouses, their children and, later, their elderly parents. Furthermore, a significant percentage of women who suffer from depression were sexually abused as children (Weiss et al., 1999).

Elder abuse is the use of physical or sexual violence against an elderly person; some researchers include verbal threats and neglect in their definitions. Physical and psychological abuse of elderly individuals takes place not only in institutional settings such as hospitals and nursing homes, but especially in family settings. Such abuse occurs in all racial and ethnic groups and at all socioeconomic levels. To determine the extent of elder abuse, sociologists Karl Pillemer and David Finkelhor (1988) interviewed more than 2000 elderly persons living in Boston. In their much cited study, nearly 4% of the aged participants reported physical or emotional abuse or neglect. As many as 2.5 million Americans over 65 years of age are abused annually (Kleinschmidt, 1997). As the average age of the American population increases, many experts expect that the prevalence of elder abuse will increase as well.

The causes of elder abuse are complex. Elderly persons are most likely to be victimized by their spouses or adult children who must care for them. Caring for frail, aged relatives can be frustrating and stressful. Furthermore, the caretaker may depend on the elderly person for his or her housing and income. In such situations, resentful caretakers may resort to abusive behavior. In severe cases, violence against the elderly is associated with certain mental illnesses and drug (usually alcohol) abuse.

incest sexual relations between family members who are not spouses.

elder abuse use of physical or sexual violence against an elderly person.

ANALYZING
Health-Related Information

COMFORTABLY NUMB

The following article promotes an herbal tea formulated to reduce a person's level of anger. Read the article and evaluate it using the model for analyzing health-related information. The main points of the model are noted below; the model is fully explained on p. 12–13.

Aunt Annie's Tranquillity Tea

As you know, I've been using herbs all my life to treat everything from acne to zinc deficiency. Most of my knowledge about herbs didn't come from books or the Internet, it was passed down to me in my Great Aunt Annie's diary. Annie had a fabulous herb garden in the back of her house. One afternoon in 1914 she made the most amazing discovery, which she later recorded in her diary. She had dug up some comfrey root and picked a bunch of pennyroyal and lobelia leaves from the garden. Since coltsfoot was blooming, she thought it might be a nice change to add some of its leaves to her usual tea recipe. She brewed up a pot of tea from the mixture and drank about 2 cups of it. The tea was delicious. Very soothing.

Less than an hour later, Great Uncle Jeb came in from the barn, tracking dirt all over Aunt Annie's new carpet. Now I need to tell you that Annie had a terrible temper—she was only 4' 8" tall, but she used to push big old Jeb around a lot. Needless to say, Uncle Jeb was expecting the worst from his wife. But this time, instead of flying off the handle and kicking Jeb, as she was prone to do, Aunt Annie laughed and hugged him. Happy as a kitten rolling in catnip, Annie cleaned up the mess. Uncle Jeb suspected Annie had added something different to her usual tea recipe, so he had her sit down and recall the herb mixture. Using her recipe, Jeb made a pot of that tea for Annie to drink every day for the rest of her life. When Uncle Jeb began making whiskey in the barn and staying out late with his friends, Annie never raised a fuss. She just sat in the bent oak rocking chair, sipping her tea.

If you want to try Aunt Annie's Tranquillity Tea on someone you know who's got a bad temper, I'll send the recipe to you. I'm the editor of this magazine, so just send $10 for shipping and handling to my address, which is on the inside of the front cover. I'd love to hear about your experiences with the tea; be sure and let me know how it worked for you.

Your friend

Herb

Herb Z. Gardenia

1. Which statements are verifiable facts; which are unverified statements or value claims?
2. What are the credentials of the person who wrote the article? Does the author's background and education qualify him as an expert in the topic area?
3. What might be the motives and biases of Mr. Gardenia? State reasons for your answer.
4. Which information is relevant to the issue or main point of the article; which information is irrelevant?
5. Is the source reliable? Does it have a reputation for publishing misinformation?
6. Does the article attack the credibility of conventional scientists or medical authorities?

Based on the above analysis, do you think that this article is a reliable source of health-related information? Summarize your reasons for coming to this conclusion.

Chapter Review

Summary

Interpersonal violence is a major public health problem because it produces staggering physical, psychological, and social consequences. A violent social incident occurs when at least one person intentionally applies or threatens physical force on other(s). Rates of violence are difficult to determine because so many of these incidents, especially rapes and domestic violence, are never reported to the authorities.

Regardless of whether physical harm occurs, violent victimization is always injurious to psychological functioning. Psychological effects of violence include emotional distress, depression, suicidal thinking, chronic physical complaints, and drug abuse. To recover from the psychological effects of violence, one should seek help from health care professionals.

Violence is complex; there is no single cause of violence, nor is violent behavior limited to a particular group of persons. Factors that contribute to violence include poverty, substance abuse, certain psychological disorders, and poor self-esteem. In many instances, violence is learned behavior.

Community violence includes acts that occur between strangers or acquaintances, usually in public places. Institutional violence occurs mainly within institutional environments, such as schools, workplaces, and prisons. Domestic violence encompasses both friends and family members and usually takes place in homes. Sexual violence involves areas of the body that are sensitive to sexual arousal. Cases of institutional, domestic, and sexual violence are seldom reported. As a result, official crime statistics underestimate the rates of such violence.

Sexual violence involves sexual activity gained through force, threat of force, or coercion. The majority of sexual assaults are committed not by strangers but by acquaintances, friends, family members, and spouses. Twenty-five percent to 36% of college students report having experienced some form of violence in at least one dating relationship.

To reduce the likelihood of becoming a victim of violence, one should limit one's exposure to risky situations. For example, avoiding high-crime districts, locking doors and windows, staying in public view, and getting along with others are actions that can reduce one's risk of violence.

Most physical violence against children is committed by adults known to the victims, such as relatives, neighbors, or baby-sitters. Girls, especially those between the ages of 8 and 10, are more likely to be targets of sexual abuse than boys. Parents should teach their young children how to recognize and report sexual abuse. Children who experience violence often suffer emotional and social injuries that remain long after physical injuries have healed.

Elder abuse occurs in all racial and ethnic groups and at all socioeconomic levels. Family members are responsible for the vast majority of abuse directed toward elderly persons. As the average age of the American population increases, many experts expect that the incidence of elder abuse will increase also.

Applying What You Have Learned

1. If your friend reports being sexually harassed by a college professor, what advice could you give to him or her? *(Application)*
2. You have to attend classes or work at a job in the evenings. Determine at least two steps you can take to reduce your risk of violence on campus or at work. *(Analysis)*
3. Plan a program to increase security in your dorm or on your campus. Consider forwarding it to an official at the university who might be interested in your plan, such as the Dean of Student Affairs. *(Synthesis)*
4. Evaluate your present security situation. Determine situations in your life that provide some risk of violence and describe ways in which you can reduce these risks. *(Evaluation)*

KEY

Application: Using information in a new situation.
Analysis: Breaking down information into component parts.
Synthesis: Putting together information from different sources.
Evaluation: Making informed decisions.

Reflecting On Your Health

1. As mentioned in this chapter, visual media can influence a person's attitudes toward violence. Choose a violent movie or television show that you watched recently. What impact, if any, did it have on your feelings about violence?
2. Do you like to play violent computer games? If so, do you think this activity has an affect on your attitudes toward violence?
3. What could you do to avoid getting into an abusive relationship with an intimate partner?
4. How safe do you feel at home or in the dorm? What worries you most about the safety of your environment? What steps could you take to make your residence more secure?
5. If you were out walking alone at night and someone was following you, what would you do to reduce your risk of being attacked? Do you think that it is safe for you to walk alone at night? Why or why not?

References

Afkhami, M. (1999). An AMEWS/MESA special session on violence against women. *Middle East Women's Studies Review, 13*(4):5+.

Brener, N. D., Simon, T. R., Krug, E. G., & Lowry, R. (1999). Recent trends in violence-related behaviors among high school students in the United States. *Journal of the American Medical Association, 282*(5):440-446.

Decker, S. H. (1997, March 27). Getting a grip on gangs. *St. Louis Post-Dispatch, 119*(86):1G-2G.

Eisenstat, S. A., & Bancroft, L. (1999). Domestic violence. *New England Journal of Medicine, 341*:887-892.

Fitzpatrick, K. M. (1999). Violent victimization among America's school children. *Journal of Interpersonal Violence, 14*(10):1055-1069.

Fox, J. A. & Zawitz, M. W. (1999). *Homicide trends in the United States.* Bureau of Justice Statistics, Washington, DC: United States Department of Justice. http://www.ojp.usdoj.gov/bjs/homicide/homtrnd.htm

Frank, J. B., & Rodowski, M. J. (1999). Review of psychological issues in victims of domestic violence seen in emergency settings. *Emergency Medical Clinics of North America, 17*(3):657-677.

Hamberger, K. L., & Ambuel, B. (1998). Dating violence. *Pediatric Clinics of North America, 45*(2):381-390.

Herman-Giddens, M. E., Brown, G., Verbiest, S., Carlson, P. J., Hooten, E. G., Howell, E., & Butts, J. D. (1999). Underascertainment of child abuse mortality in the United States. *Journal of the American Medical Association, 282*(5):463-467.

Holtzworth-Munroe, A., Bates. L., Smutzler, N., & Sandin, E. (1997). A brief review of the research on husband violence. *Aggression and Violent Behavior, 2*(1):65-99.

Hoyert, D. L., Kochanek, K. D., & Murphy, S. L. (1999). Deaths: Final data for 1997. *National Vital Statistics Reports, 47*(19).

Kleinschmidt, K. C. (1997). Elder abuse: A review. *Annals of Emergency Medicine, 30*(4):463-472.

Leventhal, J. M. (1999). The challenges of recognizing child abuse: Seeing is believing. *Journal of the American Medical Association, 281*(7):657-659.

Mullen, P. E., Pathé, M., Purcell, R., & Stuart, G. W. (1999). Study of stalkers. *American Journal of Psychiatry, 156*:1244-1249.

Pillemer, K., & Finkelhor, D. (1988). The prevalence of elder abuse: A random sample survey. *Gerontologist, 28*:51-57.

Rennison, C. M. (1999). *Criminal victimization 1998, changes 1997–98 with trends 1993–98.* (NCJ-176353) Bureau of Justice Statistics, Washington, DC: United States Department of Justice.

Schafer, J., Caetano, R., & Clark, C. L. (1998). Rates of intimate partner violence in the United States. *American Journal of Public Health 88*(11):1702-1704.

Stacy, R. D., Prisbell, M., & Tollefsrud, K. (1992). A comparison of attitudes among college students toward sexual violence committed by strangers and by acquaintances: A research report. *Journal of Sex Education and Therapy, 18*:257-263.

Tjaden, P., & Thoennes, N. (1998). *Prevalence, incidence, and consequences of violence against women: Findings from the National Violence Against Women Survey.* Atlanta: National Institute of Justice and the Centers for Disease Control and Prevention.

U.S. Department of Health and Human Services (USDHHS), Public Health Service. (1999). *Healthy people 2000 review, 1998–1999* (publication 99-1256). Washington, DC: Government Printing Office. http://odphp.osophs.dhhs.gov/pubs/hp2000/prog_rvw.htm

U.S. Department of Justice, Bureau of Justice Statistics. (1998). *Crime in the United States, 1998: Uniform Crime Reports.* http://www.fbi.gov/ucr/98cius.htm

U.S. Department of Justice, Bureau of Justice Statistics. (1999). *Drugs and Crime Facts.* Washington, DC: Government Printing Office. http://www.ojp.usdoj.gov/bjs/dcf/duc.htm

U.S. Department of Justice, Bureau of Justice Statistics. (1999). *Key crime and justice facts at a glance.* Washington, DC: Government Printing Office. http://www.ojp.usdoj.gov/bjs/glance.htm

U.S. Department of Labor. (1999). *National census of fatal occupational injuries, 1998.* Washington, DC: Government Printing Office. http://stats.bls.gov/oshhoma.htm

Weiss E. L., Longhurst, J. G., & Mazure, C. M. (1999). Childhood sexual abuse as a risk factor for depression in women: psychosocial and neurobiological correlates. *American Journal of Psychiatry, 156*:816-828.

Willis, E., & Strasburger, V. C. (1998). Media Violence. *Pediatric Clinics of North America, 45*(2):319-331.

Youth Risk Behavior Surveillance: National College Health Risk Behavior Survey—United States, 1995. (1997). *Weekly Morbidity and Mortality Report, 46*(SS-6):1-54.

chapter 5

Relationships and Sexuality

Sex is everywhere in our society. You can find sexually explicit images and information in movies, books, TV shows, online computer programs, and in the lyrics of popular music. If you browse through magazines or scan billboards, you are likely to see pictures of attractive young men and women in advertisements for clothes, perfumes, or cars. Whether their product is a movie or pair of jeans, promoters and advertisers know that "sex sells." What does sex mean to you?

The term *sex* refers to one's gender, male or female, as well as to sexual intercourse and other intimate physical activities that involve the genitals. Sexuality, however, is more than genders or reproductive organs. **Sexuality** is the aspect of personality that encompasses an individual's sexual thoughts, feelings, attitudes, and actions. Each person has a unique collection of private and public sexual experiences that shapes his or her sexuality.

Numerous biological, psychological, social, and cultural forces interact to influence one's sexual development, sexual health, and interpersonal relationships **(Figure 5-1).**

> " . . . promoters and advertisers know that 'sex sells.' "

Sexuality is woven into every aspect of human life; sex affects a person's identity, self-esteem, emotions, personality, relationships, lifestyle, and overall health.

Being knowledgeable about sexuality is important for maintaining good health and optimal well-being. Misinformation can lead to serious consequences, such as unintentional pregnancies or sexually transmitted infections. Additionally, people who are well informed about sexuality can communicate effectively with their medical practitioners or sexual partners regarding reproductive or sexual concerns.

Throughout life, you make various sexually related decisions, for example, deciding with whom to have an intimate sexual relationship. Such decisions can have serious effects on your health and well-being, as well as those of others. By considering how your actions may affect yourself and your sexual partners, you can become a more sexually responsible person. This chapter focuses primarily on the social and emotional aspects of sexuality; Chapter 6 addresses the physical aspects of sexuality.

What You'll Learn

www.jbpub.com/healthyliving

The web site for this book offers many useful tools and is a great source for supplementary health information for both students and instructors. Visit the site at www.jbpub.com/healthyliving for information on these topics:

Human Sexual Behavior
Sexual Orientation
Romantic Relationships
Across the Life Span: Sexuality

Chapter Overview

How biological and psychological factors influence sexual behavior.

How culture affects sexuality.

The nature versus nurture debate and sexual orientation.

The diversity of sexual behavior.

Definitions and theories of love and commitment.

DIVERSITY *Health* — The Virtue of Virginity

Con$umer *Health* — Ginseng and Sexual Prowess

Managing Your Health — Minding Your Sexual Manners | Tips for Better Sex

across the lifespan — Sexuality

Student Workbook

Self Assessment: The Love Attitudes Scales | Communication Patterns Questionnaire
Changing Health Habits: Would a Behavior Change Improve Your Relationships?

Do You Know?

• What are common sexual practices?
• How living together affects future marriage?
• How to communicate effectively?

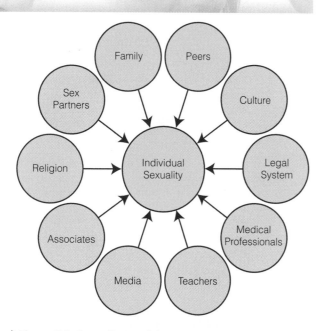

▲**Figure 5-1 Sexuality Model.** Numerous biological, psychological, social, and cultural forces interact to influence sexual development, sexual health, and interpersonal relationships.

ovaries and testes produce hormones that affect sexual functioning (▌ **Figure 5-2**). Additionally, the hypothalamus, located above the pituitary, produces hormones that trigger the secretion of pituitary hormones. During puberty in males, pituitary hormones activate the maturation of the male reproductive structures and the release of increased levels of the male sex hormone testosterone. Testosterone plays a role in the maturation of the male reproductive structures, stimulates the development of sperm, and triggers and maintains the development of the secondary sexual characteristics such as the growth of a beard and the deepening of the voice. During puberty in females, pituitary hormones cause maturation of the ovaries, which then begin secreting the female sex hormones estrogen and progesterone. Estrogen stimulates maturation of the uterus and vagina and development of the female secondary sexual characteristics such as the development of breasts and a change in the distribution of body fat.

During middle age, the production of sex hormones declines. After 40 years of age, men produce less testosterone and fewer sperm. Despite this reduction, elderly men can still father children. When women enter menopause, usually between 45 and 55 years of age, their estrogen and pro-

Human Sexual Behavior

The reproductive activity of most complex animals includes behaviors commonly referred to as courtship and mating. Unlike other animals, humans exhibit a variety of complex sexual behaviors that do not necessarily result in reproduction. People often engage in sexual activity for pleasure and relaxation or to help maintain the emotional bonds of their intimate relationships. Some individuals, however, use their sexuality to dominate, exploit, or harm others. What factors influence human sexual behavior?

The Biology of Sexual Behavior

The motivation to pursue sexual activity, the sex drive or *libido,* is an instinctual behavior moderated by the sex hormones. The ovaries and the testes, glands that make up part of the hormonal (endocrine) system secrete these chemical messengers. The endocrine system is so named because of the endocrine glands (such as the ovaries and the testes), which secrete the hormones. Glands are individual cells or groups of cells that secrete substances. They are called endocrine because they release substances within (endo-) the body, rather than secreting substances that exit the body (like sweat, for example).

The endocrine system plays an important role in sexual functioning. The pituitary (located in the brain), and the

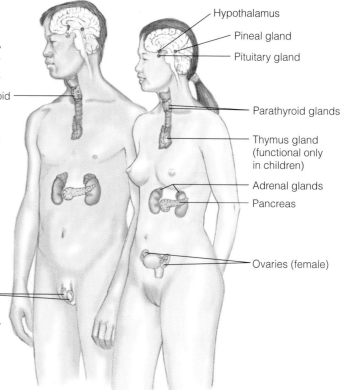

▲**Figure 5-2 Endocrine Glands.** The pituitary, ovaries, and testes produce hormones that affect sexual functioning. The hypothalamus produces hormones that trigger the secretion of pituitary hormones.

gesterone levels decrease dramatically. As a result, menopausal women are no longer fertile. However, most healthy elderly men and women continue to have an interest in sex, and they engage in sexual activity. In a recent study conducted for the American Association for Retired Persons, about 50% of those aged 45 through 59 reported having sex at least once a week. Among those aged 60 through 74, 30% of men and 24% of women reported having sex at least once a week (Jacoby, 1999).

The Psychology of Sexual Behavior

Certain thoughts, sensations, and emotions modulate sexual behavior, as do the sex hormones. Included in this psychological mix are factors such as satisfaction with one's body, good physical and emotional health, absence of beliefs that can hinder sexual responsiveness or enjoyment, previous positive sexual experiences, and high self-esteem.

Many **sexologists**, scientists who study human sexuality, think that people who have high self-esteem are more likely to have positive attitudes concerning their sexuality than persons with poor self-concepts. However, people frequently judge their bodies and sexual prowess against unrealistic standards of physical attractiveness and sexual ability that are presented in the media. As a result, some individuals develop feelings of sexual inadequacy and low self-esteem because they feel sexually unattractive or inept. People who have these feelings may be unable to enjoy their sexuality and may be unable to form fulfilling intimate relationships.

sexuality
the aspect of personality that encompasses a person's sexual thoughts, feelings, attitudes, and actions.

sexologists
scientists who study human sexuality.

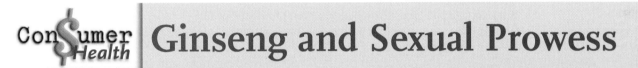

ConSumer Health | Ginseng and Sexual Prowess

You've probably seen ads for ginseng in magazines, on television, or on the Web. The ads often make claims such as "Ginseng will boost your energy and sexual stamina," or "Ginseng has been used for centuries in maintaining overall health and vitality," or "Ginseng will reduce stress and the effects of aging." "Can it do that?" you wonder. "Heck," you think, "may as well try it. What can I lose?"

Ginseng is an herb that grows wild or is cultivated in eastern Asia and North America. For hundreds of years, the root of the plant has been used in Asia for medicinal purposes as well as an aphrodisiac because it often looks like a human body. But what do we know about ginseng? Will it make you more sexually "potent?" Can it harm you or, alternatively, enhance your health?

On the positive side, studies in Taiwan show that sperm motility is enhanced after sperm are incubated with extracts of ginseng. Is sperm motility enhanced within men who take ginseng? There is still no answer to that question. Furthermore, enhancing sperm motility may have nothing to do with boosting sexual desire or "performance."

On the negative side, medical researchers know that drug interactions occur with many herbals. Ginseng, in particular, may alter bleeding (or clotting) time, the time it takes for blood to stop flowing from a tiny wound. Ginseng also interacts with anticoagulant drugs, which "thin" the blood; that is, they decrease the ability of the blood to clot. Therefore, anticoagulants and ginseng should not be taken together. Ginseng also may interfere with the heart medication digoxin (digitalis), which affects the force and rate at which the heart beats.

In addition to its interaction with anticoagulants and digoxin, ginseng should not be used if a person is taking estrogens or corticosteroid drugs such as cortisone because of possible additive effects. Ginseng may also affect blood glucose levels, so it should not taken by persons with diabetes mellitus. For those on the antidepressant drug phenelzine sulfate (Nardil), ginseng could provoke a manic episode (an extreme excited state). Its general side effects may include headache and involuntary muscular contractions.

Perhaps ginseng improves one's overall health, which in turn, enhances one's ability to perform sexually? Results of a study conducted on a group of young, healthy men in Thailand did not show a boost in their immune system function.

Additionally, medical researchers can find no improvement in peak aerobic exercise performance of people who take ginseng, and can find no identifiable effect of ginseng in the treatment and rehabilitation of geriatric patients.

With all these results in mind, you might not want to rely on ginseng for better bedroom calisthenics just yet . . .

Sources: Allen, J. D., McLung, J., Nelson, A. G., & Welsch, M. (1998). Ginseng supplementation does not enhance healthy young adults' peak aerobic exercise performance. *Journal of the American College of Nutrition,* 17:462-466.
Chen, J. C., Xu, M. X., Chen, L. D., Chen, Y. N., & Chiu, T. H. (1999). Effect of panax notoginseng extracts on inferior sperm motility in vitro. *American Journal of Chinese Medicine,* 27:123-128.
Miller, L. G. (1998). Herbal medicinals: Selected clinical considerations focusing on known or potential drug-herb interactions. *Archives of Internal Medicine,* 158:2200-2211.
Srisurapanon, S., Rungroeng, K., Apibal, S., Cherdrugsi, P., Siripol, R., Vanich-Angkul, V., & Timvipark, C. (1997). The effect of standardized ginseng extract on peripheral blood leukocytes and lymphocyte subsets: A preliminary study in young healthy adults. *Journal of the Medical Association of Thailand,* 80(Suppl 1):S81-5.
Thommessen, B., & Laake K. (1996). No identifiable effect of ginseng (Gericomplex) as an adjuvant in the treatment of geriatric patients. *Aging (Milano),* 8:417-420.

Culture and Sexuality

Society strongly influences the sexual attitudes and behaviors of a population by identifying acceptable sexual activities and placing restrictions on others. For example, some cultures value sexual abstinence before marriage; others value sexual experimentation during childhood. A **value** is a belief that an idea, object, or action has worth. The "Diversity in Health" essay "The Virtue of Virginity" provides a cross-cultural perspective concerning the value of sexual abstinence before marriage.

An individual usually formulates a personal value system before adulthood. A *value system* is a collection of beliefs that helps a person identify and classify things as being good or bad, or neither good nor bad. This value system guides the reasoning and behavior of the individual, especially in sexual decision making.

Many Americans derive their sexual values from Judeo-Christian religious teachings. However, individuals within the culturally diverse U.S. population adhere to a variety of sexual values, some of which conflict with traditional Judeo-Christian teachings. No universally accepted set of sexual values applies to Americans.

Widely accepted values can help people determine behavioral norms, but these norms often change over time and across cultures. Before World War I, for example, it was socially unacceptable for "proper" American men or women to expose much of their bodies in public. Today, most Americans think that it is acceptable for people to wear clothing that exposes much of their bodies, especially in warm weather. However, in some cultures, persons are punished severely if they appear in public dressed in revealing outfits; the only socially acceptable style of clothing is that which has been worn for centuries (Figure 5-3).

Gender Identity and Roles

Gender is the classification of the sex of a person based on many criteria, among them anatomic and chromosomal characteristics. **Gender identity** is an individual's perception of himself or herself as being male or female. Various biological, social, and environmental forces help mold a child's gender identity.

Before birth, genetic and hormonal factors influence the sexual development of the embryonic brain. After birth, social factors have a major impact on gender identity. As children interact with people, they observe and learn gender roles and sexual stereotypes. A **gender role** refers to patterns of behavior, attitudes, and personality attributes that are traditionally considered in a particular culture to be feminine or masculine. A **sexual stereotype** is the widespread association of certain perceptions with one gender. Examples of sexual stereotypes are associating the color blue with boys and pink with girls, or associating passiveness with females and aggressiveness with males.

Throughout the world, obvious biological differences between the sexes form the basis for traditional gender roles. In many cultures, for example, women are responsible for routine child-rearing and household management. This traditional gender role assignment likely developed for a variety of reasons, such as a woman's biological role in giving birth and nursing infants. It is also likely that because men, in general, are physically stronger than women, their customary roles have been protecting and providing for their families, especially in hunter-gatherer or agrarian societies.

In addition to biological factors, culture (often determined by race and ethnicity) and religion heavily influence sexual attitudes and behaviors. In many cultures, men learn to be sexually aggressive and women learn to be sexually passive. According to these sexual stereotypes, men are always eager for sex, and they are expected to demonstrate their interest and aggressiveness by initiating sexual encounters. Women are expected to be less interested in sex than men and to show their passiveness by accepting the sexual advances of men willingly.

value the belief that an idea, object, or action has worth.

gender the classification of the sex of a person based on many criteria, among them anatomic and chromosomal characteristics.

gender identity an individual's perception of himself or herself as being male or female.

gender role patterns of behavior, attitudes, and personality attributes that are traditionally considered in a particular culture to be feminine or masculine.

sexual stereotype the widespread association of certain perceptions with one gender.

▲ **Figure 5-3 Culturally Appropriate Clothing.** In most Islamic countries, the only socially acceptable style of clothing for women is that which has been worn for centuries.

DIVERSITY *in Health* | The Virtue of Virginity

Some American parents teach their children to consider virginity a gift that is given to spouses on their wedding night. Since the majority of American youth have sexual intercourse before leaving their teens, the importance of virginity before marriage appears headed for extinction. For many people, however, virginity continues to be highly valued.

Since ancient times, people from various cultures have used the condition of a bride's hymen to document her sexual history. In these cultures, an intact hymen is considered a sign of virginity. Although the hymen has no known biological function, this thin membranous tissue usually covers part of the outer entrance to the vagina. Most hymens have at least one opening that is wide enough to permit the discharge of menstrual blood. In many instances, this opening is too narrow for a penis to penetrate without tearing the hymen.

According to the Old Testament of the Bible, a man who thought that his bride was not a virgin on their wedding night was entitled to have his townspeople stone her to death. In some ancient societies, a newly wed woman who could not prove her virginity might be banished from her hometown, tortured, or killed. Her lover, if known, often received the same treatment. Today, virginity is still an important criterion for selecting a mate, especially in India, Indonesia, China, Taiwan, Iran, Turkey, and Arab nations. In most of these places, however, a new bride with sexual experience usually receives less harsh treatment than in the past. She may be rejected by her husband and returned to her family as "used goods." Facing embarrassment and ridicule from neighbors, the woman's family may disown her.

According to Islamic tradition, a woman's virginity is the basis for her honor and that of her family, her future groom, and his family. Muslims, followers of Islam, would arrange early marriages for their female children to ensure that these girls entered puberty as virgin brides. Fatima Mernissi (1987), a sociologist in the African country of Morocco, thinks that Muslim men maintain their respect and pride by controlling the sexuality of their wives, daughters, and sisters. In many Muslim communities, young women are required to be heavily veiled in the presence of strange men and in public (see Figure 5-3). If they do not wear veils, young women may be punished severely or labeled as prostitutes because their appearance is sexually tempting to men. Older Muslim women often appear unveiled in public because it is assumed that they are no longer sexually attractive.

Marriage customs in rural parts of Africa, Asia, and the Mediterranean often include some ritual that "proves" the bride has lost her virginity on her wedding night. In parts of Greece, the groom's friends gather outside the window of the newly married couple on the morning after the wedding to receive the news that the bride is no longer a virgin. After the groom makes the expected announcement, the gathering of friends celebrate by firing guns into the air. In many Middle Eastern villages that are populated with followers of Islam, it is customary for the groom to display his bride's underpants or their bloodstained sheets as evidence.

The social value of virginity is so powerful that plastic surgeons in Japan and Italy routinely reconstruct hymens so that their unmarried female patients who have been sexually active can give the impression that they are virgins. In some societies, new brides keep a small amount of chicken blood handy to smear on sheets during the wedding night, or they make a small cut near the vaginal opening that will bleed during sexual intercourse.

Economic factors are also thought to play a major role in perpetuating the value of premarital virginity. In many cultures, property is handed down from fathers to sons. Therefore, families strive to protect their financial interests and lines of inheritance by seeking virgin brides for male relatives. An unmarried woman who is not a virgin could be pregnant with a male child whose father is from another family. Without DNA testing to confirm a child's paternity, rural people in underdeveloped regions rely on an intact hymen as a sign of virginity. Along with this view of women as property, cultural norms of sexual chastity, female virginity, pure bloodlines, and family honor may also serve to control women's behavior.

Even though cultural, historical, economic, and other factors perpetuate virginity examinations, the Turkish Medical Association has deemed these exams a form of gender-based violence. Additionally, virginity examinations violate guarantees of freedom from discrimination found in the International Covenant on Civil and Political Rights, the European Convention on Human Rights, and the Convention on the Elimination of All Forms of Discrimination Against Women, all of which are international human rights standards that Turkey has ratified. Results of a recent study reveal, however, that nearly half of physicians in Turkey who conduct such examinations for reasons of alleged sexual assault, also conduct them for social reasons in spite of their belief that such examinations are inappropriate, traumatic, and often performed against a patient's will (Frank et al., 1999).

Sources: Frank, M. W., Bauer, H. M., Arican, N., Fincanci, S. K., & Iacopino, V. (1999). Virginity examination in Turkey: Role of forensic physicians in controlling female sexuality. *Journal of the American Medical Association*, 282:485-490.
Mernissi, F. (1987). *Beyond the veil: Male-female dynamics in modern Muslim society.* Bloomington, IN: Indiana University Press.

In the United States, parents, friends, teachers, and the media influence children's perceptions of gender roles. For example, mothers appear to be a primary socializing agent for their daughters. The results of studies of mothers' and daughters' attitudes over time toward children, marriage, and careers reveal that mother/daughter attitudes are similar when the girls are adolescents and young teens. When daughters become adults, their gender role attitudes still appear to be significantly similar to those of their mothers; the attitudes of both groups change over time in similar patterns (Bohannon & Blanton, 1999).

Some Americans reject traditional gender stereotypes because these attitudes and practices can create and foster sexism. **Sexism**, discrimination and bias against one sex, is common in many societies. For many women in the United States and other countries, sexist practices affect their status and health at work, school, and home. Sexual harassment and violence against women are forms of sexism. Men can experience sexism as well; white American males often feel the object of sexist practices in the workplace when hiring guidelines favor females.

Over the past two decades, societal norms in the United States have moved to a more liberal interpretation of appropriate role behaviors for women (Bohannon & Blanton, 1999). Women are now more comfortable asking men out on dates. Men and women may feel free to initiate or refuse sexual activity. Additionally, a growing number of Americans feel free to choose nontraditional careers and adopt flexible gender roles. In a few families, traditional sex roles are reversed. For example, a woman may decide to work outside of the home while her male partner chooses to stay at home to care for their children and manage household tasks.

Transsexualism

In some instances, a person's gender identity conflicts with his or her biological sex, a condition known as *gender dysphoria*. An individual with this disorder feels trapped in the body of the opposite sex, and is a **transsexual.** To satisfy their self-concepts, transsexuals often dress and act like members of the opposite sex. Experts estimate that 1 in 37,000 to 100,000 males, and 1 in 100,000 to 400,000 females in the United States are transsexuals (Greenberg et al., 2000).

Transsexuals frequently undergo psychotherapy and hormonal treatments to help them deal with their gender identity conflicts; others choose to have sex reassignment surgery to change their sexual appearances. Physicians who perform sex reassignment surgeries usually remove certain reproductive organs and reconstruct the genitals of the patient to make them resemble those of the opposite sex. After transsexual surgery, however, the newly fashioned reproductive organs do not function like the organs of people who were born with them.

Healthy LIVING PRACTICES

To help you make responsible decisions concerning your sexuality, consider how your sexual behavior affects yourself and others.

Sexual Orientation

One of the most emotionally charged aspects of human sexuality is **sexual orientation**, that is, the direction of a person's romantic thoughts, feelings, and attractions. Survey data from European and American studies indicate that about 90% to 95% of people identify themselves as **heterosexual**, sexually attracted to members of the opposite sex (Smith, 1991; Sell, Wells, & Wypij, 1995). The remainder identify themselves as **homosexual** or **bisexual.** Homosexuals are sexually attracted to members of their own sex; bisexuals engage in sexual activity with both sexes. Of the homosexual population, about 65%–75% are males, and the remaining are females, although this figure is often debated (Greenberg et al., 2000). Homosexual men and women are commonly referred to as *gay* people; homosexual women are also called *lesbians*. Sexologist Alfred Kinsey proposed that sexual orientation is a continuum with exclusively heterosexual and homosexual designations on either end; degrees of bisexuality fall within the middle region of this continuum (Kinsey et al., 1953) (■ **Figure 5-4**).

100% Heterosexual	A few homosexual fantasies or experiences	More heterosexual than homosexual	Bisexual	More homosexual than heterosexual	A few heterosexual fantasies or experiences	100% Homosexual

▲**Figure 5-4 Kinsey's Continuum of Sexual Orientation.** Sexuality researcher Alfred Kinsey thought that sexual orientation is a continuum with exclusively heterosexual and homosexual designations on either end and degrees of bisexuality in the middle region.

Nature or Nurture?

Do people, particularly homosexuals, choose their sexual orientation? Until recently, it was generally believed that homosexuality was learned behavior, and that children became homosexual by having early social and sexual experiences with gay individuals. At present, researchers cannot find a common childhood characteristic that predicts adult sexual orientation. Children may have same-sex experiences with other children, but most of them develop heterosexual orientations as they mature. Some gays and lesbians report that they knew they were different at an early age, but they did not recognize their homosexuality until they were in their teens or early 20s. Today, mental health experts generally agree that homosexuals do not decide their sexual orientation, nor can gay people alter their sexual preferences easily, if at all.

Researchers have also been studying the biological basis of homosexuality. Results of studies of the early 1990s showed physical differences in small groups of cells in the hypothalamus of the brains of heterosexual and homosexual men (LeVay, 1991). Since brains of deceased men must be used for these studies, sample sizes were small. Scientists conclude that more data are needed to confirm these findings.

In 1993 molecular geneticist Dean Hamer and his colleagues (1993) announced that they had found a genetic link to male homosexuality. The researchers stated that a particular region of the X chromosome in homosexual males was involved in male sexual orientation in some, but not all, gay men. Males inherit this sex chromosome (condensed piece of hereditary material) from their mothers. The particular region of the X chromosome, q28, was dubbed the "gay gene." However, the results of more recent research reported by a group of scientists from both the United States and Canada do not support the presence of an Xq28 gene that influences sexual orientation (Rice et al., 1999; Wickelgren, 1999). At this time the biological basis of sexual orientation remains uncertain, but research scientists and health professionals expect that homosexuality is determined by a combination of factors.

Homosexuality and Society

Since ancient times, homosexuality has existed in most societies. Homosexuals are members of every racial, ethnic, socioeconomic, religious, and occupational group. While many homosexuals choose to conceal their sexual orientation, especially from their co-workers and neighbors, others have decided to "come out," expressing their sexual preferences openly.

Homophobia is an intense fear of or hostility toward homosexuals. However, not every person who objects to homosexuality is afraid of gay people or is hostile toward them. Therefore, *antihomosexual* may be a more descriptive term than *homophobic* to describe people who harbor such fears and hostilities.

Many heterosexuals do not accept homosexuality because they think gay sexual behavior is unnatural or it contradicts their religious beliefs. Other people are afraid of contact with gays because they associate acquired immune deficiency syndrome (AIDS) with homosexuality. Results of research studies show that in general, women hold fewer negative attitudes and beliefs toward homosexuals than men do, and exhibit fewer antihomosexual behaviors (Johnson, Brems & Alford-Keating, 1997; Whitley & Kite, 1995).

Homosexuals may feel isolated and have low self-esteem as a result of hostility and rejection from their families and other members of society. Family counseling can improve relations between homosexual children and their parents. Additionally, gay people may enhance their self-concepts by forming social networks with other homosexuals.

In 1996 U.S. President Bill Clinton signed the "Defense of Marriage" bill, which does not recognize marriages between homosexuals and allows states to ignore same-sex marriages that have been performed in other states (Carney, 1996). Gay couples, however, often cohabit and form lifetime commitments, commonly called domestic partnerships. Since domestic partners often contribute to the economic survival of their households, share property, and raise children, they want the same legal rights and protections that heterosexual married couples have, such as the right to claim insurance benefits when their partners die. Some cities, such as San Francisco and Seattle, and a few states now recognize certain legal aspects of homosexual partnerships, such as the right to adopt children from one of their previous marriages. As of July 1, 2000, Vermont recognized civil unions between gays in that state.

sexism discrimination and bias against one sex.

transsexual a person who is dissatisfied with his or her biological gender.

sexual orientation the direction of a person's romantic thoughts, feelings, and attractions toward people of the same or different sex.

heterosexual a person who is sexually attracted to members of the opposite sex.

homosexual a person who is sexually attracted to members of his or her own sex.

bisexual a person who engages in sexual activity with both sexes.

homophobia an intense fear of or hostility toward homosexuals.

Healthy LIVING PRACTICES

Consider seeking professional counseling if you are confused or troubled by your sexual orientation.

Diversity in Sexual Behavior

Common Sexual Practices between Partners

Most heterosexuals are familiar with the notion of "having sex" or **sexual intercourse** as vaginal sex, the insertion of a penis into a vagina. Vaginal sex, or **coitus**, is the most common and popular form of intimate sexual activity among heterosexual adults. On average, adult Americans report that they engage in coitus about once a week. Married individuals report having vaginal sex more frequently than never-married, divorced, or widowed persons. The results of various surveys indicate that the longer a couple has been married, the less frequently they engage in coitus (Michael et al., 1994).

Couples often engage in **petting** as a pleasurable substitute for or a prelude to coitus. Petting activities include a variety of sex acts that range from kissing and fondling breasts to performing oral sex. Additionally, a heterosexual couple may rub their genital areas together, without allowing the penis to penetrate the vagina. For people who want to reduce their risk of pregnancy or sexually transmitted infections, petting can be a safer alternative to vaginal sex.

Although not as popular as vaginal sex, oral sex is becoming a common sexual activity. **Cunnilingus** is the use of the mouth and tongue to stimulate a woman's genitals; **fellatio** refers to oral stimulation of a male's genitals. In the early part of this century, heterosexuals, even those who were married, rarely practiced oral sex. By the 1970s, sex manuals and sexuality textbooks had begun to suggest that couples incorporate oral sex into their sexual routines. Currently, more than 75% of American men and nearly as many American women report that they have either received or given oral sex (Michael et al., 1994). Women who are unable to have orgasms during coitus are often able to have them while receiving oral sex.

Some couples find anal sex, the practice of stimulating the anal area with the penis, mouth, or fingers, to be pleasurable. Although anal intercourse is a common sexual practice of gay males, a growing number of heterosexual couples are experimenting with the activity; 10% to 20% of heterosexuals report having had anal sex at least once (Michael et al., 1994). When women, however, are asked to rate how much they enjoy various sexual activities, they usually rank anal sex among the least liked.

sexual intercourse penetration of the vagina by a penis.

coitus (KO-ih-tus) the act of a penis penetrating a vagina, often referred to as vaginal intercourse.

petting sexual activities that may be a substitute for or prelude to coitus.

cunnilingus (KUN-ih-LING-gus) use of the mouth and tongue to stimulate a woman's genitals.

fellatio (feh-LA-she-oh) use of the mouth and tongue to stimulate a male's genitals.

Many women find anal intercourse to be unappealing because the practice can be painful. The muscles surrounding the anal opening normally tighten when stimulated. As a result of this tightening, large hard objects have difficulty entering the anus. Forcing the object into the anus can tear its delicate tissues and produce pain.

Anal sex also can spread infection. Bacteria can be spread from the rectum into the vagina or the *urethra,* the tube that carries urine from the bladder, if anal sex is followed by coitus. These bacteria may cause troublesome vaginal and bladder infections. After anal sex, one should wash the fingers or penis thoroughly before inserting them into a vagina or another rectum to reduce the risk of spreading harmful bacteria. Women should urinate after vaginal sex to help remove some of the bacteria that have entered the urethra, reducing the risk of a bladder infection. Anal sex also increases the risk of contracting HIV and other sexually transmitted infections from an infected partner. Using latex condoms during anal sex reduces this risk.

Solitary Sexual Behavior

Sex does not necessarily require a partner for it to be a pleasurable experience. People who practice masturbation, or solitary sex, can achieve orgasms by stroking or rubbing their own sexually sensitive body parts, especially the genitals. Although people may feel guilty or shameful because they masturbate, the practice is common. In the National Health and Social Life Survey (NHSLS), nearly 60% of the male and about 40% of female respondents between 18 and 59 years of age reported that they had masturbated at least once during the past year (Michael et al., 1994). Data from other studies generally indicate that nearly all men engage in solitary sex at some point in their lives.

People often think that only adolescent boys and single men masturbate, but women and married or cohabiting individuals also practice solitary sex, especially when their partners are unavailable. Some women masturbate because they do not have orgasms during vaginal intercourse. These women may be reluctant to communicate with their partners about their most sexually sensitive body parts or about sexual practices that they think are stimulating. Whatever their reasons for masturbating, people can relieve sexual tension safely with this practice. No physiological harm comes from masturbating, nor is there evidence that it leads to an inability to establish sexual relationships (Greenberg et al., 2000).

Celibacy

Celibacy, or **sexual abstinence**, is refrainment from sexual intercourse, usually by choice. Celibacy can be a way of life; the clergy of some religions practice sexual abstinence. Some celibate individuals engage in alternative sexual practices such as petting and masturbation. Temporary sexual abstinence during the woman's peak period of fertility is a feature of natural family planning methods (see Chapter 6). Late in pregnancy, couples may decide to avoid vaginal intercourse, especially if the activity is too awkward and uncomfortable.

Celibacy is not known to be harmful; indeed, it is the most effective measure for preventing pregnancies and sexually transmitted infections. Therefore, most health experts recommend that teenagers practice sexual abstinence before marriage.

Healthy LIVING PRACTICES

- Wash after touching the anal area so as not to spread bacteria that live in the rectum to other parts of the body.
- To reduce the risk of transmitting the virus that causes AIDS, use latex condoms during vaginal or anal intercourse.
- Practicing sexual abstinence is the most reliable way to avoid pregnancy and sexually transmitted infections.

www.jbpub.com/healthyliving

Romantic Relationships

Defining Love

Giving and receiving love is so important to a person's well-being that social scientists have speculated about it and studied its origins, characteristics, and stages. What is love? Why do people fall in love?

Love is difficult to define because the term has different meanings for different people. One definition is that *love* is a collection of behaviors, thoughts, and emotions that are associated with a psychological attraction toward other individuals. There are numerous kinds or degrees of love and a variety of feelings associated with love. Liking, fondness, affection, attraction, infatuation, and lust are feelings that are related to love. Also, the love of two friends can be quite different from the feelings between parent and child or husband and wife. According to sexologists William H. Masters and Virginia E. Johnson, all forms of love involve the element of **caring**, the expression of concern for someone's well-being.

Zick Rubin, one of the first psychologists to develop a questionnaire to measure the meanings of love, attempted to differentiate between loving and liking. He found that loving had characteristics of intimacy, attachment, caring, and commitment while liking had charac-

teristics of affection and respect (Rubin, 1973). **Intimacy** is the disclosure of one's most personal thoughts and emotions to a trusted individual. **Attachment** is the desire to spend time with someone to give and receive emotional support. **Commitment** is the determination to maintain the relationship even when times are difficult. **Affection** is a feeling of fondness toward another. **Respect** is the feeling that another has value and deserves attention.

Most humans seek loving relationships with other individuals to meet their emotional needs. Love that is fulfilling is reciprocal; that is, when one loves another, he or she is loved in return. Individuals who are in love feel free to achieve self-actualization (see Chapter 2) because their relationship fosters mutual independence as well as emotional, social, and spiritual growth.

Psychologists' Theories about Love

Beginning with Sigmund Freud in 1922, psychologists have tried to explain the phenomenon of love. Early "love theorists" such as Freud were clinical psychologists, professionals who diagnose, treat, and study mental or emotional problems and disabilities. Most of their theories relied on ideas that people loved others as a remedy for their own problems or deficiencies, rather than loving others for themselves.

In recent decades, social psychologists have formulated theories on love. These professionals explore questions by examining the individual in a social context while taking into account personality, which is the distinctive pattern of behavior, thoughts, motives, and emotions that characterizes an individual.

In 1956 Eric Fromm presented his ideas about love in *The Art of Loving*. A basic idea in Fromm's book, as noted in its title, is that loving is an art and, as such, must be learned and practiced. Fromm also distinguished between types of love, such as motherly love and erotic love.

In 1973 John Alan Lee theorized that six styles of loving exist. His ideas have since been upheld by results of studies of other researchers. **Table 5-1** lists these styles with their names (derived from the Greek), meanings, and characteristics of each. To see with which of Lee's style you most closely align, take "The Love Attitudes Scale" provided in the student workbook.

In 1986 Robert Sternberg developed a triangular theory of love that incorporates three components—intimacy, commitment, and passion—as symbolized by the points

celibacy, or sexual abstinence refrainment from sexual intercourse, usually by choice.

caring the expression of concern for someone's well-being.

intimacy disclosure of one's most personal thoughts and emotions to a trusted individual.

attachment the desire to spend time with someone to give and receive emotional support.

commitment the determination to maintain a relationship even when times are difficult.

affection fondness.

respect the feeling that one's partner has value and deserves attention.

Table 5-1	Lee's Six Styles of Loving	
Name	**Meaning**	**Characteristics**
Ludus	Game-playing love	Enjoying "chasing" love interests but not "catching" them
Eros	Romantic, passionate love	Believing in "true" love and "instant" chemistry
Storge	Affectionate, friendly love	Believing that love grows out of friendship
Mania	Possessive, dependent love	Believing that your lover's attention is all that matters
Pragma	Logical, practical love	Thinking that the best lover for you will fit a predetermined set of criteria
Agape	Selfless love	Wanting to bear your lover's burdens so that he or she does not suffer

Source: Lee, J. A. (1973). *The colours of love*. Ontario, Canada: New Press.

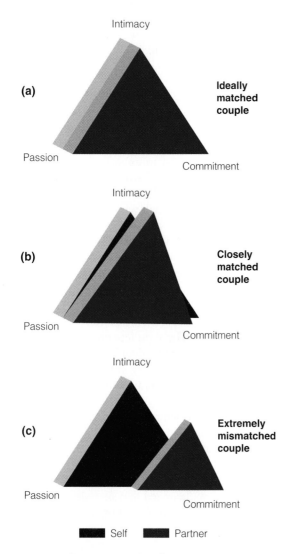

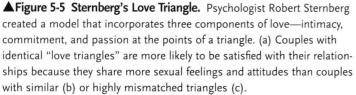

▲**Figure 5-5 Sternberg's Love Triangle.** Psychologist Robert Sternberg created a model that incorporates three components of love—intimacy, commitment, and passion at the points of a triangle. (a) Couples with identical "love triangles" are more likely to be satisfied with their relationships because they share more sexual feelings and attitudes than couples with similar (b) or highly mismatched triangles (c).

of a triangle, as ▌ **Figure 5-5(a).** shows. His intimacy component includes behaviors that foster a feeling of warmth, while the commitment component refers to the decision to love as well as to make a relationship last. Passion, in the love triangle, refers not only to sexual passion but also to the fulfillment of needs that elicit a passionate response. The balance of these three components affects the shape of the triangle. Amount of love affects the area of the triangle.

The individuals in a love relationship often have feelings of intimacy, commitment, and passion that differ from those of their partners. Although two people may be in love with each other, their "love triangles" will not match if one loves the other more than is reciprocated, and if one differs from the other in the balances of the three kinds of love. According to Sternberg, couples with similar love triangles are more likely to be satisfied with their relationships because they share more love-related feelings and attitudes, as ▌ **Figure 5-5(b)** shows, than couples with mismatched triangles, as in ▌ **Figure 5-5(c).** Sternberg has developed a questionnaire to measure love according to his love triangles theory (Sternberg, 1998; Sternberg, 1997).

Finally, Sternberg asserts that although there are only three components of love, these three components combine in various ways to produce seven kinds of love (Sternberg, 1998). For example, an absence of all three components (intimacy, commitment, and passion) results in nonlove. The presence of all three components results in consummate love. ▌ **Table 5-2** lists Sternberg's kinds of love and their components.

Love Attachments

The early bonds, or attachments, that develop between parents and their offspring may influence the ability of the children to form close, secure relationships when they are adults. Experts think that children who have emotionally distant and neglectful parents may mature into *anxious lovers*. Anxious lovers often have considerable doubts about the quality of their sexual relationships and are unable to trust their partners. Some children who have poor

Minding Your Sexual Manners

The following guidelines can help you make socially responsible decisions regarding your sexual behavior.

1. Never force sex on another person, regardless of the situation.
2. Understand that at any time in a relationship, when a person says no, that means no, not yes or maybe.
3. Avoid situations that can impair your ability to make responsible sexual decisions, especially situations that involve alcohol and other drug use.

4. Be prepared to prevent pregnancies or sexually transmitted infections. Do not engage in risky sexual behaviors. Protect yourself and your partner by using a new latex condom with each act of sexual intercourse.
5. Communicate your concerns about the risks of pregnancy and sexually transmitted infections to your partner.
6. Share the responsibility of preventing pregnancies and sexually transmitted infections with your partner.

7. Respect the sexual privacy of your partner and your relationship. It is OK to discuss your sex life with a qualified therapist, but not with friends.
8. Consider the feelings of others. Public displays of intimate behavior can offend or embarrass people.
9. Do not sexually harass others.
10. Treat your partner with care and respect.

Adapted from Hatcher, R. A., Sanderson, C. A., & Smith, K. L. (1990). Sexual etiquette 101. *SIECUS Report, 18:*9.

---

attachments to their parents may avoid becoming emotionally close to people in adulthood. Avoidant lovers may be unable to form long-term commitments with their partners. If parents meet the emotional needs of their children and frequently display affection toward them, the children are likely to mature into secure lovers. Secure lovers are more likely to form trusting and committed relationships with other adults than are anxious or avoidant lovers.

Table 5-2	Sternberg's Seven Kinds of Love		
	Components of Love		
Kind of love	**Intimacy**	**Passion**	**Commitment**
Nonlove	−	−	−
Liking	+	−	−
Infatuated love	−	+	−
Empty love	−	−	+
Romantic love	+	+	−
Companionate love	+	−	+
Fatuous love	−	+	+
Consummate love	+	+	+

Source: Sternberg, R. J. (1998). *Cupid's arrow: The course of love through time.* Cambridge, UK: Cambridge University Press, p. 17.

Love Changes over Time

Early in a relationship, when physical attraction is greatest and partners know very little about one another, their passion is high. Preoccupied with their sexual desire for each other, passionate lovers think about their partners and want to be with them constantly.

Some people experience *infatuation,* a passionate but unrealistic attraction to someone. Infatuated individuals often exaggerate the positive characteristics of their partners while ignoring their faults. A relationship that is based on infatuation may not survive, especially when one or both lovers become aware of their partners' weaknesses and find these faults unacceptable.

Eventually, the intense sexual attraction that characterizes the initial stage of a romantic relationship subsides. The couple, if sexually active, usually engages in sex less frequently than in the earlier phase of their relationship. They enjoy being together, but they can endure separations. Other aspects of their relationship, such as companionship, often deepens. Although couples in this stage of love have conflicts, committed partners usually try to resolve their problems.

Not every couple experiences the stages of love in this order. Sometimes passionate love affairs evolve from romantic companionate relationships, such as when friends become lovers. Whatever the course of a romantic relationship, however, it will have phases of growth and change. If you are involved in an intimate relationship, the "Managing Your Health" features "Minding Your Sexual Manners" above and "Tips for Better Sex" on p. 93 provide suggestions that may help you maintain the intimacy of this partnership.

Establishing Romantic Commitments

Have you ever been in love? Why did you fall in love with that person? Studies have shown that physical attraction is the most important factor that determines whether two individuals become romantically interested in one another. People often use other criteria as well, such as social status, occupation, and wealth, to select their sexual partners. Not surprisingly, Americans spend millions of dollars annually to enhance their "sex appeal" by purchasing make-up, jewelry, clothing, and expensive cars.

Initially, two people who are physically attracted to each other usually make and hold eye contact. Couples may describe this behavior as "falling in love at first sight." After two people find each other physically appealing, they need to determine if they are **compatible;** that is, if they are capable of existing together in harmony.

▲**Figure 5-6 Many Personal Characteristics Contribute to Compatibility.** Although this man and woman are not extremely close in age, they have the same racial background and may have other similarities that foster their compatibility as a couple.

Which characteristics are important for establishing long-term satisfying and compatible relationships? Individuals in such relationships are usually close in age, and they usually share similar racial, ethnic, religious, and educational backgrounds (▐ **Figure 5-6).** Members of couples who have extremely different backgrounds or dissimilar characteristics can certainly form satisfying and lasting relationships, but these situations are less common than those described previously (Michael et al., 1994).

Types of Romantic Commitments

Cohabitation In the past four decades, a growing number of unmarried people have decided to live with their het-

erosexual partners. In 1960, 439,000 adult heterosexual couples lived together; in 1998, the number rose to just over 4.2 million (U.S. Bureau of the Census, 1998). The practice of unmarried couples living together is called **cohabitation.**

Why do people live together rather than get married? Among young people, the widespread belief is that cohabitation is a way to find out if they and their partners really get along. Cohabitation is viewed as a way to avoid a bad marriage and eventual divorce (Popenoe & Whitehead, 1999d). However, results of studies show that people who cohabit before marriage (with the exception of those who are engaged and have set a wedding date) are *not* more likely to enjoy longer and happier marriages than individuals who do not live together before marrying. Studies conducted in the United States, Sweden, and Canada document higher divorce rates among couples who cohabited before marriage than among those who did not. Research results suggest that this increased risk of divorce may be due to self-selection; that is, persons who are less able to sustain long-term relationships may choose to cohabit prior to marriage, rather than to marry without first living with their partners (Lillard et al., 1995; Hall & Zhao, 1995). Additionally, research data show that multiple cohabiting experiences do *not* help people learn to have better relationships. In fact, persons with multiple cohabiting experiences are more likely to have failed future relationships than persons who do not cohabit. Although this negative correlation of cohabitation on later marriage stability is not totally understood, no positive contribution of cohabitation to marriage has been found (Popenoe & Whitehead, 1999a).

In spite of a negative correlation between cohabitation and marriage stability, cohabitation is emerging as a significant experience for young adults and is replacing marriage as the first living-together union. Researchers estimate that 25% of unmarried women in the United States between the ages of 25 and 39 are currently living with a heterosexual partner. Approximately 50% are estimated to have cohabited at one time (Bumpass & Lu, 1999).

Marriage In the United States and in most other countries, marriage is a legally binding commitment between an adult man and an adult woman. Most Americans desire marriage as a lifelong and loving partnership, and expect sexual faithfulness, emotional support, mutual trust, and lasting commitment (Popenoe & Whitehead, 1999b). However, research results show a decline in marital quality

Managing Your Health

Tips for Better Sex

1. Develop the nonsexual sides of your relationship; sharing common interests such as music, camping, or sports can help maintain the partnership outside the bedroom.
2. Communicate with your partner. Convey specific information to each other concerning the sexual activities that are the most pleasurable as well as the least desirable. If you like having your breasts kissed or you do not like having your buttocks squeezed, say so.
3. Keep sex spontaneous. The predictability of sexual activity can make it less exciting.
4. Make sex more interesting by varying the situations in which it occurs.

Be creative; find unusual locations, wear provocative sleepwear or undergarments, or try new positions for sex.
5. Allow enough time for sex. Spend some time talking, touching, caressing, and kissing before having sexual intercourse. These activities can be the prelude to a more satisfying sexual relationship.
6. Avoid worrying about orgasms or sexual performances. You may find that it is not essential to have orgasms or accomplish penetration during every sexual encounter to feel sexually satisfied.
7. Think about fulfilling your lover's needs before yours. If you are not in-

terested in receiving sexual stimulation at the same time, concentrate on satisfying your lover. Your partner may be willing to reciprocate at some other time.
8. Recognize that there are no recipes for perfect sex. Focus on the sensations and emotions surrounding the sexual experience rather than the mechanics.
9. Avoid making an issue out of your partner's occasional lack of interest in sex or inability to have sexual intercourse. Even in the best of relationships, it is normal to have times when the conditions are not right for sex. If such problems persist, seek professional advice.

---

since 1980. Couples interviewed in 1992 reported less marital interaction, more marital conflict, and more problems with their marriages than did couples interviewed in 1980 (Rogers & Amato, 1997).

Along with being less satisfied with their marriages, Americans are also marrying a bit later in life today than in recent decades. In 1975 the median age at first marriage was 21.1 years for women and 23.5 years for men. (The median is the point on a scale of measurement below which 50% of the scores fall.) By 1998 the median age of first marriage had increased to 25.0 years for women and 26.7 years for men (U.S. Bureau of the Census, 1998). Americans have also become less likely to marry; from 1970 to 1996 the annual number of marriages per 1000 unmarried women aged 15 and older has declined by one-third (Popenoe & Whitehead, 1999c).

What factors help make a marriage successful? Partners in successful marriages often demonstrate positive problem-solving and communication skills. When conflicts arise, couples with these skills can openly discuss their feelings, and they are willing to negotiate and compromise to find solutions. Additionally, partners in successful marriages share basic values, have mutual concerns, and exhibit high degrees of physical intimacy.

Extrarelational Sex Some people have sexual relationships with individuals who are not their spouses or primary sex partners. Although most Americans disapprove of such **extrarelational** sexual activity, particularly when married

couples are involved, results of a recent survey show that persons 45 to 55 are more tolerant of extramarital sex than are older people (Jacoby, 1999). (Having sex with someone other than one's spouse is commonly referred to as *extramarital sex* or *adultery*.) The majority of married Americans report that they are faithful to their spouses. Experts, however, have difficulty obtaining an accurate estimate of the number of Americans who have had extramarital sex because people may be unwilling to reveal this information. In the 1990/91 National AIDS Behavioral Survey, less than 3% of more than 1680 married respondents indicated that they had extramarital sex at least once during the previous year (Choi et al., 1994). In a 1994 study (Laumann et al., 1994), 10% of women and 25% of men reported having had an extramarital sexual relationship.

Separation and Divorce In spite of having high hopes for happiness and success during their wedding celebrations, many couples see their marriages end in separation or divorce. About 50% of marriages entered into during a year are projected to end in divorce before one spouse dies (Popenoe & Whitehead, 1999c). Accurate data concerning the number of married persons who separate permanently are unavailable. Teenage marriages are especially vulnerable to dissolution. Women who marry when they are younger

compatible
capable of existing together in harmony.

cohabitation
unmarried persons living together.

extrarelational sex
sexual relationships with individuals who are not one's spouse or primary sex partner.

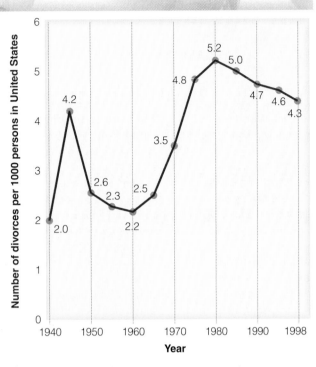

▲**Figure 5-7 U.S. Divorce Rates: 1940 to 1998.** Since 1981 the divorce rate has declined in the United States.

Sources: U.S. Bureau of the Census, Statistical Abstract of the United States (1996). Washington, DC: U.S. Government Printing Office; and National Center for Health Statistics. (1999). Births, marriages, divorces, and deaths: Provisional data for 1998. *National Vital Statistics Reports,* 47(21). Hyattsville, MD: National Center for Health Statistics.

than 20 years of age are twice as likely to be in a failed marriage as women who marry when they are 22 years of age or older.

Early in the twentieth century, divorce was uncommon in this country. In 1940 the U.S. divorce rate was 2 divorces per 1000 persons. The divorce rate rose during World War II and peaked at more than 4 divorces per 1000 at the war's end. The rate fell during the fifties to nearly prewar rates, and rose again in the 1960s and 1970s. From 1979 through 1981, the U.S. divorce rate was at its highest level of the century, slightly more than 5 divorces per 1000. The decline in the divorce rate has been modest since that time, and in 1998 was at 4.3 divorces for every 1000 persons (▌ Figure 5-7). Currently in the United States, more than 1 million divorces occur annually.

Marriages fail for numerous reasons. People frequently cite reasons for dissolving their marriages that involve problems with their spouses, particularly extramarital sexual activity, emotional immaturity, and alcoholism. Other factors that contribute to marital separation and divorce include the failure to communicate with or to understand one's spouse; gender role disagreements; personality, interest, and value differences; and the desire for more personal freedom. In most instances, more than one factor contributes to the breakup of a marriage.

After their divorces are final, many people begin to search for new partners, and they eventually remarry—men at a higher rate than women. Remarriages do not have better success rates than first marriages. Divorced people who remarry have a greater probability of subsequent divorce than do persons marrying for the first time (Ceglian & Gardner, 1999).

- To increase your child's chances of being able to form secure and trusting relationships as an adult, consider ways to be more attentive to his or her emotional needs; display your affection frequently.
- To increase your likelihood of having a happy and long-term marriage, avoid cohabitation prior to making this commitment and communicate as effectively as possible with your spouse.

Communication in Relationships

Effective communication is a cornerstone of interpersonal and sexual relationships. In order to communicate effectively, people must express themselves as accurately and as clearly as possible but also must listen with attentiveness, openness, and patience. To express yourself accurately and clearly, first, say exactly what you mean. If you avoid being straightforward so that you will not hurt someone's feelings, for example, the person with whom you're communicating may not understand your message. Second, your statements must be specific, not vague. For example, telling your partner that you would like him to be more spontaneous will probably make him question what you really mean. Do you always want him to act in a spontaneous manner? Has he never been spontaneous? Or do you really mean that you had wanted him to accept yesterday's last-minute party invitation, and wished that he could have just dropped what he was doing, changed his clothes, and dashed out the door with you? Third, avoid sending mixed messages. For example, don't tell your partner that everything is fine when she can tell from your behavior and expression that you are really feeling "down." Or, don't say, "I don't want to worry you, but I think I have a sexually transmitted infection."

Another mechanism to foster effective communication is to express your feelings using "I" statements when discussing issues with a partner. Then go on to say what you need to try to maintain (or change) the feeling. Statements that begin with "You" can hinder open communication between partners, particularly if the speaker is criticizing the listener's behavior or blaming this person for something.

For example, instead of saying "You always spend too much time with your friends," you could say "I feel lonely and miss you terribly when you are out with your friends. (Express the feeling.) Could I join you on those occasions so that we could spend more time together?" (State the remedy.) Try not to fall into the trap of "false" I statements. "I feel like you spend too much time with your friends" is really a "you" statement.

Besides being able to express oneself clearly, an effective communicator has good listening skills. Failure to hear information accurately or completely can create misunderstandings that result in conflicts. In discussions, good listeners restate or paraphrase what they have heard their partners say. This practice allows speakers, if necessary, to correct or clarify what they have said. For example, if your partner says, "When we get together with your friends or your family, you always ignore me," you could respond by saying, "I didn't realize that you feel neglected in those situations. What can I do to make you feel more included?" To evaluate your communication patterns, use the "Communication Patterns Questionnaire" in the student workbook.

In addition to words, people use nonverbal forms of communication, such as body positioning (body language) and facial gestures, to express their thoughts (▮ **Figure 5-8**). Touching is a form of nonverbal communication that can convey important information about intimate sexual feelings. Many people report that being held, kissed, massaged, or fondled by their partners is as sexually gratifying as sexual intercourse. Sensual touching does not have to involve the genitals; gently massaging your partner's back, for example, can convey your feelings of love to this individual.

Healthy
LIVING PRACTICES

- To encourage discussions between you and your partner about issues that concern the relationship, use "I" statements to express your feelings and avoid using "You" statements. "You" statements can anger or belittle your partner.
- Listen carefully to your partner during your discussions. Repeat what your partner says to avoid misunderstandings. If your partner gives unclear responses to your questions, ask for additional information.

www.jbpub.com/healthyliving

across the lifespan

Sexuality

Most preschoolers masturbate. Parents who think masturbation is a healthy and normal aspect of sexuality usually let their children know that the behavior is inappropriate in public but do not attempt to stop this behavior in private. Preschool children typically play games in which they act out adult gender roles. By this age, children have learned that there are differences between the sexes. Children are curious about sexuality; they may "play doctor" by examining each others' genitals. Additionally, young children often ask questions such as "Where did I come from?" If parents are uncertain how to answer this or other questions about sexual matters, they can usually find a collection of age-appropriate sexuality books that they can read with their children at their local libraries. Of course, parents should read these books themselves before they read them with their children.

It is not unusual for elementary school-age children to engage in mutual sex play, activities that may include rehearsing adult sexual behaviors. Sex experts consider such sex play normal behavior when it is playful, occurs infrequently, and does not involve coercion.

The ability to reproduce begins during puberty. Many teens avoid sexual activity because they fear becoming pregnant, contracting sexually transmitted infections, and losing self-esteem or parental trust. The media, however, exposes American youth to sexually explicit images that may conflict with parental values and encour-

▲**Figure 5-8 Nonverbal Communication.** Nonverbal forms of communication, such as body postures and facial gestures, can convey thoughts. What do this couple's nonverbal signals communicate?

age sexual experimentation. Additionally, peers or older persons can exert considerable pressure on teens to engage in sex. To help youth maintain their abstinence, parents and educators can teach teens how to use sexual assertiveness skills.

In spite of efforts to promote teenage abstinence, only 1 in 4 American teenagers refrains from having sex. At age 15, about one-quarter of young girls in the United States have had sexual intercourse. By age 17, about one-half have engaged in coitus, and by 19, three-quarters are no longer virgins (Abma et al., 1997).

Michael Benson from Northwestern University Medical School and Edward Torpy from Loyola University in Chicago conducted an anonymous survey of almost 1000 urban students in grades 6 to 8. After analyzing the results of their survey, Benson and Torpy (1995) concluded that, among other things, gender, age of puberty, and ethnic group are associated with virginity loss. Sex education, religious affiliation, grade average, and self-esteem were among the variables that were not associated, either positively or negatively, with virginity. By eighth grade (by approximately age 13), more boys reported sexual activity than girls. Eighty-two percent of the male African American students indicated that they were sexually active; this percentage was nearly twice that of their White or Latino peers. Additionally, the young African American males reported having more sex partners than their peers from the other racial or ethnic groups. Self-reported data on American girls and sexual intercourse indicates that by age 17, about 50% of Hispanic and Black girls have had sexual intercourse, as have about 35% of White girls (Abma et al., 1997). Results of a 1997 study conducted by the Centers for Disease Control and Prevention (CDC) across genders shows that nearly 22% of Black students, about 8% of Hispanic students, and 4% of White students have initiated sexual intercourse before 13 years of age (CDC, 1998a).

The CDC has compared behavior trends in youth from 1991 through 1997, and found that the percentage of high school students who have ever had sexual intercourse has decreased from about 54% in 1991, to about 48% in 1997. Additionally, the number of sexual partners high school students report having has dropped from nearly 19 persons to 16. More students are using condoms; in 1991 about 46% of sexually active students used a condom at their last sexual intercourse, while in 1997 nearly 57% reported having done so. The use of birth control pills declined, however. In 1991 nearly 21% of sexually active high school girls used "the pill." In 1997 about 17% used this form of birth control (CDC, 1998b). Although pill use has dropped, condom use has risen.

The teenage birth rate has declined from 1991 to 1998 (■ Figure 5-9). Compared with women in their 20s, pregnant teenagers have a greater risk of experiencing serious complications during pregnancy and delivery as well as of giving birth to premature underweight babies. Premature

infants are born before the 37th week of pregnancy. The risk of giving birth to a premature, low-birth-weight infant is especially high for pregnant adolescents between 10 and 14 years of age. Underweight premature newborns have a greater risk of serious health and developmental problems than normal-weight newborns who are born at term, that is, between the 37th and 41st weeks of pregnancy.

Most unmarried teenage girls who give birth to live infants keep their babies rather than give them up for adoption. Adolescent mothers are more likely to be unmarried, poor, and have less education than mothers who give birth when they are older. Many teenage mothers have difficulty improving their educational and socioeconomic levels when they become adults.

Some unwed teenage fathers choose to fulfill their parental responsibilities by providing financial and emotional support for their children. Many of them live with or marry the mother of their children. The long-term outlook

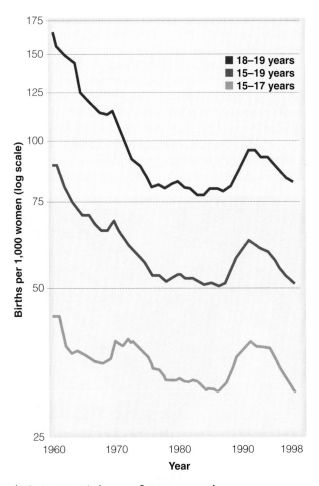

▲Figure 5-9 **Birth rates for teenagers by age: United States, 1960 through 1998.**

Source: Ventura, S. J., Mathews, T. J., & Curtin, S. C. (1999). Declines in teenage birth rates, 1991–98: Update of national and state trends. *National Vital Statistics Reports, 47*(26). Hyattsville, MD: National Center for Health Statistics.

for these cohabitations or marriages is not good. Data from one study of teenage fathers indicate that only about 16% of these individuals continue to live with their child and its mother 15 months after the baby's birth (Hardy et al., 1989).

With respect to the elderly, sex has enduring importance; sexuality does not end because a person is older (█ **Figure 5-10**). According to a 1998 survey conducted by the National Council on Aging (NCOA), nearly half of Americans age 60 or older engage in sexual activity at least once a month (NCOA, 1998). Results of this study reveal that sexual inactivity in the later years of life usually is due to medical disabilities or lack of a sexual partner, rather than to lack of desire.

Older adults experience a gradual decline in sexual functioning. Therefore, elderly individuals should recognize that their sexual responses are likely to be different from when they were young adults. For example, it usually takes longer for the older adult to become adequately sexually stimulated before sex, and orgasms are less intense. Chronic diseases such as diabetes or heart disease can further limit an aged person's sexual responses or interest in sex. Certain antihypertensive and antidepressant medications can produce side effects that impair sexual functioning; affected individuals should discuss their sexual problems with their physicians. Frequently, changing medications can be helpful. In some cases, medical treatments are available that can improve sexual functioning. Elderly individuals who have sexual impairments that do not respond to treatment can rely on noncoital forms of sexual expression such as kissing, caressing, cuddling, or oral sex to obtain pleasure and fulfillment. In fact, the results of one study of 200 older married couples reveal that affectionate behavior is more crucial to their happiness than sex (Mathias-Riegel, 1999).

Besides physical factors, significant social changes such as the loss of a spouse or moving into a nursing home can

▲Figure 5-10 **Sexuality Has No Age Limit.**

have negative impacts on the sexuality of aged individuals. Widows and widowers may have difficulty meeting sexual partners. Elderly nursing home residents may not feel free to express their sexuality because they lack privacy. As the number of elderly Americans rises, addressing sexuality needs within this age group will become an increasingly important issue.

ANALYZING Health-Related Information

Explain why you think the website reproduced below is a reliable or an unreliable source of information. Use the model for analyzing health-related information to guide your thinking; the main points of the model are noted to the right. The model is fully explained on pages 12 to 13. (Information about Johan, who maintains the website with his wife, is also shown below. If you wish to visit this site, the Web address is:

http://www.santesson.com/aphrodis/pine.htm)

1. Which statements are verifiable facts, and which are unverified statements or value claims?
2. What are the credentials of the person who wrote the information posted on the website? If this information is available, does the author's background and education qualify him or her as an expert in the topic area?
3. What might be the motives and biases of the person who wrote information on the website? State reasons for your answer.
4. Which information on the website is relevant to the topic? Which information is irrelevant?
5. Is the source reliable? Does it have a reputation for publishing misinformation?
6. Does the website attack the credibility of conventional scientists or medical authorities?

Based on the above analysis, do you think that this website is a reliable source of health-related information? Summarize your reasons for coming to this conclusion.

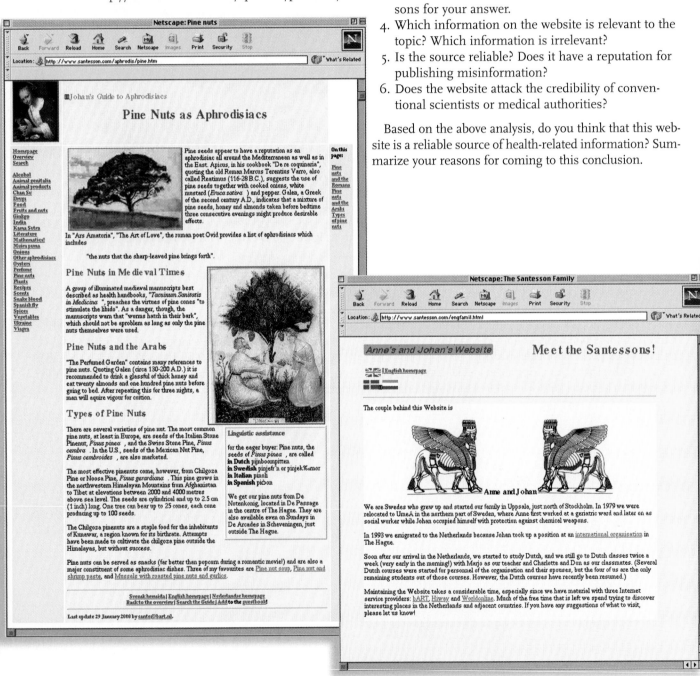

Chapter Review
Summary

Human sexuality is a complex set of thoughts, feelings, attitudes, and behaviors that are related to reproduction as well as to being a male or female. Numerous biological, psychological, social, and cultural forces interact to influence sexuality. Sexuality influences all aspects of an individual's life, including identity, self-esteem, emotions, personality, relationships, lifestyle, and health.

Being knowledgeable about sexuality is important for maintaining good health and optimal well-being. Instincts, sensations, and hormones drive reproductive behavior, but social, cultural, and religious factors heavily influence a person's sexual attitudes, values, and behaviors. Sexually responsible people consider how their sexual behavior affects themselves and others.

Gender is the classification of the sex of a person based on many criteria, among them anatomic and chromosomal characteristics. Gender identity is an individual's perception of himself or herself as being male or female. Various biological, social, and environmental forces help mold a child's gender identity. A gender role refers to patterns of behavior, attitudes, and personality attributes that, in a particular culture, are traditionally considered feminine or masculine. In the United States today, gender roles are undergoing dramatic changes and are becoming more flexible than in the past.

Sexual orientation, the direction of one's romantic thoughts, feelings, and attractions, can be toward the same sex, the opposite sex, or both sexes. Biological factors, such as genetics, and environmental influences, such as childhood experiences, probably contribute to the formation of one's adult sexual orientation.

Sexual partners may engage in a variety of intimate activities including petting as well as vaginal, oral, and anal sex. However, sex does not require a partner for it to be a pleasurable experience—most people masturbate at some point during their lives. Some people choose to refrain from sexual activity for a variety of reasons, such as health concerns or religious beliefs. Abstaining from sexual activity is not known to be harmful, and it is an effective measure for preventing pregnancies and sexually transmitted infections.

People need to establish and maintain satisfying attachments to others for optimal health and well-being. People who have high self-esteem, are satisfied with their bodies, are in good health, and have positive feelings about their sexuality are likely to form fulfilling intimate relationships. Although love is difficult to define, people in loving relationships share feelings of caring, respect, attachment, commitment, and intimacy.

Various psychologists have developed theories about love. However, experts generally agree that love changes over time. Early in a relationship, when physical attraction is greatest and partners know very little about one another, their passion is high. Eventually, the intense sexual attraction that characterizes a romantic relationship in its initial stages subsides. Other aspects of the relationship, such as companionship, often deepen. Compatibility, the ability to exist in harmony, is crucial in the development of a healthy emotional attraction between partners. Usually important for establishing a compatible relationship is the sharing of similar interests, attitudes, and values.

In the United States, about 50% of marriages now end in divorce. More couples are choosing to cohabit before marriage, but this practice results in a higher risk of divorce than not living together prior to marriage. Those who are married are less satisfied with their marriages and are marrying later in life than in recent decades. Effective communication is an essential ingredient for maintaining satisfying and successful marriages and intimate relationships.

Children are curious about sex; they frequently play sex games with other children and ask their parents questions about sex. Children's sex play is normal behavior when it is playful, occurs infrequently, and does not involve coercion.

Today, teens are becoming sexually active at an earlier age and have more sex partners than those of previous generations. About 48% of American high school students have engaged in sexual intercourse. Although the teenage birth rate has declined, it is still high. Compared with women in their 20s, pregnant teenagers have a greater risk of serious complications during pregnancy and delivery, as well as of giving birth to premature and underweight newborns. Additionally, adolescent mothers are more likely to be unmarried, poor, and have less education than mothers who give birth when they are older. Many teenage mothers have difficulty improving their educational and socioeconomic levels when they become adults.

Sexuality does not end at a particular age. Most healthy elderly men and women continue to be interested and participate in sexual activity. However, sexual functioning declines with aging; sexual responses in older persons are different from when they were young adults. As the number of elderly Americans rises, addressing sexuality needs in this age group will become an increasingly important issue.

Applying What You Have Learned

1. Develop a plan to improve the way you convey your feelings in relationships. *(Application)*
2. Analyze your present intimate relationship or a past one. Explain why you think it will be (or was) a short-term or long-term relationship. *(Analysis)*
3. Propose a checklist of characteristics that you could use to select a suitable partner. Explain why these characteristics are important. *(Synthesis)*
4. Develop a position concerning the promotion of masturbation as a safe sex alternative. How would you defend your position? *(Evaluation)*

KEY

Application: Using information in a new situation.
Analysis: Breaking down information into component parts.
Synthesis: Putting together information from different sources.
Evaluation: Making informed decisions.

Reflecting On Your Health

1. What is the source of your sexual values (e.g., your parents, your religious upbringing, etc.)? Do you feel comfortable with those values? Why or why not? Do you feel as though your peers share some or all of your values, or do you feel intimidated or pressured to change your values?
2. Do you think that "traditional" gender roles are appropriate in American society today? If you think that some are appropriate and some are not, pick one example from each category and explain your feelings about their appropriateness or inappropriateness.
3. Do you agree with former Surgeon General Joycelyn Elders' opinion that sex education in America's schools should include instruction about masturbation? Why or why not?
4. Think about a current or former intimate relationship you had. Do you think that your love relationship fits one of Lee's six styles of loving or one of Sternberg's kinds of love? How does it fit or not fit?
5. Think about the nature of your verbal interactions with someone important to you—a parent or spouse, for example. How could you communicate more effectively with that person using suggestions in this chapter?

References

Abma, J. C., Chandra, A., Mosher, W. D., Peterson, L., & Piccinino, L. (1997). Fertility, family planning, and women's health: New data from the 1995 National Survey of Family Growth. *National Center for Health Statistics, Vital Health Statistics, 23*(19). http://cdc.gov/nchs/datawh/statab/pubd/2319_19.htm

Benson, M. D., & Torpy, E. J. (1995) Sexual behavior in junior high school students. *Obstetrics and Gynecology, 85:*279-284.

Bohannon, J. R., & Blanton, P. W. (1999). Gender role attitudes of American mothers and daughters over time. *Journal of Social Psychology, 139:*173-179.

Bumpass, L., & Lu, H. (1999). *Trends in cohabitation and implications for children's family contexts.* Unpublished manuscript, Center for Demography & Ecology, University of Wisconsin, Madison.

Carney, D. (1996). GOP bill restricting gay unions clears . . . but does not yield political dividends. *Congressional Quarterly Weekly Report, 54:*(36): 2598-2599.

Ceglian, C. P. (1999). Attachment style: A risk for multiple marriages? *Journal of Divorce and Remarriage, 31:*125-139.

Centers for Disease Control and Prevention (CDC). (1998a). Youth risk behavior surveillance—United States, 1997. *Morbidity and Mortality Weekly Report, 47*(No. SS-3). http://www.cdc.gov/nccdphp/dash/yrbs/natsum97/susex97.htm

Centers for Disease Control and Prevention (CDC). (1998b). *Fact sheet: Youth risk behavior trends.* Atlanta: Author. http://www.cdc.gov/nccdphp/dash/yrbs/trend.htm

Choi, K. H., Catania, J. A., & Dolcini, M. M. (1994). Extramarital sex and HIV risk factors among U.S. adults: Results from the national AIDS behavioral survey. *American Journal of Public Health, 84:* 2003-2007.

Fromm, E. (1956). *The art of loving.* New York: Harper.

Greenberg, J. S., Bruess, C. E., & Haffner, D. W. (2000). *Exploring the dimensions of human sexuality.* Sudbury MA: Jones & Bartlett Publishers.

Hall, D. P., & Zhao, J. Z. (1995). Cohabitation and divorce in Canada: Testing the selectivity hypothesis. *Journal of Marriage and the Family, 57:*421-427.

Hamer, D. H., Hu, S., Magnuson, V. L., Hu, N., & Pattatucci, A. M. (1993). A linkage between DNA markers on the X chromosome and male sexual orientation. *Science, 261:*321-7

Hardy, J. B., Duggan, A. K., Masnyk, K., & Pearson, C. (1989). Fathers of children born to young urban mothers. *Family Planning Perspectives, 21:*159-163, 187.

Hatcher, R. A., Sanderson, C. A., & Smith, K. L. (1990). Sexual etiquette 101. *SIECUS Report,* 18, 9.

Jacoby, S. (1999). Great sex: What's age got to do with it? *Modern Maturity, 42*(5):40.

Johnson, M. E., Brems, C., & Alford-Keating, P. (1997). Personality correlates of homophobia. *Journal of Homosexuality, 34:*57-69.

Kinsey, A. C., Pomeroy, W. B., Martin, C. E., & Gebhard, P.H. (1953) *Sexual behavior in the human female.* Philadelphia: Saunders.

Laumann, E. O., Gagnon, J. H., Michael, R. T., & Michaels, S. (1994). *The social organization of sexuality: Sexual practices in the United States.* Chicago: University of Chicago Press.

Lee, J. A. (1973). *The colours of love.* Ontario, Canada: New Press.

LeVay, S. (1991). A difference in hypothalamic structure between heterosexual and homosexual men. *Science, 253:*1034-1037.

Lillard, L. A., Brien, M. J., & Waite, L. J. (1995). Premarital cohabitation and subsequent marital dissolution: A matter of self-selection? *Demography, 32:*437-57.

Mathias-Riegel, B. (1999). Intimacy 101: A refresher course in the language of love. *Modern Maturity, 42*(5):46.

Michael, R. T., Gagnon, J. H., Laumann, E. O., & Kolata, G. (1994). *Sex in America.* Boston: Little, Brown and Company.

National Council on Aging (NCOA). (1998). *Half of older Americans report they are sexually active; 4 in 10 want more sex, says new survey.* http://www.ncoa.org/news/archives/sexsurvey.htm

National Council on Aging (NCOA). (1998). Healthy sexuality and vital aging. Executive Summary. Washington, DC: Author.

Popenoe, D., & Whitehead, B. D. (1999a) *Should we live together? Part 1.* New Brunswick, NJ: National Marriage Project. http://marriage.rutgers.edu/publivet.htm

Popenoe, D., & Whitehead, B. D. (1999b) *The state of our unions.* New Brunswick, NJ: National Marriage Project. http://marriage.rutgers.edu/pubstat.htm

Popenoe, D., & Whitehead, B. D. (1999c) *The state of our unions: part 2, social indicators of marital health & wellbeing.* New Brunswick, NJ: National Marriage Project. http://marriage.rutgers.edu/bpubstat.htm

Popenoe, D., & Whitehead, B. D. (1999d) *The state of our unions: part 3: social indicators of marital health & wellbeing (continued).* New Brunswick, NJ: National Marriage Project. http://marriage.rutgers.edu/cpubstat.htm

Rice, G., Anderson, C., Risch, N., & Ebers, G. (1999). Male homosexuality: Absence of linkage to microsatellite markers at Xq28. *Science, 284:*665-667.

Rogers, S. J. & Amato, P. (1997). Is marital quality declining? The evidence from two generations. *Social Forces, 75:*1089-1100.

Rubin, Z. (1973). *Liking and loving.* New York: Hold, Rinehart, and Winston.

Sell, R. L., Wells, J. A., & Wypij, D. (1995). The prevalence of homosexual behavior and attraction in the United States, the United Kingdom, and France: Results of a national population-based sample. *Archives of Sexual Behavior, 24:*235-248.

Smith, T. W. (1991). Adult sexual behavior in 1989: Number of partners, frequency of intercourse and risk of AIDS. *Family Planning Perspectives, 23:*102-107.

Sternberg, R. J. (1986). A triangular theory of love. *Psychological Review, 93:*19-135.

Sternberg, R. J. (1997). Construct validation of a triangular love scale. *European Journal of Social Psychology, 27:*313-335.

Sternberg, R. J. (1998). *Cupid's arrow: The course of love through time.* Cambridge, UK: Cambridge University Press.

U.S. Bureau of the Census. (March, 1998 [Update]). Marital status and living arrangements. *Current Population Reports,* Series P20-514 (and earlier reports). Washington, DC: Government Printing Office. Available: http://census.gov/population.socdemo/ms-la/tabms-2.txt

Ventura, S. J., Mathews, T. J., & Curtin, S. C. (1999). Declines in teenage birth rates, 1991–98: Update of national and state trends. *National Vital Statistics Reports, 47*(26). Hyattsville, Maryland: National Center for Health Statistics.

Whitley, B. E., Jr., & Kite, M. E. (1995). Sex differences in attitudes toward homosexuality: A comment on Oliver and Hyde (1993). *Psychological Bulletin, 117:*46-154. (Discussion 155-158).

Wickelgren, I. (1999). Discovery of "gay gene" questioned. *Science, 284:*571.

Reproductive Health

This striking photograph depicts the essence of **sexual reproduction**: the fertilization of an egg (ovum) by a sperm, a process also called conception. The photograph is color enhanced; the outside of the egg is shown as orange and the sperm as blue. A layer of cells that extend from the egg cover its surface. During the maturation of the egg, these outer cells secrete a thick gellike material that covers the egg beneath. Together, the gel and the outer cells form a protective covering, which sperm must penetrate by means of digestive enzymes in their heads. Although it is difficult to see in this photograph, the head of only one sperm is making its way through these outer layers and ultimately fertilized this egg.

When the sperm enters the egg, it triggers the egg's final maturation. Following this process, the hereditary material from the sperm and the mature egg unite, forming a new cell—the zygote. This single cell has the potential to develop into a new individual.

Fertility, the ability to conceive a child, has been important to couples since the ancient civilizations. Fertility rites were

> *"This striking photograph depicts the essence of sexual reproduction: the fertilization of an egg (ovum) by a sperm . . ."*

practiced then and are still practiced in some parts of the world today. You may have seen fertility statues, with characteristically large breasts, pregnant bellies, or exaggerated penises, which are used in these ancient rites. Researchers have found that many ancient rites and customs have scientific merit. For example, if each partner of an infertile couple believes in the value of certain fertility practices, each may develop a positive emotional state, a factor that promotes fertility. In other examples, Hungarian peasant women bite their placenta after its delivery, and women in certain regions of China eat dried placenta. They believe these practices help the women remain fertile. Scientists know that the placenta contains large amounts of a hormone that is used to treat ovulatory failure. (The placenta is discussed on page 112.) This tradition, then, may be chemically beneficial to the women who practice it.

Infertility is the inability of a couple to conceive a child after 1 year of unprotected sex. Couples may have reduced fertility for a variety of reasons; it is not necessarily due to

What You'll Learn

www.jbpub.com/healthyliving

The web site for this book offers many useful tools and is a great source for supplementary health information for both students and instructors. Visit the site at www.jbpub.com/healthyliving for information on these topics:

Sexual Dysfunctions
Pregnancy and Human Development
Contraception
Managing Your Health: Genetic Counseling and Prenatal Diagnosis
Across the Life Span: Sexual Development

Chapter Overview

The functions and structures of the male and female reproductive systems.
The phases of the sexual response cycle.
Symptoms of and treatments for sexual dysfunctions.
What happens throughout the menstrual cycle.
How a woman can prepare her body for pregnancy.
How a fetus develops.
The changes in a pregnant woman from conception through the postpartum period.
The causes of and treatments for infertility.
The benefits and drawbacks of contraceptive methods.

 **DIVERSITY** in Health   Menopause

Con$umer Health   Home Pregnancy Tests

 Managing Your Health   Genetic Counseling and Prenatal Diagnosis | Enlargement of the Prostate

across the **lifespan**   Sexual Development

 Applying Concepts for Healthy Living A Workbook

Student Workbook

Self Assessment: Contraceptive Comfort and Confidence Scale | Attitudes Toward Timing of Parenthood Scale
Changing Health Habits: Do You Want to Improve Your Reproductive Health?

Do You Know?

- How well your contraceptive works compared to others?
- What causes birth defects?
- When a woman is most likely to get pregnant?

"a problem" with one partner or the other. Factors that slightly impair the fertility of both sexual partners may interact to render a couple infertile. These factors include a low sperm count, a high percentage of abnormally shaped sperm, scarring in the female genital tract, structural defects of the uterus, and hormonal imbalances. Treatments for infertility are specific to the causes and include surgical procedures, hormone therapy, medication, and lifestyle changes. In addition to these therapies, physicians can also harvest eggs and sperm to assist fertilization and implantation.

Whether physician-assisted, accompanied by ancient rites and customs, or accomplished with no intervention at all, fertilization is an event that is preceded by a variety of physiological processes that make it all possible, and that is where we begin this chapter.

The Male Reproductive System

The male reproductive system is structured for the development and maturation of sperm and for delivering sperm to the vagina. **Figure 6-1** is a diagram of a posterior view (a) and a lengthwise section of the male reproductive tract (b).

The Internal Organs of Sexual Reproduction

Sperm Development Sperm are produced in the **testes** (singular, testis), which hang outside the body (in the angle formed between the legs) encased in a sac of skin called the **scrotum.** The testes have two major functions: production of the sex hormone testosterone and production of sperm cells. The testes are packed with hundreds of feet of tubes (called *seminiferous tubules*) in which sperm are made.

Each day, the testes of an adult male produce hundreds of millions of sperm. Various conditions are necessary for proper sperm production. The testes must be cooler than body temperature to produce normal sperm; the position of the scrotum keeps the temperature of the testes below that of the rest of the body. It was formerly thought that wearing tight pants or tight undergarments held the testes so close to the body that the temperature within the tubules was raised. The results of recent research show that there are no significant differences in the scrotal temperatures of men who wear tight underwear or pants, and those who wear loose garments (Munkelwitz, & Gilbert, 1998). Scientists think that blood flow near the surface of the scrotum increases when the groin temperature rises, dissipating the heat and lowering scrotal temperature.

sexual reproduction the fertilization of an egg (ovum; plural, ova) by a sperm.

testes (TES-tease) the male reproductive organs that produce sperm (the male sex cells) and testosterone (a male sex hormone).

scrotum (SKRO-tum) the sac of skin in which the testes are enclosed and hang outside the body.

epididymis (EP-ih-DID-ih-mis) a coiled tube that lies on the back of each testis and in which sperm mature.

ductus deferens (DUCK-tus DEF-er-enz) a tube that links the epididymis and the urethra, the passageway through which sperm exit the body.

Figure 6-1 The Male Reproductive System. ◀(a) Posterior view of the internal organs, and ▼(b) lengthwise section (side view) of the internal organs.

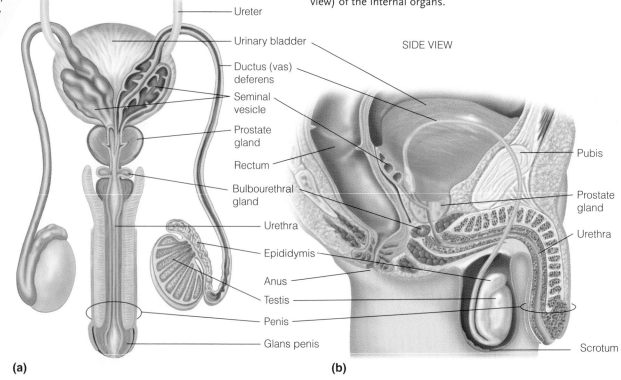

FRONT VIEW

- Ureter
- Urinary bladder
- Ductus (vas) deferens
- Seminal vesicle
- Prostate gland
- Rectum
- Bulbourethral gland
- Urethra
- Epididymis
- Anus
- Testis
- Penis
- Glans penis

(a)

SIDE VIEW

- Pubis
- Prostate gland
- Urethra
- Scrotum

(b)

Semen Formation After sperm are manufactured in the seminiferous tubules, they are gently moved along by the fluid in which they are suspended. The sperm move through a network of ducts to the **epididymis** (plural, epididymides). The epididymis is a coiled tube that lies on the back of each testis. Here is where the sperm mature, developing the ability to swim and to fertilize an egg.

Rhythmic contractions of the muscular walls of the epididymis slowly move the sperm to the **ductus (vas) deferens** when maturation is complete. The ductus deferens is a tube that links the epididymis and the urethra, the passageway through which sperm exit the body. Sperm are stored in the ductus deferens until they are released from the body during **ejaculation**, their emission from the penis during **orgasm**, the peak of sexual excitement. Sperm can be stored for a few days in these ducts. If not ejaculated within that time, the sperm die and are ingested by the body's white blood cells. Newly synthesized sperm take their place. For this reason, men who have had vasectomies (see p. 131) should not be concerned that sperm are accumulating in their bodies.

The sperm are suspended in relatively little fluid while stored in the ductus deferens. A variety of organs referred to as accessory sex glands add fluid to the sperm as they exit the body during ejaculation. This fluid contains nutrients to fuel the sperm as they journey up the female reproductive tract, alkaline substances to neutralize the acidity of the vagina, and other chemicals that aid sperm movement. The secretions of the accessory sex glands (called seminal fluid) and the sperm make up the **semen**, or *ejaculate*.

During ejaculation, sperm are swiftly propelled through the ductus deferens by the rhythmic contractions of its muscular walls. Just prior to the merging of the two ductus deferens where they meet the urethra, the secretions of the paired **seminal vesicles** flow into the ejaculate. The thick secretions of the seminal vesicles add much of the volume to the ejaculate (approximately 60%) and contain the sugar fructose, which provides nutrition for the sperm.

As the ejaculate continues traveling through the male reproductive tract, the **prostate gland** adds its secretion. This single, walnut-sized gland lies just below the bladder. It surrounds the urethra and produces a milky fluid that protects sperm from the acidic environment of the woman's vagina.

During sexual arousal, the bulbourethral glands produce a mucus-like fluid that precedes the ejaculate. The *bulbourethral glands* (also called Cowper's glands), paired glands about the size of peas, are located on either side of the urethra just below the prostate. The secretions of these glands help neutralize the acidity of the male urethra and the vagina. These glands also contribute a small amount of lubrication for sexual intercourse. However, this fluid may contain sperm. For this reason (and others), the withdrawal method of birth control is not highly reliable (see p. 125).

The External Organs of Sexual Reproduction

The scrotum and the **penis** are the external organs of sexual reproduction (external genitals) in males (see Figure 6-1). Three columns of spongy tissue in the inner structure of the penis (**Figure 6-2**) become filled with blood during sexual arousal, which causes the penis to enlarge and become firm so that it can be inserted into the vagina. During sexual intercourse the penis can become stimulated enough to result in orgasm, during which ejaculation occurs.

ejaculation the emission of semen from the penis during orgasm.

orgasm the peak of sexual excitement.

semen the ejaculate; the secretions of the accessory sex glands (called seminal fluid) and sperm.

seminal vesicles (SEM-ih-nal VES-ih-klz) paired male sex organs located near the junction of the two vas deferens, which produce thick fructose-containing secretions that are added to the ejaculate.

prostate gland a single, walnut-sized gland that lies just below the bladder surrounding the urethra. The prostate produces a milky alkaline fluid that is added to the ejaculate.

penis a cylindrical external organ of sexual reproduction in males, which hangs in front of the scrotum.

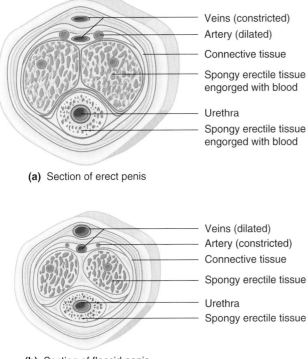

Veins (constricted)
Artery (dilated)
Connective tissue
Spongy erectile tissue engorged with blood
Urethra
Spongy erectile tissue engorged with blood

(a) Section of erect penis

Veins (dilated)
Artery (constricted)
Connective tissue
Spongy erectile tissue
Urethra
Spongy erectile tissue

(b) Section of flaccid penis

◄Figure 6-2 **The Erect and Flaccid Penis.** (a) During an erection, blood fills the spongy erectile tissue of the penis. (b) When the blood drains from this tissue, as it does after orgasm, the penis becomes flaccid.

▼**Figure 6-3 The Female Reproductive System.** (a) Side view (lengthwise section) of the internal organs, and (b) posterior view of the internal organs.

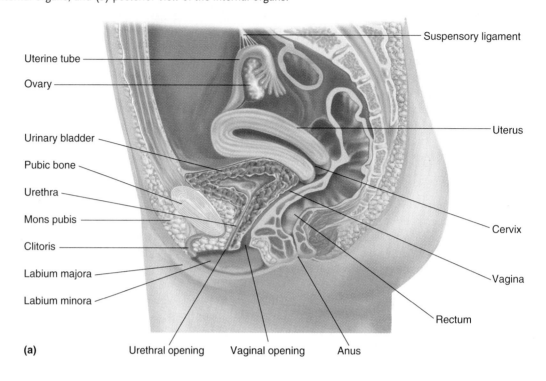

(a)

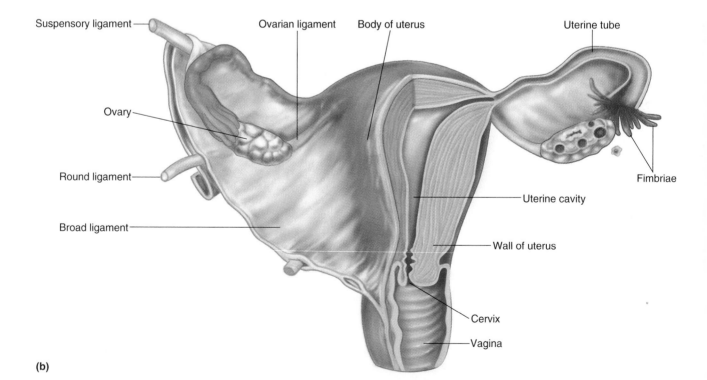

(b)

The Female Reproductive System

The female reproductive system is structured for the development and maturation of ova, for receiving sperm, for providing an environment in which a fertilized ovum can develop and mature, and for giving birth to the developed fetus. ▮ **Figure 6-3** is a diagram of a lengthwise section of the female reproductive tract (a) and a posterior view (b).

The Internal Organs of Sexual Reproduction

Egg Development Ova are produced in the **ovaries**, which are two oval organs suspended by ligaments (a type of connective tissue) in the pelvic cavity. The almond-sized ovaries contain **follicles**, which are masses of cells that contain immature ova in various stages of development (▮ **Figure 6-4**). Each follicle contains one ovum.

Unlike male sex cells, *all* female sex cells begin to develop before birth. This process stops before birth and the potential eggs remain dormant throughout childhood. Each month after the onset of sexual maturity, or *puberty,* but prior to menopause (see p. 134), a few ova continue their development. Most of the time one ovum matures and bursts from an ovary each month; this process is **ovulation**. The ovulation of two ova can lead to the development of fraternal twins, if both are fertilized. Identical twins result when the two cells formed from the fertilized ovum's first division continue development as independent organisms. A woman's reproductive life span lasts from puberty to age 50 (on average), so only about 400 ova mature during this period.

Where Eggs Are Fertilized and Then Develop During ovulation, the egg is released into the pelvic cavity. Lying close to the ovaries are the *fimbriae,* the fringed edges of the **uterine tubes** (see Figure 6-3), also called *fallopian tubes* or

oviducts. The uterine tubes are shaped somewhat like trumpets, with their wider ends near the ovaries and their narrower ends connected to the uterus. As the fimbriae move, they create a current of fluid that gently sweeps the ovum into the tube. If sperm are present, the uterine tube is also the site of fertilization. The fertilized ovum moves through the uterine tube as it journeys to the uterus.

The **uterus** is a hollow, muscular, pear-shaped organ that protects and nourishes the developing organism. The fertilized egg implants in the wall of the uterus and grows and develops during pregnancy, which will be discussed shortly.

The uterus opens into the vagina at the **cervix**, the narrow neck of the uterus. The cervix produces mucus. At certain times of the month the consistency of the cervical mucus changes, facilitating sperm movement into the uterus around the time of ovulation and hindering it at other times. The **vagina** is a tube about 10 cm (approximately 4 in.) long. It receives the penis during intercourse, allows the passage of the menstrual flow, and is a birth canal.

The External Organs of Sexual Reproduction

The female external genitals (see Figure 6-3a) collectively are called the **vulva**. The vulva surrounds the vaginal opening. The urethra, the tube that carries urine from the bladder to the outside, lies anterior to the vagina.

Although the urethra is shared by the urinary and reproductive systems in men, it has no reproductive or sexual function in women. Because it is close to the anal area, the urethra can become infected by digestive tract microorganisms during sexual intercourse if these bacteria become lodged in this tube. If microorganisms are not washed from the urethra by urine, they may multiply and cause urethritis (also commonly known as cystitis, a urinary tract infection, or a bladder infection). Health-care providers recommend that women who develop such infections easily urinate after sexual intercourse and drink plenty of fluids to keep the urethra washed free of bacteria.

Located under a protective hood of tissue, the **clitoris** lies anterior to the urethra. This tiny structure has spongy tissue like that of the penis and becomes

ovaries internal organs of female sexual reproduction within which eggs (ova) develop.

follicles masses of cells in the ovaries that contain immature ova (eggs) in various stages of development. Each follicle contains one ovum.

ovulation the maturation and release of an egg from an ovary, usually each month from puberty to menopause.

uterine tubes passageways that extend from each ovary to the uterus.

uterus a hollow, muscular, pear-shaped organ that protects and nourishes the embryo/fetus during development.

cervix the narrow neck of the uterus.

vagina a tube about 10 cm (approximately 4 in.) long that receives the penis during intercourse, allows the passage of the menstrual flow, and is a birth canal.

vulva the collective term for the external female genitals. The vulva surrounds the vaginal opening.

clitoris (KLIT-oh-ris) a female organ of sexual arousal. Located under a protective hood of tissue, the clitoris lies in front of the urethra.

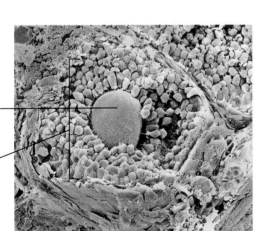

Developing egg

Ovarian follicle

▲**Figure 6-4** A highly magnified, colorized photograph of a developing ovarian follicle with developing egg (ovum).

engorged with blood during sexual arousal. Like the penis, it has numerous nerve endings that send messages to the brain, which are interpreted as sensations of sexual pleasure when this organ is stimulated indirectly during sexual activity. (Rubbing the clitoris directly may result in discomfort.)

Extending from over the clitoris to an area behind the vagina, two thin hairless folds of skin called the **labia minora** (meaning "small lips") cover and protect the vaginal opening and urethra. Within the area bounded by the labia minora, lying near the vaginal and urethral openings and the clitoris, are various glands that secrete lubricating substances during sexual activity. Next to these skin folds are the hairy, more rounded, and thicker **labia majora** ("large lips"). The labia majora extend forward to unite in a mound of fatty tissue called the **mons pubis**. The mons pubis provides a cushion over the pubic bone, a portion of the pelvic bones that is in front of the genitals.

The breasts are also external organs of sex and reproduction in women. Breasts primarily consist of fat and glandular tissue (■ **Figure 6-5**). Exercise will not increase breast size; it can develop only the underlying pectoral muscles. Although their major purpose is the production of milk to sustain an infant after birth, the breasts are also sensitive to sexual stimulation. The nipples contain nerve endings that are sensitive to touch; smooth muscles in the nipples contract during sexual arousal, causing the nipples to become erect.

labia minora (LAY-bee-ah my-NOR-ah) two thin, hairless folds of skin that extend from over the clitoris to an area behind the vagina. The labia minora cover and protect the vaginal opening and urethra.

labia majora (LAY-bee-ah mah-JOR-ah) hairy, rounded, and thick folds of skin that lie adjacent to the labia minora and extend forward to unite at the mons pubis.

mons pubis a mound of fatty tissue that lies over the pubic bone, cushioning it.

testosterone a male sex hormone (androgen) that plays a role in the development of functionally mature sperm and is responsible for the development and maintenance of male secondary sexual characteristics such as the deepening of the voice and the growth of facial hair.

vasocongestion a condition in which the spongy tissue of the penis and clitoris expands with blood during sexual arousal.

myotonia an increase in muscle tension throughout the body during sexual arousal.

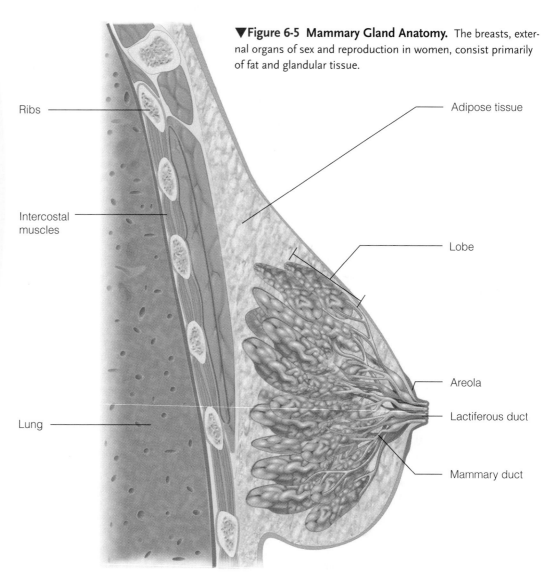

▼**Figure 6-5 Mammary Gland Anatomy.** The breasts, external organs of sex and reproduction in women, consist primarily of fat and glandular tissue.

Ribs

Intercostal muscles

Lung

Adipose tissue

Lobe

Areola

Lactiferous duct

Mammary duct

The Sexual Response

The sexual response in both males and females is governed primarily by the nervous system rather than by hormones. Hormones are chemicals secreted in one part of the body that have an effect in another. **Testosterone**, the "male" hormone (women also secrete testosterone), helps maintain the sex drive, or libido.

The two major physical changes that occur during sexual arousal are vasocongestion and myotonia. **Vasocongestion** occurs as blood flow away from the sexual organs is reduced. The spongy tissue of the penis and clitoris expands with blood and these structures become erect. **Myotonia**, an increase in muscle tension, occurs throughout the body.

Both sexes have broader responses than just these events. This pattern of responses is termed the *sexual response cycle*. It is usually thought of as having four phases: excitement, plateau, orgasm, and resolution (■ **Figure 6-6**).

During the *excitement phase* of the sexual response cycle, both men and women have a heightened sexual awareness. Certain thoughts, sights, touches, and even sounds or odors lead to a rush of blood to the clitoris and vaginal opening in women and to the penis in men.

In men, the penis expands as blood fills spaces in its columns of spongy tissue. As a result, the penis becomes erect, and the expansion of the tissue compresses the veins that take blood away from this organ (see Figure 6-2). Consequently, as blood flow into the penis increases, blood flow out of the penis decreases. This decrease in blood flow maintains the erection.

In women, glands in the vulvar area secrete mucuslike fluid. The congestion of blood in the vulvar area and in the vagina swells the labia and pushes fluid through the vaginal wall. These fluids are lubricants for sexual intercourse. Blood also rushes to the breasts. In response, the breasts swell. The nipples become erect as smooth muscles contract. Many women also exhibit a *sex flush* at this time, a reddening of the skin as blood flow through it increases.

As sexual excitement continues, the *plateau phase* begins. The heart rate, blood pressure, respiration rate, and level of muscle tension all increase. During the plateau phase, the erection of the male intensifies as the penis is massaged rhythmically by intercourse (anal or vaginal), manual stimulation, or oral stimulation. Sensory impulses from tactile sensations in both sexes reinforce their sexual sensations. In women, the lower third of the vagina constricts around the penis. The upper two-thirds of the vagina widens as the uterus and cervix lift up, creating a space for the semen. Continued stimulation of the clitoris and penis leads to the next phase of the sexual response—the orgasmic phase.

In men, ejaculation occurs during the *orgasmic phase*. This involuntary response (over which men can exert some

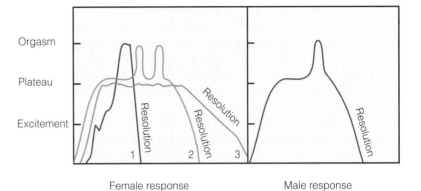

▲ Figure 6-6 The Female and Male Human Orgasmic Responses. The female response is much more variable than is the male response, as shown by the three female patterns and one male pattern illustrated here.

voluntary control) results when the nervous system sends messages to muscles in the walls of the ductus deferens and urethra to contract. At the same time, the seminal vesicles and prostate receive messages to release their secretions. The pelvic muscles also rhythmically contract. Orgasm in women is characterized by rhythmic contractions of the pelvic muscles and vaginal walls. Both sexes experience a peak of sexual pleasure at orgasm. Erection and ejaculation are the two primary components of the male sex act. The clitoris of the female becomes erect during sexual activity and she achieves orgasm, but women do not ejaculate like men.

During the *resolution phase* the body returns to its pre-arousal state. The heart rate, blood pressure, and respiration slow; the muscles relax. In males, the erection subsides (the penis becomes flaccid) and sometimes fatigue sets in. Depending on the man and his age, he will not be able to develop another erection for a few minutes to a few hours. This time is the *refractory period*. Unlike men, women have the capacity to reach the orgasmic phase again (have multiple orgasms) in sequence or rather quickly after dropping to the plateau phase.

Sexual Dysfunctions

A *dysfunction* is an impaired bodily process or a behavior that hinders the development or maintenance of healthy relationships. *Sexual dysfunctions* relate to the psychological and physical conditions that interfere with the sexual response.

Erectile Dysfunction (Impotence)

A common problem with the sexual response that occurs in men, particularly middle-aged and older men, is *impotence*. More properly called **erectile dysfunction (ED)**, impotence is the inability of a man to develop and/or sustain an erection firm enough for penetration. The incidence of ED rises as men age, from 7% in men aged 18 to 29, to 18% in men aged 50 to 59 (Laumann et al., 1999). Some men with various degrees of erectile dysfunction are able, with proper stimulation, to reach orgasm and ejaculate.

Until the last decade, impotence was thought to be primarily a psychological problem, a conclusion based on research studies conducted by well-known sex therapists Masters and Johnson. However, medical researchers have discovered that approximately 70% to 80% of cases of impotence are due to physical problems. The most common cause of physically based impotence is blood vessel disease.

In order to develop and maintain an erection, blood must fill the spongy tissue of the penis and compress the veins that bring blood away from the penis. If a man has fatty deposits clogging his penile arteries, blood flow to the penis may be insufficient to develop and maintain an erection. In fact, physicians note that ED is often the first sign that a man has vascular disease, which can also affect the arteries that supply his heart with blood and the vessels that supply blood to his brain. Therefore, to maintain sexual potency throughout mid-life and old age, men are encouraged to eat a low-fat diet, exercise regularly, and stop smoking. A more detailed look at maintaining vascular health (and therefore sexual health) is described in Chapter 12.

Erectile dysfunction can also be caused by a variety of other conditions, such as diabetes mellitus; damage to the spinal nerves or other nerves involved in erection; damage to the arteries that bring blood to the penis; certain medications used to control high blood pressure, anxiety, or depression; illness or injury that damages the penis; and hormonal imbalances. Alcohol and illegal drugs such as marijuana, heroin, and cocaine have also been shown to affect penile function negatively. In addition, stress can be a cause of impotence. Epinephrine (adrenaline), a chemical released by the body during the stress reaction, impedes a man's ability to have an erection.

Physicians warn that minor physical problems can cause problems with erection that can worry a man and lead to psychological problems with erection. A significant finding to help distinguish between a physical and psychological cause for impotence is whether the man has a normal pattern of erections while asleep but not while engaged in sex with his partner. Men are encouraged to seek medical help for impotence immediately so that underlying, and possibly serious, physical problems can be diagnosed and treated promptly. If physical problems are not the cause, the psychological health of the patient as well as the health of his relationships should be explored.

Premature Ejaculation

Premature ejaculation is another common male sexual dysfunction. The phrase "premature ejaculation" means that a man consistently attains orgasm shortly after intercourse begins (in less than 2 minutes more than 50% of the time) and before he wishes it to occur. The prevalence of this dysfunction is difficult to determine, but data from the National Health and Social Life Survey (NHSLS), a study of adult sexual behavior in the United States, shows that premature ejaculation affects approximately one-third of men between the ages of 18 and 59 (Laumann et al., 1999).

The cause of premature ejaculation is a controversial topic among medical researchers and psychologists who study sex-related disorders. One hypothesis suggests that premature ejaculation is related to anxiety. Another hypothesis is that men who exhibit premature ejaculation may be physically more sensitive to sexual stimulation. However, the results of a recent study refute this claim (Paick et al., 1998).

Whatever its cause, premature ejaculation usually can be overcome with proper treatment, which may include medication (Evanoff & Newton, 1998). The most common treatment is the "squeeze" technique, which helps a man learn to delay orgasm. To employ this technique, the man's partner uses her fingers to squeeze the front and back (not sides) of the penis where the glans meets the shaft (see Figure 6-1) or the base of the penis when the man feels as though he will ejaculate. After a few seconds, she releases her fingers. The couple waits 30 seconds and then resumes sexual activity until his orgasm is once again imminent. The squeeze is once again applied. This process is repeated as often as the couple desires. After a few sessions of using this technique, the male usually is able to delay ejaculation without help (Greenberg et al., 2000); however, the squeeze technique shows poor long-term success (Evanoff & Newton, 1998). In some cases, a couple may need to seek counseling from a qualified sex therapist to help them adjust their sexual techniques or to address other issues that may relate to the problem.

Hypoactive Sexual Desire Disorder

Hypoactive sexual desire disorder (HSDD) refers to a low interest in sex. This disorder affects both men and

---

erectile dysfunction a sexual dysfunction in which a man is unable to develop and/or sustain an erection firm enough for penetration of the vagina. Also called impotence.

premature ejaculation a common male sexual dysfunction in which a man consistently attains orgasm shortly after intercourse begins and before he wishes it to occur.

vaginismus (VAJ-in-NIZ-mus) a sexual dysfunction of women in which the lower portion of the vagina contracts involuntarily at the anticipation of penetration, preventing it.

menstrual cycle (MEN-stroo-al) the monthly changes in the levels of the female sex hormones that orchestrate physiological changes in the ovaries and uterus.

menses (MEN-seez) the menstrual period; the sloughing of the endometrium.

women, although HSDD occurs more often in women. (The term *frigid* was formerly used to refer to women with HSDD, but this term is no longer used because of its negative connotations.)

It is difficult to estimate accurately the prevalence of HSDD because no criteria have been established that define abnormal (or normal) levels of sexual desire. Additionally, desire varies among individuals and between partners, and decreases as people age. However, when interviewed for the NHSLS, approximately 30% of women and 15% of men between the ages of 18 and 59 reported that they lacked interest in sex over the prior year.

Hypoactive sexual desire disorder has a variety of psychological and physical causes such as restrictive views regarding sex, a history of sexual abuse, relationship problems, certain chronic diseases such as rheumatoid arthritis, fatigue, stress, illness, and abnormal hormone levels. Treatment includes the identification and elimination of the cause. Problems within the relationship or those rooted in long-held, deep-seated feelings and beliefs require counseling and therapy for resolution. Other treatments include rest, relaxation, hormone treatments, and changes in medications that a patient may be taking. Additionally, many therapists suggest that couples practice *sensate focus,* a type of sex therapy developed by Masters and Johnson. This technique involves lovers caressing, touching, and exploring the sensual areas of each other's bodies in ways that produce pleasure, promote trust and communication, and reduce anxiety. Neither partner pressures the other for sex.

Vaginismus

Vaginismus is a sexual dysfunction of women in which the muscles of the lower third of the vaginal canal contract involuntarily (and often painfully) at the anticipation of sexual intercourse, the insertion of tampons, or a pelvic examination. The muscular contractions are strong enough to prevent penetration. Women with vaginismus do not usually have other sexual dysfunctions and can achieve orgasm by stimulating the clitoris. Vaginismus appears to have both physical and psychological causes. A recent review of the literature (Reissing et al., 1999) suggests that vaginismus is a neglected health problem of women, and that this sexual dysfunction has not been studied adequately since its name was first coined in 1861.

A variety of physical conditions can cause pain during intercourse *(dyspareunia)* and result in vaginismus. Causes of dyspareunia include a poorly healed episiotomy (an incision made to widen the vaginal opening during the birth process); infections, sores, or lesions of the vagina or vulva; sexually transmitted infections (STIs); or inadequate lubrication during intercourse. If a woman experiences pain during intercourse because of one or more of these conditions, involuntary vaginal contractions may occur as the body attempts to protect itself from penetration and subse-

quent pain. If the cause of the pain eventually subsides, the contractions may still occur as a conditioned response.

Psychogenic vaginismus usually begins without a physical cause. The results of studies show that this type of vaginismus occurs as a protective response to perceived pain or violation of the body, with the most common cause being child sexual abuse (Greenberg et al., 2000).

Treatments for vaginismus have high success rates and include desensitization through exercises with dilators (Schnyder et al., 1998). Treating physical causes may resolve the condition. If a psychological cause exists, treatment usually includes behavioral therapy and counseling.

If you are a middle-aged man who does not develop or maintain erections during sleep or sexual activity, your problem may be related to vascular disease rather than to psychological problems. Your health-care provider can evaluate your condition and provide treatment.

The Menstrual Cycle

Women, unlike men, experience a cyclic waxing and waning of their sex hormones each month. These hormonal changes orchestrate physiological changes in the ovaries and uterus. These changes are collectively called the **menstrual cycle**, which literally means "monthly cycle." The average length of a cycle is 28 days (see Figure 6-16).

The menstrual cycle is usually described as beginning on the first day of the **menses** (menstrual period). The menses are the sloughing of the inner lining of the uterus, which is the **endometrium.** This lining develops gradually during the month, preparing for the implantation of a fertilized egg. If fertilization and implantation do not occur, the ovum dissolves and hormonal changes result in the lining being cast from the body. Each month a new lining develops.

What happens to the uterine lining is controlled by the hormones estrogen and progesterone. **Estrogen** is a hormone secreted by ovarian follicles, the groups of cells within which ova mature (see Figure 6-4); **progesterone** is secreted by the **corpus luteum,** the remnant of a follicle that has released its ovum.

endometrium (EN-doe-ME-tree-um) the inner lining of the uterus.

estrogen (ES-tro-jen) a hormone secreted by ovarian follicles, the groups of cells within which ova mature. With progesterone, estrogen stimulates the continued development and thickening of the uterine lining.

progesterone (pro-JES-te-rone) a hormone secreted by the corpus luteum. With estrogen, progesterone stimulates the continued development and thickening of the uterine lining.

corpus luteum (KOR-pus LOO-tea-um) the ruptured follicle left behind after ovulation.

Each month during her childbearing years, a woman's body prepares for a pregnancy. Usually only one ovarian follicle reaches the final stage of development in any particular cycle. About mid-cycle, hormonal changes trigger ovulation, the release of the egg from the ovary. The corpus luteum (meaning "yellow body") secretes high amounts of progesterone and lesser amounts of estrogen, which cause the uterine lining to grow, thicken, and develop a rich blood supply in preparation for the implantation of a fertilized ovum. If fertilization does not occur, the corpus luteum degenerates and stops producing hormones. Without hormonal stimulation, the uterine lining degenerates and is passed out of the body through the vagina during the menses.

If fertilization occurs, the corpus luteum does not degenerate. It produces estrogen and progesterone throughout pregnancy, maintaining the lining of the uterus. As the pregnancy develops, so does the **placenta**, a structure consisting of maternal and fetal tissues that also secretes hormones that help maintain the pregnancy.

Premenstrual Syndrome

Approximately 95% of American women in their reproductive years report mild to moderate discomfort during the week prior to menstruation as their hormonal levels drop. Up to 40% report that premenstrual symptoms such as depression, anxiety, irritability, mood swings, headaches, and bloating interfere with their relationships and their daily activities. Approximately 5% of these women report severe impairment (Daugherty, 1998; Ugarriza et al., 1998). This debilitating condition, originally termed premenstrual tension syndrome because most women experiencing it reported tension and anxiety among their symptoms, is now simply referred to as **premenstrual syndrome**, or **PMS**. Many people refer loosely to more minor symptoms of premenstrual distress as PMS, but medically the term refers to symptoms that *significantly* interfere with daily life.

Most women with PMS are helped by one or more of the following treatments: counseling, lifestyle modification such as including exercise in their daily regimen; or medications prescribed for specific symptoms. Fluoxetine (Prozac) has shown usefulness in the treatment of PMS, acting to reduce symptoms of depression and anxiety that are linked to problems with the proper regulation of serotonin, a brain neurotransmitter. Additionally, many women are helped by using low-dose, combined oral contraceptives (see p. 130). Nutritional treatments include a diet low in salt, fat, caffeine, and sugar (Ugarriza et al., 1998). Taking calcium supplements has been shown to reduce the physical and psychological symptoms of PMS by almost 50% (Thys-Jacobs et al., 1998).

Toxic Shock Syndrome

A disease called *toxic shock syndrome (TSS)* is associated with the menses. This disease became well known in the 1980s, when hundreds of women who used certain high-absorbency tampons during their menstrual periods were stricken. In TSS, staphylococcal (STAFF-ih-low-KAH-kul) bacteria grow in the blood-soaked tampon and in vaginal tissues, producing toxins that can enter the woman's bloodstream. Although TSS is associated with a wide variety of surgical conditions unrelated to the menses (such as skin, bone, and soft tissue infections), about two-thirds of all cases are related to tampon use during the menses. Additionally, TSS can occur from use of contraceptive diaphragms and sponges (see pp. 127–129), but such occurrences are rare. Although TSS is an uncommon disease, women from 15 to 34 years old are at the highest risk. Approximately 3% of women who contract TSS die from its effects (Rivlin, 2000).

The most common symptoms of TSS are fever, muscle pain, headache, dizziness, diarrhea, vomiting, and a sunburnlike rash. One to two weeks after the onset of the disease, the skin of the palms, fingers, toes, and soles of the feet begins to peel. Generally TSS patients are hospitalized and treated with fluids and antibiotics.

To avoid contracting TSS from tampon use, women who use tampons should change them often and alternate their use with pads throughout the menses. Although high-absorbency tampons have been removed from the market, women should use only the level of absorbency they require. If during tampon use, a woman experiences fever, rash, dizziness, or diarrhea, she should remove the tampon and seek medical attention immediately.

Pregnancy and Human Development

www.jbpub.com/healthyliving

Pregnancy is the gestational process, that is, the process of development of a new individual from fertilization until birth. What can a woman do to prepare her body for pregnancy? What can she do during the *prenatal* period, the time during which she is pregnant, to increase her chances of delivering a healthy baby?

Prepregnancy and Prenatal Care

Various **teratogens**, environmental influences such as drugs, alcohol, viruses, and dietary deficiencies, can damage the embryo or fetus. The highly sensitive periods of the developing structures of the embryo and fetus to teratogens occur primarily during the first 8 weeks after conception, possibly before a woman knows that she's

placenta
(plah-SEN-tah) a structure that develops after implantation of a fertilized ovum in the uterine wall and consists of maternal and fetal tissues that secrete hormones that help maintain the pregnancy.

premenstrual syndrome (PMS) symptoms such as depression and anxiety that occur prior to the menses and that significantly interfere with daily life.

pregnancy the gestational process; the process of development of a new individual from fertilization until birth.

teratogens various environmental influences such as drugs, alcohol, viruses, and dietary deficiencies that can damage the embryo or fetus early in pregnancy.

pregnant. Therefore, if you are trying to become pregnant, to help avoid birth defects you should take care of your body as if you were pregnant. The "Analyzing Health-Related Information" feature on page 136 discusses folic acid (folate), a B vitamin critical to proper neural tube development of the embryo. ▌ Table 6-1 lists various teratogens and their detrimental effects on the embryo/fetus.

A woman preparing for pregnancy should have a medical checkup to determine if her level of antibodies against rubella (German measles) is sufficient. She should also be screened for STIs, especially AIDS, and should avoid changing the cat's litter box to help protect herself from contracting toxoplasmosis (infection with a microscopic parasite found in cat feces). Additionally, a woman preparing for pregnancy should seek her health-care provider's advice regarding the use of medications.

It is important that a woman contemplating pregnancy eat a well-balanced and nutritious diet to enter this critical

Table 6-1 Selected Teratogens Known to Cause Birth Defects

Teratogen	Explanation
Maternal Infectious or Noninfectious Disease	
Cytomegalovirus	A herpes-type virus that can cross the placenta and infect the embryo. Found in about 1% of newborns. Most defects affect the nervous system. Risk of brain damage is 50% after infection early in pregnancy. One in ten affected fetuses die.
Diabetes mellitus	Risk of major malformations is about 18%. Heart malformations and neural tube defects are most frequent. Risk is greatest in uncontrolled or poorly controlled diabetes.
Phenylketonuria (PKU) untreated	Excess phenylalanine, not the defective gene, causes birth defects such as mental retardation and malformations of the heart.
Rubella	The German measles virus can cross the placenta and infect the embryo. Infection during the first 3 months of pregnancy is likely to result in abnormalities such as deafness, heart defects, and mental retardation.
Drugs, Other Chemicals, and Radiation	
Alcohol (chronic alcoholism—6 oz or more per day—constitutes high risk)	Main characteristics of the birth defects caused by maternal chronic alcoholism are growth deficiency, hyperactivity, distractibility, small head, underdevelopment of the brain, and mental retardation. Moderate maternal drinking can affect the IQ and learning ability of offspring.
Anticonvulsant medication	Probability of birth defects varies with medications, dosage, and stage of pregnancy.
Chemotherapeutic agents	Drugs used to treat cancer can also harm the embryo or fetus.
Cocaine	Some possible birth defects from cocaine use during pregnancy are bleeding in the brain, death of part of the brain tissue, underdeveloped head and brain, prematurity, and seizures.
Diethylstilbestrol (DES)	A drug formerly prescribed for women who were in danger of having a miscarriage. This drug affected some of their female offspring, causing unusual vaginal, cervical, and uterine changes beginning in adolescence. Increased risk for developing a certain type of vaginal and cervical cancer.
Ionizing radiation	Extremely high exposure to x-rays or exposure to radiation used in cancer therapy can affect the embryo or fetus and result in an underdeveloped head and brain.
Accutane	This synthetic form of vitamin A is used to treat certain types of acne. Birth defects that may result from use during pregnancy (when taken by mouth) include malformations of the ear, brain, and heart. Health-care providers also suggest avoiding megadoses (above 10,000 I.U.) of vitamin A during pregnancy.
Thalidomide	A drug taken for morning sickness in the 1960s. Taking this drug between 20 days and 36 days after conception resulted in major anatomical deformities of the limbs and heart.

Genetic Counseling and Prenatal Diagnosis

You and your spouse have decided it's time to have a baby. You are both worried that a genetic disease may run in either of your families. (A genetic disease is caused by problems with the hereditary, or genetic, material.) Also, you're worried about the risk of birth defects because "mom" will be far past age 35 when she gives birth, and the likelihood of genetic diseases is higher than at younger ages. What can you both do to ensure the genetic health of your baby?

Your first step might be to discuss your concerns with an obstetrician/gynecologist. Your health-care practitioner may send both of you to a genetic counselor to explore the incidence of genetic disease in your families and to determine the probability of you and your spouse having a child with a genetic disorder.

There are many reasons to seek genetic counseling. Parents with a child who has a genetic disease often choose genetic counseling to determine the probability that future children will be affected. In populations at high risk for certain genetic diseases, such as African Americans and sickle-cell anemia, or Ashkenazi Jews and Tay-Sachs disease, families or prospective parents may visit genetics centers to undergo screening tests. Once screening has been done and the carriers and noncarriers of the disease have been identified, the genetic counselor can then advise them of their probability of passing on any problem genes to children.

After the baby is conceived and prior to birth, various techniques are available to tell for sure if the baby is affected with a wide variety of disorders. Tests performed on the fetus (or related tissues) to determine its health are called prenatal diagnoses. Methods that are frequently used are ultrasound, amniocentesis, and chorionic villus sampling. These methods can detect many, but not all, fetal abnormalities.

Ultrasound scanning, or sonography, is a common, painless, safe, and relatively inexpensive procedure for prenatal diagnosis that has been used since the 1960s. Ultrasound uses high-frequency sound waves to visualize the fetus, which can be seen as early as 7

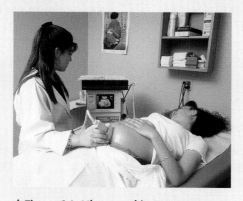

▲Figure 6-A **Ultrasound in Pregnancy.**
The ultrasound probe produces sound waves that bounce off fetal tissues. As the probe is moved across a pregnant woman's abdomen, images are visualized on a screen that provide information about the position, size, and physical condition of the fetus.

weeks of development. The ultrasound probe is moved over the woman's abdomen. Sound waves enter the uterus and bounce off fetal structures in ways that reflect their density and makeup. The reflected waves are projected on a monitor screen **(Figure 6-A)** and their patterns are interpreted by a health-care provider. Using this technique, a health-care provider can detect many structural abnormalities, estimate the age of the fetus, confirm if multiple fetuses are present, and confirm fetal position. In addition, ultrasound is often used to help guide needle placement in amniocentesis, fetal blood sampling, and chorionic villus sampling (CVS).

Another common type of prenatal diagnosis is **amniocentesis,** which was developed in the 1960s and was widely used by the 1970s. Amniocentesis involves the removal of some of the amniotic fluid that surrounds the fetus. This watery fluid protects the baby from jarring movements and contains waste products and some cells from the fetus. Geneticists observe these cells to determine whether the fetus will be born with a genetic abnormality. In addition, medical technicians can perform tests on the fluid to determine the presence of substances that are indicators of

various conditions, such as certain neural tube defects and Rh disease (a blood incompatibility problem between mother and fetus).

To extract some amniotic fluid and cells from around the fetus, the physician inserts a thin, long needle through the abdominal and uterine walls of the mother until the needle pierces the amniotic sac **(Figure 6-B).** (The physician guides the needle using ultrasound so that it will not injure the fetus, and anaesthetizes the abdominal wall with a local anesthetic.) After the fluid is withdrawn, the cells must be grown, or cultured, which takes approximately 4 weeks. This technique is now performed as early as 11 weeks of gestation, but is routinely performed between 15 and 18 weeks, so diagnosis is generally completed by the 19th to 22nd week. Physicians are studying even earlier amniocentesis testing. This procedure is considered safe; the risk of miscarriage due to amniocentesis is 0.25% to 0.5% (1 in 200 to 400).

Fetal blood sampling was developed in the 1970s. Extracting blood from the fetus is risky; however, blood can be withdrawn safely from the umbilical vein. With this technique, physicians can screen infants for various blood disorders such as sickle-cell anemia and hemophilia. The risk of miscarriage with this technique is approximately 2% (2 in 100). This technique is least risky when performed between weeks 18 and 21 of pregnancy.

Chorionic villus sampling (CVS) was also developed around 1970 but came into wide use in the 1980s. The chorion is the outermost of the fetal membranes **(Figure 6-C)** that facilitate the exchange of nutrients, gases, and other materials such as waste products between the fetus and the mother. The umbilical cord extends from the fetus to the chorion. Fingerlike projections called villi (singular, villus) extend from the chorion into maternal tissues at the placenta, the pancake-shaped part of the chorion that joins mother and fetus. In this way the blood of the fetus, circulating through blood vessels in the chorion and its villi, comes into close contact (but does not mix) with maternal blood vessels. To perform CVS, a physician inserts a thin tube or a nee-

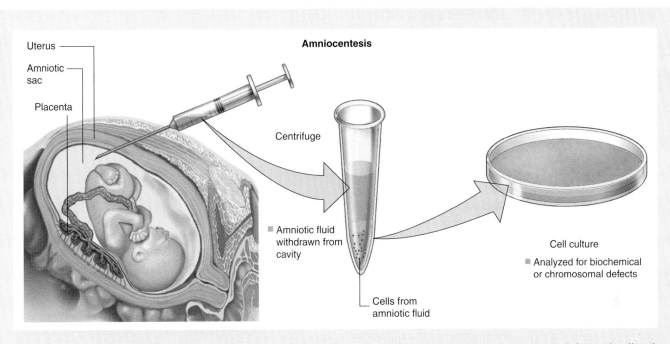

Amniocentesis

Uterus

Amniotic sac

Placenta

Centrifuge

■ Amniotic fluid withdrawn from cavity

Cells from amniotic fluid

Cell culture

■ Analyzed for biochemical or chromosomal defects

▲**Figure 6-B Amniocentesis.** In the amniocentesis procedure, a long thin needle is used to pierce the mother's abdominal wall and uterus, and withdraw amniotic fluid. Free fetal cells are found in this fluid and can be analyzed for the fetus's gender, age, and indications of chromosomal abnormalities.

dle into the vagina and up into the uterus. The instrument vacuums up a tiny sample of villi. Although this technique has the advantages of early testing (weeks 9 to 11) and quicker analysis of cells (no culturing is needed), the risk of miscarriage is 2% to 4% (2 to 4 in 100). Additionally, in the early 1990s medical researchers discovered that CVS can cause birth defects of the limbs. If this procedure is conducted prior to 10 weeks of pregnancy, the risk is 20%, but drops to 7% at 10 weeks or more of gestation. The defects when CVS is performed at 10 weeks or later involve only the fingers or toes.

Today, using ultrasound to guide them, physicians are able to sample fetal skin and certain other tissues. In addition, some conditions can be treated before birth. Amazingly, the fetus can be given a blood transfusion while in the uterus. Open fetal surgery, a highly risky but potentially life-saving procedure, is new and experimental at this time. The choices that remain are terminating the pregnancy or carrying the fetus to term. If the second choice is made, prenatal diagnosis is extremely helpful to ensure that the baby receives the best possible medical care for its condition, beginning from its first breath.

www.jbpub.com/healthyliving

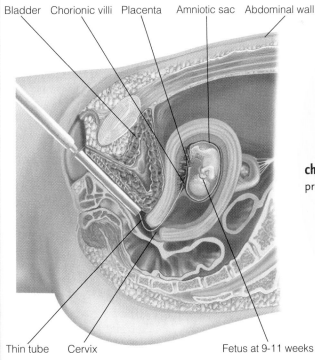

Bladder   Chorionic villi   Placenta   Amniotic sac   Abdominal wall

Thin tube   Cervix   Fetus at 9-11 weeks

▲**Figure 6-C Chorionic Villus Sampling.** This illustration of chorionic villus sampling shows the thin tube, or catheter, that is inserted into the vagina, up through the cervix, and into the uterus. This tube is used to collect pieces of chorionic villi, which are part of the outer fetal tissue called the chorion (not part of the fetus). These cells are analyzed for chromosomal abnormalities.

amniocentesis a prenatal test performed generally between the 15th and 18th weeks of gestation, in which some of the amniotic fluid that surrounds the fetus is removed and studied to determine whether the fetus has a genetic abnormality.

chorionic villus sampling a prenatal test performed generally between the 9th and 11th weeks of gestation, in which some of the fetal extra-embryonic tissue is removed and analyzed to determine whether the fetus has a genetic abnormality.

period with sufficient nutrient stores and blood levels to meet needs of the pre-embryo and embryo before the placenta is established. (The body has both short-term and long-term nutrient storage capabilities.) Chapter 9 describes some nutritional guidelines for a prepregnancy diet; a woman should also consult her health-care practitioner regarding proper nutrition during pregnancy. A pregnant women should not assume that she is "eating for two" in the sense that she should double her food intake. Her need for calories, protein, and calcium are only somewhat greater than her prepregnancy needs. Excessive weight gain during pregnancy may mean excess body fat retained long after pregnancy. Although certain nutrients are extremely important (such as folate, which helps prevent neural tube defects), a pregnant woman should take only the vitamin supplements that her health-care provider prescribes. Some nutrients, such as vitamin A, are teratogens in certain quantities.

human chorionic gonadotropin (hCG) in a pregnant woman, a hormone produced by embryonic tissues destined to become the placenta. Pregnancy tests rely on the detection of this hormone in the blood.

pre-embryo the first 2 weeks of gestational development.

embryo the third through the eighth weeks of gestational development.

fetus the 9th through 38th weeks of gestational development.

labor (parturition) (PAR-too-RISH-un) the process of childbirth.

It is critical that a woman avoid drinking alcohol, smoking cigarettes, and taking any drugs (unless they have been prescribed) when preparing for pregnancy and during pregnancy. Chronic alcohol consumption can cause fetal alcohol syndrome (see pp. 192–193), which can result in a variety of birth defects including mental retardation, growth deficiency, and hyperactivity. Smoking a pack or more of cigarettes per day can result in a low-birth-weight baby who is weak and vulnerable to illness. If a pregnant woman is addicted to drugs, her baby will be born addicted as well. In addition, she is more likely to experience complications during pregnancy and have a baby with severe birth defects. Taking drugs and drinking alcohol occasionally can also damage the embryo or fetus. No safe level of these teratogens has been determined.

Women older than 35 years of age have a higher risk of having babies with Down syndrome (a genetic abnormality resulting in mental retardation) than younger women. Older women may choose to have diagnostic tests such as amniocentesis or chorionic villus sampling during pregnancy to detect possible genetic disease or other abnormalities in the fetus. In addition, couples often seek genetic counseling before becoming pregnant. If anyone in a couple's family has a genetic disease, seeking genetic counseling may be prudent. (The "Managing Your Health" essay "Genetic Counseling and Prenatal Diagnosis" discusses prenatal tests and counseling.)

Many women want to know if exercising during pregnancy will hurt the fetus. Generally, if a woman was exercising before she became pregnant, she can continue exercising while she is pregnant. However, a health-care provider may suggest modifications in a pregnant woman's workout regimen. Also, some health-care providers recommend that their previously sedentary patients start a mild exercise program to help them become stronger and develop stamina for the birth process. Chapter 11 discusses exercising and pregnancy in more detail in its "Life Span" section.

Healthy LIVING PRACTICES

- Women preparing for pregnancy should have a medical checkup, eat a well-balanced and nutritious diet, and avoid drinking alcohol, smoking cigarettes, or using any other drugs.
- Women and men concerned about the possibility of passing a genetic condition on to their offspring can seek genetic counseling when considering pregnancy.

Determining If You or Your Partner Is Pregnant

How do you know if you or your partner is pregnant? By noticing certain physical signs, you may become aware of this condition. A pregnant woman will not menstruate, so a missed menstrual period may be the first sign. However, a pregnant woman may experience *implantation bleeding* about a week before the expected time of the menstrual period. This small amount of blood flow from the uterus occurs when the fertilized ovum nestles into the uterine wall. Additionally, the breasts may feel sore, she may feel nauseated at certain times during the day or all day, and she may feel tired, moody, or both. These signs are bodily reactions to changes in hormone levels during pregnancy.

If a woman suspects that she is pregnant, she may choose to conduct a home pregnancy test or visit her gynecologist/obstetrician for such a test. The "Consumer Health" feature "Home Pregnancy Tests" discusses how pregnancy tests work and provides guidelines for conducting such a test.

If a woman has missed more than one menstrual period and is certain that she is not pregnant, she should see her health-care provider. *Amenorrhea* (ah-MEN-oh-REE-ah), or abnormal stoppage of the menses, is most often caused by stress, weight loss, or strenuous exercise regimens. However, it can have more serious causes, such as hormonal imbalances or tumorous growths.

Pregnancy and Fetal Development

Pregnancy usually lasts 38 weeks, or approximately 9 months. The delivery date is calculated to be 40 weeks from a woman's last menstrual period because *conception* (fertilization) usually occurs in the middle of the cycle.

Con$umer Health | Home Pregnancy Tests

Most pregnancy tests rely on the detection of the hormone **human chorionic gonadotropin (hCG).** This hormone is produced by embryonic tissues destined to become the placenta, the organ that allows the exchange of nutrients, gases, and wastes between the fetus and a pregnant woman. Pregnancy tests to detect hCG can be conducted on either blood or urine. Urine tests are most frequently used to detect hCG because urine is easier to collect than blood. This is the type of test in home test kits.

The way pregnancy tests work is that hCG binds with specific antibodies present in the test. If a woman is *not* pregnant, hCG will not be present in her urine, binding will not occur, and the test will be negative. If a woman *is* pregnant, hCG will be present in her urine, binding will occur, and the test will be positive.

Home pregnancy tests are easy to use. These tests contain either a plastic stick with an absorbent part that is placed in the urine flow, or a plastic device with an opening containing absorbent material into which drops of urine are placed. While a woman waits, the urine moves though the absorbent material inside either type of device, and the hCG (if present) attaches to antibody that has a color label such as blue or red. The hCG-antibody complex then moves to another window where it binds to a second antibody attached to the absorbent material in either a line or a circle. Therefore, if hCG is present in a woman's urine, a colored line or circle appears, indicating that both antibodies have attached to the hCG and that the woman is pregnant.

It is important to follow the directions of a home test carefully and wait the prescribed length of time to "read" the result. Testing the first urine of the day is best because hCG is most concentrated in the first urine. However, today's home pregnancy testing kits are quite sensitive and you can use any urine of the day. You may conduct a home test on the day of a missed period or after that time; the results are 99% accurate. Be sure to check the expiration date on the package and only use tests that have not expired. Virtually all tests marketed today in the United States are reliable, but ask your pharmacist for help if you are unsure which test to choose. A woman who has a positive test should see her health-care provider immediately for a confirmatory test (false positives occur rarely) and appropriate prenatal care.

Typically pregnancy is described in terms of trimesters, or 3-month periods, during which certain developmental events take place. (Because months are more than 4 weeks, the month-to-week correlations given here are approximate.)

The first trimester is a crucial time of development when all the organ systems of the body are forming and becoming functional. Cells in the embryo migrate to key developmental positions, shaping the individual as it takes on a human form. In contrast, the second and third trimesters are periods of growth and refinement of the organ systems. ▌**Figure 6-7** through ▌**Figure 6-11** depict the development of the **pre-embryo** (the first 2 weeks of development), the **embryo** (weeks 3 through 8), and the **fetus** (weeks 9 through 38).

While the embryo and fetus is developing, changing, and growing over 9 months, changes also take place in the mother's body. ▌**Figure 6-12** summarizes these changes. In addition, the pregnant woman may experience nausea, vomiting, frequent urination, leg cramps, vaginal discharge, fatigue, and constipation during the first trimester. Nausea, vomiting, and leg cramps (if present) usually subside by the second trimester. At that time, additional changes may take place. In her last two trimesters,

a pregnant woman may experience swelling of the legs and feet, varicose veins, backache, heartburn, and shortness of breath, in addition to continuing vaginal discharge, frequent urination, fatigue, and constipation. ▌**Table 6-2** lists various problem conditions that may occur during pregnancy.

The Birth Process

No one is certain what events signal the beginning of **labor,** the process of childbirth. Labor is also called parturition and takes place in three stages: cervical dilation, fetal delivery, and placental delivery. The birth process normally takes about 13 hours for the woman who is giving birth for the first time. In women who have previously given birth, the time shortens considerably and is about 8 hours.

Two main events occur during dilation: rhythmic contractions of the uterine muscles cause the cervix (the opening of the uterus) to dilate (widen) and to efface (thin out). In the nonpregnant state, the cervix is hard and tubelike with an extremely narrow opening. During the first stage of labor, the cervix becomes soft. The opening widens and the tissue stretches so that by the end of the first stage of labor the cervical opening is 3 1/2 in. to 4 in. wide and the tubular cervix no longer exists as such—it flattens

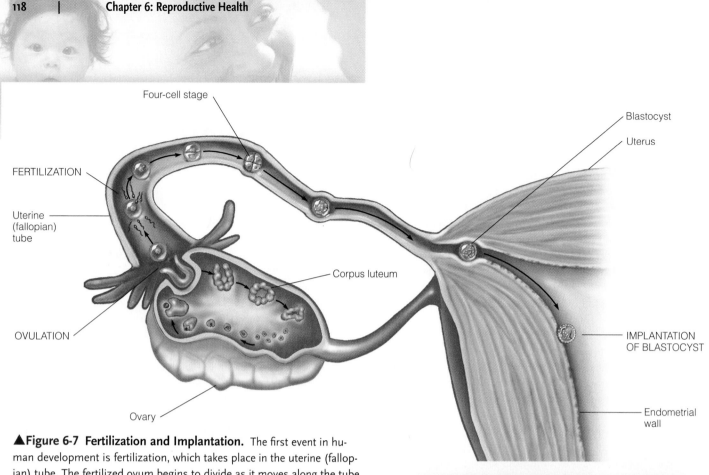

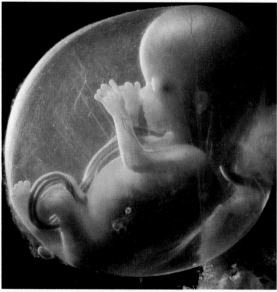

Figure labels: Four-cell stage, Blastocyst, Uterus, FERTILIZATION, Uterine (fallopian) tube, Corpus luteum, OVULATION, IMPLANTATION OF BLASTOCYST, Ovary, Endometrial wall

▲**Figure 6-7 Fertilization and Implantation.** The first event in human development is fertilization, which takes place in the uterine (fallopian) tube. The fertilized ovum begins to divide as it moves along the tube to the uterus, and is now referred to as a pre-embryo. At 4 days after fertilization, the developing ball of cells begins to fill with fluid, a stage of pre-embryonic development termed the blastocyst. Approximately 6 days after fertilization, the blastocyst implants in the back wall of the uterus. During implantation, the embryo attaches firmly to the inner lining of the uterus. This illustration shows the journey of the fertilized ovum from the fallopian tube to the uterus. Occasionally implantation takes place outside of the uterus, a condition known as ectopic pregnancy. Pre-embryos may implant on an ovary, on the intestine, or in a fallopian tube. All ectopic pregnancies endanger the mother's life.

▶**Figure 6-8 Human Embryo between 4 and 5 Weeks of Development.** As the pregnancy moves into the third week, the pre-embryo is only one-tenth of an inch long. The flattened pre-embryo develops into a cylindrical embryo. Some of the organs, such as the heart, begin to develop. This four-and-a-half-week-old embryo has established the

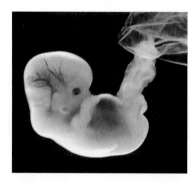

beginnings of most of the major organ systems of the body. Its C-shaped body has a featureless head, a middle with the heart and liver bulging from the body, and a tail. During the fifth week, the embryo doubles in length from 4 mm (3/16″) to 8 mm (3/8″). The brain grows rapidly. Wrists, fingers, and ears begin to form during the sixth week of development. Although development has been rapid, growth has not. By the end of the sixth week, the embryo is a mere half-inch long.

▲**Figure 6-9 Human Fetus about 11 to 12 Weeks of Development.** During the seventh week, eyelids begin to cover the eyes, and the face begins to look somewhat human. By the eighth week, the last week in the embryonic period, the embryo grows to about an inch. Most of the body systems are functional by this time. The fetal period begins at week 9, lasts throughout the rest of the pregnancy, and is characterized by growth and functional maturation of the organs. During weeks 9 through 13 (the third month), facial features become more well developed, with eyelids completely covering the eyes and then fusing shut. (The eyes can be seen through the thin eyelids.) The genitals begin to develop, and the heart is now a four-chambered structure.

▲ **Figure 6-10 Human Fetus about 5 Months (20 Weeks) of Development.** The second trimester comprises the fourth, fifth, and sixth months of development, or weeks 14 through 26. The organs that developed during the first trimester mature and grow during this trimester. As the fourth month passes, the genitals become fully formed. The sensory organs nearly finish their development and refinements of body structures occur. The mother becomes aware of fetal movements around the fifth month of pregnancy, the stage of development of the fetus in the photo. By the end of the fifth month, as fat deposits are laid down, the fetus begins to look more like a baby. Only 12 inches long and weighing 1 pound, it probably could not survive on its own. However, if born by the end of the sixth month, the fetus has a chance of surviving with special medical care.

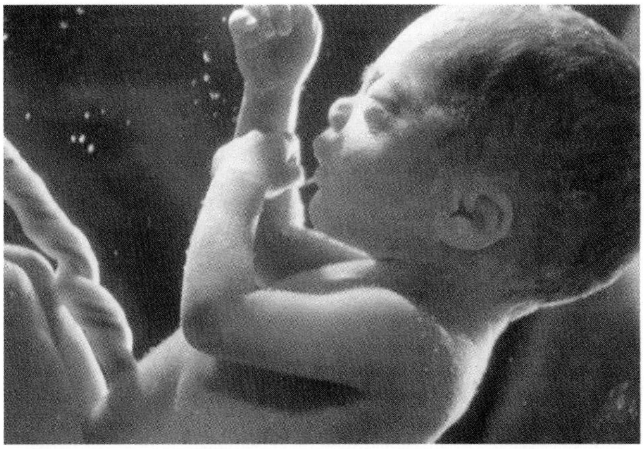

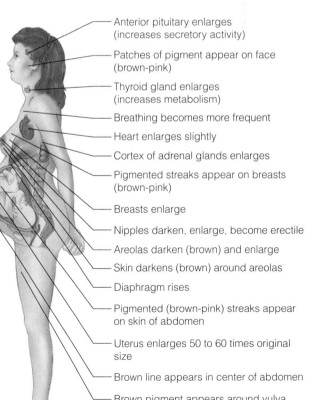

▲ **Figure 6-11 Human Fetus Nearly Full Term—8 to 9 Months.** During the third trimester, months seven through nine or weeks 27 through 38, the fetus primarily gains weight. Its lungs develop more fully, eyelids open, and the nervous system undergoes further development. However, the nervous system is not fully developed and its maturation continues after birth. At the end of the third trimester, the average fetus weighs about 7 1/2 pounds and is 20 inches long.

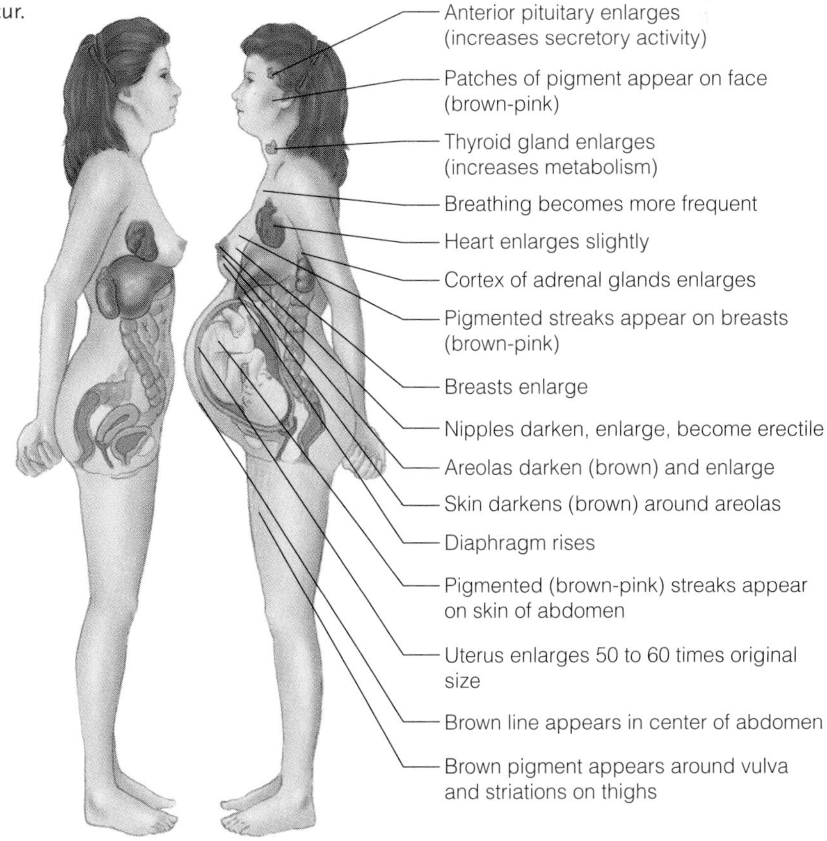

Anterior pituitary enlarges (increases secretory activity)

Patches of pigment appear on face (brown-pink)

Thyroid gland enlarges (increases metabolism)

Breathing becomes more frequent

Heart enlarges slightly

Cortex of adrenal glands enlarges

Pigmented streaks appear on breasts (brown-pink)

Breasts enlarge

Nipples darken, enlarge, become erectile

Areolas darken (brown) and enlarge

Skin darkens (brown) around areolas

Diaphragm rises

Pigmented (brown-pink) streaks appear on skin of abdomen

Uterus enlarges 50 to 60 times original size

Brown line appears in center of abdomen

Brown pigment appears around vulva and striations on thighs

▶ **Figure 6-12 A Summary of the Physical Changes That Take Place during Pregnancy.** (*Left*) The unpregnant female body; (*Right*) Changes that appear by 30 weeks of fetal development.

Table 6-2 Pregnancy Problems and Symptoms

Name of Condition (Alternative or former names)	Definition	Cause	Symptoms	Treatment
Ectopic pregnancy	Fertilized egg implants outside the uterus. Majority occur in the uterine tube.	Problems with anatomy of uterine tubes, possibly due to PID (see p. 362) or uterine surgery. Use of IUD (see pp. 130–131).	Loss of menses, pelvic or abdominal pain, abnormal vaginal bleeding.	Surgery to remove embryo. Nonsurgical treatments may be used in certain situations.
Pregnancy-induced hypertension [PIH] (Preeclampsia) (Toxemia of pregnancy)	A group of metabolic disturbances.	Unknown.	High blood pressure, water retention, and an excess of protein in the urine, occurring in the third trimester. Primarily a disease of first pregnancy. Occurs with higher frequency in adolescent women and those older than 35 years.	Bed rest. Medication to reduce blood pressure and prevent seizures. Delivery usually cures the condition.
Eclampsia	An extension of PIH to the point of seizure, coma, or both.	Unknown.	Increase in blood pressure from that in PIH, abdominal pain, blurry vision, headache, shakiness. May occur in third trimester or postpartum (see p. 122).	Convulsions and high blood pressure are treated with medication. Delivery takes place as soon as patient is stabilized.
Diabetes mellitus associated with pregnancy (Gestational diabetes mellitus [GDM])	A metabolic disorder that leads to high glucose levels in the blood (see Chapter 9). In pregnancy, poor control of blood glucose levels can lead to fetal abnormalities.	Hormonal changes of pregnancy often result in a display of diabetes in women with risk factors for the disease.	See Table 9-3. Women with risk factors for diabetes (obesity and family history) should be screened prior to and during pregnancy for this disease.	Control of blood sugar level with diet and/or insulin injections.

Sources: Rivlin, M. E., & Martin, R. W. (2000). *Manual of clinical problems in obstetrics and gynecology*, 5th ed. Philadelphia, PA: Lippincott, Williams & Wilkins. Zuspan, F. P., & Quilligan, E. J. (1998). *Handbook of obstetrics, gynecology, and primary care*. St. Louis, MO: Mosby.

and becomes continuous with the lower portion of the uterus (**Figure 6-13**). During this time (or prior to labor in some cases) the amniotic sac ruptures (the water breaks), releasing the amniotic fluid. (This fluid cushions the fetus during development.) The baby must be born within 24 hours of the rupture, or serious infection could occur.

In the beginning of her labor, a woman's uterine contractions may last for 30 seconds and be 15 to 20 minutes apart. As labor progresses, the contractions become stronger, longer, and more closely spaced. By the end of the first stage of labor, during a period called transition, contractions occur every 1 to 2 minutes and last up to a minute each.

Some women experience preparatory contractions that are not a part of labor, which are called **Braxton-Hicks contractions**, or *false labor*. False labor contractions can be distinguished from the contractions of true labor in that they occur irregularly, the intervals between contractions do not shorten, and the contractions do not increase in strength. A woman experiencing these contractions should consult her physician to confirm that she is not in labor.

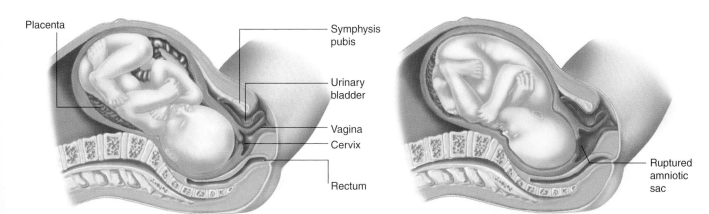

(a) Early first-stage labor

(b) Later first-stage labor: the transition

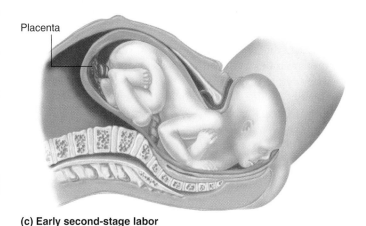

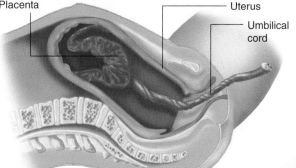

(c) Early second-stage labor

(d) Third-stage labor: delivery of afterbirth

▲**Figure 6-13 The Stages of Labor.** (a) The position of the fetus at the beginning of labor. (b) Dilation, the cervix (the opening to the uterus) widens and thins. (c) Expulsion, the baby is born. (d) Placental delivery.

During the second stage of labor, the baby is born. The average time for this stage is 30 to 60 minutes. Uterine contractions continue and move the baby into the birth canal (vagina). The woman pushes and bears down, aiding this process. The head usually appears first, but some babies are born in the breech position, feet or buttocks first. A **breech birth** is a more complicated delivery than a head-first delivery and may require surgical removal of the baby through the abdominal wall—a cesarean section. During a vaginal delivery, the physician may perform an **episiotomy**, making a cut in the tissue surrounding the vaginal opening to widen the opening. (This cut is usually made in the direction of the anus.) Without this procedure, the skin and surrounding tissues may sustain more damage and heal with more difficulty than surgically cut tissue.

After the baby is born, its nose and mouth are cleared of mucus by suctioning. The umbilical cord is clamped in two places and cut between the clamps to prevent bleeding. Health-care practitioners assess the baby's ability to adjust to life outside the uterus at 1 minute and then 5 minutes after birth.

Within 15 and 30 minutes after delivery of the baby, the uterus continues to contract, separating the fetal placental tissues from maternal tissues. During this third stage of labor, the placenta is expelled from the uterus. Figure 6-13 summarizes the birth process, showing the three stages of labor (a–d).

Circumcision

Although few data are available, they show that from about 45% to 70% of male newborns are circumcised in the United States (American Academy of Pediatrics [AAP], 1999). In some groups, such as followers of the Jewish and Islamic faiths, circumcision rates approximate 100% because the procedure is practiced for religious and cultural reasons. *Circumcision* is a surgical procedure to remove the foreskin of the penis, which is a fold of skin covering the end of the penis. The photos in ▌**Figure 6-14** show both an uncircumcised and a circumcised penis.

Braxton-Hicks contractions false labor; preparatory contractions that are not a part of labor.

breech birth a delivery in which the baby presents feet or buttocks first instead of the usual head-first position.

episiotomy (eh-PIZ-ee-OT-oh-me) a cut in the tissue surrounding the vaginal opening to widen it during a vaginal delivery so that the surrounding skin and tissues will be less likely to tear.

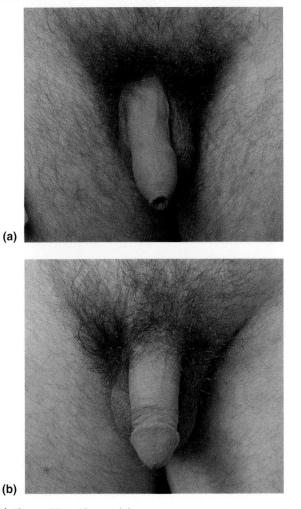

▲**Figure 6-14 Circumcision.** (a) Uncircumcised penis. (b) Circumcised penis.

Existing scientific evidence demonstrates potential medical benefits of newborn male circumcision, such as lowered risk of urinary tract infections especially in infants younger than 1 year of age, lowered risk of penile cancer, and lowered risk of STIs, especially syphilis and HIV infection. However, the policy statement of the American Academy of Pediatrics notes that, in general, the differences in risk are small and the data are not sufficient to recommend routine circumcision of male newborns at this time. Additionally, circumcision has some risks as does any surgical procedure, though complications are rare and usually minor. Therefore, the AAP suggests that parents, in conjunction with their pediatricians, decide what is in the best interest of the child. If the decision is made for circumcision, the Academy strongly recommends giving the infant pain relief medication (AAP, 1999).

The Postpartum Period

The *postpartum period* is the 6 weeks after childbirth during which a mother's body returns to its prepregnant state.

One of the areas of the body affected greatly, of course, is the reproductive system. The uterus returns nearly to its original size, remaining slightly larger because of the cells that were added during pregnancy. Within 2 weeks, the cervical opening closes to a slit, and tissue damage that occurred to it during the birth process heals. The vagina, bruised and swollen from the newborn traveling through it, returns to normal after about 3 weeks. The episiotomy and any torn tissues surrounding the vaginal opening heal within 1 week.

A variety of other organ systems and tissues in the mother's body change during pregnancy and return to their prepregnant state during the postpartum period and beyond. For example, muscles in the pelvic region gradually regain their original tone, but this process may take up to 6 months. During the first few days after delivery, a woman may have trouble urinating due to bruising of the bladder, the effects of anesthetics, and swelling of the ureters, tubes that lead from the kidneys to the bladder. The ureters may remain swollen for up to 3 months, although problems with urination usually last only a few days. During the birth process and the expulsion of the placenta, a woman loses blood. Her blood plasma and red blood cell volumes usually return to the normal nonpregnant state by the end of the postpartum period, but may take a few additional weeks. Hormonal changes are comparatively rapid after delivery; some return to normal levels by the end of the first postpartum day, but others take 1 to 2 weeks to normalize.

Many women experience *postpartum depression,* especially in the week after delivery. Approximately 40% to 85% of women experience mild depression, often referred to as "the blues." This mild form of depression, often accompanied by mood swings, is thought to be a result of the physical and mental stresses of childbirth, as well as the variety of physical (including hormonal) changes that take place during that time. Symptoms include periods of crying, sleep disturbances, loss of appetite, and confusion. The blues usually subside during the second postpartum week. Severe depression is rare (Glass & Bruner, 2000). Physicians usually recommend that a woman consult her health-care provider to discuss treatment with a mild sedative if she is experiencing sleep problems, since a lack of sleep may contribute to her depression.

At the beginning of the postpartum period, many women also start breastfeeding their infants. The benefits of breastfeeding are discussed in the "Across the Life Span" section of Chapter 9.

Healthy LIVING PRACTICES

- If you are female and have missed a period, are nauseated at times, feel tired often, and are experiencing

moodiness, check with a health-care provider; you may be pregnant.

- A home pregnancy test can be used on the day of a missed period or thereafter to determine pregnancy. A health-care practitioner can provide laboratory testing to confirm pregnancy.

Infertility

Infertility is the inability of a couple to conceive a child after 1 year of unprotected sex. Some infertility experts suggest that couples wait for 2 years before seeking help for infertility. Couples may have reduced fertility for a variety of reasons. Infertility is not necessarily due to "a problem" with one partner or the other. Factors that slightly impair the fertility of both sexual partners may interact to render a couple infertile.

One reason for male infertility is faulty sperm production. In normal sperm production, the semen contains approximately 80 to 120 million sperm per milliliter (ml). Since the ejaculate volume ranges from 2 to 8 ml (slightly less than a teaspoon to nearly 2 teaspoons), the total sperm ejaculated ranges from about 200 million to 800 million. A sperm count lower than 20 million sperm per ml (40 million to 160 million total in the ejaculate) may impair fertility.

In addition to a low sperm count, a high percentage (usually more than 40%) of abnormally shaped sperm can affect male fertility. Abnormally shaped sperm such as those with two heads or abnormally shaped heads or tails (■ **Figure 6-15**) may not be able to swim well. These defects may reduce their chances of reaching the egg.

Male infertility is often related to a variety of environmental factors or diseases. Cigarette smoking, chronic alcoholism, various medications, and prolonged illnesses with accompanying fever all affect sperm production. Infection with the mumps virus can render a man sterile.

A man can also have a problem with sperm transport, which can cause infertility even if the sperm count is adequate for conception. Infections caused by certain STIs can block the ductus deferens and injure these tubes. Erectile dysfunction is also a common cause of infertility if a man is unable to ejaculate.

There are a variety of causes of infertility in women. In some instances, the vagina cannot be penetrated due to an intact hymen or to vaginismus (see p. 111). Some abnormalities in the structure of the vagina, which may be present at birth or caused by scarring from STIs or trauma, allow only partial penetration. Unfortunately, couples having trouble with penetration often use lubricants that kill sperm. For example, one type of the popular K-Y jelly has spermicidal properties.

Once sperm travel up the vagina, they must pass through the cervix to reach the uterus and the fallopian tubes. Secretion of mucus by the cervix is important to sperm motility. During the few days prior to ovulation, the cervical mucus changes consistency, which facilitates the movement of sperm. Infection can damage the glands that secrete mucus or result in the presence of white blood cells. The properties of this mucus also change if a woman has an estrogen deficiency. Such changes in the quality and quantity of mucus can impair the sperm's ability to reach an egg.

infertility
inability to conceive a child after 1 year of unprotected sex.

Structural defects of the uterus do not usually cause infertility; usually such problems result in repeated miscarriage. However, the uterine (fallopian) tubes can be another fertility trouble spot. Infection with *N. gonorrhoeae* or *C. trachomatis* (see Chapter 14) can result in severe tissue destruction, completely blocking the tubes and causing sterility. Infections of other origins, such as from appendicitis or IUD complications, may result in less severe blockage. Pregnancy may occur, but the risk is increased for ectopic pregnancy. Endometriosis is another cause of sterility, ectopic pregnancy, or both.

The ovaries can be the source of impaired fertility. Hormonal imbalances can interfere with ovulation, and a mumps infection, radiation, and chemotherapy can damage the ovaries. Additionally, function of the ovaries declines as a woman ages, reducing her ability to conceive. Dietary deficiencies and strenuous exercise, such as jogging 10 or more miles per week, have also been shown to affect ovary function.

To treat infertility, a physician skilled in this practice begins with extensive histories of the couple's health. This may be followed by a series of relatively simple tests such as a sperm count to rule out common causes of infertility. Other, more extensive, physical examinations may be necessary to determine the cause. In some instances, the cause cannot be determined. Treatments are specific to the known causes of the infertility and include surgical procedures, hormone therapy, medication, and lifestyle changes.

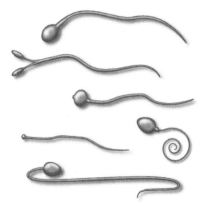

▲ **Figure 6-15 Abnormal Sperm.** Abnormal sperm exhibit various types of malformations.

In addition to these therapies, physicians can harvest ova and obtain semen to assist fertilization and implantation. For example, if a couple has problems with sperm reaching the cervix, cervical conditions that are hostile to sperm, or the health of the sperm themselves, a physician may suggest artificial insemination, which has been practiced in the United States for more than 50 years. During this procedure, semen (the husband's or a donor's) is placed in the cervical opening. The couple must use the methods of natural family planning discussed in this chapter to determine the best time for this procedure.

Women who have no uterine tubes or blocked tubes that do not respond to surgery often choose in vitro fertilization (IVF) to conceive. ("In vitro" means "in a test tube" or "in the laboratory.") In vitro fertilization involves fertilization of ova with sperm in laboratory glassware, with subsequent implantation of zygotes (fertilized eggs) in the woman's uterus. In some cases the couple's own ova and sperm are used for this procedure. If this is not possible, donor gametes for one or the other are used. In vitro fertilization may also be used for other fertility problems. The birth of the first baby conceived through in vitro fertilization took place in 1978.

In 1983 the first pregnancy was reported in which embryos derived from in vitro fertilization had been frozen. During IVF, fertilization is attempted with many eggs because not all eggs become fertilized. Freezing some of the resultant zygotes allows physicians to save ova that have been fertilized but cannot be implanted. (Only three to five eggs can be implanted safely at a time.)

In 1986 an alternative procedure to IVF was introduced: gamete intrafallopian tube transfer (GIFT). This procedure can be used only in women who have normal uterine (fallopian) tubes. The procedure is similar to IVF, but the fertilized ova are inserted into the tubes by means of a fine tube threaded through a needle hole in the abdominal wall. (In IVF, the zygotes are implanted in the uterus.) GIFT is twice as successful as IVF in producing pregnancies and live births, but it is more invasive and more costly than IVF.

birth control (contraception) methods to avoid pregnancy.

abstinence a method of birth control that involves refraining from vaginal intercourse.

natural family planning (fertility awareness) formerly called the rhythm method; a group of birth control techniques in which a couple abstains from sexual intercourse during the time of the month when a woman is most likely to conceive.

sess your attitude toward the timing of parenthood by using the self-assessment scale in the student workbook.) Therefore, couples usually use some form of **birth control**, or contraception, which are methods to avoid pregnancy.

Couples and individuals have many factors to consider when choosing a birth control method. They might consider its cost, effectiveness, reversibility, side effects, ease of use, convenience, and effectiveness against STIs. They must also consider their age and whether they need contraception on a regular basis or if they have only infrequent contraceptive needs. Many people are also concerned about the ways in which a contraceptive interferes with or fits in with their lovemaking. Some people have religious considerations to think about when making this choice.

Because a woman has a long reproductive life lasting some 30 to 35 years (from her teenage years until age 50 on average), the form of contraception she chooses may vary to meet her needs throughout the stages of her life. A variety of contraceptive methods are available, each with its own risks, benefits, and level of effectiveness. Most methods are based on the female reproductive cycle and rely on a woman's taking action. However, many methods can rely on the action of both partners and be incorporated into lovemaking.

The effectiveness of a contraceptive method is an important factor to consider. The *theoretical effectiveness* of a contraceptive refers to the number of women who will not become pregnant out of 100 couples using a method consistently and properly as their only means of birth control for 1 year. For example, if a method is 80% effective, 80 of 100 women using this method will not become pregnant over a year; 20 women will become pregnant. *Actual effectiveness* refers to the number of women who will not become pregnant of 100 couples using a method under usual conditions. Many people forget to use the method or use it improperly, lowering its effectiveness. (Unprotected sex has an effectiveness rate of 15%. Put simply, having unprotected sex is not an effective means of birth control.) ▌ **Table 6-3** lists the effectiveness of the various forms of birth control.

The "Contraceptive Comfort and Confidence Scale" in the student workbook will help you assess whether the method of contraception that you are using or considering is or will be effective for you.

Abstinence and Natural Methods

With respect to contraception, **abstinence** means refraining from vaginal intercourse. Without this act, a woman cannot get pregnant (unless sperm are introduced artificially into her reproductive tract by a physician). Abstinence is 100% effective and is an excellent alternative for young men and women who feel they are not ready to have sex. Also, people choose to abstain from sex during various periods of their lives for varied reasons.

www.jbpub.com/healthyliving

Contraception

Most of the time, people engage in sexual intercourse for nonreproductive reasons. The timing may not be right for a pregnancy or their family may be complete. (You can as-

Natural family planning, or fertility awareness (formerly called the *rhythm method*), is a group of birth control techniques in which a couple abstains from sexual intercourse during the time of the month when a woman is most likely to conceive. The actual effectiveness of these methods is about 80% because it is often difficult to determine when ovulation has occurred and fertilization can take place.

Ovulation usually takes place in the middle of a woman's reproductive cycle. If she has sex up to 72 hours before ovulation, she can become pregnant because sperm live approximately this long. The egg survives for 24 hours, so fertilization can occur for 1 day after ovulation also. In summary, fertilization can take place up to 3 days before and 1 day after ovulation.

The time of ovulation varies with the length of a woman's cycle and may vary within cycles of a consistent length. In fact, a woman can ovulate anytime during her cycle and can even become pregnant during her menstrual period. There are four ways to determine (but without 100% certainty) when ovulation takes place: the temperature method, the calendar method, mucus inspection, and the mucothermal method. All but the calendar method are based on changes that take place in a woman's body around the time of ovulation.

To use the *temperature method,* a woman takes her temperature with a special basal thermometer before she gets out of bed every day for a few months. Since the body temperature dips just before and rises just after ovulation (■ **Figure 6-16),** charting body temperature for a few months can help a woman determine when she ovulates and if ovulation is regular.

To use *mucus inspection,* a woman notes when her cervical mucus changes consistency. Four days before ovulation, cervical mucus (which flows to the vagina) becomes clearer and thinner. She should avoid intercourse from this time until the mucus changes back to its cloudier, thicker appearance. The *mucothermal method* combines this method with the temperature method described in the previous paragraph.

To use the *calendar method,* the woman records the length of her menstrual cycles for a year, beginning on day 1 of menstrual bleeding. After determining the length of her shortest and longest cycles, she uses a chart or formula to determine which days of the month she could become pregnant (■ **Table 6-4).** This method works best when a woman has cycles that are consistently the same length. If a woman's cycle varies greatly, "safe" times within her cycle will be shorter than if her cycles are more regular.

Coitus interruptus, or withdrawal, is another natural form of birth control. To use this method, the man senses when he is close to ejaculation, then removes his penis from his partner's vagina and genital area, interrupting intercourse. There are many problems with this method, however. A man must exercise a great deal of self-control, removing his penis from the vagina at a time when his desire may be to thrust more deeply. Also, he must be able to sense when he has enough time to remove himself before

coitus interruptus (withdrawal) (KO-ih-tus in-ter-RUP-tus) a form of birth control in which the man removes his penis from his partner's vagina and genital area, interrupting intercourse before ejaculation.

Table 6-3	Effectiveness of Various Birth Control Methods	
Method	**Actual Effectiveness (%)**	**Theoretical Effectiveness (%)**
Abstinence	—	100
Fertility awareness	80	91–99
Coitus interruptus (withdrawal)	81	96
Spermicides	74	94
Diaphragm	80	94
Contraceptive sponge (women who have not given birth)	80	91
Contraceptive sponge (women who have given birth)	60	80
Cervical cap (women who have not given birth)	80	91
Cervical cap (women who have given birth)	60	74
Male condom	86	97
Female condom	79	95
Combined oral contraceptives (the pill)	97	99.9
Progestin-only pill (the mini-pill)	97	99.5
Depo-Provera	99.7	99.7
IUDs (across types)	98–99.9	98.5–99.9
Female sterilization	99.5	99.5
Male sterilization	99.85	99.9

Source: Hatcher, R. A., et al., (1998). *Contraceptive technology* (17th ed.). New York: Ardent Media.

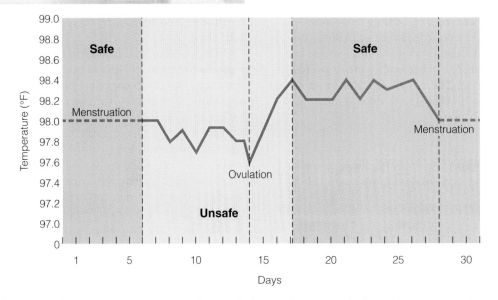

▲ **Figure 6-16 Basal Body Temperature Variations during the Menstrual Cycle.** In this graph, basal body temperature is shown to vary during this "model" menstrual cycle. The time of ovulation is determined by noting the fall in temperature just before ovulation and the rise over three days just after. Remember, most menstrual cycles are not as regular as this "model" cycle. Safe days vary widely among women and may vary widely among an individual's cycles. The days prior to ovulation are considered "unsafe" because a woman does not yet know whether ovulation has occurred.

Table 6-4 How to Calculate Your Fertile Period

If Your Shortest Cycle Has Been (no. of days)	Your First Fertile (Unsafe) Day Is	If Your Longest Cycle Has Been (no. of days)	Your Last Fertile (Unsafe) Day Is
21*	3rd Day	21*	10th Day
22	4th	22	11th
23	5th	23	12th
24	6th	24	13th
25	7th	25	14th
26	8th	26	15th
27	9th	27	16th
28	10th	28	17th
29	11th	29	18th
30	12th	30	19th
31	13th	31	20th
32	14th	32	21st
33	15th	33	22nd
34	16th	34	23rd
35	17th	35	24th

*Day 1 = First day of menstrual bleeding
Source: Hatcher, R. A., et al., (1998). *Contraceptive technology.* (17th ed.). New York: Ardent Media, Inc., p. 317.

ejaculation. Additionally, sperm from a recent ejaculation may be present in the urethra and may be carried to the tip of the penis with drops of pre-ejaculatory fluid and result in pregnancy. To reduce the possibility of sperm in the pre-ejaculate, a man should urinate after ejaculation and carefully clean all semen from the penis. With perfect use, coitus interruptus is 96% effective. However, during actual use this form of contraception is only 81% effective. None of the natural methods of birth control protects against the transmission of STIs.

Chemical and Barrier Methods

Spermicides are chemicals that kill sperm. The most common active ingredient in spermicides marketed in the United States is nonoxynol-9. The inactive ingredients make up the carrier, or base, of the spermicides, which are sold as foams, creams, jellies, films, suppositories, or tablets. (Spermicides are also added to many brands of condoms.) The carrier distributes the spermicide in the vaginal canal. Shortly before vaginal sex, foams, creams, and jellies are placed high in the vagina near the cervix using an applicator, as shown in ▌ **Figure 6-17.** Spermicidal films are placed near the cervix. Suppositories and tablets are placed in the vagina and given time to dissolve. Correct placement of the spermicide and timing of insertion are critical

▼**Figure 6-17 Jelly and Foam Spermicides with Applicator.**
Diaphragm with contraceptive jelly (*Top right*) and cervical cap
(*Bottom right*).

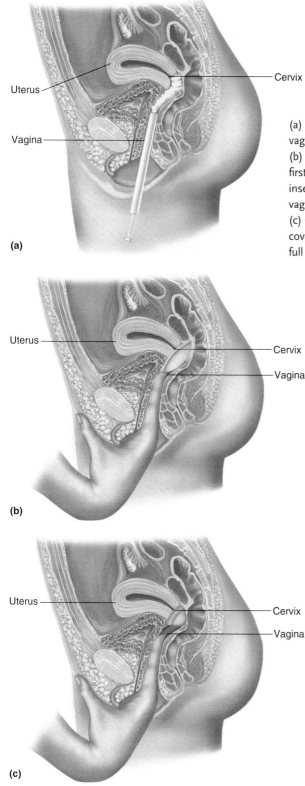

(a)

(a) Spermicide is being placed in the
vagina using a plunger-type applicator.
(b) Diaphragm is being inserted. It is
first ringed with spermicide, pinched for
insertion, and then placed high in the
vagina, covering the cervix.
(c) Cervical cap is being inserted to
cover the cervix. It is first filled one-third
full with spermicide.

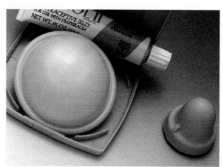

(b)

(c)

to the spermicide's effectiveness, which is 94% if these
products are used correctly and consistently.

A benefit of using spermicides for contraception is that
they decrease the risk for contracting certain STIs such as
gonorrhea and chlamydial infection (Cook & Rosenberg,
1998) and they decrease the risk for developing
cervical cancer related to infection with certain
types of human papillomavirus (HPV). Evidence suggests that the risk for the sexual
transmission of hepatitis B virus might
also be reduced, although condom use or
abstinence is still the best method for
reducing the risk of HIV infection (see
Chapter 14). Within the next decade,
spermicides are likely to be developed
that have more effective disease-
preventing properties. Other advantages to using spermicides are that
the side effects (such as allergy and
vaginal irritation or infection) are minimal, they are used only when birth control is needed, and they are easy products
to obtain over the counter.

Barrier methods of contraception block the
path that sperm must take to reach the ovum.
These forms of contraception include male condoms, female condoms, diaphragms, and cervical caps
(see Figure 6-17). The Today Vaginal Contraceptive Sponge,
an over-the-counter **sponge** that contained spermicide and
was used like a diaphragm, was taken off the market in the

spermicides
chemicals that
kill sperm.

barrier methods types
of birth control that block
the path that sperm must
take to reach the ovum;
these forms of contraception include male condoms, female condoms,
diaphragms, and
cervical caps.

sponge an over-the-counter product containing spermicide
that is used like a
diaphragm.

United States in 1995. The Food and Drug Administration discovered that the water system used in the manufacture of the product was contaminated with bacteria that cause diarrhea, although the sponges were never shown to be contaminated with this pathogen. A New Jersey pharmaceutical company purchased the Today Sponge from its original manufacturer in 1999, and plans to market this product in 2000.

male condom a sheath used to cover the penis during sexual intercourse to help prevent pregnancy or sexually transmitted infections.

female condom a polyurethane sheath with a ring at each end used to line the vagina during sexual intercourse to help prevent pregnancy or sexually transmitted infections.

Male condoms, the only form of birth control presently available for men other than vasectomy (see p. 131), are one of the most popular forms of birth control in the United States. The use of male condoms is also described in Chapter 14. Used for the prevention of pregnancy, condoms are 86% effective with actual use and 97% effective with consistent and proper use. Scientists are currently developing new methods of birth control for men, including hormonal contraceptives that would stop sperm production (Swerdloff et al., 1998) and an antifertility drug called triptolide, which has been isolated from the plant *Tripterygium wilfordii* used in traditional Chinese medicine to treat inflammation (Lue, 1998).

Figure 6-18 illustrates the correct procedure for putting on a male condom: Put the condom on after the penis has become erect but before there is genital contact with a partner. Hold the top half-inch of the condom, squeezing the air out. (This space will form a reservoir for semen. If air is not removed from this space, the semen cannot collect at the condom tip.) Place the rolled-up condom over the head of the penis (■ **Figure 6-18a).** While still holding the tip, unroll the condom to cover the penis to its base (■ **Figure 6-18b and c).** Gently smooth out any air that may have been trapped between the condom and the penis. After ejaculation, hold the condom firmly at its base to prevent slippage while you withdraw the still-erect penis from your partner's body. Remove the condom from the penis (■ **Figure 6-18d),** being careful not to spill semen on your partner and not to touch the exterior of the condom to your genital area. (The outside of the condom may have become contaminated from an infected partner.) Discard the used condom.

Approved by the FDA in 1993 the Reality **female condom,** a polyurethane sheath with a ring at each end, lines the vagina. Its use is also described in Chapter 14. Female condoms, used consistently and properly as a form of birth control, are approximately 95% effective. Their actual effectiveness, however, is 79%.

Figure 6-19 shows a female condom and the correct procedure for inserting one: Holding the closed end of the condom, squeeze the ring inside the condom so that it flattens and can

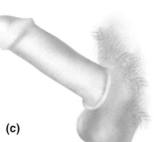

(a)

(b)

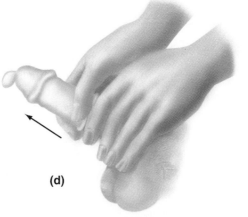

(c)

(d)

◀Figure 6-18 **How to Put on a Male Condom.** The text explains each step.

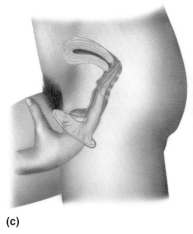

Inner ring   Index finger

Open end

(a)

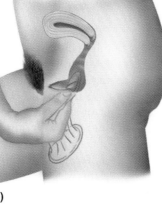

(b)

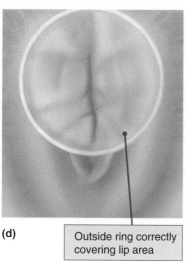

(c)

(d)

Outside ring correctly covering lip area

◀Figure 6-19 How to insrt a Female Condom. The text explains each step.

collapsing the diaphragm so that it can be inserted into the vagina. When the diaphragm reaches the cervical area, its spring pops open, causing the diaphragm to assume its dome shape and to be held firmly in place over the cervix.

After insertion, a diaphragm is effective for 6 hours, so that a woman could insert the diaphragm well before sexual intercourse. However, spermicide must be added before each additional act of intercourse. After the last intercourse, the diaphragm must be left in place for at least 6 hours but must not be worn for more than 24 hours because of risk of infection. Used properly and consistently, the diaphragm is 94% effective. Currently under development are disposable, single-use diaphragms.

The **cervical cap** (Figure 6-17c) works much the same way as the diaphragm, but it is smaller and covers only the cervix. The cervical cap has not been in use in the United States until relatively recently; the Prentif cavity-rim cervical cap was approved by the FDA in 1988.

Before inserting a cervical cap, fill it one-third full with spermicide. When in place, it fits snugly around the base of the cervix and provides protection for 48 hours. Additional spermicide is not necessary with repeated intercourse, unlike the diaphragm. The cervical cap is 91% effective; however, its effectiveness is lowered to 74% in women who have given birth. In the future, silicone rubber cervical caps that release spermicide will become available.

Some women use **douching** as a contraceptive method. Douching is the use of specially prepared solutions to cleanse the vagina. *Douching is not effective for contraception.* By the time a woman can douche after sexual intercourse, sperm have already reached the cervix and uterus and cannot be washed away. Additionally, if a woman has used a contraceptive product containing spermicide, or has used spermicide alone as a contraceptive, douching may wash away the chemical and render it inactive.

be inserted into the vagina (▌ **Figure 6-19a).** Insert the flattened ring and condom into the vagina (▌ **Figure 6-19b),** gently pushing it up to the cervix as shown in ▌ **Figure 6-19c.** You should be able to feel the ring positioned past the pubic bone. Straighten out the part of the condom lining the vagina if it is twisted. The outside ring should cover the labia, as shown in ▌ **Figure 6-19d.** After intercourse, first twist the condom to close it at the vaginal opening, which will prevent sperm and pathogens from touching your genital area. Remove the condom with gentle pulling and discard. Female and male condoms are intended for one-time use.

The diaphragm has been in use in the United States longer than 60 years. Shown in Figure 6-17b, a **diaphragm** is a dome-shaped rubber cup bordered by a flexible spring that is designed to cover the cervix and surrounding area. This prescription item must be fitted by a health-care practitioner.

Before inserting a diaphragm, place spermicide on both its sides and around its rim. Compress the spring,

diaphragm a dome-shaped rubber cup bordered by a flexible spring that covers the cervix and surrounding area during sexual intercourse to help prevent pregnancy.

cervical cap a dome-shaped rubber cup, smaller than a diaphragm, that covers the cervix during sexual intercourse to help prevent pregnancy.

douching (DOOSH-ing) the use of specially prepared solutions to cleanse the vagina; not an effective birth control method.

Hormonal Methods

Hormonal methods of birth control prevent pregnancy by suppressing ovulation. There are four types of hormonal contraceptive products: combined oral contraceptives (the pill), Norplant (recently discontinued), Depo-Provera, and progestin-only pills (mini-pills).

Combined oral contraceptives suppress ovulation through the combined actions of estrogen and progestin (a synthetic form of progesterone). During the month there is a pill-free time when menstruation occurs.

The pill has numerous advantages. It is highly effective (97% to 99.9%), decreases menstrual cramps, decreases the length of the menses and the amount of blood lost, has a protective effect against pelvic inflammatory disease, reduces the risk for ovarian and endometrial cancer (cancer of the uterine lining), reduces the risk for benign (noncancerous) breast disease, and helps prevent osteoporosis (thinning of the bones). The pill is a readily reversible form of contraception and, since 1965, has consistently been the contraceptive choice of approximately 25% of U.S. women who use contraceptives (Jones, 1999).

The pill has been available for nearly 40 years and is one of the best-studied prescription medications. The amount of estrogen and progestin in pills has decreased over the years, so today's pills are much safer than pills of the past. Cardiovascular disease is the most serious complication of the pill. Women at high risk for developing this complication of combined oral contraceptive use are those who are older than 50 years of age or who are older than 35 years of age and smoke cigarettes. Women who are sedentary, overweight, and have high blood pressure, diabetes mellitus, or an elevated serum cholesterol level are also at high risk. Along with the risk of developing cardiovacular disease, women who take the pill may develop headaches, may have mood changes, and are at increased risk for chlamydial infection. Although pill-takers are not at increased risk for other STIs, they are not protected against them. Women who have coronary artery disease, a history of developing blood clots, or a family history of breast cancer should not use combined oral contraceptives.

Women who have had a stroke or cancer of the reproductive organs should also choose another birth control method.

Norplant (recently discontinued), Depo-Provera, and mini-pills are all forms of progestin-only contraceptives. Progestin works to suppress ovulation in much the same way as combined oral contraceptives.

In use in the United States from 1990 to 1999, Norplant consisted of matchstick-sized contraceptive capsules that were surgically placed just under the skin of the upper arm. Usually six capsules were implanted, which conferred contraception for about 5 years. Although Norplant was an effective and widely used contraceptive, many women discontinued its use due to abnormal uterine bleeding (Vincent et al., 1999). Additionally, women reported a range of other side effects including acne, hair loss, mood swings, migraines, blurred vision, and difficulties in removal (Dyer, 1999). In April, 1999, the manufacturer of Norplant discontinued its manufacture after many complaints and legal suits were filed by women in the United States and Britain, claiming that they were not adequately warned about the product's side effects. A similar product called Implanon has been shown to be extremely effective in clinical trials (Croxatto & Makarainen, 1998). This product is a single matchstick-sized implant, and is approved for use in Europe. As of June, 2000, Implanon has not been approved for use in the United States by the Food and Drug Administration (FDA).

Depo-Provera, which has been used in the United States since 1992, is an injection of progestin that inhibits ovulation for 3 months. **Mini-pills** are progestin-only pills that are taken continually; menstruation does not occur. They have been in use in the United States for approximately 25 years.

Although highly effective, progestin-only contraceptives have a few serious disadvantages. These contraceptives change a woman's menstrual cycle. In addition to amenorrhea, these changes can include opposite effects: an increased number of days of menstruation with light bleeding or an increased number of days with heavy bleeding. Women find some of these changes unacceptable. Another disadvantage is that long-term use of progestin-only contraceptives may cause thinning of the bones due to low estrogen.

Within a few years, vaginal rings will likely become available that will contain progestin only or a combination of progestin and estrogen. These doughnut-shaped contraceptives will fit in the vagina much like a diaphragm but will work by releasing hormones. Instead of taking a pill every day, a woman will keep the ring in place for 3 weeks, then remove it for 1 week, during which time she will menstruate (Roumen & Dieben, 1999; Weisberg et al., 1999).

Intrauterine Devices

An **intrauterine device (IUD)** is a small apparatus that a health-care practitioner inserts into the uterus (▮ **Figure**

---

combined oral contraceptives "the pill"; suppress ovulation through the combined actions of estrogen and progestin.

Depo-Provera an injection of progestin that inhibits ovulation for 3 months.

mini-pills progestin-only contraceptive pills that are taken continually; menstruation does not occur.

intrauterine device (IUD) a small contraceptive device that either is covered with copper or contains a reservoir of progestin and is inserted into the uterus.

sterilization a permanent form of birth control that requires a surgical procedure.

tubal ligation female sterilization that is performed by cutting and tying off the uterine tubes so that the sperm and egg cannot unite.

vasectomy male sterilization that is performed by cutting and tying off the ductus (vas) deferens to prevent sperm from becoming part of the ejaculate.

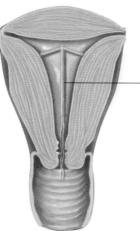

- Uterus
- Applicator
- Cervix
- Vagina

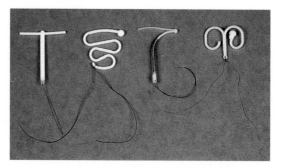

◀**Figure 6-20** The Intrauterine Device (IUD) is a small apparatus that is inserted into the uterus. ▼The active ingredient of an IUD is either copper or progestin.

▪ IUD in place

6-20). A string hangs from the base of the IUD and extends into the vagina; the presence of the string is an indication that the IUD is still in place. The active ingredient of the IUD is either copper, which covers the IUD, or progestin, which is contained in a reservoir within the IUD.

Although IUDs have a high rate of effectiveness (98% to 99.9%), the way in which they work has been a source of controversy. Results of several studies suggest that IUDs interfere with the movement of sperm through a woman's reproductive tract. There is little evidence to suggest that IUDs make it difficult for a fertilized ovum to implant, thereby aborting it (Dardano & Burkman, 1999).

The greatest risk of IUD use is pelvic inflammatory disease (PID). (PID is also discussed in Chapter 14.) PID can occur if the uterine lining becomes contaminated with bacteria during insertion of the IUD. Also, women who have multiple sex partners or whose partner has multiple partners are more likely to develop PID with IUD use. Such women should consider a form of birth control, such as male or female condoms, that also protects against sexually transmitted infections and consequent PID. Since PID may result in infertility, young women who have not given birth may choose another form of birth control. (Today, most women who use IUDs are older than 35 years.) Disadvantages of IUD use are increased blood loss during menstruation or spotting between periods, and expulsion of the IUD. If a woman becomes pregnant while the IUD is in place, the chance of miscarriage (spontaneous abortion) is about 50%. If the IUD is not removed when she be-

comes pregnant, a woman could contract a severe infection and die.

The IUD may be a good choice for the woman older than 35 who is in a monogamous relationship, cannot use hormonal types of birth control, and needs a long-term form of contraception. Once the IUD is inserted, it does not need to be changed for 1 to 8 years, depending on the IUD used.

Sterilization

Sterilization is a permanent form of birth control that requires a surgical procedure. Although it may be possible to reverse the procedure and regain fertility, this operation is much more difficult than the sterilizing procedure and has only a 45% to 80% chance of success. Female sterilization is a **tubal ligation** and involves cutting and tying off the uterine tubes by means of clips, rings, or burning so that the sperm and egg cannot unite. Male sterilization is a **vasectomy** and involves cutting and tying off the ductus deferens to prevent sperm from becoming part of the ejaculate. (The name of this procedure refers to the older name for this structure, the vas deferens.) ▮ **Figure 6-21** illustrates both procedures.

Tubal ligation is a medically more complicated and more costly procedure than vasectomy, but both are highly

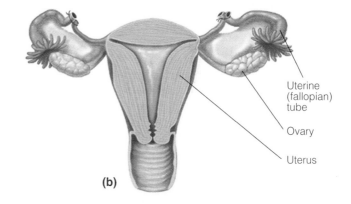

▶**Figure 6-21 Sterilization Methods.**
Male sterilization (a), or vasectomy, involves cutting and tying off the ductus (vas) deferens. Female sterilization (b), or tubal ligation, involves cutting and tying off of the fallopian tubes.

(a)

- Uterine (fallopian) tube
- Ovary
- Uterus

(b)

effective. Failure is most often due to surgical error or to the spontaneous rejoining of the tubes. Both procedures are reversible, but restored fertility is not guaranteed and varies widely among persons. Physicians suggest that patients consider both tubal ligation and vasectomy permanent procedures (Hatcher et al., 1998).

Healthy LIVING PRACTICES

- The most effective means to prevent an unwanted pregnancy are sexual abstinence and sterilization, followed closely by hormonal methods and IUDs.
- To reduce the risk of contracting or transmitting sexually transmitted infections, use a condom during sexual intercourse. The best way to protect yourself against STIs is to practice sexual abstinence.

Abortion

Sometimes contraceptive methods fail and an unplanned pregnancy occurs that a woman or a couple chooses to terminate. Sometimes pregnancy seriously jeopardizes a woman's health and ending the pregnancy is the only means of saving her life. There are numerous other reasons why women and couples choose to terminate a pregnancy.

A controversial 1973 United States Supreme Court decision (*Roe v. Wade*) ruled that induced abortion is a legal medical procedure. States may regulate abortions in the second trimester to protect the health of the pregnant woman, but the decision to end a pregnancy during the first trimester is the private concern of a woman and her health-care practitioner.

An **abortion** is the removal of the embryo or fetus from the uterus before it is able to survive on its own. During a *spontaneous abortion,* the body expels the embryo, usually because of serious genetic defects, although there may be other causes. Spontaneous abortions (miscarriages) generally occur during the first trimester. Ten to twenty percent of pregnancies end in spontaneous abortion.

During an *induced abortion,* a physician performs medical procedures that remove the embryo/fetus from the uterus. There are three principal ways to perform an induced abortion: vacuum aspiration, dilation and evacuation (D&E), and induction; the choice of method depends on the stage of development of the embryo/fetus.

abortion removal of the embryo or fetus from the uterus before it is able to survive on its own.

vacuum aspiration a method of early first-trimester induced abortion in which embryonic tissue is drawn out of the uterus by a suction device.

mifepristone (MIFF-ih-PRIS-tone) (RU486) a drug that induces early first-trimester abortions; this drug blocks progesterone, which is necessary for the adequate development of the uterine lining and implantation.

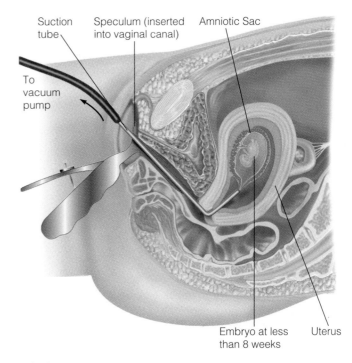

▲**Figure 6-22 Suction Curettage.** During this procedure, a thin, hollow tube is inserted through the vagina and cervix to the uterus. A suction aspirator (vacuum pump) draws tissue out of the uterus and into a container.

The safest time to have an abortion is between 7 and 10 weeks of gestation. If an abortion is performed before 6 to 7 weeks or after 10 weeks, there is an increased risk of complications. Nevertheless, elective abortion in the United States is safe; less than 1% of women who have abortions experience serious complications.

The abortion procedure used when the embryo is at less than 8 weeks of development is **vacuum aspiration,** or *suction curettage.* (*Curettage* means clearing material from a surface.) It can be performed in the physician's office in approximately 10 to 20 minutes with the use of a local anesthetic. To perform a vacuum aspiration, the physician inserts a slender, hollow plastic tube through the vagina and cervix into the uterus. The tube is connected to a suction aspirator, which draws the tissue out of the uterus and into a container (▮ **Figure 6-22**). After this procedure is completed, a narrow metal rod is inserted through the tube, and the uterine wall is scraped to be certain that all the tissue has been removed. Vacuum aspiration is used for 50% of abortions, and are performed within the first 8 weeks of embryonic development. The embryo is less than an inch long at this time.

Mifepristone (formerly known as RU486 or the French abortion pill) is also a method to terminate early first-trimester pregnancies. In July of 1996, the FDA Advisory Committee on Reproductive Health Drugs determined that mifepristone is safe and effective; approval of the drug for use in the United States is pending as of June, 2000.

It is approved for medical abortions in France, China, Sweden, and the United Kingdom. This drug, taken within 3 weeks of a missed period, induces abortion in 95% of pregnant women by blocking progesterone, which is necessary for the adequate development of the uterine lining. Without the buildup of this lining, implantation does not occur, and therefore, pregnancy is not established.

Abortions that are performed during 8 to 12 weeks of development use vacuum aspiration (suction curettage), but the cervix is also dilated (widened) to reduce the risk of damage to the uterus. This variation of suction curettage is called *dilation and curettage*, or *D&C*. Occasionally, general anesthesia is used for this procedure. Forty percent of all abortions are performed this way. In summary, 90% of abortions are performed in the first trimester by suction curettage or by dilation and curettage.

Early second-trimester abortions (13 to 16 weeks) are performed by **dilation and evacuation (D&E)**, also referred to as a *surgical abortion*. A D&E is performed somewhat like a D&C, except that there is greater dilation of the cervix and a larger suction device is used. In addition, the physician uses a special forceps to remove fetal parts.

Induction is used between 16 and 24 weeks of development, although D&E procedures are replacing induction as a safer, faster, and less expensive method of abortion at this stage of gestation. Induction means that labor is artificially induced (started). *Saline abortions* are one method of induction: A physician inserts a long needle through the abdominal wall and into the amniotic sac. A salt solution is injected into the sac, which causes the quick death of the fetus. The uterus begins contractions within 12 and 24 hours, and the woman delivers a dead fetus. This procedure is performed using a local anesthetic. Other types of solutions and prostaglandins (hormonelike substances that cause the uterus to contract) are also used for induction.

A special type of D&E procedure (the so-called partial birth abortion) is used to abort fetuses after 24 weeks. Only 1% of abortions are performed this late in a pregnancy. The U.S. House of Representatives and Senate voted to ban such late-term abortions in both 1997 and 2000. President Clinton vetoed the 1997 bill and is expected to veto the Partial-Birth Abortion Ban Act of 2000.

www.jbpub.com/healthyliving

Sexual Development

The gender of an individual is set at the time of fertilization and is determined by the type of sex chromosomes (genes) it receives from its parents. Females have two X chromosomes; males have an X and a Y.

During the 7th week of development, the embryo with a Y chromosome begins to develop testes. The developing testes secrete male hormones called *androgens*. (The powerful male hormone testosterone is an androgen.) These hormones direct the development of a male reproductive system. Embryos and fetuses without a Y chromosome begin to develop ovaries during the 9th week. The absence of androgens results in the development of a female reproductive system.

After birth, the secretion of testosterone in male babies nearly ceases and does not resume until puberty, the time of sexual maturation. The female reproductive system does not become active until that time as well.

Puberty is a stage of development during which the endocrine (hormone) and reproductive systems mature. Puberty begins at approximately 10 to 11 years of age and concludes about 5 or 6 years later. Girls usually enter puberty about 2 years earlier than boys. Scientists do not know what triggers this developmental process.

During childhood, the production of a hormone that stimulates the release of male and female sex hormones is suppressed. At the onset of puberty, the suppression ceases and the brain begins releasing the hormone that regulates the production of testosterone in males and estrogen in females. As puberty proceeds, the brain secretes greater and greater amounts of this hormone; thus more and more testosterone or estrogen is secreted. It is these hormones that stimulate the physical changes of puberty. These changes include growth spurts due to the growth of the skeleton (especially the long bones), the development of pubic and underarm hair, and the growth and maturation of the reproductive tract.

In males, building levels of testosterone result in an enlarging of the testes and penis, deepening of the voice due to an enlargement of the voice box, development of facial hair, broadening of the shoulders, and enlargement of the arm, chest, and leg muscles. Under the direction of testosterone, the seminiferous tubules begin manufacturing sperm. A significant developmental event in pubertal boys is semen emission during sleep (nocturnal emissions or wet dreams). Initially, sperm are not present in the semen.

In females, estrogen results in the development of the breasts and the rounding of the hips. Females experience **menarche**, the first menstruation, at around 12 years of age. (The normal range for menarche is 8 to 15 years of age.) A delay of the menarche may occur in girls with chronic diseases (such as diabetes mellitus) or those with disorders that affect their nutritional status (such as anorexia nervosa).

When a woman reaches 45 to 55 years of age, most of her ovarian follicles (eggs) have matured, and the remaining

dilation and evacuation (D&E) surgical abortion; a technique used for early second-trimester abortion in which the cervix is dilated (widened) and the fetal tissues are suctioned from the uterus.

induction an abortion technique used between 16 and 24 weeks of gestation in which labor is artificially started.

puberty (PEW-ber-tea) a stage of sexual development during which the endocrine (hormone) and reproductive systems mature.

menarche (meh-NAR-key) the first menstruation.

follicles are old. During some months, these aging follicles do not reach maturity and ovulation does not take place. Without mature egg follicles, the normal cyclic secretion of estrogen and progesterone does not occur, and the menses become irregular. Eventually, all follicles stop maturing, estrogen and progesterone are no longer secreted, and the menses cease. The cessation of the menses is called **menopause.** This term means the final menstrual period, but it is widely used to refer to the few years of transition when a woman passes from her reproductive years to her nonreproductive years. The "Diversity in Health" essay discusses menopausal symptoms and attitudes across cultures.

As the hormonal changes of menopause take place, women usually experience symptoms such as hot flashes and physiological changes such as thinning of the vaginal walls and vaginal dryness. In addition, the loss of estrogen results in an increased risk of osteoporosis and

menopause

(MEN-oh-pawz) the cessation of the menses; a term widely used to refer to the few years of transition during which a woman passes from her reproductive years to her nonreproductive years.

heart disease. Therefore, many health-care practitioners suggest hormone replacement therapy (HRT) for their patients. The hormones prescribed are either estrogen alone or estrogen in combination with progestin. HRT is controversial, however, because estrogen increases the risk of endometrial and breast cancers. The addition of progestin in HRT reduces the risk of endometrial cancer, but the combination further increases the risk of breast cancer.

Men also undergo changes in their reproductive systems during middle age. Men are fertile throughout their lives, although the number of healthy, active sperm they produce decreases as they grow older. Middle-aged men experience a decline in testosterone, ejaculate with less force and less volume, and take longer to regain an erection after orgasm. In addition, the prostate gland usually enlarges (see the "Managing Your Health" essay "Enlargement of the Prostate").

Although both men and women undergo changes in their reproductive systems beginning at middle age, these changes do not have to impair their ability to have a healthy, enjoyable sex life extending into their elderly years.

DIVERSITY in Health | Menopause

Menopause is a time of transition for every woman who reaches her 50s, but transition is about the only thing women universally experience during this time. The symptoms of menopause and attitudes regarding this process vary extensively among women across cultures. Why do these differences exist?

One hypothesis is that if a society regards the menopause as a positive time, then the symptoms of menopause reported by its women will decrease in number and severity. Certain evidence seems to support this hypothesis. For example, during their childbearing years, the Rajput women of Northern India are socially constrained and cannot move about freely in their villages. Those who no longer menstruate are freed of this constraint. Interestingly, these women report no symptoms of menopause. Similarly, Mayan women look upon the menopause as a lifting of the burden of childbearing. They, too, report no symptoms of hot flashes or cold sweats such as are typically reported by North American women. Additionally, Yanomamo women (forest-dwellers who live near the border between Brazil and

Venezuela) eagerly await menopause, which is considered the time of "older age," for this time of life brings increased status and decision-making power in their society.

Many researchers point out that it is difficult to form conclusions concerning symptoms and behaviors across cultures because the definition of terms such as *menopause* vary from culture to culture. In some cultures, there are no words in the language to identify particular menopausal symptoms or the menopause itself. Additionally, some symptoms are not recognized in Western medical literature as signs of menopause, but they are reported frequently by menopausal women in non-Western cultures. For example, Japanese women commonly report menopausal symptoms of shoulder stiffness and dizziness; Nigerian women frequently report having menopausal joint pains.

The diversity of the symptoms and experiences of women of various cultures regarding menopause cannot be attributed solely to differences in cultural beliefs. Their menopausal symptoms and experiences must also be evaluated in the

context of their differences with respect to risk factors for death and disease. Peoples of different cultures have different lifestyles that affect their health, which may account for some of the differences in the symptoms and perceptions of menopause across cultures.

Menopause is a significant time in a woman's life, and her attitude about and bodily response to "the change" is crucial to her susceptibility to disease, quality of life, and aging process. Currently, medical researchers are debating the significance of menopause to healthy aging. The experts disagree about the extent to which the decline in ovarian function contributes to physiological and psychological symptoms of menopause. Researchers are unanimous in their opinion that more research is needed to answer many of the questions we are just beginning to ask about this middle-life transition.

Sources: Mercer, C. (1999). Cross-cultural attitudes to the menopause and the ageing female, *Age and Ageing*, 28-S2, 12-17.
Lock, M. (1994). Menopause in cultural context. *Experimental Gerontology*, 29:307-317.
Woods, N. F. (1994). Menopause—challenges for future research, *Experimental Gerontology*, 29:237-243.

Enlargement of the Prostate

If you are male and over 45, your prostate may be enlarging slowly. This process of enlargement is common for men your age; it is part of the aging process and may never be a cause for concern. However, about 50% of men in their 60s and about 90% of men in their 70s and 80s complain of problems caused by an enlarged prostate gland, also known as prostatic hyperplasia, or benign prostatic hypertrophy (BPH).

Medical researchers are not sure why the prostate enlarges with age. The testes appear to play some role in the development of BPH because men whose testes were removed in childhood do not develop this condition. In addition, men who have the condition and have the testes removed find that their BPH regresses.

How can an enlarged prostate affect your health? Notice in Figure 6-1 that the prostate gland surrounds the urethra beneath the urinary bladder. As the prostate enlarges, it may squeeze the urethra, hampering the flow of urine through this tube. Therefore, the symptoms that may appear first as a result of BPH are difficulty in beginning to urinate, a decrease in the force of the urine stream, a dribbling of urine after urinating, a sensation of a full bladder after urinating, and a need to urinate 5 or 10 minutes after urinating.

As the prostate squeezes the urethra more and more, the muscles of the bladder wall respond by thickening as they forcefully push urine through the constricted urethra. This thickened bladder is irritated easily, however, and contracts more readily. Therefore, the following symptoms develop: an urgency to urinate and/or leaking of urine, more frequent urination, especially at night, and painful urination. Eventually, urine flow can be blocked to the point that emergency treatment is necessary.

There are several treatments for BPH. Surgery is usually undertaken when symptoms are severe: when a man is retaining urine, experiencing repeated bladder infec-

tions, bleeding from the urethra, or developing kidney problems due to the BPH. During the surgery, the portion of the prostate squeezing the urethra is removed.

One new treatment is balloon dilatation. During this procedure, an inflatable device is inserted into the urethra though the opening at the tip of the penis. The device is inflated at the area of constriction and is then removed. This procedure widens the urethra to alleviate symptoms.

Various medications also ease the symptoms of BPH. Certain drugs act on the smooth muscle of the urethra to help urine flow. Hormone treatments can often cause the gland to shrink. However, all treatments have significant side effects that patients should discuss thoroughly with their health-care practitioners. If symptoms are minimal, watchful waiting may be an appropriate course of action (Wasson et al., 1995).

Benign prostatic hypertrophy is not the only reason the prostate may be enlarged. Enlargement of this gland may also be caused by prostate cancer. This cancer is the second most common cause of cancer deaths in men (lung cancer being the first). However, it usually does not appear in men younger than 55, and it is generally a slow-growing form of cancer. Its symptoms

overlap with those of BPH and include difficult, frequent, and painful urination, and blood in the urine.

The symptoms of BPH and prostate cancer are more than just a nuisance. The restriction or blockage of urine flow can damage the kidneys; prostate cancer can spread, resulting in death. To avoid the discomforts and possible serious consequences of these conditions, therefore, the prostate should be examined regularly. The American Cancer Society recommends that men older than 50 have a digital rectal examination every year. During this examination, the physician inserts a gloved, lubricated finger into the rectum. Because the prostate lies next to the rectum **(Figure 6-D),** the physician can palpate (feel by pressing lightly) the size of the prostate.

Newer diagnostic techniques include transrectal ultrasound, in which the physician inserts an ultrasound probe into the rectum that results in an image of the prostate on a monitor. Ultrasound is a technique that visualizes internal soft tissues by means of sound waves. As the sound waves travel through tissues, some waves are bounced back to the probe and some are transmitted through the tissue. Tissues are visualized as a three-dimensional pattern of shaded areas, which physicians can interpret.

Recently, a blood test has been developed to help detect prostate cancer. This test is known as prostate specific antigen (PSA) and helps find many prostate cancers years before they would otherwise be detected. See Chapter 13 for a discussion of prostate cancer and the PSA test.

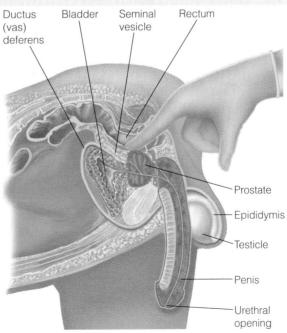

Ductus (vas) deferens · Bladder · Seminal vesicle · Rectum · Prostate · Epididymis · Testicle · Penis · Urethral opening

◀ **Figure 6-D Digital Examination of the Prostate.** The physician can feel an enlargement of the prostate gland by inserting a gloved finger into the rectum.

ANALYZING | *Health-Related Information*

Explain why you think this website about folic acid is a reliable or an unreliable source of information. Use the model for analyzing health-related information to guide your thinking; the main points of the model are noted below. The model is fully explained on pages 12 to 13.

1. Which statements are verifiable facts, and which are unverified statements or value claims?
2. What are the credentials of the agency that created the website? If this information is available, is the agency qualified as an expert in the topic area?
3. What might be the motives and biases of the agency that created the website? State reasons for your answer.
4. Which information in the website is relevant to the topic? Which information is irrelevant?
5. Is the source reliable? Does it have a reputation for publishing misinformation?
6. Does the website attack the credibility of conventional scientists or medical authorities?

Based on the above analysis, do you think that this website is a reliable source of health-related information? Summarize your reasons for coming to this conclusion.

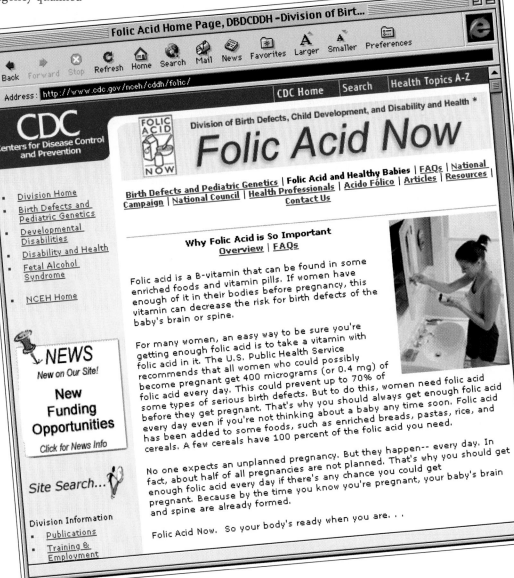

Chapter Review

Summary

Sexual reproduction involves the fertilization of an egg by a sperm, forming the first cell of a new individual. The male reproductive system produces sperm (male sex cells) and delivers them to the vagina of the female. Sperm are produced in the testes and are moved along the male reproductive tract with the seminal fluid secreted by accessory sex glands during ejaculation.

Eggs (ova; female sex cells) develop and mature in the female reproductive system, which also receives sperm and provides an environment in which a fertilized ovum can develop. Eggs mature in the ovaries, are fertilized in the uterine tubes, and develop in the uterus during pregnancy.

The sexual response of individuals engaging in sexual activity is usually described in phases. During the excitement phase, both men and women have a heightened sexual awareness. During the plateau phase, the heart rate, blood pressure, respiration rate, and level of muscle tension all increase and the erection of the male intensifies. During the orgasmic phase, men ejaculate, while women's vaginal walls contract rhythmically. During the resolution phase the body returns to its prearousal state.

Some people have sexual dysfunctions that interfere with their sexual response. Common sexual dysfunctions include erectile dysfunction, the inability of a man to develop and/or sustain an erection firm enough for penetration; premature ejaculation, consistently attaining orgasm shortly after intercourse begins and before a man wishes it to occur; hypoactive sexual desire, a low interest in sex (which occurs in both sexes but is more prevalent in women); and vaginismus, a sexual dysfunction of women in which the muscles of the lower third of the vaginal canal contract involuntarily at the anticipation of vaginal penetration.

Women experience cyclic monthly hormonal changes that orchestrate physiological changes that take place in the ovaries and uterus. The changes are collectively called the menstrual cycle. During the menstrual cycle an ovum matures and is released from the ovary while the lining of the uterus thickens in preparation for the implantation of a fertilized ovum. If pregnancy does not occur, the uterine lining sloughs off during the menses.

If fertilization takes place, the embryo/fetus develops in the uterus of the female. This developmental process is termed pregnancy, or gestation. Various environmental influences (teratogens) such as drugs, alcohol, viruses, and dietary deficiencies can damage the embryo or fetus early in pregnancy. A woman preparing for pregnancy should have a medical checkup; eat a well-balanced and nutritious diet; avoid drinking alcohol, smoking cigarettes, and taking drugs; and possibly seek genetic counseling.

Women who become pregnant may notice physical signs of this condition such as a missed period, nausea, fatigue, and moodiness. A woman can conduct a home pregnancy test after a missed period or have a laboratory test performed to determine if she is pregnant.

Pregnancy lasts 38 weeks and is typically described in terms of trimesters, or 3-month periods. During the first trimester, all the organ systems of the body form and become functional. The second and third trimesters are periods of growth and refinement of the organ systems.

The process of childbirth (labor) takes place in three stages: dilation, expulsion, and placental delivery. During dilation, the uterine muscles contract, causing the cervix to widen (dilate) and thin out (efface). During the second stage of labor the baby is born. Within 15 to 30 minutes after delivery of the baby, the placenta is expelled from the uterus.

Couples often want to avoid pregnancy for various reasons, so they choose some form of birth control, or contraception. Contraceptive methods are varied and can be grouped into five categories: abstinence and natural methods, chemical and barrier methods, hormonal methods, intrauterine devices, and sterilization. Each method has different advantages, disadvantages, and levels of effectiveness. Abstinence and sterilization are the most effective means of contraception, followed closely in effectiveness by hormonal methods and IUDs. Using condoms or practicing abstinence are the best ways to prevent the transmission of sexually transmitted infections while at the same time preventing pregnancy.

Sometimes contraceptive methods fail and an unplanned pregnancy occurs that a woman or a couple chooses to terminate. There are other reasons why women and couples choose to terminate a pregnancy, including health concerns of the mother. Terminating a pregnancy involves the removal of the embryo or fetus from the uterus before it is able to survive on its own. This process is called an induced abortion. In the United States today, there is great controversy over a woman's right to choose induced abortion. Ninety percent of abortions are performed during the first trimester using a procedure called suction curettage. The drug RU486, which is also effective in inducing abortion during the first trimester, is not yet approved for use in this country.

The gender of an individual is set at the time of fertilization and is determined by the type of sex chromosomes (genes) that it receives from its parents. The male and female reproductive tracts develop during gestation. Further maturation does not continue until puberty, the time of sexual maturation, which begins at approximately 10 to 11 years of age and concludes about 5 or 6 years later. Men and women both undergo changes to their reproductive function during middle age. Women have a cessation of the menses as a result of physiological and hormonal changes and can no longer reproduce. Men can reproduce throughout their lives but at middle age experience a decline in testosterone and sexual functioning.

Applying What You Have Learned

1. A woman is 42 years old, unmarried, and has sex regularly with a single sexual partner. She has been using an intrauterine device but has developed an infection with the insertion of her most recent IUD. She must change to another method of birth control. If you were this woman, which method would you choose? Provide evidence that your choice is prudent. *(Application)*

2. In this chapter, much attention is given to the theoretical and actual effectiveness of various types of birth control. When you look at Table 6-3, which column should carry more weight in your decision making—the theoretical or the actual effectiveness? Give reasons for your answer. *(Analysis)*

3. You have been asked to lead a discussion in your health class about the pros and cons of legalized abortion. You may discuss any information in this chapter relevant to this issue. (You may add other topics not mentioned in this chapter as well.) List the topics you will discuss and briefly describe the importance of each to the issue of abortion. *(Synthesis)*

4. Devise an assessment that will help people evaluate their attitudes toward abortion. Explain why you think that your assessment tool will accurately evaluate these attitudes. *(Evaluation)*

KEY

Application: Using information in a new situation.
Analysis: Breaking down information into component parts.
Synthesis: Putting together information from different sources.
Evaluation: Making informed decisions.

Reflecting On Your Health

1. Contracting sexually transmitted infections can endanger your health and your ability to have children. What is the relationship between responsible sexual behavior and reproductive health in your life?

2. If you are a man, what did you learn in this chapter about female reproductive health that was new to you? If you are a woman, what did you learn in this chapter about male reproductive health that was new to you? How will this new knowledge affect your behavior toward the opposite sex? How might it affect your attitudes?

3. Most contraceptive methods focus on the female reproductive system. Because of this focus, should women have the primary responsibility for contraception? Why or why not?

4. In the United States, a woman's right to choose to have an abortion is protected by law. Do you think that the law should be changed to criminalize abortion? If so, why? Should abortion be legal only in certain circumstances? If so, when?

5. Table 6-1 lists selected teratogens. If a woman knowingly exposes her embryo/fetus to teratogenic drugs such as alcohol, should she be prosecuted in the criminal justice system? Why or why not?

References

American Academy of Pediatrics (AAP). (1999). Circumcision policy statement. *Pediatrics, 103*:686-693.

Cook, R. L., & Rosenberg, M. J. (1998). Do spermicides containing nonoxynol-9 prevent sexually transmitted infections? A meta-analysis. *Sexually Transmitted Diseases, 25*:144-150.

Croxatto, H. B., & Makarainen, L. (1998). The pharmacodynamics and efficacy of Implanon. An overview of the data. *Contraception, 58*:(6 Suppl), 91S-97S.

Dardano, K. L., & Burkman, R. T. (1999). The intrauterine contraceptive device: An often-forgotten and maligned method of contraception. *American Journal of Obstetrics and Gynecology, 181*:1-5.

Daugherty, J. E. (1998). Treatment strategies for premenstrual syndrome. *American Family Physician, 58*:183-192, 197-198.

Dyer, C. (1999). Legal suit over Norplant collapses. *British Medical Journal, 318*:485.

Evanoff, A., & Newton, W. P. (1998). Treatment of premature ejaculation. *Journal of Family Practice, 46*:280-281.

Glass, C. A., & Bruner, J. P. (2000). Postpartum depression. In M. E. Rivlin & R. W. Martin (Eds.), *Manual of clinical problems in obstetrics and gynecology*, 5th ed. (pp. 204-208). Philadelphia, PA: Lippincott, Williams & Wilkins.

Greenberg, J. S., Bruess, C. E., & Haffner, D. W. (2000). *Human sexuality*. Sudbury, MA: Jones and Bartlett Publishers.

Hatcher, R. A., Trussel, J., Stewart, F., Cates, W. Jr., Stewart, G. K., Guest, F., & Kowal, D. (1998). *Contraceptive technology.* (17th ed.). New York: Ardent Media.

Jones, K. P. (1999). Oral contraception: current use and attitudes. *Contraception, 59*(1 Suppl):17S-20S.

Laumann, E. O., Paik, A., & Rosen, R. C. (1999). Sexual dysfunction in the United States: Prevalence and predictors. *Journal of the American Medical Association, 281*:537-544.

Leu, Y, Sinha Hikim, A. P., Want, C., Leung, A., Baravarian, S., Reutrakul, V., Sangsawan, R., Chaichana, S., & Swerdloff, R. S. (1998) Triptolide: A potential male contraceptive. *Journal of Andrology, 19*:479-486.

Lock, M. (1994). Menopause in cultural context. *Experimental Gerontology, 29*:307-317.

Munkelwitz, R., & Gilbert, B. R. (1998). Are boxer shorts really better? A critical analysis of the role of underwear type in male subfertility. *Journal of Urology, 160*:1329-1333.

Paick, J. S., Jeong, H., & Park, M. S. (1998). Penile sensitivity in men with premature ejaculation. *International Journal of Impotence Research, 10*:247-250.

Reissing, E. D., Binik, Y. M., & Khalife, S. (1999). Does vaginismus exist? A critical review of the literature. *Journal of Nervous and Mental Disease, 187*:261-274.

Rivlin, M. E. (2000). Toxic shock syndrome. In M. E. Rivlin & R. W. Martin (Eds.), *Manual of clinical problems in obstetrics and gynecology*, 5th ed. (pp. 306-310). Philadelphia, PA: Lippincott, Williams & Wilkins.

Roumen, F. J., & Dieben, T. O. (1999). Clinical acceptability of an ethylene-vinyl-acetate nonmedicated vaginal ring. *Contraception, 59*:59-62.

Schnyder, U., Schnyder-Luthi, C., Ballinari, P., & Blaser, A. (1998). Therapy for vaginismus: In vivo versus in vitro desensitization. *Canadian Journal of Psychiatry, 43*:941-944.

Swerdloff, R. S., Bagatell, C. J., Wang, C., Anawalt, B. D., Berman, N., Steiner, B., & Bremner, W. J. (1998). Suppression of spermatogenesis in man induced by Nal-Glu gonadotropin releasing hormone anatagonist and testosterone enanthate (TE) is maintained by TE alone. *Journal of Clinical Endocrinology and Metabolism, 83*:3527-3533.

Thys-Jacobs, S., Starkey, P., Bernstein, D., & Tian, J. (1998). Calcium carbonate and the premenstrual syndrome: Effects on premenstrual and menstrual symptoms. Premenstrual Syndrome Study Group. *American Journal of Obstetrics and Gynecology, 179*:444-452.

Ugarriza, D. N., Klingner, S., & O'Brien, S. (1998). Premenstrual syndrome: Diagnosis and intervention. *Nurse Practitioner, 23*(9):40, 45, 49-52.

Vincent, A. J., Malakooti, N., Zhang, J., Rogers, P. A., Affandi, B., & Salamonsen, L. A. (1999). Endometrial breakdown in women using Norplant is associated with migratory cells expressing matrix metalloproteinase-9 (gelatinase B). *Human Reproduction, 14*:807-815.

Wasson, J. H., Reda, D. J., Bruskewitz, R. C., Elinson, J., Keller, A. M., & Henderson, W. G. (1995). A comparison of transurethral surgery with watchful waiting for moderate symptoms of benign prostatic hyperplasia. *New England Journal of Medicine, 332*(2):75-79.

Weisberg. E., Fraser, I. S., Lacarra, M., Mishell, D. R. Jr., Alvarez, F., Bracher, V., & Nash, H. A. (1999) Efficacy, bleeding patterns, and side effects of a 1-year contraceptive vaginal ring. *Contraception, 59*:311-318.

chapter 7

Drug Use and Abuse

Drugs. For many people, this word produces thoughts of shadowy characters secretively injecting illegal and dangerous compounds into their veins. This word may also evoke images of boarded-up crack houses, young people "zoned out" like this girl after inhaling paint fumes, and women being assaulted while under the influence of date rape drugs. To others, the word *drugs* brings positive thoughts, such as physicians prescribing medicines to relieve the signs and symptoms of illness. Other images might include your sitting comfortably in the dentist's chair while drugs block the pain of the drill, or a person with cancer being treated with powerful chemical therapies to eliminate deadly, abnormal cells. What are drugs? Why do drugs elicit both negative and positive images?

Drugs are nonfood chemicals that alter the way a person thinks, feels, functions, or behaves. For thousands of years, people have taken naturally occurring drugs that produce medicinal benefits or **psychoactive** (mood-altering or mind-altering) effects. Nearly everyone uses drugs, for a variety of reasons. Most people have taken aspirin or other pain relievers to treat

"Drugs . . . can have serious negative effects on the health and well-being of individuals when used improperly."

headaches, sipped cups of coffee or caffeinated soft drinks to stay awake, or drunk alcoholic beverages to celebrate special occasions or to complement meals. Each of these familiar products contains drugs that have beneficial uses, but they can have serious negative effects on the health and well-being of individuals when used improperly. Additionally, inappropriate drug use contributes to numerous social problems that plague our society, such as crime, unemployment, and family violence and dissolution.

This chapter examines the effects of certain drugs on the functioning of the brain, the general nature of drug use and abuse, and the various problems associated with the use of these chemicals. ▌ **Table 7-1** lists the major types of drugs that affect brain functioning and provides examples of each. Since many Americans use alcoholic beverages and tobacco, Chapter 8 focuses on the effects of these products on health. Some people take steroid hormones to improve their appearance; see pages 260–261 in Chapter 11 for more information concerning the effects of steroids on health.

What You'll Learn

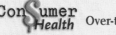

www.jbpub.com/healthyliving

The web site for this book offers many useful tools and is a great source for supplementary health information for both students and instructors. Visit the site at www.jbpub.com/healthyliving for information on these topics:

Drug Use, Misuse, and Abuse
Illegal Drug Use in the U.S.
Drug Dependence
Depressants
Drug Treatment and Prevention

Chapter Overview

Differences between drug use, misuse, and abuse.
The effects of psychoactive drugs on the mind and body.
Why people use psychoactive drugs.
Patterns of drug use in the United States.
How physiological and psychological drug dependence develops.
The risk factors for drug dependence.
The long-term effects of drug abuse.
How the FDA regulates over-the-counter drugs.
Goals and strategies for drug treatment and prevention.

DIVERSITY *Health*   Khat

Con$umer *Health*   Over-the-Counter Medicines

Managing Your Health   Falling Asleep without Prescriptions

across the lifespan   Drug Use and Abuse

Student Workbook

Applying Concepts for Healthy Living · A Workbook

Self Assessment: Are You Dependent on Drugs?
Changing Health Habits: Are You Using Drugs Inappropriately?

Do You Know?

• How drugs can affect the brain?
• If smoking marijuana is safer than smoking cigarettes?
• Which dietary supplements contain drugs that may be dangerous?

Table 7-1 — Psychoactive Drugs: Effects on the Body

Drug Category	Examples: Trade or Other Names	Physical Dependence	Psycho-Logical Dependence	Tolerance	Possible Side Effects	Overdose Effects	Withdrawal Effects
Opiates	Heroin (China white), morphine, codeine-containing products, nethadone, Demerol, Talwin, Darvon, Percodan	Moderate to high	Moderate to high	Yes	Euphoria, sleepiness, depressed breathing, nausea	Slowed breathing, convulsions, coma, death	Teary eyes, watery nose, yawning, tremors, anxiety, abdominal cramps
Depressants	Alcohol*, barbiturates (Goofballs), Valium, Halcion, Quaalude, "roofies" (Rohypnol)	Varies	Varies	Yes	Slurred speech, drunken behavior	Depressed breathing, dilated pupils, coma, death	Depression, anxiety, sleeplessness, convulsions, death
Stimulants	Caffeine, cocaine (snow, Big C), methamphetamine, crystal meth (crystals), Preludin, Ritalin, Dexadrine or "dex", Black beauties, Black hollies	Possible	High	Yes	Alertness, euphoria, increased pulse rate and blood pressure, sleeplessness, lack of appetite	Fever, hallucinations, convulsions, death	Prolonged sleep, irritability, depression, anxiety, moodiness
Hallucinogens	LSD blotters, mescaline, STP, psilocybin, high doses of PCP, Peyote, Psychedelic mushrooms	None (LSD and mescaline) Others: unknown	Unknown	Yes	Euphoria, hallucinations, poor time perception	Anxiety, psychotic behavior	None reported
Marijuana (cannabis)	Pot, hash, hashish oil, Acapulco gold, blunts, buds, Colombo	Unknown	Moderate	Possible	Euphoria, relaxation, increased appetite, distorted time perception	Anxiety, paranoia	Anxiety, depression
Inhalants	Gasoline, paint thinners and removers, freon, aerosols, butyl nitrate	None	Possible	No	Euphoria, sleepiness, confusion, slurred speech	Brain, kidney, or liver damage; headaches; death	Anxiety
Drugs with mixed effects	Nicotine†, PCP, MDMA (Ecstasy)	Unknown	High (PCP) Unknown (MDMA)	Yes	Hallucinations and altered perceptions (PCP)	Psychosis, possible death (PCP)	Unknown

*See Chapter 8.
†See Chapter 9.
Sources: *Drugs of abuse* (1996). Washington, DC: U.S. Department of Justice, Drug Enforcement Administration; Goldberg, R. (1997). *Drugs across the spectrum*. Englewood, CO: Morton Publishing Co.; and Hanson, G. & Venturelli, P. J. (1998). *Drugs and Society*. Sudbury, MA: Jones & Bartlett Publishers.

Drug Use, Misuse, and Abuse

The typical American household has a supply of pain relievers, cold remedies, cough syrups, and other medications. *Medications* are drugs that have beneficial uses such as treating diseases or correcting physiological abnormalities. Medicinal drugs are frequently misused. **Drug misuse** is the temporary and improper use of a legal drug. ▌**Table 7-2** lists some typical misuses of drugs.

A physician's prescription is necessary to legitimately purchase the most powerful and potentially hazardous medications. Most of the active compounds contained in prescription drugs have been tested scientifically for safety and effectiveness. However, people can buy thousands of medicines without prescriptions, commonly called over-the-counter, or OTC, drugs. Many over-the-counter remedies contain chemicals that have not been evaluated scientifically. Although people often think that OTC drugs are completely safe, any substance that has druglike effects can be dangerous if used improperly. Aspirin and antihistamines, for example, are toxic (poisonous) when ingested in high doses. A later section of this chapter examines problems associated with the use of certain OTC drugs.

Foods are not considered drugs, but many foods contain substances such as caffeine that affect the body. Furthermore, when some vitamins and minerals are consumed in large doses, they have druglike activity in the body. For example, physicians occasionally prescribe large doses of niacin (a B vitamin) to lower the blood cholesterol levels of certain patients. Many people, however, take massive doses of vitamins and minerals without consulting physicians because they think nutrients are safe to ingest. These individuals are not aware that many vitamins and minerals are toxic when taken in such high doses. Chapters 9 and 16 discuss hazards associated with consuming large amounts of nutritional supplements.

In some instances, drug use becomes **drug abuse**, the intentional improper or nonmedical use of any drug. Drug abuse occurs whenever the use of a substance negatively affects the health and well-being of the user, his or her family, or society. People are more likely to abuse psychoactive drugs than other drugs because of their effects on the mind.

The government controls the use of most psychoactive drugs because of their potential for abuse. Title II of The Comprehensive Drug Abuse Prevention and Control Act of 1970, usually referred to as the Controlled Substances Act, is the legal foundation of narcotics enforcement in the United States. It classifies many psychoactive substances into five drug schedules according to their potential for abuse and degree of medical usefulness (▌**Table 7-3**). Schedule I drugs are commonly abused and have little medicinal value. In the United States, it is illegal to use, possess, or sell Schedule I drugs. Schedule V drugs are infrequently abused and have important medicinal uses. Schedule II, III, IV, and V drugs are available by prescription.

Officials with the Drug Enforcement Administration (DEA) evaluate medical and scientific information from the U.S. Department of Health and Human Services (HHS) before classifying a drug as a controlled substance. The placement of a drug into one of the five schedules does not necessarily reflect its potential for being abused or producing harmful effects. Heroin, PCP, and marijuana are Schedule I drugs, but the effects of abusing heroin or PCP are more serious than those of abusing marijuana. Alcohol and nicotine are not scheduled drugs, yet the widespread abuse of these addictive substances is responsible for disabling and killing more people each year than the combined use of all controlled drugs.

drugs nonfood chemicals that alter the way a person thinks, feels, functions, or behaves.

pyschoactive having mind-altering or mood-altering effects.

drug misuse the temporary and improper use of a legal drug.

drug abuse the intentional improper or nonmedical use of any drug.

Table 7-2 Typical Drug Misuse Behaviors

Behavior	Example
Discontinuing the use of prescribed medications prematurely even though you have been instructed to take it for a longer period	Taking an antibiotic only until symptoms disappear
Mixing drugs	Taking barbiturates and drinking alcohol at a party (combining these depressant drugs can have deadly consequences)
Taking more than the recommended dosage	Consuming ten multiple vitamin and mineral supplements instead of one daily
Saving and using medications past their expiration date	Taking a pain reliever that was prescribed 5 years ago
Sharing medicines	Giving your prescribed allergy medicine to a friend

Table 7-3 Drug Schedules

Schedule	Examples of Drugs
I	Heroin, LSD, mescaline, methaqualone, peyote, PCP, psilocybin, THC, hashish, marijuana, Rohypnol ("roofies" or the "date-rape drug")
II	Ritalin, opium, Percodan, Dilaudid, cocaine, Methadone, Marinol, Demerol, morphine, amphetamines, barbiturates (fast-acting)
III	Paregoric, anabolic steroids, tylenol with codeine, vicodan
IV	Valium, Librium, Serax, Halcion, Darvon, Placidyl, phenobarbital, Miltown
V	APC with codeine, Robitussin A–C, Lomotil

Sources: *Physicians' desk reference.* (1996). Oradell, NJ: Medical Economics Company, Inc.; and *Drugs of abuse.* (1996). Washington, DC: U.S. Department of Justice, Drug Enforcement Administration.

People abuse illegal drugs such as cocaine, legally available psychoactive substances such as alcohol, some prescription drugs, and OTC remedies. Many individuals abuse a combination of legal and illegal drugs. Regardless of its legal status, no drug is completely safe. The risk that a drug will cause serious side effects largely depends on the type of drug, the amount taken over time, and the health of the person using the drug.

Healthy
LIVING PRACTICES

Since no drug is completely safe, consider the effects a drug can have on your health and well-being before using it.

Psychoactive Drugs: Effects on the Mind and Body

How Psychoactive Drugs Affect the Brain

Psychoactive drugs affect the nervous system, the communications network of the body, by changing the way the brain perceives and processes information received from the environment. Chapter 2 describes the nervous system, which includes the brain and spinal cord (central nervous system, or CNS) and the sensory and motor nerves that transmit messages to and from the central nervous system.

Psychoactive drugs interact with nerve cells in the brain, altering the activity of chemical transmitters that carry messages from one nerve to another. As a result, these drugs influence perceptions, thought processes, feelings, and behaviors. Many commonly abused drugs affect specific regions of the brain, referred to as reward centers because they have a positive influence on mood and alertness. As a result, when used initially, these drugs often produce **euphoria**, an intense feeling of well-being commonly called a "high." Although altering the normal internal chemical environment of the brain affects a person's mood and behavior, external conditions can modify these responses.

What Happens to Drugs in the Body?

After being taken, psychoactive drugs enter the bloodstream and eventually reach the brain, where they produce their characteristic effects. As drugs circulate, the body may eliminate small amounts of these substances in urine, feces, or exhaled breath. In most instances, the remaining drugs undergo **detoxification**, the process of converting harmful substances into less dangerous compounds that can be excreted. Detoxification usually occurs in the liver. The body stores some drugs, primarily in fat, for days and possibly weeks after exposure, particularly when detoxification occurs slowly. Until the body completely eliminates a drug, small amounts of the substance may be detectable in blood or urine.

A state of **intoxication** occurs when the amount of a substance reaches poisonous levels in the body. This level varies among individuals, but genetic factors, body size, physical health, and prior drug exposure influence a person's ability to metabolize, or process, a drug. The signs and symptoms of intoxication include slurred speech, poor muscular coordination, and mental confusion.

An *overdose* occurs when an excessive amount of a drug circulates in the bloodstream and overwhelms the ability of the body to detoxify or eliminate the substance rapidly. Overdoses of OTC, prescription, and illegal drugs can damage or destroy tissues. In some instances, drug overdoses can be fatal. Table 7-1 describes some signs and symptoms of overdoses of various psychoactive drugs.

Polyabuse, abusing more than one drug at a time, is a common practice. For example, individuals often drink alcoholic beverages while they use heroin, barbiturates, cocaine, or other drugs. When people take different drugs that have similar actions, the effects of each drug may be greatly multiplied. This phenomenon, called **synergism**, can be deadly. Alcohol and barbiturates, for example, are depressant drugs that slow the functioning of the central nervous system. If a person drinks a few alcoholic beverages while taking barbiturates, the combined effects of these substances can depress respiration severely, producing coma or death. Polyabuse can cause drug interactions in addition to synergism that can have serious and even fatal outcomes. Many people are not aware that drinking alcohol while taking acetaminophen, a compound contained in popular over-the-counter pain relievers such as Tylenol, can cause liver failure and death.

Healthy
LIVING PRACTICES

To avoid the effects of drug synergism or interactions, do not combine drugs, including alcohol and OTC medicines, without consulting a physician or registered pharmacist.

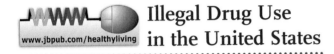

Illegal Drug Use in the United States

www.jbpub.com/healthyliving

The Prevalence of Illegal Drug Use

Researchers conduct surveys and interviews to estimate the prevalence of illegal (illicit) drug use in the United States. For example, the 1998 National Household Survey on Drug Abuse sampled 25,500 Americans 12 years of age or older. From the data they collected, researchers concluded that in 1998 an estimated 13.6 million Americans were illicit drug users, meaning they had used an illicit drug in the month prior to interview. Although the 1998 figure represents essentially no change from the number of illicit drug users during 1997, far fewer Americans were using these substances than in the late 1970s. In 1979 researchers estimated that 25 million people in the United States used illegal drugs (Substance Abuse and Mental Health Services Administration [SAMHSA], 1999).

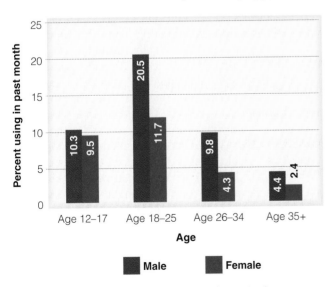

▲Figure 7-1 **Percentage of People in the United States Who Were Illicit Drug Users in 1998.** Source: U.S. Department of Health and Human Services (1999). *National Household Survey on Drug Abuse. Population Estimates, 1998.* Rockville, MD: U.S. Public Health Service.

According to the 1998 National Household Survey on Drug Abuse, certain segments of the American population use illicit drugs more than do other groups, and more men than women take drugs (█ Figure 7-1). Slightly over 18% of unemployed adults were current users of illicit drugs in 1998; only 6.4% of employed adults took these substances. Among people between 26 and 34 years of age, those who lacked high school diplomas had higher rates of illicit drug use (9.8%) while college graduates had the lowest rate of use (4.8%). In 1998 nearly three-fourths of U.S. drug users were White (SAMHSA, 1999).

Rates of illegal drug use are especially high among teenagers and young adults. Since 1975 researchers at the University of Michigan's Institute for Social Research have conducted Monitoring the Future, an annual survey of American high school and college students, to ascertain their use of drugs. Data from the 1999 survey indicate that approximately 38% of full-time college students took one or more illegal drugs during 1998, up from 33% in 1994. In 1998, 36% of college students used marijuana, up from 29% in 1994, and 26% in 1991. Additionally, the use of LSD ("acid") rose in the mid-90s from 1989, and has since begun to fall. In 1998, 4.4% of college students reported taking LSD during the previous 12 months. In 1994 this figure was about 5%, while in 1989 it was 3.4% (Johnston et al., 1995, 1999b).

Why Do People Use Psychoactive Drugs?

Drug users often provide numerous reasons to explain why they began taking psychoactive substances. Most people begin taking mood-altering drugs for nonmedical purposes. Some individuals use alcohol or other drugs simply as a pleasurable experience. Others use drugs to cope with their psychological problems, reduce stress, or escape from unpleasant aspects of their lives. Curiosity often motivates many teenagers and young adults to experiment with drugs. Movies and advertisements may stimulate this curiosity by showing sophisticated and attractive people smoking cigars or drinking alcoholic beverages, for example, while engaging in enjoyable activities (█ Figure 7-2). Additionally, teenagers may use drugs to impress their peers and gain social acceptance (Hanson & Venturelli, 1998).

Patterns of Psychoactive Drug Use

Drug experimentation and illicit use often occur during the teen years and peak between the ages of 18 and 25 (see Figure 7-1). Most drug abusers in this age group begin by

euphoria (you-FOR-ee-a) an intense feeling of well-being commonly called a "high."

detoxification the process of converting harmful substances into less dangerous compounds.

intoxication the state of being poisoned by a drug or other poisonous substance.

polyabuse abusing more than one drug at a time.

synergism (SIH-ner-jism) the multiplied effects produced by taking combinations of certain drugs.

ijuana use declined among eighth, tenth, and twelfth graders in the United States in 1998, its use was still prevalent. Twenty-two percent of eighth graders and nearly half of twelfth graders surveyed in the Monitoring the Future study reported that they had tried marijuana (Johnston et al., 1999a).

Any combination of stimulants, depressants, or hallucinogens may follow marijuana use. After trying these drugs, some young people move on to use opiates. However, not every youthful drug user follows this stepping-stone pattern of drug experimentation. For example, many teenagers who experiment with alcohol or marijuana do not try other psychoactive drugs.

Most people who use illegal drugs recreationally discontinue taking these substances by the time they reach their mid-thirties (see Figure 7-1). By this age, the majority of adults have adopted traditional adult roles that include marriage, parenthood, and careers. These individuals usually recognize that abusing alcohol, tobacco, or illicit drugs can be self-destructive. However, people over age 30 are more likely than younger individuals to abuse their prescribed medications. In fact, abuse of prescription drugs is rare in 14- to 24-year-olds (Lieb et al., 1998).

Drug Dependence

www.jbpub.com/healthyliving

Most people who use psychoactive drugs such as alcohol or marijuana take them for pleasure, to relax, or to feel comfortable in social settings, which is termed *recreational drug use*. To assess your use of drugs, complete the questionnaire in the student workbook entitled "Are You Dependent on Drugs?"

Drug dependence or **addiction** occurs when users develop a habitual pattern of taking drugs that produces a compulsive need, which is both physical and psychological, to use these substances. The terms *dependency* and *addiction* are often used interchangeably to describe any compulsive behavior that interferes with one's health, work, and relationships.

Dependent individuals are unable to avoid using drugs; most have a history of unsuccessful attempts to stop. Over time, these people escalate their intake of drugs even as they recognize that their actions are harmful to themselves and others. People who are dependent on drugs are so preoccupied with the need to obtain and use these substances that other aspects of their lives, such as handling the responsibilities of family and work, become less important.

Physiological and Psychological Dependence

When people take certain psychoactive drugs repeatedly over an extended period, their bodies make various physiological adjustments to function as normally as possible. For

▲**Figure 7-2 The Media and Drugs.** Academy Award–winning actress Mira Sorvino looking trendy by smoking a cigar. The media frequently portray sophisticated and attractive young people using drugs while engaging in enjoyable activities. As a result, young people may copy such behaviors.

drug dependence or addiction a state in which one develops a habitual pattern of taking drugs that usually produces a compulsive need to use these substances, tolerance, and withdrawal.

tolerance an adaptation to drugs in which the usual dose no longer produces the anticipated degree of physical or psychological effects.

withdrawal a temporary physical and psychological state that occurs when certain drugs are discontinued.

smoking cigarettes, then they consume alcoholic beverages like beer or wine. Some youth inhale chemicals such as those in aerosols and plastic cements to obtain their mind-altering effects. Alcohol, nicotine, and inhalants are often referred to as "gateway" drugs because adolescents use these substances before moving on to other psychoactive drugs (Hansen & Venturelli, 1998). Many adolescents stop experimenting with new drugs after using alcohol or nicotine. If they continue trying drugs, teenagers are likely to use marijuana next. Although mar-

example, dramatic chemical changes occur in the brains of chronic drug users that influence their thought processes and behaviors. As a result, these individuals display the characteristic signs and symptoms of *physical dependence* or *physical addiction:* drug tolerance and withdrawal.

After chronic exposure to certain drugs, the body develops **tolerance**, the ability to endure larger amounts of these substances while the adverse effects decrease. When this occurs, users discover that their usual dose of drugs no longer produces the desired degree of physical or psychological effects. To increase tolerance, addicted individuals must take larger quantities of these substances, increasing the risk of overdose.

Withdrawal is a temporary physical and psychological state that occurs when certain drugs are discontinued. The signs and symptoms of withdrawal include trembling, anxiety, and pain. In cases of barbiturate addiction, withdrawal symptoms are so severe they can cause death. Table 7-1 indicates psychoactive drugs' potentials for producing tolerance, withdrawal, and addiction.

Psychological dependence is a person's need to use certain psychoactive drugs regularly to obtain their pleasurable effects and to relieve boredom, anxiety, or stress. Psychologically dependent people experience powerful cravings for these substances, which motivates drug-seeking behavior. However, it may be difficult to distinguish psychological dependence from physical dependence. As mentioned earlier, psychoactive drugs produce physiological changes in the brain that influence behavior. Thus, these changes may affect a person's emotional responses, including feelings about the need to take psychoactive substances.

Not everyone who habitually uses or abuses psychoactive substances becomes dependent on their use. For example, individuals who drive after becoming drunk at bars or parties are abusing alcohol, but they are not necessarily alcoholics. It is difficult to determine when the habitual use of a psychoactive substance becomes a dependency. Scientists are interested in determining why some people seem to be more susceptible to drug dependency and addiction than others.

Risk Factors for Drug Dependency

Like many other health problems, there is no single risk factor for drug dependency. Substance addiction results from complex interactions among biological, personal, social, and environmental factors. Results of research conducted by the National Institute of Drug Addiction (NIDA) (1997) suggest that certain conditions in the home are probably the most crucial risk factors for children becoming drug abusers. Such factors include home environments in which parents abuse drugs or suffer from mental illness; ineffective parenting, particularly with children who have difficult temperaments or conduct disorders; and a lack of mutual child-parent attachments and parental nurturing. Risk factors for drug abuse that relate to a child's behavior outside of the home include inappropriately shy or aggressive behavior in the classroom; poor school performance; poor social skills; friendships with peers who use drugs; and a belief that parents, the school, peers, and the community approve of drug use. Conversely, *protective factors*, those associated with reduced potential for drug abuse, include strong family and school ties; parental monitoring of behavior with clear rules of conduct; involvement of parents in the lives of children; academic success in school; and the belief that parents, the school, peers, and the community do not approve of drug use.

To avoid the destructive effects of a drug dependency or addiction, do not use psychoactive substances unless you are under a physician's care.

Stimulants

Throughout the world, people have used various stimulant drugs for thousands of years to relieve fatigue, suppress appetite, and improve mood. (See the "Diversity in Health" essay, "Khat.") Stimulants enhance chemical activity in parts of the brain that influence emotions, sleep, attention, and learning. Within minutes after taking stimulants, users are more alert, excitable, and restless. Additionally, these drugs increase blood pressure levels and heart rates.

Amphetamines and Methamphetamines

Synthetic stimulants are amphetamines, methamphetamines, and nonamphetamines (see Table 7-1). Amphetamines such as Dexedrine increase energy and alertness, lessen the need to sleep, produce euphoria, and suppress appetite. Amphetamines and chemically related stimulants have few medicinal uses. Physicians may prescribe these drugs to treat narcolepsy, an uncommon condition characterized by episodes of falling asleep during the day. Although the practice is controversial, some physicians prescribe amphetamines to suppress the appetites of people who are trying to lose weight. Stimulants suppress appetite, but the effects are usually short-lived.

Methamphetamines ("speed") are more powerful forms of amphetamines that have few medically approved uses. In the early 1980s, 21% to 22% of college students reported using amphetamines within the past year. Their use dropped significantly each year from 1983 to 1992, when only 3.6% of college students reported using this drug. From 1993 to 1998, its use rose again, ranging from 4.2% to 5.7% (Johnston et al., 1999).

Methamphetamine is taken orally (usually as a pill) or the powder is snorted. It can also be injected or smoked. In

DIVERSITY in Health | Khat

Which psychoactive drug is associated with weddings and weekends? If your answer is alcohol, you may be wrong. In the East African countries of Somalia and Ethiopia, people chew *khat*, the leaf buds and leaves of the native bush *Catha edulis*, to celebrate weddings and other special events. For centuries, people from these cultures have chewed or smoked khat or drunk tea brewed from its leaves as a socially acceptable and enjoyable pastime. Many homes in Somalia have a special room in which family members and their friends gather to munch khat and chat. Like alcohol and other psychoactive substances that are more familiar to Americans, khat contains chemicals that are known to produce both pleasurable and harmful side effects.

Khat contains cathionine and cathine, compounds that are chemically similar to amphetamines. Not surprisingly, khat produces psychological and physiological responses that resemble those produced by amphetamines and other stimulants. After using khat, people report feeling euphoric and alert; they have little desire to eat, sleep, or engage in sex. Additionally, khat users experience elevated blood pressures and heart rates. After the stimulating and mood-elevating effects of the drug subside, khat users feel anxious and irritable.

Khat impairs thought processes such as mental concentration and judgment; therefore, driving while under its influence can be hazardous. Men who use khat regularly may develop permanent impotence; women who use khat during pregnancy are at risk of giving birth to underweight newborns. Over time, chewing khat damages teeth, contributing to dental decay. During Somalia's recent civil war, reports appeared in the Western press that khat-chewing members of the country's warring militia displayed aggressive, paranoid, and psychotic behavior. These responses usually result from overdoses of khat.

In the early 1990s thousands of Somalians and Ethiopians fled the civil unrest raging in their homelands and sought refuge in Western countries, including England and the United States. After settling in the West, many of these immigrants maintained their habit of using khat. To satisfy their demand, the immigrants purchase khat leaves that have been flown into North America or the United Kingdom from East Africa.

Concerned about the drug's effects on the central nervous system, officials at the U.S. Drug Enforcement Administration added cathine to its list of controlled substances in 1988. In 1993 the Food and Drug Administration issued an import alert that recommended detention of khat by Customs officials to prevent its entry into the United States. Currently, khat use does not pose a major drug enforcement problem. However, the problem of illegal khat use may become more widespread in the United States as more East African immigrants settle in this country.

Sources: Randall, T. (1993). Khat abuse fuels Somali conflict, drains economy. *Journal of the American Medical Association, 269*:12–15; and Wisnisowski, L. A. (1993). Import alert 66-23-*Catha edulis* (khat). Internal Memo, Division of Import Operations & Policy, Food and Drug Administration.

small doses, methamphetamines produce euphoria, appetite loss, excessive perspiration, and pounding heartbeats. The effects of taking larger doses can be frightening: chest pains, irregular heartbeat, fever, hallucinations, and convulsions. People who drive while on methamphetamines exhibit erratic driving patterns such as weaving and drifting off the road. They are also prone to exceeding the speed limit and being involved in high speed collisions (Logan, 1996). Overdoses of methamphetamines can be deadly by resulting in cardiovascular collapse or strokes. When taken by pregnant women, the drug can result in birth defects such as cleft lip and palate, and heart defects. Fetal growth is also stunted (Plessinger, 1998). Withdrawal from methamphetamines often results in anxiety, fatigue, sleeplessness, paranoia, delusions, and severe depression.

In the 1980s drug suppliers from Korea, Taiwan, and the Philippines introduced an illegal crystalline form of methamphetamine called *crystal meth* (also referred to as *meth, crank, ice,* and *glass*). Using crystal meth can produce violent behavior and damage the liver, kidneys, and lungs.

To meet the rapidly growing demand for the substance in the United States, amateur chemists are producing crystal meth in crude laboratories in their homes. The use of such "homemade" drugs is extremely dangerous.

Amphetamines and methamphetamines are two drugs in a group called *club drugs* or *party drugs*. Club drugs include alcohol, LSD (Acid), MDMA (Ecstasy), GHB, GBL, Katamine (Special K), Fentanyl, Rohypnol, amphetamines, and methamphetamines. (We discuss these drugs in this chapter, with the exception of alcohol, which is discussed in Chapter 8.) Adolescents, teenagers, and young adults use these drugs at raves (all-night parties) and in other social situations to reduce anxiety, induce euphoria, or build energy to keep on dancing or partying. However, these drugs are not harmless "fun" drugs and can have long-lasting negative effects on the brain. Therefore, in December of 1999 the NIDA announced a commitment of $54 million for research into these drugs (a funding increase of 40%) and plans to work with a variety of other national groups to educate the public about club drugs (Reuters, 1999).

Cocaine

Cocaine is a white powdery substance extracted from the leaves of the coca bush, which is not the same plant as the cacao tree from which cocoa and chocolate are derived. This potent stimulant has some medical uses, particularly as an **anesthetic**, a substance that interferes with normal sensations. However, cocaine was the most widely used illegal stimulant in the United States during the late 1970s and early 1980s, a time during which the public was misinformed about the drug and its dangers. Additionally, many health-care practitioners did not understand the dangers of cocaine use or its addictive nature, and, as a consequence, cocaine was viewed as glamorous and was used by many celebrities as well as millions of Americans. The popularity of cocaine declined dramatically between 1985 and 1992, most likely from public understanding that accompanied increased knowledge about this drug and its dangerous effects (Hanson & Venturelli, 1998). The level of cocaine use has not changed significantly since 1992. Nevertheless, experts estimate that approximately 600,000 Americans used cocaine frequently in 1998 (SAMHSA, 1999).

Cocaine is highly addictive. In laboratory studies of the drug's effects, animals prefer to self-administer cocaine rather than engage in reproductive behavior or obtain food. Many people who are dependent on cocaine demonstrate similar responses. Cocaine abusers often dissociate themselves from their families, friends, and associates.

Chronic cocaine abuse produces serious health problems (see Table 7-1). People who snort cocaine regularly often suffer from chronic irritation of their nasal passages. This irritation causes nosebleeds, and it can destroy the septum, the cartilaginous tissue that divides the area between the two nostrils. Additionally, snorting cocaine and smoking crack damage lung tissue and increase susceptibility to respiratory tract infections.

Long-term use of cocaine may interfere with normal sexual functioning. Men who use cocaine regularly often experience an inability to achieve erections and a reduced sexual drive. Women who are chronic users may experience difficulty achieving orgasms, infertility, and menstrual problems.

Cocaine use can have deadly consequences. People infected with hepatitis or AIDS can spread these diseases by sharing their used hypodermic needles with uninfected drug users. Additionally, cocaine use increases the risk of dy-ing suddenly from life-threatening disorders of the circulatory system such as irregular and rapid heartbeat, high blood pressure, stroke, and heart attacks. Death is especially likely when people take cocaine with other psychoactive substances such as alcohol and heroin. During the past two decades, several well-known individuals have died as a result of using cocaine (■ **Figure 7-3**).

While under the influence of cocaine, some individuals experience severe psychotic reactions, including paranoia, that may result in violent behavior. It is not uncommon for cocaine abusers to report having delusions such as the sensation that bugs are crawling beneath their skin. The psychological symptoms of cocaine intoxication also leads some users to attempt suicide, and a number of them succeed.

anesthetics drugs that interfere with normal sensations.

Caffeine

Worldwide, caffeine is the most widely used psychoactive substance (Nehlig, 1999). Caffeine and its related chemical compounds occur naturally in several varieties of plants that we use to make foods and beverages, including coffee, tea, and cocoa. People may ingest caffeine when they consume caffeinated soft drinks or they take certain over-the-counter

▲ **Figure 7-3 Celebrities Who Have Died as a Result of Using Cocaine.** Cocaine use increases the risk of dying suddenly from life-threatening disorders of the circulatory system, such as irregular and rapid heartbeat, stroke, and even heart attacks. During the past two decades, several well-known individuals have died as a result of using cocaine, including comedian/actor John Belushi, actor River Phoenix, and comic Chris Farley (shown above left).

medications. ▊ **Table 7-4** lists the amounts of caffeine contained in certain beverages, foods, and over-the-counter products.

Caffeine has been generally recognized as a stimulant that causes limited dependence. People often benefit from

Table 7-4	Caffeine Content of Popular Beverages, Foods, and Products	
Food, Beverage, or Product		**Typical Amount/ Range (mg)**
Coffee		
Cappuccino (2 oz)		100
Espresso (2 oz)		100
Brewed, drip method (5 oz)		60–180
Brewed, percolator (5 oz)		40–170
Instant (5 oz)		30–120
Decaffeinated, brewed (5 oz)		2–5
Decaffeinated, instant (5 oz)		1–5
Tea		
Brewed, U.S. brands (5 oz)		20–90
Brewed, imported brands (5 oz)		25–110
Instant (5 oz)		25–50
Iced (5 oz)		28–32
Cocoa-Containing Products		
Cocoa (5 oz)		2–20
Chocolate milk (5 oz)		1–4
Milk chocolate (1 oz)		1–15
Dark chocolate, semi-sweet (1 oz)		5–35
Chocolate flavored syrup (1 oz)		4
Soft Drinks (12 oz)		
Dr. Pepper		40
Cola-type beverages		
Regular		30–46
Diet		2–58
Caffeine-free		0
Mountain Dew, Mello Yello		52
Jolt		75–100
Over-the-Counter Medications		
Vivarin (1 pill)		200
Nodoz (1 pill)		100
Anacin, Empirin, or Midol (2 pills)		64
Excedrin (2 pills)		130

Sources: Based on Caffeine: Grounds for concern? (1994). *University of California at Berkeley Wellness Letter, 10*(6):5; and Goldberg, R. (1997). *Drugs across the spectrum*, Englewood, CO: Morton Publishing Co.; and Sizer, F., & Whitney, E. (1997). *Nutrition, concepts and controversies.* Belmont, CA: Wadsworth Publishing Co.

taking small amounts of caffeine (less than 250 milligrams per day) because the stimulant improves work capacity, level of alertness, and mood. However, after abstaining from caffeine for about half a day, a person who is accustomed to taking the drug typically experiences withdrawal symptoms that include headache, tiredness, irritability, and depression.

The average American consumes about 200 mg of caffeine daily—the equivalent of about 2 cups of coffee or 5 cola beverages. People who drink a few cups of caffeine-containing beverages daily usually do not suffer ill effects. However, individuals who consume more than 600 mg per day often experience psychological as well as physical problems known as *caffeinism*. The manifestations of caffeinism include nervousness, trembling, irritation of the stomach lining, insomnia, increased urine production, diarrhea, sweating, and rapid heart rate. People who do not regularly consume caffeine or who are sensitive to it may develop caffeinism after taking as little as 250 mg of the drug daily.

Most research data indicate that typical patterns of caffeine consumption are not harmful (Hanson & Venturelli, 1999). Since caffeine stimulates the heart, people with heart disease should consult their physicians about the need to restrict their intake of this drug. If you want to lower your level of caffeine intake or abstain from it, reduce your intake gradually to avoid withdrawal symptoms, especially headaches.

Healthy
▊ LIVING PRACTICES ▊

If you have ill effects such as anxiety or sleep disturbances from consuming too much caffeine, gradually wean yourself from the drug to avoid its withdrawal symptoms

www.jbpub.com/healthyliving

Depressants

Depressants produce **sedative** (calming) and **hypnotic** (trancelike) effects as well as drowsiness. These drugs slow the activity of the cerebral cortex, the part of the brain that is responsible for thought processes. Depressant drugs include alcohol, barbiturates such as phenobarbital (Luminal), and minor tranquilizers such as diazepam (Valium).

Physicians frequently prescribe sedatives and minor tranquilizers, especially for people suffering from insomnia or mild anxiety. In many instances, people can treat their mild anxiety or insomnia without powerful depressants. Anxious individuals can try to reduce their feelings of stress by practicing the relaxation techniques described in Chapter 3. The "Managing Your Health" feature entitled "Falling Asleep without Prescriptions" provides sugges-

Falling Asleep without Prescriptions

If you experience occasional sleepless nights, the following self-treatment tips for insomnia may be helpful.

1. Take a warm bath or shower before bedtime.
2. Practice progressive muscular relaxation while in bed (see Chapter 3 for details).
3. Don't eat big meals or drink large amounts of fluids in the evening.

Have a light snack before bedtime, but avoid alcohol or caffeine-containing foods.

4. Reserve time for vigorous regular exercise earlier in the day and engage in lighter physical activity at least 2 hours before bedtime.
5. Don't stay in bed if you can't fall asleep; get out of bed, read a dull book, or watch a boring TV show.

Return to bed when you begin to feel sleepy.

6. Take an over-the-counter (OTC) sleep aid only as a last resort. Recognize that most of these medications contain antihistamines that lose their effectiveness if used regularly.
7. Avoid bedtime doses of OTC pain relievers that contain caffeine.

tions that may induce sleep without the use of depressants or other drugs.

Dangerous side effects can result when people misuse depressants. All of these drugs slow the heart and respiratory rate, which increases the risk of dying from respiratory failure after taking an overdose. Combining depressants—for example, drinking alcohol while taking Valium—produces synergistic effects. Such synergism of depressants can be life threatening.

Tolerance and dependency occur with regular use of depressants. Withdrawal from these drugs can cause *delirium* (mental confusion and disorientation), and *seizures* (abnormal brain activity that results in uncontrollable muscular movements). Some addicted people die while undergoing withdrawal from depressants.

Rohypnol

Rohypnol (row-HIP-nole), commonly called roofies (along with a variety of other street names), is one of a few "date-rape drugs." (See "GHB and GBL.") While under the influence of Rohypnol, women are unable to resist rapists, and they cannot recall, for various lengths of time, what happened to them while under the influence (Anglin et al., 1997). Because of concern about Rohypnol and other similarly abused sedative-hypnotics, Congress passed the "Drug-Induced Rape Prevention and Punishment Act of 1996" to increase federal penalties for use of any controlled substance to aid in sexual assault (NIDA, 1999c).

Although not approved for use in the United States, this drug is widely available in Mexico, Colombia, and Europe where it is used for the treatment of insomnia. Like other depressants, its effects include sedation, muscle relaxation, and anxiety reduction. It also causes dizziness, loss of mo-

tor control, lack of coordination, slurred speech, confusion, and gastrointestinal disturbances, all of which can last 12 hours or more. Abuse of Rohypnol is a growing public health problem, especially among teenagers in the United States (Drug Enforcement Administration [DEA], 1996).

GHB and GBL

Gamma hydroxybutyrate, better known as *GHB,* was formerly sold in health food stores as a dietary supplement to induce sleep and build muscle. (Its over-the-counter sale was banned by the FDA in 1990.) The longer periods of sleep it induced were supposed to allow release of human growth hormone, which has been linked with increased muscle mass. However, GHB users reported unpleasant side effects such as nausea and shaking. More dangerously, this drug has induced seizures and coma in some users (Kam & Yoong, 1998).

The United States Food and Drug Administration (FDA) considers GHB an unapproved new drug. As a result of the increased abuse of GHB in the United States as well as its use as a date-rape drug, the DEA requested the United States Department of Health and Human Services to conduct a scientific and medical evaluation of GHB and submit a scheduling recommendation (FDA, 1999b).

In January 1999 the FDA warned consumers about a drug related to GHB: gamma butyrolactone, or *GBL.* After ingestion, the body converts GBL to GHB. Some products labeled as dietary supplements contain GBL, and claim to build muscles, improve physical performance, enhance sex, reduce stress, and induce sleep. However, GBL-related products have been associated with

sedatives a group of drugs that produce calming effects.

hypnotics drugs that produce trance-like effects and drowsiness.

reports of at least 55 adverse health effects, including seizures, vomiting, slowed breathing, slowed heart beat rate, and coma. One death had been reported from GBL at the time of the FDA warning (FDA, 1999a). The FDA considers GBL an unapproved new drug, as it does GHB. After the FDA warning, all but one manufacturer of GBL-related products agreed to recall these drugs and to stop their manufacture and distribution (FAD, 1999b).

Healthy
■LIVING PRACTICES■

- Do not accept drinks from casual acquaintances or strangers; they may contain dangerous drugs.
- Do not drive or operate machinery while under the influence of depressant drugs because these substances can impair your thought processes and muscular coordination.
- Do not drink alcohol while taking other depressants. The synergistic effect of combining these compounds can be deadly.

Opiates

analgesics
(an-al-GEEZ-iks) a group of drugs that alleviate pain.

narcotics a group of drugs that induce euphoria and sleep as well as alter the perception of pain.

Opiates include *opium,* the dried sap extracted from seedpods of opium poppies shown in ■ **Figure 7-4,** and drugs such as codeine, morphine, heroin, and Percodan that are derived from opium. Synthetic opiates include Darvon and Demerol. These compounds have important medical uses as sedatives, analgesics, and narcotics. **Analgesics** alleviate pain; **narcotics** alter the perception of pain and induce euphoria and sleep. (Many people incorrectly use the term *narcotic* to describe any illegal drug.)

In addition to relieving pain, opiates slow the activity of the intestinal tract, so they are useful in treating severe diarrhea. Physicians frequently prescribe codeine-containing syrups to subdue severe coughing. Despite their medicinal value, opiates are extremely dangerous

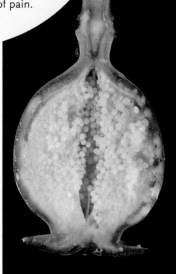

◄**Figure 7-4 Longitudinal Section Through a Seedpod of the Opium Poppy.** The dried sap extracted from opium poppy seedpods is used to make the narcotic opium. Some white sap can be seen on the cut edge of this seedpod.

when taken in an uncontrolled manner. These drugs are highly addictive; people who use opiates daily develop dependence and tolerance within a few weeks.

After it enters this country, opium is chemically converted to heroin by drug dealers. They also add various materials, such as quinine or cornstarch, to dilute the drug's concentration. Substances that dilute the concentration of a drug are called *adulterants.* Since heroin abusers lack information concerning the potency of their drug purchases after chemical conversion by drug dealers, they risk taking overdoses or having allergic reactions to the adulterants.

Heroin is the most widely abused illegal drug worldwide (Hansen & Venturelli, 1998). Survey data indicate that approximately 2% of American high school students have used heroin at least once, approximately 1% used it in the year prior to the survey, and approximately 0.5% are current users (Johnston et al., 1999a). These percentages are higher than from 1990 to 1996. Since heroin imported from Colombia and Mexico is cheaper than it used to be and is very potent, teenagers are able to snort heroin rather than inject it, making it easier for them to use this drug for the first time (Schwartz, 1998). However, heroin use is increasing in all age groups. Experts estimate that about 500,000 to 750,000 Americans are addicted to heroin (Hanson & Venturelli, 1998).

Using opiates, especially heroin, can cause a variety of serious health problems. Excessive doses of opiates depress the CNS, slowing respiration and reducing mental functioning. Such overdoses require immediate medical attention and can be deadly. Sharing needles that are used to inject heroin intravenously can cause life-threatening bacterial infections and viral diseases, such as AIDS and hepatitis.

Marijuana

Marijuana is the most widely used illicit drug in the United States. An estimated 11 million Americans over 12 years of age use marijuana. This represents 5% of the population age 12 and older (SAMHSA, 1999).

The marijuana plant *(Cannabis sativa)* contains the psychoactive compound delta-9-tetrahydrocannabinol, or THC. *Hashish* is a dried resin made from marijuana flowers, which contain a higher concentration of THC than the leaves of the plant. Also extracted from marijuana flowers, hashish oil contains a greater percentage of THC than hashish. A few drops of hashish oil added to a cigarette produce psychoactive effects that are the same as smoking a marijuana cigarette, or *joint.*

When people smoke marijuana or hashish, THC enters the brain rapidly. THC alters muscular coordination and normal thought processes such as mental concentration, problem solving, time perception, and short-term memory. Like the effects of alcohol, these alterations can have serious consequences for drivers. Results of a study on the effects of marijuana on driving abilities reveal that smoking one marijuana cigarette affects drivers' equilibrium and ability to brake quickly during the hour following ingestion of the drug (Liguori et al., 1998). Additionally, an analysis of the blood and urine from fatally injured drivers indicate that drug use (including alcohol) is a factor in 52% of motor-vehicle fatalities. After alcohol, the most common drug found in the blood was marijuana, and marijuana was most prevalent in the 15- to 30-year age group (Logan & Schwilke, 1996).

Marijuana and hashish smoke contain numerous irritants that can damage the bronchial tubes and lungs. Some of these irritants are the same cancer-causing substances found in cigarette smoke (Fung et al., 1999). Compared to smoking filter-tipped cigarettes, smoking marijuana results in about a fivefold increase in the amount of carbon dioxide in the blood, about a threefold increase in the amount of tar inhaled, and retention in the respiratory tract of one-third more inhaled tar (Wu et al., 1988). Results of studies also show that smoking marijuana has effects on the respiratory system that may increase risk for the development of lung infections and lung cancer (Barsky et al., 1998; Baldwin et al., 1997).

Although many users think that marijuana enhances their sexual responsiveness, results of some studies have found that the drug interferes with reproductive functioning. Men who use marijuana may experience a temporary reduction of their normal testosterone levels. *Testosterone* is a sex hormone that maintains sex drive and sperm production. This effect may decrease the sperm count, but there is no evidence that marijuana is responsible for male infertility. Some women who use marijuana fail to ovulate regularly, which can negatively affect their fertility (Hanson & Venturelli, 1998).

Most Americans who smoke marijuana use the drug occasionally, particularly while they are in social settings. Although low-THC cannabis (the form generally available in the United States) rarely produces physical dependence, it can cause psychological dependence; some people who smoke marijuana or hashish daily become compulsive users. Compulsive users, particularly teenagers and college students, may lose their ambition to achieve goals or their motivation to work. After discontinuing marijuana use, however, these individuals generally regain their ambition and motivation (Hanson & Venturelli, 1998).

Among marijuana's medical uses is that it reduces the fluid pressure in the eyes of people with glaucoma. However, physicians usually prescribe other medications to treat this disorder. Marinol, a drug that contains synthetic THC, eases the side effects of nausea and vomiting that often accompany chemotherapy during cancer treatment. Other drugs are available to control these side effects. Marijuana is also used to ease the symptoms of wasting syndrome in AIDS patients, muscle spasms in patients with muscle disorders such as multiple sclerosis, and the pain

of migraine headaches. It can also help control seizures (Taylor, 1998).

Marijuana has been approved for medical use in Arizona, California, Oregon, Nevada, Maine, Washington, Alaska, Hawaii, and the District of Columbia. However, the federal government still considers any use of marijuana illegal, and its laws supersede state laws. In 1999 a bill was introduced in the U.S. House of Representatives that would allow states to determine their own policies regarding medical marijuana use, and that decision is pending at this time.

Most opponents of using smoked marijuana for medical purposes are not against the medical use of synthetic THC as pills or injectable drugs. Since most supporters of the medical use of smoked marijuana are against using synthetic THC, many suggest that their motivation for support is not scientific or medical but rather a "back door" method of legalization (DuPont, 1999).

Smoking marijuana can impair your thought processes and ability to drive, damage your lungs, reduce your fertility, and lessen your motivation to work. Therefore, abstain from using this drug to avoid these serious effects.

Hallucinogens

When taken internally, hallucinogens produce *hallucinations,* abnormal and unreal sensations such as seeing distorted and vividly colored images. Many people report feeling pleasantly detached from their bodies or united with their environment while using hallucinogens. Hallucinogens, however, can produce frightening psychological responses such as anxiety, depression, and the feeling of losing control over your mind. The physical side effects of hallucinogens include elevated blood pressure, dilated pupils, and increased body temperature. Although chronic users of these drugs may develop psychological dependence and tolerance, physical addiction and withdrawal do not occur.

In the United States, the most potent and commonly abused hallucinogens are LSD, mescaline, psilocybin (SIGH-low-SIGH-bin), and PCP. These drugs have no approved medical uses, and their recreational use is illegal. Native Americans, however, are permitted to use *peyote,* a cactus that contains mescaline, in certain religious rites.

LSD

LSD (lysergic acid diethylamide) is a colorless, odorless, flavorless compound that is manufactured in pill, solution, and powder form. It is an extremely potent drug; taking very small amounts produces vivid hallucinations that can last up to 12 hours. While taking LSD, some people have severe psychotic reactions, such as paranoid delusions. Additionally, for days or weeks after taking LSD, users may have "flashbacks" in which they experience mild hallucinations. Medical practitioners usually reassure these people that flashbacks are harmless and subside over time and that few, if any, long-term psychological problems result from hallucinogen use (Halpern & Pope, 1999). Although no scientific evidence clearly links use of LSD with the development of fetal abnormalities, LSD can stimulate uterine contractions so pregnant women should avoid it (Goldberg, 1994).

analogs
drugs that are chemically similar but have different effects in the body.

During the early 1980s, LSD use by college students declined dramatically, from 6.3% in 1982 to 2.2% in 1985. By 1992, however, LSD use among college students had climbed to 5.7% and remained at that level until 1997. By 1998, use began to decline again (Johnston et al., 1999b).

Mescaline

A small, round, spineless cactus that grows in Mexico and Texas produces the hallucinogen mescaline, or peyote (◾ Figure 7-5). After eating peyote, people have hallucinations that last 1 to 2 hours. These "trips" are milder and easier to control than LSD trips. Since pure mescaline is difficult to produce for illicit sale, most mescaline sold on the streets contains LSD as the psychoactive agent.

Psilocybin

Many mushrooms, including several wild-growing varieties that are found throughout the United States, contain psilocybin. After eating these fungi, sometimes called *magic mushrooms*, people experience elevated blood pressure, body temperature, and pulse rate. Psilocybin produces euphoria and hallucinations, but these psychoactive effects are not as intense or long-lasting as those produced by LSD. Unpleasant responses to psilocybin ingestion include wide mood swings and uncontrollable movements of arms and legs. Although fatal overdoses from psilocybin have not been reported, users may die if they eat other wild mushrooms that are poisonous.

PCP

Along with LSD, PCP (phencyclidine) is one of the most commonly abused hallucinogens (NIDA, 1999c). PCP (commonly called *angel dust* or *rocket fuel*) is difficult to classify because the drug produces hallucinogenic, depressant, stimulant, or anesthetic effects depending on the dose in which it is taken. Within a few minutes after taking PCP, users begin to experience its psychoactive effects, which can last up to 6 hours.

Unlike other hallucinogenic drugs, high doses of PCP can cause severe toxic reactions. Taking 1 mg to 5 mg of PCP produces confusion and loss of muscular coordination; users also feel warm, sweaty, relaxed, and euphoric. As the level of intake increases to about 10 mg, users become confused, paranoid, and agitated; they act drunk, have hallucinations, and report numbness in their arms and legs. Taking 10 mg to 25 mg produces the signs and symptoms of PCP toxicity, including trancelike or psychotic behavior. Doses that exceed 25 mg to 50 mg can produce fever, convulsions, coma, elevated blood pressure, and death. People who survive the acute toxic effects of PCP often feel depressed and anxious. Additionally, they may show signs of brain damage such as confusion and disorientation that can take weeks to disappear.

In the 1960s drug researchers developed ketamine, a PCP analog that has fewer troublesome side effects than PCP. An **analog** is chemically similar to another drug and may or may not produce similar responses. Today, legally manufactured PCP analogs such as Ketalar (ketamine hydrochloride) have limited human and veterinary medical use as anesthetics. People who take ketamine may experience dangerous side effects such as high blood pressure and rapid pulse rate. The long-term risks of abusing ketamine are unknown.

Healthy
◾ LIVING PRACTICES ◾

Do not eat wild mushrooms. Some are poisonous and can cause death.

Inhalants

Inhalants are gases that produce euphoria, dizziness, confusion, and drowsiness shortly after they are inhaled, or *huffed*. Numerous household products release toxic fumes; these include paints and fingernail polishes that contain acetone, and lighter fluids that contain butane (◾ Table 7-5). Freon, a refrigerant used in many air conditioners, is a toxic gas also.

▲ Figure 7-5 Peyote Cactus (*Lophophora williamsii*). This small, round, spineless cactus grows in Mexico and Texas and produces the hallucinogen mescaline, or peyote.

Table 7-5	Common Products that Contain Toxic Inhalants

Glues
Aerosols
Cleaning solutions
Fingernail polishes and fingernail polish removers
Fuels and lighter fluids
Paints and paint thinners
PVC cement
Hair spray
Typing correction fluid

Inhalants irritate the mucous membranes lining the eyes, mouth, nose, throat, and lungs. Inhalant abusers often develop watery, reddened eyes and a persistent cough. Some users experience double vision, nausea, vomiting, fainting, and a ringing sensation in their ears. Many teenagers are unaware of the serious health effects of inhalant use: brain damage, irregular heartbeat, anemia, liver damage, kidney failure, coma, or death. Only 39% of eighth graders and 46% of tenth graders think that experimentation with inhalants is dangerous, which may explain the widespread use of inhalants at these ages (Johnston et al., 1999a).

Healthy LIVING PRACTICES

Use household products that release toxic fumes, such as paints, glues, and lighter fluids, in well-ventilated areas to avoid inhaling these chemicals.

Designer Drugs

People who have some knowledge of chemistry can alter the chemical structure of a controlled substance to make a new compound that is not classified as a controlled drug. The new compound, called a *designer drug,* usually produces psychoactive responses similar to the drug from which it was produced. Designer drugs are relatively easy and inexpensive to produce. Thus, people who make these drug analogs can reap considerable profits from selling them.

After officials with the DEA determine that a designer drug has the potential to be abused, they can classify the compound as a controlled substance. However, underground chemists often avoid prosecution by continuing to modify the substance, producing new generations of the drug that the DEA does not control. ▌**Table 7-6** lists some of the best-known designer drugs, their psychoactive effects, and potential health risks.

Designer drugs are often more toxic than the compounds from which they are derived. China white, for example, is 1000 times more potent than its parent drug, fentanyl. China white and other fentanyl analogs have been responsible for at least 100 deaths (Hanson & Venturelli, 1998).

Ecstasy

The illegal designer drug *Ecstasy,* or *MDMA* (3,4-methylenedioxymethamphetamine), became a controlled substance in 1985. Chemically similar to mescaline and methamphetamine, Ecstasy produces both hallucinogenic and stimulant effects. Ecstasy users report that the drug improves their self-esteem and increases their desire to have intimate contacts with other people. However, users may experience panic and anxiety, hallucinations, tremors, rapid heart rate, loss of coordination, and psychotic behav-

Table 7-6	Popular Designer Drugs		
Designer Drug	**Original Drugs**	**Psychoactive Effects**	**Possible Health Risks**
MPPP MPTP	Meperidine (Demerol)	Heroinlike euphoria (depressant)	Parkinsonian syndrome: drooling, uncontrollable skeletal muscle movements, muscle rigidity (permanent).
China white	Fentanyl (Sublimaze)	Euphoria, respiratory depression	Death from respiratory failure
Ecstasy, XTC, Adam, M & M, MDMA	Mescaline–methamphetamine	Euphoria, CNS stimulant, hallucinations	Panic, anxiety, paranoia, increased and irregular heart rate, fever, hypertension, brain damage, seizures, death
Love drug (MDA)	Mescaline–methamphetamine	Euphoria, talkativeness, increased need to make friends	Fever, rapid heart rate, hypertension, seizures, death

ior. Some users report more serious side effects such as irregular heartbeat, hypertension, fever, and seizures. Since the 1980s several people have died after taking this drug. In 1998 relatively few respondents to the Monitoring the Future survey reported any use of MDMA. Among all 19- to 32-year-olds combined, 6.8% say they have tried it at some time, compared to 5.8% of high school seniors. The number of persons who used this drug at least once during the year prior to the survey decreased substantially after age 22 (Johnston et al., 1999b).

Over-the-Counter Drugs

If you walk down the aisles of a pharmacy or discount department store, you are likely to see a huge array of over-the-counter (OTC) medicines. Television advertisements promote a variety of OTC products that "shrink hemorrhoids," "promote regularity," or "kill germs." The demand for these products is growing as more Americans practice self–health care to reduce their health-care costs.

The FDA regulates the production and marketing of prescription and nonprescription medications in the United States. To be sold in this country, an OTC medicine must be effective and safe when people follow the product information that comes with it (in packages or on labels). Although the FDA does not evaluate the safety or effectiveness of every OTC product that is marketed, the agency requires that active ingredients in products be evaluated for safety and usefulness. *Active* ingredients have an effect on the body; *inert* ingredients do not affect the body. Products that contain unsafe or ineffective ingredients or that have dishonest labeling cannot be sold. Herbal products that are sold as food supplements in health food stores are not regulated by the FDA. Some of these products contain substances that produce druglike effects and are toxic (see Chapter 1; the "Consumer Health" box on the next page discusses the role of the FDA in protecting consumers from unsafe and ineffective health care products).

Misuse and abuse of OTC medicines is common. As mentioned in the beginning of this chapter, the improper use of these medications can be harmful. Furthermore, some OTC products contain substances such as alcohol that can produce serious psychoactive effects, especially when they are taken in large doses.

Look-Alike Drugs

The active ingredient in "stay-awake" pills is the stimulant caffeine. Some manufacturers produce caffeine-containing capsules or pills that look like prescription amphetamines or related prescribed stimulants. The production and sale of these look-alike drugs are difficult to regulate because they contain caffeine, an allowed substance. Frequently, people who sell street drugs misrepresent look-alike stimulants as amphetamines to unsuspecting users.

Weight Loss Aids

Nearly anyone who has tried to lose weight knows that it is frustrating and that hunger seems to be constant. Many overweight people have taken various pills, powders, beverages, and foods for years to promote weight loss and prevent hunger. The "Consumer Health" box in Chapter 10 describes the potential harmful effects of these products and the drugs they contain.

Ephedrine

During asthma attacks, affected people often use prescription or over-the-counter products containing ephedrine or pseudoephedrine to dilate their bronchial tubes. Since ephedrine and pseudoephedrine act as mild stimulants, some individuals misuse medicines that contain these compounds as "pep pills." Ephedrine and pseudoephedrine can produce high blood pressure, sleeplessness, irregular and rapid heart rate, and restlessness; taking high doses of either substance may evoke psychotic symptoms. FDA officials have discussed banning ephedrine-containing OTC products because of their dangerous side effects and because amateur chemists can use them to make methamphetamines.

The Chinese herb *ephedra*, or *ma huang*, is a natural source of ephedrine that can be purchased in health food stores. It is often used in dietary supplements and body-building products. People who use ephedra as a stimulant think that it is safe and not addictive. However, the drug can cause heart attacks, seizures, and even death. Since 1997 the FDA has required warning and dosage restrictions on products that contain ephedrine. In addition to ephedra, numerous herbs or plant extracts—such as lobelia, comfrey, yohimbe, *Ginkgo biloba*, or sassafras—contain substances that can produce harmful side effects when ingested as supplements or teas (■ Figure 7-6).

◀Figure 7-6 **Hazardous Herbs.** Numerous plants can be toxic. Lobelia induces vomiting; overdoses can result in convulsions, loss of consciousness, and death.

ConSumer Health

Over-the-Counter Medicines: Safety and the FDA

The FDA reports that Americans spend more than $18 billion annually on the estimated 300,000 drugs that are available without prescriptions. According to the American Pharmaceutical Association, people initially use self-care practices, such as OTC drugs, to treat 60% to 90% of all ailments. Painkillers and cold, sinus, and cough remedies are among the best-selling OTC products. The demand for these and other OTC products will continue to grow as more American consumers practice self–health care to reduce their health-care costs.

Some OTC drugs are useful, but others are ineffective. To protect consumers, the Food and Drug Administration (FDA) regulates the testing, production, marketing, and labeling of medical devices and medications; the safety of foods and truthfulness of information on their labels; and the safety of cosmetics. A medical device or OTC medicine that is sold in the United States must be effective for its intended use and safe when its instructions are followed.

The FDA also requires that the active ingredients in OTC products be evaluated for safety and usefulness. Active ingredients have an impact on the body; inert ingredients do not affect the body. The FDA allows manufacturers of OTC products to use ingredients that are generally recognized as safe (GRAS), generally recognized as effective (GRAE), and generally recognized as honestly labeled (GRAHL). The FDA employs investigators who review information that appears on the labels of OTC products. Products that contain unsafe or ineffective ingredients, or that have labels displaying dishonest information, cannot be sold.

In 1998 the FDA proposed a new, easy-to-read and easy-to-understand labeling format for OTC drugs. Figure 7-A shows the information that must appear on the labels of an OTC medicinal product. Note that the new label clearly displays warnings concerning the safe use of the product. Always follow instructions on the package or label concerning the use of any OTC medication.

Individuals, physicians, and staff of health-care facilities can report cases of harm that result from using medicinal and nutritional products. If you have any problem with a medication, medical device, or dietary supplement, report the problem to the FDA's MedWatch hotline by calling 1-800-332-1088.

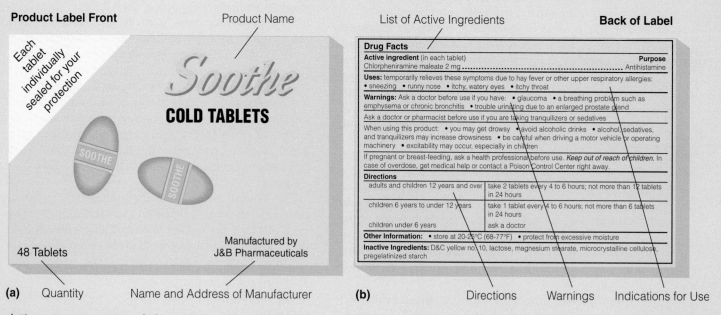

Product Label Front   Product Name   List of Active Ingredients   **Back of Label**

Each tablet individually sealed for your protection

Soothe
COLD TABLETS

SOOTHE

48 Tablets   Manufactured by J&B Pharmaceuticals

(a)   Quantity   Name and Address of Manufacturer

Drug Facts

Active ingredient (in each tablet)	Purpose
Chlorpheniramine maleate 2 mg	Antihistamine

Uses: temporarily relieves these symptoms due to hay fever or other upper respiratory allergies: • sneezing • runny nose • itchy, watery eyes • itchy throat

Warnings: Ask a doctor before use if you have: • glaucoma • a breathing problem such as emphysema or chronic bronchitis • trouble urinating due to an enlarged prostate gland

Ask a doctor or pharmacist before use if you are taking tranquilizers or sedatives

When using this product: • you may get drowsy • avoid alcoholic drinks • alcohol, sedatives, and tranquilizers may increase drowsiness • be careful when driving a motor vehicle or operating machinery • excitability may occur, especially in children

If pregnant or breast-feeding, ask a health professional before use. *Keep out of reach of children.* In case of overdose, get medical help or contact a Poison Control Center right away.

Directions

adults and children 12 years and over	take 2 tablets every 4 to 6 hours; not more than 12 tablets in 24 hours
children 6 years to under 12 years	take 1 tablet every 4 to 6 hours; not more than 6 tablets in 24 hours
children under 6 years	ask a doctor

Other Information: • store at 20-25°C (68-77°F) • protect from excessive moisture

Inactive Ingredients: D&C yellow no. 10, lactose, magnesium stearate, microcrystalline cellulose, pregelatinized starch

(b)   Directions   Warnings   Indications for Use

▲**Figure 7-A New OTC Label.** Certain information must appear on the labels of an OTC medicinal product: (a) Front of label, and (b) back of label.

Healthy LIVING PRACTICES

- Ask your physician about the need to use over-the-counter medications. If it is necessary for you to take these drugs, follow the labels' instructions concerning their safe use. Your pharmacist is also a source of reliable information concerning the safe use of OTC drugs.
- Obtain reliable information concerning the safety and effectiveness of herbal products before you ingest them.

Drug Treatment and Prevention

www.jbpub.com/healthyliving

Treating Drug Dependency

When some people recognize that they have a problem controlling their use of drugs, they voluntarily discontinue abusing drugs without the assistance of specialized treatment programs. Other people seek treatment after realizing that they cannot stop abusing substances on their own. Many of these individuals require medical supervision in special clinical settings to manage withdrawal signs and symptoms safely. In some instances, people do not want treatment for their substance abuse because the behavior is too gratifying for them or they deny that they have a drug problem. In cases involving criminal activities, legal authorities may require that addicted individuals either complete drug treatment or serve prison sentences.

The goal of drug treatment is to reduce the likelihood that abusers will return to their previous drug use behaviors. Most abusers prefer *outpatient drug-free programs* that provide medical care and a wide variety of counseling and psychotherapy approaches while patients continue to live with their families and work in their communities. (These programs do not include use of the medication/drug methadone.)

Self-help groups are a popular and useful adjunct to professional outpatient drug treatment. Individuals recovering from drug dependency attend regular meetings to receive encouragement and social support from other former substance abusers. Alcoholics Anonymous (AA) is one of the oldest, most effective self-help programs (see Chapter 8). Many other community-based self-help programs that treat drug abuse, such as Narcotics Anonymous, are modeled after AA.

In severe cases, drug abusers may undergo detoxification and then live for several months in controlled environments called *residential therapeutic communities* or *group homes*. Living in these communities reduces the likelihood that patients will be exposed to drugs while they resocialize, or readjust to general society. While in group homes, patients also receive medical care, social services, and psychological counseling. After they leave residential therapeutic communities, individuals usually attend community- or hospital-based counseling sessions to prevent *relapse*, the return to drug abuse. For people who lack health insurance, the high cost of medical care is a major barrier to obtaining treatment in a therapeutic community.

Most drug treatment programs that last fewer than 90 days have limited long-term effectiveness (NIDA, 1999a). Results of studies show that length of time in drug treatment is the best single predictor of positive post-treatment outcomes (DesJarlais & Hubbard, 1999). Many drug-dependent people need more than 3 months of outpatient care or living in controlled environments to change their substance-related behaviors and attitudes. Additionally, recovering addicts often need to acquire job skills while they are in therapy to improve their chances of becoming drug-free, productive members of society.

A considerable number of patients finish treatment but relapse within a few weeks or months of abstinence. Former addicts are more likely to relapse if they have severe mental illness or polyabuse, and if they return to communities where illicit drugs are available and are widely used. Recovering drug addicts are more likely to abstain from using drugs if they are married or in stable relationships, supported by their families, and employed. In 1998 nearly 1 million Americans received treatment or counseling for their drug use (SAMHSA, 1999).

Preventing Drug Misuse and Abuse

The U.S. government devotes much of its drug prevention efforts to reducing the supply of illicit drugs. These efforts include destroying crops such as marijuana and coca plants; stopping the flow of illegal substances through U.S. borders; and prosecuting individuals who manufacture, sell, and purchase drugs illegally. Such measures, however, are not effectively reducing the demand for illicit drugs in this country. Many people think that social and economic programs to reduce poverty and unemployment would decrease the demand for illegal drugs. Additionally, educational programs that promote drug-free lifestyles, especially among children and young adults, may help reduce the prevalence of drug abuse.

The National Institute on Drug Abuse conducted research for 20 years to determine which drug prevention programs have the highest degree of long-term effectiveness. They found that successful prevention programs:

- enhance protective factors and to reverse or reduce known risk factors (see p. 147),
- use interactive methods such as peer discussion groups,
- target all forms of drug use,
- teach skills to resist drugs when offered,
- strengthen personal commitments against drug use,
- increase social skills and assertiveness, and
- reinforce attitudes against drug use.

ANALYZING *Health-Related Information*

The following ad promotes a book that describes how to eliminate addictive urges. Read the advertisement and evaluate it using the model for analyzing health-related information. The main points of the model are noted below; the model is fully explained on pages 12–13.

1. Which statements are verifiable facts, and which are unverified statements or value claims?
2. What are the credentials of the person who wrote the ad? If this information is available, does the author's background and education qualify him or her as an expert in the topic area?
3. What might be the motives and biases of the person who wrote ad? State reasons for your answer.
4. Which information in the ad is relevant to the product? Which information is irrelevant?
5. Is the source reliable? Does it have a reputation for publishing misinformation?
6. Does the ad attack the credibility of conventional scientists or medical authorities?

Based on the above analysis, do you think that this ad is a reliable source of health-related information? Explain why you would or would not buy the book. Summarize your reasons for coming to this conclusion.

Escape from the Personal Prison of Addiction

Dr. W. S. Davis-Crocker

Is your life being ruined by chemical addictions? Wouldn't it be wonderful to say "no" to drugs and to stick to it? Now you can learn a simple technique to take control of your destructive behaviors.

After years of scientific research, Dr. W. S. Davis-Crocker has unlocked the neurobiochemical secrets of addiction. In her newest book, *Escape from the Personal Prison of Addiction,* Dr. Davis-Crocker, world-reknowned author and founder of the Davis-Crocker Institute for the Study of Habituation, describes how to rid yourself of addictions painlessly.

Finally, there is hope for addicts. In just three days of practicing the advice in her book, your cravings for alcohol, cigarettes, heroin, and even chocolate will vanish! There is no need for you to use special medications or costly psychotherapy.

To order your copy of *Escape from the Personal Prison of Addiction,* call ███████. All major credits cards accepted.

Also register to attend Dr. Davis-Crocker's next seminar in your area. Enrollment is limited, so call the toll-free number now to reserve your seat, and we'll send you our informative pamphlet *Why Me?* at no charge.

Additionally, drug education programs that involve parents, media, and the community are more successful than programs that limit educational activities to classrooms. The research-based programs for general populations of students that are effective include Project STAR, the Life Skills Training Program, and Project Family (NIDA, 1999c).

Healthy LIVING PRACTICES

If you or someone you know is abusing drugs, obtain help from local substance abuse programs or from your health-care practitioner.

across the lifespan

Drug Use and Abuse

Pregnant drug users are at risk for miscarriage, *ectopic* ("tubal") pregnancy, and stillbirth (giving birth to a dead infant). Babies born to women who used cocaine, opiates, amphetamines, or marijuana regularly during pregnancy are more likely to be premature (born too soon) and smaller than infants who were not exposed to these drugs before birth. Compared with other infants, premature or underweight newborns are more likely to have serious

Table 7-7	Adolescents: Risk Factors for Drug Use

Experiences that increase risk of drug use:
Academic failure
Early antisocial behavior
Early drug experimentation

Personality characteristics that increase risk of drug use:
Rebelliousness
Low self-esteem
Sensation seeking

Environmental situations that increase risk of drug use:
Family disorganization
Family history of drug use
Drugs readily available
Drug use among friends/peers
Poor socioeconomic status of community

Source: Based on Gilchrist, L. D. (1991). Defining the intervention and target population. In C. G. Leukefeld & W. J. Bukoski (Eds.), *Drug abuse prevention intervention research: methodological issues.* NIDA Research Monograph No. 107; Washington, DC: U.S. Government Printing Office.

health problems early in life. Drug-exposed newborns also tend to have smaller than normal head circumferences, a sign that brain growth has been negatively affected. Pregnant women should consult their physicians before taking any drug.

The news media have reported that many children who were exposed to drugs before birth experience various developmental problems, such as motor movement impairments and learning delays. Research studies do not uphold these ideas, and some researchers think that such problems are the result of the environment in which these young children are raised. Children from low socioeconomic backgrounds are at risk of having developmental problems for a variety of reasons. Before they are born, their mothers are less likely to obtain adequate prenatal medical care. Lack of prenatal care increases a woman's risk of having problems during pregnancy that can affect her health and that of her infant. Additionally, low-income parents may not have the financial resources or parenting skills to provide effective intellectual stimulation for their preschool children. Studies are needed to monitor the drug use of pregnant women and follow their children for several years. The results of such long-term research may clarify the extent to which prenatal drug exposure influences the mental and physical development of children (Eyler & Behnke, 1999; Tronick & Beeghly, 1999).

Adolescents who have certain characteristics are more likely to use alcohol and other drugs than adolescents without these characteristics. These drug use risk factors include gender, family income, parents' use of drugs, latchkey status, and peer drug use. Adolescent males are more likely to use psychoactive drugs and in higher amounts than adolescent females. In general, teenagers from low-income families are more likely to use psychoactive substances than youth from high-income families. Adolescents whose parents use mind-altering drugs have a higher risk of using these substances than the children of non-drug users. Latchkey kids have a higher risk of using drugs than children who have adult supervision when they come home after school. Teenagers whose closest friends are drug users are more likely to take psychoactive substances than children without drug-using friends. **Table 7-7** lists risk factors associated with illicit drug use among children and teenagers. Approximately 55% of high school seniors have used illegal drugs at some time in their lives (Johnston et al., 1999a).

In spite of living in situations that promote substance use and abuse, many young people abstain from taking psychoactive drugs. Teenagers who stay in high school, attend classes regularly, make good grades, and get along well with their parents generally avoid using drugs. These children have personality traits that are collectively referred to as *resiliency*. Resilient children accept responsibility, adapt to change, manage stress, solve problems, and are achievement- and success-oriented. Resilient young people have the ability to remain psychologically, socially, and spiritually healthy even though their families are dysfunctional or not supportive.

The abuse of illicit drugs is not a widespread problem among the elderly in the United States. However, many elderly take a variety of prescribed medications to treat problems such as insomnia, depression, hypertension, and heart disease. These aged individuals have a higher risk of becoming intoxicated from taking medications because their bodies do not detoxify and eliminate the substances as effectively as younger ones. More research is needed to determine medication levels that are safe and effective for elderly individuals.

The risk of serious drug interactions and drug synergism is high among aged people who take more than one prescribed drug. In many instances, elderly persons appear to have suffered a stroke, developed Alzheimer's disease, or become severely depressed when actually their confusion and weakness are the side effects of taking numerous prescribed medicines.

Do not use any drugs during pregnancy without the approval of your physician.

Chapter Review

Summary

Drugs are nonfood chemicals that alter the way a person thinks, feels, functions, or behaves. Many drugs have beneficial uses as medicines, but these substances can have serious negative impacts on the health and well-being of individuals when they are used improperly. People often abuse psychoactive, or mood-altering, drugs. Drug abuse contributes to numerous social problems that plague our society such as crime, unemployment, and family violence and dissolution.

By interacting with nerve cells in the brain, psychoactive drugs influence perceptions, thought processes, feelings, and behaviors. Additionally, environmental factors can affect how people act and feel while under the influence of psychoactive drugs.

In most instances, the liver converts drugs into less dangerous compounds that can be eliminated in urine, feces, or exhaled breath. When the body is unable to detoxify and eliminate excessive amounts of a drug rapidly, the characteristic signs and symptoms of intoxication occur. Drug overdoses and polyabuse may produce serious, even deadly, effects.

In 1998 an estimated 13.6 million Americans over 12 years of age were illegal drug users. Rates of illegal drug use are especially high among teenagers and young adults. Initially, these individuals typically use alcohol, nicotine, or inhalants; they then may move on to marijuana. Some persons experiment with or use other illegal drugs after marijuana. Most illegal drug users discontinue taking these substances by the time they reach their mid-30s.

Dependency and addiction describe any habitual behavior that interferes with a person's health, work, and relationships. Drug dependence or addiction occurs when users develop a pattern of taking drugs that usually produces a compulsive need to use these substances, a tolerance for them, and withdrawal when they are discontinued. The type of substance taken, the social environment of the person, his or her personality, and genetics influence an individual's chances of developing a drug dependency.

Depressants such as alcohol and barbiturates slow the activity of the cerebral cortex, producing sedative and hypnotic effects as well as drowsiness. Thus, people should not drive or operate machinery while under the influence of depressants. Misusing depressants can be deadly.

Stimulants enhance chemical activity in parts of the brain that influence emotions, sleep, attention, and learning. Caffeine is the most commonly consumed legal stimulant in this country. Stimulants such as Ritalin and cocaine have few medical uses. Cocaine is addictive and frequently abused. In the United States, the use of illegal methamphetamines is growing rapidly.

Opiates have important medical uses as sedatives, analgesics, and narcotics. When misused, opiates are highly addictive and extremely dangerous.

Marijuana, which contains THC as its major psychoactive compound, is the most widely used illicit drug in the United States. Although marijuana does not produce physiological dependence, some individuals become compulsive users. Marijuana smoke contains numerous irritants that can damage the bronchial tubes and lungs. Some of these compounds are the same cancer-causing substances found in cigarette smoke.

Hallucinogens alter the brain's ability to perceive sensory information, producing abnormal and unreal sensations. In the United States, the most potent and commonly abused hallucinogens are LSD, mescaline, psilocybin, and PCP. High doses of PCP can be deadly.

Many common household products release toxic fumes that can produce psychoactive effects when inhaled. Teenagers may use inhalants before they move on to other psychoactive drugs. Inhalants can depress respiration, resulting in coma or death.

Amateur chemists make designer drugs by altering the chemical structures of controlled substances. In some cases, these drug analogs are more toxic than the compounds from which they were derived.

The FDA regulates the production and marketing of all medications in the United States. Some health food and OTC products contain substances that are harmful or that produce psychoactive effects, especially when they are misused or abused.

The primary goal of drug treatment is to help abusers become drug-free. Drug treatment usually involves participation in outpatient treatment programs and self-help groups. Drug prevention programs that target school-age children typically provide information about drugs and teach drug resistance and refusal skills.

Drug use during pregnancy increases the risk of miscarriage, ectopic pregnancy, and stillbirth. Women who use cocaine, opiates, amphetamines, and marijuana regularly during pregnancy are more likely to give birth to premature and smaller infants than pregnant women who do not use these drugs. The extent to which prenatal drug exposure influences the long-term mental and physical development of children is unclear.

Approximately 55% of American high school seniors have experimented with illicit drugs. Although drug abuse is rare among the aged, these individuals may experience harmful effects from taking prescribed medicines because they do not detoxify and eliminate drugs as effectively as younger individuals or because they misuse or become confused by multiple prescriptions.

Applying What You Have Learned

1. Why do people abuse certain drugs such as cocaine and not others such as aspirin? *(Application)*
2. Have you ever used a medication improperly? If your answer is yes, describe your misuse of the drug. *(Analysis)*
3. Plan an educational program for fifth-grade students that discourages illicit drug use. *(Synthesis)*
4. One of your friends thinks that marijuana is safe and that its use should be decriminalized. Evaluate this person's position by considering the health effects on the population if marijuana were legalized. *(Evaluation)*

KEY

Application: Using information in a new situation.
Analysis: Breaking down information into component parts.
Synthesis: Putting together information from different sources.
Evaluation: Making informed decisions.

Reflecting On Your Health

1. Do you use drugs responsibly? Explain why you do or do not.
2. Under what circumstances would you intervene to stop a friend from abusing drugs?
3. What are you currently doing or what would you do to encourage your children not to use illegal drugs?
4. What kinds of over-the-counter drugs do you use? Do you think that your use of these drugs is helpful or harmful to your health?
5. If you abuse drugs, do you think that your health or the health of others is adversely affected by your behavior? Why or why not? After reading this chapter and learning about the health effects of illegal drugs, are you motivated to stop your drug abuse? Why or why not?

References

Anglin, D., Spears, K. L., & Hutson, H. R. (1997). Flunitrazepam and its involvement in date or acquaintance rape. *Academic Emergency Medicine, 4:*323-326.

Baldwin, G. C., Tashkin, D. P., Buckley, D. M., Park, A. N., Dubinett, S. M., & Roth, M. D. (1997). Marijuana and cocaine impair alveolar macrophage function and cytokine production. *American Journal of Respiratory & Critical Care Medicine, 156:*1606-1613.

Barsky, S. H., Roth, M. D., Kleerup, E. D., Simmons, M., & Tashkin, D. P. (1998). Histopathic and molecular alterations in bronchial epithelium in habitual smokers of marijuana, cocaine, and/or tobacco. *Journal of the National Cancer Institute, 90:*1198-1205.

DesJarlais, D. C., & Hubbard, R. (1999). Treatment for drug dependence. *Proceedings of the Association of American Physicians, 111:*126-130.

Drug Enforcement Administration [DEA]. (1996). *Drugs of abuse.* Washington, DC: U.S. Department of Justice.

Dupont, R. L. (1999). Examining the debate on the use of medical marijuana. *Proceedings of the Association of American Physicians, 111:*166-172.

Eyler, F. D., & Behnke, M. (1999). Early development of infants exposed to drugs prenatally. *Clinics in Perinatology, 26:*107-150.

Food and Drug Administration (FDA). (1999a). FDA warns about products containing gamma butyrolactone or GBL and asks companies to issue a recall. *FDA Talk Paper.* Available: http://vm.cfsan.fda.gov/~lrd/tpgbl.html.

Food and Drug Administration (FDA). (1999b). *Statement by Nicholas Reuter, MPH Associate Director for Domestic and International Drug Control, Office of Health Affairs Food and Drug Administration, Department of Health and Human Services, before the subcommittee on oversight and investigations Committee on Commerce U.S. House of Representatives.* Available: http://www.fda.gov/ola/substance.htm

Fung, M., Gallagher, C., & Machtay, M. (1999). Lung and aerodigestive cancers in young marijuana smokers. *Tumori, 85:* 140-142.

Goldberg, R. (1994). *Drugs across the spectrum.* Minneapolis/St. Paul: West Publishing Company.

Halpern, J. H., & Pope, H. G. (1999). Do hallucinogens cause residual neuropsychological toxicity? *Drug & Alcohol Dependence, 53:* 247-256.

Hanson, G., & Venturelli, P. J. (1998). *Drugs and Society.* Sudbury, MA: Jones and Bartlett Publishers.

Johnston, L. D., O'Malley, P. M., & Bachman, J. G. (1995). *National survey results on drug use from the Monitoring the Future study, 1975–1994.* Rockville, MD: National Institute on Drug Abuse.

Johnston, L. D., O'Malley, P. M., & Bachman, J. G. (1999a). *National survey results on drug use from the Monitoring the Future study, 1975–1998: Vol. I. Secondary school students.* Rockville, MD: National Institute on Drug Abuse (NIH Pub. No. 99-4660).

Johnston, L. D., O'Malley, P. M., & Bachman, J. G. (1999b). *National survey results on drug use from the Monitoring the Future study, 1975–1998: Vol. II. College students and young adults.* Rockville,

MD: National Institute on Drug Abuse (NIH Pub. No. 99-4661).

Kam, P. C., & Yoong, F. F. (1998). Gamma-hydroxybutyric acid: an emerging recreational drug. *Anaesthesia, 53:*1195-1198.

Lieb, R., Pfister, L. R., & Wittchen, H. U. (1998). Use, abuse and dependence of prescription drugs in adolescents and young adults. *European Addiction Research. 4:*67-74.

Liguori, A., Gatto, C. P., & Robinson, J. H. (1998). Effects of marijuana on equilibrium, psychomotor performance, and simulated driving. *Behavioral Pharmacology, 9:*599-609.

Logan, B. K. (1996). Methamphetamine and driving impairment. *Journal of Forensic Sciences, 41:*457-464.

Logan, B. K., & Schwilke, E. W. (1996). Drug and alcohol use in fatally injured drivers in Washington State. *Journal of Forensic Sciences, 41:*505-510.

National Institute on Drug Abuse (NIDA) (1999a). *Principles of Drug Addiction Treatment: A Research-Based Guide.* Washington, DC: National Institutes of Health, National Institute on Drug Abuse. (NIH Pub. 99-4180).

National Institute on Drug Abuse (NIDA). (1999b). Rohypnol and GHB. Available: http://165.112.78.61/Infofax/RohypnolGHB.html

National Institute on Drug Abuse (NIDA). (1999c). *The Sixth Triennial Report to Congress from the Secretary of Health and Human Services. Drug Abuse & Addiction Research: 25 Years of Discovery to Advance the Health of the Public.* Washington, DC: National Institutes of Health, National Institute on Drug Abuse.

National Institute on Drug Abuse (NIDA). (1997). *Preventing drug use among children and adolescents: A research-based guide.* Washington, DC: U.S. Government Printing Office.

Nehlig, A. (1999). Are we dependent upon coffee and caffeine? A review on human and animal data. *Neuroscience and Biobehavioral Reviews, 23:*563-576.

Plessinger, M. A. (1998). Prenatal exposure to amphetamines: Risks and adverse outcomes in pregnancy. *Obstetrics and Gynecology Clinics of North America, 25:*119-138.

Reuters Health Information (1999, December 4). *National Initiative Takes Aim at 'Club Drugs.'*

Schwartz, R. H. (1998). Adolescent heroin use: a review. *Pediatrics, 102:*1461-1466.

Substance Abuse and Mental Health Services Administration (SAMHSA). (1999). *Summary of Findings from the 1998 National Household Survey on Drug Abuse.* (DHHS Publication No. SMA 99-3328). Washington, DC: U.S. Government Printing Office.

Taylor, H. G. (1998). Analysis of the medical use of marijuana and its societal implications. *Journal of the American Pharmaceutical Association, 38:*220-227.

Tronick, E. Z., & Beeghly, M. (1999). Prenatal cocaine exposure, child development, and the compromising effects of cumulative risk. *Clinics in Perinatology, 26:*151-171.

Wu, T. C., Tashkin, D. P., Djahed, B., & Rose, J. E. (1988). Pulmonary hazards of smoking marijuana as compared with tobacco. *New England Journal of Medicine, 318:*347-351.

chapter 8

Alcohol and Tobacco

WARNING

CIGARETTES HURT BABIES

Tobacco use during pregnancy reduces the growth of babies during pregnancy. These smaller babies may not catch up in growth after birth and the risks of infant illness, disability and death are increased.

Health Canada

WARNING

CIGARETTES CAUSE MOUTH DISEASES

Cigarette smoke causes oral cancer, gum diseases and tooth loss.

Health Canada

WARNING
TOBACCO USE CAN MAKE YOU IMPOTENT

Cigarettes may cause sexual impotence due to decreased blood flow to the penis. This can prevent you from having an erection.

Health Canada

WARNING
CIGARETTES CAUSE LUNG CANCER

lung cancer

85% of lung cancers are caused by smoking. 80% of lung cancer victims die within 3 years.

Health Canada

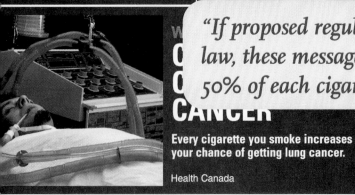

W...
C... C... CANCER

Every cigarette you smoke increases your chance of getting lung cancer.

Health Canada

"If proposed regulations are passed into law, these messages will cover more than 50% of each cigarette pack . . ."

Canada is getting tough on smokers. During a press conference on "Weedless Wednesday," January 19, 2000, Health Minister Allan Rock unveiled 16 new visual warnings for cigarette packages, some of which are seen here. If proposed regulations are passed into law, these messages will cover more than 50% of each cigarette pack, containing images and words that are larger and much more graphic than the four surgeon general's warnings currently printed on cigarette packs in the United States. They will be difficult to ignore each time a smoker pulls out a pack to light up. Canada's health minister will also introduce legislation requiring tobacco manufacturers to report the toxic emissions of the approximately 50 chemical compounds in cigarettes. Current regulations require reporting only tar, nicotine, and carbon monoxide. Along with these new warnings and emissions listings, Canadians will likely pay a higher cigarette tax, which the health minister suggests is an effective deterrent to youth smoking. Although smoking among all Canadians older than 15 years fell from 30% to 25% from 1991 to 1999, smoking among Canadian youths aged 15 to 19 years rose from 21% to 28% (Statistics Canada, 2000). Smoking among American youths rose in a similar manner. In 1998, over 1/3 of American young people were smokers by the time they completed high school, and the smoking rate was substantially higher among those who dropped out before graduating (Johnston et al., 1999a).

Smoking cigarettes and drinking alcohol are behaviors that often begin in adolescence. Most adolescents view these behaviors as acceptable because advertisements encourage such thinking, especially ads that target this age group, such as the Joe Camel advertisement shown in **Figure 8-1a.** Launched in 1987, the Joe Camel campaign was very attractive to young children as well as adolescents. Although a 12-year decline in adolescent smoking had occurred prior to the Joe Camel campaign, the decline stopped with its introduction and the incidence of smoking in the 14- to 17-year-old age group increased (Pierce, 1998). Joe Camel ads were finally banned as part of the 1998 tobacco settlement with the states and five territories (Ebnet, 1998).

Figure 8-1 Joe Camel. ▶(a) Such cigarette advertisements are criticized because they appear to target preteens and teens. ▼(b) To counter Joe Camel advertising, Tobacco Free Washington placed a "Joe Chemo" billboard above a busy highway in Seattle. Here, they show the tobacco icon turned cancer patient.

(a)

(b)

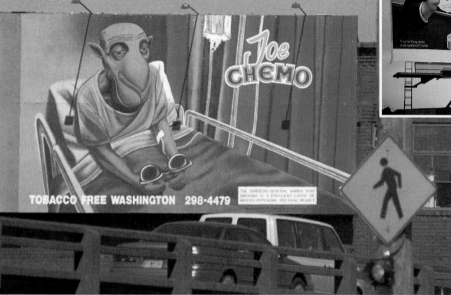

Although advertising tobacco products to young people is on the decline, certain celebrities, viewed as authority figures by many adolescents, teens, and young adults, still promote the use of alcohol. Many medical researchers and health-care professionals think that advertising alcohol and other drug-related products such as cigarettes encourages the use of all drugs. The practice of promoting alcohol and tobacco use is particularly dangerous because they are two primary "gateway" drugs. That is, most people follow a pattern of progression in drug use from alcohol and/or tobacco to marijuana to "hard" drugs (Hansen & Venturelli, 1998).

Both tobacco and alcohol can have devastating effects on health. Before you read this chapter, consider taking one or both of the self-assessments for this chapter in the student workbook. Clinicians use the CAGE screening test to detect alcohol abuse or alcoholism. The National Cancer Institute's quiz "Why Do You Smoke?" will help you understand the roots of your smoking behavior. If you do not smoke cigarettes or drink alcoholic beverages, you probably know family members, co-workers, or friends who may benefit from these self-assessments. Taking these tests could be their first steps to healthier lifestyles.

www.jbpub.com/healthyliving

Alcohol

Alcohol Use, Abuse, and Dependence

Alcohol use is quite prevalent in the United States, probably more prevalent than you might think. If every man, woman, and child over the age of 14 drank alcohol, each would have to consume 576 12-ounce cans of beer per year to account for the annual consumption of alcohol in this country! Of course, not everyone over 14 years of age consumes alcoholic beverages; therefore, some who drink alcohol consume much more than this amount. Some consume less.

According to the 1998 National Household Survey on Drug Abuse, approximately 52% of Americans older than 12 years are current alcohol users, which means that they had at least one drink in the month before they took the survey. This group includes binge alcohol users and heavy alcohol users. For the purposes of the survey, *binge alcohol users* had five or more drinks on the same occasion at least once in the month prior to the survey. *Heavy alcohol users* had five or more drinks on the same occasion on at least five days in the month prior to the survey (Substance Abuse and Mental Health Services Administration [SAMHSA], 1999). (All heavy alcohol users are also binge alcohol users.) ■ **Table 8-1** lists the number of drinks consumed by very light to very heavy drinkers as measured in standard drinks per week.

Many people who consume alcoholic beverages use alcohol responsibly. Responsible drinkers do not allow drinking alcoholic beverages to threaten their physical or psychological health or interfere with their relationships or interactions with others. Additionally, their behavior while drinking does not threaten the health or well-being of others.

Alcohol use becomes **harmful use** when a person drinks alcoholic beverages while knowingly damaging his or her physical and/or psychological health. A person who sustains injuries from accidents while drinking or becomes depressed from drinking, for example, is engaging in harmful use.

Alcohol abuse encompasses the symptoms of harmful use but also includes a social dimension. When drinking, the alcohol abuser has problems interacting with people in his or her family, in social settings, or at work. Typically, the

Table 8-1	Drinking Levels as Shown in Standard Drinks per Week

Drinking Level	Standard Drinks Per Week*
Abstainer	0
Very light	1 to <3 1/2
Light	3 1/2 to <7
Moderate	7 to <14
Heavy	14 to <28
Very heavy	28+

*One standard drink is 0.5 oz absolute alcohol, 12 oz beer, 5 oz wine, or 1.25 oz liquor.
Source: Adapted from Jacobson, J. L., & Jacobson, S. W. (1994). *Alcohol Health & Research World, 18*(1):30–35.

abuser uses alcohol in physically dangerous situations, such as when driving a car. However, he or she does not develop tolerance to the drug, exhibit withdrawal symptoms when not drinking (see Chapter 7), or compulsively use alcohol. Both harmful use and alcohol abuse are patterns of behavior, not just one-time occurrences, and are usually considered to be present if the behavior has occurred for at least one month or has occurred repeatedly over a longer period of time.

Alcohol abuse becomes **alcohol dependence**, or **alcoholism**, when certain other symptoms occur that are part of the *alcohol dependence syndrome*. ▌**Table 8-2** lists the

Table 8-2	Alcohol Dependence Syndrome

Three or more of the following symptoms over a year usually indicates alcohol dependency syndrome:

- A strong desire or compulsion to drink
- Difficulty in controlling the amount of alcohol consumed and when it is consumed
- Withdrawal symptoms when alcohol is not consumed, or consuming alcohol to avoid withdrawal symptoms
- Evidence of tolerance, that is, increased amounts of alcohol are needed to achieve the effects originally produced by lower amounts
- Progressive neglect of other interests because of drinking, while spending an increased amount of time obtaining and drinking alcohol, and recovering from its effects
- Continuing to use alcohol despite clear evidence of its physical and/or psychological effects on the user

symptoms of this syndrome. A diagnosis of dependence is usually made if a person exhibits three or more of these symptoms over a year's time. Approximately 10% of those who drink alcohol experience problems related to their alcohol use. These people account for 50% of all alcohol consumed in the United States (Goldberg, 1994). Currently, 14 million Americans are dependent on alcohol and approximately 105,000 people die each year from their addiction (McGinnis & Foege, 1999).

Factors Related to Alcohol Abuse and Dependence

About 100 years ago, alcoholics were thought simply to have a "weak character" or to suffer from "moral weakness." Since that time, especially within the past 50 years or so, scientists have gathered evidence showing that alcoholism has a variety of origins, many of them biological. In addition, research results show the importance of the interactions among biology, psychology, and the environment in the development of alcoholism. A cause of alcoholism is unknown, however.

Heredity For centuries, people have observed that alcoholism runs in families. Researchers have explored environmental and hereditary (genetic) factors of alcoholics to determine which are significant in the development of alcoholism.

By studying the family history of alcoholics, scientists determined that people who have a first-degree relative (parent, brother, or sister) with alcoholism have a higher risk of developing alcoholism than people in the general population. Scientists estimate this risk to be from 4 to 7 times higher. Sons of alcoholic fathers are at greatest risk. Additionally, data from adoption, twin, and animal studies indicate that there is a genetic component to alcoholism.

Scientists also study the reactions of people at risk for developing alcoholism (those who have a first-degree alcoholic relative) in comparison with those not at risk for alcoholism. In general, those at risk do not react to the consumption of alcohol with the same intensity as those not at risk. Some scientists think that persons at risk for alcoholism may not perceive that they are becoming intoxicated until they have had far more to drink than those not at risk for alcoholism.

harmful use drinking alcoholic beverages while knowingly damaging one's physical and/or psychological health.

alcohol abuse includes the symptoms of harmful use, but when drinking the abuser exhibits long-term social interaction problems and uses alcohol in physically dangerous situations.

alcohol dependence (alcoholism) a syndrome characterized by at least three of the following symptoms: a compulsion to drink, difficulty in controlling the amount of alcohol consumed, withdrawal symptoms when alcohol is not consumed, evidence of tolerance, progressive neglect of other interests because of drinking, and continuing to use alcohol despite its physical and psychological effects on the user.

Two other genetically linked factors are thought to influence the development of alcoholism: temperament and behavior. *Behavior* is the way people act—what they do. *Temperament* means disposition—the characteristic way in which people emotionally respond to the things and people around them. Temperament and behavior are thought to be inherited traits that are modified by interactions with the environment (see Chapter 2). Certain characteristics of temperament and behavior appear to be associated with enhanced risk for alcoholism: hyperactivity, impulsivity, aggression, short attention span, quickly changing emotions, slowed ability to calm oneself following stress, thrill-seeking behavior, and inability to delay gratification.

intoxication
impairment of the functioning of the central nervous system as a result of ingesting toxic substances like alcohol.

tolerance a physiological response in chronic users of drugs in which increased amounts of the drug are required to achieve effects previously produced by lower amounts.

Brain Effects When a person drinks alcoholic beverages, various behavioral changes occur that are commonly called **intoxication**, impairment of the functioning of the central nervous system (the brain and spinal cord). ▌ **Table 8-3** lists the changes that characteristically take place as a person consumes more and more alcohol. In this table, alcohol consumption and blood alcohol concentrations (BACs) are listed as ranges because the number of drinks as related to the body weight determines the concentration of alcohol in the blood. That is, in general, the larger the person, the greater the amount of alcohol that must be consumed for a specific blood alcohol concentration. Blood alcohol concentrations also rise more quickly in women than in men. One of the reasons for this occurrence is that women have proportionally more fat and less water in their bodies than

do men. Alcohol is more soluble in water than in fat; therefore, if a woman drinks the same amount as a man, her generally smaller size and lower water content results in a higher concentration of alcohol in watery body tissues such as the blood. Additionally, the stomach enzyme that breaks down alcohol before it reaches the bloodstream is less active in women than it is in men.

Why do certain changes take place in the body when a person consumes alcoholic beverages? The answer has to do with how alcohol affects interactions among nerve cells in the brain. As discussed in Chapter 7, psychoactive drugs (including alcohol) act at communication points among nerve cells. Psychoactive drugs interfere with the normal activity of the chemicals that carry nerve impulses from one nerve cell to another. The manner of this interference varies among drugs.

Alcohol acts on parts of the brain that are responsible for drives and emotions, as well as the part of the brain that coordinates skeletal muscle movements. It also affects the "thinking" part and reward centers in the brain.

Many people drink alcohol to "get drunk," but other factors often contribute to excessive alcohol consumption. Anxious people, for example, may use alcohol to relieve their anxieties. Researchers think that persons with a family history of alcoholism are more likely to be motivated to drink alcohol to get "high," while persons with no family history of alcoholism are more likely to be motivated by anxiety.

At high doses, alcohol also has effects that are aversive; that is, they are sufficiently unpleasant (such as nausea and vomiting) that people often lose their desire to drink. Severe aversive effects, such as unconsciousness, result in a person being unable to continue drinking. Therefore, aversive effects help curb excessive alcohol consumption.

Table 8-3	Effects of Various Levels of Alcohol Consumption on Inexperienced Drinkers	
Number of Standard Drinks	Blood Alcohol Concentration (BAC)*	Effects
1–2	0.02 to 0.06%	Euphoria; reduction in anxiety
3–5	0.08 to 0.15%	Impairment of judgment, motor coordination, and emotional control; involuntary rapid eye movements; double vision; speech disorders; may be accompanied by aggressive behavior as alcohol level rises
7–8	0.20 to 0.25%	Sedation; impairment of ability to learn and remember information
12–18	0.40 to 0.50%	Loss of adequate respiration; dangerously low blood pressure; dangerously low internal body temperature; coma or death may result

*Blood alcohol concentration is expressed in percentages: A BAC of 0.05% means an alcohol concentration of 5 milliliters (ml) for every 10,000 ml of blood.

Chronic drug users develop **tolerance** to the drug; that is, increased amounts of alcohol are required to achieve effects previously produced by lower amounts. Tolerance develops because the chronic use of the drug stimulates liver enzymes to break down the drug with increasing swiftness. Also, brain cells become less responsive to the drug over time. Tolerance develops for both the pleasant and unpleasant effects of alcohol consumption, so chronic drinkers do not experience the aversive effects as quickly as do occasional drinkers. Therefore, their alcohol consumption is not curbed as quickly.

Psychological, Social, and Developmental Factors People drink for reasons other than to experience the "brain effects" of feeling good or reducing anxiety. Similarly, people curb their drinking or abstain from drinking for reasons other than aversive brain effects that may stimulate nausea and vomiting. Many of these reasons are *psychological,* having to do with thoughts, feelings, attitudes, and expectations about alcohol. Some of the reasons are *social,* relating to interactions with friends, relatives, and co-workers. Still other reasons are *developmental,* relating to the psychological, social, and biological changes in individuals over time and as they mature.

People often consume alcoholic beverages because they expect positive psychological effects from their drinking, such as enhancing social interactions, feeling pleasurable effects, or producing sedation. People develop their expectations concerning alcohol from experience, observation, and what they are told. In fact, a person's beliefs about alcohol can be predictive of their future drinking habits: Heavy drinkers tend to view the positive effects of alcohol as arousing, while light drinkers tend to view the positive effects as sedating.

Individuals often consume alcohol to ease their social interactions or because it's the thing to do in a particular social setting. With adolescents and young adults, peers may pressure one another to drink alcohol. The section "Alcohol and College Students" explores the role of peer pressure in the drinking patterns of college students. Cultural factors are additional important social reasons for drinking alcohol. In many cultures, people consume alcohol with meals or as a part of other traditional social activities.

Abusive and alcohol-dependent drinking patterns often begin in adolescence. A wide variety of factors affect children as they mature and influence the development of patterns of drinking alcoholic beverages. The biggest early risk factor for alcohol abuse and dependence is having a parent who is an alcoholic or who abuses alcohol. Adolescent children of alcoholics have significantly higher levels of alcohol use than adolescent children of nonalcoholics. Additionally, a child reared in an alcoholic family has a 50% greater risk of developing alcoholism then a child who is not reared in such an environment (Hanson & Venturelli, 1998; Pullen, 1994).

Another way in which parents influence their children is by their parenting practices. Teenagers who report receiving high levels of nurturing and support from their parents also report fewer alcohol-related problems than teenagers who report little parental nurturing and support. Teenagers who report feeling close to their parents drink alcoholic beverages less frequently than teenagers who report that they do not feel close to their parents. Children are more likely to use alcohol if their parents are not involved in their activities, there is a lack of or inconsistent discipline, and the parents have low educational aspirations for the children. Positive family relationships, involvement, and attachment appear to discourage youths' initiation into alcohol use.

Psychological, social, and developmental factors all interact with genetic factors to result in behavior. These interactions explain why not all alcoholics have a family history of alcoholism, and why not all persons with a family history of alcoholism become alcoholics. These dynamic interactions occur throughout life, with varying contributions from genes and environment at different times.

Alcohol and College Students

Alcohol abuse is a serious problem that often appears to begin or accelerate during the college years. In fact, the most commonly abused drug among college students is alcohol. Studies show that college students drink alcohol for a variety of reasons. █ **Table 8-4** lists the primary reasons that students give to explain why they drink. An interesting study conducted by Hugh Klein (1992) at Indiana University of Pennsylvania shows, however, that there are differences between moderate and heavy drinkers with regard to their reasons for drinking.

Moderate drinkers who do not abuse alcohol do not cite many reasons for their drinking. They state that they drink to celebrate important occasions (such as a friend's birthday or the completion of an exam) or because they enjoy

Table 8-4	College Students: Major Reasons for Drinking

College students report that they drink alcohol because

- it helps them celebrate special occasions.
- they enjoy the taste of alcohol.
- they want to relieve tension.
- it helps them relax.
- it helps them feel more comfortable in social settings.
- they want to get drunk.
- it relieves boredom.
- it just seems like the thing to do.
- they want to forget about schoolwork.

Source: Adapted from Klein, H. (1992). Self-reported reasons for why college students drink. *Journal of Alcohol and Drug Education,* 37(2):14–27.

Date Rape Drugs: Safety Tips for Women

- Drink from tamper-proof bottles or cans, and insist on opening them yourself.
- Be cautious about drinking from glasses in bars.
- Don't leave your drink unattended or trust someone to watch your drink while you dance or use the bathroom. Even a friend could get distracted.
- Accept drinks at a bar or club only from the bartender or server. If you can, watch your drink being prepared.
- Don't exchange or share drinks.
- Don't take a drink from a punch bowl or container that is passed around.
- Don't drink anything that has an unusual taste or appearance.
- Don't mix drugs with alcohol.

Source: Munz, M. (2000, Feb. 3). Arrest is first in Missouri involving date-rape drug. *St. Louis Post-Dispatch, 122*(34):A1, A-11. Data compiled from rape treatment centers.

---

the taste of alcohol. They do not drink with any goal in mind such as getting drunk.

Heavy drinkers who abuse alcohol, however, often state many reasons for their drinking, including the reasons listed in Table 8-4. They also differ from moderate, non-problem drinkers in that their drinking tends to be escapist and goal-oriented, as shown in the table. College men are more likely to be in this category than women. College men who belong to fraternities, especially those who live in fraternity houses, make up a large proportion of students who drink heavily (Pullen, 1994).

Fraternities are one campus institution in which drinking is particularly evident and is promoted. Within such social groups as fraternities, there is heavy peer pressure to drink. One reason for this peer pressure is that drinking in fraternities, as in other campus social groups, is perceived as promoting a feeling of unity and cohesiveness among their members. The consumption of alcoholic beverages, therefore, is deemed integral to many of the social and institutional aspects of college.

Certain student characteristics correlate with alcohol abuse. Although any student may abuse alcohol, abusers are more likely to be younger students with low self-esteem, high levels of anxiety, a mildly assertive personality, and at least one alcoholic parent. Men are more likely than women to abuse alcohol, and the freshman and sophomore years are the most likely times for students to exhibit alcohol abuse. Additionally, students who have a GPA of less than 2.0 are more likely than students with higher GPAs to abuse alcohol (Pullen, 1994).

Drinking alcohol during the college years poses many risks for students, including health problems; accidents; social embarrassment due to unusual behavior, vomiting, or urinating in public; and performance problems at school or work. In fact, many students who abstain from alcohol do so because they want to avoid such risks. Alcohol can also be a vehicle for date rape drugs (see Chapter 7). The "Managing Your Health" box "Date Rape Drugs: Safety Tips for Women" provides guidelines to help women avoid ingesting these dangerous substances in alcoholic beverages. ❚ **Table 8-5** lists the primary reasons some students abstain from drinking alcohol.

How the Body Processes Alcohol

When an alcoholic beverage is consumed, the alcohol in the drink is absorbed into the bloodstream from the stomach and intestinal tract. The blood transports alcohol to the "detoxification center" of the body—the liver. The liver degrades harmful substances such as drugs by changing them into compounds that are safer or easier to excrete.

The stomach also degrades some alcohol. Eating food while drinking alcoholic beverages results in the alcohol be-

Table 8-5	College Students: Major Reasons for Not Drinking

College students report that they abstain from drinking alcohol because

- they adhere to certain religious or moral convictions.
- they fear alcohol will harm their health.
- they dislike the taste of alcohol.
- it interferes with their jobs, school, personal relationships, or finances.
- they do not wish to conform to peer pressure to drink.
- their parents disapprove.
- they fear legal problems (e.g., drinking and driving).

Source: Adapted from Vogler, R. E., Webber, N. E., Rasor, R., Bartz, W. R., & Levesque, J. (1994). What college students need to know about drinking. *Journal of Alcohol and Drug Education, 39*(3):99–112.

ing held in the stomach for a longer time with the food. Therefore, more of it gets broken down in the stomach, and less alcohol enters the bloodstream. A person who drinks while eating will have a slower rise in the blood alcohol level than will a person who drinks on an empty stomach. Conversely, aspirin and cimetidine (an ulcer drug) inhibit the breakdown of alcohol in the stomach. A person who takes either of these drugs along with alcohol will have a quicker rise in the blood alcohol level than will a person who does not take these drugs when drinking alcohol.

Consequences of Alcohol Abuse and Dependence

Diseases and Conditions The harmful use and abuse of alcohol result in multiple effects on the body that are serious threats to health. Alcohol consumption does not affect all individuals in the same way; various effects result from differences among abusers' genetic makeup, general health, and drinking patterns. In spite of these differences, however, excessive alcohol consumption exerts its most serious effects on the liver, cardiovascular system, immune system, reproductive system, and brain. It also affects how vitamins are used by the body and can result in vitamin deficiencies. In pregnant women, it has devastating effects on the fetus.

Diseases of the Liver Because the liver is the major detoxification site for alcohol, it is particularly prone to harm by chronic alcohol consumption. Years of drinking can result in three types of liver disease: fatty liver, alcoholic hepatitis, and cirrhosis of the liver. The symptoms of each may overlap, and a person can have more than one of these conditions simultaneously. Women tend to develop these conditions at lower levels of alcohol intake than men (see p. 170).

Nearly 90% of heavy drinkers develop a *fatty liver* because alcohol induces the accumulation of fat in liver cells. This process begins immediately upon drinking: Fat accumulation has been found in the livers of young men after only one night of heavy drinking. Most liver cells are not specialized for fat storage, and their ability to perform their normal functions declines when they store fat. These liver cells eventually die; the scar tissue that remains produces cirrhosis.

Approximately 15% to 30% of alcoholics develop *liver cirrhosis* (■ **Figure 8-2**). This disease develops as alcohol begins to kill liver cells. Liver cells have the ability to regenerate, much like skin heals from a small cut. However, if cell damage is extensive, the liver cannot produce new cells quickly enough to replace destroyed ones. Connective tissue cells fill the spaces left by the dead cells, similar to the way scar tissue may fill the gap of tissue caused by a severe cut. However, connective tissue is not functional liver tissue, and the liver's ability to perform its many important functions declines. Eventually the person must have a liver transplant or he or she will die.

Approximately 40% of chronic abusers develop *alcoholic hepatitis*. Hepatitis is an inflammation of the liver, which can be caused by hepatitis viruses or by toxic chemicals such as alcohol. A severe case of hepatitis can result in death.

The majority of individuals who develop cirrhosis of the liver have been drinking heavily for 10 to 20 years. Women, however, are more at risk than men for liver disease. Because women detoxify alcohol less efficiently than men, the concentration of alcohol in their blood rises more quickly than in men when both consume the same number of drinks. Therefore, serious forms of alcoholic liver disease occur more frequently in women than in men. Additionally, women are more likely than men to develop these conditions at lower levels of alcohol consumption and after shorter periods of alcohol dependence. Hereditary factors and body weight, as well as sex, appear to play a role in susceptibility to liver disease. Results of recent studies also show that obese alcoholics have a two to three times higher risk of having alcoholic liver disease than non-obese alcoholics (Bunout, 1999).

Cardiovascular Disease and Cancer There is considerable evidence that limiting alcohol consumption to 1 oz or less of ethanol per day (two drinks or less) decreases the risk of death from coronary artery disease and stroke (see Chapter 12). However, heavier drinking is associated with cardiovascular diseases such as cardiomyopathy (heart muscle disease), hypertension (high blood pressure), arrhythmias (disturbances in heart rhythm), and stroke. In fact, very heavy drinking (about five drinks per day) is associated with a fourfold increase in the risk of stroke (Hillbom et al., 1999).

Alcohol abuse is a risk factor for certain cancers. The heavy consumption of alcohol can cause cancers of the esophagus and liver. It is also associated with the development of stomach cancer and increases the likelihood of larynx and mouth cancer in smokers. People who smoke cigarettes and drink alcohol, even in moderate amounts,

▲**Figure 8-2 An Unhealthy Liver with Cirrhosis.** Healthy liver tissue is smooth and dark red/brown.

ANALYZING Health-Related Information

The following article appeared in the *FDA Consumer,* the July/August 1998 issue. Read the article and explain why you think it is a reliable or an unreliable source of information. Use the model for analyzing health information to guide your thinking; the main points of the model are noted below. A full explanation of the model can be found on pages 12 to 13.

1. Which statements are verifiable facts; which are unverified statements or value claims?
2. What are the credentials of the person writing the article? If this information is available, does the author's background and education qualify him or her as an expert in the topic area?
3. What might be the motives and biases of the person writing the article? State reasons for your answer.
4. Which information is relevant to the issue or main point of the article; which information is irrelevant?
5. Is the source reliable? Does it have a reputation for publishing misinformation?
6. Does the article attack the credibility of conventional scientists or medical authorities?

Based on the above analysis, do you think that this article is a reliable source of health-related information? Summarize your reasons for coming to this conclusion.

Bottoms Up? The Benefits and Drawbacks of Alcoholic Beverages

by Liz Applegate, Ph.D.

You fought hard for that PR, and it wasn't easy. The course featured a couple of hills in the last miles, and the day was hot. But you did it, and now you want to celebrate with a couple of cold brews. You feel you deserve it.

Some postrace celebrations offer beer among their beverages. And runners gladly toast their victories or heal their race wounds with a bottle or two. Why not? What's the harm? Besides, a drink now and then may actually be good for you: moderate alcohol consumption has been shown to lower cholesterol levels, lessen the risk of heart disease, and perhaps even prevent age-related memory loss. All the more reason to quench your thirst with a drink or two.

However, while the latest news on booze makes it sound like a veritable nutritional beverage, drinking can be devastating to both your health and your running performance. Before you say "bottoms up," you need to know the harmful, as well as the healthful, effects of alcohol; then you can decide whether or not you should imbibe.

Here's to Your Health

Throughout history, alcohol has been considered a powerful elixir and has often been used medicinally. The Gaelic word for whiskey, *uisce beatha,* means "water of life." Today, scientists are finding there may be some truth to these beliefs.

The recent buzz about alcohol's potential health benefits began when researchers discovered that people of the Mediterranean region have low rates of heart disease despite a diet higher in fat—both vegetable and animal fat—than the average American diet. What researchers also noted is that Mediterranean people drink wine, usually red wine, with their meals. (Much less research has been done on white wine, so little is known of its health benefits.)

Since then, studies have shown that moderate drinking reduces the risk of strokes due to blocked arteries. It appears that alcohol raises artery-clearing HDL cholesterol while lowering artery-clogging LDLs. This combined with certain lifestyle differences and a lower risk of cardiovascular disease among moderate drinkers results in a 20% lower risk of death compared to that of nondrinkers.

And there may be an added benefit to having a little wine with dinner: it seems that moderate drinkers retain mental sharpness with age better than nondrinkers. A recent study that tracked the drinking habits of nearly 4,000 twins for 20 years found that

those who drank one to two drinks daily maintained better reasoning powers, problem-solving and other mental skills than those who abstained. The theory behind this goes back to alcohol's effects on cholesterol levels: clearer arteries, better blood flow to the brain, clearer thinking.

The antioxidant antidote. As researchers continued to explore the reasons for alcohol's health benefits, they discovered that the antioxidants in wine and other alcoholic beverages (we don't yet know whether beer contains antioxidants) may explain why alcoholic drinks protect against heart disease. Called phenolic flavonoids, these antioxidants come from grape skins during winemaking.

The theory of their effect is this: As LDL cholesterol circulates in the bloodstream, it oxidizes. This oxidation, or "rusting," of LDLs leads to vessel damage and, ultimately, blockage of the arteries. Antioxidants prevent oxidation of LDLs, thus lessening artery damage and helping to prevent heart disease and stroke.

Recent research at the University of California at Davis supports this theory. Studies there showed that 2 to 3 hours after drinking two glasses of red wine, levels of phenols peak in the bloodstream. These higher levels of phenols likely mean greater protection against LDL oxidation.

Sobriety Check

Though the latest news certainly implies that a little imbibing may help you live longer, don't be lulled into a blissful ignorance of alcohol's harmful effects. Drinking alcoholic beverages can take a toll on your body—and a very serious one if you overdo it.

Your body treats alcohol like a VIP. From the moment of absorption to final processing, alcohol gets top priority over other nutrients, thereby interfering with other important bodily functions. Let's take a look at alcohol's route through the body.

When you drink, about a fifth of the alcohol is absorbed quickly by the stomach. The rest moves into the intestines and soon into the bloodstream. Some of the alcohol in your stomach is immediately metabolized and never gets into the bloodstream (*note:* women have less of the enzyme responsible for this metabolism, which is one reason why they often feel the effects of a drink more readily than men). The remainder of the alcohol circulates in your bloodstream to different tissues and organs of the body.

Because alcohol is soluble in water, it first goes to the more watery parts of your body, such as the brain. Another reason that women are more readily affected by alcohol than men is that they have lower body water content due to higher body fat percentages. As a result, the concentration of alcohol in women's blood rises more rapidly.

Once in the blood, alcohol gets transported to the liver, where it is metabolized—broken down—at a rate of about 10 grams (a little less than what's contained in a standard drink) an hour. As you drink, your liver gets busy "detoxifying" alcohol, and the other vital duties of this organ are put on hold.

One of the functions of the liver is to process fat and ship it out into the bloodstream for transport to muscle and fat cells. The presence of alcohol delays this process, and as a result, small droplets of fat accumulate in the liver and remain there until all the alcohol is metabolized. Once you've stopped drinking and the alcohol has left your system, the liver can process fat and get rid of it. However, if you drink a lot and frequently, the accumulation of fat droplets can damage liver function and may eventually lead to liver disease.

Drinking and Running Don't Mix

When it comes to running, drinking alcoholic beverages can sap your body of the two substances it needs most to perform well: food and water.

Another function of your liver is to store glycogen that your body can then use for energy. Again, if your liver is busy processing alcohol, this interferes with carbohydrate metabolism, and blood sugar levels drop. A night of drinking can leave you feeling weak and hungry and none too ready for your morning run. And if you do decide to give it that old college try, you'll probably find that your pace is sluggish and your endurance subpar.

Also be aware that alcohol is a diuretic, meaning that it speeds water loss from your body, making dehydration a real threat. Part of the reason for a hangover is that your brain, a very watery organ, shrinks somewhat through dehydration after drinking. This shrinkage causes a headache. Along with water, several vitamins and minerals are lost from your body, including zinc, a mineral critical to healthy immune function.

As all runners know, dehydration affects your running performance and can become a serious problem if too much water is lost. Furthermore, you lose water as you sweat during a run or race. So drinking alcohol during postrace celebrations sends blood alcohol concentrations soaring. You become further dehydrated, and you get drunk on less alcohol.

And if you think a postrace beer helps to replenish carbohydrates, consider this: a 12-ounce can of beer contains only between 5 and 11 grams of carbohydrates. This means you would need to drink a half to a full case of beer in order to get the 125 grams of carbohydrates you need in the first few hours after a tough effort.

So What's Right for You?

Let me begin by saying that even moderate alcohol consumption isn't right for everyone. For many, the health risks of drinking far outweigh any possible health benefits. Approximately 100,000 Americans die prematurely each year from misuse of alcohol.

Those who should abstain from alcohol altogether include pregnant women, women trying to get pregnant, persons on medications such as antidepressants (combining alcohol and drugs can accentuate the effects of both), recovering alcoholics, individuals operating machinery or driving a car, and those under the legal drinking age. If you have any questions about whether alcohol may be particularly harmful to your health, check with your doctor.

For those who can consume alcoholic beverages healthfully, the key is moderation. An accepted definition of moderate alcohol consumption is one to two drinks daily for most men and one drink for most women. A standard drink is 12 ounces of beer, 5 ounces of wine or 1 1/2 ounces of hard liquor. And remember, for each drink you have, your body needs an hour to process the alcohol. So if

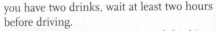

you have two drinks, wait at least two hours before driving.

And as for mixing running and drinking, avoid alcohol the night before a race or a tough workout. If it's a big race for you, consider abstaining for two nights beforehand.

After your race, it's okay to have one or two to celebrate, but be sure to drink plenty of water or sports drinks, too. Drink 16 ounces of fluid for every pound lost from sweat. And eat plenty. Bananas, bagels, and muffins will replenish spent carbohydrates and help to stave off the effects of alcohol.

Source: Applegate, L. (May 1995). "Bottoms up? The benefits and drawbacks of alcoholic beverages," *Runner's World*, 26–29.

Note: Liz Applegate is a nutritionist who teaches at the University of California, Davis. She writes a monthly column for *Runner's World*.

multiply their risk of cancer of the esophagus 12 to 19 times, because together these drugs have a multiplier affect. That is, when people take both drugs routinely, their risk of cancer is much higher than if the risk of each was added (Castellsague et al., 1999).

Even when not abused, alcohol can raise the risk of cancer. Consuming three or more drinks per week raises a woman's risk for developing breast cancer. Additionally, data suggest that women who drink alcohol while taking estrogen in postmenopausal estrogen replacement therapy may increase their breast cancer risk more than if they used either one alone (Ginsberg, 1999).

Immune System Suppression The immune system (see Chapter 14), which protects the body from invasion by pathogens, also suffers as a result of chronic alcohol abuse. This behavior impairs the functioning of the immune system, predisposing the drinker to infectious diseases such as colds, pneumonia, and tuberculosis. Chronic alcohol abuse even suppresses the activity of certain immune system cells that defend the body against the spread of cancer.

Detrimental Effects on the Reproductive System Alcohol affects the reproductive systems of both men and women. It affects the functioning of the testes, decreasing the amount of the sex hormone, testosterone, these organs produce. Alcoholic men often experience shrinking of the testicles, impotence, and loss of libido, or sex drive. In women, alcohol affects the functioning of the ovaries. The menstrual periods of alcoholic women are often irregular or cease altogether. As a result, alcoholic women often have difficulty becoming pregnant. Alcoholic women also have a higher rate of early menopause than nonalcoholic women. During pregnancy, alcohol consumption can have devastating effects on the fetus. This topic is discussed in the "Life Span" section of this chapter (see pages 192–193).

Detrimental Effects on the Brain Alcohol consumption has multiple effects on the brain. Chronic alcoholics may experience brain disorders. One of the most serious is the Wernicke-Korsakoff syndrome. This syndrome includes mental confusion, abnormal eye movements, and an inability to coordinate skeletal muscles, which results in abnormal posture and a staggering gait. Scientists have discovered that this syndrome may be due to the alcoholic's inability to use the B vitamin thiamin properly. Some alcoholics are deficient in this vitamin (and many other nutrients) because their diets consist primarily of alcohol rather than food. In either case, if given thiamin, the abstinent alcoholic can be cured of the abnormal eye movements, posture, and gait. However, the person is left with anterograde amnesia—the inability to remember new information for more than a few seconds.

Another effect of alcohol on the brain is intoxication, the impairment of the central nervous system (see Table 8-3). *Withdrawal* is another brain effect of alcohol, but only in alcohol-dependent individuals who stop drinking or reduce their alcohol intake. Withdrawal symptoms usually occur about 24 to 36 hours after an alcoholic stops drinking. Typically, the alcoholic experiences mild agitation, shaking, anxiety, loss of appetite, restlessness, and insomnia. Five to 15% of alcoholics experience grand mal seizures (convulsions) during withdrawal. Additionally, a small percentage of alcoholics have severe withdrawal symptoms that include hyperactivity, hallucinations, disorientation, and confusion. This severe withdrawal syndrome is called *delirium tremens*, or *DTs*.

Some researchers suggest that a *hangover* is a mild form of withdrawal that can occur in anyone who consumes alcoholic beverages heavily during a session of drinking. The signs of a hangover include headache, diarrhea, loss of appetite, blackouts, anxiety, stomach pains, tremors, and thoughts of suicide. If the "mild withdrawal" explanation is true, it explains why consuming additional alcohol temporarily relieves hangover effects.

Other physiological effects of drinking alcohol may cause hangovers, however. Alcoholic beverages contain certain acidic compounds that have toxic effects on the body. These compounds differ among types of alcoholic beverages and affect whether someone will experience a hangover. Another compound called formaldehyde (a preservative of dead animals) is produced by the body when it cannot keep up with the breakdown of alcohol being consumed. The buildup of formaldehyde contributes to a hangover. Additionally, alcohol causes the body to lose water. This dehydration occurs in brain cells as well as other body cells. Pain accompanies their rehydration.

Whatever the causes of a hangover, home remedies such as taking vitamins, getting in a cold shower, or drinking coffee will not cure the "morning-after" pain of drinking too much. Time alone will cure a hangover.

Effects on Behavior and Safety

Serious and Fatal Injuries Statistics show that alcohol use and abuse is related to serious and even fatal injuries. Alcohol frequently contributes to water-related accidents, motor-vehicle accidents, general aviation crashes, domestic and nondomestic violence including sexual assault and rape, suicides, and homicides.

Data from a variety of studies show that one-third to one-half of drivers hurt or killed in motor-vehicle accidents are intoxicated at the time of the accident (Centers for Disease Control and Prevention [CDC], 1999a; Hansen et al., 1996; Mancino et al., 1996; Mercer & Jeffery, 1995). Approximately one-third of all victims of homicide and unintentional-injury death (excluding those in car crashes) are intoxicated at the time of their deaths as well. Additionally, about one-fifth of suicide victims are intoxicated when they take their own lives (Smith et al., 1999). In comparison, less than one-tenth of individuals in a London study who died of natural causes had alcohol in their blood at the time of death (Cox et al., 1997).

Automobile Accidents Drinking and driving is potentially deadly because alcohol impairs the perceptual, intellectual,

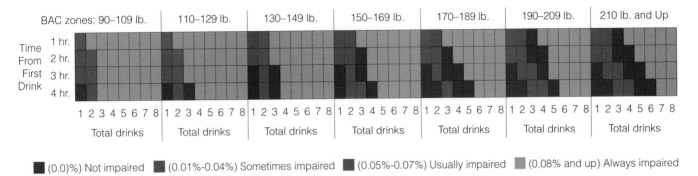

BAC zones:	90–109 lb.	110–129 lb.	130–149 lb.	150–169 lb.	170–189 lb.	190–209 lb.	210 lb. and Up

Time From First Drink: 1 hr. / 2 hr. / 3 hr. / 4 hr.

1 2 3 4 5 6 7 8 | 1 2 3 4 5 6 7 8 | 1 2 3 4 5 6 7 8 | 1 2 3 4 5 6 7 8 | 1 2 3 4 5 6 7 8 | 1 2 3 4 5 6 7 8 | 1 2 3 4 5 6 7 8

Total drinks (for each zone)

■ (0.0)%) Not impaired   ■ (0.01%–0.04%) Sometimes impaired   ■ (0.05%–0.07%) Usually impaired   ▨ (0.08% and up) Always impaired

▲**Figure 8-3 Blood Alcohol Concentration by Body Weight.**
These graphs show the approximate BACs of people in various weight ranges. The BAC of each group is calculated using the number of drinks consumed over measured points of time. The BACs are denoted by various colors. Source: Adapted from the California Department of Motor Vehicles.

and motor skills needed to operate motor vehicles safely. Traffic accidents are the leading cause of death among people aged 5 to 24 years, and the second leading cause of death in children under the age of 5 (Hoyert et al., 1999). Researchers estimate that eliminating alcohol would reduce overall traffic fatalities by about 47%. In most states, the legal BAC limit for operating an automobile is 0.10%. Thirteen states have reduced their BAC limits to 0.08%, and 38 states have a lower unlawful BAC threshold for youth under 21, and in some cases, under 18 (National Transportation Statistics, 1998). ■ **Figure 8-3** shows approximate blood alcohol concentration by body weight and

the time from the first drink. Note the number of drinks a person can have over a period of time before he or she is considered legally drunk. Also realize that some impairment occurs after a person consumes only one drink.

Alcohol-related fatal automobile accidents occur more frequently at certain times of the day and during certain days of the week than others. Approximately 50% of drivers killed during the weekend had BACs of at least 0.01% compared to 29% of drivers killed during weekdays. Similarly, 62% of drivers killed during nighttime hours had BACs of 0.01% or more compared to only 18% of drivers killed during daytime hours (U.S. Department of Transportation [DOT], 1998). ■ **Figure 8-4** shows that alcohol-

▼**Figure 8-4 Percentage of Fatal Alcohol-Related Automobile Accidents Graphed According to the Time of Day They Occurred.** Source: U.S. Department of Transportation (April 1998). *Final report. Alcohol highway safety: Problem update.* Washington, DC: National Highway Traffic Safety Administration.

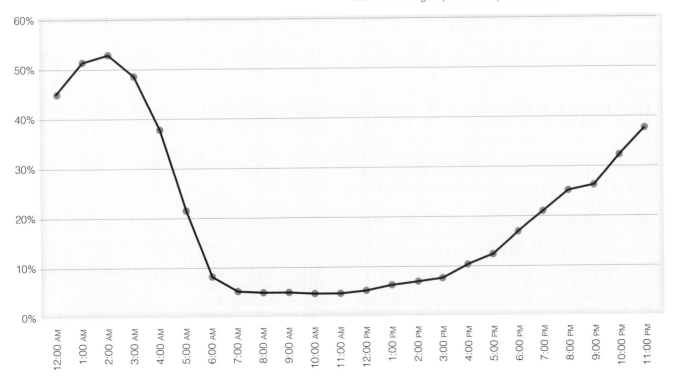

related fatal car crashes peak between midnight and 3 A.M. Few alcohol-related crashes occur between 7 A.M. and 3 P.M., but the percentage rises throughout the late afternoon and evening until the midnight peak. These statistics together show that a person driving at night and in the early morning hours, especially on a weekend, is more likely to be involved in a fatal alcohol-related motor vehicle accident than driving during the day and during the week. Taking public transportation or cabs on weekend nights is safer than driving for both drinkers and nondrinkers alike.

One *Healthy People 2000* goal is to reduce alcohol-related automobile deaths. The *Healthy People 2010—Conference Edition* report (2000) shows such deaths to have dropped from 9.8 per 100,000 Americans in 1987 to 6.5 per 100,000 in 1997. (Automobile fatalities are defined as alcohol-related when at least one automobile driver or nonoccupant of the car[s] involved in the crash [such as a pedestrian or cyclist] has a BAC of 0.01% or higher.) Drivers aged 18 years and younger have experienced the greatest decline in alcohol-related automobile fatalities, from 22 deaths per 100,000 in 1982 to 10 per 100,000 in 1996. The National Highway Traffic Safety Administration suggests that this decline is at least partly due to enforcement of minimum drinking age laws ("Healthy People 2010", 2000). The 1998 National Household Survey on Drug Abuse (SAMHSA, 1999) also shows that alcohol use among youth aged 12 to 17 years dropped from 50% in 1979 to 21% in 1992, and has remained relatively stable at this lower level since then.

Women who drink and drive must remember that their BACs rise more quickly than the BACs of males who consume the same number of drinks. Recent data indicate that females are increasingly involved in fatal automobile accidents. In 1982, 12.3% of drivers in fatal crashes with a BAC of 0.10% or more were female, and this percentage has grown steadily to 15.7% in 1996, an increase of 28% (DOT, 1998). Both sexes must also remember that the risk of fatal crashes rises rapidly with increasing BAC. As you can see in ▌ **Figure 8-5,** the risk of having a fatal car crash is about 11 times greater for drivers with BACs between 0.05% and 0.09% than for persons with no alcohol in their blood. This risk increases dramatically, to nearly 50 times greater, for drivers with BACs between 0.10% and 0.14%. For drivers with BACs equal to or higher than 0.15%, the risk is almost 400 times greater.

Airplane Accidents Alcohol also impairs the ability of pilots to fly aircraft. Alcohol has not been directly implicated in U.S. commercial airline crashes; however, it appears to play a more prominent role in general aviation crashes. Experimental research indicates that hangover effects (see page 176) may impair pilot performance for several hours even after alcohol has been eliminated from the blood (Yesavage & Leirer, 1986).

Water-Related Accidents Alcohol is also a significant factor in water-related accidents. Researchers estimate that alcohol consumption is associated with between 41% and 79% of adult drownings. The highest percentages are associated with males older than 25 years (Plueckhahn, 1975; Wintemute et al., 1990.). Most alcohol-related drownings are associated with motor-vehicle accidents, but alcohol is also present in the blood of more than half the drowning victims who were swimming, boating, or rafting when they died. Alcohol also contributes to diving accidents that leave victims with serious spinal cord injuries.

Prevention

Because many people begin drinking alcoholic beverages during adolescence, prevention programs often target younger children to educate them about alcohol before they reach their teenage years. Prevention efforts include school-based programs for children in grades 5 through 10, but most target fifth and sixth graders. Because this time is developmentally critical as students move from elementary school to middle school or junior high, those who have experimented with alcohol may begin to misuse it at this time.

There are a variety of school-based programs. *Affective education* seeks to influence students' feelings about them-

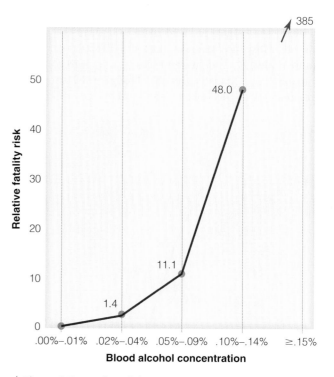

▲**Figure 8-5 Fatality Risk at Various Levels of Blood Alcohol Concentration.** This graph shows that as the BAC rises, the likelihood of being killed while driving a car increases. As the BAC approaches the legal limit for drunkenness (0.08% to 0.10%), the risk of being killed rises dramatically. Source: Zador, P. L. (1991). Alcohol-related relative risk of fatal driver injuries in relation to driver and age and sex. *J. Stat. Alcohol* 52(4), 302–310.

selves and alcohol by helping them develop self-esteem as well as problem-solving and decision-making abilities. In addition, these programs promote an understanding of how alcohol use can interfere with personal values and goals. Results of research show that such programs have limited effectiveness. *Life skills programs* emphasize the development of communication, conflict resolution, and assertiveness skills to help students cope with peer pressure to drink alcohol, smoke cigarettes, or take other drugs. Results of research show that life skills programs reduce alcohol use primarily among females. *Resistance training*—the "Just say no" approach—shows mixed results. *Normative education* aims to correct erroneous beliefs about the prevalence and acceptability of alcohol use among peers. (Results of survey research show that young people believe that alcohol use among their peers is more common than it really is.) Adding normative components to alcohol education programs for adolescents appears useful. More recent school-based programs have been shown to be more effective than early programs in reducing alcohol use and abuse by young people because many have been redesigned to incorporate research-based aspects shown to work (National Institute of Alcohol Abuse and Alcoholism [NIAAA], 1997).

Prevention efforts that focus on the entire population of drinkers are called *environmental approaches*. Such approaches are important because approximately 52% of Americans are current alcohol users (SAMHSA, 1999), and many drinkers experience moderate to severe alcohol-induced impairment at least occasionally. These drinkers are all at risk for alcohol-related injuries and health problems.

One prevention strategy for the general population was the requirement by the U.S. government to place warnings on alcoholic beverage containers beginning in 1989. How-ever, survey data show that only about one-fourth of adults realize that the labels exist. Researchers have not found evidence that warning labels reduce alcohol consumption and its health-related effects. Another prevention strategy was the establishment of 21 as the minimum age for purchase and consumption of alcohol. Evidence suggests that this strategy significantly reduced youth drinking and related problems such as alcohol-related traffic accidents in those under the age of 21 (NIAAA, 1997).

How to Control Your Alcohol Consumption

Studies show that light drinkers have certain behavior patterns that help them curb their drinking. These attributes are listed in the "Managing Your Health" box below and are effective rules for controlling alcohol consumption.

Diagnosis and Treatment of Alcoholism and Alcohol Abuse

According to the 1997 National Household Survey on Drug Abuse (SAMHSA, 1998), approximately 3.1 million Americans received treatment for alcohol abuse during the year prior to the survey. Of Americans treated, the majority were between the ages of 18 and 34 years. Also, males were twice as likely as females to have received treatment. Various types of treatment are available for those who need help. Screening techniques help identify those persons who need treatment.

The CAGE screening test, printed in the student workbook, is considered one of the most effective screening devices for alcohol abuse or alcoholism. A variety of other screening instruments are available also.

Health-care professionals who determine that their patients are alcohol dependent refer them to substance abuse specialists for evaluation and possible treatment. Patients

Guidelines for Safer Drinking

1. Think about your alcohol drinking behaviors beforehand and plan how you will drink.
2. Drink slowly, and alternate alcoholic beverages with nonalcoholic beverages.
3. Eat before or while drinking.
4. Set a limit on the amount of alcohol you can drink at one time. Base this limit on the number of drinks someone with your body weight can drink and still remain below a BAC of 0.05% (see Figure 8-3); count drinks to stay within this limit.
5. Set a limit on how long you will drink; ideally, drink for an hour or less.
6. Drink only to enhance a good time and not to combat stress or to avoid dealing with problems.
7. Become skillful at assertively refusing drinks.
8. Don't drink daily (to avoid developing tolerance).
9. Cultivate alternatives to drinking that compete with its benefits (such as relaxing or socializing).
10. Practice social skills such as approaching people and engaging them in conversation while sober so you won't need alcohol to feel comfortable in social settings.

Source: Adapted from Vogler, R., Webber, N. E., Rasor, R., Bartz, W. R., & Levesque, J. (1994). *Journal of Alcohol and Drug Education, 39*(3):99-112.

that show nondependent problem drinking are often encouraged to participate in brief intervention programs.

In the past, physicians and substance abuse practitioners thought that an alcoholic could not be helped until he or she "hit bottom" and then asked for help. A person who did not ask for help was considered to be denying his or her alcoholism and lacking motivation to change. Current thinking regards motivation as a process of behavioral change rather than a trait that people have or do not have.

Before treatment, the role of clinical intervention is to help the patient understand the serious dangers inherent in his or her abusive or dependent drinking behavior. Once the alcoholic realizes the need to change his or her behavior, he or she tries to decide what course of action to take.

Table 8-6	The Twelve Steps of Alcoholics Anonymous

1. We admitted we were powerless over alcohol—that our lives had become unmanageable.
2. Came to believe that a Power greater than ourselves could restore us to sanity.
3. Made a decision to turn our will and our lives over to the care of God as we understood Him.
4. Made a searching and fearless moral inventory of ourselves.
5. Admitted to God, to ourselves, and to another human being the exact nature of our wrongs.
6. Were entirely ready to have God remove all these defects of character.
7. Humbly asked Him to remove our shortcomings.
8. Made a list of all persons we had harmed, and became willing to make amends to them all.
9. Made direct amends to such people wherever possible, except when to do so would injure them or others.
10. Continued to take personal inventory and when we were wrong promptly admitted it.
11. Sought through prayer and meditation to improve our conscious contact with God, as we understood Him, praying only for knowledge of His will for us and the power to carry that out.
12. Having had a spiritual awakening as the result of these Steps, we tried to carry this message to alcoholics, and to practice these principles in all our affairs.

Source: The Twelve Steps are reprinted with permission of Alcoholics Anonymous World Services, Inc. Permission to reprint the Twelve Steps does not mean that AA has reviewed or approved the contents of this publication, nor that AA agrees with the views expressed herein. AA is a program of recovery from alcoholism only—use of the Twelve Steps in connection with programs and activities which are patterned after AA, but which address other problems, or in any other non–AA context, does not imply otherwise.

The clinician helps the patient select a course of action, or treatment program, that best suits his or her needs.

Both inpatient and outpatient programs exist. *Inpatient treatment,* in which the alcoholic resides at a treatment facility, is sometimes used for the early phases of treatment, particularly acute detoxification. During this time, the patient abstains from alcohol and experiences withdrawal symptoms (see page 176). Approximately 10% to 13% of patients need medication during this time to help them reduce potentially life-threatening effects of withdrawal. During the detoxification period, patients participate in group therapy and alcohol education sessions for several hours daily. Recovering alcoholics usually live with patients to help them through the process. Such programs usually last 28 days. Near the end of this process the alcoholic's family is usually asked to participate in treatment.

Due to rising medical costs, acute detoxification, as well as further treatment, may take place in *outpatient programs.* Such programs, developed over the past 25 years, have been extremely successful. Approximately 90% of patients are now treated in outpatient facilities. In these programs, the patient spends a specific amount of time at the treatment facility but lives at home.

After a person has sought treatment for alcohol abuse or dependence, the next stage in behavior change is *maintenance.* For long-term maintenance treatment, recovering alcoholics take part in group meetings and attend individual counseling sessions once or twice a week at outpatient facilities, participate in self-help group meetings, and sometimes participate in family therapy. The maintenance period usually lasts one year.

Sometimes *relapse* occurs. During a relapse, a recovering alcoholic returns to his or her drinking habits. Relapse can be triggered by a variety of factors such as stress, depression, alcohol craving, negative life events, and interpersonal tensions. To recover once again, the patient goes through the stages of behavior change. Treatment to prevent an initial or repeated relapse often involves self-help groups.

Alcoholics Anonymous (AA) is the best-known and most widely available of the self-help groups. Governed by its own members, the organization's philosophy is that alcoholism is a physical, emotional, and spiritual disease for which there is no cure. Recovery is a lifelong process that involves attention to AA's Twelve Steps, which are listed in ▌ **Table 8-6.** AA also has related support groups for family members and friends of alcoholics such as Alateen and Al-Anon.

Although not as well known, other self-help groups exist. The Secular Organization for Sobriety (SOS) is a group similar to AA, except its program does not include spiritual aspects. Neither does the Rational Recovery (RR) program, which emphasizes the importance of alcoholics becoming aware of their irrational beliefs, self-perceptions, and expectancies in order to be successful in changing their behavior. These groups suggest abstinence as a preferred drinking goal but emphasize personal choice. One self-help approach for women is Women for Sobriety. This group emphasizes women's issues such as assertiveness, self-confidence, and autonomy as part of the change process.

Healthy
LIVING PRACTICES

- To be a responsible drinker, do not allow your drinking to threaten your health, endanger the safety of others, or interfere with business or personal relationships.
- If drinking alcohol is damaging your physical and/or psychological health, you should seek medical help.
- If you use alcohol in physically dangerous situations, have developed a tolerance to alcohol, exhibit withdrawal symptoms when you are not drinking, and compulsively use alcohol, you are probably alcohol dependent and should seek medical help.
- Be sure to eat while drinking alcoholic beverages so that less alcohol will enter the bloodstream.
- If you consume alcohol, drink only 1 oz of ethanol per day or less to decrease the risk of coronary artery disease and stroke. Heavier alcohol consumption is associated with a variety of heart and blood vessel diseases.
- Do not drive after consuming alcoholic beverages. Alcohol impairs many of the skills needed to operate motor vehicles safely. As your blood alcohol concentration increases, your risk of having a car crash increases dramatically.

www.jbpub.com/healthyliving

Tobacco

Types of Tobacco Products

Cigarettes are the most prevalent type of tobacco product in the United States. In 1998 an estimated 60 million Americans were cigarette smokers, representing 27.7% of the population age 12 and older (SAMHSA, 1999). Although this rate is a decrease of about 16% since 1965 (one of the peak years for cigarette smoking in the United States), the decline has leveled off in recent years. Scientists think that the United States will not make the goal of *Healthy People 2000*—to reduce the percentage of smokers to 15% by the year 2000 (CDC, 1999b). That data, not available at this writing, will be available in late 2001. Additionally, the rate of smoking among young adults aged 18 to 25 has increased dramatically in recent years, from 34.6% in 1994 to 41.6% in 1998 (SAMHSA, 1999). The "Consumer Health" box "Kreteks and Bidis: Unwrapping

the Facts" on page 182 describes types of cigarettes that are becoming popular with young Americans.

Smoking cigars and pipes is not as prevalent in the American population as smoking cigarettes. In 1998 approximately 12% of men smoked cigars, versus 2.3% of women (SAMHSA, 1999). Most cigar or pipe smokers are men over the age of 35 years. Generally, women do not smoke pipes.

In 1998 nearly 6% of American men but only 0.5% of American women used *smokeless tobacco*, which includes *snuff* and *chewing tobacco* (SAMHSA, 1999). Snuff, the most popular form of smokeless tobacco, is powdered or finely cut tobacco. It may be used loose or wrapped in a paper pouch. Although snuff can be inhaled, most users in the United States today place snuff between the cheek and gum. This practice is called *dipping*.

Chewing tobacco is loose leaf tobacco or a plug of compressed tobacco, which is sometimes called a *quid*. It is placed in the cheek. It can be chewed, as its name suggests, or, more often, it is sucked. During the time that snuff or chewing tobacco remains in the mouth, it forms a liquid that smokeless tobacco users usually spit out. For this reason smokeless tobacco is often called spitting tobacco.

Worldwide, a variety of other tobacco products exist besides those mentioned here. Additionally, methods of tobacco use vary among cultures. "The Diversity in Health" essay "Tobacco Drinking???" on page 183 describes a few tobacco-related practices of various South American cultures.

Who Uses Tobacco and Why?

As mentioned earlier, most people who smoke cigarettes began this habit when they were adolescents. ▌ **Figure 8-6** shows the ages at which adults say they started smoking. Only 11% of adult smokers started this habit after age 18. Smokeless tobacco use usually begins in early adolescence or in childhood also.

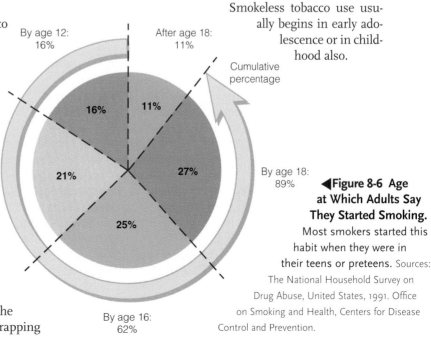

◄ **Figure 8-6 Age at Which Adults Say They Started Smoking.** Most smokers started this habit when they were in their teens or preteens. Sources: The National Household Survey on Drug Abuse, United States, 1991. Office on Smoking and Health, Centers for Disease Control and Prevention.

Data show that during the 1990s there was an increase in the percentage of high school students who smoke cigarettes daily (■ **Figure 8-7**). More than a quarter of high school students responded that they were current cigarette smokers on the National Youth Tobacco Survey, and more than one-third reported using some form of tobacco in the month prior to the survey (CDC, 2000). Despite all that is known today about the health consequences of cigarette smoking, nearly one-third of twelfth-grade students still do not believe that there is a great risk in smoking a pack or more of cigarettes per day (Johnston et al., 1999a). The *Healthy People 2000* objective is to reduce the number of new, young smokers to 15%.

The use of snuff among adolescent boys has risen dramatically since 1970. Overall use of smokeless tobacco (chewing tobacco or snuff) among adolescent males re-

Con$umer *Health* | Kreteks and Bidis: Unwrapping the Facts

Kreteks (clove cigarettes) and bidi cigarettes are becoming increasingly popular among American youth. Clove cigarettes, developed in Indonesia in the early 1900s and presently manufactured there, have been imported into the United States since 1968. Bidis, manufactured primarily in India and other Southeast Asian countries, were not widely used in the United States until the mid-1990s.

Clove cigarettes look much like tobacco cigarettes and are made with or without filter tips. Most are wrapped with white paper, but some have brown or black coverings. Clove cigarettes contain approximately 40% ground cloves and 60% tobacco, although the specific amount varies among manufacturers and brands. Clove oil is added as well, often discoloring the cigarette paper. As these cigarettes burn, the cloves make a crackling sound. (*Kretek* means "crackle" in Indonesia.)

Many users of clove cigarettes think that they are less dangerous to smoke than regular cigarettes because 40% of their content is cloves rather than tobacco. However, they are making an incorrect, and possibly deadly, assumption. Clove cigarettes are rolled tighter than regular cigarettes, resulting in a denser product. Put simply, there's less air in clove cigarettes than in regular cigarettes, so the tobacco content of kreteks is similar to that of regular cigarettes. Additionally, tests show that clove cigarettes deliver, on aver-

age, twice as much tar, nicotine, and carbon monoxide as do moderate tar-containing American cigarettes.

Clove cigarettes also contain an anesthetic called eugenol (a natural component of the cloves), which can cause allergic reactions in some. This anesthetic numbs the backs of smokers' throats and windpipes. Researchers think that this numbing effect is the reason that smokers inhale kretek smoke more deeply and retain it in their lungs longer than when smoking regular cigarettes. They also suspect that this numbing effect may encourage smoking by people who might otherwise find smoking cigarettes harsh and distasteful. In a 1999 survey nearly 2% of middle school students and 6% of high school students responded that they had smoked clove cigarettes on one or more occasions during the previous month.

Bidis are small, strong-smelling brown cigarettes wrapped in leaves (much like cigars) and are tied with a string. They are smaller and thinner than regular cigarettes and come in flavors such as cherry, mango, chocolate, and strawberry. Results from a 1999 survey of students in grades 7 through 12 conducted in Massachusetts reveal that young people smoke bidis because they like the flavor and find bidis cheaper and easier to buy than regular cigarettes. Additionally, they perceived bidis to be safer than smoking regular cigarettes. How-

ever, as with clove cigarettes, this assumption is false. Tests show that bidis produce approximately 3 times the amount of carbon monoxide and nicotine as American cigarettes, and about 5 times the amount of tar. Additionally, smokers inhale more often and more deeply when smoking bidis than when smoking regular cigarettes because the leaf wrapper does not burn well. In a 1999 survey more than 2% of middle school students and about 5% of high school students responded that they had smoked bidi cigarettes on one or more occasions during the previous month.

So, are smoking kreteks and bidis safe alternatives to smoking regular cigarettes? The answer is an emphatic no! In fact, the data show that these alternative smoking products pose even greater health risks than regular cigarettes. Additionally, their appeal to adolescents and teenagers adds to an already alarming trend of increased cigarette smoking nationwide among high school students.

Sources: Centers for Disease Control and Prevention. (2000). Tobacco use among middle and high school students—United States, 1999. *Morbidity and Mortality Weekly Report,* 49:49-53.

Centers for Disease Control and Prevention. (1999). Bidi use among urban youth—Massachusetts, March–April 1999. *Morbidity and Mortality Weekly Report,* 48:796-799.

Centers for Disease Control and Prevention. (1985). Epidemiologic notes and reports illnesses possibly associated with smoking clove cigarettes. *Morbidity and Mortality Weekly Report,* 34:297-299.

mains high. In general, females show little use of smokeless tobacco compared to males. However, in certain populations of Native Americans, up to 28% of the females use smokeless tobacco products (Spangler et al., 1995).

Psychosocial Reasons for Using Tobacco Products Adolescents initially try tobacco products for a variety of reasons. Adolescents who have family members or friends who

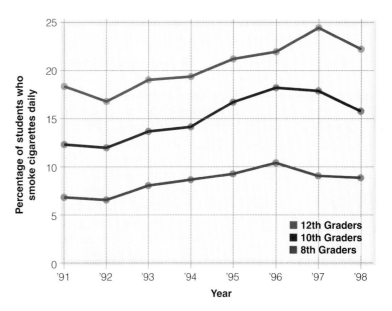

▶Figure 8-7 **Cigarettes: Trends in Daily Use by 8th-, 10th-, and 12th-Graders.** Source: Johnston, L. D., O'Malley, P. M., & Bachman, J.G. (1999). *National Survey Results on Drug Use from the Monitoring the Future Study, 1975–1998. vol 1: Secondary School Students.* Rockville, MD: National Institute on Drug Abuse (NIH pub. no. 99-4660).

DIVERSITY in Health | Tobacco Drinking??

To North Americans, the phrase "using tobacco" usually means smoking cigarettes, cigars, or pipes. Occasionally we might envision a person using chewing tobacco or placing a pinch of snuff between the gums and cheek. (This practice is called "dipping" snuff.) But various cultures use tobacco in other ways—including some ways that may be new to you.

Drinking liquid tobacco is one of the oldest methods of tobacco use. The members of certain tribal populations in South America, particularly those living in Guiana, the upper Amazon, and the mountainous regions of Ecuador and Peru, drink tobacco juice. The drinking of tobacco has also been reported in other South American regions, including northwestern coastal Venezuela, northwestern Colombia, and a few scattered places in Bolivia and Brazil.

The various groups of people who drink tobacco juice prepare it in different ways. The leaves may be first pounded, chewed, or shredded. Sometimes they are left untreated. Then the tobacco leaves are placed in water; sometimes other ingredients are added such as salt, pepper, or plant materials such as tree bark. The mixture is boiled and then strained to obtain the liquid. Usually it is then set aside to allow much of the water

to evaporate. The remaining material has the consistency of a paste, syrup, or jelly. The syrups and jellies are usually liquid enough to drink by mouth or pour in the nose. People from some areas squirt the juice from one person's mouth to another.

Various tribes of the northernmost extension of the Andes in Colombia and Venezuela and in parts of the northwest Amazon make a thick extract of tobacco called ambil that they rub across their teeth, gums, or tongue. This thick, black gelatin is made by boiling tobacco leaves for hours or days and then thickening the extract with starch. Recipes vary; some tribes add pepper, avocado seeds, sugar, or tapioca. Ambil is sometimes ingested with other tobacco products or hallucinogenic drugs.

Using chewing tobacco is practiced by about 2% to 3% of the population in the United States. It is more widely practiced in South America and the West Indies. A person who uses tobacco in this way usually sucks or sometimes chews tobacco quids, which are simply pieces of tobacco made for this purpose. However, the South American and West Indian practices of preparing quids may seem unusual to North Americans. South American and West Indian recipes may

include soil, ashes, salt, or honey with the finely crushed tobacco leaves. (North American quids are also flavored in various ways.) South American Indians generally swallow the juices from the tobacco, rather than spit them out.

Another practice among South American Indians that may seem unusual to North Americans is the use of tobacco as an enema or suppository. Generally, these native people use tobacco in this manner to treat constipation or worm infestations. Various tribes of Indians who reside in the mountains of Peru also use tobacco in this way during certain rituals.

People in different cultures often adopt different health-related behaviors. What seems unusual to persons in one culture may not seem unusual at all to individuals from another. People who drink tobacco juice, for example, might think that smoking the leaves of the plant is a strange practice! However, each practice engenders its own benefits or problems and contributes to diversity in health around the world.

Source: Adapted from U.S. Department of Health and Human Services. (1992). *Smoking and health in the Americas: A 1992 report of the Surgeon General, in collaboration with the Pan American Health Organization* (DHHS Publication No. CDC 92-8419). Atlanta, GA: U.S. Department of Health and Human Services, pp. 19–31.

nicotine an addictive psychoactive drug found in tobacco.

acute bronchitis a temporary inflammation of the mucous membranes of the bronchi.

chronic bronchitis a persistent inflammation and thickening of the lining of the bronchi.

emphysema (EM-fih-SEE-mah) a chronic condition in which the air sacs of the lungs lose their normal elasticity, impairing respiration.

smoke cigarettes or use smokeless tobacco are more likely to begin these habits than teenagers who do not observe these behaviors in people close to them. Many adolescents try smoking, chewing, or dipping simply to experiment. Others use tobacco as a way to feel older and more independent, as a response to advertising, or as a response to social pressure. The influence of peers is the most important factor in determining when and how adolescents first try cigarettes.

Certain characteristics of adolescents make them more likely to use tobacco: low self-esteem, susceptibility to peer pressure, a sensation-seeking nature, a rebellious personality, depression or anxiety, low academic achievement, and a low level of knowledge about the immediate health risks of smoking. Additionally, adolescents who think that their parents do not care about them or adolescents who are alone much of the time are more likely to try smoking. Girls are significantly less likely to begin smoking if they are involved in an organized sport. However, participation in sports does not affect boys' initiation into smoking.

Nicotine Addiction Why do teenagers and adults continue smoking and using smokeless tobacco? Most people continue because they are addicted to **nicotine.** Nicotine is a psychoactive drug that acts at communication points among nerve cells in the brain, as do other psychoactive drugs. It becomes addicting during the first few years of use.

The many reasons that people say they continue to smoke (other than craving or being addicted to cigarettes) include:

- It is arousing and gives them energy.
- It helps concentration.
- It lifts the mood.
- It reduces anger, tension, depression, and stress.
- It is a habit.
- It is a pleasurable activity.

However, some of the pleasure of smoking (as well as using smokeless tobacco) is really the relief of the symptoms of nicotine withdrawal. During the day, as a person smokes, he or she builds up tolerance to nicotine. Nicotine withdrawal symptoms become more pronounced between each successive cigarette. To relieve these symptoms (■ **Table 8-7),** most cigarette addicts smoke more as the day goes on. Overnight, the level of nicotine in the blood drops and tolerance decreases; thus, the smoker is resensitized to the effects of nicotine. The first cigarette of the day is usually quite satisfying to the smoker as the cycle of tolerance and then resensitization begins once again.

The Health Effects of Tobacco Use

In 1964, U.S. Surgeon General Luther Terry issued a landmark report that linked cigarette smoking with the development of lung cancer and other diseases. Since that famous report, scientists have learned a great deal about the health consequences of smoking and smokeless tobacco use, and the Surgeon General's Office has issued more than 20 reports on smoking and health. In these reports, cigarette smoking is recognized as the leading source of preventable illness and death in the United Sates. Every year, approximately 430,000 people die in the United States as a result of using tobacco products (CDC, 1999c). ■ **Figure 8-8** shows how smoking affects risk for various diseases.

Immediate Effects of Nicotine and Carbon Monoxide After entering the body, nicotine produces a variety of effects. It increases the heart rate and the amount of blood that the heart pumps in a single beat. However, nicotine also constricts, or narrows, the blood vessels. As a result, the blood pressure rises. Nicotine also increases the metabolic rate—the speed at which all the chemical reactions of the body take place. These effects increase the body's demand for oxygen. However, the carbon monoxide in cigarette smoke binds to hemoglobin in the red blood cells, reducing its ability to carry oxygen.

Table 8-7	**Typical Symptoms of Nicotine Withdrawal**

Restlessness
Eating more than usual
Anxiety/tension
Impatience
Irritability/anger
Difficulty concentrating
Excessive hunger
Depression
Disorientation
Loss of energy/fatigue
Dizziness
Stomach or bowel problems
Headaches
Sweating
Insomnia
Heart palpitations
Tremors
Craving cigarettes

Source: Adapted from Gritz, E. R., Carr, C. R., & Marcus, A. C. (1991). The tobacco withdrawal syndrome in unaided quitters. *British Journal of Addiction*, 86(1):57–69.

Nicotine and carbon monoxide are not the only components of cigarette smoke that affect the body. There are more than 4000 chemical compounds in the gases and particles that make up cigarette smoke. Some are poisonous, such as hydrogen cyanide; some are irritating to the lungs and mucous membranes, such as particulate matter; and some cause cancer, such as the tars—sticky substances similar to road tar. The rest of this section describes specific health effects of smoking tobacco and using smokeless tobacco products.

Respiratory Illnesses The windpipe and its major subdivisions are lined with microscopic hairlike structures called *cilia,* which are embedded in a layer of sticky mucus. This mucus traps inhaled particles and microbes. As the cilia beat, the mucus moves upward, sweeping this debris up and out of the air passageways.

Inhaled cigarette smoke paralyzes the cilia. With continued smoking, the cilia are damaged. Cigarette smoke also irritates the airways and tar builds up on the cilia, causing excess mucus to be produced. The chronic cough of smokers, usually called *smoker's cough,* is a result of the body's attempt to remove this excess, stationary mucus.

Acute bronchitis is an inflammation of the mucous membranes of the bronchi, which is usually caused by a viral infection. However, smokers are more susceptible than nonsmokers to acute bronchitis because of their impaired and irritated bronchi. The signs and symptoms of this disease are soreness or tightness in the chest, slight fever, cough, chills, and a vague feeling of weakness or discomfort. Bronchitis with accompanying high fever, breathlessness, and yellow, gray, green, or bloody sputum is serious and the person should seek medical attention immediately.

Chronic bronchitis is usually caused by cigarette smoking, but cigar and pipe smoking may also be causes. Chronic bronchitis is a persistent inflammation and thickening of the lining of the bronchi caused by the constant irritation of smoke. As the lining of these airways thickens, breathing becomes more difficult and coughing increases. The cells lining the bronchi produce additional mucus, causing congestion in the lungs and further hampering breathing. The signs and symptoms of chronic bronchitis are shortness of breath and a chronic cough that produces considerable amounts of mucus. Chronic bronchitis is a serious disease that can result in death. In addition to bronchitis, smoking is also a risk factor for *pneumonia,* an in-

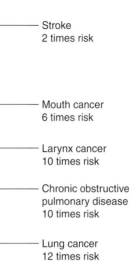

- Stroke
  2 times risk

- Mouth cancer
  6 times risk

- Larynx cancer
  10 times risk

- Chronic obstructive
  pulmonary disease
  10 times risk

- Lung cancer
  12 times risk

- Coronary heart
  disease
  2 times risk

◀**Figure 8-8 The Risk of Smoking Cigarettes.** This illustration compares the increased risk of a smoker to develop certain diseases to the risk of a nonsmoker. Sources: Adapted from U.S. Department of Health and Human Services, *Reducing the health consequences of smoking: 25 years of progress. A report of the surgeon general.* Rockville, MD: Office of Smoking and Health, 1989. NIH Publication No. 92-2962, "Nurses: help your patients stop smoking." Department of Health and Human Services, 1992.

flammation of the lungs that is caused by a variety of bacteria and viruses.

Smoking is also the main cause of **emphysema (■ Figure 8-9),** a condition in which the air sacs of the lungs lose their normal elasticity. Some air sacs become overstretched and eventually rupture, resulting in larger air sacs with less surface area over which gas exchange can take place. Under these conditions, the lungs can no longer accommodate normal amounts of air. Also, without the normal elasticity of the lungs, a person can no longer inhale and exhale normally. Breathing becomes a continual effort.

The lung damage of emphysema can never be repaired. As the disease progresses, the heart becomes increasingly

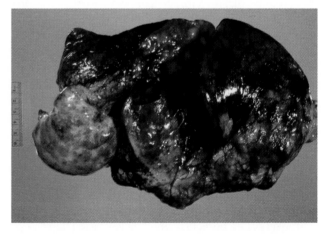

▲**Figure 8-9 Lung from a Person with Emphysema.** Due to this disease, some of the alveoli have ruptured, creating tiny craters within the lung, which are difficult to see in this picture. Note the blackened tissue due to years of smoking.

overworked. Because the blood it is pumping is oxygen poor, the body sends signals to the heart to pump more blood more quickly. Eventually the person with extensive lung damage dies, usually from heart failure. However, if emphysema is detected early (especially before symptoms develop), its destructive effects can be halted by stopping smoking.

People with chronic bronchitis and emphysema are said to have **chronic obstructive pulmonary disease (COPD)**. Cigarette smoking is the major cause of COPD; it would probably be a minor health problem if people did not smoke (National Heart, Lung, and Blood Institute [NHLBI], 1995). Smoking is thought to be responsible for approximately 61,000 deaths from COPD per year, or about 82% of all COPD deaths.

Cardiovascular Disease Forty-three percent of people who die from smoking-related causes die from **cardiovascular disease (CVD)**, or dysfunction of the heart and blood vessels. Cardiovascular disease is the number one cause of death in the United States. There are a variety of cardiovascular diseases, including *coronary artery disease* (CAD), *hypertension* (chronic high blood pressure), and stroke (blood vessel disease of the brain). *Atherosclerosis,* the buildup of fatty deposits in the arteries, is an important cardiovascular disease process that is an underlying cause in CAD and stroke. These diseases are discussed in detail in Chapter 12.

Cigarette smokers are more than twice as likely as nonsmokers to have a heart attack or stroke, and up to four times as likely to die from a heart attack because of smoking's effects on the cardiovascular system. As many as 30% of CAD deaths in the United States each year are attributable to cigarette smoking (Ockene & Miller, 1997). Using smokeless tobacco is a significant CVD risk factor also, but cigar and pipe smoking are less significant (American Heart Association [AHA], 1999).

Women who take oral contraceptives (birth control pills) and who smoke cigarettes increase their risk of heart attack several times. Oral contraceptives increase the risk of developing blood clots, which can block already narrowed arteries in persons with atherosclerosis, a disease that smokers have an increased risk of developing. For these reasons, smoking while taking oral contraceptives also increases the risk of peripheral vascular disease and stroke.

Smokers often think that smoking low-yield ("light") cigarettes poses fewer health risks than smoking regular-strength cigarettes. Light cigarettes, which began to be marketed in the 1960s in response to health concerns, are lower in tars and nicotine. However, research data show that smokers generally puff on these cigarettes longer and inhale more deeply than when smoking regular cigarettes. Also, they often smoke more light cigarettes than they would regular cigarettes, so they may actually take in more tars, nicotine, and other noxious and cancer-causing compounds than if they smoked regular cigarettes. Scientists have found no evidence that smoking low-tar and low-nicotine cigarettes reduces the risk of coronary heart disease.

When a smoker quits, his or her risk of heart disease begins dropping immediately. The time it takes for a former smoker's risk of death from heart attack to reach that of a nonsmoker's varies from 3 to 9 years. The recovery time depends on the number of years a person smoked and how many cigarettes he or she smoked per day. However, if a smoker has already developed heart disease before quitting, the risk of heart attack will not return to that of a nonsmoker, although it will be lower than if he or she had continued smoking.

Cancer Cancer is a group of diseases in which certain cells exhibit abnormal growth. Cancers can arise in various locations in the body and then spread to others. The most prevalent forms of cancer in the United States are discussed in Chapter 13, which also describes lifestyle changes you can make in addition to quitting smoking that will reduce your chances of developing these cancers. Guidelines for early detection are listed in Chapter 13 (see p. 303).

Cancer is the second biggest killer of Americans, and tobacco use is responsible for about 30% of cancer deaths annually in the United States (American Cancer Society [ACS], 1999). Tobacco use causes or is related to cancers of the lungs, larynx, oral cavity, esophagus, kidneys, bladder, pancreas, stomach, and cervix. Lung cancer is the most prevalent form of cancer caused by tobacco use.

Periodontal Disease Smoking tobacco and using smokeless tobacco can have serious effects on the oral cavity. These effects can range from embarrassing problems such as bad breath and stained teeth to life-threatening conditions such as oral cancer (Figure 8-10). People who use tobacco products regularly, often develop **periodontal disease**, commonly known as gum disease. Periodontal disease is actually more than just disease of the gums. It is a disease of all the supporting tissues around the teeth, which include the gums, the bone in which the teeth are embedded, and the ligaments that hold the teeth to the bone.

People can develop periodontal disease for a variety of reasons, such as poor dental hygiene, overzealous brushing that damages the gums, and clenching and grinding of the teeth. Using tobacco products is especially destructive to the gums and often is a cause of severe periodontal disease. Nicotine narrows the blood vessels in the gums, reducing the amount of oxygen that reaches these tissues. As a result, the gum tissue becomes less resistant to infection. Additionally, good oral hygiene and proper periodontal treatment are often ineffective when a person with periodontal disease continues to use tobacco.

Young people who use smokeless tobacco products often develop periodontal disease. Gum recession most often oc-

chronic obstructive pulmonary disease (COPD) a syndrome that includes chronic bronchitis, asthma, and emphysema and that is characterized by extreme difficulty in breathing.

cardiovascular disease (CVD) disorders of the heart and blood vessels.

periodontal disease (PER-ee-oh-DON-tal) a disorder of the tissues that support the teeth.

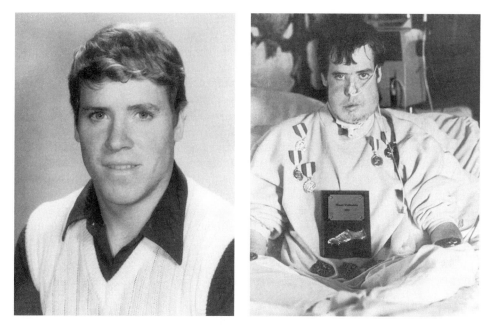

▶**Figure 8-10 Sean Marsee, Before and After Using Smokeless Tobacco.** Sean, an Oklahoman and award-winning high school athlete, died of oral cancer caused by his habit of chewing tobacco. His disease developed and killed him in about one year.

curs at places where smokeless tobacco is held in the mouth. Additionally, *leukoplakia,* a disease characterized by precancerous white patches that develop on the mucous membranes of the mouth (▋ **Figure 8-11),** is common in adolescents who use these products. Approximately 5% of these lesions become cancerous within 5 years. However, if a smokeless tobacco user discontinues use, the leukoplakia regresses and may disappear.

Osteoporosis Osteoporosis, or a loss of bone density, occurs most frequently in postmenopausal White women.

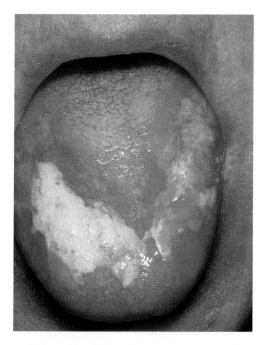

▲**Figure 8-11 Leukoplakia.** This precancerous condition often develops on the mucous membranes of the mouths of those who use smokeless tobacco products.

This disease is serious because it places women at risk for bone fractures, back pain, and other accompanying problems. Hip fractures are particularly serious; the death rate for women who sustain hip fractures is 15% to 20% higher than for women who do not sustain this injury. (Osteoporosis is discussed in more detail in Chapter 9.)

Smoking cigarettes causes a loss of bone density in women and reduces the age at which menopause occurs by about 2 years. Therefore, women who smoke a pack of cigarettes a day throughout their adult lives reach early menopause with bones that are up to 10% less dense than those of nonsmokers.

Environmental Tobacco Smoke

In the past two decades, nonsmokers have become increasingly aware that smoke in their indoor environments could pose a health risk. This smoke, termed **environmental tobacco smoke (ETS)** or *secondhand smoke,* is made up of the sidestream smoke emitted from a lit cigarette, cigar, or pipe and the smoke exhaled by smokers.

In 1986 the National Research Council (NRC) and the United States Surgeon General's Office compiled research data to assess the health effects of exposure to ETS (CDC, 1986; NRC, 1986). Both reports conclude that ETS can cause lung cancer in adult nonsmokers. Researchers estimate that approximately 3000 lung cancer deaths per year in the United States are attributable to the chronic inhalation of secondhand smoke. The reports also acknowledge that ETS contains the same carcinogenic compounds that have been identified in the mainstream smoke inhaled by smokers. These conclusions have prompted the designation of governmental and other public buildings, many workplaces,

environmental tobacco smoke (ETS) the smoke emitted from a lit cigarette, cigar, or pipe and the smoke exhaled by smokers.

and restaurants in many states as smoke-free environments to reduce the effects of ETS on the public. By 1993 nearly 82% of indoor workers were restricted from smoking in their workplaces (Farrelly et al., 1999).

Recent analyses of research data (National Safety Council, 1999) show that chronic exposure to ETS is also a risk factor for cardiovascular disease and heart attack. Breathing environmental tobacco smoke has other negative effects on nonsmoking adults, such as coughing, mucus production, chest discomfort, and reduced lung function. A person with reduced lung function might become short of breath while performing physical activities.

The 1986 reports of the NRC and the Surgeon General additionally conclude that children, particularly infants and young children, suffer significant consequences from breathing secondhand smoke. Children of parents who smoke have an increased frequency of respiratory symptoms such as coughing and wheezing, and of lower respiratory tract infections such as bronchitis, influenza, and pneumonia.

Environmental tobacco smoke is also a risk factor for the development of asthma in children. Exposure to ETS can cause asthmatic attacks and an increased severity of asthma in children who already have the disease. (Chapter 14 discusses asthma in more detail.)

Avoiding secondhand smoke will help you stay healthier. The "Managing Your Health" box includes tips on how to say no to secondhand smoke.

Managing Your Health

How to Say No to Secondhand Smoke

If you live with a smoker:

- Ask him or her not to smoke in your home. Discuss how his or her habit puts you and others living there at risk.
- If he or she is unwilling to go outside, suggest ways to limit the exposure to smoke for you and others. Maybe a room could be set aside for smoking—one that is seldom used by other members of the household. Some smokers protect others at home by smoking near an open window or when no one is around.
- Keep rooms well ventilated. Open windows.
- Support smokers who decide to quit.

When visitors come:

- Ask all smokers who visit not to smoke in your house or apartment, but to please smoke outside.
- Do not keep ashtrays around.

In others' homes:

- Tell friends and relatives politely that you would appreciate their not smoking while you are there.

- Let people know when their smoke is causing immediate problems. If it is making your allergies worse, making you cough or wheeze, or making your eyes sting, say so. Some smokers put their cigarettes away when they see the discomfort it causes.

If you have children:

- Insist that babysitters, grandparents, and other caregivers not smoke around your children.
- Help children avoid secondhand smoke if smokers do use tobacco around them. Have them leave the room or play outside while an adult is smoking. Air rooms out after smoking occurs.
- Keep smokers away from places in which children sleep.

When smoking is allowed at the workplace:

- Talk to your employer about the company's smoking policy. Give your employer copies of the Environmental Protection Agency (EPA) report on the harmful effects of environmental tobacco smoke. Call 1-800-438-4318 to obtain this report.

- Ask to work near other nonsmokers and as far away from smokers as possible.
- Ask smokers if they would not smoke around you.
- Use a fan and open windows (if possible) to keep air moving.
- Hang a Thank You for Not Smoking sign in your work area.
- Volunteer to help develop a fair company policy that protects nonsmokers.
- Contact the local Lung Association, the American Cancer Society, or the National Cancer Institute (1-800-4-CANCER) for information concerning smoking cessation programs that can be conducted at your workplace.

When you are in public places:

- Always take the nonsmoking options that are available in rental cars, hotels, and restaurants.
- If a restaurant puts you at a table near smokers (even if you are in a nonsmoking section), ask to move.
- Keep children out of smoking areas.

Source: Adapted from National Cancer Institute. (1993). *I mind very much if you smoke* (NIH Publication No. 93-3544). Washington, DC: National Institutes of Health.

Quitting

Most smokers want to quit. In a recent Gallup poll, 76% of smokers told Gallup interviewers that they would like to give up cigarettes. Sixty-five percent said that they had made a serious effort to stop smoking in the past. And 95% of smokers reported that they think smoking is harmful to their health. Eighty-three percent of smokers reported that they wish they had never started smoking (Gillespie, 1999).

Benefits of Quitting At any age, there are many reasons to stop smoking cigarettes. Five primary reasons to quit are cited in the 1990 report of the Surgeon General (U.S. Department of Health and Human Services [DHHS]) *The Health Benefits of Smoking Cessation*:

1. Smoking cessation has major and immediate health benefits.
2. Former smokers live longer than continuing smokers.
3. Smoking cessation decreases the risk of lung cancer, other cancers, heart attack, stroke, and chronic lung disease.
4. Women who stop smoking before pregnancy or during the first 3 to 4 months of pregnancy reduce their risk of having a low birth weight baby to that of women who never smoke.
5. The health benefits of smoking cessation far exceed any risks from the average weight gain of 6 to 9 pounds or any adverse psychological effects that may occur after quitting.

One of the health effects of smoking discussed earlier in this chapter is nicotine addiction. On quitting, an addicted smoker experiences some or all of the nicotine withdrawal symptoms listed in Table 8-7. These unpleasant psychological and physiological conditions peak 1 to 2 days following quitting but subside during the following weeks. The two withdrawal symptoms that last the longest are the urge to smoke and an increased appetite. However, using a nicotine patch, nicotine gum, nicotine inhaler, or buproprion (an antidepressant now being used to treat nicotine dependence) during the early cessation period may help reduce these symptoms and make quitting easier (Hurt, 1998). As these withdrawal symptoms subside, former smokers report that favorable psychological changes occur over time, such as enhanced self-esteem and an increased sense of self-control.

Because smoking cigarettes has negative effects on the respiratory system, a person who quits notices that it is easier to breathe. Smoking cessation reduces the rate at which symptoms such as cough, mucus production, and wheezing occur. It also reduces the incidence of respiratory infections such as bronchitis and pneumonia. (Pneumonia can be deadly for people who have chronic diseases.) Also, after sustained abstinence from smoking cigarettes, persons with COPD have less chance of dying from this disease than they did before they quit.

Quitting also has positive effects on the cardiovascular system. Data show that the smoker who quits cuts his or her elevated risk of cardiovascular disease in half only 1 to 2 years after quitting. The degree of risk that remains then declines gradually. Some data show that a former smoker reaches the risk level of a nonsmoker from 5 to 9 years after quitting. Other data show that the former smoker must wait from 10 to 15 years to achieve this goal. The more cigarettes a person smokes and the earlier a person started to smoke, the longer the recovery time (Kawachi et al., 1994). Since the risk of cardiovascular disease increases as the number of cigarettes smoked increases, smoking fewer cigarettes can be a way to lower CVD risk if an individual has little success quitting. However, smoking low-yield (low tar and nicotine) cigarettes does not appear to reduce risk. Among persons diagnosed with cardiovascular disease, smoking cessation markedly reduces the risk of additional heart attacks and cardiovascular death. The benefits of quitting exist for people of all ages. Older individuals should not think that it is "too late" to quit (DHHS, 1990).

Quitting smoking substantially decreases the risk of lung, laryngeal, esophageal, oral, pancreatic, bladder, and cervical cancers (DHHS, 1990). However, data suggest that the decrease in risk for cancer is not as rapid as for cardiovascular disease. There appears to be a lag between the time a person quits smoking and the lowering of risk of cancer (Enstrom, 1999; Enstrom & Heath, 1999; Ockene et al., 1990). ■ **Figure 8-12** is a visual summary of the health benefits of quitting smoking.

The Process of Quitting Cigarette smoking is an addiction, and an addicted smoker who is quitting goes through the same process of behavioral change as does anyone addicted to any drug. For a smoker to contemplate quitting, he or she must understand and accept that cigarette smoking is dangerous or must have other reasons for quitting that are important to him or her. Then the smoker begins to see the potential benefits and negative effects associated with quitting. For example, the smoker may realize that nicotine is a drug and that he or she is addicted to this drug. Quitting will stop the addiction. However, along with this positive behavior (stopping the addiction) comes negative consequences: withdrawal symptoms. To be prepared to quit, the smoker should analyze both the negative and positive aspects of change and prepare to deal with the negative aspects. Often, discussion with a medical practitioner is helpful. Also, if a smoker analyzes the reasons he or she smokes (see "Why Do You Smoke?" in the student workbook), the smoker will be better equipped to handle the consequences of quitting (see "Tips for Quitters" on p. 191).

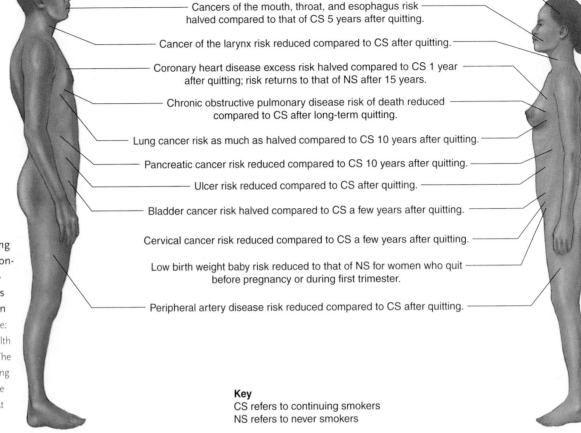

▶Figure 8-12 The Health Benefits of Quitting Smoking. The risks of developing many diseases and conditions drop dramatically, in varied lengths of time, after a person quits smoking. Source: U.S. Department of Health and Human Services, "The health benefits of smoking cessation: A report of the surgeon general 1990. At a glance."

Stroke risk reduced compared to that of CS 5 to 15 years after quitting.

Cancers of the mouth, throat, and esophagus risk halved compared to that of CS 5 years after quitting.

Cancer of the larynx risk reduced compared to CS after quitting.

Coronary heart disease excess risk halved compared to CS 1 year after quitting; risk returns to that of NS after 15 years.

Chronic obstructive pulmonary disease risk of death reduced compared to CS after long-term quitting.

Lung cancer risk as much as halved compared to CS 10 years after quitting.

Pancreatic cancer risk reduced compared to CS 10 years after quitting.

Ulcer risk reduced compared to CS after quitting.

Bladder cancer risk halved compared to CS a few years after quitting.

Cervical cancer risk reduced compared to CS a few years after quitting.

Low birth weight baby risk reduced to that of NS for women who quit before pregnancy or during first trimester.

Peripheral artery disease risk reduced compared to CS after quitting.

Key
CS refers to continuing smokers
NS refers to never smokers

Once the smoker realizes the need to quit, he or she should decide what course of action to take. Should it be quitting "cold turkey" or cutting down at first? (If a person is addicted to nicotine, stopping "cold turkey" may be best. The assessment activity "Why Do You Smoke?" can help identify addiction.) Will the smoker join a smoking cessation program or stop without group support? Again, the advice of a medical practitioner may be helpful at this stage. A smoker can also call the American Lung Association, the American Heart Association, the American Cancer Society, or the National Cancer Institute for free literature on quitting and information on smoking cessation programs. Many programs are available, and the smoker needs to select the program that suits his or her needs best. Medication may also be helpful at this stage, such as a nicotine patch or nicotine gum to lessen the withdrawal symptoms from nicotine. Also, the smoker may enlist the support of family and friends through the quitting process.

After the first 6 months, which is considered the *quitting period*, the former smoker enters the period of *maintenance*, which lasts 6 months also. Some quitters who join smoking cessation programs continue to attend group meetings for support. Others get continued support from friends, family members, or other former smokers.

As with other addictions, sometimes *relapse* occurs. During a relapse, a former smoker returns to smoking habits. Relapse can be triggered by a variety of factors such as stress, depression, a craving for cigarettes, negative life events, and interpersonal tensions. To quit, the relapsed smoker goes through the stages of behavior change once again.

One barrier to quitting is the smoker's fear of gaining weight. In fact, about 25% of smokers cite this possibility as the reason for not quitting. Likewise, about 25% of people who quit relapse because they begin to gain weight and are afraid of gaining more. This fear is not unfounded—80% of persons who quit smoking gain weight. Data show, however, that the average weight gain is only 6 to 9 pounds and the risk of large weight gain is extremely low. Individuals who smoke heavily gain the most weight after quitting (Heishman, 1998).

People gain weight when they stop smoking for two reasons: They eat more (often to put something other than a cigarette into their mouths) and their metabolism slows slightly. To combat this effect, as part of your smoking cessation plan be sure to include an exercise program to maintain your metabolic rate. Also, keep lots of fat-free, low-calorie snacks handy, such as slices of vegetables with low-fat dip, fruits, pretzels, and sugar-free gelatin.

Prevention

Prevention programs developed in the 1980s reflect an understanding that smoking begins in early adolescence and that young people go through stages in the development of smoking behavior (see the section entitled "Psychosocial Reasons for Using Tobacco Products" on pp. 183–184). To-day's programs also recognize that a child's social environment is the most important determinant of whether he or she will smoke. Therefore, prevention programs now target seventh and eighth graders, reaching children before most start smoking. Their focus is on helping young people develop skills to identify and resist social influences to

Tips for Quitters

If you smoke and have not responded to the questions in the assessment activity in the student workbook titled "Why Do You Smoke?" do so now. Then read the suggestions for quitting that specifically address each reason you smoke. If you tailor your plan to quit smoking to match the reasons that you smoke, the cessation process will be easier.

Reason: "Smoking gives me energy."

- Get enough rest to feel refreshed and alert.
- Exercise regularly to raise your overall energy level.
- Take a brisk walk instead of smoking if you start feeling sluggish.
- Eat regular, nutritious meals for energy.
- Drink lots of cold water to refresh you.
- Avoid getting bored, which can make you feel tired.

Reason: "I like to touch and handle cigarettes."

- Pick up a pen or pencil when you want to reach for a cigarette.
- Play with a coin or handle nearby objects.
- Put a plastic cigarette in your hand or mouth.
- Hold a real cigarette if the touch is all you miss.
- Eat regular meals to avoid confusing the desire to eat with the desire to put a cigarette in your mouth.
- Take up a hobby like knitting or carpentry that keeps your hands busy.
- Eat low-fat, low-sugar snacks like carrot sticks or bread sticks.
- Suck on sugar-free hard candy.

Reason: "Smoking gives me pleasure."

- Enjoy the pleasures of being tobacco-free, such as how good foods taste; how much easier it is to walk, run, and climb stairs; and how good it feels to be in control of the urge to smoke.
- Spend the money you save on cigarettes on another kind of pleasure, such as a shopping spree or a night out.
- Remind yourself of the health benefits of quitting. Giving up cigarettes can help you enjoy life's other pleasures for many years to come.

Reason: "Smoking helps me relax when I'm tense or upset."

- Use relaxation techniques to calm down when you are angry or upset. Deep breathing exercises, muscle relaxation, and imagining yourself in a peaceful setting can make you feel less stressed.
- Exercise regularly to relieve tension and improve your mood.
- Take action to alleviate situations that cause stress.
- Avoid stressful situations.
- Get enough rest and take time to relax each day.
- Enjoy relaxation. Take a long, hot bath. Have a massage. Lie in a garden hammock. Listen to soothing music.

Reason: "I crave cigarettes and am addicted to nicotine."

- Ask your medical practitioner about using a nicotine patch or nicotine gum to help you avoid withdrawal symptoms.

- Go "cold turkey." Tapering off probably won't work for you, because the moment you put out one cigarette you begin to crave the next.
- Keep away from cigarettes completely. Get rid of ashtrays. Destroy any cigarettes you have. Try to avoid people who smoke and smoke-filled places like bars.
- Tell family and friends you've quit smoking.
- Remember that physical withdrawal symptoms last about 2 weeks. Hang on!

Reason: "Smoking is a habit."

- Cut down gradually. Smoke fewer cigarettes each day or only smoke them halfway down. Inhale less often and less deeply. After several months it should be easier to stop completely.
- Change your smoking routines. Keep your cigarettes in a different place. Smoke with your opposite hand. Do not do anything else while smoking. Limit smoking to certain places, such as outside or in one room at home.
- When you want a cigarette, wait one minute. Do something else instead of smoking.
- Be aware of every cigarette you smoke. Ask yourself, Do I really want this cigarette? You may be surprised at how many you can easily pass up.
- Set a date for giving up smoking altogether and stick to it.

Source: Adapted from "Learning Why You Smoke Can Teach You How to Quit." The National Cancer Institute. (1993). U.S. Department of Health and Human Services.

www.jbpub.com/healthyliving

Table 8-8 — Proposed FDA Regulations to Reduce Access and Appeal of Tobacco Products to Minors

The regulations would:

1. Require retailers to verify the age of persons who appear to be younger than 27 years of age and want to purchase cigarettes or smokeless tobacco products.
2. Eliminate "impersonal" methods of sale and distribution that do not readily allow age verifications (e.g., mail orders, self-service displays, free samples, and vending machines).
3. Limit advertising to which minors may be exposed to a text-only format.
4. Ban outdoor advertising of tobacco products within 1000 feet of schools and playgrounds.
5. Prohibit the sale or distribution of brand-identifiable nontobacco items and services.
6. Prohibit the sponsorship of events in the brand name.

Sources: Centers for Disease Control and Prevention. (1996). Accessiblity of tobacco products to youths aged 12–17 years—United States, 1989 and 1993. *Morbidity and Mortality Weekly Report, 45*(6):125–130.
Centers for Disease Control and Prevention. (1999, June 25). State laws on tobacco control—United States, 1998. *Morbidity and Mortality Weekly Report, 48*(SS03):21-62.

smoke, such as advertising and peer pressure. Additionally, they educate adolescents about the short-term negative effects of tobacco use. Understanding short-term consequences positively affects adolescent behavior more than knowledge of long-term effects. Data show that several types of prevention programs delay or reduce youth tobacco use for periods of 1 to 5 years and more. Effective prevention programs engage the school, parents, and media (Pentz, 1998).

Other programs have been developed that focus on smokeless tobacco use. The goal of these programs is to counter the perception that smokeless tobacco is a safe alternative to smoking cigarettes.

Reducing the availability of cigarettes to adolescents is another prevention measure. Unfortunately, adolescents can get cigarettes quite easily even though the sale of tobacco products to minors is illegal in all states and the District of Columbia. One of the goals of *Healthy People 2000* is to enforce laws that prohibit sales to minors to reduce the percentage of minors who successfully purchase cigarettes to 20%. In August 1995 the Food and Drug Administration proposed regulations that would reduce the availability of cigarettes to minors as well as reduce their appeal.
▌ **Table 8-8** lists these regulations. On March 21, 2000, the U.S. Supreme Court ruled that the FDA does not have

fetal alcohol syndrome FAS)
a group of abnormal physical and behavioral traits exhibited by babies born to women who consumed alcohol heavily during pregnancy.

the authority to regulate tobacco products. On that same date, President Clinton called for Congress to enact statutes that would mirror the FDA regulations.

Healthy LIVING PRACTICES

- If you have or plan to have children, consider discussing the health effects of smoking with them when they are very young to discourage them from starting the habit.
- If you are a smoker, do not smoke near children. Children are particularly susceptible to the damaging effects of tobacco smoke.
- If you have bronchitis with accompanying high fever, breathlessness, and yellow, gray, green, or bloody sputum, seek medical attention immediately.
- If you have a smoker's cough that produces considerable amounts of mucus and shortness of breath, seek medical attention immediately because you may have chronic bronchitis, a serious disease.
- If you choose to smoke, see your health-care provider regularly for an evaluation of your respiratory system.
- If you are a nonsmoker, avoid areas where cigarette smoke is present. Breathing in this smoke increases your risk of developing heart disease, lung cancer, and various respiratory diseases and conditions.
- If you use tobacco products, you can reduce your risk of developing various cancers, cardiovascular disease, and periodontal disease by quitting.
- If you are female and smoke cigarettes, you have a higher risk of developing osteoporosis than nonsmoking women and you may reach menopause early. To reduce this risk, stop smoking.
- If you decide to quit smoking cigarettes, plan your quitting process. Expect quitting to be difficult at times. Consider using an organized program, medication, or both to help you quit. To combat weight gain when quitting, exercise and keep lots of fat-free, low-calorie snacks handy.

across the lifespan

The Effects of Alcohol and Tobacco Use

Fetuses and infants are significantly affected by the alcohol and tobacco use of their mothers. Approximately 30 years ago, scientists discovered that babies born to alcoholic women exhibited a group of certain abnormal physical and behavioral traits. This combination of traits is not found in babies born to women who do not drink heavily during pregnancy. Together these abnormalities are called **fetal alcohol syndrome (FAS)**.

The predominant feature of FAS is mental retardation. This syndrome is also characterized by (a) retarded growth both before and after birth; (b) central nervous system defects (in addition to mental retardation) such as behavioral problems, and skull or brain malformations; and (c) characteristic facial features that include small eye openings, a broad thin upper lip, and a flattened nose bridge and mid-face (■ Figure 8-13). Thirty to forty percent of FAS babies are also born with heart defects.

Some babies who were exposed to alcohol before birth are born with only a few FAS abnormalities; these children are said to have fetal alcohol effects (FAE) or alcohol-related birth defects (ARBD). The severity and extent of the abnormalities appear to be related to the amount a woman drinks during her pregnancy and whether she drinks for the duration of her pregnancy. Scientists have not determined a threshold level beneath which no effects will occur. However, many studies show that in the period prior to learning that they are pregnant, women who drank three alcoholic beverages per day, on average, were more likely to deliver babies with birth defects. Also, binge drinking appears to have high potential for harming an embryo or fetus (Jacobson & Jacobson, 1994; Nevitt, 1996).

Maternal smoking during pregnancy can harm not only the fetus, but the pregnant woman as well. Pregnant women who smoke cigarettes are at risk of developing serious conditions, including abruptio placentae and placenta previa. *Abruptio placentae* occurs when the placenta separates from the uterus, resulting in hemorrhage (life-threatening bleeding). (The placenta is an organ through which the fetus obtains nutrients and oxygen, and excretes wastes.) The hemorrhage can be severe and occur suddenly, putting the lives of both the mother and fetus at risk. Maternal smoking is also associated with *placenta previa,* in which the placenta implants abnormally and covers the opening of the cervical canal. As this opening dilates at the beginning of the birth process, bleeding and severe hemorrhage can occur. Other complications of pregnancy associated with cigarette smoking are uterine bleeding and premature delivery.

Smoking during pregnancy also retards fetal growth and causes an average reduction in birth weight. Some infants do not survive the effects of maternal smoking during pregnancy. Data show that fetuses and infants from 28 weeks of gestation to 4 weeks after birth, carried by and born of women who smoke during pregnancy, have a 25% to 30% higher rate of death than those of women who do not smoke. Babies born of mothers who smoke also have a higher than average incidence of death from *Sudden Infant Death Syndrome (SIDS)* and from respiratory diseases. The sudden, unexpected death of an apparently healthy infant, SIDS occurs while the baby is sleeping. It is the most common cause of death of children between the ages of 2 weeks and 1 year.

Another age group of persons strongly affected by alcohol and tobacco use is the elderly. Because the elderly are more physically vulnerable to the effects of alcohol, they

▼**Figure 8-13 Child with Fetal Alcohol Syndrome (FAS).** This adopted boy exhibits features characteristic of FAS: small eye openings, a broad thin upper lip, and a flattened nose bridge and mid-face.

may develop alcohol problems even though their formerly unproblematic patterns of drinking have not changed. Alcohol also reacts adversely with many medications. Elderly persons taking medications for various conditions may appear to be reacting adversely to their medications rather than experiencing an alcohol problem. Additionally, if alcohol worsens their health, their health-care providers may prescribe additional or different medications. A vicious cycle of drug interactions and health complications may continue until the health-care practitioner recognizes that the patient has an alcohol problem.

The elderly face special harm from smoking because most people older than 65 years of age who smoke have been doing so for 30, 40, or 50 years. As a result, a disproportionate number of elderly develop life-threatening diseases such as cancer and emphysema, because these diseases usually take decades to develop.

Among those older than 65, the death rate of current smokers is twice that of people who never smoked. Smoking is associated with a variety of other ailments that are often seen in the elderly, such as cataracts (a loss of transparency of the lens of the eye), delayed healing of broken bones, periodontal problems, ulcers, high blood pressure, brain hemorrhages, and skin wrinkles. From prenatal development to the elderly years, no one who uses alcohol or tobacco products, or breathes in smoke from others' use, can escape their health effects.

Healthy
■ LIVING PRACTICES ■

Do not consume alcoholic beverages when pregnant because alcohol can harm the unborn fetus and is a risk factor for developing life-threatening hemorrhage.

Chapter Review

Summary

Drinking alcohol and smoking cigarettes are behaviors that often begin in adolescence. Alcohol use is quite prevalent in the United States; approximately 52% of Americans use alcohol. Some people use alcohol responsibly, not allowing their drinking to threaten their health nor interfere with their relationships. In contrast, the harmful user drinks alcoholic beverages while knowingly damaging his or her health. The alcohol-dependent person, or alcoholic, additionally develops tolerance to the drug, exhibits withdrawal symptoms when not drinking, compulsively uses alcohol, and may exhibit other behaviors that are a part of the alcohol-dependence syndrome.

A cause of alcoholism is unknown. However, studies suggest that alcoholism has a genetic (hereditary) component. People abuse alcoholic beverages and become alcohol dependent for psychological, social, and developmental reasons as well.

When a person drinks alcoholic beverages, various behavioral changes that are commonly called intoxication result from impairment of the central nervous system. The harmful use and abuse of alcohol results in multiple effects on the body that are significant threats to health. Excessive alcohol consumption exerts its most dangerous effects on the liver, cardiovascular system, immune system, reproductive system, and brain. Alcohol use and abuse is also related to serious and even fatal injuries.

Approximately 3.1 million Americans were treated for alcohol abuse and dependence in 1997. Most of those individuals were 18 to 34 years old. Alcohol abuse and dependence are often detected by the use of screening tests. Health-care professionals who determine that their patients are alcohol dependent refer them to substance abuse specialists for evaluation and possibly treatment. Patients who show nondependent problem drinking are often encouraged to participate in brief intervention programs. Self-help groups support the alcoholic on a long-term basis to help prevent relapse into abusive or dependent behaviors.

Cigarettes are the most prevalent type of tobacco product used in the United States today. Approximately 28% of Americans smoke cigarettes. Most people who smoke cigarettes and use smokeless tobacco began this habit when they were adolescents. Adolescents initially try tobacco products for a variety of reasons: to do what parents or peers do, to experiment, to feel older and more independent, or to join certain social groups. Adolescents most likely to use tobacco have particular characteristics such as low self-esteem, high susceptibility to peer pressure, and a sensation-seeking nature.

Most teenagers and adults continue to smoke and use smokeless tobacco because they are addicted to the psychoactive drug nicotine. Nicotine, like all psychoactive drugs, acts on certain communication points among nerve cells in the brain.

Cigarette smoking is the leading source of preventable illness and death in the United States because many of the 4,000 chemical compounds in cigarette smoke affect the body adversely. Every year, approximately 430,000 people die in the United States as a result of using tobacco products.

Inhaled cigarette smoke affects the airways by damaging the cilia that sweep debris from this region, by causing the airways to secrete excess mucus, and by irritating and inflaming the airways. As a result, smokers suffer chronic cough and are at high risk for a variety of respiratory infections such as acute and chronic bronchitis, and pneumonia. Smoking is also the main cause of emphysema, a condition in which the air sacs of the lungs have lost their usual elasticity so that a person cannot inhale and exhale normally.

Forty-three percent of persons who die from smoking-related causes die from cardiovascular disease. Scientists have found no evidence that smoking low-tar and low-nicotine cigarettes reduces the risk of coronary heart disease.

Cancer is the second-biggest killer of Americans, and tobacco use is responsible for about 30% of cancer deaths annually in the United States. Lung cancer is the most prevalent form of cancer caused by tobacco use. Smokeless tobacco use does not cause lung cancer, but it does cause cancers of the larynx, oral cavity, and esophagus. These cancers are also caused by smoking cigarettes, cigars, and pipes.

People who use tobacco products regularly often develop periodontal disease, which is a disease of the supporting structures of the teeth. Eventually, if periodontal disease is not treated and controlled, the teeth become loose and fall out.

Smoking cigarettes causes a loss of bone density in women. This condition is serious because it places women at risk for bone fractures, back pain, and other accompanying problems. Smoking also reduces the age at which menopause occurs by about two years.

Environmental tobacco smoke (ETS), the sidestream smoke emitted from a lit cigarette, cigar, or pipe and the smoke exhaled by smokers, can cause lung cancer in adult nonsmokers. Chronic ETS exposure is also a risk factor for cardiovascular disease and heart attack. Additionally, children of parents who smoke have an increased frequency of respiratory symptoms such as coughing and wheezing, and lower respiratory tract infections such as bronchitis and pneumonia.

Sixty-five percent of smokers have, at one time, tried to quit smoking. Quitting has major and immediate health benefits, for people of all ages.

Cigarette smoking is an addiction, and an addicted smoker who is trying to quit goes through the same process of behavioral change as does anyone addicted to any drug. Quitting is easier if the smoker analyzes why he or she smokes, and develops or chooses a method of quitting that addresses these reasons.

Successful smoking-prevention programs reflect an understanding that smoking begins in early adolescence and that a child's social environment is the most important determinant of whether he or she will smoke. Prevention programs help young people develop the skills to identify and resist social influences to smoke.

Fetuses and infants are significantly affected by the alcohol and tobacco use of their mothers. The syndrome of effects from heavy alcohol consumption during preg-

nancy is called fetal alcohol syndrome. The predominant feature of FAS is mental retardation. Maternal smoking during pregnancy can harm the pregnant woman as well, placing her at risk for developing several life-threatening conditions.

Another age group of persons strongly affected by alcohol and tobacco use is the elderly. The elderly are more physically vulnerable to the effects of alcohol and are more likely to be taking a variety of medications that may interact negatively with alcohol.

Smoking is associated with a variety of ailments in the elderly. Among those older than 65, the death rate of current smokers is twice that of people who have never smoked.

Applying What You Have Learned

1. Using the information in this chapter, write a paragraph that would describe what you might say to a friend to discourage him or her from abusing alcohol. *(Application)*

2. Analyze your reasons for smoking or those of a smoking friend or relative by using the assessment "Why Do You Smoke?" located in the student workbook. Then list the essential elements of a smoking cessation program for yourself or for that individual. *(Synthesis)*

3. For the past 15 years or so, researchers have viewed alcoholism from a "biomedical" point of view. Many researchers thought that it was only a matter of time before a gene for alcoholism would be found. Recently, many researchers have agreed that biology plays a role in addiction, but have suggested that biology is only one factor in the devel-

opment of alcoholism. What other factors are involved? Does Alcoholics Anonymous appear to address this variety of factors in its twelve steps to recovery? State the reasons for your answers. *(Evaluation)*

4. List all the places where you are regularly exposed to environmental tobacco smoke. Decide whether you should change any of your activities to reduce your exposure to ETS. State the reasons for your answer. *(Evaluation)*

KEY

Application: Using information in a new situation.
Synthesis: Putting together information from different sources.
Evaluation: Making informed decisions.

Reflecting On Your Health

1. Describe your attitudes toward alcoholics before reading this chapter. Have your attitudes changed after reading this chapter? Why or why not?

2. If you drink alcohol, what motivates your use of this drug? Are you comfortable with your patterns of drinking and reasons for doing so? Why or why not? If you are uncomfortable with your drinking patterns, what can you do to change them?

3. If you were out with friends who were drinking, would you attempt to stop someone from driving who was clearly unfit to get behind the wheel? If not, why not? If so, what strategy might be successful? Why do you think this strategy would work?

4. If you are a smoker, what do you do to avoid having others breathe your secondhand smoke? If nothing, what might you do in the future? If you are a nonsmoker, what do you do to avoid breathing others' secondhand smoke? If nothing, what might you do in the future?

5. Do you smoke bidis or clove cigarettes? If so, why did you start smoking these products? After reading the "Consumer Health" feature in this chapter, do you think you will continue this practice? Why or why not?

References

American Cancer Society. (1999). *1999 Facts and Figures.* Atlanta: American Cancer Society.

American Heart Association. (1999, December). *Cigarette Smoking and Cardiovascular Disease: AHA Scientific Position.* Available: http://www.americanheart.org/Heart_and_Stroke_A_Z_Guide/cigcvd.html

Bunout, D. (1999). Nutritional and metabolic effects of alcoholism: Their relationship with alcoholic liver disease. *Nutrition, 15:*583-589.

Castellsague, X., Munox, N., DeStefani, E., Victora, C. G., Castelletoto, R., Rolon, P. A., & Quintana, M. J. (1999). Independent and joint effects of tobacco smoking and alcohol drinking on the risk of esophageal cancer in men and women. *International Journal of Cancer, 82:*657-664.

Centers for Disease Control and prevention (CDC). (1986). *The health consequences of involuntary smoking—a report of the Surgeon General.* Rockville, MD: U.S. Department of Health and Human Services, Public Health Service. DHHS Publication No. (CDC)87-8398.

Centers for Disease Control and Prevention (CDC). (1999a). Alcohol involvement in fatal motor-vehicle crashes—United States, 1997–1998. *Morbidity and Mortality Weekly Report, 48:*1086-1087.

Centers for Disease Control and Prevention (CDC). (1999b). Cigarette smoking among adults—United States, 1997. *Morbidity and Mortality Weekly Report, 48:*993-996.

Centers for Disease Control and Prevention (CDC). (1999c). Tobacco use—United States, 1900–1999. *Morbidity and Mortality Weekly Report, 48:*986-993.

Centers for Disease Control and Prevention (CDC). (2000). Tobacco use among middle and high school students—United States, 1999. *Morbidity and Mortality Weekly Report, 49:*49-53.

Cox, D. E., Sadler, D. W., & Pounder, D. J. (1997). Alcohol estimation at necropsy: Epidemiology, economics, and the elderly. *Journal of Clinical Pathology, 50:*197-201.

Ebnet, M. (1998, Nov. 20). Tobacco deal wins unanimous OK by states. *The Seattle Times,* p. A1.

Enstrom, J. E. (1999). Smoking cessation and mortality trends among two United States populations. *Journal of Clinical Epidemiology, 52:*727-729.

Enstrom J. E., & Heath, C. W., Jr. (1999) Smoking cessation and mortality trends among 118,000 Californians, 1960–1997. *Epidemioloyg, 10:*500-512.

Farrelly, M. C., Evans, W. N., & Sfekas, A. E. (1999). Impact of workplace smoking bans: Results from a national survey. *Tobacco Control, 8:*272-277.

Gillespie, M. (1999, November 18). *Majority of smokers want to quit, consider themselves addicted.* Princeton, NJ: Gallup News Service. Available: http://www.gallup.com/poll/releases/pr991118.asp

Ginsberg, E. S. (1999). Estrogen, alcohol, and breast cancer risk. *Journal of Steroid Biochemistry & Molecular Biology, 69:*299-306.

Goldberg, R. (1994). *Drugs Across the Spectrum.* St. Paul, MN: West Publishing Company.

Hanson, A. C., Kristensen, I. B., Dragsholt, C., Brangstrup, V., & Hansen, J. P. (1996). Alcohol and drugs (medical and illicit) in fatal road accidents in a city of 300,000 inhabitants. *Forensic Science International, 79:*49-52.

Hanson, G., & Venturelli, P. J. (1998). *Drugs and Society.* Sudbury, MA: Jones and Bartlett Publishers.

Healthy People 2010. (2000). Chapter 26, Substance Abuse. In *Healthy People 2010—Conference Edition,* pp. 3–56. Available: http://www.health.gov/healthypeople/document/html/volume2/26substance.htm

Heishman, S. J. (1998). *Behavioral-cognitive effects of smoking.* A paper presented at National Institutes of Health conference Addicted to Nicotine: A National Research Forum at the Natcher Conference Center in Bethesda, MD, July 27–28.

Hillbom, M., Juvela, S., & Numminen, H. (1999). Alcohol intake and the risk of stroke. *Journal of Cardiovascular Risk, 6:*223-228.

Hoyert, D. L., Kochanek, K. D., & Murphy, S. L. (1999). Deaths: Final data for 1997. *National Vital Statistics Reports, 47*(19):1–105.

Hurt, R. D. (1998). *New medications for nicotine dependence treatment.* A paper presented at the National Institutes of Health conference Addicted to Nicotine: A National Research Forum at the Natcher Conference Center in Bethesda, MD, July 27–28.

Jacobson, J. L., & Jacobson, S. W. (1994). Prenatal alcohol exposure and neurobehavioral development: Where is the threshold? *Alcohol Health & Research World, 18*(1):30-35.

Johnston, L. D., O'Malley, P. M., & Bachman, J. G. (1999a). *National survey results on drug use from the Monitoring the Future study, 1975–1998: Vol. I. Secondary school students.* Rockville, MD: National Institute on Drug Abuse (NIH Publication No. 99-4660).

Johnston, L. D., O'Malley, P. M., Bachman, J. G. (1999b). *National survey results on drug use from the Monitoring the Future study, 1975–1998: Vol. II. College students and young adults.* Rockville, MD: National Institute on Drug Abuse (NIH Publication No. 99-4661).

Kawachi, I., Graham, A., Stampfer, M., Willett, W., Manson, J., Rosner, B., Speizer, F., & Hennekens, C. (1994). Smoking cessation and time course of decreased risks of coronary heart disease in middle-aged women. *Archives of Internal Medicine, 154:*169-175.

Klein, H. (1992). Self-reported reasons for why college students drink. *Journal of Alcohol and Drug Education, 37*(2):14-27.

Mancino, M., Cunningham, M. R., Davidson, P., & Fulton, R. L. (1996). Identification of the motor vehicle accident victim who abuses alcohol: An opportunity to reduce trauma. *Journal of Studies on Alcohol, 57:*652-658.

McGinnis, J. M., & Foege, W. H. (1999). Mortality and morbidity attributable to use of addictive substances in the United States. *Proceedings of the Association of American Physicians, 111:*109-118.

Mercer, G. W., & Jeffery, W. K. (1995). Alcohol, drugs, and impairment in fatal traffic accidents in British Columbia. *Accident Analysis and Prevention, 27:*335-343.

National Heart, Lung, and Blood Institute (NHLBI). (1992). *Nurses: Help your patients stop smoking.* Washington, DC: National Institutes of Health (NIH Publication No. 92-2962).

National Heart, Lung, and Blood Institute (NHLBI). (1995). *Chronic obstructive pulmonary disease.* Washington, DC: National Institutes of Health (NIH Publication No. 95-2020).

National Institute on Alcohol Abuse and Alcoholism. (1997). *Ninth special report to the U.S. Congress on alcohol and health. Chapter 9. Prevention of alcohol problems.* Washington, DC: National Institutes of Health.

National Research Council (NRC). (1986). *Environmental Tobacco Smoke: Measuring Exposure and Assessing Health Effects.* Washington DC: National Academy Press.

National Safety Council. (1999, November 16). *Fact Sheet: Environmental Tobacco Smoke.* Available: http://www.nsc.org/ehc/indoor/ets.htm

National Transportation Statistics. (1998). Chapter 3, Transportation safety, Table 3-25. Available: http://www.bts.gov/btsprod/nts/chp3/tbl3x25.html

Nevitt, A. (1996). *Fetal alcohol syndrome.* New York: Rosen Publishing Group.

Ochene, I. S., & Miller, N. H. (1997). Cigarette smoking, cardiovascular disease, and stroke. *Circulation, 96:*3243-3247.

Ockene, J. K., Kuller, L. H., Svendsen, K. H., & Meilahn, E. (1990). The relationship of smoking cessation to coronary heart disease and lung cancer in the Multiple Risk Factor Intervention Trial (MRFIT). *American Journal of Public Health, 80:*954-958.

Pentz, M. A. (1998). *Effective prevention programs for tobacco use.* A paper presented at the National Institutes of Health conference Addicted to Nicotine: A National Research Forum at the Natcher Conference Center in Bethesda, MD, July 27–28.

Pierce, J. P. (1998, July). *Advertising and Promotion.* Paper presented at the conference Addicted to Nicotine: A National Research Forum, Bethesda, MD. Available: http://www.nida.nih.gov/MeetSum/Nicotine/Pierce.html

Plueckhahn, V. D. (1975). Death by drowning? Geeling 1959 to 1974. *Medical Journal of Australia, 2:*904-906.

Pullen, L. M. (1994). The relationships among alcohol abuse in college students and selected psychological/demographic variables. *Journal of Alcohol and Drug Education, 40*(1):36-50.

Smith, G. S., Brana, C. C., & Miller, T. R. (1999). Fatal nontraffic injuries involving alcohol: A metaanalysis. *Annals of Emergency Medicine, 33:*659-668.

Spangler, J. G., Dignan, M. B., & Michielutte, R. (1995). Smokeless tobacco use among American Indian Women—Southeastern North Carolina, 1991. *Morbidity and Mortality Weekly Report, 44:*113-117.

Statistics Canada. (2000, January 20). Tobacco use. *The Daily,* p. 6-7. Available: http://www.statcan.ca/Daily/English/000120/d000120b.htm

Substance Abuse and Mental Health Services Administration (SAMHSA). (1998). *Summary of Findings from the 1997 National Household Survey on Drug Abuse.* Washington, DC: U.S. Government Printing Office.

Substance Abuse and Mental Health Services Administration (SAMHSA). (1999). *Summary of Findings from the 1998 National Household Survey on Drug Abuse.* (DHHS Publication No. SMA 99-3328). Washington, DC: U.S. Government Printing Office.

U.S. Department of Health and Human Services (DHHS). (1990). *The health benefits of smoking cessation: A report of the surgeon general.* Atlanta, GA: U.S. Department of Health and Human Services. DHHS Publication No. (CDC) 90–8416.

U.S. Department of Transportation (DOT) (1998, April). *Final report. Alcohol highway safety: Problem update.* Washington, DC: National Highway Traffic Safety Administration. Available: http://www.nhtsa.dot.gov/people/injury/alcohol/alcupdate/alcprobupd.html

Wintemute, G. J., Teret, S. P., Kraus, J. F., & Wright, M. (1990). Alcohol and drowning: An analysis of contributing factors and a discussion of criteria for case selection. *Accident Analysis & Prevention, 22:*291-296.

Yesavage, J. A., & Leirer, V. O. (1986). Hangover effects on aircraft pilots 14 hours after alcohol ingestion: A preliminary report. *American Journal of Psychiatry, 143:*1546-1550.

Nutrition

Hamburger, cola, french fries, pizza, potato chips, tofu, yogurt, olive oil, nonfat milk, mango, and wheat germ—which of these foods do you eat regularly? Do you eat chutney, trifle, black beans, calimari, sushi, or borscht regularly? Why do you eat certain foods and not others? Before deciding what to eat, do you consider the nutritional value of food? When asked if they care about what they eat, two young men who were enrolled in a college health class responded:

Do I care about what I eat? Well, it depends on how hungry I am. If I am hungry enough, I'll eat anything, except some processed meats. I don't care about the amount of fat, calories, or nutritional value in foods. All I care about is how much the food costs and how much it takes to fill me up. I'm young and healthy and have hardly any body fat—I've been eating greasy, cheap, fast foods for years.

I care about what I eat, but my diet doesn't show it. When I wake up, I don't have time to eat. After class I eat burritos or pizza rolls before going to work. After work, I usually stop at a fast food place. . .I eat lots of french fries. I do

Which of these foods do you eat regularly?

want to eat better, but it's hard when you're always on the go.

The term **diet** refers to one's usual pattern of food choices. Poor diet is a major risk factor for chronic diseases such as heart disease, diabetes, stroke, obesity, and some forms of cancer. Good lifelong dietary habits play important roles in maintaining good health and preventing chronic diseases. By making specific dietary changes, young people with poor diets may reduce their chances of developing chronic disorders later in life.

This chapter highlights information concerning nutrients, their major food sources and roles in the body, and the benefits of choosing a nutritious diet. The information in this chapter will help you evaluate the nutritional adequacy of your diet and plan nutritious menus.

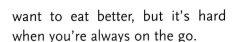

What You'll Learn

www.jbpub.com/healthyliving

The web site for this book offers many useful tools and is a great source for supplementary health information for both students and instructors. Visit the site at www.jbpub.com/healthyliving for information on these topics:

Basic Nutrition Principles
The Energy Supplying Nutrients
The Non-Energy Nutrients
Planning a Nutritious Diet
Nutrition for Optimal Physical Performance

Chapter Overview

The basic principles of nutrition.

How your body digests and uses the food you eat.

The functions and sources of nutrients.

How to plan a nutritious diet.

How malnutrition affects health.

DIVERSITY *Health* Asian-American Food

Con$umer *Health* Dietary Supplements

Managing Your Health Trimming the Fat from Your Diet

across the lifespan Nutrition

Student Workbook

Applying Concepts for Healthy Living

A Workbook

Self Assessment: Assessing the Nutritional Quality of Your Diet / Diabetes Mellitus Test

Changing Health Habits: Deciding to Change Your Diet

Do You Know?

• Which foods might help prevent cancer?

• How to judge the nutritional adequacy of your diet?

• If any vitamins are poisonous?

www.jbpub.com/healthyliving

Basic Nutrition Principles

What Are Nutrients?

Nutrition is the study of the way the body processes and uses **nutrients**, substances in food that the body needs for growth, repair, and maintenance of cells. In addition to these functions, some nutrients regulate cellular activity or supply energy. ▌Table 9-1 lists the six classes of nutrients, describes some of their roles in the body, and identifies their major food sources. In general, carbohydrates and fats supply energy; vitamins and minerals participate in chemical reactions that regulate body processes; and proteins provide the material for tissue growth, repair, and maintenance. Water transports materials in the body and also participates in numerous chemical reactions.

The human body can *synthesize* (produce) certain nutrients. For example, by exposing your skin to sunlight for about 20 minutes, your body can make a day's supply of vitamin D. Other nutrients are essential; that is, the diet must supply nutrients that the body does not make or does not make in

diet one's usual pattern of food choices.

nutrients substances in food that are necessary for growth, repair, and maintenance of tissues. Some nutrients regulate cellular activity or supply energy.

phytochemicals a group of non-nutrients that are produced by plants and may have beneficial effects on the body.

the amounts needed for good health. Nutritional deficiency diseases can develop when diets contain inadequate amounts of certain nutrients.

What Are Non-Nutrients?

Some foods contain substances that you can live without; therefore, they have no nutritional value. Many of these *non-nutrients,* such as fiber, are naturally found in plants and have beneficial effects on the body. Other non-nutrient substances, such as pesticide residues or lead, enter food unintentionally and can be hazardous to health.

Plants produce a large number of **phytochemicals**, a group of non-nutrients that may have beneficial effects on the body. For example, phytochemicals such as *sulforaphane* and *beta carotene* may prevent the development of cancerous tumors ("Beyond Vitamins," 1999). Recently, scientists observed that people who eat several servings of fruits and vegetables each day are less likely to develop certain cancers and heart disease than those who do not consume these foods daily. There is no scientific evidence, however, that individuals benefit from taking pills that contain phytochemicals. Nutrition experts recommend that people eat a variety of fruits, vegetables, and whole grains daily to obtain the various phytochemicals. ▌Table 9-2 lists some phytochemicals as well as their food sources and possible effects on the body.

Table 9-1 — The Six Classes of Nutrients

Nutrient Class	Major Roles in the Body	Rich Food Sources
Carbohydrates	Energy	Grain products, beans, vegetables, fruits, honey, and candy
Lipids	Triglycerides: Energy Cholesterol: certain steroid hormones, bile production, skin maintenance, nerve function	Vegetable oils, margarines, fatty meats, cheeses, cream, butter, and fried foods
Proteins	Growth, repair, and maintenence of all cells; production of enzymes, antibodies, and certain hormones	Dried beans, peas, nuts, soy products, meats, shellfish, fish, poultry, eggs, and dairy products (except cream and butter)
Vitamins	Metabolism, reproduction, development, and growth	Widespread in foods: nuts, beans, peas, fruits and vegetables, whole grains; meats
Minerals	Metabolism, development, and growth	Widespread in foods: nuts and whole grains; meats, fish, and poultry; dairy products, vegetables, and fruits
Water	Essential for life: many chemical reactions require water; it helps maintain normal body temperature, and dissolves and transports nutrients	Water, nonalcoholic and caffeine-free beverages, fruits, vegetables, and milk (nearly every food contributes water to the diet)

Table 9-2	Phytochemicals	
Phytochemicals	**Major Plant Sources**	**Possible Disease-Fighting Properties**
Allium	Garlic, onions, leeks	Enhances immune function
Indoles, isothiocyanates (sulforaphane)	Broccoli, cabbage, watercress, cauliflower, bok choy, collard and mustard greens, brussels sprouts	Inhibit cancer tumor growth
Ellargic acid	Nuts (especially walnuts), grapes, apples, strawberries, raspberries, cranberries, blackberries	Antioxidant activity: Protects cells from the damaging effects of free radicals; inhibits tumor growth
Flavonoids	Soy products, apples, artichokes, red wines, tea, onions	Prevent cancer, antioxidant activity, reduce risk of heart disease
Polyphenols	Black and green tea, red wine	Inhibit tumor growth, reduce heart disease risk
Monoterpenes	Citrus peel oils, citrus fruits, cherries	Anticancer agents
Carotenoids	Dark orange, yellow, and green fruits and vegetables	Prevent cancer

Source: Dietary flavonoids and risk of coronary heart disease. (1994). *Nutrition Reviews, 52*(2), 59–68; Marwick, C. (1995). Learning how phytochemicals help fight disease. *Journal of the American Medical Association. 274,* 1328–1330; A garden of phytochemicals. (1995). *University of California of Berkeley Wellness Letter, 12*(1), 6–7.

Natural, Health, Organic, and Functional Foods

Food manufacturers can label their products as *natural* if they contain no artificial additives such as synthetic colors or flavors. So-called natural foods are not necessarily more nutritious than foods that do not carry this description. For centuries, people in many cultures regarded natural foods such as honey, cider vinegar, or herbal teas as *health foods.* Many consumers still think these foods have healthful or medicinal properties. Although plants often contain beneficial phytochemicals, many herbs are natural sources of highly toxic chemicals.

Food producers can describe their fruits, vegetables, and meat and poultry products as *organic* if they meet certain standards. Fruits and vegetables, for example, must be grown without the use of synthetic pesticides and fertilizers. Currently, the *United States Department of Agriculture (USDA)* is developing national standards for the labeling of meat and poultry as organic.

Advertisers sometimes refer to their products as organic to imply that these items are superior. Although organically grown foods may contain less pesticide residue, they are not nutritionally superior than foods that have been grown using conventional farming methods. Chemists classify most compounds as organic if they contain carbon. Carbohydrates, fats, proteins, and vitamins contain carbon; therefore, they are organic compounds. Since foods consist of these nutrients, all foods are organic.

Functional foods, sometimes called *nutraceuticals,* are manufactured foods that have scientifically established medicinal benefits that are not provided by nutrients (Parisa, 1999). A person must eat a certain amount of these foods to obtain the desired effects. For example, a chemical from a plant that can lower blood cholesterol levels has been added to certain margarines and salad dressings recently. In the future, consumers may be able to buy specially formulated foods that reduce body fat or the risk of cancer.

What Happens to the Food You Eat?

Humans eat a wide variety of plants, animals, and animal products to obtain nutrients and other beneficial substances. In their natural state, many nutrients are in complex forms that the body cannot use. During the process of **digestion**, the digestive system breaks down complex nutrients into basic forms (**Figure 9-1**). Various *enzymes,* compounds that speed up chemical changes, participate in the process of digestion.

Absorption is the passage of nutrients through the walls of the intestines and eventually into the blood. After nutrients enter the bloodstream, many circulate to the liver, where they are processed or stored.

digestion the process of breaking down large food molecules into smaller molecules that the intestinal tract can absorb.

absorption the passage of nutrients through the walls of the small and large intestines and eventually into the general circulation of the body.

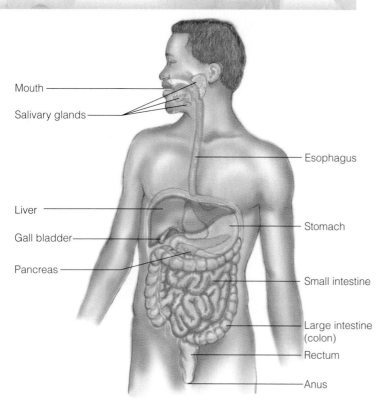

Mouth

Salivary glands

Esophagus

Liver

Stomach

Gall bladder

Pancreas

Small intestine

Large intestine (colon)

Rectum

Anus

▲**Figure 9-1 The Digestive System.** The stomach and small intestine breaks down large compounds in foods into smaller molecules that can be absorbed through the intestinal walls.

By the time any remaining food material enters the large intestine, most of its nutrients have been absorbed. This residue, the *feces* or *stool*, remains in the rectum until the individual has a bowel movement to eliminate the waste. The entire process of digesting the food, absorbing its nutrients, and eliminating fecal residue generally takes about 1 to 3 days.

The kidneys play an important role in maintaining normal nutrient levels by filtering excess water-soluble nutrients from the blood so they can be eliminated in the urine. A *water-soluble* nutrient dissolves in water. Many nutrients such as proteins, B vitamins, and vitamin C are water-soluble. *Fat-soluble* nutrients such as cholesterol and vitamin A do not dissolve in water, and the kidneys cannot eliminate them easily. Since blood has a high water content, the body attaches proteins to fat-soluble nutrients, which enables them to travel in the bloodstream. The kidneys usually do not filter proteins out of the blood, so the fat-soluble nutrients circulate until the liver or fat cells remove them for storage. Health problems occur when the body cannot use or store excess nutrients, especially those that are fat-soluble.

Energy from Foods **Metabolism** refers to all of the chemical reactions that take place in the body. These reactions are necessary to power muscular movements, synthesize and repair tissues, release and use energy, and produce enzymes and hormones. To carry out metabolic activities, cells need the energy stored in certain nutrients. Oxygen, which enters the body from the lungs, is needed to *metabolize* (break down) these substances, releasing the stored energy. This energy powers cell activities and helps maintain body temperature.

The amount of energy in foods is expressed as a number of *Calories*, commonly referred to as "calories." A **calorie** is a unit of energy. Foods containing carbohydrates, fats, proteins, and the non-nutrient alcohol provide calories. Carbohydrates and proteins supply 4 calories per gram, alcohol provides 7 calories per gram, and fat provides 9 calories per gram. The body cannot extract energy from water, vitamins, and minerals; therefore, these nutrients do not provide calories. Food composition tables such as those in Appendix C list the caloric value and nutrient content of commonly eaten fast foods.

The Energy-Supplying Nutrients

www.jbpub.com/healthyliving

Carbohydrates

Plant foods supply most of the **carbohydrates**—*sugars* and *starches*—in the diet. The simplest carbohydrates are sugars called monosaccharides. *Glucose,* commonly referred to as "blood sugar," is the most important monosaccharide in the human body. All cells, especially nerves, metabolize glucose for energy. *Starches* are long chains of glucose molecules. During digestion, large starch molecules are broken down to release glucose molecules for absorption.

Fruits, vegetables, and corn syrup are rich sources of monosaccharides. Grains, beans, and certain vegetables such as potatoes are rich sources of starch. Except for honey and milk, most animal foods do not contain carbohydrates.

Carbohydrates and Health Sucrose (table sugar) and *lactose* (milk sugar) form when two monosaccharides bond. During digestion, sucrose and lactose are broken down, releasing their component simple sugars. Many adults, however, cannot digest lactose. Such lactose-intolerant people may experience intestinal bloating, cramps, and diarrhea if they consume milk or other products that contain lactose. *Lactose intolerance* affects about 25% of the adult population in the United States (Inman-Felton, 1999). Members of minority groups, especially of Asian and African ancestry, are more likely to be affected than Caucasians.

Because milk is an excellent source of the mineral nutrient calcium, it is important that lactose-intolerant people consume alternative calcium-rich foods, such as buttermilk, cheese, regular yogurt, and some types of tofu. People with this condition can add a special enzyme to milk and other foods that contain lactose just before consuming them. The enzyme breaks down lactose, reducing the risk of unpleasant side effects. Affected individuals, however, can often consume small amounts of lactose-containing foods without experiencing discomfort.

Table sugar is a primary ingredient in candies, desserts, soft drinks, and many processed foods. Sugar is blamed for numerous health problems, including allergies, diabetes mellitus (diabetes), hyperactivity, mental illness, and criminal behavior. Some people even think sugar is toxic. Does evidence exist to support these claims? Does a preference for sugary foods pose any health dangers?

Tooth decay is the only disorder that is clearly associated with sugar consumption. Although eating sugary foods is not dangerous, this practice often displaces other, more nutritious foods from the diet. According to the USDA, the average American consumed about 90 pounds of carbohydrate sweeteners, primarily as corn syrup and sucrose, in 1996 (Kanton, 1999). Most nutrition experts recommend that Americans reduce their intake of these sweeteners to about one-half of its present level by consuming fewer candies, sugar-sweetened soft drinks, and bakery items. Artifical sweeteners such as Nutrasweet and Sucralose are added to sugar-free chewing gum, soft drinks, and "dietetic" foods. Consumed in normal amounts, these sweeteners contribute few or no calories to one's diet.

Some people avoid eating white sugar, which is made from sugar beets or sugar cane, but will use honey as a sweetener because they think it is more "natural" and nutritious than sugar. Although it may contain very small amounts of phytochemicals, honey has essentially the same nutritional value as table sugar.

Honey should not be added to baby foods because it may contain spores of *Clostridium botulinum,* a bacterium that produces a dangerous *toxin* (poison). This toxin affects nerves, causing loss of muscle functioning, which can be life threatening when it impairs breathing. Infants who eat contaminated honey are at risk of developing infantile botulism because their stomachs do not produce enough acid to kill the bacterial spores. Children older than 1 year of age and adults produce sufficient amounts of stomach acid, so they can eat honey safely (Wardlaw, 1999).

Carbohydrates represent about 44% to 47% of the typical American's calories. Many nutrition experts think Americans should increase their carbohydrate intake to 55% to 60% of their calories, primarily from starchy foods. Sugar intake should be limited to no more than 15% of calories (Wardlaw, 1999). To meet this recommendation, people who consume 2000 calories daily would need to limit their sugar intake to 300 calories. In view of the fact that a 12-ounce can of a cola-type soft drink sweetened with sugar or corn syrup contributes about 140 calories, this level of sugar consumption may be too restrictive for many Americans.

Diabetes Mellitus Diabetes mellitus, often called diabetes, is a group of common chronic diseases characterized by an inability to metabolize carbohydrates properly. This abnormality also affects protein and fat metabolism. A person with diabetes produces no insulin, or insufficient amounts of insulin, or has cells that do not respond normally to insulin. *Insulin,* a hormone that is produced in the pancreas (see Figure 9-1), helps glucose (blood sugar) enter cells. Without the normal action of insulin, the cells cannot carry out their metabolic activities properly, and glucose builds up in the blood.

High blood glucose levels can lead to major chronic health disorders, including vision problems, kidney disease, hypertension, nerve damage, and heart disease. The two most prevalent forms of the disease are *type I diabetes,* formerly called insulin-dependent diabetes mellitus, and *type II diabetes,* formerly referred to as non–insulin-dependent diabetes mellitus. **Table 9-3** lists the common signs and symptoms of each type.

Persons with type I diabetes require daily injections of insulin because the pancreas does not produce the hormone. Medical experts think an inappropriate immune system response to an infection causes this type of diabetes. Although type I diabetes is often called juvenile diabetes, the label is misleading because type I diabetes can strike at any age. The majority of cases, however, are diagnosed in childhood.

Most people with diabetes have type II. They are usually older than 40 years, overweight, and have a family history of diabetes. Since 1982 the prevalence of type II cases

metabolism all the chemical reactions that take place in the body.

calorie a unit of energy.

carbohydrates a class of nutrients that includes sugars and starches.

Table 9-3 Common Symptoms of Diabetes Mellitus

Type I Diabetes
(Generally develops in childhood and young adulthood)
- lack of energy
- listlessness
- frequent urination
- excessive thirst
- "fruity" odor in breath
- increased appetite with weight loss
- vision problems

Type II Diabetes
(Generally develops in adulthood)
Usually few symptoms, but when they exist:
- excessive thirst
- frequent urination
- vision problems
- In women, recurrent vaginal infections
- skin sores that do not heal

among American children has increased dramatically, particularly among Black and Hispanic youth (Libman & Arslanian, 1999). Obesity, physical inactivity, and poor diet contribute to the development of the disease in both adults and children.

Type II diabetes can often be controlled by dietary modifications and regular exercise, but many affected people need to take medications that increase the production of insulin by the pancreas. Some people with type II need daily insulin injections. By carefully controlling their blood sugar levels through diet, exercise, and if necessary, medication, diabetics can often lessen the long-term damaging effects of the disease.

Table 9-4	Fiber-Rich Foods
Whole-grain products	Wheat flour
	High-fiber wheat bran cereals
	Shredded wheat cereal
	Oat bran
	Oatmeal
	Brown rice
	Whole-grain crackers
	Buckwheat groats
	Barley
	Wheat germ
Dried beans and peas	Lentils
	Pinto beans
	Lima beans
	Kidney beans
	Navy beans
	Split peas
Fruits	Bananas
	Berries
	Oranges
	Figs
	Grapefruits
	Fruits with edible peels (e.g., apples, peaches, pears)
Vegetables	Vegetables with edible peels (e.g., potatoes)
	Brussels sprouts
	Broccoli
	Okra
	Cabbage
	Peas
	Turnips
	Spinach
	Sweet potatoes

According to the *Healthy People 2000 Review, 1998–1999* (USDHHS, 1999) the incidence of diabetes in the United States increased from 2.9 per 1,000 people in 1988 to 3.1 per 1,000 in 1994. The year 2000 target was 2.5 per 1,000 people. It is important to have routine health checkups because many people with type II diabetes are not aware that they have the disorder. You may want to take the diabetes quiz in the student workbook to assess your risk of developing this disease.

Fiber and Health Plants make certain carbohydrates and other substances that the human small intestine cannot digest. This material is called **dietary fiber,** or simply fiber. Soluble forms of fiber swell or dissolve in water; insoluble forms remain relatively unchanged in water. Apples, bananas, citrus fruits, carrots, kidney beans, psyllium seeds, and oats are rich sources of soluble fiber. Brown rice, wheat bran, and whole-grain wheat products are rich sources of insoluble fiber. Plants usually contain mixtures of these forms of fiber. ■ **Table 9-4** lists fiber-rich foods; note that none is from animal sources.

Although fiber is a non-nutrient, it provides some important health benefits. Soluble fiber slows the absorption of glucose from the digestive tract, which is beneficial for people with diabetes. Furthermore, increasing the amount of soluble fiber in the diet lowers blood cholesterol levels by reducing cholesterol absorption in the small intestine. Lower levels of blood cholesterol are associated with a lower risk of heart disease.

Insoluble fiber contributes to the formation of softer, larger stools that stimulate the muscles of the colon, producing the urge to have bowel movements more frequently. As a result, eating high-fiber foods can prevent *constipation,* infrequent or difficult bowel movements.

In the early 1970s, scientists observed that populations that consume foods rich in fiber have much lower rates of cancer of the large intestine and rectum *(colorectal cancer)* than populations who eat low amounts of fiber. As a result, some medical researchers thought that a high-fiber diet reduced the risk of this cancer. Recently two teams of scientists investigated whether eating high-fiber diets prevents the recurrence of precancerous growths in the colon and rectum (Alberts et al., 2000; Schatzkin et al., 2000). Results showed that such diets did not reduce the risk of the growths. These studies, therefore, do not support the concept that high-fiber diets lower the risk of colorectal cancer. Although a high-fiber diet can reduce the risks of heart disease, type II diabetes, and certain intestinal disorders, more research is needed to determine the role, if any, that dietary fiber plays in protecting against colorectal cancer.

Many Americans are concerned about their bowel habits; instead of eating more fiber-rich foods, they spend millions of dollars every year on laxatives that promise "regularity." Constipation results when stools are too small and hard to stimulate the colon regularly. A constipated in-

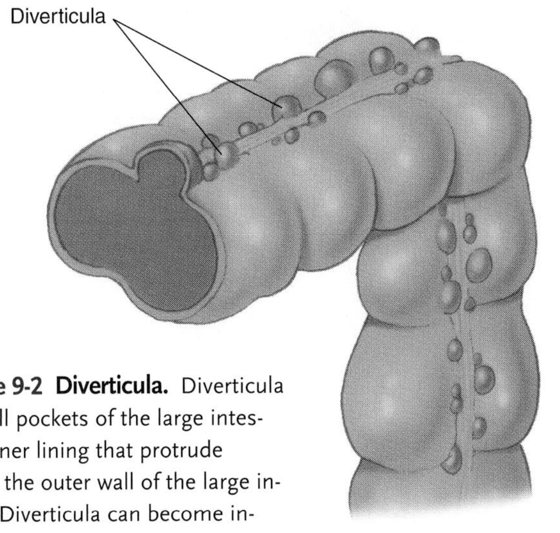

Diverticula

▶**Figure 9-2 Diverticula.** Diverticula are small pockets of the large intestine's inner lining that protrude through the outer wall of the large intestine. Diverticula can become infected and rupture.

dividual often has to strain while having bowel movements, increasing the pressure on veins in the rectum. This pressure can result in **hemorrhoids**, which are painfully swollen veins in the rectal and anal areas. Straining during bowel movements causes the colon lining to form small pouches called *diverticula* (▊ **Figure 9-2**). This chronic condition is called **diverticulosis**. Fecal material that becomes lodged in some of these little pouches can cause serious bleeding and inflammation *(diverticulitis)*. Diverticulitis can be life threatening if an inflamed pouch ruptures and spills fecal material into the abdominal cavity. Diverticulosis commonly occurs in Americans over 50 years of age, but the condition often produces no serious symptoms.

In addition to eating more fiber-rich foods, consuming adequate amounts of water helps prevent constipation. Regular exercise is often recommended to improve bowel functioning. Current research, however, indicates that it is not a useful treatment for chronic constipation (Meshkinpour et al., 1998). If constipation persists, or if you have intestinal pain, blood in your stools, or rectal bleeding, check with a qualified health-care practitioner to rule out serious health problems.

The typical American consumes less than 20 grams of fiber a day. Medical experts think individuals should consume at least 25 grams of fiber by eating more fruits, vegetables, beans, and whole-grain cereal products each day. During processing, grains often lose their vitamin, mineral, and fiber-rich parts. White flour, for example, is a refined grain product made from wheat kernels. Compared to whole-wheat flour, white flour contains very little fiber.

Jacobs and his colleagues (1999) analyzed data collected from the Iowa Women's Health Study to determine the relationship between whole-grain consumption and health.

According to their findings, women who ate more whole-grain products practiced healthier lifestyles and had a lower risk of premature deaths than women who ate more refined grains. Replacing refined flour products, such as white bread, with whole-grain breads is an easy way to increase the fiber content of your diet. Some brown breads contain little fiber; use the nutrient label to compare the fiber content of breads. Too much dietary fiber can interfere with the absorption of essential minerals; therefore, avoid consuming more than 35 grams of fiber daily.

Lipids

Dietary **lipids** include cholesterol and triglycerides. About 95% of the lipid content in foods are **triglycerides**, commonly called *fats* and *oils.* Since each cell contains triglycerides, it is not surprising that a small amount of fat is necessary for health. Compared to carbohydrates, fat is a more concentrated source of calories. The body stores energy in its fat deposits, which insulate the body from cold temperatures, give the body shape, and protect internal organs from jarring movements.

Each triglyceride has three fatty acids. Scientists classify fatty acids into three types: *saturated, monounsaturated,* and *polyunsaturated,* according to their chemical structures. Although the triglycerides found in foods contain mixtures of these three types of fatty acids, one type usually predominates. ▊ **Table 9-5** indicates the amounts of lipid as well as the percentages of saturated, monounsaturated, and polyunsaturated fatty acids in a tablespoon of various fats and oils.

Animal foods generally contain more saturated fat than plant foods. Olive, peanut, and canola oils are rich sources of monounsaturated fat; corn, safflower, cottonseed, and walnut oils are high in polyunsaturated fat. Oils from palm kernels or coconuts, commonly called tropical oils, are unusual in that they are from plants but contain large amounts of saturated fat.

Animal foods also contain **cholesterol**, a compound that is structurally different from a triglyceride. In spite of its reputation for being a troublemaker, cholesterol has several very important functions in the body. Cell membranes contain cholesterol, and the body uses this lipid to produce steroid hormones, vitamin D, and *bile,* a substance needed for proper fat digestion. Even if you could avoid eating foods that contain cholesterol, your liver and small intestine would make this essential compound.

dietary fiber indigestible substances produced by plants.

hemorrhoids painfully swollen veins that can form in the rectal and anal areas.

diverticulosis an intestinal disorder that occurs when the colon lining forms small pouches that protrude through the outer wall of the colon.

lipids a class of nutrients, which includes triglycerides and cholesterol, that do not dissolve in water.

triglycerides the most prevalent form of lipids in foods; often called fats or oils.

cholesterol a type of lipid found only in animals.

Table 9-5 Fatty Acid Content of Common Fats and Oils*

Source or Type of fat/oil	Total Lipid/ Tablespoon (g)	% Saturated	% Monounsaturated	% Polyunsaturated
Safflower oil	14	9	12	74
Sunflower oil	14	11	19	66
Corn oil	14	13	24	59
Soybean oil	14	14	23	59
Soybean/cottonseed oil	14	18	29	48
Olive oil	14	13	73	8
Canola oil	14	7	59	29
Peanut oil	14	17	46	31
Chicken fat	13	30	45	21
Lard (pork fat)	13	39	45	12
Beef fat	13	50	42	4
Coconut oil	14	90	5	1
Hydrogenated vegetable shortening	13	25	45	26
Margarine (hard)	11	20	45	33
Butter	11	65	30	4

*Fatty acid totals are not 100% because other lipids are present in the fat or oil.

Table 9-6 Cholesterol in Foods

Food	Serving Size	Cholesterol (mg)
Beef Liver	4 oz	545
Egg	1 large	212
Yolk		212
White		0
Shrimp	3 oz	167
Turkey, ground cooked	4 oz	116
Beefsteak	4 oz	94
Ice cream (rich = 16% fat)	1 cup	90
Sherbet (2% fat)	1 cup	10
Yogurt, plain low-fat	1 cup	14
Whole milk	1 cup	33
Reduced-fat (2%) milk	1 cup	18
Nonfat milk	1 cup	4
Butter	1 tablespoon	31
Swiss cheese	1 oz	26
Cream cheese	1 oz	10
Bacon	3 slices	16

Only animals produce cholesterol; therefore, the compound is found in animal and not plant foods. Meats, whole-milk products, and egg yolks supply most of the cholesterol in the typical American diet. Table 9-6 lists cholesterol-rich foods and the amount of cholesterol in each serving.

Lipids and Health The fat contained in or added to foods makes them taste rich and flavorful. How did you react when you first tasted nonfat milk? Did you think the milk was watery or "thin" when compared to whole or reduced-fat (2%) milk? Although most people do not eat pure fat, they often have difficulty resisting foods that combine fat with sugar or salt, as in candy bars, cake frostings, or tortilla chips. Diets that supply too much fat or excessive amounts of saturated fat are associated with an increased risk of obesity, heart disease, and some cancers. Eating large amounts of saturated fat can result in higher-than-normal blood cholesterol levels. High intakes of cholesterol may raise blood levels of this lipid also.

Diets that contain high amounts of certain unsaturated fatty acids, such as those in olive oil and canola oil, may reduce the risk of heart disease. Furthermore, diets that include fatty fish from cold water such as salmon, herring, tuna, and mackerel may lower the risk of heart disease and stroke. These fish are rich sources of *omega-3 fatty acids*, types of polyunsaturated fatty acids that the body cannot make. Fish oil supplements, however, are not recommended because high intakes of omega-3 fatty acids can interfere too much with blood clotting, making excessive

DIVERSITY in Health | Asian-American Food

For centuries, the Chinese culture has had a major influence on other Asian populations. These populations consume large quantities of rice, wheat noodles, and vegetables combined with eggs or a small amount of meat (usually poultry, fish, or pork). The traditional Asian diet is high in starch and fiber and usually low in fat, especially saturated fat. Stir-frying vegetables and meats in a lightly oiled wok or steaming foods are popular Oriental cooking methods that add fewer calories than deep-fat frying and preserve more vitamins and minerals than boiling. To season their foods, most Asian cooks use low-fat items such as garlic, ginger, and sauces made from mustard and soybeans.

Not all features of the traditional Asian diet are healthful. Asian meals contain little or no dairy products; therefore, the amount of calcium in these diets is usually low. Compared to Caucasians and Africans, people of Asian ancestry have a higher risk of osteoporosis. Among the residents of northern Japan, the consumption of soy sauce as well as fermented and pickled foods may contribute to the relatively high incidence of certain cancers and hypertension.

After immigrating to the United States, many Asians adopt Western food preferences and preparation practices. For example, American-style Chinese meals often include larger portions of meat and breaded, deep-fat fried foods. Eventually, Asian-Americans began to experience the same chronic health problems as do populations living in the United States for longer periods.

Some people experience an adverse reaction when they eat Asian or other foods to which the flavor enhancer *monosodium glutamate (MSG)* has been added. After eating food that contains MSG, persons who are sensitive to the compound may report a "tight" sensation in the face and chest, headache, and pain and reddening of skin, especially on the face. The Food and Drug Administration refers to this condition as the *MSG symptom complex* (Yang et al., 1997).

You can still enjoy eating meals in Chinese, Japanese, Thai, and other Asian-American restaurants by selecting menu items carefully. Choose plenty of steamed vegetables and rice or noodles to accompany the entrée. Avoid dishes containing foods that have been dipped in batter and fried; avoid or limit your intake of fried won-tons and egg rolls; and do not add soy sauce to your food. If you react adversely to MSG, many cooks, upon request, will prepare your food without it.

bleeding likely. Instead of taking fish oil supplements, try to include a couple of cold-water fish items in your diet every week.

Unlike the typical American diet, the traditional diet of Mediterranean populations contains smaller amounts of meat and sweets and larger amounts of plant foods, fish, and olive oil (see the inside back cover). The risk of heart disease is lower for individuals who consume the traditional Mediterranean diet ("Eating Mediterranean," 1999). The Diversity in Health essay above discusses the traditional Asian diet, which also contains less animal protein and saturated fat than Western diets.

Not all foods made with vegetable oil have healthful properties. *Hydrogenation* is a food-processing technique that partially hardens the oil so it can be made into shortening and sticks of margarine. This process alters the natural chemical structure of some unsaturated fatty acids in vegetable oils, making them more saturated. Hydrogenation also changes some of the remaining unsaturated fat into an unusual form: *trans fatty acids*. In the body, trans fatty acids behave like saturated fats, raising blood cholesterol levels (Ascherio et al., 1999). Late in 1999 the Food and Drug Administration (FDA) proposed new labeling regulations concerning the trans fatty acid content of foods. The amount of trans fat in a serving of food will be shown on the label, and the total amount of fat will include trans fats. (See Figure 9–6.) To reduce your intake of trans fatty acids, use soft or liquid margarines and avoid baked goods and fried foods, which are often made with hydrogenated fats. Other factors besides dietary lipids contribute to heart disease; Chapter 12 discusses in depth this number one killer of Americans.

Fat Substitutes Engineered compounds such as *Olestra, Oatrim,* and *Simplesse* are used to replace some or all of the fat in certain processed foods. Olestra, for example, supplies no calories because it cannot be digested and absorbed. A one-ounce serving of regular tortilla chips supplies 130 calories and contains 6 grams of fat; the same amount of chips fried in Olestra contains 76 calories and no fat. For consumers demanding a variety of fat-free snack foods that taste good, Olestra seems to be a good fat substitute. However, eating foods made with Olestra may produce some unpleasant side effects (Nestle, 1998). Additionally, the substance interferes with the absorption of certain vitamins. Food scientists are currently developing fat replacers that taste good, do not cause side effects, and are chemically stable when heated.

Setting Limits The typical American diet contains too much fat, especially saturated fat. Dairy products, meat, and processed snack foods contribute much of the saturated fat in the typical American's diet. College students and other busy people often have difficulty restricting their

Trimming the Fat from Your Diet

Americans are reducing the amount of fat in their diets by changing the ways they select and prepare their food. The following tips can help you trim much unnecessary and unwanted fat out of your diet.

- Stir fry or steam vegetables, or eat them raw.
- Avoid breaded and fried vegetables, chicken, fish, and meats.
- Avoid sausage, bacon, and fatty luncheon meats.
- Eat boiled or baked instead of fried potatoes.
- Trim all visible fat from meats before cooking them.
- Bake, roast, boil, or broil meats instead of frying them.

- Remove and discard the skin before cooking poultry (about one-half of the fat is in the skin).
- Chill cooked chili, stews, soups, sauces, and gravies. Then, skim off the fat before reheating and serving these foods.
- Substitute nonfat milk for whole or reduced-fat (2%) milk.
- Substitute reconstituted, nonfat dry milk in recipes that use milk or cream.
- Eat low-fat or fat-free frozen yogurt, ice milk, and cheese made from nonfat milk.
- When making omelets, use only one egg yolk.

- Use a light coating of an oil spray when baking, instead of large amounts of fats or oils.
- Eat more chicken and fish and less beef.
- Use low-fat or fat-free salad dressings.
- Substitute plain low-fat or fat-free yogurt for sour cream in recipes.
- Skim frostings from cakes; frosting is made with hydrogenated shortening, which is 100% fat.
- When eating two-crust pies, eat the filling and only one crust; discard the remaining crust.
- Reduce by one-fourth the amount of fat (margarine, butter, oils, or shortening) in recipes.

---

intake of saturated fat, especially if they eat greasy snacks and fast foods regularly. Popular fast foods, such as cheeseburgers, pizza, fried chicken, beef tacos, and milk shakes, contain large amounts of saturated fat. Many fast-food restaurants, however, offer less fatty items such as roast chicken, low-fat yogurt, bean burritos, and meatless salads.

Health experts recommend that adults reduce their fat consumption to less than 30% of their calories, limit their saturated fat consumption to no more than 10% of calories, and limit their cholesterol intake to no more than 300 milligrams per day. According to the latest *Healthy People 2000* progress report (USDHHS, 1999), many Americans are eating less fat. In 1991, 34% of the calories in the average adult American's diet were from fat. Currently, 33% of the calories in the average adult's diet are provided by this nutrient. The Managing Your Health feature above, "Trimming the Fat in Your Diet," provides some practical ways to reduce your intake of fat.

Most food labels provide nutrition information concerning the amounts of total fat, saturated fat, and cholesterol in food products. A later section of this chapter will show you how to use this information to control the amount and type of fat in your diet.

Proteins

Your body needs **proteins** to build, maintain, and repair cells; to form structural components such as hair and nails; and to make enzymes, antibodies, and numerous hormones. Although carbohydrates and fats are its primary fuels, the body derives a small amount of energy from protein. Most foods contain some protein.

Proteins consist of **amino acids.** During digestion, proteins in plant or animal foods are broken down, releasing amino acids for absorption. Human cells use about 20 different amino acids to synthesize the thousands of proteins in the body. The cells can make 11 of these amino acids; the other 9 amino acids are essential and must be supplied by the diet. If the diet lacks the essential amino acids, the body is unable to grow properly or carry out vital functions.

Most animal foods contain adequate amounts of each essential amino acid; these foods are *complete* protein sources. Plants are sources of *incomplete* protein because they either contain insufficient amounts or lack one or more of the essential amino acids. The best plant sources of essential amino acids are soybeans, whole grains, seeds, nuts, peas, and lentils. Fruits do not contain appreciable amounts of essential amino acids.

Proteins and Health Most adult Americans consume about 14 to 18% of their calories from protein. This percentage is about twice the amount required by the body. Although high protein intakes do not harm most healthy individuals, eating generous portions of animal foods contributes excessive amounts of cholesterol and saturated fat to the diet.

Many athletes and bodybuilders think it is necessary to consume large quantities of protein-rich animal foods and take protein supplements to increase their muscle mass. This practice does not build bigger muscles; instead, their bodies metabolize the extra amino acids for energy or convert them into body fat. Additionally, the kidneys need more water to eliminate the excess metabolic by-products. The most effective way to enhance muscle mass is to combine a nutritionally adequate diet with a program of muscle-strengthening exercises.

Animal products, especially meat, fish, poultry, and dairy foods, contribute about 70% of the protein in the American diet (Smit et al., 1999). A growing number of Americans are consuming plant-based, or *vegetarian,* diets that contain little or no animal foods.

There are several types of vegetarian diets. The *vegan,* or total vegetarian, diet consists of plant foods only. Other vegetarian diets include some animal foods. For example, the *lacto-vegetarian* diet contains dairy products, and the *lacto-ovo-vegetarian* diet includes eggs as well as dairy products. Some people who eat fish or poultry still call themselves vegetarians because they do not eat *red* meats. There are so many different plant-based diets, it is difficult to estimate the number of Americans practicing some form of vegetarianism.

Are vegetarian diets nutritious? Plant-based diets may promote health because they contain more fiber, antioxidants, and phytochemicals and less saturated fat and cholesterol than the traditional meat-rich Western diet. Generally, the nutritional adequacy of a vegetarian diet varies according to the degree of its dietary restrictions. Animal foods are rich sources of essential amino acids and often contain minerals in forms that are easy to absorb. By eating a variety of plant foods and consuming dairy products, however, vegetarians can obtain adequate amounts of most essential amino acids and minerals. Thus, with careful planning, most plant-based diets can be nutritionally adequate (American Dietetic Association, 1997). If you are interested in learning specific details about vegetarian cookery and menu planning, you can obtain this information from hospital dietitians or University Extension nutritionists in your area.

Healthy
LIVING PRACTICES

- To reduce your risk of obesity, heart disease, type II diabetes, and certain digestive tract disorders, consume 25 to 35 grams of fiber each day by eating more fruits, vegetables, beans, and whole-grain cereal products.
- To lower your risk of diabetes and heart disease, reduce your fat intake to less than 30% of your daily calories, limit your intake of saturated fat to less than 10% of daily calories, and reduce your cholesterol intake to 300 or fewer milligrams per day.

- You can reduce the amount of cholesterol and saturated fat in your diet by consuming low-fat yogurt and nonfat milk and by eating less cheese, fatty meat, fried food, and fat-laden bakery goods and snack foods.
- Many fast foods are high in fat. If you eat at fast-food restaurants regularly, reduce your intake of fried foods by selecting salads or grilled chicken items.
- If you eat large amounts of red meat and other animal foods, consider eating less of it and consuming more beans, nuts, and whole-grain cereals instead.

www.jbpub.com/healthyliving

Non–Energy-Supplying Nutrients

Vitamins

The human body needs **vitamins** to regulate growth; release energy from carbohydrates, fats, and proteins; and maintain tissues. Although many vitamins participate in the chemical reactions that release energy, they do not provide calories.

Scientists classify vitamins according to their ability to dissolve in water or fat. Vitamin C and the eight B vitamins are water-soluble; vitamins A, D, E, and K are fat-soluble. The body does not store most water-soluble vitamins to any appreciable extent, whereas fat-soluble vitamins are stored in the liver and body fat and can accumulate. **Table 9-7** lists most of the vitamins as well as their major roles in the body and rich food sources.

Compared to the energy-supplying nutrients and water, the body requires very small amounts of vitamins. Diets that include a wide variety of foods can meet the vitamin needs of healthy individuals. Some persons, however, take nutrient supplements that provide several times the recommended levels of vitamins to treat or prevent illness. More of a nutrient is not necessarily better. Cells use limited amounts of each vitamin daily. In many instances, excessive amounts of these nutrients accumulate in the body and cause harmful side effects. Table 9-7 provides information concerning the signs and symptoms of vitamin toxicity disorders.

Antioxidants The chemical structures of certain compounds, particularly polyunsaturated fatty acids, make them vulnerable to damage by free radicals. A **free radical** is an unstable and highly reactive atom or compound that removes electrons from other substances, which destroys them. Under certain conditions, oxygen becomes a free radical. Free radical formation produces chemical changes

proteins a class of nutrients that build, maintain, and repair cells.

amino acids the molecules that comprise proteins.

vitamins a class of nutrients that participates in a variety of chemical reactions such as energy production, growth regulation, and tissue maintenance.

free radical an unstable, highly reactive substance that can damage cells.

Table 9-7 Major Vitamins

Vitamin	Major Functions	Rich Food Sources	Deficiency Signs/Symptoms	Toxicity Signs/Symptoms
A and provitamin A (beta carotene)	Vision in dim light, growth, reproduction, maintains immune system and skin, antioxidant	Liver, milk, green and yellow fruits and vegetables	Poor vision in dim light, dry skin, blindness, poor growth, respiratory infections	Intestinal upset, hair loss, headache, birth defects
D	Bone and tooth development and growth	Few good food sources other than fortified milk and eggs	Weak, deformed bones (rickets)	Growth failure, loss of appetite, weight loss
E	Antioxidant: protects cell membranes	Vegetable oils, whole grains, wheat germ, asparagus	Anemia (rarely occurs)	Intestinal upsets, may interfere with the metabolism of other vitamins
C	Scar formation and maintenance, immune system functioning, antioxidant	Fruits and vegetables	Frequent infections, bleeding gums, bruises, poor wound healing	Intestinal upsets, headache, weakness, kidney stones
Thiamin	Energy metabolism	Pork, liver, nuts, dried beans and peas, whole-grain cereals	Heart failure, mental confusion, depression, paralysis (beriberi)	Unknown
Riboflavin	Energy metabolism	Milk and yogurt, meat, greens, whole-grain and enriched breads and cereals	Enlarged, purple tongue; fatigue	Unknown
Niacin	Energy metabolism	Protein-rich foods, whole-grain and enriched breads and cereals	Skin rash, diarrhea, weakness, dementia, death (pellagra)	Painful skin flushing, intestinal upsets, liver damage
Vitamin B_6	Protein and fat metabolism	Protein-rich foods, leafy vegetables, whole grains	Anemia, skin rash, irritability	Weakness, depression, nerve damage
Folate (folic acid)	DNA production	Leafy vegetables, oranges, nuts, liver, enriched breads and cereals	Anemia, depression, spina bifida in developing embryo	Unknown
B_{12}	DNA production	Animal products	Anemia, fatigue, paralysis	Unknown

Source: Adapted from Sizer, F., & Whitney, E. (1997) *Nutrition: Concepts and controverises.* Belmont, CA: Wadsworth Publishing Co.

Table 9-8 — Rich Fruit and Vegetable Sources of Antioxidants*

Fruits	Vegetables
Prunes	Kale
Raisins	Spinach
Blueberries	Brussel sprouts
Blackberries	Alfalfa sprouts
Strawberries	Broccoli florets
Raspberries	Beets
Plums	Red bell peppers
Oranges	Onions
Red grapes	Corn
Cherries	Eggplant

*The fruits and vegetables in the table are ranked according to their score of the ORAC (Oxygen Radical Absorbance Capacity) assay.

Source: Antioxidant foods: Foods that score high in antioxidant assay ORAC (Oxygen Radical Absorbance Capacity) (1999). *Food and Nutrition Research Briefs*. U.S. Department of Agricultural Research Service. www.ars.usda.gov/is/np/fnrb/

in cells that may contribute to the development of cardiovascular disease (diseases of the heart and blood vessels), certain cancers, degenerative changes in the eye, and other chronic health conditions.

Many foods contain **antioxidants** that can protect cells by preventing or reducing the formation of free radicals. These antioxidants include a variety of phytochemicals and vitamins E and C, and beta carotene, a yellow pigment in plants that the body converts to vitamin A. Table 9-2 lists some phytochemicals and their food sources; ▌ Table 9-8 lists fruits and vegetables with high antioxidant activity.

Since the 1980s, scientists have been investigating the possible risks and benefits of eating diets rich in antioxidants or taking antioxidant vitamin supplements. Although there is no strong scientific data to support the popular belief that vitamin C prevents colds, evidence is mounting that vitamins C and E may reduce the risk of developing heart disease and certain cancers (Hercberg et al., 1999). Results of the most recent Health and Nutrition Examination Survey indicate that nearly 30% of Americans have low blood levels of vitamin E (Ford & Sowell, 1999). Of the major race/ethnic groups studied, Black Americans had the lowest levels of this vitamin in their blood. Although Blacks also have high rates of heart disease and cancer, factors other than low blood levels of vitamin E may be responsible.

Should you take large doses of vitamins, especially antioxidant vitamins, to prevent disease? Nutrition experts are divided over the issue of antioxidant vitamin supplementation. The cells in your body make antioxidants. Some scientists think modern humans are exposed to much higher levels of environmental hazards, such as air pollution and pesticide residues, than their ancestors. These conditions may increase the body's need for antioxidants beyond the amounts that are made or can be obtained from food, making supplementation necessary. Other scientists think plant foods are the best source of antioxidants. Unlike supplements, plant foods contain mixtures of vitamins and phytochemicals that collectively may provide healthful benefits. Some medical experts are concerned that taking large doses of antioxidant vitamins can have harmful side effects, including promoting the growth of cancer cells (Herbert, 1999; Hercberg et al., 1999).

Many Americans take vitamin supplements. In a recent study, Hensrud and his colleagues (1999) found that more than 40% of 200 randomly selected clinic patients took multivitamin supplements regularly. Some subjects reported taking high doses of supplements containing only one vitamin; supplements containing vitamins E or C were the most popular. In 1997 American adults spent an estimated $3.3 billion on high-dose vitamin products (Eisenberg et al., 1998). Unless medically necessary, these supplements are an economically wasteful and risky practice. By eating a variety of fruits and vegetables daily, you are less likely to encounter toxicity problems because these foods naturally supply the antioxidant vitamins in smaller quantities.

Minerals

Minerals are a group of elements such as calcium, iron, and sodium that can function as free atoms or as parts of *inorganic* compounds. Most inorganic compounds do not contain carbon atoms. Many mineral elements such as magnesium regulate chemical reactions; others are structural components contained in certain organic molecules, like the calcium in bones. The body needs very small amounts of minerals, compared to the energy-supplying nutrients and water. Excesses of any mineral can create imbalances with other minerals or can be toxic.

▌ Table 9-9 lists some essential minerals, describes their major physiological roles, and identifies foods that contain high amounts of these substances. The following section provides information about calcium and iron, two minerals that have considerable health importance.

Calcium Calcium is the most plentiful mineral in the body. You may be aware that calcium is necessary for the development of strong bones and teeth, but this mineral

antioxidants compounds that prevent or reduce the formation of free radicals.

minerals a class of inorganic nutrients that includes several elements such as iron, calcium, and zinc, which have a wide variety of functions in the body.

Table 9-9	Some Essential Minerals

Mineral	Roles	Rich Food Sources	Deficiency Signs/Symptoms	Toxicity Signs/Symptoms
Calcium	Builds and maintains strong bones and teeth, regulates muscle and nerve function, regulates blood pressure and blood clotting	Milk products, fortified tofu and soy milk, fish with edible small bones such as sardines and salmon, broccoli, hard water	Poor bone growth, weak bones	Kidney stones
Potassium	Maintains fluid balance, necessary for nerve function	Whole grains, fruits, and vegetables	Muscular weakness, confusion, death	Heart failure
Sodium	Maintains fluid balance, necessary for nerve function	Salt	Muscle cramping	Hypertension
Magnesium	Regulation of enzyme activity, necessary for nerve function	Green leafy vegetables, nuts, whole grains, chocolate	Muscular weakness, convulsions, confusion	Unknown
Zinc	Component of several enzymes and the hormone insulin, maintains immune function, necessary for sexual maturation and reproduction	Meats, fish, poultry, whole grains, vegetables	Poor growth, failure to mature sexually, improper healing of wounds	Gastrointestinal upsets, anemia, heart and blood vessel diseases
Selenium	Component of an enzyme that functions as an antioxidant	Seafood, liver, and vegetables and grains grown in selenium-rich soil	May protect against heart disease and certain cancers	Nerve damage
Iron	Component of hemoglobin, involved in the release of energy	Liver, red meats, and enriched breads and cereals	Anemia	Hemochromatosis

Source: Adapted from Sizer, F., & Whitney, E. (1997). *Nutrition: Concepts and controversies.* Belmont, CA: Wadsworth Publishing Co.

has other important roles such as regulating blood pressure and participating in muscular movements. The body carefully maintains the level of calcium in the blood within a specific range. When the level is too high, the bones can remove and store the excess. If the amount of calcium in the blood begins to drop below normal levels, the bones release some of the mineral from storage, returning the level to normal.

As it adjusts to the demands of bearing the body's weight, bone tissue undergoes a continual process of being built, torn down, and rebuilt. After about 40 years of age, the bones of most people begin to break down at a faster rate than they rebuild. As bones gradually lose mineral density, they become weak and brittle. Fragile bones break easily, and sometimes shatter due to being unable to support the body. Although any bone can be affected, bones in the hip, spine, and wrist are most likely to break. This condition, **osteoporosis**, threatens the health of millions of aging Americans, especially menopausal women. One of every 2 women and 1 in 8 men over 50 years of age will have a fracture that is the result of osteoporosis (National Institutes of Health [NIH], 1999). Men usually have denser bones than women, which may explain why most aging men are not affected by osteoporosis to the same extent as aging women.

Fractures are associated with an increased risk of permanent disability or death, particularly if the fracture immobilizes the person; immobility increases the likelihood that fatal blood clots or pneumonia develop. A painful and disabling condition known as "dowager's hump" can occur when bones in the upper spine are so weak that they experience small compression fractures over time while trying to support the weight of the skull. As these bones heal into wedge shapes, the upper spine assumes an abnormal curvature (■ Figure 9-3). As a result, people with spinal osteoporosis often "shrink"—they lose some of their height.

As one ages, a calcium-rich diet and weight-bearing physical activity help build and maintain strong bones. After menopause, however, such practices may not be enough to prevent osteoporosis or slow its progress. Within the first 5 to 10 years after menopause, even healthy women are susceptible to losing a large percentage of their bone mass. Why?

The hormone *estrogen* stimulates bones to maintain their mass and retain calcium. A sign of normal estrogen production is regular menstrual cycles. A woman has reached *menopause* when her estrogen levels drop dramatically and her menstrual cycles have ceased. As women approach this time of life, those who have a history of regular menstrual cycles are more likely to maintain their bone mass than those who had irregular or absent menstrual cycles.

Besides being a postmenopausal woman, other characteristics increase one's risk of osteoporosis. The condition may be inherited, and members of certain racial groups are more susceptible to osteoporosis than others. African Americans tend to have larger bone masses that afford some protection against osteoporosis. On the other hand, slender small-boned people of European and Asian ancestry are more likely than people with large bones to develop osteoporosis.

Certain lifestyle choices can increase a person's risk of osteoporosis. Young people with low-calcium diets are likely to have less dense bones that are susceptible to osteoporosis as they grow older. Cigarette smoking and alcohol consumption can accelerate bone loss. Furthermore, young women who exercise excessively may disrupt their body's normal estrogen production and menstrual cycles. This reduction in estrogen levels can lead to premature bone loss.

Special x rays are used to diagnose bone loss clinically. To treat menopausal women who are at risk of osteoporosis, physicians often prescribe hormone replacement therapy, that is, synthetic hormones that contain estrogen or a combination of estrogen and progesterone. Nonhormonal treatments are available also. Women who are approaching menopause should consult their physicians about their risks of developing osteoporosis and their treatment options.

Most medical experts recommend that young men and women adopt behaviors that maximize their bone mass. If you are concerned about your risk of developing osteoporosis, consume foods that supply calcium such as those shown in ■ Figure 9-4. If you do not consume dairy products or foods fortified with calcium, ask your physician about alternative ways to obtain this mineral, such as calcium-containing supplements or antacids. In addition

▲Figure 9-3 Dowager's Hump. In people with osteoporosis, the bones in the upper spine develop small compression fractures. These bones heal into wedge shapes, and the upper spine assumes a deformed, curved shape known as "dowager's hump."

to calcium, vitamin D and the mineral magnesium are important for bone health. Adopting healthful lifestyles, such as refraining from smoking, reducing alcohol consumption, and engaging in physical activities that place stress on your bones, such as walking, weight lifting, or jogging, can help maintain your skeleton's structural integrity (Katz & Sherman, 1998).

Osteoporosis can occur at any age. If you think your risk of developing this condition is high, ask your doctor to perform a bone density test. By treating osteoporosis in its early stages, substantial bone loss can be prevented.

osteoporosis an age-related condition in which bones lose density, becoming weak and breaking easily.

Iron Most of the body's iron is found in the *hemoglobin* molecules within the red blood cells. Hemoglobin combines with oxygen in the lungs and transports it to cells throughout the body. Oxygen is necessary to release the energy stored in glucose.

Anemia results when the body produces abnormal red blood cells. In cases of iron-deficiency anemia, the bone marrow forms red blood cells that are smaller and contain less hemoglobin than normal cells. Without sufficient hemoglobin, the red blood cells carry less oxygen than usual as they circulate. Anemic individuals often report feeling tired because their cells are unable to obtain adequate amounts of energy.

Iron-deficiency anemia is one of the most prevalent nutritional disorders in the United States. This anemia may occur in people who experience significant losses of blood

▲ **Figure 9-4 Calcium-Rich Foods.** Some of the richest food sources of calcium are low-fat milk and yogurt, and greens. Although most cheeses are high in fat, they are good sources of calcium.

or consume diets that lack iron. Many individuals, especially premenopausal women, are at risk of becoming iron-deficient because they do not consume enough iron-rich food to replace the iron lost each month in menstrual blood. Individuals undergoing rapid growth, such as infants, children, teenagers, and pregnant women, have high needs for iron and are at risk of iron-deficiency anemia.

To ensure adequate iron intake, you can eat the iron-rich foods listed in Table 9-9. Normally, the small intestine does not absorb much of the iron in foods, especially the iron in plants. You can enhance the absorption of plant sources of iron by eating them with meat or vitamin C–rich foods. In addition to eating more foods that contain iron, people with iron-deficiency anemia may need to take iron supplements.

Annually, thousands of young children unintentionally poison themselves, a few of them fatally, after ingesting toxic amounts of iron-containing nutritional supplements. Many of these cases involve unsupervised young children who take overdoses of flavored vitamin/mineral supplements, thinking they are candy. To prevent such tragedies, store nutrient supplements like other medications, making them inaccessible to children.

As many as 1 in 250 Americans have a genetic condition that increases their intestinal absorption of dietary iron (McDonnel & Witte, 1997). The iron accumulates in their bodies and reaches toxic levels by the time they are middle-aged. These persons are often unaware that they have the potentially fatal condition called hemochromatosis, or iron overload, until it causes serious conditions such as diabetes, liver damage, and heart disease. A simple blood test can detect this treatable disorder. People with hemochromatosis should not take supplements that contain iron and should limit their intake of iron-rich foods.

Water

Water is essential for life on earth. You can survive weeks, months, and even years without one of the other nutrients, but you cannot survive for more than a few days without water. Water has many functions in the body: dissolving and transporting materials, eliminating wastes, lubricating joints, and participating in numerous chemical reactions.

About 60% of an adult's body is water. To function properly, the body maintains its fluid levels within specific limits, generally by increasing or decreasing urine production. Although it carefully conserves water, the body loses water when one perspires, urinates, exhales, and defecates. Drinking plain water and fluids such as milk, juices, and soft drinks replenish the body's water. Most foods, especially fruits and vegetables, also supply water.

Advertisements often promote beer as a thirst quencher; however, drinking alcoholic beverages does not replace body water. Alcohol acts as a *diuretic,* a compound that increases urinary losses of water. Caffeine is also a diuretic.

Many people do not realize that they need to obtain adequate amounts of water each day. Nutrition experts generally recommend that people drink at least 8 cups of water daily. *Dehydration* occurs when the normal level of body water declines, and the affected individual does not consume replenishing fluids. The symptoms of dehydration include weakness, confusion, and irritability. During prolonged fevers or bouts of diarrhea or vomiting, the body can lose substantial amounts of water, causing dehydration. These conditions cause the loss of minerals such as sodium and potassium as well. If untreated, severe dehydration is usually fatal. Chapter 11 provides more information about dehydration and heat-related illnesses.

Healthy people can become dehydrated while working or exercising in hot conditions. Is it helpful to consume sports drinks under these situations? In addition to water and glucose, sports drinks contain small amounts of the minerals sodium and potassium; therefore, these beverages may be beneficial for individuals engaging in prolonged, strenuous physical activities in which considerable sweating occurs. Most people, however, can maintain their fluid and mineral balance by eating a variety of foods and by drinking plenty of water before and during the activity.

Healthy ▬ **LIVING PRACTICES** ▬

- To obtain all of the vitamins and minerals you need, eat a wide variety of foods each day; include whole grains, dairy products, fruits, and vegetables.
- Store nutrient supplements like other medications, making them inaccessible to children.
- If you are hot or exercising heavily, to prevent dehydration, drink plenty of water and other beverages that do not contain caffeine or alcohol.

- To increase the likelihood that you will maintain your bone mass as you age, consume more calcium-rich foods, drink less alcohol, do not smoke, and engage in weight-bearing exercise regularly.

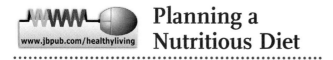

Planning a Nutritious Diet

The Keys to a Nutritious Diet

When you eat a milk-chocolate candy bar or some french-fried potatoes, you probably know that these foods contain carbohydrate and fat, but you may be surprised to learn that they also supply some protein, water, and even vitamins and minerals. Most foods are mixtures of nutrients that contain relatively large quantities of water, carbohydrate, fat, or protein, with much smaller quantities of vitamins and minerals. Nutrition experts recommend that people eat a variety of foods each day to ensure the nutritional quality of their diets.

A nutritious diet has two key features: nutrient adequacy and nutrient balance. The foods in a nutritionally adequate and balanced diet contain all essential nutrients in the proper proportions. By selecting a wide variety of foods, you can usually obtain the essential nutrients. Many people upset the nutritional balance of their diets by consuming more food than they need, by making poor food choices, or by taking massive doses of nutrient supplements. Eating too much food can make one overweight; eating too much saturated fat may clog one's arteries, ingesting too many supplements can create nutrient toxicity disorders. "Everything in moderation" is the best approach to planning nutritionally adequate and well-balanced diets. The Consumer Health feature below provides information about dietary supplements.

How much of each nutrient do you need for optimal health? How can you be certain that your diet is nutritionally adequate? The following information provides answers to these questions.

Nutrient Requirements

A **nutrient requirement** is the amount that prevents an average person from developing the nutrient's deficiency disease. For example, the average person requires 8 to 10 milligrams of vitamin C a day to prevent *scurvy,* the vitamin C deficiency disease. One-half cup of orange juice supplies 60 milligrams of vitamin C, more than enough vitamin C to prevent most cases of scurvy.

A required level of a nutrient, however, is not necessarily an optimal amount. By obtaining only the required levels of most vitamins, for example, the body does not have amounts to store in various tissues. The body relies on its nutrient reserves if nutritious food becomes unavailable.

Consumer Health | Dietary Supplements

The federal Supplement and Health Education Act allows manufacturers to classify nutrient supplements, herbal products, and certain hormones as "dietary supplements." As a result of this legislation, the FDA cannot regulate dietary supplements to the same extent as it regulates foods, cosmetics, and medicinal drugs. Many dietary supplements contain ingredients that have not been scientifically tested for safety or effectiveness. In some instances, the supplement is known to produce serious side effects. Nevertheless, these products can be sold in health food stores, pharmacies, and supermarkets without a prescription.

The FDA does not permit vague claims that a supplement will prevent or cure diseases, but it does allow manufacturers to indicate how their products affect the body's structures or functions (Nesheim, 1998). For example, a manufacturer can state on the label that a product is an "antioxidant," "improves urine flow," or "boosts energy." Many supporters of the dietary supplement industry, however, insist that the FDA's regulation of health claims on labels is unconstitutional. Recent legal court action against the FDA may limit the agency's ability to control health claims on labels.

In some instances, the distinction between a dietary supplement and a medicinal drug is unclear. For example, promoters of the hormone dehydroepiandrosterone, commonly called DHEA, claim that it is a miraculous "antidote for aging." Although DHEA is not found in foods, the hormone is sold as a dietary supplement. The adrenal glands produce DHEA and blood levels tend to decline as one ages, but scientists are not certain that taking supplements of this hormone is beneficial. Preliminary studies indicate that excessive doses of the hormone can interfere with normal liver function, masculinize women, and increase the risk of certain cancers.

Dietary supplements that contain melatonin are also popular among some consumers. Like DHEA, melatonin is produced by the human body and is not found in foods. People take melatonin primarily for its purported abilities to induce sleep and relieve jet lag.

Until large-scale controlled studies provide evidence that synthetic DHEA and melatonin are safe and beneficial, consumers should not take supplements that contain these compounds.

Thus, nutrition experts recommend that people consume more than just the required amounts of many nutrients.

The Recommended Dietary Allowances

To determine whether a population's diet supplies amounts of certain nutrients that can prevent deficiency diseases, nutritionists use standards called the **Recommended Dietary Allowances (RDAs)**. The latest edition of these standards is Appendix B.

To establish the recommendation for a nutrient, scientists take the required level and add a certain amount to provide a margin of safety. For example, the current RDA for vitamin C (adults, nonsmokers) is 60 milligrams, about 50 milligrams greater than the average person's vitamin C requirement. Since most people need much less vitamin C, they will not show the signs and symptoms of scurvy even if their intake does not meet 100% of the RDA.

To evaluate the nutritional adequacy of your diet, complete the assessment activity "Assessing the Nutritional Quality of Your Diet" in the student workbook. If your usual intake of any nutrient is less than 100% of the RDA, you can use food composition tables such as in the one in Appendix C to identify which foods are rich sources of that nutrient, and eat more of them. In most instances, vitamin and mineral supplements are not necessary, unless recommended by your physician.

Scientists are in the process of establishing a new set of recommendations, the **Dietary Reference Intakes (DRIs)** that will replace the RDAs. Although they are based on RDAs, the DRIs go a step farther by recommending levels of certain nutrients that ensure optimal health and well-being (King, 1999). Unlike RDAs, the DRIs include recommendations for people over 51 years of age. The DRIs provide four sets of recommendations, including the *Tolerable Upper Intake Levels (ULs)* for certain nutrients. Limiting one's intake to less than the ULs can reduce the chances of developing nutritional toxicities. Appendix B includes the latest list of DRIs.

The Dietary Guidelines

The United States Department of Agriculture (USDA) and the Department of Health and Human Services (HHS) issue the *Dietary Guidelines for Americans,* a list of general recommendations that focus attention on the association between diet and chronic disease. ▌ **Table 9-10** is the 2000 version of these Dietary Guidelines.

nutrient requirement
the amount of a nutrient that prevents an average person from developing a particular deficiency disease.

Recommended Dietary Allowances (RDAs) standard amounts of various nutrients that experts use to evaluate the nutritional adequacy of a population's diet.

Dietary Reference Intakes (DRIs) a new set of standards for evaluating the nutritional quality of diets

nutrient-dense food that contains a higher proportion of vitamins, minerals, and proteins than calories from fats and sugars.

Table 9-10	**The Dietary Guidelines for Americans, 2000**

1. Aim for a healthy weight.
2. Be physically active each day.
3. Let the Pyramid guide your food choices.
4. Choose a variety of grains daily, especially whole grains.
5. Choose a variety of fruits and vegetables daily.
6. Keep foods safe to eat.
7. Choose a diet that is low in saturated fat and cholesterol and moderate in total fat.
8. Choose beverages and foods to moderate your intake of sugars.
9. Choose and prepare foods with less salt.
10. If you drink alcoholic beverages, do so in moderation.

Source: *Dietary guidelines for Americans.* 5th ed. Washington, DC: U.S. Departments of Agriculture and Health and Human Services. Home and Garden Bulletin No. 232.

The Food Guide Pyramid

The *Food Guide Pyramid* is a menu-planning guide developed by the USDA that incorporates recent medical evidence concerning the role of diet in disease (▌ **Figure 9-5**). In addition to grouping foods according to their nutritional value, the Food Guide Pyramid includes a range of daily recommended servings for nearly every food category (see ▌ **Table 9-11**). Nutritionists modify the Food Guide Pyramid to meet cultural and philosophical differences. For example, see the food guide pyramids for vegetarians and Mediterranean populations on the inside back cover.

As you can see in Figure 9-5, six food groups compose the four-level Food Guide Pyramid. Most of the various foods in each group contain similar nutrients. Cereal products form the base of the pyramid; fruits and vegetables form the next level. Cereals, fruits, and vegetables are rich in carbohydrates, vitamins, minerals, and fiber. The bulk of the diet should consist of foods selected from these two levels. Protein-rich foods, including meats and dairy products, compose the third level of the pyramid. Although these are nutritious foods, they often contain too much saturated fat; therefore, fewer servings are recommended.

A **nutrient-dense** food contains a higher proportion of vitamins, minerals, and proteins than calories from fats and sugars. Many nutrient-dense foods also contain fiber. During processing, sugar, fat, and salt are often added to raw foods, which reduces their nutrient density.

Fatty and sugary foods form the top of the pyramid. Since these foods are not nutrient-dense, the Food Guide Pyramid does not include a recommendation to eat a minimum number of servings daily. Foods that add a considerable amount of calories from fat and sugar to the diet are

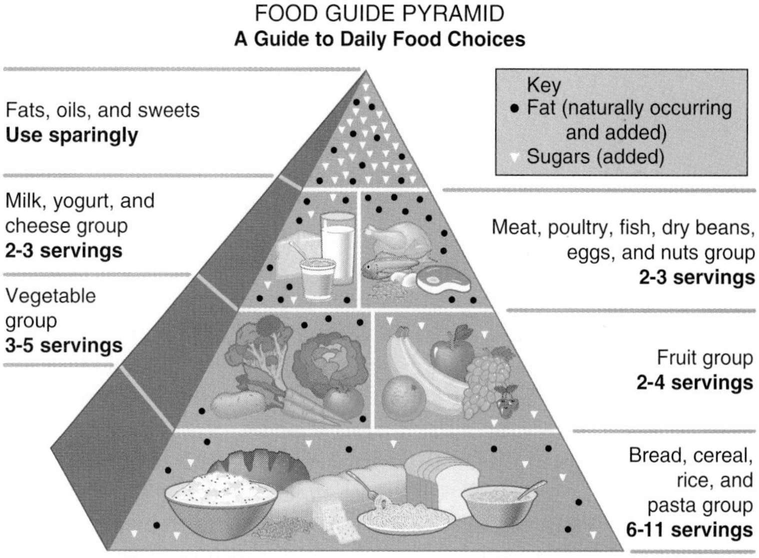

▶**Figure 9-5 The USDA Food Guide Pyramid.** The Food Guide Pyramid incorporates recent medical evidence concerning the role of diet in disease. Foods rich in fiber and complex carbohydrates form the large base of the pyramid; foods high in sugar and fat form its small top.

FOOD GUIDE PYRAMID
A Guide to Daily Food Choices

Fats, oils, and sweets
Use sparingly

Key
● Fat (naturally occurring and added)
▼ Sugars (added)

Milk, yogurt, and cheese group
2-3 servings

Meat, poultry, fish, dry beans, eggs, and nuts group
2-3 servings

Vegetable group
3-5 servings

Fruit group
2-4 servings

Bread, cereal, rice, and pasta group
6-11 servings

often referred to as "junk" or "empty-calorie" foods. If one's overall diet is nutritionally adequate, and one can "afford" the extra calories to fuel physical activity, eating a reasonable amount of foods rich in sugar and fat may be acceptable. Many people, however, eat too many sugary or fatty foods, displacing more nutrient-dense foods from their diets. By avoiding foods at the top of this guide and eating the minimum number of servings of the other foods, adults can control their caloric and fat intake while obtaining nutritionally adequate diets.

Using Nutritional Labeling

The FDA requires nearly every packaged food to have nutritional labeling. Consumers can use food labeling to determine and compare the nutritional value of most packaged foods. ▌ **Figure 9-6** illustrates the "Nutrition Facts" portion of a food label.

Many consumers want to know how many grams of fat and calories are in a serving of food. This information appears at the top of the Nutrition Facts label. People should also monitor the amounts of cholesterol, sodium, and fiber

in packaged foods. The Nutrition Facts label indicates these amounts by weight and as percentages of established nutrient labeling standards called the Daily Values (DVs).

Health officials at the FDA used various sources of nutritional information to determine the DVs for many nutrients and for fiber. As you can see in Figure 9-6, the lower part of the Nutrition Facts label shows two sets of DVs. One set of DVs is for people who consume 2000 calories each day; the other set is for those who consume 2500 calories daily. The DVs for total fat, saturated fat, cholesterol, and

Table 9-11 — The Food Guide Pyramid: Recommended Servings of Foods

Food Groups	Servings*		
	Sedentary Women	Children, Teenage Girls, Active Women, and Sedentary Men	Teenage Boys and Active Men
Breads, cereals, rice, and pasta	6	9	11
Vegetables	3	4	5
Fruits	2	3	4
Milk	2–3†	2–3†	2–3†
Meat, fish, poultry, nuts, dry beans, and eggs	2 (total 5 oz)	2 (total 6 oz)	3 (total 7 oz)

*Serving Sizes:
Breads, Cereals, Rice, and Pasta
  1 slice of bread
  $1/_2$ cup of cooked rice or pasta
  $1/_2$ cup cooked cereal
  1 oz ready-to-eat cereal
Vegetables
  $1/_2$ cup of chopped raw or cooked vegetables
  1 cup of leafy raw vegetables
Meat, Poultry, Fish, Dry Beans, Eggs, and Nuts
  $2^1/_2$ to 3 oz of cooked lean meat, fish, or poultry = 1 serving
  $1/_2$ cup of cooked beans, 1 egg, or 2 Tbsp. peanut butter = $1/_3$ serving

Fruits
  1 piece of fruit or melon wedge
  $1/_2$ cup of canned fruit
  $3/_4$ cup of juice
  $1/_4$ cup of dried fruit
Milk and Milk Products
  1 cup of milk or yogurt
  $1^1/_2$ to 2 oz of cheese

†Pregnant or breast-feeding women, teenagers, and young adults to 24 years of age need 3 servings.
Source: *The Food Guide Pyramid*. Washington, DC: U.S. Department of Agriculture, Human Nutrition Information Service, 1992. Home and Garden Bulletin No. 252.

sodium are maximum amounts. You should keep your daily intake of these nutrients *below* these amounts.

Specific information concerning the nutritional content per serving of the food product appears on the upper half of the label. In addition to showing amounts of fat, saturated fat, cholesterol, sodium, and total carbohydrate, fiber, sugar, and protein by weight, the Nutrition Facts label displays most of this information as percentages of the DVs for a 2000 calorie diet. Percentages of the DVs for key vitamins and minerals are shown below the second bold line.

According to the information near the top of Nutrition Facts, a serving of the product supplies 361 calories, 117 of which are from fat. To determine the percentage of calories from fat, divide the calories from fat (117) by the number of calories in the serving (361). Almost one-third of the calories in this food (32%) are from fat. Since most health experts recommend that Americans eat no more than 30% of their total calories from fat, you might decide to purchase a similar product that contains a lower percentage of its calories from fat.

Nutrition Facts

Serving size 10 1/2 oz (298 g)
Servings per Container 2

Amount per serving

Calories 361	Calories from Fat 117

	% Daily Value*
Total Fat 13 g	20%
Saturated Fat **8 g	40%
Cholesterol 60 mg	20%
Sodium 800 mg	33%
Total Carbohydrate 37 g	12%
Dietary Fiber 0 g	
Sugars 10 g	
Protein 24 g	

Vitamin A 10% • Vitamin C 15%

*Percent Daily Values are based on a 2,000-calorie diet. Your daily values may be higher or lower depending on your calorie needs.
**Includes 2 g trans fat.

	Calories	2,000	2,500
Total Fat	Less than	65 g	80 g
Sat Fat	Less than	20 g	25 g
Cholesterol	Less than	300 mg	300 mg
Sodium	Less than	2,400 mg	2,400 mg
Total Carbohydrate		300 g	375 g
Dietary Fiber		25 g	30 g

Calories per gram: Fat 9 • Carbohydrate 4 • Protein 4

▲**Figure 9-6 Nutrient Facts.** Most packaged foods have nutrient facts on their labels. People can use this information to evaluate the nutritional quality of their food.

Another approach to controlling your fat intake is to eat foods with a variety of fat contents, but your intake should not exceed 65 grams of fat per day, the DV for a 2000-calorie diet. For example, you might eat a 1-oz. serving of corn chips that contains 6 grams of fat and supplies 40% of its calories from fat. The other foods eaten on this day should provide no more than 59 grams of fat.

Not everyone thinks that the Nutrition Facts label is easy to use or helpful. Since the percentage of total calories from fat is not listed, people cannot easily compare the fat content of packaged food products. Additionally, many adult Americans need to consume lower amounts of calories and fat than the DVs. Furthermore, most people eat a variety of foods, some of which is fresh, or prepared in restaurants. As a result, these persons will probably underestimate the amounts of calories and nutrients in their diet if they rely only on the information provided by food labels.

Do You Need Nutritional Supplements?

By carefully selecting a variety of foods from the five major groups of the Food Guide Pyramid, healthy adults should obtain enough vitamins and minerals (Denny, 1998). Some people, however, need to supplement their diets with certain nutrients. Pregnant and breastfeeding women need more iron, calcium, and folic acid than what is available in foods. Some vegetarians need more calcium, iron, zinc, and vitamins B_{12} and D. Elderly persons may benefit from extra vitamin D and B_{12}.

Nutrient supplements do not contain all of the substances found in food that benefit health; therefore, do not take them in place of eating nutrient-dense foods. If your diet is nutritious, and you still want to take a multiple vitamin and mineral supplement as an "insurance policy," choose a reasonably priced product that contains no more than 100% of the DV for each of the vitamins and minerals listed on the label. The supplement should meet United States Pharmacopeia (USP) standards for strength, purity, and ability to dissolve. Vague advertising statements or labeling declarations, such as "meets laboratory standards for quality," do not guarantee product quality.

Healthy LIVING PRACTICES

- To plan well-balanced, nutritious daily menus, follow the recommendations of the Food Guide Pyramid.
- Use the Nutrition Facts on food labels to compare the nutritional content of packaged foods and plan nutritious meals and snacks.
- If you want to take a multiple vitamin and mineral supplement, choose a product that meets USP standards and supplies no more than 100% of each nutrient's DV.

ANALYZING *Health-Related Information*

Garlic Grace Notes

The following advertisement promotes garlic oil tablets to relieve fatigue. Read the ad and evaluate it using the model for analyzing health-related information. The main points of the model are noted below; the model is fully explained on pages 12–13.

1. Which statements are verifiable facts, and which are unverified statements or value claims?
2. What are the credentials of the person who wrote the ad? Does the author appear to have appropriate background and education in the topic area? If it is difficult to tell if the author has specific health expertise, what can you do to check his/her credentials?
3. What might be the motives and biases of the author?
4. What is the main point of the ad? Which information is relevant to the issue or main point; which information is irrelevant?
5. Is the source reliable, or does it have a reputation for publishing misinformation? Does the ad present both the pros and cons of the product?
6. Does the ad attack the credibility of conventional scientists or medical authorities?

Based on the above analysis, do you think that this ad is a reliable source of health-related information? Summarize your reasons for coming to this conclusion.

RUSSIAN SCIENTISTS DISCOVER NEW TREATMENT FOR FATIGUE!

Kiev, Russia—Russian researchers working under the direction of famed doctor Igor X. Ivanamiraculsky of Minsk have discovered that Russian garlic oil is a safe and effective treatment for chronic fatigue. In hundreds of double-blind studies performed at the Minsk Institute of Food Research, college students, athletes, and even elderly persons who took the garlic oil capsules reported having 25% more energy than those persons taking placebos. These results are nothing short of amazing!

Now, you can benefit from Dr. Ivanamiraculsky's discovery. For the first time, the doctor's energy-boosting garlic oil pills are available in the United States. No prescription is needed for this 100% completely natural energizer. Just ask for odor-free GARGOIL at your local pharmacy or health-food store. Satisfaction guaranteed! If you are not completely satisfied after taking GARGOIL, return the unused portion to the place of purchase for a refund. Remember to be careful and follow the label's instructions; some people report feeling too energized after taking GARGOIL! Accept no garlic oil substitutes—ask for GARGOIL.

Nutrition for Optimal Physical Performance

Most athletes are on the lookout for something—a diet, supplement, or drug—that may give them the competitive edge. The best advice for all athletes is to use the Food Guide Pyramid to choose a well-balanced diet composed of a variety of foods. By eating more servings of fruits and vegetables, athletes can obtain safe quantities of vitamins and minerals without taking supplements. There is no scientific evidence that protein-rich diets build bigger muscles, so eating large servings of meat or taking protein supplements is unnecessary. High protein intakes may cause dehydration and ac-celerate the loss of calcium from bones. Furthermore, protein-rich foods often contain a lot of fat, especially saturated fat. Fat intake should be no more than 30% of total calories.

Carbohydrate is the preferred fuel of the body, therefore, a diet that supplies plenty of carbohydrates from starchy foods is recommended (Wardlaw, 1999). Some athletes practice "carbohydrate loading" to maximize the amount of carbohydrate stored in their muscles. Several days before an event, for example, the athlete gradually increases the amount of carbohydrate eaten and gradually decreases the amount of time working out. Two to four hours before the competitive event, the athlete eats a light meal composed of starchy foods such as bagels, pasta, or breads and cereals. Not all athletes find that carbohydrate loading helps their performance. Thus, one should test the effects of the diet when not preparing for competition. Chapter 11 discusses physical fitness, including the use of *ergogenic* (performance-enhancing) aids, in detail.

malnutrition

overnutrition or undernutrition that results when diets supply improper amounts of nutrients.

Malnutrition: Undernutrition and Overnutrition

Malnutrition results when a person's usual food intake supplies inadequate or excessive amounts of nutrients. *Under*nutrition occurs when a diet does not contain enough nutrients; *over*nutrition results from consuming excessive amounts of nutrients. Undernutrition can be especially devastating for children. Undernourished youngsters often develop nutritional deficiency diseases; as a result, they may not grow properly or perform physical and mental tasks optimally. Undernutrition exists in the United States. According to the 1998 Current Population Survey, Americans living in nearly 4 million impoverished households experience hunger on a monthly basis ("Hunger," 1999). Even some people with adequate incomes are marginally nourished because they choose diets that supply barely enough calcium, zinc, iron, vitamin E, and the B vitamin folate. Such individuals may experience more frequent infections and take longer to recover from illnesses than those who are well nourished.

People living in countries with high standards of living are more likely to suffer from the ill effects of overnutrition rather than undernutrition. Individuals who eat too much fat, for example, may develop obesity, diabetes, and heart disease. The following chapter discusses obesity and weight management.

across the lifespan

Nutrition

From conception until birth, the developing embryo/fetus depends on its mother to supply the nutrients it needs for development and growth. Women often become more health-conscious during pregnancy, and as a result, they may select more nutritious diets. A woman's nutritional status prior to conception, however, has a significant impact on the health of her baby. By consuming a nutritious diet before becoming pregnant, a woman can build optimal nutrient reserves that prepare her body for the nutritional demands of pregnancy. During pregnancy, undernourished women have a higher risk than well-nourished mothers-to-be of miscarrying, having premature or underweight infants, and delivering babies with birth defects.

Consuming diets that supply adequate folate is critical, especially during the first four weeks of pregnancy when the *neural tube,* the embryonic region that forms the brain and spinal cord, develops. Occasionally, the neural tube fails to develop properly, resulting in *spina bifida* and related defects. Spina bifida occurs when a section of the spinal bones do not fuse to form the channel that encases and protects the spinal cord. In severe cases, the spinal cord protrudes from the infant's back, seriously impairing the child's ability to control the lower part of its body.

Many pregnant women are not even aware of their pregnancy when the neural tube is forming. To maximize the amount of folate in their tissues, women should eat plenty of folate-rich foods, especially enriched breads and cereals, lentils, fruits, and green leafy vegetables (see Table 9-7), before pregnancy.

During pregnancy, women should eat nutritious diets, obtain medical care, and take their *prescribed* doses of prenatal vitamin and mineral supplements. Before taking other supplemental nutrients, pregnant women should always check with their physicians or qualified health-care providers. Consuming excessive amounts of nutrient supplements during pregnancy increases the risk of certain birth defects.

Current infant feeding recommendations include the following: provide breastmilk and a supplement that contains vitamin D and iron for at least the first 12 months of life; do not feed solid foods before 4 months of age; and do not feed fresh whole or reduced-fat cows' milk before the first birthday. Iron-fortified infant formulas are acceptable alternatives to fresh cows' milk, but every healthy pregnant woman should consider the benefits of breastfeeding her baby. Breastmilk is the most suitable food for infants.

Breastmilk offers many advantages to infants and their mothers ("Breastfeeding," 1997). It is formulated properly and requires no bottles. Breastfed infants have fewer intestinal and respiratory tract infections (Wilson et al., 1998). The proteins in human milk will not cause allergies like those in formulas. Additionally, breastfeeding is economical and convenient; mothers can breastfeed anywhere they feel comfortable doing so. Individuals who are interested in breastfeeding can obtain educational materials and advice from members of the La Leche League, an organization with groups in many U.S. communities.

Many women do not breastfeed because they want to return to a job, they lack the support of family and friends, or they are uncomfortable with this practice. These women should follow their pediatrician's advice concerning the use of commercially prepared infant formulas. Formulas are nutritionally acceptable alternatives for human milk.

Parents often describe their preschool-aged children as picky eaters because they do not seem to be as hungry or interested in eating as when they were infants. However, most children eat enough calories to maintain their normal growth pattern. During this period, children often establish their food preferences and eating habits; well-informed responsible adults can serve as role models, teaching youngsters how to choose nutrient-dense foods.

Eating a nutritious breakfast is an important habit to develop early in life. The child who routinely skips breakfast and eats too many sugary snacks can develop borderline or overt nutritional deficiencies. This child often lacks energy, has difficulty concentrating on school work, and experiences behavioral problems. In severe cases, a malnourished child fails to grow properly.

Adolescents experience rapid growth during puberty, and their appetites increase accordingly. Teenagers often become overly concerned with their body size and shape. As a result, boys may experiment with dietary supplements to increase muscle mass. To lose weight, girls may skip meals or choose diets that limit nutritious foods, such as calcium-rich dairy products. Growing adolescents require plenty of calcium to maximize bone mass. An obsession with body size can foster poor eating practices and eating disorders that last into adulthood.

Aged persons who consumed a nutritious diet and have exercised regularly since their youth are more likely to enjoy good health than those who ate poor diets and were inactive. However, physical, psychological, social, and economic factors often influence the quality and quantity of the elderly person's food intake. As one ages, production of

▲Figure 9-7 Many elderly Americans participate in congregate meal programs within their community.

acid and other stomach secretions decreases, reducing the ability of the small intestine to absorb calcium, iron, and vitamins D and B_{12} ("Translating the Science," 1998). Therefore, older adults should ask their physicians about the need to take certain nutrient supplements.

Many elderly persons are unable to shop for groceries or prepare foods because of arthritis and strokes. Older individuals who are psychologically depressed, socially isolated, or financially impoverished often lack the interest or the resources to prepare nutritious meals. These people are at risk of becoming malnourished. Many communities offer federally subsidized nutrition programs such as Meals-on-Wheels and congregate meals for those who are at least 60 years old. The Meals-on-Wheels program relies on community volunteers to deliver a hot meal, milk, and fresh fruit to homebound people as often as five days a week. More mobile aged individuals can participate in congregate meal programs in which they visit community centers where hot meals are served five days a week (▌ Figure 9-7). Besides providing a nourishing meal, these sites enable elderly participants to interact socially. Frequent contact with other people can reduce an elderly person's risk of depression, a health problem that often affects isolated aged people.

Healthy
■LIVING PRACTICES■

- To increase your chances of having a healthy baby, improve the quality of your diet before you become pregnant.
- Excesses of certain nutrients can produce birth defects, so ask your health-care practitioner for advice before you take nutrient supplements during pregnancy.
- If you are a woman who plans to have children, consider the benefits of breastfeeding, especially during their first 6 to 12 months of life.

Chapter Review

Summary

Nutrients are substances in foods that supply energy; regulate body processes; and provide material for growth, maintenance, and repair of tissues. The six classes of nutrients are carbohydrates, lipids, proteins, vitamins, minerals, and water. Many foods also contain non-nutrients, substances that are not essential but may have healthful benefits.

During digestion, food is broken down into nutrients that can be absorbed. Cells metabolize carbohydrates, fats, and proteins, which releases energy stored in the compounds. The amount of energy stored in food is measured in calories. Cells cannot release energy from water, vitamins, and minerals.

Carbohydrates, the sugars and starches, are a major source of energy for the body. The only disorder that is clearly associated with excessive carbohydrate consumption is tooth decay. Plant foods supply dietary fiber and phytochemicals. Diets rich in fiber may reduce the risks of diverticulosis, hemorrhoids, constipation, and heart disease. Phytochemicals may prevent various chronic diseases including certain cancers.

Many medical experts think Americans eat too much fat, saturated fat, and cholesterol. Eating excessive amounts of these lipids is associated with an increased risk of obesity, heart disease, and certain cancers.

Protein is essential for tissue growth, repair, and maintenance; and for producing enzymes, antibodies, and certain hormones. The average American consumes more than twice the amount of protein needed, particularly from animal foods. One way to reduce the amount of animal foods in the diet is to eat more protein from plants. Vegetarian diets are associated with lower risks of chronic conditions such as heart disease.

Vitamins and minerals regulate body processes; some minerals are structural components of tissues. Over-doses of many vitamins and most minerals can cause nutritional imbalances and be toxic; therefore, unless medically indicated, people should avoid taking high doses of nutrient supplements.

A lifetime of inadequate calcium intake coupled with low estrogen levels after menopause increase a woman's risk of osteoporosis. Iron-deficiency anemia is a common nutritional problem, especially among women of childbearing ages. Dehydration is a serious condition that results when water intake is inadequate or water losses are excessive.

The key features of a nutritious diet are nutrient adequacy and nutrient balance. By selecting a variety of foods and by avoiding the indiscriminate use of nutrient supplements, one's diet can be nutritionally adequate and balanced.

A requirement for a nutrient is the smallest amount that prevents a deficiency disease. Eventually, Dietary Reference Intakes (DRIs) will replace the RDAs as standards for determining the nutritional adequacy of diets. The Food Guide Pyramid is a practical daily menu-planning guide. Nutrient labeling can help consumers select nutritious foods. Malnutrition occurs when diets supply too little or too many nutrients.

The quality of a woman's diet before and during pregnancy has an impact on the health of her developing child. During the first year of life, human milk is the best food for infants; solid foods should not be fed to babies until they are 4 months old. Without proper supervision, children and teenagers may skip meals or select inadequate diets. Physical, psychological, economic, and social factors contribute to the risk of malnutrition in the elderly.

Applying What You Have Learned

1. Explain how you would use nutrient labeling information to choose food products that are low in fat. (*Application*)
2. Keep a food record for one day. Analyze this day's food choices by using the Food Guide Pyramid. (*Analysis*)
3. Plan a menu for a day (meals, snacks, and beverages) that meets the Food Guide Pyramid's minimum recommended number of servings. (*Synthesis*)
4. Use a computer dietary analysis program to evaluate the nutritional quality of your diet. Which foods can you eat to improve your diet? (*Evaluation*)

KEY

Application: Using information in a new situation.
Analysis: Breaking down information into component parts.
Synthesis: Putting together information from different sources.
Evaluation: Making informed decisions.

Reflecting On Your Health

1. Have you changed your diet as a result of taking this course? How is your present diet different from what you ate in the past? Why do you think your present diet is better or worse than your past diet?

2. What factors influence your food choices? How willing are you to try new foods? What new foods have you eaten in the past year?

3. Do you use nutrition labels? If you do, which information do you think is most important? How does nutritional labeling help you be a better consumer? If you don't use nutrition labels, why not?

4. Do you take nutritional supplements? If you do, which supplements do you take? Why do you take them?

5. Females: Would you or did you breastfeed your children? Males: Would you want or did the mother of your children breastfeed them? Why or why not?

References

Alberts, D. S., Martínez, M.E., Roe, D. J., Guillén-Rodríguez, J. M., Marshall, J. R., Van Leeuwen, J. B., Reid, M. E., Ritenbaugh, C., Vargas, P. A., Bhattacharyya, A. B., Earnest, D. L., Sampliner, R. E., & the Phoenix Colon Cancer Prevention Physician's Network (2000). Lack of effect of a high-fiber cereal supplement on the recurrence of colorectal cancer. *The New England Journal of Medicine*, 342:1156-1162.

American Dietetic Association Reports: Position of the American Dietetic Association: vegetarian diets. (1997). *Journal of the American Dietetic Association*, 97(11):1317-1321.

Ascherio, A., Katan, M. B., Zock, P. L., Stampher, M. J., & Willett, W. C. (1999). Trans fatty acids and coronary heart disease. *New England Journal of Medicine*, 340(25):1994-1998.

Beyond vitamins: the new nutrition revolution. (1999). *Berkeley Wellness Letter*, 15:Suppl.

Breastfeeding and the use of human milk (1997). American Academy of Pediatrics. *Pediatrics*, 100(6):1035-1039.

Denny, S. (1998). About vitamin-mineral supplements. *Nutrition Today*, 33(2):69-70.

Eating Mediterranean (1999). *Mayo Clinic Health Letter*, 17(6):4.

Eisenberg, D. M., Davis, R. B., Ettner, S. L., Appel, S., Wilkey, S., Rompay, S. V., & Kessler, R. C. (1998). Trends in alternative medicine use in the United States, 1990–1997. *Journal of the American Medical Association*, 280:1569-1575.

Ford, E. S. & Sowell, A. (1999). Serum α-tocopherol status in the United States population: findings from the Third National Health and Nutrition Examination Survey. *American Journal of Epidemiology*, 150(3):290-300.

Hensrud, D. D., Engle, D. D., & Scheitel, S. M. (1999). Underreporting the use of dietary supplements and nonprescription medications among patients undergoing a periodic health examination. *Mayo Clinic Proceedings*, 74(5):443-447.

Herbert, V. (1999). Underreporting of dietary supplements to health-care providers does great harm. *Mayo Clinic Proceedings*, 74:531-532.

Hercberg, S., Galan, P., & Preziosi, P. (1999). Antioxidant vitamins and cardiovascular disease: Dr. Jekyll or Mr. Hyde? *American Journal of Public Health*, 89(3):289-291.

Hunger still a widespread problem in U.S. (1999). *Reuters Health News*. http://dailynews.yahoo.com/h/nm/19991014/hl/hun19_1.html

Inman-Felton, A. E. (1999). Overview of lactose maldigestion (lactase nonpersistence). *Journal of the American Dietetic Association*, 99(4):481-489.

Jacobs, D. R., Meyer, K. A., Kushi, L. H., & Folsom, A. R. (1999). Is whole-grain intake associated with reduced total and cause-specific death rates in older women? The Iowa Women's Health Study. *American Journal of Public Health*, 89:322-329.

Kanton, L. S. (1999). A comparison of the U.S. food supply with the Food Guide Pyramid recommendations. In *America's Eating Habits: Changes and Consequences*. In E. Frazão (Ed.), Food and Nutrition Rural Economics Division, Economic Research Service. United States Department of Agriculture. *Agricultural Bulletin* No. 750 (AIB-750).

Katz, W. A., & Sherman, C. (1998). Osteoporosis: The role of exercise in optimal management. *Physician and Sportsmedicine*, 26(2):33-35, 39-42.

King, J. C. (1999). Food choices for the 21st century: A word to our colleagues. *Nutrition Today*, 34(4):170-173.

Libman, I., & Arslanian, S. A. (1999). Type II diabetes mellitus: No longer just adults. *Pediatric Annals*, 28(9):589-593.

McDonnel, S. M., & Witte, D. (1997). Hereditary hemochromatosis. *Postgraduate Medicine*, 102(6):83-5, 88-91, 94.

Meshkinpour, H., Selod, S., Movahedi, H., Nami, N., James, N., & Wilson, A. (1998). Effects of regular exercise in management of chronic idiopathic constipation. *Digestive Disease Science*, 43(11):2379-2383.

National Institutes of Health (NIH), Osteoporosis and Related Bone Diseases-National Resource Center. (1999). *Osteoporosis overview*. Washington, DC: NIHORBDNNRC. www.osteo.org

Nesheim, M. C. (1998). Regulation of dietary supplements. *Nutrition Today*, 33(2):62-68.

Nestle, M. (1998). The selling of Olestra. *Public Health Reports*, 113:509-520.

Parisa, M. W. (1999). Functional foods: Technology, functionality, and health benefits. *Nutrition Today*, 34:150-151.

Schatzkin, A., Lanza, E., Corle, D., Lance, P., Iber, F., Caan, B., Shike, M., Weissfeld, J., Burt, R., Cooper, M. R., Kikendall, J. W., Cahill, J., & the Polyp Prevention Trial Study Group (2000). Lack of effect of a low-fat, high-fiber diet on the recurrence of colorectal adenomas. *The New England Journal of Medicine*, 342:1149-1155.

Smit, E., Nieto, F. J., Crespo, C. J., Mitchell, P. (1999). Estimates of animal and plant protein intake in U.S. adults: Results from the Third National Health and Examination Survey, 1988–1991. *Journal of the American Dietetic Association*, 99:813-820.

Translating the science behind the Dietary Reference Intakes. (1998). *Journal of the American Dietetic Association*, 98(7):756.

U.S. Department of Health and Human Services (USDHHS), Public Health Service. (1999). *Healthy people 2000 review, 1998–1999* (publication 99-1256). Washington, DC: Government Printing Office. http://odphp.usophs.dhhs.gov/pubs/hp2000/prog_rvw.htm

Wardlaw, G. M. (1999). *Nutrition perspectives*. St. Louis: McGraw-Hill.

Wilson, A. C., Forsyth, J. S., Greene, S. A., Irvine. L., Hau, X., & Howie, P. W. (1998). Relation of infant diet to childhood health: Seven-year follow-up of cohort of children in Dundee infant feeding study. *British Medical Journal*, 316:21-25.

Yang, W. H., Drouin, M. A., Herbert, M., Mao, Y., & Karsh, J. (1997). The monosodium glutamate symptom complex: Assessment in a double-blind, placebo-controlled, randomized study. *Journal of Allergy Clinical Immunology*, 99(6 Pt 1):757-762.

chapter 10

Body Weight and Its Management

As you can see in the picture, college student Matt Schicker is half the man he used to be. Well, he's *almost half* the man he used to be. As a child, Matt could have been described as "pudgy." By the time he entered high school, his weight reached 240 pounds, far too much for his 5'8" frame. Matt grew taller and continued to gain weight, but he is not sure how much he gained because he stopped getting on the scales after 265 pounds. His pants, the ones he is shown wearing, had a 44" waistline. Although girls teased him about his weight, his male friends were impressed with his baseball skills. His pitching was tough to hit and he could easily swat home runs. Nevertheless, the high school coaches would not select him for the baseball team because he could not keep up with the other boys when running during practice. "I was tired of being fat," says Matt. "And there is a lot of diabetes in my family. I didn't want to get it." What did he do? He stopped eating most fast foods and began lifting weights, practicing martial arts, and playing tennis, softball, and inline hockey. Physical activity became the cornerstone of his daily routine. Within a year and a half, Matt lost at least 100

His pants—the ones he is shown wearing—had a 44" waistline!

pounds. What is more remarkable, Matt has kept his weight down for three years by continuing to control his appetite and being physically active. Now, Matt is 6′ tall and weighs 190 pounds. If he maintains his current lifestyle, he should avoid obesity in the future.

Obesity is a condition characterized by an excessive and unhealthy amount of body fat. People who do not have "weight problems" often think overweight individuals lack the willpower to control their eating and weight. It is true that one gains body fat by eating more calories than needed. Many fat people, however, may have inherited genes for conserving food energy as fat instead of wasting it as body heat. For these people, gaining weight may be a normal metabolic process that is difficult to alter. Most medical experts now view obesity as a chronic metabolic disease that results from complex interactions among biological, psychological, and environmental influences.

According to former U.S. Surgeon General C. Everett Koop (1999), excess body fat contributes to 300,000 preventable deaths each year in the United States. The

What You'll Learn

www.jbpub.com/healthyliving

The web site for this book offers many useful tools and is a great source for supplementary health information for both students and instructors. Visit the site at www.jbpub.com/healthyliving for information on these topics:

Defining Overweight and Obesity
The Caloric Cost of Living
Weight Management

Chapter Overview

The definitions of overweight and obesity.
How your body uses the energy from foods.
How to determine your percentage of body fat.
The causes of obesity.
How to manage your weight .

DIVERSITY *Health* The Plight of the Pima

Con$umer *Health* Over-the-Counter Weight Loss Aids

Managing Your Health General Features of Reliable Weight Reduction Plans

across the lifespan Weight Management

Student Workbook

Self Assessment: How Much Energy Do You Use Daily?
Changing Health Habits: Altering Caloric Intake and Physical Activity

Do You Know?

- How to shed fat and gain muscle?
- What causes "middle-age spread?"
- How to lose weight and keep it off?

estimated annual cost of treating health conditions associated with obesity is more than $100 *billion*. This chapter examines factors that contribute to the development of excess body fat, identifies health problems associated with this condition, and discusses various weight loss methods. Some individuals are underweight and want to increase their muscle mass; therefore, this chapter also provides information concerning healthy ways to gain weight.

www.jbpub.com/healthyliving

Defining Overweight and Obesity

A healthy body is not fat-free; a small amount of fat is essential for the normal functioning of all cells. Too much body fat, however, is detrimental to health and well-being. How much extra fat must a person have to be considered overweight? At what point does an overweight person become obese? Definitions for these terms often rely on the idea that a *healthy* or *desirable* range of weights exists for a particular height. **Overweight** individuals have excess body fat and weigh 10% to 19% more than their healthy weights. **Obese** persons are also overweight, but they weigh 20% or more above what is thought to be healthy. Adult Americans can use a height/weight table to determine if their weights are within a healthy range (■ Table 10-1).

Defining *overweight* and *obese* as certain percentages of weight above a desirable weight can produce inaccurate impressions. For example, athletic individuals may be overweight according to the height/weight table. Since muscle is more dense than fat, muscular athletic persons can be heavier but healthier than physically inactive *(sedentary)* individuals. A later section of this chapter provides other definitions of *overweight* and *obesity*, including those based on the body mass index.

The Prevalence of Overweight in the United States

The prevalence of excess body fat has reached epidemic proportions in the United States. In the 1980s, 25% of American adults were overweight. Today, 55% of American adults are too fat; nearly 1 in 5 are obese (Mokdad et al., 1999). More American children are overweight than in the past also. More than one-fourth of children between 6 and 17 years of age are too fat ("Update," 1997). An objective of *Healthy People 2000* (USDHHS, 1991) is to reduce the prevalence of overweight to 20% of the population who are over 20 years of age. It is unlikely this objective will be met by 2010.

How Does Being Overweight Affect Health?

Overweight people have greater risks than lean people of developing osteoarthritis, sleep apnea, gallbladder disease,

carpal tunnel syndrome, gout, hypertension, diabetes, and heart disease. Cancers of the gallbladder, cervix, uterus, and breast are more prevalent in overweight women; cancers of the colon and rectum are more likely to occur in overweight men. Surgery is riskier for obese people because physicians have more difficulty estimating the amount of anesthesia needed. Obese men and women are more likely to experience fertility problems than people whose weights are in the healthy range. Furthermore,

Table 10-1	Height/Weight Table: U.S. Department of Health and Human Services, 1995
Height*	**Range of Weight in Pounds†**
5'0"	97–128
5'1"	101–132
5'2"	104–137
5'3"	107–141
5'4"	111–146
5'5"	114–150
5'6"	118–155
5'7"	121–160
5'8"	125–164
5'9"	129–169
5'10"	132–174
5'11"	136–179
6'0"	140–184
6'1"	144–189
6'2"	148–195
6'3"	152–200
6'4"	156–205
6'5"	160–211
6'6"	164–216

*Measured without shoes
†Measured without clothing
Source: U.S. Department of Health and Human Services. (1995) *Dietary guidelines for Americans*, 4th ed. Washington, D.C.: Government Printing Office.

being overweight can interfere with one's ability to perform daily activities that require walking, carrying, kneeling, and stooping (Han et al., 1998). Few obese individuals are free of physical health problems.

An overweight person does not have to become slim to reap some physical benefits of weighing less. Losing 10% of body weight and maintaining the loss often reduce risks of heart disease and stroke. Additionally, losing modest amounts of weight can save thousands of dollars that would have been spent on treating medical conditions related to obesity (Oster et al., 1999).

Besides affecting physical health, excess body fat can have a negative impact on psychological health. Obese people often suffer from depression and low self-esteem (Rippe & Hess, 1998). An obese individual may develop these psychological problems after being discriminated against or having humiliating and embarrassing experiences while obtaining an education or seeking a job. Additionally, lean people often perceive obese individuals as physically unattractive, lacking willpower, and lazy. Not surprisingly, many obese individuals are dissatisfied and preoccupied with their body size (Parham, 1999).

What are the factors that contribute to the development of excess body fat? Why are so many Americans too fat? Is it possible to control one's weight?

The proportion of muscle and fat tissue also influences the metabolic rate. Muscle cells use more energy than fat cells; therefore, people with greater amounts of muscle mass have higher metabolic rates than those with more fat tissue. Testosterone is a hormone that stimulates muscle mass development. Since men normally produce more testosterone than women, they usually have more muscle and less fat. On average, men have higher metabolic rates than women.

Age also influences the metabolic rate. Because they are growing rapidly, infants and children have higher metabolic rates than adults. After 20 years of age, metabolic rates decline about 1% to 2% each decade. As a result of this gradual slowdown, aging people need less energy. If older people continue to eat the same amount of food as they did when younger, they gain weight. Between the ages of 20 and 50, the average American gains 20 to 30 pounds! Although the declining metabolic rate is a contributing factor, many health experts think physical inactivity is more responsible for "middle-age spread" than is overeating. As one grows older, exercising can help retain muscle mass and slow the decline in the metabolic rate.

obesity a condition in which the body has unhealthy amounts of fat. Obese people weigh 20% or more above their desirable weights.

overweight a condition in which the body has too much fat. Overweight people weigh 10% to 19% more than desirable.

metabolic rate the amount of energy the body requires to fuel vital activities during a specified time.

metabolism all chemical reactions that take place in the body.

The Caloric Cost of Living

www.jbpub.com/healthyliving

Energy for Metabolism

Most metabolic reactions in the body require the input of energy (calories) from foods. Each day, the body expends the largest portion of energy (50% to 70%) to maintain its metabolic activities such as building new tissue, maintaining body temperature, circulating blood, and transporting material in and out of cells. The **metabolic rate** is the amount of energy required to fuel vital activities within a specified time.

Individual metabolic rates vary; genetics probably plays a major role in setting these rates. Hormones, especially thyroid hormone produced in the thyroid gland, regulate **metabolism (Figure 10-1).** The vast majority of overweight people, however, have normal blood levels of thyroid hormone.

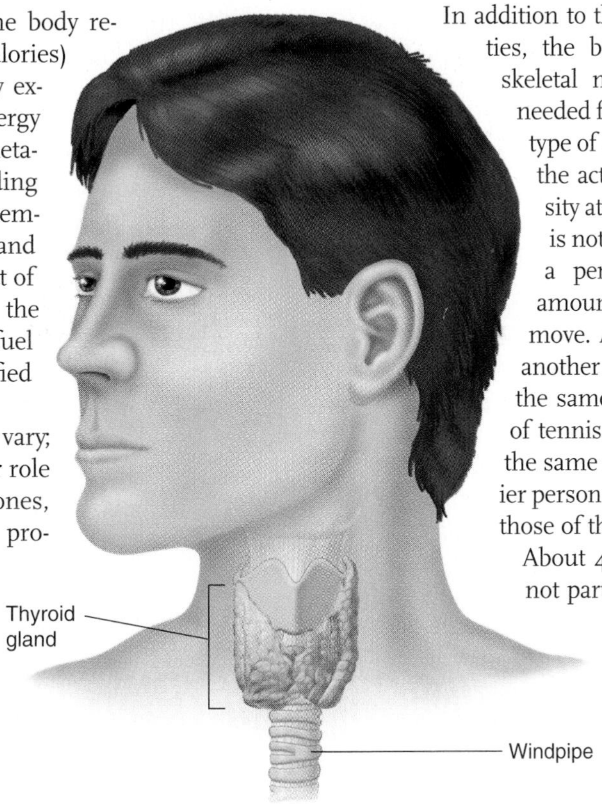

Energy for Physical Activity

In addition to the caloric cost of metabolic activities, the body expends energy to contract skeletal muscles. The amount of energy needed for physical activity depends on the type of activity, the time spent performing the activity (its duration), and the intensity at which it is performed. Although it is not related directly to physical activity, a person's body size influences the amount of physical effort needed to move. A person who weighs 100 lb and another who weighs 175 lb might spend the same amount of time playing a game of tennis. If both of them play tennis with the same intensity, the muscles of the heavier person require more energy to move than those of the lighter person.

About 4 in 10 overweight individuals do not participate in physical activities, even

Thyroid gland

Windpipe

◀Figure 10-1 The Thyroid Gland. The thyroid gland produces hormones that control the metabolic rate.

when they have the time to do so ("Prevalence of Physical Inactivity," 1996). Health experts recommend that adults should perform at least 30 minutes of moderate or intense physical activity, nearly every day. Chapter 11 identifies physical activities that are moderate or intense.

People can increase the amount of energy expended during physical activity by increasing its duration or intensity. Furthermore, the metabolic rate often remains elevated for several hours after one discontinues vigorous physical activity. This elevation may result from an increase in the metabolic activity of muscle cells that occurs after physical exertion. Therefore, individuals may be able to raise their resting metabolic rates by engaging in regular physical activity (Rippe & Hess, 1998).

Table 10-2 lists some common physical activities and the number of calories people expend per minute of performing each activity. Note that the number of calories used for an activity varies according to body weight. For most people, the number of calories expended for physical activity is *less* than the number expended for metabolism.

Energy for Other Needs

Together, metabolic and physical activity energy needs comprise more than 90% of a person's energy expenditure. After eating a meal, the body requires a small amount of energy to digest, absorb, and process the nutrients from food. This use of energy, the **thermic effect of food (TEF)**, accounts for a very small portion, less than 10%, of one's total energy expenditures.

Some medical researchers classify spontaneous muscle movements, fidgeting for example, as a minor category of energy expenditure called *non-exercise activity thermogenesis (NEAT)*. As a result of NEAT, some restless people may metabolize hundreds of calories daily, which reduces their likelihood of gaining body fat (Levine et al., 1999). At present, the amount of calories expended for specific types of movements that waste energy as NEAT has not been determined.

How many calories does your body need daily? To estimate your daily caloric expenditures, you can add the number of calories needed for metabolism, physical activity, and TEF. The assessment activity in the student workbook can help you estimate the number of calories you expend in a day.

The Basics of Energy Balance

In general, people maintain, gain, or lose body weight according to the basic principles of energy balance, as illustrated in Figure 10-2. When the caloric intake from food equals the number of calories expended for energy needs, no change in body weight occurs. When caloric intake is less than caloric expenditures, the body loses weight as cells burn stored fat. If caloric intake is more than caloric expenditures, the body conserves much of the excess calories as fat, and weight gain occurs. Each pound of body fat represents about 3500 calories of potential energy; therefore, consuming as little as 100 extra calories per day for a year can result in a 10-lb weight gain.

Body Composition

How Much Fat Is Normal?

When you step on a scale, you can determine your body weight as a number of pounds or kilograms. That weight, however, does not specify how much water, muscle, or fat

| Table 10-2 | Approximate Energy Costs of Various Physical Activities |

Physical Activity	Calories per Pound of Body Weight per Minute	
	Range for Women	Range for Men
Sedentary Sitting quietly, playing a musical instrument	up to .017	up to .017
Light Playing pool, bowling, golf, volleyball, walking (3 mph)	.017 to .033	.017 to .035
Moderate Badminton, canoeing, gymnastics, hockey, cycling, swimming, dancing, tennis, skiing	.033 to .050	.035 to .052
Heavy Basketball, climbing, cross-country running, rowing	.050+	.052+

To estimate the number of calories you expend while performing a particular physical activity, multiply the calories per pound per minute by your weight. Use the figures in the left-hand column if you are a woman, and in the right-hand column if you are a man. Then multiply that number by the number of minutes spent performing the activity. For example, if you are a woman who weighs 120 lb, and you spent 40 min cycling: .033 × 120 = 3.96 calories per minute; 3.96 × 40 minutes = about 158 calories spent. (The rates of caloric expenditure per minute are given as ranges. For example, if you cycled intensely, use a rate at the high end of the range.)

Source: Adapted from Durnin, J. V. G. A., & Passmore, R. (1967). *Energy, work, and leisure*. London: Heinemann.

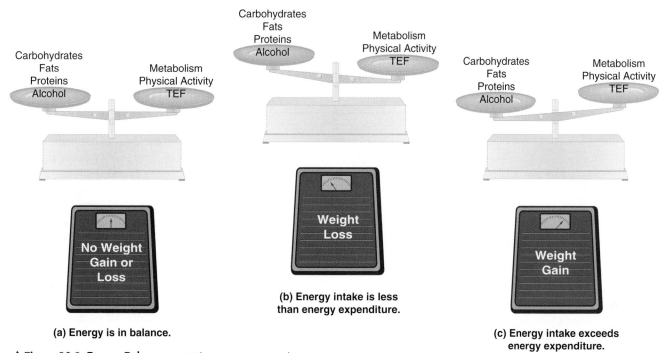

(a) Energy is in balance.

(b) Energy intake is less than energy expenditure.

(c) Energy intake exceeds energy expenditure.

▲**Figure 10-2 Energy Balance.** (a) When energy expenditure equals energy intake, the body maintains its weight; (b) When energy expenditure is greater than energy intake, the body loses weight; (c) when energy expenditure is less than energy intake, the body gains weight.

is in your body. Fat-free body weight consists of water, proteins, and minerals found in the bones, muscles, and organs *(lean tissues)*. About 60% of an adult's weight is water; 6% to 22% is protein, and 3% is minerals. Most of the remaining weight is fat.

About one-half of an average person's body fat is located in a layer under the skin *(subcutaneous* fat). Small amounts of fat are stored in muscles, which rely on the fat for energy. Besides subcutaneous and muscle fat, regions of the abdomen, thighs, hips, and buttocks store considerable amounts of fat.

Every year Americans spend money on useless treatments to eliminate "cellulite." Many people think cellulite is an abnormal type of fat that appears as lumpy dimpled skin on the buttocks and thighs. Cellulite fat, however, does not exist. There is no difference between the fat cells in so-called cellulite and those in other parts of the body (Rosenbaum et al., 1998). Strands of connective tissue hold subcutaneous fat in place. If these strands hold the fat in an irregular pattern, the fat tissue can extend into layers of skin, giving the skin a lumpy appearance. Women are more likely than men to have irregular connective tissue under their skin. The best way to improve the appearance of thighs and buttocks is to exercise and lose excess weight.

Obesity can begin at any age. However, the number and size of fat cells increase dramatically when this condition occurs during childhood and other periods of rapid growth

(Robertson et al., 1999). People who become overweight in adulthood usually have normal numbers of fat cells, but their fat cells are larger than normal (Wardlaw, 1999). The number of fat cells, however, can increase when extreme obesity occurs during the adult years.

Once fat cells form, there is little evidence that they can disappear with short-term weight reduction efforts. Under these conditions, most fat cells shrink as they release stored fat to meet the energy needs of other tissues. After shrinking, fat cells may send chemical signals to the nervous system that stimulate the urge to eat, making it difficult for people to maintain their reduced body weights.

Determining Percentages of Body Fat

Many health experts use the percentage of body fat to define obesity. A healthy adult man consists of about 6% to 18% fat; a healthy adult woman is about 12% to 25% fat (Williams, 1999). Men are obese if their percentage of body fat exceeds 25%; this level is 30% for women. ▮ Table 10-3 shows a set of standards for classifying people as excessively lean, lean, normal, overweight, and obese according to sex and percentage of body fat.

Hydrostatic weighing (underwater weighing) is one of the most reliable methods to estimate an individual's percentage of body fat. Body fat is less dense than lean tissues or water; therefore, extra fat makes the body more buoyant. Underwater weighing, however, is not a practical or convenient way to determine one's percentage of body fat.

thermic effect of food (TEF) the small amount of energy that the body uses to digest, absorb, and process the nutrients from foods.

Table 10-3	Body Fat Classifications Based on Body Composition or BMI		

| | Percentages of Body Fat | | |
Classification	Men	Women	BMI
Excessively lean	<5%	<10%	—
Lean	5–12%	10–18%	<18.5
Normal	13–19%	19–25%	18.5–24.9
Overweight	20–24%	26–32%	25.0–29.9
Obese	25% and more	33% and more	30.0–34.9
Extreme obesity	—	—	≥35

Source: Adapted from Williams, M. H. (1999). *Nutrition for health, fitness, & sport.* Boston: McGraw-Hill; *Clinical guidelines on the identification, evaluation, and treatment of overweight and obesity in adults.* (1998). Bethesda, MD: National Institutes of Health, National Heart, Lung, and Blood Institute.

Bioelectrical Impedance and Near-Infrared Interactance
Bioelectrical impedance uses electrical currents to estimate the percentage of body fat. Water and certain mineral elements conduct electrical currents, whereas fat is a poor conductor of electricity. The equipment shown in ▊ **Figure 10-3** safely measures the body's electrical conductivity to determine the percentage of body fat. When subjects have normal amounts of body water, bioelectrical impedance provides reliable estimates of their percentage of body fat.

Near-infrared interactance testing estimates the percentage of body fat by using a small device to pass infrared light quickly through the biceps muscle of the upper arm. Near-infrared testing, however, often underestimates percentage of body fat, especially as body fatness increases. This error limits its usefulness as a reliable measurement (Wagner & Heyward, 1999).

Skinfold Thicknesses Several years ago, advertisements for a breakfast cereal asked people to "pinch an inch" as a method of determining their amount of body fat. If people could pinch a fold of abdominal skin that was more than an inch wide, they were too fat. This crude technique of measuring skinfold thicknesses relied on the principle that one-half of an average person's fat is located beneath the skin.

Using skinfold thicknesses to assess body composition is not as accurate as the underwater weighing and bioelectrical impedance techniques, but it is more practical and less costly. Instead of using fingers to pinch a section of skin and its underlying layer of fat, a trained person uses special calipers to measure skinfold thickness more precisely. Skinfold measurements should be taken at three or more body sites; averaging these measurements accounts for individual differences in body fat distribution.

The reliability of using skinfolds to estimate the percentage body fat depends on the accuracy of the calipers, the number of skinfolds measured, and the skill of the person performing the measurements. Although measuring skinfolds is a popular technique, some health experts challenge the value of skinfold thicknesses to determine the degree of body fat in obese individuals. Unlike average persons, obese individuals have less than half of their body fat under their skin, and they store considerable amounts of fat in their abdomens. Therefore, other assessment methods such as bioelectrical impedance may provide more accurate information concerning the body composition of obese individuals.

Assessing Healthy Body Weights

Height/Weight Tables In 1995 the U.S. Departments of Agriculture and Health and Human Services issued a set of weight guidelines indicating a *range* of weights that are healthy for a particular height (see Table 10-1). For exam-

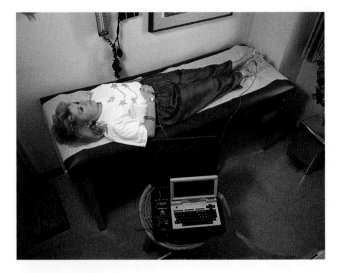

▲**Figure 10-3 Bioelectrical Impedance.** This individual is having her percentage of body fat determined by the bioelectrical impedance method.

ple, the healthy weight range for people who are 5'10" is 132 lb to 174 lb. This table does not distinguish weights of men and women; women usually have smaller bones and less muscle than men, so they should use the lower end of the range. Men and large-boned, muscular women should use the higher end of the weight ranges to find their healthy body weights.

You can use Table 10-1 to determine if your weight is healthy for your height. Find your height, without shoes, and note the weight range for that height. Is your weight, without clothing, within the healthy range?

Body Mass Index Most health experts use the **body mass index (BMI)** to determine a range of healthy body weights. Unlike height/weight tables, the BMI correlates body weight with the risk of developing chronic health condi-tions associated with excess body fat. To estimate your BMI, multiply your weight in pounds by 705. Then divide that number by your height in inches squared. For example, if you weigh 150 lb and are 67" tall, multiplying your weight times 705 equals 105,750 and squaring your height equals 4,489. Dividing 105,750 by 4,489 produces approximately 23.56. Thus, your BMI is 23.56.

Persons with BMIs between 25.0 and 29.9 are overweight; people with BMIs of 30 or more are obese (see Table 10-3). Using BMIs as a guide, you can determine if your weight is normal for your height. Weights at which a person would be considered overweight or obese are shown in ▌ **Table 10-4**. The median BMI for adult Americans is 25.5, which is in the overweight range (Kuczmarski et al., 1997).

Eugenia Calle and her colleagues (1999) exam-ined the medical histories of more than 200,000 Americans who had died between 1982 and 1996. According to those findings, men with BMIs greater than 26.5 and women with BMIs greater than 25.0 have significantly greater risks of dying from chronic conditions, especially heart disease, than men and women with lower BMIs. The risk for Whites, however, is much greater than for Blacks. The reason for this difference is unclear.

Waist-to-Hip Circumference The distribution rather than the percentage of body fat may be a more important risk factor for the health condi-tions that are associated with excess body fat. Men and women who have large body fat depots cen-trally located in their waists and backs tend to have higher blood cholesterol levels and a greater risk of developing gallstones, diabetes, hypertension, and heart disease than individuals with the same amount of fat located below the waist. Why? Ab-dominal fat cells are more likely to release their stores of fatty acids into the blood than fat cells found in the hips and thighs. Excessive amounts of fatty acids in the blood may promote cardiovas-cular disease, increase blood pressure, and inter-fere with normal blood glucose metabolism, re-sulting in diabetes (Wickelgren, 1998). As men grow older, they usually add body fat in their ab-dominal regions, which increases their **waist-to-hip circumference ratio (WHR)** to unhealthy levels. Unlike men, aging women tend to add fat to regions below the waist. ▌ **Figure 10-4** shows a man with central obesity ("apple-shaped") and a woman whose excess body fat is located primarily below the waistline ("pear-shaped").

body mass index (BMI) a stan-dard that corre-lates body weight with the risk of de-veloping chronic health conditions as-sociated with obe-sity. The formula for BMI is weight (kg) divided by height² (m).

Table 10-4	Classifying Body Weight Based on BMIs	
Height (in.)	**Overweight (BMI 25.0 to 29.9) Lower limit (lb)**	**Obese (BMI 30 or more) Lower limit (lb)**
58	119	143
59	124	148
60	128	153
61	132	158
62	136	164
63	141	169
64	145	174
65	150	180
66	155	186
67	159	191
68	164	197
69	169	203
70	174	207
71	179	215
72	184	221
73	189	227

Source: *Clinical guidelines on the identification, evaluation, and treatment of overweight and obesity in adults.* (1998). Bethesda, MD: National Institutes of Health, National Heart, Lung, and Blood Institute.

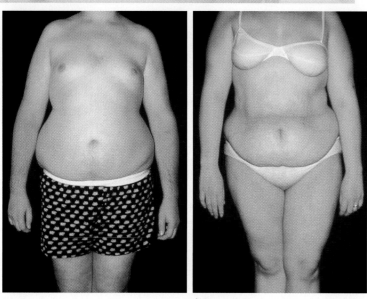

(a)   (b)

◀Figure 10-4 **Typical Fat Distribution in Overweight Persons.** Men and women who have large body fat depots centrally located in their waists and backs tend to have a higher risk of chronic health problems than individuals with the same amount of fat located below the waist. (a) Overweight males typically have central fat deposits ("apple-shaped bodies"); (b) Overweight females often have excess body fat below the waist ("pear-shaped bodies")

What Causes Obesity?

In most cases, there is no single cause for obesity. According to the principles of energy balance, the body gains fat when it has an excess of energy; the body loses weight when energy intake does not meet its needs. Overweight people often claim that they gain weight by eating small amounts of food. Underreporting caloric intake, however, is common, especially by overweight individuals (Kretsch et al., 1999). The following section examines factors that contribute to weight gain.

Biological Influences

Genes control the development of many physical characteristics, including height, fat distribution, and body frame size. Genes may also code for weight gain by determining the production of hormones that regulate one's metabolic rate and appetite. As a result, cases of obesity are more likely to occur in certain families. When one or both parents are obese, they are more likely to have offspring who gain excessive amounts of body fat than two parents of normal weights. Could a person benefit from inheriting genes that code for gaining weight easily?

Thousands of years ago, "fat" genes were vital to human survival. Our early ancestors probably endured long periods of fasting, interrupted by shorter periods of feasting. When food was plentiful, our ancestors thrived on the bounty. Some members of the population may have inherited metabolisms that "burned off" the excess food energy as body heat. Others had "thrifty" metabolisms that enabled them to store much of the excess energy as body fat. When food was scarce, individuals with thrifty metabolisms were more likely to survive than those with metabolisms that stored as much energy as fat. Today, most Americans have access to a steady supply of tasty fattening food. Therefore, persons who have thrifty metabolisms find it difficult to control their weight in such environments. The "Diversity in Health" essay "The Plight of the Pima" discusses the harmful effects that ge-

The only equipment you need to determine your WHR is a flexible tape measure. ▌ **Figure 10-5** illustrates where to place the tape measure according to guidelines used in the third National Health and Nutrition Examination Survey (Carson et al., 1994). To measure your waistline, place the tape around your body at the top of the hipbone, which is usually just below the navel. The proper way to measure your hip circumference is to place the tape around your buttocks at the widest point. Divide your waist measurement by the hip measurement to calculate the ratio of your waist circumference to your hip circumference. What is your WHR? Men who have WHRs greater than .90 and women with WHRs greater than .80 have increased risks of developing the health problems associated with being overweight. According to a report published by the National Institutes of Health ("Clinical Guidelines," 1998), high-risk waistlines measure greater than 40 inches for males and 35 inches for females.

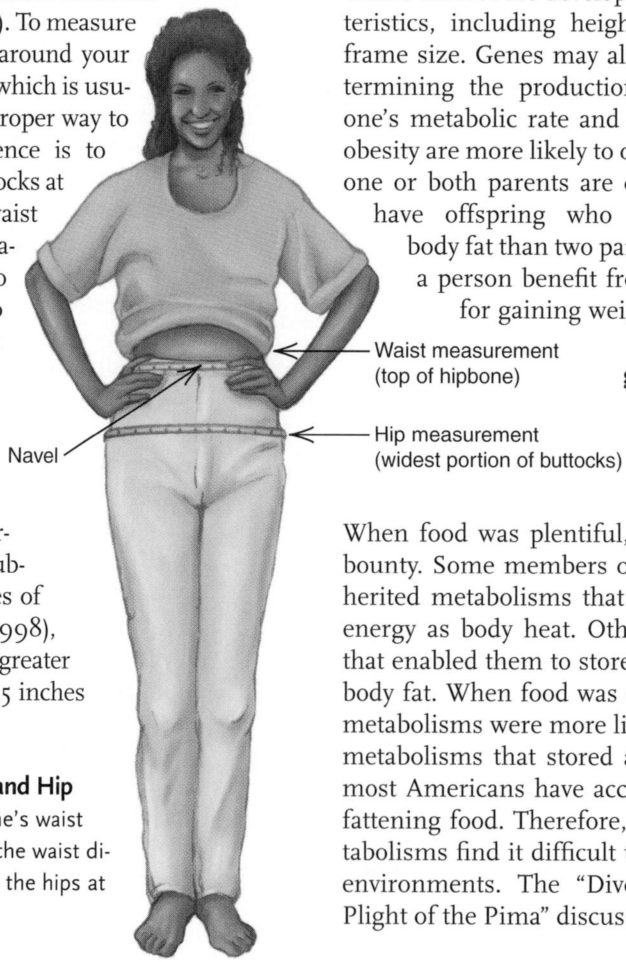

Waist measurement (top of hipbone)

Hip measurement (widest portion of buttocks)

Navel

▶Figure 10-5 **Measuring Waist and Hip Circumferences.** To determine one's waist and hip circumferences, measure the waist directly above the hipbone; measure the hips at the widest point of the buttocks.

netic and environmental factors have had on the Pima Indian population of southern Arizona.

The Set Point Theory Although body weight usually fluctuates slightly from day to day, most people report that their weight remains fairly stable for months, even years. This observation led some medical experts to propose that the level of body fat is genetically preset. Once the level of body fat reaches this **set point**, the metabolic rate and other internal mechanisms maintain the degree of fatness, like a thermostat can be set to maintain the temperature of a room. Lean persons may have lower set points than overweight individuals. For example, when lean people deliberately overeat to gain weight, they usually lose the extra weight after resuming their normal eating habits. Although having a high set point may result in an unhealthy percentage of body fat, that amount of fat may be normal for the person. As a result, the person's fat cells may resist efforts to lose storage fat.

Appetite Regulation Nearly everyone knows what it feels like to be hungry. **Hunger** is the physiological drive to seek and eat food. **Appetite** is the psychological desire to eat specific foods, which is not the

waist-to-hip circumference ratio (WHR) the relationship between waist and hip circumferences that is used to predict the health risks associated with excess body fat.

set point a level of body fat that is predetermined genetically. Once body fat reaches this level, internal mechanisms, such as the metabolic rate, maintain this degree of fatness.

hunger the physiological drive to seek and eat food.

appetite the psychological desire to eat foods that are appealing.

DIVERSITY in Health   The Plight of the Pima

After the July rains, the Sonora Desert of southwestern Arizona becomes transformed for a brief time into a natural fast-food restaurant. For hundreds of years, the Pima Indians residing in this harsh environment harvested the seasonal bounty of mesquite pods, acorns, wolfberries, prickly pears, tepary beans, and cholla blossoms to supplement their regular diet of hunted animals and cultivated maize (corn) and lima beans. The Pima were slim, but they flourished while enduring this cycle of feast and famine.

By the 1930s, the Arizona Pima had discontinued eating most of their ancient fare and adopted Western foods that provided generous amounts of lard (pork fat), refined starches, and sweets. Within a couple of decades, an alarming number of Pima had become obese and developed non–insulin-dependent diabetes mellitus (type 2 diabetes). Today, nearly 70% of Arizona Pima are obese (Valencia et al., 1999). Obesity is a risk factor for type 2 diabetes; more than 40% of Arizona Pima suffer from this condition. This is the highest known incidence of the disease in the world. Why are the Pima so severely affected by obesity and type 2 diabetes?

Medical experts suspect certain biological and environmental factors influence the development of obesity and diabetes in this population. Experts think the Pima have thrifty metabolisms that allow them to survive their harsh desert environment with its natural cycles of feast and famine. Although their current dietary habits have made the need for such metabolisms obsolete, the Pima are still genetically programmed to conserve a major share of their food intake as fat. Additionally, most Arizona Pima lead more sedentary lives than their ancestors or relatives living in Mexico. The typical Mexican Pima Indian has fewer labor-saving devices and performs more physical work than the typical Arizona Pima.

The Arizona Pima's abandonment of ancient dietary practices may contribute to their current health problems. Besides being lower in fat, traditional Pima foods provide more complex carbohydrates than typical modern menus. Furthermore, the ancestral diet supplied substances that may have protected the Pima from type 2 diabetes. Many desert plants contain significant amounts of amylose, a digestible carbohydrate, as well as gums and mucilages, two forms of soluble fiber. Eating foods rich in these substances slows digestion and delays the absorption of glucose from the small intestine. This delay prevents sharp increases in blood levels of insulin, the hormone that signals cells to remove glucose (blood sugar) from the blood. Under normal circumstances, the body can prevent sharp increases or decreases of blood glucose. However, individuals who suffer from type 2 diabetes are unable to avoid dramatic fluctuations in blood glucose or insulin levels, which can damage the body.

Today medical experts are studying the Pima to determine what steps can be taken to reduce their prevalence of obesity and diabetes. Some scientists think tribal members should return to their former dietary practices; many of these ancestral foods are still available. By eating desert plant foods rich in amylose and soluble fibers, the Pima may reduce their risk of developing type 2 diabetes. If the Pima are to survive as a population, they may need to recover their traditional "roots."

Sources: Boyce, V. L., & Swinburn, B. A. (1993). The traditional Pima Indian diet: Composition and adaptation for use in a dietary intervention study. *Diabetes Care, 16*(51):369-371.
Cowen, R. (1990). Seeds of protection: Ancestral menus may hold a message for diabetes-prone descendants. *Science News, 137*:350-351.
Valencia, M. E. Bennett, P. H., Ravussin, E., Esparza, J., Fox, C., & Schultz, L. O. (1999). The Pima Indians of Sonora, Mexico. *Nutrition Reviews, 57*(5):S55-S58.

same as being hungry. **Satiety** is the feeling that enough food has been eaten to relieve hunger and turn off appetite.

The digestive system, brain, and fat cells play important roles in controlling hunger and satiety. While a person is eating, the intestinal tract releases several chemicals that accumulate and signal the brain to eat less food (Woods et al., 1998). Additionally, the sensation of stomach fullness results in termination of eating. Leptin, a hormone produced by fat cells, affects the *hypothalamus,* a region of the brain that regulates eating behavior (■ Figure 10-6). In animal studies, one area of the hypothalamus initiates eating behavior when activated by leptin; the other area reduces the urge to eat when activated by the hormone. Although some humans lost weight when given injections of leptin, more research is needed to determine if obese persons can benefit from this treatment (Heymsfield et al., 1999).

Composition of the Diet Americans are eating a smaller proportion of their calories as fat, but they are eating about 100 *more* calories per day than 20 years ago ("Position of the American Dietetic Association" [ADA], 1998). An excess of calories from carbohydrate, protein, fat, and alcohol can result in weight gain. However, diets that contain high amounts of fat are associated with the development of obesity. An ounce of fat supplies more than twice the number of calories as an ounce of carbohydrate or protein. Furthermore, the body stores more fat when the excess of calories is supplied by dietary fat rather than carbohydrate or protein. (Hill & Peters, 1998).

No specific calorie-restricted diet has been shown to enhance weight loss and maintenance (Ryan et al., 1999). However, overweight people often lose weight when following a low-fat, high-carbohydrate diet because the food plan includes generous servings of fruits, vegetables, beans, and whole-grain cereals. These nutrient-dense, high-fiber foods are quite filling, and dieters may fail to eat enough to meet their total permissible number of calories. Why do overweight people blame carbohydrates for their weight problem?

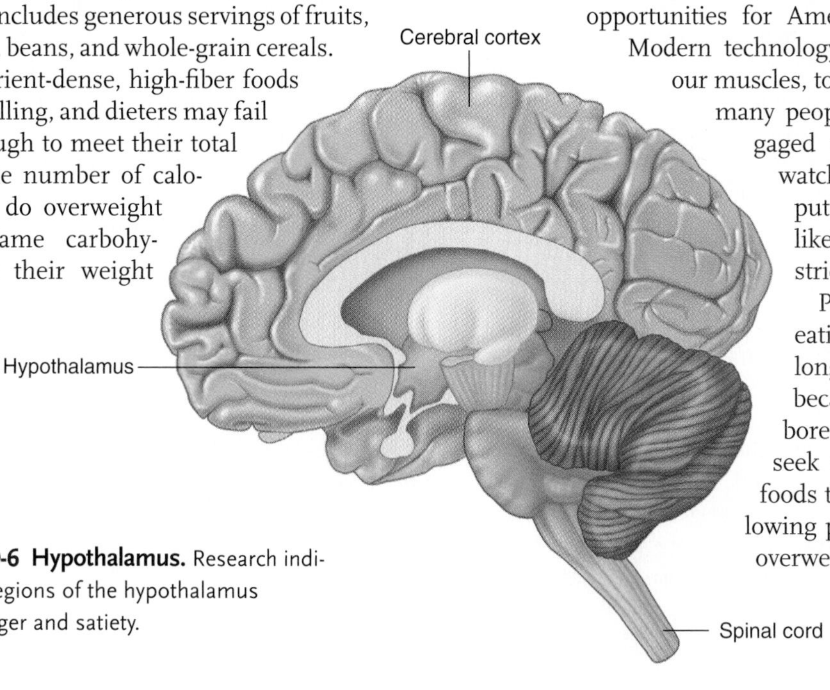

satiety
the feeling that enough food has been eaten to relieve hunger and turn off appetite.

fad diets eating plans that are popular for a time, then quickly lose their widespread appeal.

Carbohydrate-rich foods often taste better when they are fried or when fats such as butter, sour cream, or gravy are added to them. Most desserts and snack foods contain carbohydrate and fat; mixtures of sugar and fat are almost irresistible. Thus, the typical American diet promotes overeating because it provides an interesting, tasty, and enjoyable variety of fatty foods.

So, do not throw away your calorie and fat-counting guides if you are trying to control your weight. By eating more fruits and vegetables and fewer fatty foods, you can control your caloric intake.

Environmental, Social, and Psychological Influences

Some environmental conditions promote overeating. Many people respond to certain social situations by overeating. For example, you may be "stuffed" after eating a Thanksgiving dinner, but when you see pumpkin pie topped with whipped cream, you can find "room" in your stomach for dessert. Additionally, events that mark important milestones of life usually include big meals and special foods. Imagine a birthday party or wedding celebration that does not include a frosted layer cake!

Advertisers know the value of making foods look appealing. To stimulate sales, for example, fast-food restaurants show hamburgers topped with crisp lettuce and bacon extending beyond the bun. Actors or models in food ads appear to be happy and pleased with their food choices. Additionally, some fast-food restaurants offer "super-size" portions that encourage overeating. Many of these restaurants as well as supermarkets are open 24 hours. You do not even have to leave home to buy food; pizza, Chinese, and other food can be delivered to your front door.

Work and home environments often do not provide opportunities for Americans to be physically active. Modern technology enables machines, instead of our muscles, to do much of our work. At home, many people spend their leisure time engaged in sedentary activities such as watching a television or using a computer. Physically inactive people are likely to gain weight unless they restrict their food intake.

Psychological state can influence eating behavior. Some people eat long after satisfying their hunger, because they are excited, anxious, or bored. Many depressed individuals seek comfort from eating, especially foods that are fatty and sugary. The following personal reflection written by an overweight young woman illustrates how emotions can affect eating behavior:

▶**Figure 10-6 Hypothalamus.** Research indicates that regions of the hypothalamus control hunger and satiety.

Cerebral cortex

Hypothalamus

Spinal cord

I gained 20 pounds between the ages of 16 and 18. At the time I was in an abusive relationship with my boyfriend. I felt like dirt and the only thing that made me feel good was food. I was totally devastated when he was killed in a car accident when I was 18. I ate even more. I went to a nutritionist for a diet. I tried to stay on it but failed. Looking back, every time I gained weight it was due to stress. When I am stressed, I need to get out of the house, take my mind off things.

In developed nations, disorders such as bulimia nervosa and compulsive overeating affect considerable numbers of people, especially girls and women. These conditions are associated with serious psychological disturbances; therefore, they are discussed in Chapter 2.

Weight Management

In 1996 almost 30% of American men and 45% of American women reported that they were trying to lose weight (Serdula et al., 1999). Dissatisfaction with body size is common, particularly among women. Almost one-third of the women who wanted to lose weight had body weights that were in the healthy range. The majority of people trying to lose weight indicated that they ate less fat, but not fewer total calories. Only 20% of the people reported using a combination of diet and exercise to lose weight. In a survey of American college students, nearly 60% of females and 30% of males reported that they were attempting to lose weight at the time of the survey ("Youth Risk," 1997).

Even though they may have gained the weight gradually, overweight individuals who want to lose weight often seek methods that promise quick and dramatic results. These people are likely to believe advertisements for weight loss methods or products that guarantee pounds will "melt fast without sweating or dieting." As a result, most people lose more than just body fat by using various weight loss products and services. Each year, Americans spend about $35 billion on weight loss or weight maintenance efforts (Cleland et al., 1998). These efforts include joining weight loss programs or spas; and buying special foods, books, pills, and gadgets. Do these products and services enable people to lose weight? How can you judge the value of a weight loss method? The following sections answer these questions.

Weight Reduction Diets

As mentioned earlier, the body loses weight when its caloric intake is less than its energy needs. In this situation, the body relies primarily on stored fat for energy. To lose weight, overweight individuals should eat fewer calories than they need or expend more calories. Most reliable weight reduction regimens incorporate both of these features by combining a low-calorie diet with a plan that increases physical activity.

Some of the more popular weight loss diets of the last three decades have included a variety of recommendations such as fasting, counting calories, not counting calories, avoiding certain food combinations, eating plenty of protein and little carbohydrate, or eating only a few foods (**Table 10-5**). Such diets are often referred to as **fad diets** because they remain popular for a few months then quickly lose their widespread appeal. Fad diets usually have one common feature—severe caloric restriction. Very low-calorie diets may provide fewer than 800 calories per day and be nutritionally inadequate because they limit food choices.

Diets that provide 400 or fewer calories daily are often called fasts. Fasts are essentially starvation regimens. Some fasts permit only fruit juices and nutrient supplements. Fasting accelerates the loss of fat and lean body tissue, creating unhealthy metabolic by-products. Healthy individuals should not fast for more than a day without medical supervision.

Initially, obese people typically lose substantial amounts of weight while following a low-calorie diet or fast. When caloric intake is very low, the body burns fat as well as lean tissue for energy. Since fat and lean tissue store water, using these tissues for energy creates a surplus of water in the body. The kidneys eliminate the excess water, causing a dramatic loss of weight that often encourages dieters during the early phase of their weight reduction efforts. Within a few weeks, however, the body regains its normal water balance, and the rate of weight loss slows.

Very low-calorie diets or fasts trigger energy-conserving mechanisms in the body that are designed to help people survive starvation. The metabolic rate decreases with caloric restriction, especially when individuals consume fewer than 800 calories a day. Thus, dieters must cut their caloric intakes even further to continue losing weight, which often makes adhering to their diets even more difficult.

In spite of their efforts, most individuals experience a decline in their rate of weight loss after several weeks of following a calorie-reduced diet. Some of this slowdown occurs because the body expends fewer calories to maintain the new weight. As the body adjusts to the reduced caloric intake, it metabolizes less fat and lean tissue for energy, slowing the rate of weight loss. Additionally, dieters who follow restrictive diet plans for more than a few weeks often become bored with the regimens and gradually return to their old eating habits. Most people who have lost weight regain some or all of it—and often, even more weight—after a period of caloric restriction. Frustrated dieters often blame themselves for lack of self-control. Episodes of losing and regaining weight are referred to as yo-yo dieting or *weight cycling*. Some medical experts think weight cycling is more harmful to one's health than maintaining an excessive but stable amount of body fat. Current research, however, indicates that yo-yo dieting does not increase the risk of hypertension or heart disease (Field et al., 1999; French et al., 1999). Obesity clearly poses more health risks than weight cycling. Rather than endure periodic dieting, overweight people should consider other, more successful methods of losing weight—changing eating and exercise patterns for life.

Physical Activity

Many American adults are less active physically than when they were younger, partly because they have occupations that require little physical effort. Men who had trim, athletic builds during adolescence often develop bulging waistlines by the time they are 40. As they reach middle age, women often blame "gravity" or pregnancy for the expanding dimensions of their waists, hips, and thighs. Can adopting more physically active lifestyles reverse these changes?

> I gained 20 pounds before my wedding. My husband bought me a stepper for a wedding present (that's what I wanted), and I use it with an exercise video. Now, I exercise more than ever, but I haven't lost much weight.

This student has discovered that exercising to lose body fat often does not produce the desired change in body weight. Physical activity alone is not as effective as low-calorie diets for treating obesity, because most overweight individuals cannot perform enough exercise to create a significant deficit of calories. This does not mean that overweight people should abandon physical activity as a means of losing excess body fat.

Exercise retains lean tissue and builds muscle mass, which may stabilize or even increase one's body weight. Thus, what appears to be a lack of progress while restricting food intake and exercising may be the result of a healthy increase in muscle mass. Rather than tracking changes in body weight, physically active overweight individuals can keep weekly records of waist and chest circumferences (men) or waist and hip circumferences (men and women). People who become more physically active while dieting often report that their clothing fits better, or they can wear smaller sizes, even though they have not lost

Table 10-5 — Some Fad Diets

Diet	Approach	Possible Problems
Dr. Atkins Diet Revolution Enter the Zone The Doctor's Quick Weight Loss Diet Protein Power Healthy For Life The Complete Scarsdale Medical Diet	Restrict carbohydrate intake	High animal fat intake may contribute to heart disease.
Pritikin Diet Macrobiotic Diet (certain types) The Rice Diet The Mayo Clinic Diet (Not associated with the Mayo Clinic) T-Factor Diet Stop the Insanity The Pasta Diet The McDougall Plan The Maximum Metabolism Diet	Limit food choices; very low fat	Boredom with limited food choices; May result in nutritional deficiencies if followed for long periods; High fiber intake results in increased intestinal gas and may interfere with mineral absorption; Dieter often feels deprived and hungry.
Cabbage Soup Diet The New Beverly Hills Diet Dr. Berger's Immune Power Diet Bloomingdale's Diet Eat to Win Two-Day Diet Spirulina Diet Vinegar Diet Grapefruit Diet	May promote certain nutrients, substances, foods, or food combinations as having "fat-burning" abilities	Boredom with limited food choices; may result in nutritional deficiencies if followed for long periods.

Source: Adapted from Wardlaw, G. M. (1999). *Perspectives in Nutrition.* Boston: McGraw-Hill.

much weight. Besides improving physical appearance, exercise reduces elevated blood pressures and lipid levels. Furthermore, individuals who exercise daily are more likely to maintain their weight loss than those who are less active (Ryan et al., 1999).

Most overweight individuals can safely increase their physical activity by walking, bicycling, or swimming for at least 30 minutes, preferably on a daily basis. Regardless of the activity, it should be enjoyable and practical to perform on a year-round basis. Before beginning a vigorous physical activity program, inactive people over 40 years of age should obtain the approval of their health-care practitioners.

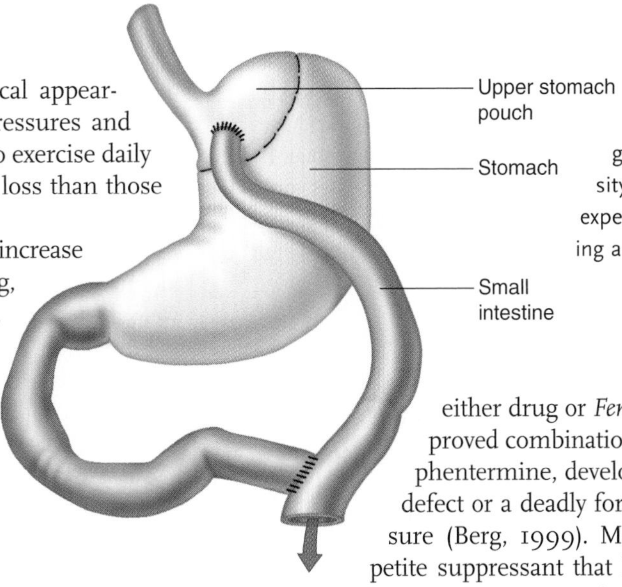

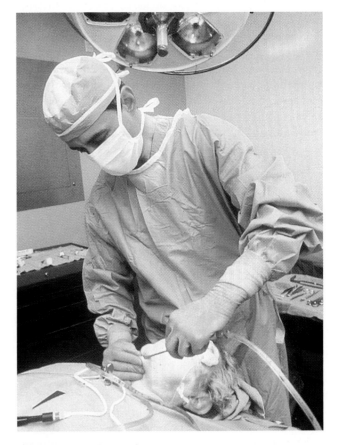

Upper stomach pouch

Stomach

Small intestine

◀ **Figure 10-7 Gastric Bypass Surgery.** Gastric bypass is a surgical procedure used to treat obesity. After surgery, the obese person experiences discomfort after overeating and is less likely to overeat.

Surgical Procedures

Most severely obese individuals experience little success following low-calorie diet plans and exercising to lose weight. *Gastric bypass* surgeries are sometimes used to treat extremely obese individuals. ▌ **Figure 10-7** illustrates the appearance of the stomach and small intestine after one type of gastric bypass surgery. A surgeon drastically reduces the capacity of the stomach by creating a small pouch in the upper part of the stomach for food to enter. After having this procedure, the overweight person can no longer eat large portions of food without vomiting or uncomfortable feelings of fullness. Most people who have had gastric bypasses are able to lose as much as 50% of their presurgery weight, achieving long-term weight maintenance and improving their overall health (Balsiger et al., 1997).

Liposuction, vacuuming subcutaneous fat out of the body, is the most common type of plastic surgery (Troilius, 1999). Before removing the fat, the area is injected with an anesthetic-containing fluid or treated with ultrasound *(ultrasound assisted lipoplasty).* This technique has cosmetic value when used to remove small areas of fat that create unsightly bulges such as "saddlebag thighs" or double chins (▌ **Figure 10-8).** Liposuction can be hazardous; infections, blood clots, disfigurement, and even death can result. For most overweight individuals, liposuction is not an acceptable weight loss method.

Medications

Overweight persons who try to follow low-calorie diets often lose control over their appetites and as a result overeat. For decades, medical researchers have been testing various medications to determine if they can help people adhere to their diet plans more easily or lose weight faster. Ideally, weight loss medications should be effective and safe, and not addictive.

Like all drugs, diet suppressants can cause serious side effects. In 1997 fenfluramine and dexfenfluramine *(Redux)* were withdrawn from the market after persons using

either drug or *Fen/Phen,* a non-FDA-approved combination of fenfluramine and phentermine, developed a rare heart valve defect or a deadly form of high blood pressure (Berg, 1999). Meridia is the only appetite suppressant that has FDA approval for long-term use (Ryan et al., 1999). Meridia, however, can increase blood pressure in some patients. The FDA recently approved Xenical, a drug that does not suppress appetite but interferes with fat absorption. Weight loss drugs are not useful unless added to a plan that includes a calorie-reduced diet and an exercise regimen. Furthermore, people who have lost weight with the help of

▲ **Figure 10-8 Liposuction.** Liposuction is a medical procedure in which a special instrument is inserted into body fat through an incision made in the skin, and the fat is vacuumed from the body.

"diet drugs" usually regain it when they discontinue taking the medications.

The "Consumer Health" feature below describes the risks associated with over-the-counter weight loss products. The "Analyzing Health-Related Information" feature examines an advertisement for an over-the-counter weight loss product.

Strategies for Successful Weight Loss

Overweight individuals can lose body fat and maintain their new weight by following sensible and safe weight loss plans, which have three major characteristics:

1. They are medically and nutritionally sound.
2. They include practical ways to engage in regular physical activity.
3. They are adaptable to one's psychological and social needs.

Nutritionally sound weight reduction diets emphasize nutrient-dense foods, and they are nutritionally well balanced and adequate. Without being overly restrictive, such diets supply fewer calories than overweight people need. No special foods are necessary; the recommendations of the Food Guide Pyramid (see inside covers) form the basis of calorie-reduced daily menus.

Reasonable and reliable diet plans recommend ways to increase physical activity such as by adding 30 to 60 minutes of walking, swimming, or bicycling to one's daily routine. Additionally, weight loss plans should meet the psychological and social needs of overweight persons. A reliable plan, for example, helps a person set an achievable weight loss goal, recognize faulty eating habits, build self-esteem, and obtain family or group support. You can use the criteria listed in the Managing Your Health tips "General Features of Reliable Weight Reduction Plans" to judge the effectiveness of most weight-reduction methods.

Effective weight loss plans usually emphasize *behavior modification*. Behavior modification involves learning to identify behaviors that contribute to one's inability to lose weight, such as eating too much fatty food and not engaging in enough physical activity. Additionally, the overweight person learns to modify inappropriate behaviors so that weight loss and its maintenance are possible. ▌ Table 10-6 lists key behaviors, such as not watching television while eating, that can help overweight people achieve their weight loss goals.

To avoid regaining weight, successful dieters must make lifestyle changes they can follow throughout their lifetimes, such as exercising regularly and controlling caloric intake. Small incremental changes that are implemented gradually are easier to adopt than extreme exercise regimens and overly restrictive diets. Most fad diets do not focus on behavior modification. However, even reliable weight loss programs that promote behavior modification do not offer guarantees for long-term success. The process of changing behaviors takes education, practice, time, and perseverance.

The majority of people who have lost weight through nonsurgical methods experience relapse, regaining all of the weight within 1 to 5 years ("Position of the ADA," 1997). Relapses occur when overweight persons fail to modify eating behaviors and physical activity patterns permanently and have unrealistic weight loss expectations. Individuals who lose weight while following fad diets are

Con$umer Health | Over-the-Counter Weight Loss Aids

Nearly anyone who has tried to lose weight knows that it can be frustrating. Hunger seems to be a constant companion. For years, overweight people have taken various pills, powders, beverages, and foods to promote weight loss and prevent hunger. Several brands of diet pills are available over the counter (without prescription), but taking them can be harmful.

Over-the-counter diet pills usually contain phenylpropanolamine (PPA) as the active ingredient. Phenylpropanolamine is a mild stimulant that suppresses appetite over a short period. Large amounts of PPA elevate one's mood, a response that makes abuse of diet pills appealing. However, PPA can also produce unpleasant and sometimes dangerous side effects such as rapid pulse, headaches, and increased blood sugar and blood pressure. In high doses, PPA may destroy muscle tissue. As a result of their concern over the safety and abuse of PPA, FDA officials do not approve dosages that exceed 75 mg per day.

Individuals should not take any weight loss drug, prescription or over-the-counter, without the advice and monitoring of their health-care practitioners. If you have any problem with a weight loss medication or product, report the problem to the FDA's *MedWatch* hotline by calling 1-800-332-1088.

ANALYZING *Health-Related Information*

The following advertisement promotes a weight loss product. Read the ad and evaluate it using the model for analyzing health-related information. The main points of the model are noted below; the model is explained fully on pages 12–13.

1. Which statements are verifiable facts, and which are unverified statements or value claims?

2. What are the credentials of the person who wrote the ad? Does the author appear to have appropriate background and education in the topic area? If it is difficult to tell if the author has specific health expertise, what can you do to check his/her credentials?

3. What might be the motives and biases of the author?

4. What is the main point of the ad? Which information is relevant to the issue or main point; which information is irrelevant?

5. Is the source reliable, or does it have a reputation for publishing misinformation? Does the ad present both the pros and cons of the product?

6. Does the ad attack the credibility of conventional scientists or medical authorities?

Based on the above analysis, do you think that this ad is a reliable source of health-related information? Summarize your reasons for coming to this conclusion.

FINALLY!

Pond scum, grapefruit pills, cabbage soup, stimulants, prepackaged foods, cellulite creams—you name the diet or diet product—you probably have tried it and have been disappointed. The fat didn't budge, and what's worse, you may have gained even more weight as a result of your efforts. You are not alone. There are millions of victims of diet failure—people, like you, who wasted their money and hope of diets and diet products that promised so much and delivered so little.

a weight-loss product that lives up to your expectations!

New and improved FLAB-BE-GONE speeds up your cells' natural fat-burning potential by 68%.

Now you can stop dieting and get the slim, trim figure that you've always wanted.

HOW? Take FLAB-BE-GONE, the revolutionary new method of weight loss that uses your cells' own fat-burning ability to shed unwanted pounds of ugly fat from your body. FLAB-BE-GONE enables you to lose weight effortlessly, while you sleep or watch TV. There's no need to exercise that makes you sweat and damages your joints. You don't have to count calories, grams of carbs or fat, or starve yourself. Just take two FLAB-BE-GONE tablets with meals or snacks. Want an ice cream sundae? Go ahead, eat it. Just take FLAB-BE-GONE with it! Within hours, watch as those pounds of fat and cellulite melt off your body!

Can you believe it? Yes, it's true.
The unique formulation of FLAB-BE-GONE makes it possible to lose up to 10 pounds overnight. Guaranteed!
If you don't lose weight after 1 week of using FLAB-BE-GONE as directed, we will refund your money. You can't lose!

For a month's supply, send $59.95 to:

LOSE UP TO: 10 inches off your waistline
6 inches off your hips
8 inches off your thighs.

Warning: We must ask you to consult your physician before taking this product. If your weight drops too quickly while taking FLAB-BE-GONE, simply reduce the dose.

General Features of Reliable Weight Reduction Plans

Use the following features to judge the quality of weight loss programs.

The diet plan is medically sound if it

- provides recommendations that are safe and supported by scientific evidence.
- suggests receiving a physician's approval prior to initiating the plan.
- encourages gradual weight loss.

The diet is nutritionally sound if it

- meets nutritional needs.
- includes foods from each group of the Food Guide Pyramid.
- encourages eating smaller portions of nutritious foods.
- encourages self-control over problem foods such as sweets.
- considers individual food preferences.
- includes reasonable amounts of fiber and complex carbohydrates.
- reduces caloric intake to no lower than 1000 calories per day.
- recommends losing 1/2 lb to 2 lb per week.

- avoids requiring special or costly supplements and foods.
- avoids claims about the superiority of the plan.
- avoids guarantees concerning weight loss.

The diet plan considers physical fitness needs if it

- recommends an exercise plan that is tailored to the individual's needs, time constraints, interests, and capabilities.
- includes practical suggestions for altering sedentary behaviors.
- encourages daily aerobic activities that last at least half an hour.
- avoids promoting costly exercise equipment, joining exercise clubs, or buying special gadgets to shed pounds.
- recommends physical activities that are safe and enjoyable.
- considers special health concerns of the individual.

The diet plan meets psychological and social needs if it

- provides practical suggestions for modifying food-related attitudes and behaviors.
- educates about the need to set realistic weight loss goals.
- includes techniques to monitor progress (such as weekly recording of waist-to-hip ratios).
- builds self-esteem.
- includes tips to control eating in social situations.
- includes foods that family and friends eat.
- provides strategies for coping with setbacks, difficult situations, and non-supportive people.
- offers opportunities for group support.

Source: Adapted from Dwyer, J. T. (1992). Treatment of obesity: Conventional programs and fad diets. In P. Björntorp, & B. N. Brodoff (Eds.), *Obesity* (pp. 662–676). Philadelphia: Lippincott.

prone to relapse when they return to their usual food habits.

Presently, there is no safe or effective treatment that "cures" being overweight. Therefore, one should strive to prevent excessive weight gain by making permanent lifestyle changes that include reducing the size of food portions, especially fatty foods, and increasing physical activity (Rippe & Hess, 1998; Willett et al., 1999).

Weight Gain

Although it may seem nearly everyone is on a diet to lose weight, some people are underweight and trying to gain weight. Many health experts think underweight individuals should avoid gaining body fat, unless their condition is the result of chronic illness. Nevertheless, thin individuals are often just as dissatisfied with their body sizes as overweight people.

To gain lean tissue, underweight persons need to consume at least 700 to 1000 more calories per day than they usually eat and perform muscle-building exercises. To obtain the extra calories, underweight people can eat more than three meals a day and snack on nutrient-dense foods such as dried fruit, whole-wheat muffins, granola bars, peanut butter, and nuts. You can find other nutritious foods that are high in food energy by consulting food composition tables such as those in the Appendix. Since fatty foods are a source of considerable calories, physically active underweight individuals can eat up to 30% of their caloric intake from these items. Because of the association with cardiovascular disease, people trying to gain weight should avoid eating excessive amounts of saturated fats. Peanut butter, olives, and walnuts are high in unsaturated fat, which is healthier than saturated fat. For people trying to gain weight, the effort must be main-

Table 10-6	Examples of Behavior Modification for Weight Management

Behavior	Actions to Modify Behavior
Eliminate or ignore improper eating cues.	• Keep daily food records to identify problem foods. • Use a shopping list and do not buy problem foods. • Eat fruit or a meal before shopping for food. • Discard problem foods. • While at home, restrict eating to the kitchen or dining room. • Do not eat while watching TV. • Avoid places with vending machines. • Avoid fast-food restaurants that do not sell low-fat foods.
Reduce caloric intake.	• Serve meals on smaller plates. • Prepare smaller amounts of foods to reduce the likelihood of "seconds." • Avoid buffet-style or all-you-can-eat restaurants. • Eat a low-fat snack or watery soup before a meal. • Keep fruit and vegetables on hand to snack on when hungry. • Ask for salad dressing "on the side" at restaurants. • Prepare low-calorie lunches and snacks to take to work or school. • Substitute fresh fruit or yogurt for rich desserts. • Read nutrition labels to identify high-calorie foods. • Learn to leave some food on your plate.
Stay focused on your goal.	• Set incremental goals, such as losing 5 pounds in 5 weeks. • Place a picture of yourself on the refrigerator or pantry door. • Measure your waistline once a week. • Place exercise equipment and walking shoes where you can see them. • Buy a new outfit that is one size smaller and hang it where you can see it. • Ask your friends and family to support your efforts. Give them examples of how they can help.
Practice appropriate behaviors.	• Find ways to move around while at work, school, or home. For example, take the stairs instead of the elevator. • If you relapse, tell yourself that this is normal. Do not label yourself a failure. Ask yourself what you can learn from the experience, so it less likely to affect your eating again. Minor occasional deviations will not affect your weight. Continue with your objectives. • Set aside at least 30 minutes each day to engage in an enjoyable physical activity.
Use non-food rewards for appropriate behaviors.	• Praise yourself frequently for exercising or taking smaller servings of high-calorie foods. • Buy a desired item such as a new CD or an item of clothing. • Take a walk or ride a bike through a park.

tained over the long-term, just as it is for people trying to lose weight.

If you are thinking about losing or gaining weight, complete the "Changing Health Habits" activity for this chapter in the student workbook. This activity can help you decide if you are ready to make the lifestyle changes needed to modify your weight and maintain a new, healthier weight for the rest of your life.

Healthy
LIVING PRACTICES

• If you want to lose weight, modify your lifestyle. For example, eat less fat by replacing high-fat snacks with more nutrient-dense foods.

• To lose or control your body weight, engage in vigorous physical activity such as jogging, brisk walking, cycling, or swimming for at least 30 minutes, preferably every day.

- To judge whether a weight loss plan or program is sensible and safe, determine if it is medically and nutritionally sound, includes a plan to increase regular physical activity, is adaptable to your psychological and social needs, and can be followed for a lifetime.
- If you want to gain weight, add at least 700 to 1000 calories to your usual daily intake and exercise to build muscle mass. To boost the caloric content of meals and snacks, eat more nutrient-dense foods such as dried fruit, whole-wheat muffins, granola bars, peanut butter, and nuts.

across the lifespan

Weight Management

The amount of weight a woman gains during pregnancy affects the health of her baby. The average woman should gain about 25 to 35 pounds by the end of pregnancy (Wardlaw, 1999). This weight gain includes not only the fetus's weight, but also the weight of the pregnant woman's additional body fluids, fat stores, and breast and uterine tissues. Women who are underweight when they become pregnant can expect to gain more weight; those who are overweight may gain a few pounds less than average.

Some pregnant women restrict their food intake to limit their weight gain because they do not want to struggle with losing the extra pounds after the baby arrives. However, caloric restriction during pregnancy may be hazardous to the developing fetus. The time to lose weight is before or after pregnancy and not during this period. Nevertheless, within two years after giving birth, many women remain several pounds heavier than those who have not been pregnant.

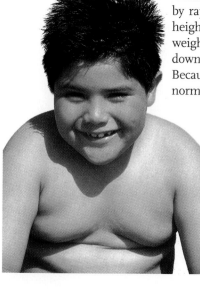

Infancy is a period characterized by rapid gains in both weight and height. Many babies who are overweight at their first birthday, slim down by the time they enter school. Because dietary fat is essential for normal growth and development,

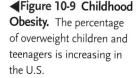

◀Figure 10-9 Childhood Obesity. The percentage of overweight children and teenagers is increasing in the U.S.

low-fat or calorie-restricted diets are not recommended for children under 2 years of age.

As in the adult population, the number of overweight school-age children is increasing in the United States. More than 25% of children 6 to 17 years old are overweight (▊ Figure 10-9). Children and adolescents need adequate amounts of energy for physical development and activity, but they typically eat more calories and fat than recommended in the U.S. Dietary Guidelines. Some experts think that, besides dietary factors, preoccupation with sedentary activities such as watching television and playing video games contributes to the increase of childhood obesity (Robinson, 1999). No one can predict whether an overweight child will become an overweight adult. However, obese adolescents are about six times likely to remain obese as young adults (Robertson et al., 1999).

Childhood and adolescent obesity often becomes a problem that affects the entire family. Overweight children may develop eating disorders and low self-esteem when parents, other adults, or peers treat them negatively. An effective program that helps overweight children lose weight should not interfere with their normal physical development and should not encourage the development of eating disorders. Successful treatment involves teaching children and their parents how to make appropriate dietary modifications, increase physical activity, and resolve conflicts that may involve eating habits.

By 65 years of age, most people have experienced a decline in their lean mass and an increase in their fat mass. This change occurs to a lesser extent in individuals who maintain a high degree of physical activity as they grow old. Some elderly persons may benefit from having moderate amounts of body fat, particularly if they lose their appetites during illness. In most instances, however, the same health problems that plague younger overweight individuals can affect the overweight elderly.

Overweight elderly persons can follow the same recommendations for losing weight as do younger overweight individuals: select nutrient-dense foods, reduce intakes of fatty and sugary foods, and become more physically active. Even modest increases in physical activity, such as walking, swimming, or light exercise, can benefit most elderly people (Jensen & Rogers, 1998).

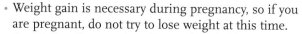

Healthy LIVING PRACTICES

- Weight gain is necessary during pregnancy, so if you are pregnant, do not try to lose weight at this time.
- Restrictive diets can interfere with a child's normal development. Check with a health-care practitioner before placing your child on a fat- or calorie-restricted diet.

Chapter Review

Summary

Recent health surveys indicate that more Americans are overweight than in previous decades. More than one-half of the adult U.S. population is too fat. Excess body fat is associated with low self-esteem and increased risks of chronic health conditions such as osteoarthritis, sleep apnea, gallbladder disease, gout, hypertension, diabetes, certain cancers, and heart disease.

The body uses the energy in foods to power metabolic activity, to move skeletal muscles, and to process nutrients after meals. According to the principles of energy balance, the body requires a certain number of calories to maintain its weight. When one consumes more calories than needed, weight gain occurs; when one ingests fewer calories than needed, weight loss occurs. Since each pound of body fat represents about 3500 calories, consuming 500 fewer calories a day than needed should result in a weight loss of one pound per week.

Methods of determining the percentage of body fat include measuring subcutaneous fat (skinfold thicknesses), hydrostatic weighing, bioelectrical impedance, and near-infrared interactance. To determine if they are overweight, many people rely on height/weight tables, waist-to-hip ratios (WHR), and body mass indices (BMI). Risks of chronic health problems and death increase as the WHR and BMI increase.

Obesity is not simply the result of a lack of willpower. The development of obesity is a complex process involving interactions among biological, psychological, social, and environmental factors. These factors include genetics, responses to social situations, food availability and composition, and levels of physical activity.

Obesity is a chronic condition. Most people who have lost weight will regain much or all of it within 5 years. To lose weight and maintain the loss, overweight individuals need to decrease their caloric intake by eating less food and increase their caloric expenditures by increasing their levels of physical activity. A reliable weight loss regimen should include a well-balanced, nutritionally adequate but calorie-reduced diet and an exercise regimen that can be followed for life.

To increase her chances of having healthy babies, an average pregnant woman needs to gain about 25 to 35 pounds. While pregnant, women should not consume low-calorie diets because caloric restriction may harm the fetus. After birth, infants need some fat in their diets; therefore, physicians do not recommend that parents restrict the fat intake of children under 2 years of age.

Children and adolescents need adequate amounts of energy for physical development and activity. In the United States, the percentage of children and teenagers who are overweight is growing. Experts think that this increase is primarily the result of sedentary lifestyles and poor eating habits. It is difficult to predict whether an overweight child will become an overweight adult. Overweight adolescents, however, are at risk of remaining overweight when they reach adulthood. Overweight elderly individuals tend to experience the same health problems as younger overweight adults.

Applying What You Have Learned

1. Develop a day's menu, including meals and snacks, for a nutritionally adequate, low-fat weight loss plan. Your plan should follow the minimum number of recommended servings from the Food Guide Pyramid (see Figure 9-5). *(Application)*

2. You see an advertisement for a special drink that is supposed to eliminate excess body fat while you sleep. According to the ad, this product helps you lose weight "fast" by increasing your metabolic rate; there is no need to eat less food or exercise more often. Explain why you think this ad is a source of reliable or unreliable health-related information. *(Synthesis)*

3. A man has been maintaining his weight by consuming 2500 calories a day. If he does not alter his physical activity level, how many calories should he consume daily to lose four pounds in a month? *(Application)*

4. Compare your present weight to your weight of two years ago. If you have gained or lost weight over the past couple of years, explain how you reached your present weight by evaluating your lifestyle. What factors might account for the weight change? If you have not gained or lost weight during this period, explain why this situation has occurred. *(Evaluation)*

KEY

Application: Using information in a new situation.
Synthesis: Putting together information from different sources.
Evaluation: Making informed decisions.

Reflecting On Your Health

1. "Fat people could lose weight if they would just push themselves away from the dinner table." After reading this chapter, what have you learned about obesity and weight control that might cause you to react differently to this statement than you might have prior to reading this chapter?

2. As mentioned in this chapter, normal weight people often have negative feelings toward obese individuals. What were your feelings about obese people before you read this chapter? After reading this chapter, have your feelings about obese persons changed? If so, describe how your feelings changed.

3. Do you think there is too much emphasis on dieting in the United States? How would you respond if your best friend tells you that he or she is "on a diet?"

4. Do you think obese people should be given special privileges such as those given to people who have physical disabilities?

5. How does the media influence your satisfaction with your body size and shape? Do you think the media should encourage people to be more satisfied with their body sizes and shapes? If you think the media should take such steps, how could this affect people's health?

References

Balsiger, B. M., Luque-de Leon, E., & Sarr, M. G. (1997). Surgical treatment of obesity: Who is an appropriate candidate? *Mayo Clinic Proceedings, 72*:551-558.

Berg, F. M. (1999). Health risks associated with weight loss and obesity treatment programs. *Journal of Social Issues, 55*(2):277-297.

Calle, E. E., Thun, M. J., Petrelli, J. M., Rodriguez, C., & Health, C. W. (1999). Body-mass index and mortality in a prospective cohort of U.S. adults. *New England Journal of Medicine, 341*:1097-1105.

Carson, C. A., Meilahn, E. N., Caggiula, A. W. (1994). Comparison of waist measurements: A methodologic issue in longitudinal studies. *Journal of the American Dietetic Association, 94*:771-772.

Cleland, R., Graybill, D. C., Hubbard, V., Khan, L. K., Stern, J. S., Wadden, T. A., Weinsier, R., & Yanovski, S. (1998). Commercial weight loss products and programs: What consumers stand to gain and lose. Washington, DC: Federal Trade Commission, Bureau of Consumer Protection. www.ftc.gov/os/1998/9803/weightlo.rpt.htm

Clinical guidelines on the identification, evaluation, and treatment of overweight and obesity in adults (1998). National Institutes of Health, National Heart, Lung, and Blood Institute. Bethesda, MD.

Field, A. E., Byers, T., Hunter, D. J., Laird, N. M., Manson, J. E., Williamson, D. F., Willett, W. C., & Colditz, G. A. (1999). Weight cycling, weight gain, and risk of hypertension in women. *American Journal of Epidemiology, 150*(6):573-579.

French, S. A., Folsom, A. R., Jeffery, R. W., & Williamson, D. F. (1999). Prospective study of intentionality of weight loss and mortality in older women: The Iowa Women's Health Study. *American Journal of Epidemiology, 149*(6):504-514.

Han, T. S., Tijhuis, M. A. R., Lean, M. E. J., & Seidell, J. D. (1998). Quality of life in relation to overweight and body fat distribution. *American Journal of Public Health, 88*:1814-1820.

Heymsfield, S. B., Greenberg, A. S., Fujioka, K., Dixon, R. M., Kushnew, R., Hunt, T., Lubina, J. A., Patane, J., Self, B., Hunt, P., & McCamish, M. (1999). Recombinant leptin for weight loss in obese and lean adults. *Journal of the American Medical Association, 282*(16):1568-1575.

Hill, J. O., & Peters, J. C. (1998). Environmental contributions to the obesity epidemic. *Science, 280*:1371-1374.

Jensen, G. L., & Rogers, J. (1998). Obesity in older persons. *Journal of the American Dietetic Association, 98*:1308-1311.

Koop, C. E. (1999). General information. http:/www.shapeup.org

Kretsch, M. J., Fong, A. K. H., & Green, M. W. (1999). Behavioral and body size correlates of energy intake and underreporting by obese and normal-weight women. *Journal of the American Dietetic Association, 99*(3):300-306.

Kuczmarski, R. J., Carroll, M. D., Flegal, K. M., & Troiano, R. P. (1997). Varying body mass index cutoff points to describe overweight prevalence among U.S. adults: NHANES III (1988 to 1994). *Obesity Research, 5*:532-548.

Levine, J. A., Eberhardt, N. L., & Jensen, M. D. (1999). Role of nonexercise activity thermogenesis in resistance to fat gain in humans. *Science, 283*(5399):212-214.

Mokdad, A. H., Serdula, M. K., Dietz, W. H., Bowman, B. A., Marks, J. S., & Koplan, J. P. (1999). The spread of the obesity epidemic in the United States, 1991–1998. *Journal of the American Medical Association, 282*(16):1519-1522.

Oster, G., Thompson, D., Edelsberg, J., Bird, A. P., & Colditz, G. A. (1999). Lifetime health and economic benefits of weight loss among obese persons. *American Journal of Public Health, 89*(10):1536-1542.

Parham, E. S. (1999). Promoting body size acceptance in weight management counseling. *Journal of the American Dietetic Association, 99*(8):920-925.

Position of the American Dietetic Association: Weight management. (1997). *Journal of the American Dietetic Association, 97*(1):71-74.

Prevalence of physical inactivity during leisure time among overweight persons—behavior risk factor surveillance system, 1994. (1996). *Morbidity and Mortality Weekly Report, 45*(9):185-188.

Rippe, J. M., & Hess, S. (1998). The role of physical activity in the prevention and management of obesity. *Journal of the American Dietetic Association, 98*(Suppl. 2):S31-S38.

Robertson, S. M., Cullen, K. W., Baranowski, J., Baranowski, T., Hu, S., & de Moor, C. (1999). Factors related to adiposity among children aged 3 to 7 years. *Journal of the American Dietetic Association, 99*(8):938-943.

Robinson, T. N. (1999). Reducing children's television viewing to prevent obesity. *Journal of the American Medical Association, 282*(16):1561-1567.

Rosenbaum, M., Prieto, Y., Hellmer, J., Boschmann, M., Krueger, J., Leibel, R. L., & Ship, A. G. (1998). An exploratory investigation of the morphology and biochemistry of cellulite. *Plastic and Reconstructive Surgery, 101*(7):1934-1939.

Ryan, D. H., Bray, G. A., Rössner, S., & Galasso, G. J. (1999). Conference report—Obesity: New directions, June 27–29, 1998, Charleston, South Carolina. *Obesity Research, 7*(3):303-308.

Serdula, M. K., Mokdad, A. H., Williamson, D. F., Galuska, D. A., Mendlein, J. M., & Heath, G. W. (1999). Prevalence of attempting weight loss and strategies for controlling weight. *Journal of the American Medical Association, 282*(14):1353-1358.

Troilius, C. (1999). Ultrasound-assisted lipoplasty: Is it really safe? *Aesthetic Plastic Surgery, 23*(5):307-311.

Update: Prevalence of overweight among children, adolescents, and adults—United States, 1988–1994. (1997). *Morbidity and Mortality Weekly Report, 46*(9):199-202.

U.S. Department of Health and Human Services (USDHHS), Public Health Service. (1991). *Healthy people 2000: National health promotion and disease prevention objectives.* Washington, DC: Government Printing Office.

Wagner, D. R., & Heyward, V. H. (1999). Techniques of body composition assessment: A review of laboratory and field methods. *Research Quarterly for Exercise and Sport, 70*(2):135-149.

Wardlaw, G. M. (1999). *Nutrition Perspectives.* St. Louis: McGraw-Hill.

Wickelgren, I. (1998). Obesity: How big a problem? *Science, 280*:1364-1367.

Willett, W. C., Dietz, W. H., & Colditz, G. A. (1999). Guidelines for healthy weight. *New England Journal of Medicine, 341*:427-434.

Williams, M. H. (1999). *Nutrition for Health, Fitness, & Nutrition.* Boston: McGraw-Hill.

Woods, A. C., Seeley, R. J., Porte, D., & Schwartz, M. W. (1998). Signals that regulate food intake and homeostasis. *Science, 280*:1378-1383.

Youth Risk Behavior Surveillance: National College Health Risk Behavior Survey—United States, 1995. (1997). *Weekly Morbidity and Mortality Report, 46*(SS-6):1-54.

chapter 11

Physical Fitness

If you look around your home, you will see many devices and products that make your life easier: electric can-openers, permanent-press clothes, dishwashers, garage-door openers, and remote controls. Outside of your home, there are more labor-saving machines. You can ride a lawn mower instead of push one, you can drive a car rather than walk to places, use elevators and escalators rather than climb stairs, and take moving walkways rather than walk through some of the larger airports. You can even make your leisure time less physically demanding by using a motorized cart to get around a golf course or a motorboat to get around a lake. Besides using labor-saving products, you can have other people perform your physical work. For example, you can pay a team of people to wash your car or clean your house.

A hundred years ago Americans often performed hard physical work at home and on the job. By the end of the twentieth century, a variety of machines, products, and services had become available that made our daily lives less physically demanding. Today, we generally have more leisure time than our great-grandparents, but many of us spend it performing

> *". . . you can . . . use elevators and escalators rather than climb stairs. . ."*

activities that do not contribute to our physical health.

Regardless of age and physical condition, nearly everyone can achieve health benefits by exercising regularly and becoming more physically active. Many people are aware of the beneficial effects of exercise on the functioning of the heart and skeletal muscles. Nevertheless, more than 60% of U.S. adults do not exercise routinely, and 25% are sedentary ("Physical Activity and Health," 1996). Of those adults who exercise regularly, only 15% describe their physical activity levels as "vigorous." An objective of *Healthy People 2000* was that at least 30% of Americans who are 6 years of age and older would be engaging in light-to-moderate exercise for a minimum of 30 minutes, preferably every day, by the year 2000. In 1985, 22% of Americans who were at least 6 years old engaged in light-to-moderate exercise regularly. According to the latest *Healthy People 2000* update (USDHHS, 1999), 23% of this population were performing light-to-moderate exercise regularly in 1995. Thus, Americans are making little progress toward meeting this objective.

What You'll Learn

www.jbpub.com/healthyliving

The web site for this book offers many useful tools and supplementary health information for both students and instructors. Visit the site at www.jbpub.com/healthyliving for information on these topics:

Physical Activity and Health
The Health-Related Components of Physical Fitness
Physical Fitness and Athletic Performance
Consumer Health: Choosing a Fitness Center
Across the Life Span: Physical Fitness

Chapter Overview

The principles of physical fitness.
The health-related components of fitness.
Exercising for optimal health.
Developing your own exercise program.
Preventing and managing exercise injuries.

DIVERSITY *Health* New Interest in an Ancient Approach to Fitness

Con$umer *Health* Choosing a Fitness Center

Managing *Your Health* Assessing the Intensity of Your Workout

across the *Lifespan* Physical Fitness

Student Workbook

Self Assessment: Cardiorespiratory Fitness: The Walkport Fitness Walking Test
Changing Health Habits: Do You Want to be More Physically Active?

Do You Know?

- How to calculate your target heart rate?
- How to bulk up safely?
- If muscles can turn into fat?

This chapter discusses the basic principles of fitness, including the health benefits of exercise and a physically active lifestyle, and how to design a basic fitness program that you can follow for the rest of your life.

Principles of Physical Fitness
The Body in Motion

Physical movement involves the interrelated functioning of the muscular and skeletal systems. The functioning of the muscular system is so closely associated with the skeletal system that the two are often referred to as the *musculoskeletal system*.

The *skeletal muscles* provide shape, support, and movement for your body. ▌**Figure 11-1** identifies the major skeletal muscle groups of the human body. A skeletal muscle consists of hundreds of muscle cells called *muscle fibers*. Movement occurs when the muscle fibers contract, shortening the length of the muscle. **Tendons**, tough bands of fibrous tissue, connect skeletal muscles to bones and play an important role in muscular movement. **Joints** are places where two or more bones come together. Most joints are movable; therefore, such joints permit the movement be-

▼**Figure 11-1 Major Skeletal Muscles of the Human Body.**
(a) Front view; (b) Back view

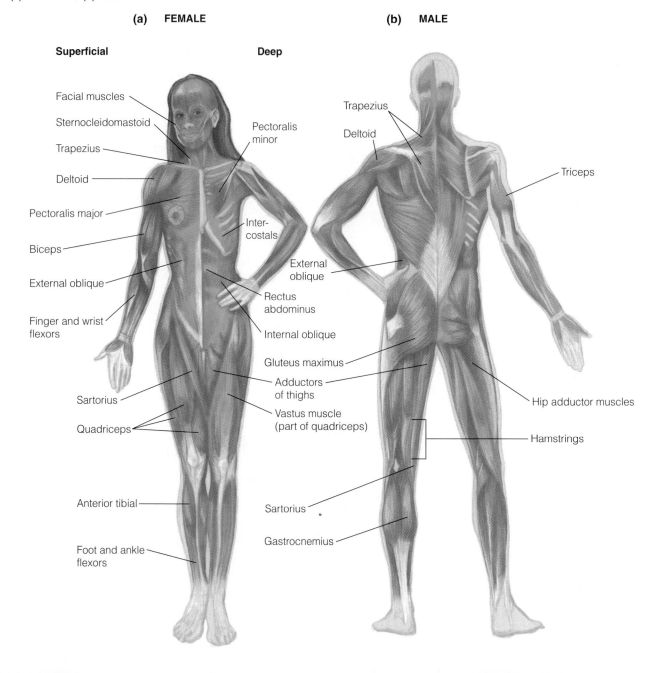

(a)   FEMALE

Superficial   Deep

- Facial muscles
- Sternocleidomastoid
- Trapezius
- Deltoid
- Pectoralis major
- Biceps
- External oblique
- Finger and wrist flexors
- Sartorius
- Quadriceps
- Anterior tibial
- Foot and ankle flexors

- Pectoralis minor
- Inter-costals
- External oblique
- Rectus abdominus
- Internal oblique
- Gluteus maximus
- Adductors of thighs
- Vastus muscle (part of quadriceps)
- Sartorius
- Gastrocnemius

(b)   MALE

- Trapezius
- Deltoid
- Triceps
- External oblique
- Hip adductor muscles
- Hamstrings

tween bones. **Ligaments** are tough bands of connective tissue that hold bones together at the joints.

The Circulatory and Respiratory Systems

Optimal functioning of the circulatory and respiratory systems (sometimes referred to as the *cardiorespiratory system*) is necessary to achieve a high degree of physical fitness. The circulatory system includes the heart, blood, and blood vessels. The lungs are the major structures of the respiratory system. As ▌ **Figure 11-2** illustrates, the functioning of the heart and lungs is interrelated.

The heart is a muscular pump that usually beats about 70 to 80 times each minute. Its job is to circulate blood throughout the body's vast network of blood vessels: the arteries, veins, and capillaries. Blood transports oxygen and nutrients to cells and carries waste products such as carbon dioxide away from them.

Cells need oxygen to release the energy stored in glucose and fats. As the heart pumps blood through microscopic blood vessels in the lungs, carbon dioxide leaves the blood and is exhaled. While in the lungs, hemoglobin in the red blood cells picks up oxygen from the inhaled air. The oxygen-rich blood returns to the heart, which pumps it to the rest of the body. As the blood moves through tiny capillaries in tissues, oxygen and nutrients move out of the bloodstream and into the cells. Waste products move out of the cells and into the blood. The blood then circulates through veins back to the heart. This cycle repeats itself with every heartbeat and breath.

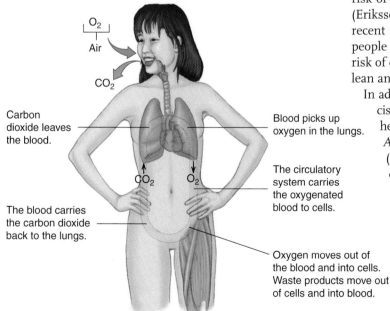

▲**Figure 11-2 Cardiorespiratory System.** The functioning of the heart and lungs is interrelated. The heart pumps blood to the lungs where it picks up oxygen. The oxygenated blood returns to the heart, which pumps it throughout the body.

Defining Physical Activity and Exercise

Physical activity is movement that occurs when skeletal muscles contract; everyone engages in some physical activity. **Exercise** is physical activity that is usually planned and performed to improve or maintain one's physical condition. For example, doing biceps curls is an exercise that develops upper arm strength.

Physical Activity and Health

Being physically active can substantially reduce your risks of serious chronic diseases including heart *(coronary artery)* disease, certain forms of cancer, type II diabetes, hypertension, and osteoporosis (Lee et al., 1999; Thune et al., 1997; Wei et al., 1999). Increased physical activity also reduces your risk of obesity (Rippe & Hess, 1998) and improves the functioning of your immune system ("Physical Activity and Health," 1996). Regular physical activity helps maintain muscle strength and joint function. Furthermore, elderly people may improve their balance and reduce their risk of falls by performing certain exercises regularly. Making small lifestyle adjustments that increase your level of physical activity can lower your risk of premature death significantly (Erikssen et al., 1998). The results of recent research indicate that overweight people who are physically fit have a lower risk of dying prematurely than people who are lean and unfit (Wei et al., 1999).

In addition to improving physical health, regular exercise and physical activity can enhance psychological health and sense of well-being. According to *Physical Activity and Health: A Report of the Surgeon General* (1996), physical activity "reduces symptoms of anxiety and depression and fosters improvements in mood and feelings of well-being." This does not mean that physical inactivity *causes* mental health problems or that exercising will cure these conditions. However, many people who routinely engage in moderate levels of physical activity report that it makes them "feel better" (Shephard & Balady, 1999). Additionally, regular physical activity can improve the quality of sleep (Artal, 1998), which helps people feel more energetic during the day.

Many people experience short-term psychological benefits during or immediately after exercising. Strenuous physical activity produces chemical changes in the body that can improve psychological

tendons tough bands of tissue that connect many skeletal muscles to bones.

joints the places where two or more bones come together.

ligaments tough bands of connective tissue that hold bones together at joints.

physical activity movement that occurs when skeletal muscles contract.

exercise physical activity that is usually planned and performed to improve or maintain one's physical condition.

health. For example, the central nervous system releases *beta-endorphins* during exercise. Beta-endorphins are pain-killing substances that may provide natural relaxing and mood-elevating effects. Also, exercise can divert a person's attention away from distressing thoughts and negative emotions, which relieves anxiety. Long-term psychological benefits of exercise may include boosting self-esteem; physically fit people often perceive themselves as more capable of managing their health (Artal, 1998). Additionally, people who exercise with others can experience psychological benefits from the social interaction.

The Health-Related Components of Physical Fitness

Cardiorespiratory fitness, muscular strength, muscular endurance, flexibility, and body composition are the health-related components of physical fitness. These physical characteristics provide support for the body, sustain its effective and efficient movement, and influence overall health and well-being.

Assessing the Intensity of Your Workout: Target Heart Rates

To maximize the cardiorespiratory benefits of aerobic activity, you should work out at the level of intensity that raises your heart rate to within your target heart rate zone. To estimate your target heart rate zone, you need to take your pulse. **Figure 11-A** illustrates where you can feel your pulse using the carotid artery in your neck or radial artery in your wrist. Although locating the carotid artery pulse can be easier than the radial pulse, applying pressure to the carotid artery can reduce the heart rate, which interferes with obtaining a reliable measurement. For some people with cardiovascular diseases, applying pressure to the carotid artery can be dangerous. Many medical experts advise using gentle pressure on your carotid artery to measure your pulse. Practice finding your radial pulse, so you can take it quickly while exercising.

To obtain the most accurate heart rate, measure your pulse while you are still engaging in the physical activity or within 10 seconds after discontinuing the muscular movement. This timing is necessary because your pulse declines rapidly when you stop exercising. Count your pulse for 10 seconds, then multiply that number by 6 to obtain your heart rate per minute.

To estimate your target heart rate zone, obtain your *age-predicted maximum heart rate* by subtracting your age from 220. For example, if you are 21 years old and healthy, your age-predicted maximum heart rate is 199 beats per minute. Exercising at your age-predicted maximum heart rate is undesirable and uncomfortable; this extreme level of intensity is unnecessary for achieving cardiorespiratory fitness. Healthy people should exercise with enough intensity to raise their heart rates to within 65% and 90% of their age-predicted maximum heart rates. This interval is the *target heart rate zone*. People in excellent physical condition may calculate their target heart rates at the 85% to 90% intensity level. Most experts, however, do not recommend that individuals raise their heart rates more than 90% of their age-predicted maximum levels.

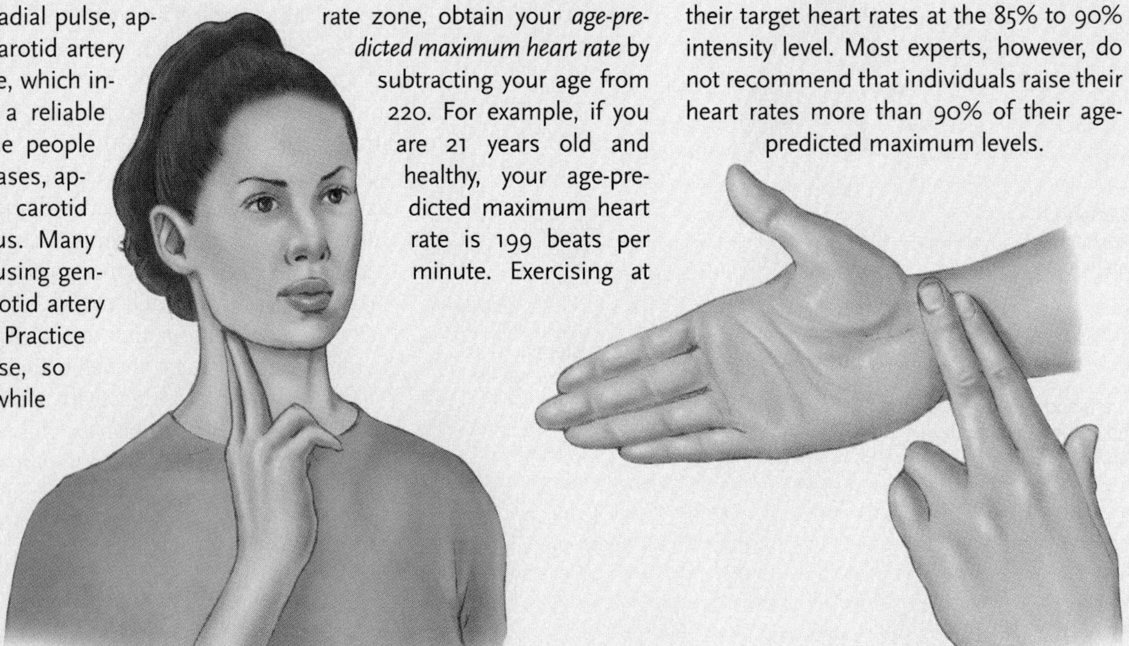

▶Figure 11-A
Taking Your Pulse.
(a) Carotid site and
(b) Radial site   **(a)**

(b)

Cardiorespiratory Fitness

During intense physical activity, skeletal muscles need large quantities of oxygen to release enough energy to sustain movement. To supply more oxygen for working muscles, the heart and breathing rates increase as the intensity of physical activity increases. However, the lungs and heart have a maximum capacity to distribute an adequate supply of oxygen throughout the body within a certain time. Once the lungs and heart reach this maximum capacity, the skeletal muscles cannot obtain the additional oxygen needed to sustain their intense level of activity, and they become fatigued.

Individuals with high degrees of **cardiorespiratory fitness** (or *endurance*) can perform muscular work more intensely and longer without becoming fatigued than persons with low levels of cardiorespiratory fitness. Young physically fit individuals can raise their heart rates to about 200 beats per minute while engaging in intense aerobic activities. As people grow older, their maximum heart rates decline. In addition to physical condition and age, other personal characteristics, including heredity, gender, and body composition, influence the

cardiorespiratory fitness the ability to perform muscular movements intensely and for long periods without becoming fatigued.

If you are healthy and exercise regularly, multiply your age-predicted maximum heart rate by 0.65 and 0.90 to obtain a heart rate interval that is 65% to 90% of your maximum. For example, a healthy 21-year-old person would multiply 199 by 0.65 to determine the lowest heart rate (65% level) and by 0.90 (90% level) to find the highest rate. If you are out of shape, multiply your age-predicted maximum heart rate by 0.55 (55% of the maximum). ▌**Figure 11-B** illustrates target heart rate zones for fit and unfit people. If you are sedentary and just starting an exercise program, strive for a maximum heart rate at the low end of your target zone. As your physical condition improves, you will need to recalculate your target heart rate so that it is in "the zone."

While exercising, if you can raise your heart rate to a value in your target zone, and maintain this rate for 30 to 60 minutes, you are giving your heart and lungs a beneficial aerobic workout. During aerobic activity, you should measure your pulse about every 10 minutes without stopping the activity. If your heart rate is higher than the maximum value of your target heart rate zone, it is possible that you underestimated your zone, or you may be overexerting yourself at your present level of fitness. You may need to reduce your muscular work load. On the other hand, if your heart rate during aerobic exercise is less than the target range, you may not be working hard enough to achieve cardiorespiratory benefits.

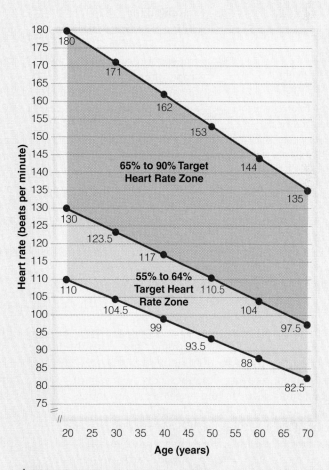

▲**Figure 11-B Target Heart Rate Zones.** The shaded areas include pulse rates within the 55% to 64% and 65% to 90% intensity ranges.

maximum degree to which a person's lungs and heart can function.

During vigorous physical activity, the heart of a physically fit person pumps more blood with each beat. When the activity ceases, the fit person's heart and breathing rates rapidly return to normal. Even while resting, such an individual's heart is efficient; each minute, it can pump the same amount of blood with fewer heartbeats than the heart of an unfit person.

aerobic
oxygen-requiring.

muscular endurance a muscle's ability to contract repeatedly without becoming fatigued.

muscular strength the ability to apply maximum force against an object that is resisting this force.

hypertrophy a condition in which muscles become larger and stronger.

atrophy a condition in which muscles lose size and strength.

detraining a condition characterized by atrophied and weak muscles, which occurs when skeletal muscles are not used regularly.

To develop cardiorespiratory fitness, you need to perform **aerobic** (oxygen-requiring) activities. An aerobic activity lasts longer than 2 minutes, increases heart and breathing rates, and involves vigorous movements of large muscles. Popular aerobic activities include running, jogging, race-walking, lap swimming, cycling, stair-stepping, aerobic dancing, cross-country skiing, and rope skipping. While performing aerobic activities, people can use their heart rates to determine if the intensity of the activities is high enough to provide cardiorespiratory benefits. To be very effective, a physical activity should be vigorous enough to raise your heart rate to within a certain range, the *target heart rate zone*. After raising your heart rate to the target zone, you should continue performing the aerobic activity, maintaining the level of intensity for at least 20 minutes. According to the American College of Sports Medicine (ACSM), healthy adults should perform moderate-intensity aerobic activities 3 to 5 days a week, from 55% to 90% of their maximum heart rates, continuously for 20 to 60 minutes (Pollock et al., 1998). The "Managing Your Health" box "Assessing the Intensity of Your Workout: Target Heart Rates" on pp. 250–251 describes how to measure your heart rate and calculate your target heart rate zone.

You do not have to jog 6 miles daily to reap the health benefits of a physically active lifestyle; most people can improve their health by performing a minimum of 30 minutes of moderately intense physical activity, preferably every day (Stofan et al., 1998). People can even benefit from intermittent episodes of aerobic activity that last 8 to 10 minutes and accumulate to at least 30 minutes in one day. Most sedentary and overweight people can integrate more physical activity into their daily routines, for example, by climbing stairs instead of taking elevators and walking to nearby places instead of driving. By exercising more vigorously, however, people can achieve even greater health

benefits. ▌ **Table 11-1** lists some physical activities classified as light, moderate, and intense.

If you have heart disease or other serious chronic conditions, are out of shape, or are 40 years old or older, obtain the approval of a qualified health-care practitioner before beginning an exercise program, especially if the program includes aerobic activities.

Assessing Cardiorespiratory Fitness You can judge your level of cardiorespiratory fitness by answering the following questions. When engaging in strenuous exercise, can you carry on a conversation with others, or are you panting for air and unable to talk? How long does it take you to catch your breath or for your heart to stop racing after you stop the activity? If you are unable to talk while exercising and it takes you a long time to recover your normal breathing and heart rates when you finish the physical activity, you probably have a relatively low degree of cardiorespiratory fitness. The assessment activity for this chapter involves a simple test that you can perform to determine your level of cardiorespiratory fitness (see student workbook).

Many formerly out-of-shape people discover that their resting heart rates have declined after a few months of regular aerobic exercise. Observing such a decline in resting heart rate not long after beginning a regular aerobic exercise program is usually an indication that cardiorespiratory fitness has improved.

To track your aerobic fitness progress, record your resting heart rates before and after initiating an exercise regimen. Determine your resting heart rate by measuring your pulse when you first wake up, before getting out of bed, on 3 consecutive days. Calculate your average resting heart rate over this 3-day period, and record it and the date. After a few months of engaging in a vigorous exercise program, repeat the procedure to determine your resting heart rate and compare the before and after measurements.

Muscular Endurance

Muscular endurance is one important aspect of muscular fitness. **Muscular endurance** is the ability of a muscle to contract repeatedly without becoming fatigued easily. For example, many people perform "crunches" to strengthen their abdominal muscles. A sedentary person may experience muscular fatigue after the third crunch and not be able to do another one. If this person, however, continues to perform crunches regularly and increases the number performed during each exercise session, he or she will develop muscular endurance in their abdominal muscles. As a result, this person can do numerous crunches with ease.

Muscular Strength

Muscular strength is another important aspect of muscular fitness. **Muscular strength** is the ability of muscles to apply maximum force against an object that is resisting this force. Many individuals perform specific exercises to increase muscular strength because they want to lift heavy

Table 11-1	Physical Activities: Intensity Levels	
Light Activity (less than 3 calories/kg/hr)	**Moderate Activity (3 to 6 calories/kg/hr)**	**Intense/Vigorous Activity (more than 6 calories/kg/hr)**
Walking slowly (1–2 mph)	Walking briskly (3 to 4 mph)	Walking briskly uphill with a load
Cycling, stationary bike	Cycling for pleasure or transportation	Cycling, fast or racing
Swimming, slow treading	Swimming, moderate effort	Swimming, fast treading, or crawl
Conditioning exercises: Light stretching	Conditioning exercises: general calisthenics	Conditioning exercises: ski or stair-climbing machine
—	Racket sports: table tennis	Racket sports: racketball, singles tennis
Golf, using power cart	Golf, pulling cart or carrying clubs	—
Bowling	—	—
Fishing, sitting	Fishing, standing and casting	—
Boating (power boat)	Canoeing leisurely (2 to 3.9 mph)	Canoeing rapidly (≥4 mph)
Carpet sweeping	General housecleaning	Moving furniture
Carpentry	Housepainting	—

Source: Adapted from Pate, R. R., et al. (1995). Physical activity and public health. *Journal of the American Medical Association, 273:402-407.*

objects with ease or improve their appearance. Other people are interested in developing larger, more well-defined muscle groups because they want to compete in body-building events (■ **Figure 11-3**). How does the strength and size of a muscle increase?

To develop a high degree of strength, muscles need to be overloaded by moving heavy objects repeatedly, particularly objects that become progressively heavier over time. For example, using a weight-lifting machine regularly can increase the size and strength of the biceps muscle in the upper arm. This response is called the *training effect*. Under these conditions, the individual fibers of the biceps muscle can enlarge, or **hypertrophy**, making the entire muscle stronger and larger. Once muscle cells enlarge, they require a regular program of resistance exercise to maintain their size and strength.

The saying, "Use it, or lose it" generally applies to skeletal muscles. Muscular **atrophy**, a condition of a muscle that has lost size and strength, results from a few weeks of **detraining**. If you have ever had a broken arm or leg, you

▶**Figure 11-3 Body Builders.** Some individuals perform specific exercises to develop larger, more well-defined muscle groups. This woman competes in bodybuilding events.

may recall that after the cast was removed, the muscles of the recovered limb were atrophied and weak. When you first used the limb, the weakened muscles ached for a brief time, but within days they became stronger. Eventually, using these muscles enabled them to regain their full strength and original size.

Exercising for Muscular Strength A safe and effective way to increase muscle strength and size is to perform repetitive exercises that overload a particular muscle group, such as lifting weights. A *repetition* is the completion of a particular exercise, for example, lifting a hand-held weight one time and returning to the resting position. A *set* involves performing the same resistance exercise movement usually 8 to 12 times. During a workout session, healthy people can train their major muscle group by performing a single set of exercises for each group of muscles (Feigenbaum & Pollock, 1999). For best results, a person should do the resistance workout 3 times a week.

Two forms of exercise that increase muscular strength are isometric and isotonic exercises. In an **isometric** exercise an individual exerts muscular force against a fixed, immovable object of resistance. For example, applying a constant amount of force while pushing against an immovable door frame is an isometric exercise. During isometric contraction, the muscle does not shorten, so it does not bulge. Although isometric exercises can increase muscular strength, they do not increase muscular endurance or flexibility effectively. Furthermore, muscles can apply excessive pressure on certain arteries during isometric contractions, raising blood pressure. Therefore, many medical practitioners do not recommend isometric exercises for people older than 35 or those suffering from cardiovascular disease.

When performing **isotonic** exercises, a person exerts muscular force against a movable but constant source of resistance. During isotonic exercise, the muscle shortens and bulges. Isotonic exercises include lifting barbells, performing push-ups, or using weight machines (■ **Figure 11-4**). Instead of describing the exercises as isotonic, some fitness experts prefer to use the term, *dynamic constant external resistance,* because it reflects the nature of these movements more accurately. An exercise is dynamic if the skeleton moves during the activity.

Flexibility

A third aspect of muscular fitness is flexibility. Movement is limited if joints are damaged or muscles cannot extend themselves fully. **Flexibility** refers to the ability to extend muscles, enabling a person to position a movable joint anywhere in its normal range of motion. Flexibility allows people to perform a variety of skeletal movements with ease, including bending, gliding, rotating, and twisting. Many daily tasks require the ability to extend muscles and move joints easily: reaching for an item stored on a high shelf, stretching to pull up a back zipper, or bending to pick up a tennis ball. Having fully extendible muscles and flexible joints enables you to care for yourself and to participate in enjoyable activities.

People can develop flexibility by performing stretching exercises such as those shown in ■ **Figure 11-5**. The proper stretching technique, *static stretching,* involves slowly and fully extending the muscle and nearby joints throughout their natural ranges of motion. When performing a static stretch, gently extend the muscle until you feel tension; if you feel discomfort, relax the muscle slightly. While stretching, breathe normally, do not hold your breath. You should be comfortable holding this position for 15 seconds. Roberts and Wilson (1999) determined that maintaining the stretched position for 15 seconds during 3 separate stretching intervals achieves greater improvements in flexibility of the leg muscles than holding the stretch for only 5 seconds during 9 separate intervals.

Most fitness experts do not recommend *ballistic stretching* activities that involve bouncing. Additionally, you should not use unnatural stretching motions that injure muscles and tendons or extend joints beyond their normal ranges of motion. If pain occurs while stretching, discontinue the activity immediately. The "Analyzing Health-Related Information" activity on p. 256 describes safe alternatives to outdated stretching exercises.

isometric
a type of exercise in which the individual exerts muscular force against a fixed, immovable object.

isotonic a type of exercise in which the individual exerts muscular force against a movable but constant source of resistance.

flexibility the ability to move a muscle to any position in its normal range of motion.

▲**Figure 11-4 Isotonic Contraction.** While performing isotonic exercise, the muscle contracts, shortening in length.

▶Figure 11-5 Stretching to Improve Flexibility.
Flexible muscles enable one to make a variety of skeletal movements to occur with ease. People can develop flexibility by performing stretching exercises such as the: (a) Low Back Stretch, (b) Calf Stretch, (c) Modified Hurdle, (d) Lunge Stretch, (e) Supine Hamstring Stretch, and (f) Groin Stretch.

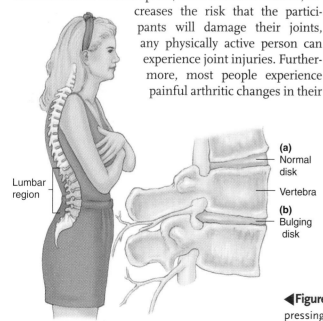

Healthy joints control the ability of muscles to move bones. Joints are susceptible to *dislocation,* that is, becoming displaced by force. Dislocation can result when joints and their supportive tissues are torn or worn after engaging in certain strenuous physical activities. When a joint becomes damaged, the injury reduces its normal range of motion, and movement often becomes painful. Although involvement in certain sports, like American football, increases the risk that the participants will damage their joints, any physically active person can experience joint injuries. Furthermore, most people experience painful arthritic changes in their joints as they age. A later section of this chapter describes injuries that can occur to the muscles, joints, and related structures.

Low Back Pain Eight out of 10 adult Americans encounter low back pain during their lives (Lewis, 1998). As its name implies, low back pain occurs in the lumbar region of the spine (the lower back, above the hips), and it can be disabling (█ **Figure 11-6).** People with this condition are unable to perform activities essential to daily living comfortably, if at all. Furthermore, low back pain is responsible for a significant percentage of worker absenteeism and workers' medical compensation claims.

Weak abdominal, back, and leg muscles as well as worn *spinal disks* often contribute to the development of low back pain. The spinal disks are flexible pads that separate the bones of the spine and act as shock absorbers, protecting the bones from striking each other. As people age, their spinal disks become worn and sometimes bulge out of their normal position. Pounding, twisting, and lifting place physical stress on the spine and are likely responsible for displacing or damaging some disks. Such movements include jogging on a sidewalk, swinging a golf club, carrying

Lumbar region

(a) Normal disk

Vertebra

(b) Bulging disk

◀Figure 11-6 Spinal Disks. (a) Normal disk position; (b) Bulging disk pressing on nerves.

ANALYZING *Health-Related Information*

The accompanying article describes safe alternatives to outdated exercises. Read the article and evaluate it using the model for analyzing health-related information. The main points of the model are noted below; the model is explained fully on pages 12 to 13.

Safe Alternatives for Outdated Exercises

Bryant Stamford, Ph.D.

Stretching and strengthening exercises are, of course, good for you. As a part of a complete fitness program, they help you stay flexible and avoid injury.

Not all exercises, though, are good for all people. Healthy young people can do almost any exercise with little risk. And older people who have exercised all their lives can exercise safely under most circumstances. But middle-aged and older people who have been inactive need to know that some of the old standbys—such as sit-ups and toe touches—can result in injury.

So how do you get the important benefits of stretching and strengthening but avoid the injuries? You need to choose exercises carefully, especially if you are getting up in years and haven't exercised regularly. To help you, potentially troublesome exercises are cited below, with recommended alternatives.

If you aren't very flexible or have had back problems, it's best to consult a doctor before starting an exercise program. You may be more susceptible to injury because of a number of factors, including past injuries, fitness, body type, flexibility, technique, and age.

Regardless of the exercises you select, apply the following principles for maximum safety:

- Use strict technique. Stop using an exercise when physical limitation prevents you from performing it well. Also stop when you are tired.
- Use a slow, deliberate approach. Never bounce: The momentum can make a safe exercise dangerous.
- Hold stretches at least 6 seconds initially, building gradually to 30 seconds, then to 2 minutes. Holding a stretched position is more effective than doing many repetitions.
- Reject the "no pain, no gain" philosophy. Pain means something is wrong, so stop immediately.

Many popular exercises stress the lower back. High on the list is the standing toe touch, which stretches the hamstring muscles at the back of your thighs. This is a bad exercise even if done slowly, but it's even worse if you bounce. A safer option is the one-legged stretch (Figure 1).

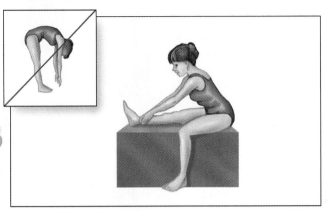

Figure 1: One-legged stretch.

Sit-ups are popular, supposedly for stomach toning. But full sit-ups stress the lower back, and they work the hip muscles more than the abdominal muscles. The "crunch" is better (Figure 2).

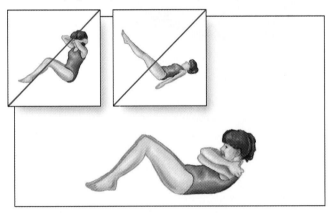

Figure 2: The crunch.

The double-leg lift while lying on your back places tremendous stress on the lower back. Movements of this type cause your back to arch, placing your lower spine and back muscles in a vulnerable position. Scissoring the legs while in this position also places the lower back in a dangerous position. Again, the crunch is a safe alternative.

The donkey kick can also be dangerous, especially to your neck and lower back. It involves being on all fours and lifting one leg as high as possible in a kicking fashion. An alternative to the donkey kick is the rear-thigh lift (Figure 3).

Exercises that involve twisting can be especially dangerous. Windmills, in which you bend over and try to touch one hand to the opposite foot, are very stressful on the lower back. But in some sports—like golf—twisting plays a major part. Therefore, when recovering from a low-back injury, perform mild, pain-free twisting movements under professional supervision.

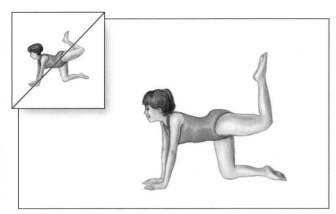

Figure 3: Rear-thigh lift.

Some exercises can harm the neck. Head rolls, in which you roll your head in a complete circle, are very stressful to the upper spine. Do neck stretches instead (Figure 4).

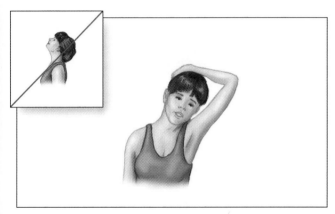

Figure 4: Neck stretch.

People do the yoga plow to stretch upper and lower back muscles by lying on their back and bringing their feet up and over until they touch the floor beyond their head. Unfortunately, this forces the disks in the neck to bulge, risking injury. For the same reason, avoid the "bicycle," in which you lie on your back, raise your hips, and "pedal" your feet. An excellent alternative is the fold-up stretch (Figure 5).

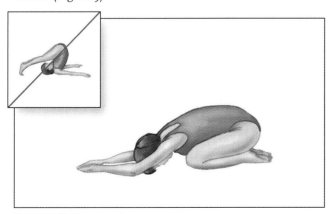

Figure 5: Fold-up stretch.

Full squats or deep knee bends can damage your knees, especially when you bounce out of the squat. Partial squats done slowly and under control are safer.

Jumping jacks involve considerable forces on your legs, particularly the knees. If you land on your toes, the Achilles tendons at the back of your heels bear a major load and could rupture if your legs aren't in the best of shape. Gently running in place provides a lower-impact way to warm up.

Less Risky Business

No matter what your age or physical condition, choosing safer exercise options will lower your risk of injury. And remember that whatever the exercise, good technique is essential.

Remember: This information is not intended as a substitute for medical treatment. Before starting an exercise program, consult a physician.

Dr. Stamford is director of the Health Promotion and Wellness Center and Professor of Allied Health in the School of Medicine at the University of Louisville, Kentucky.

Source : Stamford, B. (1995). How to warm up and cool down your workout. *The Physician and Sportsmedicine*, 23:97–98.

1. Which statements are verifiable facts, which are unverified statements or value claims?
2. What are the credentials of the person who wrote the article? If this information is available, does the author's background and education qualify him as an expert in the topic area?
3. What might be the motives and biases of the person who wrote the article? State reasons for your answer.
4. Which information in the article is relevant to the topic? Which information is irrelevant?
5. Is the source reliable? Does it have a reputation for publishing misinformation?
6. Does the article attack the credibility of conventional scientists or medical authorities?

Based on the above analysis, do you think this article is a reliable source of health-related information? Explain why you would or would not use the information. Summarize your reasons for coming to this conclusion.

a heavy backpack, and picking up a heavy box or a child. Additionally, people who sit for hours in awkward positions, wear high-heeled shoes, or have too much body fat, are susceptible to low back pain, especially if they have weak abdominal muscles.

Although medical experts agree that exercising to strengthen the abdominal, hip, upper leg, and back muscles can prevent or treat many cases of low back pain, they do not agree on which exercises to recommend. Some health-care practitioners recommend aerobic exercises; others promote various stretching activities. ▌**Figure 11-7** shows various exercises designed to strengthen the weak muscles that contribute to low back pain and improve the flexibility of the spinal joints.

You can reduce your risk of developing low back pain by changing some behaviors; for example, lose excess body fat and wear shoes with low or no heels. Additionally, you can often prevent low back pain by following the practices recommended in ▌**Figure 11-8.**

Over-the-counter pain medicines and heat treatments can often relieve low back pain. After the discomfort subsides, people should perform exercises that strengthen the lower back, hip, and abdominal muscles. If the pain persists, however, the person should obtain a complete medical evaluation to determine the source of the pain. In some cases, surgery may be necessary.

Body Composition

As mentioned in Chapter 10, the body contains large quantities of water and relatively small amounts of fat and lean tissues (bones, muscles, and organs). Body composition, the percentages of body weight contributed by lean tissue and fat mass, is a major factor in health. Although a small amount of body fat (about 4% in men and 10% in women) is essential, too much fat contributes to a variety of chronic diseases, including cardiovascular disease, hypertension, and diabetes. Regular exercise builds and maintains muscle mass and helps keep the amount of body fat at healthy levels.

The cells that comprise lean tissues, particularly muscle cells, are more metabolically active than fat cells. Therefore, muscle cells burn more calories than fat cells. By exercising and increasing muscle mass, you can increase your metabolic rate.

Aging muscle cells eventually wear out and die. Unfortunately, the body does not

▼**Figure 11-7 Exercises to Prevent Low Back Pain**

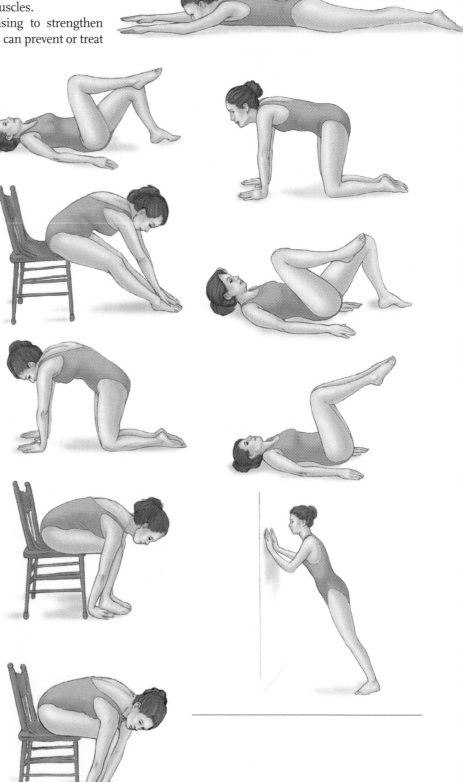

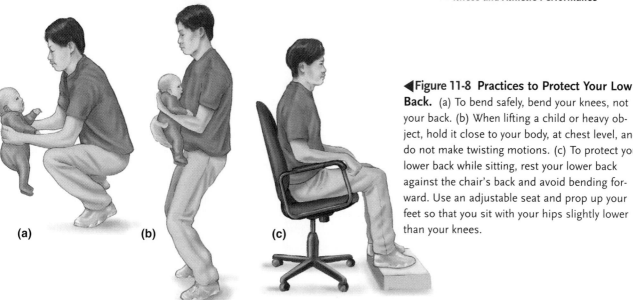

◀Figure 11-8 Practices to Protect Your Low Back. (a) To bend safely, bend your knees, not your back. (b) When lifting a child or heavy object, hold it close to your body, at chest level, and do not make twisting motions. (c) To protect your lower back while sitting, rest your lower back against the chair's back and avoid bending forward. Use an adjustable seat and prop up your feet so that you sit with your hips slightly lower than your knees.

replace these cells. As a result, people usually lose muscle mass and gain fat as they age. Many people think that unused or dying muscle cells can "turn into" fat cells. Muscle cells, however, do not transform themselves into fat cells. A muscle cell is very different from a fat cell; each type of cell has specific structures and functions. Nevertheless, you can preserve more of your muscle mass as you get older if you continue to follow a regular exercise program.

Although regular physical activity can help a person maintain muscle mass while losing weight, "spot" exercising such as performing 100 crunches daily to shrink the abdominal area, does not reduce the amount of fat stored there. During physical activity, fat deposits throughout the body release fatty acids into the bloodstream to supply energy for the vigorously moving muscles. Exercising a specific muscle group, however, can improve physical fitness and appearance by increasing the strength of the exercised muscles and improving their ability to hold in the underlying fat mass.

Engaging in an intense aerobic activity for 30 to 60 minutes daily is an effective method of "burning" body fat for energy. Even performing 30 minutes of moderate-intensity physical activity each day can help you control your weight. For example, walking 2 miles at a brisk pace expends about 200 calories, which is about the number of calories in four chocolate chip cookies (2 1/4" diameter) or 1 plain cake doughnut (3 1/4" diameter). This may seem to be a small amount of energy, but a person who consumes 200 more calories a day than necessary can gain more than 20 lb in a year. As mentioned in the previous chapter, increasing physical activity and eating a sensible calorie-restricted diet is the most effective way to control weight (Rippe & Hess, 1998).

Healthy
LIVING PRACTICES

- Engaging in intense aerobic activity regularly can improve the your cardiorespiratory fitness and the other health-related components of fitness.

- Engaging in regular resistance exercises, such as lifting weights, can increase the size and strength of your muscles.
- Stretching muscles can improve their flexibility.

Physical Fitness and Athletic Performance

www.jbpub.com/healthyliving

The Sports-Related Components of Fitness

Although genetic factors contribute to cardiorespiratory fitness, training is essential for athletes to develop their inborn physical capabilities and compete successfully in sports. The sports-related components of fitness include *speed, power, coordination, agility, balance,* and *reaction time.* Speed is the rate of movement; power is the ability to concentrate a considerable amount of force, usually from a particular group of muscles, when performing work. Coordination is the ability to perform a series of complicated muscular movements in a continuous manner. Agility enables a person to make quick precise movements, such as changing direction, with ease. Balance enables one to maintain a poised upright body position. Reaction time is the time it takes a person to adjust his or her body position to a changing environment. Although athletes often focus on improving the sports-related components of fitness that are associated with their specific sports, they also need to develop the health-related components of fitness.

ergogenic aid a product or device that enhances physical development or performance.

Ergogenic Aids

Ergogenic (work-producing) **aids** include a variety of products such as dietary supplements, stimulant drugs, and mechanical devices that supposedly enhance physical development or performance. Some of these aids are beneficial and harmless, but others are dangerous and illegal. Chromium picolinate, for example, is a popular dietary supplement that some people use to build lean body mass. The results of numerous scientific studies, however, fail to provide evidence that it improves physical performance (Williams, 1999). Furthermore, high doses of chromium picolinate may damage DNA, which increases the risk of cancer (Speetjens et al., 1999). Creatine, an amino acid, is another popular ergogenic aid. Although people can gain small amounts of body weight while taking creatine supplements, scientific studies do not support claims that the amino acid improves endurance or performance; indeed, such supplements may have negative health effects (Demant & Rhodes, 1999; Wardlaw, 1999). ▌ **Table 11-2** lists some dietary supplements, claims about their ergogenic effects, and informa-

anabolic steroids a group of synthetic drugs that have muscle-building effects on the body.

tion concerning whether scientific studies support these claims.

Both men and women may lift weights during their workout sessions to build stronger, more well-defined muscles. Men, however, are capable of developing larger muscles and having greater overall strength because their testosterone levels are higher than those of women. Testosterone is an *anabolic* (tissue-building) hormone.

Some men and women abuse **anabolic steroids**—a group of synthetic substances that are chemically related to testosterone—or other chemicals that are promoted for their muscle-building properties. These drugs can have serious irreversible effects on the body (▌ **Figure 11-9).** Male anabolic steroid users often experience shrunken testicles and infertility. Women who use these drugs may become bald, grow facial hair, and experience menstrual irregulari-

Table 11-2	**Dietary Supplements as Ergogenic Aids**	
Aid	**Claim**	**Current Findings**
Caffeine	Improves strength Enhances fat metabolism	Increases alertness, but at high doses causes nervousness; raises free fatty-acid levels during exercise; might provide modest improvement of performance.
Creatine	Enhances release of energy during exercise	May enhance performance during resistance exercise; more research is needed.
Carnitine	Enhances fat metabolism	No significant improvement in performance, but more research is needed.
Wheat-germ oil	Increases oxygen uptake by cells, improving stamina	Results of well-designed studies do not support ergogenic claims.
Lecithin and choline	Increase production of a neurotransmitter, resulting in more muscular strength	Results of well-designed studies do not support ergogenic claims.
Omega-3 fatty acids	Makes blood flow better, stimulates muscle growth	Results of well-designed studies do not support ergogenic claims; large doses may increase the risk of stroke.
Spirulina, brewer's yeast, enzymes, and DNA supplements	General performance-enhancing effects	Results of well-designed studies do not support ergogenic claims; large doses of amino acids can inhibit amino acid absorption and increase water requirement.
CoQ_{10} (coenzyme Q or ubiquinone)	Improves heart function	Results of well-designed studies do not show consistent improvement in performance; more research is needed. Long-term safety is unknown.
Bee pollen	Shortens recovery time	Results of well-designed studies do not support ergogenic claims; may cause allergic responses in some individuals.
Ginseng	Increases body's resistance to excessive physical and psychological stress	Results of well-designed studies do not support ergogenic claims; many brands contain little or no active compounds from the herb.

Male

Premature balding
Severe acne, greasy
   skin
Nausea, vomiting
Sleep disturbances
More distractible,
   aggressive, hostile,
   and irritable

Blood pressure increases
HDL levels decline, increasing
   the risk of heart disease
Risk of liver tumors and
   liver failure increases

Testosterone secretion declines
Sperm production
   declines
Testicles shrink

Female

Premature balding
Severe acne, greasy skin
Nausea, vomiting
Sleep disturbances
More distractible, aggressive,
   hostile, and irritable
Body hair, including
   facial hair, increases

Blood pressure increases
Breasts shrink
HDL levels decline, increasing
   the risk of heart disease
Risk of liver tumors and
   liver failure increases

Ovaries fail to function
properly resulting in
menstrual irregularities

▲**Figure 11-9 Possible Effects of Anabolic Steroids on the Body.** To increase their muscle mass, some men and women abuse anabolic steroids or other chemicals that are promoted for their muscle-building properties. These drugs can have serious irreversible effects on the body.

ties. Anabolic steroids increase the risks of developing heart and kidney diseases, certain cancers, and liver tumors. In some cases, damage to the liver or kidneys is so severe that death occurs. Additionally, anabolic steroids can affect personality. People who abuse anabolic steroids may act more aggressive than usual. Regular resistance exercise is the only safe way to increase the size and strength of a muscle.

Healthy
LIVING PRACTICES

- Do not use anabolic steroids to build your muscles; they can be very harmful.

Exercising for Health

People often engage in a particular *type* of exercise because of its healthful benefits. Aerobic activities increase cardiorespiratory fitness and muscular endurance. Although isometric and isotonic exercises develop muscular strength, these activities may not increase cardiorespiratory fitness significantly. Many people combine aerobic and muscle-strengthening activities in their daily workouts to improve their overall physical condition; others perform isotonic and aerobic workouts on alternate days. For example, one day's workout session would be devoted to weight-lifting; the following day's session would involve race-walking.

The frequency, duration, and intensity of exercise also influence the degree of health benefits a person derives from it. Exercise *frequency* is the number of times an individual exercises, usually reported as the number of days or exercise sessions in a week. People who exercise at least three times a week generally experience more rapid improvements to their overall fitness than people who exercise less often.

The *duration* of exercise refers to the total time the person is physically active during each exercise session. For example, people who jog for 40 minutes, 3 days a week, experience more cardiorespiratory benefits than those who jog for 10 minutes, 3 days a week. Sedentary people can develop cardiorespiratory fitness if they engage in an aerobic exercise program that gradually increases the duration of the activity, usually over several weeks.

The *intensity* of an exercise reflects the amount of physical exertion a person uses while performing the activity. Fitness experts use several methods to estimate the intensity of exercise, including the rate of oxygen consumption during exercise, heart rate, and personal perceptions of physical exertion. For the average person, playing nine holes of golf while using a power golf cart or bowling for 30 minutes are light activities; playing tennis or walking briskly for a half-hour are moderate activities; and jogging for 6 miles or playing racquetball for 30 minutes are intense activities (see Table 11-1).

The frequency, duration, and intensity of aerobic physical activities influence fitness. For example, you can exercise intensely for 20 minutes or moderately for 30 minutes and achieve similar cardiorespiratory benefits.

The Exercise Session

People should *warm up* before and *cool down (warm down)* after intense exercise. Warming up reduces the physical stress that vigorous exercise can place on the body. While warming up, the person's skeletal muscles become warm and extend easily, joints become more flexible, and heart and breathing rates increase gradually. Cooling down facilitates the circulation of blood, especially in the leg muscles, enabling the body to recover from intense physical activity. Warming up and cooling down may reduce the likelihood of injuries (Williams, 1999).

To warm up the entire body before engaging in a vigorous physical activity, you can walk at an easy pace, then gradually increase your speed until you have walked for 5 to 10 minutes. At this point, your muscles should be warm enough to perform stretching exercises such as those shown in Figure 11-5. Stretching muscles before the warm-up session is usually not recommended because extending "cold" muscles may injure them.

After stretching, many persons perform *active, task-specific* activities to warm up specific muscles. For example, a jogger would jog slowly for a few minutes, gradually increasing the pace until reaching his or her usual training speed.

Warming up before exercising is essential for people with heart disease. Abnormal functioning of the heart may occur when sedentary, middle-aged people begin to exercise suddenly without warming up. Warm-up activities increase the blood flow to the heart gradually, reducing the risk of heart attack during physical exertion.

After exercising vigorously, people should cool down by gradually reducing the intensity of their activity and by stretching. Many types of strenuous exercise increase the blood supply to the leg muscles; suddenly stopping these intense muscular movements can cause blood to accumulate in the leg veins, which can reduce the blood flow to the brain, causing dizziness, faintness, or loss of consciousness. Cooling down by engaging in 5 to 10 minutes of light exercise gradually decreases the blood flow to the leg muscles. ▌ Figure 11-10 illustrates a 50-minute workout session that consists of 10 minutes of warm-up activities, 30 minutes of jogging, and 10 minutes of cool-down exercises.

Exercise Danger Signs

Exercise improves the functioning of the heart and reduces the risk of heart disease. Sudden and intense physical exertion, however, can strain the heart, especially the

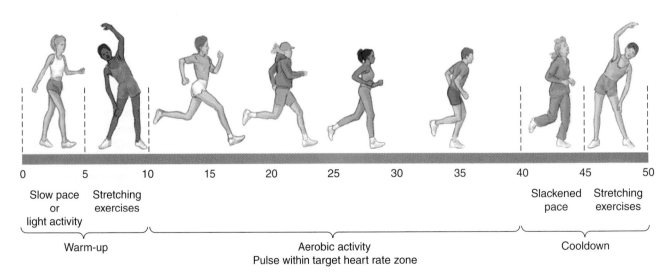

| 0 | 5 | 10 | 15 | 20 | 25 | 30 | 35 | 40 | 45 | 50 |

Slow pace or light activity — Stretching exercises

Slackened pace — Stretching exercises

Warm-up

Aerobic activity
Pulse within target heart rate zone

Cooldown

▲**Figure 11-10 A Suggested Workout Session.** A reasonable 50-minute workout session may consist of 10 minutes of warm-up activities, 30 minutes of jogging, and 10 minutes of cool-down exercises.

heart of an unfit individual or someone with cardiovascular disease.

To reduce the risk of overtaxing your cardiovascular system during vigorous exercise, warm up first, then exercise at a reduced intensity level for about 10 to 15 minutes. Keep records of your activity level and any discomfort that you experience. Discontinue the activity and consult a health-care practitioner if any of the following signs or symptoms of heart disease occur during or after exercising:

- Heart abnormalities, such as irregular rhythms, a feeling that your heart is pounding in your throat, or fluttering in your chest
- Pain or pressure in your chest, throat, or arms
- Shortness of breath, dizziness, sudden loss of coordination, cold sweating, or fainting

Developing a Personal Fitness Program

A basic personal physical fitness program should include activities that enhance cardiorespiratory fitness, muscular strength and endurance, and flexibility. To develop an effective program, determine your needs, interests, and limitations (Holly & Shaffrath, 1998). Answering the following questions can help you accomplish this step:

- How can I schedule my day's activities so I have time to exercise?
- Which physical activities am I most likely to enjoy and practice regularly for the rest of my life?
- Do I want to develop or enhance specific sports-related skills?
- Would I rather work out alone or with others?
- Where will I exercise?
- Do I have physical limitations that require special equipment or rule out certain activities?

The "Changing Health Habits" activity for this chapter can help you determine if you are ready to improve your level of physical fitness (see student workbook).

After completing the first step, make a list of your general fitness goals. One of them should be to enhance the health-related components of fitness, for example, improving your cardiorespiratory fitness or flexibility. Other goals may be changing your appearance or building agility. Although your list may include several goals, choose 1 or 2 to work on at a time.

At this point, you need to choose enjoyable physical activities that will help you meet your fitness goals. As mentioned earlier, aerobic exercise is necessary for achieving cardiorespiratory fitness. Resistance training is important for increasing lean body mass and maintaining muscular strength and endurance. Warm-up and cool-down stretching exercises can improve range of motion. Faculty who conduct personal fitness classes in the physical education department at your college can answer your questions concerning the need for special equipment or how to perform activities safely.

If you are overweight or have been sedentary, give your body time to adapt to the fitness program. For the first 2 weeks, do not try to exercise at a high intensity level or for more than 15 minutes. Some people keep an exercise log or diary to track their progress. Stop when you experience signs of exercise intolerance, such as pain or breathlessness, and note this in your log. A common problem encountered by enthusiastic but out-of-shape people is trying to do too much too soon.

When you do not experience fatigue or discomfort as a result of the activity, you are ready to move on to the improvement stage of the program. By gradually increasing the intensity and duration of your physical activity, you can progressively overload your muscles and achieve your fitness goals. For example, add 5 minutes to the time of your aerobic workout each week, until you are exercising for 45 to 60 minutes at a time. If you are walking at 2 mph, gradually increase the pace until you are able to walk between 3 and 4 mph without effort. To acquire the fitness benefits of aerobic exercise, a person must engage in the activity for at least 10 minutes at a time, at least 2 days a week, and at a minimum of 55% to 64% of his or her maximum heart rate (Pollock et al., 1998). However, engaging in aerobic exercise more often, for longer periods, and at higher intensity levels develops much higher degrees of fitness.

You can enhance muscular size and strength with a weight-lifting program that gradually overcomes the resistance of progressively heavier weights. As your muscles adapt to the workload, you should be able to develop strength by adding resistance while performing fewer repetitions. After each bout of heavy training, muscles engaged in resistance exercises need about 48 hours to recover, to repair themselves and to grow (Williams, 1999). Thus, experts often recommend alternating the days of the week in which you perform cardiorespiratory and strength training activities. ▌ **Table 11-3** shows a sample aerobic and weight resistance program that includes stretching exercises. By the end of 6 months, you should be ready to move on to the maintenance stage of the program.

A major feature of the maintenance stage of your fitness program is sustaining your fitness level and interest. Adding new activities prevents boredom with the workout program and develops different muscle groups or skills. **Cross-training,** incorporating a variety of aerobic activities into a fitness program, is an excellent way to maintain enthusiasm and interest. Working out in different environments can also add interest. Walking in parks or hiking on trails, for example, can be more interesting than walking around indoor tracks. By working out with friends or family members, you can enhance your physical as well as social health.

cross-training incorporating a variety of aerobic activities into a fitness program.

Table 11-3 — A Sample Four-Week Combined Workout Program

Week 1	Warm Up* (min.)	Workout	Cool Down* (min.)	Week 3	Warm Up* (min.)	Workout	Cool Down* (min.)
Monday	5 to 10	Brisk walking 15 min.	5 to 10	Monday	5 to 10	Brisk walking 25 min.	5 to 10
Tuesday	5 to 10	Resistance training, beginning load Reps: 5 Sets: 4	5 to 10	Tuesday	5 to 10	Resistance training, beginning load Reps: 5 Sets: 4	5 to 10
Wednesday	5 to 10	Brisk walking 15 min.	5 to 10	Wednesday	5 to 10	Brisk walking 25 min.	5 to 10
Thursday	5 to 10	Resistance training, beginning load Reps: 5 Sets: 4	5 to 10	Thursday	5 to 10	Resistance training, beginning load Reps: 5 Sets: 4	5 to 10
Friday	5 to 10	Brisk walking 15 min.	5 to 10	Friday	5 to 10	Brisk walking 25 min.	5 to 10
Saturday	5 to 10	Resistance training, beginning load Reps: 5 Sets: 4	5 to 10	Saturday	5 to 10	Resistance training, beginning load Reps: 5 Sets: 4	5 to 10
Sunday	5 to 10	Brisk walking 15 min.	5 to 10	Sunday	5 to 10	Brisk walking 25 min.	5 to 10

Week 2	Warm Up* (min.)	Workout	Cool Down* (min.)	Week 4	Warm Up* (min.)	Workout	Cool Down* (min.)
Monday	5 to 10	Brisk walking 20 min.	5 to 10	Monday	5 to 10	Brisk walking 30 min.	5 to 10
Tuesday	5 to 10	Resistance training, beginning load Reps: 5 Sets: 4	5 to 10	Tuesday	5 to 10	Resistance training, beginning load Reps: 10 Sets: 4	5 to 10
Wednesday	5 to 10	Brisk walking 20 min.	5 to 10	Wednesday	5 to 10	Brisk walking 30 min.	5 to 10
Thursday	5 to 10	Resistance training, beginning load Reps: 5 Sets: 4	5 to 10	Thursday	5 to 10	Resistance training, beginning load Reps: 10 Sets: 4	5 to 10
Friday	5 to 10	Brisk walking 20 min.	5 to 10	Friday	5 to 10	Brisk walking 30 min.	5 to 10
Saturday	5 to 10	Resistance training, beginning load Reps: 5 Sets: 4	5 to 10	Saturday	5 to 10	Resistance training, beginning load Reps: 10 Sets: 4	5 to 10
Sunday	5 to 10	Brisk walking 20 min.	5 to 10	Sunday	5 to 10	Brisk walking 30 min.	5 to 10

*Slow walking and stretching

Once people achieve high degrees of physical fitness, they need to continue exercising to maintain the healthful benefits gained during their training program. Sometimes physically fit individuals discontinue intensive regular exercise regimens for a variety of reasons, such as experiencing injuries or losing motivation. Detraining can occur within a couple of weeks after exercise sessions are discontinued. Even if they have to reduce the frequency of their exercise sessions, people can usually maintain their high level of physical fitness, as long as they do not stop working out.

Healthy
LIVING PRACTICES

- When you perform isometric or isotonic exercises to increase muscular strength, also engage in aerobic exercises to enhance your cardiorespiratory fitness.
- You can enhance your muscular strength, muscular endurance, and flexibility by increasing the frequency, duration, and intensity of your exercise sessions.
- If you have heart disease or other serious chronic conditions, you are out-of-shape, or you are over 40 years of age, obtain the approval of a qualified health-care practitioner before beginning an exercise program, especially if the program includes aerobic activities.

Preventing and Managing Exercise Injuries

Everyone should be concerned about personal safety while exercising. People should check their exercise equipment for defects and wear the proper clothing, shoes, and protective gear for the activity. Additionally, people should use some common sense about when and where they exercise. Bicyclists and joggers, for example, should obey traffic signals and avoid busy roads that have narrow or rocky shoulders. Engaging in physical activity outdoors at night is especially dangerous; people should wear clothing with reflective strips to become more visible.

Although engaging in regular physical activity is essential for optimal health, some activities are likely to result in musculoskeletal injuries. Suddenly raising the intensity level or duration of a physical activity may damage muscles or supportive tissues or aggravate existing injuries. Physically active people can use some general precautions to minimize their risk of musculoskeletal injury. Sudden, awkward movements are likely to injure muscles, tendons, and joints; therefore, people should avoid physical activities that involve exaggerated twisting or high-impact movements, like jumping.

Strains and Sprains

Almost everyone who is physically active has experienced muscle soreness or musculoskeletal injuries such as strains and sprains. Although there are no clear clinical definitions for strain or sprain, a **strain** generally refers to the damage that a muscle or tendon sustains when overextended rapidly. A **sprain** usually refers to a damaged ligament. Although these two types of injuries often occur together, a sprain tends to be more serious than a strain. The sprained ligament may be partially or completely torn, and the nearby muscle, joint, or bones may be damaged; therefore, severe sprains generally require immediate medical attention.

RICE, the acronym for rest, ice, compression, and elevation, is often effective for treating strains and sprains.

- *Rest* can reduce the pain, but light exercise or activity that uses the injured muscles is usually recommended, as long as the discomfort is tolerable.
- *Ice* treatments should be limited to 20-minute sessions and can be repeated every 2 hours (while the injured person is awake) for 2 to 3 days. Do not place ice directly on the skin.
- *Compression,* an external source of pressure, can prevent swelling. Apply a pressure bandage on the injury to produce compression. Make sure the bandage is not tight enough to interfere with circulation.
- *Elevation* also reduces swelling. When an injured limb is elevated, gravity helps the veins of the limb return blood to the heart, reducing the amount of blood and other fluids that accumulates in the damaged tissue.

With RICE and over-the-counter pain medicines, muscle soreness usually disappears within a day or two. If an injured area does not improve with RICE and the pain persists or worsens, consult a physician.

Temperature-Related Injuries

When exercising in sunny weather, the body gains heat from the environment and from its active muscles. To cool itself, the body perspires heavily, transferring heat to the environment. *Dehydration* (lack of body water) can occur if a person does not replace the fluid lost by perspiration. The muscles of a person suffering from dehydation are less able to work efficiently. It is essential that people replace the water lost in sweat by consuming adequate amounts of fluids, especially plain water. Soups, fruits, vegetables, and noncaffeinated nonalcoholic drinks contribute water to the diet also.

Hyperthermia, higher than normal body temperature, often results from dehydration. If a person becomes hot and dehydrated, heat cramps, heat exhaustion, or heat

sprain generally refers to an injured ligament.

strain generally refers to an injured muscle or tendon.

hyperthermia a condition that occurs when body temperature rises above the normal range.

stroke may occur. The signs and symptoms of **heat cramps** include muscular tightening and pain in the limbs or abdomen. The affected individual usually recovers after stopping the activity, resting in a shady area, stretching the cramped muscles, and drinking several ounces of water. After recovering, this person should not exercise for the remainder of the day.

Heat exhaustion and **heatstroke** are more serious conditions than heat cramps. People suffering from heat exhaustion have pale and clammy skin; sweat profusely; and feel nauseated, tired, and weak. They need to move to a cooler area and drink plenty of cool water. If heat exhaustion is not recognized and treated, heatstroke can develop. The signs and symptoms of heatstroke include hot, dry, reddened skin; rapid pulse; fever; and loss of consciousness. Heatstroke is a life-threatening emergency; victims should be removed from the heat and receive immediate medical attention.

When the weather is hot and humid, avoid exerting yourself outdoors during the hottest time of the day. If you must be outdoors when it is hot, follow a few precautions to reduce the likelihood of heat-related injury. Two hours before exercising, drink about 16 oz. of water; during exercise, drink 4 to 8 oz. of water every 15 to 20 minutes (Convertino et al., 1996). Even if you are not thirsty, drink plenty of water before, during, and after physical activity. Thirst is *not* a good indicator of body fluid status; many people do not feel thirsty until they are already dehydrated and have lost 2% of their body weight as water (Kleiner, 1999).

When the weather first becomes hot, individuals should begin working or exercising outdoors at a reduced intensity, then gradually increase the intensity over a 2-week period to become *acclimatized,* that is, physically adjusted to the extreme temperature change. Wearing light-colored, loose clothing in sunny, hot, and humid weather helps people stay comfortable because light colors reflect sunlight and loose clothing allows perspiration to evaporate more easily.

People who perspire excessively can lose considerable amounts of sodium chloride in their sweat. Most of these individuals can consume more water, fruit juices, and foods to replace the lost nutrients. While engaging in strenuous exercise that lasts an hour or more, people can consume sports drinks for fluid replacement (Convertino et al., 1996). In addition to water, these drinks contain sodium chloride and energy-supplying carbohydrate. Most physically active people do not need to take salt tablets (Williams, 1999). Individuals should not consume bever-

ages that contain caffeine or alcohol to replenish body fluids, because these substances are *diuretics.* A diuretic increases urine production; therefore, people lose even more body water when they drink beverages containing these substances.

Participating in outdoor activities during the winter months increases the risk of cold injury. Exposed to cold temperatures, the body reduces its blood flow to the skin, conserving body heat. The chilled person shivers and feels tingling, numbness, or burning in exposed skin or body parts. *Frostbite* occurs when ice crystals form in the deeper tissues of the skin, damaging them. Blood flow to the affected area slows, causing clots to form. Unable to obtain oxygen and nutrients, the tissue dies. The damage may be so extensive that the frostbitten areas must be amputated. A person's fingers, toes, nose, ears, and face are most susceptible to frostbite, but any exposed skin can become frostbitten. Frostbite requires immediate and proper medical treatment. Avoid rubbing frostbitten skin because it can further damage cold tissues. To prevent frostbite, people need to wear gloves or mittens, thick socks, hats that can be pulled down over the ears, and scarves when outdoors in cold weather.

Hypothermia occurs when the body's core temperature drops below 95° F (Kanzenbach & Dexter, 1999). (You use a rectal thermometer to measure core body temperature.) As body temperature declines, the person shivers, feels tired, displays poor judgment, acts disoriented, and eventually loses consciousness. Death can occur when the core temperature falls below 82° F, and breathing and circulation are too weak to support life.

As in cases of frostbite, hypothermia requires prompt medical treatment. It is important to shelter people suffering from hypothermia from the cold and remove their wet clothing. Covering them in dry blankets keeps them warm until they can be taken to a hospital. To protect against hypothermia, wear a hat and layers of warm, dry clothing.

heat cramps in a dehydrated and hot person the signs and symptoms of heat cramps include muscular tightening and pain in the limbs or abdomen.

heat exhaustion extreme fatigue that results from exercise or work in hot temperatures.

heatstroke a life-threatening condition that can occur when people exercise or work in hot temperatures.

hypothermia a condition that occurs when the body's core temperature drops below 95° F.

Healthy LIVING PRACTICES

- If you have musculoskeletal injuries, use RICE as treatment. If pain and swelling persists, contact your health-care practitioner.
- If you develop heat cramps or heat exhaustion while working or exercising, stop the activity immediately, get out of the heat, and drink plenty of water.
- If you plan to exercise or work in hot conditions, wear loose light clothing and take an ample supply of water, fruit juices, or sports drinks with you.
- When you exercise or work in cold conditions, protect yourself against hypothermia and frostbite by wearing layers of warm dry clothing, a hat or ski mask, gloves or mittens, and thick socks.

- Avoid drinking beverages that contain alcohol or caffeine to replace body water that is lost during exercise or exposure to hot temperatures.

Active for a Lifetime

People are more likely to engage in physical activity regularly if they enjoy it, recognize the health benefits, and make it a priority. Some sedentary people dislike vigorous exercise because they do not feel competent performing the activity; others may associate the activity with sweating, strain, and pain. Adults who enjoy being physically active make exercise an integral part of their daily routines.

Many people find it easier to be physically active while in college than when they are out of school and working full-time. In a nationwide survey, nearly 40% of college students reported participating in vigorous physical activities during the week prior to the survey (Youth Risk, 1997). Male students were more likely to engage in vigorous physical activity than female students, and students between 18 and 24 years old were more active than students 25 years of age and older. Additionally, black students were more likely than white students to engage in moderate physical activities and muscle-strengthening exercises.

Most college and university campuses have physical education departments that offer a variety of sports and fitness courses; some of these departments have well-equipped fitness centers. Additionally, the staff of the physical education department may conduct intramural athletic programs that are open to students, and at certain times, they may open the college's gyms and athletic fields to all students. While in school, students should take advantage of the fitness opportunities available on their college or university campuses.

After leaving college, individuals can continue to build or maintain their fitness level by exercising at home or by joining fitness centers or clubs. Although large resistance exercise machines are highly effective for building muscular strength, their expense and size make them unlikely to be found in most homes. However, you can buy barbells and smaller handheld weights at most department or sporting goods stores for use at home. To improve cardiorespiratory fitness, rowing machines, stationary bikes, and cross-country skiing machines can be purchased for home fitness centers. Before buying any large piece of fitness equipment, you should visit a gym or fitness club to test the machine and discuss its value with qualified fitness experts. For additional information, check popular consumer magazines that occasionally rate exercise equipment.

Building or maintaining physical fitness does not require a long-term commitment with a gym or fitness club, but many people enjoy the social aspects of exercising at these facilities. The quality and cost of gyms and fitness clubs vary, so you may want to consider the points listed in the "Consumer Health" feature "Choosing a Fitness Center" before joining one.

Unless you have a job that requires physical exertion or you work at a company that provides a worksite fitness center for its employees, you need to find ways to be more

Con$umer Health | Choosing a Fitness Center

Every year millions of Americans join health clubs, gyms, and exercise and fitness centers. Thousands of these people complain about their membership to states' attorneys general, Better Business Bureaus, and other consumer protection groups. The following tips can help you avoid becoming another dissatisfied health and fitness center consumer:

- Determine if you can afford to join the center.
- Inspect the center for cleanliness, type and quality of equipment, and especially, staff qualifications. Ask if staff are certified as aerobics instructors, weight trainers, or athletic trainers.

Are they trained in cardiopulmonary resuscitation (CPR) and first aid?

- Ask current members if they are satisfied with the center's facilities; and why or why not.
- Ask your local Better Business Bureau the number and nature of complaints against the organization.
- Ask for a trial period to use the facilities before joining.
- Never sign a contract under pressure at the center. Many centers use confusing and misleading advertising, including prizes or special short-term offers to spark your interest. Once you are in the facility, aggressive sales

staff engage in high-pressure sales tactics to convince you to sign a contract.

- Before signing, take a few days to read the contract carefully. Make certain that you understand the details concerning payment options, membership restrictions, cancellation terms, and the membership period. If a staff member makes additional promises, have the individual record it in writing, on the contract.

www.jbpub.com/healthyliving

physically active at work. If your office building has stairways, climb the stairs rather than ride the elevators. Instead of eating lunches in restaurants, bring your lunches from home to eat at your desk, and use the remaining time to go outside and walk. You might consider buying two pairs of athletic shoes—one for your office and one for home. You may like walking with others better than walking alone; ask someone to walk with you. Colleagues, spouses, or friends can provide the valuable social support you may need to maintain your motivation to exercise at work or home.

Like many people, you may want to be more active, but you cannot seem to find the time to exercise. It is important to remember that you do not have to spend hours each day engaging in strenuous exercises to improve your health. Even 10 to 20 minutes of vigorous aerobic activity can boost your fitness level. Determine how you spend your leisure time. Each day, how much time do you spend engaging in sedentary activities such as watching TV, communicating with others in a chat room, or playing computer games? Can you set aside at least 30 minutes each day to engage in some moderately intense physical activities?

Many aerobic activities do not require extensive time, complex skills, or special and costly equipment. For example, people can exercise by dancing to music or videos, or by performing tai chi in the privacy of their homes. The main objective is to select physical activities that you enjoy and can perform regularly for the rest of your life

As mentioned earlier, if you are out-of-shape or older than 40 years, you should consult a physician before beginning a physical fitness program that includes moderate-intensity activities. This precautionary measure can determine whether you have serious health problems. If you have a chronic condition, consult your physician for an exercise prescription. Most adults can begin a regular walking program to get into shape; after a few weeks, they can add more intense forms of physical activity to boost their cardiorespiratory fitness.

Healthy LIVING PRACTICES

- To become physically fit or to maintain a high degree of fitness, design a personal fitness program that includes activities that you enjoy and can perform regularly while you are in college and throughout your lifetime.
- If you have a sedentary job, find ways to become more physically active at work, such as walking some of the way to work, using the stairs instead of elevators, and walking during lunchtime.

www.jbpub.com/healthyliving

a c r o s s the **lifespan**

Physical Fitness

The health habits that a person adopts in childhood, including physical and sports activities, are likely to be practiced and enjoyed for a lifetime. Children who are physically active have better measures of all health-related fitness components than those who are sedentary. Since sedentary lifestyles are associated with heart disease in adults, many health-care practitioners are concerned that children may begin to develop this disease, especially if they do not engage in physical activities regularly. To improve the overall health and well-being of children, parents and schools need to find ways to encourage youngsters who are physically unfit to increase their fitness levels.

Another major concern of health and fitness experts is the proportion of American children and adolescents who spend a considerable amount of time engaged in sedentary activities, such as playing computer games or viewing television. Between 1991 and 1995, the percentage of high school students who participated daily in physical education classes declined by more than 40% (USDHHS, 1996). By 1995, only 25% of American high school students were enrolled in daily physical education classes. More research is needed to determine the long-term effects of childhood and adolescent activity habits on their future health.

Regular exercise is just as important during pregnancy as in the other times of a woman's life. Healthy, physically fit women can continue engaging in a program of mild to moderate physical activity throughout their pregnancies (Artal, 1999). If their physicians approve, women who jogged or ran before pregnancy can usually continue to do so during pregnancy. However, the ability to engage comfortably and safely in many physical activities often becomes limited in the latter stage of pregnancy. During this time, a woman's weight usually increases dramatically, especially in the center and front part of her body. As a result, she often feels awkward while engaging in many physical activities and her risk of injury increases.

A pregnant woman should avoid certain activities if they pose a risk to her health and that of her developing fetus. Physical activities that might result in injuries to the abdominal area and exhaustive exercises such as scuba diving, contact sports, heavy weight lifting, or competitive events are not recommended for pregnant women. Additionally, exercising while lying down may interfere with blood flow to the uterus and is not recommended. It is important for pregnant women to be well hydrated before, during, and after exercise and to avoid overheating. Physicians do not recommend that pregnant women exercise in hot humid conditions or use hot tubs and saunas because

▼**Figure 11-11 Exercising During Pregnancy.** If their physicians approve, many physically fit women can continue their usual exercise regimen throughout their pregnancy.

these activities can raise the woman's body temperature, endangering the fetus.

It is a good idea for pregnant women to discuss their physical activity with their physicians. Nearly all pregnant women can safely walk, swim, or ride a stationary bicycle (█ **Figure 11-11**). Those who are obese or severely underweight, are sedentary, or have histories of health problems should consult their physicians before following an exercise program.

As people age, they experience numerous changes that indicate a decline in their physical conditions. For example, the maximum heart rates of elderly people are lower during exercise, and their hearts pump less blood with each beat. Compared to when they were young adults, most aged persons have more body fat. Although exercise training of the elderly does not prevent these physical changes, it can limit the extent of the decline.

Most Americans become less active as they age. By 75 years of age, about 33% of men and 50% of women do not engage in exercise (USDHHS, 1996). It is important for people to continue exercising as they age. Physically fit aged persons usually have healthier hearts and body compositions than unfit persons of the same age. Even by performing light physical activities regularly, elderly people can reduce their blood pressure, resting heart rate, and body mass index (Mensink et al., 1999). Additionally, physical activity helps maintain or improve the flexibility of joints as well as the strength and endurance of muscles. The results of some studies suggest that regular exercise improves the cognitive functioning and mood of elderly people (Mazzeo et al., 1998). Older adults can enjoy the social aspects of exercising by joining mall-walking, dancing, or fitness classes that are designed for the elderly (█ **Figure 11-12**).

People lose their ability to maintain their balance as they age, which increases their risk of falling (Mazzeo et al., 1998). A minor fall that would not injure a healthy 23-year-old person can have dire consequences for a frail 85-year-old one. An elderly person who falls is more likely to suffer a disabling bone fracture or die from the injury than a younger person. Aged people who survive falls often experience some degree of immobility and pain that limits their ability to care for themselves and interact socially. By participating in exercise classes that improve balance and muscular strength, elderly people can reduce their risk of falls (Mazzeo et al., 1998). The "Diversity in Health" essay on page 270 describes the benefits of *tai chi,* a form of martial arts that helps some elderly people become healthier.

It is never too late to become physically fit. By increasing physical activity, even very old people can gain healthful benefits such as improved muscular strength and endurance, flexibility, and psychological well-being. To achieve these benefits, participation in strenuous formal exercise programs is not necessary; most elderly people can improve their overall health by engaging in light-to-moderate physical activities regularly such as walking, gardening, or mall-walking every day.

Healthy
█ LIVING PRACTICES █

- If you have children, consider limiting the amount of time they spend watching television or playing computer games. Encourage your children to be physically active.
- If you are pregnant, consult your health-care practitioner to determine which physical activities are safe to perform during this time.
- As you age, exercise regularly and be physically active.

▲**Figure 11-12 Exercise Is for Everyone.** Older adults can enjoy the social aspects of exercising in fitness classes.

DIVERSITY in Health | New Interest in an Ancient Approach to Fitness

In motion
all parts of the body must be
light,
nimble,
and strung together.

From T'ai chi ch'uan
by Chang San-feng (1279–1386 A.D.)

To people outside of China, it may seem difficult to believe that the graceful dancelike movements of t'ai chi chu'uan (tie-JEE-chwahn), commonly called "tai chi," is a form of exercise. Unlike Western physical activities that often require rapid, forceful, and extensive motions, tai chi involves gentle gliding muscular movements that do not overextend body parts. According to its promoters, tai chi promotes good health, physical fitness, and longevity.

The exact origins of traditional tai chi are unknown. For more than 2000 years, Chinese have practiced qigong (ch'i-kung), a series of simple exercises that focus on breathing, maintaining certain body postures, and relaxing. These features are also emphasized in tai chi. In fact, the word *chi* means "breath energy." Thus, the ancient practice of qigong may have set the stage for the development of tai chi.

In addition to qigong, the Chinese martial arts probably contributed to the development of tai chi ch'uan. Ch'uan means "the joy of fighting with bare fists." Originally tai chi ch'uan may have been used for self-defense or boxing. However, a major principle of tai chi ch'uan is to overcome brute force and harshness with softness, gentleness, and smoothness.

Chang San-feng, the thirteenth century Taoist priest whose writing appears above, is usually credited with creating tai chi. Taoism is an ancient Chinese religion and philosophy that emphasizes living in harmony with nature. To Taoists, the harmonious functioning of the body is important if one is to achieve good health and live a long life. Today, tai chi is growing in popularity with Western exercise enthusiasts who are interested in achieving its potential health benefits (⬛ Figure 11-C). Promoters of tai chi claim that the physical exercises improve digestion and circulation, as well as increase alertness. People who practice tai chi often report that the exercises are relaxing (see Chapter 3).

While performing the specific sequential exercises, the upper part of the body remains loose; the knees are slightly bent, but firmly supporting the weight of the body. Movements flow from one to another. Opposing arms and legs move in harmony; for example, as one arm gracefully arches upward, the other moves down in the same fashion. According to those who teach tai chi, if one body part does not follow another, the body is not in harmony. The series of vertical and horizontal movements continue until the sequence of exercises has been completed.

An important aspect of tai chi is mental concentration. As individuals engage in these exercises, they focus their attention on the sensations associated with the sequential movements; such attention requires silence.

As with other physical activities, practicing tai chi every day improves flexibility, muscular strength, and balance. Since tai chi does not require rapid, forceful muscular movements, it is a beneficial form of physical activity for elderly people or anyone who cannot engage in aerobic exercises.

A specially trained instructor is necessary to teach the proper posture, sequences of coordinated movements, and breathing technique of tai chi. Therefore, if you are interested in learning the exercises, check with the physical education department at your college or university to see if it offers tai chi instruction. Fitness centers in your community such as the YMCA might also offer tai chi classes.

Source: Lie, F. T. (1988). *T'ai chi ch'uan: the Chinese way.* New York: Sterling.
The essence of t'ai chi ch'uan. (1979). Translated and edited by Lo, B. P. J., Inn, M., Amacker, R., & Foe, S. Richmond, CA: North Atlantic Books.

▲Figure 11-C **Tai Chi.** An important aspect of t'ai chi is mental concentration.

Chapter Review

Summary

Regardless of age and physical condition, nearly everyone can achieve numerous health benefits by engaging in physical activity and exercise. Performing regular, vigorous exercise and physical activity can build, maintain, and preserve skeletal muscles; improve the circulation and functioning of the heart; and regulate the amount of body fat. Additionally, weight-bearing exercises such as walking, dancing, and jogging strengthen bones, which can prevent or delay the development of osteoporosis.

Besides improving physical health, exercise can have short-term and long-term psychological benefits. Physical activity can reduce symptoms of anxiety and depression and improve mood and well-being.

The health-related components of physical fitness are cardiorespiratory fitness, muscular strength, muscular endurance, flexibility, and body composition. Many fitness experts consider cardiorespiratory fitness the most important health-related element of physical fitness.

When planning an effective overall fitness regimen, people need to consider the type, frequency, duration, and intensity of their exercise activities. Additionally, individuals should design personal fitness programs that provide health benefits, satisfy their needs and interests, and can be followed for a lifetime.

Regular aerobic exercise enhances cardiorespiratory fitness, increasing the stroke volume of the heart and reducing the resting heart rate. To develop cardiorespiratory fitness, a person needs to perform aerobic activities for 30 to 60 minutes at least 3 times a week. Examples of popular aerobic activities include running, jogging, race-walking, lap swimming, cycling, stair-stepping, aerobic dancing, cross-country skiing, and rope skipping.

To develop muscular strength, muscles need to be overloaded by repeatedly moving objects that become progressively heavier. When muscles are overloaded, they hypertrophy; when muscles are not used, they atrophy or detrain. Detraining can occur within a couple of weeks after people discontinue their exercise training regimen. Thus, people must maintain their exercise programs to avoid detraining.

Immediate first aid for most musculoskeletal injuries includes RICE, the combination of rest, ice, compression, and elevation. Hypothermia and hyperthermia are serious temperature-related injuries that can occur when the body is unable to maintain its temperature in the normal range. Exercising in hot weather can produce heat cramps, heat exhaustion, or heatstroke. If untreated, heat cramps or heat exhaustion can lead to heatstroke, which can be fatal. To avoid frostbite or hypothermia, people should dress warmly while outdoors in cold and windy conditions, keeping their skin well covered.

To achieve or maintain physical fitness, people need to select physical activities or exercise programs that they enjoy and will be able to continue throughout their lives. Before beginning fitness regimens that include aerobic activities, people with heart disease or other serious chronic conditions, people who are out-of-shape, or older than 40 years should obtain the approval of their healthcare practitioners.

Regular physical activity is just as important for youngsters as for adults. Performing certain activities may be risky during pregnancy; therefore, pregnant women should discuss their physical activity with their healthcare practitioners. In most cases, it is never too late for people to begin fitness programs. By engaging in light-to-moderate physical activities regularly, such as walking or gardening every day, elderly individuals can improve their overall health.

Applying What You Have Learned

1. Calculate your target heart rate zone. *(Application)*
2. For three days, record the amount of time you spend engaging in various physical activities, such as walking to class, playing racquetball, or riding a bike. Use Table 11-1 to classify your physical activities as being light, moderate, or intense. *(Analysis)*.
3. Plan an exercise program that you can follow for a lifetime. *(Synthesis)*
4. Use the step test in the assessment activity to evaluate your current level of cardiorespiratory fitness. *(Evaluation)*

KEY

Application: Using information in a new situation.
Analysis: Breaking down information into component parts.
Synthesis: Putting together information from different sources.
Evaluation: Making informed decisions.

Reflecting On Your Health

1. Are you satisfied with your level of physical fitness? Why or why not? If you are dissatisfied, what ideas did you get from reading this chapter that will help you improve your fitness? If you are satisfied, how will you maintain your fitness?
2. What benefits would you derive from adopting a more physically active lifestyle? What factors interfere with and what factors reinforce your efforts to become more physically fit?
3. Before reading this chapter, how did you feel about ergogenic aids such as dietary supplements or anabolic steroids to enhance athletic performance? Based on what you have read in this chapter, has your attitude changed? Why or why not?
4. According to the information in this chapter, American children are less physically active than children of prior generations. If you have children or are thinking about having children, how would you encourage them to maintain a balance between the time they spend engaging in sedentary activities such as watching TV and in activities that develop physical fitness?
5. Which labor-saving devices would you be willing to stop using so you could use your muscles to do the work? Why did you choose these devices or machines? What benefits do you think you will derive from this strategy?

References

Artal, M. (1998). Exercise against depression. *The Physician and Sportsmedicine, 26*(10):55-60, 70.

Artal, R. (1999). Exercise during pregnancy: safe and beneficial for most. *The Physician and Sportsmedicine, 27*(8):51-52, 54, 57-58, 60.

Convertino, V. A., Armstrong, L. E., Coyle, E. F., Mack, G. W., Sawka, M. N., Senay, L. C., Jr., & Sherman, W. M. (1996). Exercise and fluid replacement. *Medicine & Science in Sports & Exercise, 28*:i-vii.

Demant, T. W., & Rhodes, E. C. (1999). Effects of creatine supplementation on exercise performance. *Sports Medicine, 28*(1):49-50.

Erikssen, G., Liestøl, K., Bjørnholt, J., Thaulow, E., Sandvik, L., & Erikssen, J. (1998). Changes in physical fitness and changes in mortality. *The Lancet, 352*:759-762.

Feigenbaum, M. S., & Pollock, M. L. (1999). Prescription of resistance training for health and disease. *Medicine & Science in Sports & Exercise, 31*(1):38-45.

Holly, R. G., & Shaffrath, J. D. (1998) Cardiorespiratory endurance. In: *ACSM's Resource Manual for Guidelines for Exercise Testing and Prescription,* 3rd ed. American College of Sports Medicine. Baltimore: Williams & Wilkins.

Kanzenbach, T. L., & Dexter, W. W. (1999). Cold injuries: Protecting your patients from the dangers of hypothermia and frostbite. *Postgraduate Medicine, 105*(1):72-78.

Kleiner, S. M. (1999). Water: An essential but overlooked nutrient. *Journal of the American Dietetic Association, 99*(2):200-206.

Lee, I. M., Sesso, H. D., & Paffenbarger, R. S., Jr. (1999). Physical activity and the risk of lung cancer. *International Journal of Epidemiology, 28*(4):620-625.

Lewis, C. (1998). What to do when your back is in pain. *FDA Consumer, 32*(2):26-29.

Mazzeo, R. S., Cavanagh, P., Evans, W. J., Fiatarone, M., Hagberg, J., McAuley, E., & Startzell, J. (1998). ACSM position stand on exercise and physical activity in older adults. *Medicine & Science in Sports & Exercise, 30*(6):992-1008.

Mensink, G. B., Ziese, T., & Kok, F. J. (1999). Benefits of leisure-time physical activity on the cardiovascular risk profile at older age. *International Journal of Epidemiology, 28*(4):659-666.

Pollock, M. L., Gaesser, G., A., Butcher, J. D., Després, J., Dishman, R. K., Franklin, B. A., & Garber, C. E. (1998). American College of Sports Medicine Position Stand: The recommended quantity and quality of exercise for developing and maintaining cardiorespiratory and muscular fitness, and flexibility in healthy adults. *Medicine & Science in Sports & Exercise, 30*(6):975-991.

Rippe, J. M., & Hess, S. (1998). The role of physical activity in the prevention and management of obesity. *Journal of the American Dietetic Association, 98*(suppl. 2):S31-S38.

Roberts, J. M., & Wilson, K. (1999). Effect of stretching duration on active and passive range of motion in the lower extremity. *British Journal of Sports Medicine, 33*(4):259-263.

Shephard, R. J., & Balady, G. J. (1999). Exercise as cardiovascular therapy. *Circulation, 99*:963-972.

Speetjens, J. K., Collins, R. A., Vincent, J. B., & Woski, S. A. (1999). The nutritional supplement chromium (III) tris (picolinate) cleaves DNA. *Chemical Research Toxicology, 12*(6):483-487.

Stofan, J. R., DiPietro, L., Davis, D., Kohl, H. W., III, & Blair, S. N. (1998). Physical activity patterns associated with cardiorespiratory fitness and reduced mortality: The Aerobics Center Longitudinal Study. *American Journal of Public Health, 88*(12):1807-1813.

Thune, I., Brenn, T., Lund, E., & Gaard, M. (1997). Physical activity and the risk of breast cancer. *New England Journal of Medicine, 336*(18):1269-1275.

Wardlaw, G. M. (1999). *Nutrition Perspectives.* St. Louis: WCB McGraw-Hill.

Wei, M., Kampert, J. B., Barlow, C. E., Nichaman, M. Z., Gibbons, L. W., Paffenbarger, R. S., Jr., & Blair, S. N. (1999). Relationship between low cardiorespiratory fitness and mortality in normal-weight, overweight, and obese men. *Journal of the American Medical Association, 282*(16):1547-1553.

Williams, M. H. (1999). *Nutrition for Health, Fitness, & Sport.* Boston: WCB McGraw-Hill.

U.S. Department of Health and Human Services (1996). *Physical activity and health: a report of the Surgeon General.* Atlanta, GA: Centers for Disease Control and Prevention, National Center for Chronic Disease Prevention and Health Promotion.

U.S. Department of Health and Human Services (USDHHS), Public Health Service. (1999). Healthy people 2000 review, 1998-1999 (publication 99-1256). Washington, DC: Government Printing office. http://odphp.osophs.dhhs.gov/pubs/hp2000/prog_rvw.htm

Youth Risk Behavior Surveillance: National College Health Risk Behavior Survey: United States, 1995. (1997). *Weekly Morbidity and Mortality Report, 46*(SS-6):1-54.

Cardiovascular Health

Although we all want to maintain cardiovascular health without medical intervention, thousands of individuals each year do not attain this goal. However, heart surgeons perform amazing medical feats daily, helping patients recover their cardiovascular health and live longer, productive, and pain-free lives. The procedures physicians use vary depending on the patient and his or her condition. One technique that is used frequently is bypass surgery. In the United States in 1996 an estimated 598,000 of these procedures were performed on 367,00 patients (American Heart Association [AHA], 1998).

The phrase *bypass surgery* usually means coronary artery bypass graft surgery (CABG). The coronary arteries are blood vessels that supply oxygen-rich blood to the heart muscle. When these vessels become blocked, blood flow is slowed and the heart muscle does not get enough oxygen. A person with blocked coronary arteries is said to have **coronary artery disease (CAD)**, one type of cardiovascular disease. (Coronary artery disease is also commonly called coronary heart disease [CHD].) Coronary artery

> "... *heart surgeons perform amazing medical feats daily, helping patients recover their cardiovascular health*..."

disease may result in a heart attack in which a portion of the heart muscle dies, or in **angina pectoris** (chest pain).

People who have chronic angina, blockage in the vessels that supply the left side of the heart (the side that pumps blood to the body), or blockage in multiple coronary arteries, are often candidates for bypass surgery. To perform this operation, surgeons first open the chest cavity. Using a blood vessel taken from another part of the patient's body (usually the leg), they graft one end of the new vessel to the aorta, the major artery that carries blood away from the heart and to the body. Heart surgeons graft the other end of the new vessel to the damaged coronary artery, past the area of blockage (**Figure 12-1**). The grafted vessel thus bypasses the blocked portion of the diseased vessel.

A new, experimental procedure aimed at increasing blood flow to the heart muscle is transmyocardial revascularization (TMR). In TMR, surgeons use a laser to bore narrow channels from the heart chamber into the heart muscle. The original but controversial idea behind this

www.jbpub.com/healthyliving

The web site for this book offers many useful tools and supplementary health information for both students and instructors. Visit the site at www.jbpub.com/healthyliving for information on these topics:

The Cardiovascular System and How it Works
Cardiovascular Diseases
Risk Factors for Cardiovascular Disease
Maintaining Cardiovascular Health

Chapter Overview

How the cardiovascular system works.

Symptoms of and treatments for cardiovascular disease.

Risk factors for cardiovascular disease.

How to maintain your cardiovascular health.

DIVERSITY in Health   The Italian Gene

Con$umer Health   Vitamin Pills for a Healthier Heart?

Managing Your Health   Heart Attack Symptoms

across the lifespan   Cardiovascular Health

Student Workbook

Self Assessment: Check Your Cholesterol and Heart Disease IQ
Changing Health Habits: Reducing Your Risk of Cardiovascular Disease

Do You Know?

- What to do to keep your heart and blood vessels healthy?
- What to do if you or someone you know is having a heart attack?
- If you are likely to have a heart attack or stroke?

What You'll Learn

▶Figure 12-1 **Vessel Position in a Coronary Artery Bypass Graft.** In a coronary artery bypass graft, blood vessels taken from another part of the body are grafted to the aorta, the large artery emerging from the heart. The other ends of these vessels are grafted to the coronary arteries (those that serve the heart) past the area of blockage.

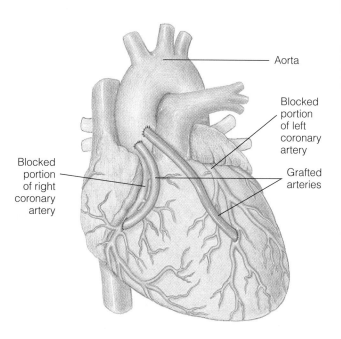

technique was that blood would flow through the heart muscle via these channels. Medical researchers now think that this procedure may work by stimulating the growth of new vessels (Galli et al., 1999; Korkola et al., 1999).

Coronary artery disease is the leading cause of death in the United States. Each year in this country, approximately 1.5 million people are diagnosed with CAD and nearly 500,000 die from it (AHA, 1999a). That means that coronary artery disease accounts for approximately 1 out of every 5 deaths in the United States.

Coronary artery disease is only one type of **cardiovascular disease (CVD)**, or dysfunction of the heart and blood vessels. Other major cardiovascular diseases are hyperten-

sion (chronic high blood pressure), stroke (blood vessel disease of the brain), and rheumatic heart disease (a complication of strep throat). Atherosclerosis (blood vessel disease) is an important cardiovascular disease process that is an underlying cause of CAD and stroke. Other cardiovascular diseases are described throughout this chapter. More than 60 million Americans (more than 1 in 4) have one or more forms of CVD. As ▌ **Figure 12-2** shows, cardiovascular disease kills more people in the United States than any other disease.

This chapter describes the causes of atherosclerosis, CAD, stroke, and hypertension—noninfectious diseases in which hereditary, environmental, and lifestyle factors interact to create an individual's risk level for developing any one of them. It also describes the interrelatedness of these diseases and how the development of one affects the development of another. Last, it explores the factors critical to maintaining cardiovascular health, to help you preserve the fitness of your heart and blood vessels throughout your lifetime. First, however, let us explore the cardiovascular system and how it works as a foundation for understanding cardiovascular health.

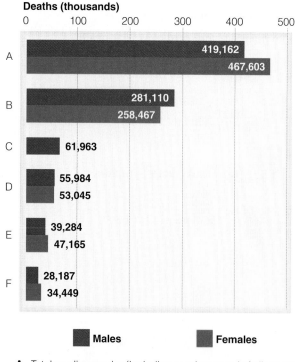

Deaths (thousands)

A Total cardiovascular (including cerebrovascular) diseases
B Cancer
C Accidents
D Chronic obstructive pulmonary disease
E Pneumonia/influenza
F Diabetes mellitus

▲Figure 12-2 **Leading Causes of Death.** This graph shows that cardiovascular disease is the number one cause of death for both men and women (all races, all ages). Source: National Center for Health Statistics. (1999). Deaths: Final data for 1997. *National Vital Statistics Reports, 47*(19).

www.jbpub.com/healthyliving

The Cardiovascular System and How It Works

You may have heard the cardiovascular system also referred to as the circulatory system. These terms are often used interchangeably. The term *cardiovascular* refers to the heart (*cardio-*) and blood vessels (*vascular*). The term *circulatory* refers to the circulation of the blood. In practical use, both terms describe a body system that pumps blood enclosed in blood vessels to all parts of the body.

Blood is a somewhat viscous fluid made up of cells suspended in a liquid. Blood performs many functions:

- It contains red blood cells and fluid (plasma) that transport the respiratory gases (oxygen and carbon dioxide), nutrients, hormones, enzymes, and waste products.
- It helps regulate body temperature by distributing the heat generated by chemical reactions in the body.
- It contains blood clotting factors (including pieces of cells called *platelets*) that protect the blood supply from excessive losses and help in tissue repair.
- It contains white blood cells (including the lymphocytes of the immune system) that help protect the body from infection (see Chapter 14).

The blood is pumped by the heart, a muscular, fist-sized organ that lies in the chest cavity about midway between the shoulders and the waist, and slightly to the left of the midline (■ Figure 12-3). The heart consists of four chambers: two upper chambers called *atria* and two lower chambers called *ventricles*. The upper chambers receive blood and then push it into the lower chambers, which pump blood to the lungs and the rest of the body.

Blood flows within a vast network of blood vessels. **Arteries** carry blood away from the heart. They have muscular, elastic walls that bulge slightly when the left ventricle contracts and pushes blood through them, and they recoil at the end of the beat. Arteries branch into smaller vessels called *arterioles*. When these vessels become so small that they allow the passage of only one blood cell at a time, they are called **capillaries**.

The capillaries permeate tissues. These tiny blood vessels have walls that are only one cell thick. The thinness of capillary walls allows substances such as nutrients and oxygen to move out of the blood and other substances such as waste products and carbon dioxide to move into the blood. Capillaries join to form larger vessels called *venules,* which in turn join to form still larger vessels, the veins.

Veins return blood to the heart. By the time the blood reaches the veins it has lost most of the force (pressure) of its push from the heart. Therefore, veins have thinner walls than do arteries; they contain less muscle and elastic tissue. In addition, veins have one-way valves along their length, which help prevent the backflow of blood. Blood returning to the heart from the head, neck, and shoulders is helped along by the force of gravity. Blood returning to the heart

▼Figure 12-3 **The Major Arteries of the Body.** The heart is located to the left of the midline in the chest cavity. The arteries take blood away from the heart and are shown in red. Veins are shown in blue.

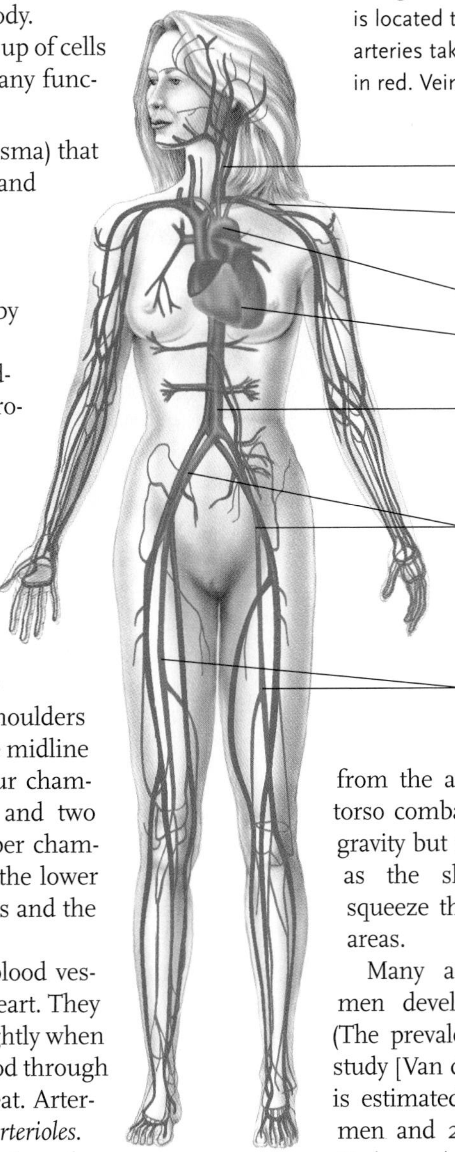

Left common carotid artery
Left subclavian artery
Aorta
Heart
Abdominal aorta
Iliac arteries
Femoral arteries

from the arms, legs, and torso combats the force of gravity but is pushed along as the skeletal muscles squeeze the veins in these areas.

Many adult women and men develop varicose veins. (The prevalence in one Belgian study [Van den Oever et al., 1998] is estimated to be 10% to 15% of men and 20% to 25% of women.) *Varicose veins* are distended or stretched veins and are found most frequently in the legs or the trunk (■ **Figure 12-4**). They have a variety of causes, including defective valves, continual and prolonged sitting or standing, pregnancy, and obesity. Therapy for varicose veins includes elevating the legs, wearing elastic stockings, and, in severe cases, surgery. Recently, lasers have been used successfully to shrink a type of varicose veins called spider leg veins (McDaniel et al., 1999). Spider veins are groups of stretched, small blood vessels that form a spiderlike pattern on the skin.

Certain blood vessels called **coronary arteries** are involved in the development of coronary artery disease. These vessels arise from the base of the aorta and bring freshly oxygenated blood to the heart muscle itself. (Although blood flows in and out of the heart's chambers, the heart muscle is not nourished by the blood while it is in the chambers.) There are two main coronary arteries: the

coronary artery disease (CAD) a condition in which the coronary vessels are blocked partially or completely by fatty deposits, blood clots, or both. Also commonly called coronary heart disease (CHD).

cardiovascular disease (CVD) (KAR-dee-oh-VAS-ku-lar) disorders of the heart and blood vessels.

arteries blood vessels that carry blood away from the heart.

capillaries (KAP-ih-LAIR-eez) microscopic blood vessels that permeate tissues, connecting small arteries to small veins.

veins blood vessels that return blood to the heart.

coronary arteries blood vessels that arise from the base of the aorta and bring freshly oxygenated blood to the heart muscle.

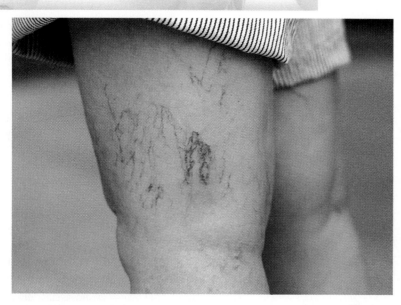

▲Figure 12-4 **Close-up of Varicose Veins on a Woman's Thigh.**

Atherosclerosis may begin with an injury to the lining of a blood vessel. Factors such as high blood pressure, for example, can damage this lining, or the immune system may play a role. Lipids, especially cholesterol, accumulate at injury sites and cling to the interior of blood vessel walls. These plaques thicken blood vessel walls, which narrows the interiors of arteries (■ **Figure 12-5)** and interferes with arterial cells' ability to obtain nutrients. Eventually, the wall beneath a plaque degenerates. Scar tissue forms and calcium is often deposited there, "hardening" the artery. Blood clots sometimes develop there, too, and may be the ultimate cause of a heart attack or stroke.

Although the incidence of atherosclerosis increases with age, not all elderly people have extensive plaques. Conversely, some young people do. In one large multicenter study (McGill & McMahan, 1998), medical researchers examined the relationship of the risk factors for adult coronary artery disease (such as smoking, obesity, poor diet, and lack of exercise) to atherosclerosis in nearly 3,000 persons, aged 15 to 34 years, who died from accidents, homicides, and suicides. The results of the study revealed that young persons with risk factors for CAD began developing fatty streaks within their arteries in their teenage years. By age 25, young persons with risk factors also had developed raised lesions in the aorta and right coronary artery. The results of this and other studies (Berensen et al., 1998; Oalmann et al., 1997) show that maintenance of cardiovascular health involves controlling risk factors early in life.

left and the right coronary arteries (see Figure 12-1). Both of these arteries branch into multiple vessels that supply the entire heart with blood.

Cardiovascular Diseases

After coronary artery disease, stroke and hypertension (in that order) produce the next highest death rates due to cardiovascular diseases. Stroke is the third leading cause of death in the United States (National Center for Health Statistics [NCHS], 1999). (Cancer is second; see Chapter 13.) These big killers—coronary artery disease and stroke—result from the development of yet another cardiovascular disease: atherosclerosis.

plaques
(plaks) fatty deposits in artery walls.

atherosclerosis (ATH-er-oh-skle-ROW-sis) disease of large and medium-sized arteries in which the inner lining has areas that are deteriorated, thickened, and inelastic.

Atherosclerosis

In 99% of CAD cases, the blood supply to portions of the heart is reduced because the coronary arteries are blocked by fatty deposits. These fatty deposits, or **plaques**, develop as part of a disease of the arteries called **atherosclerosis.** (Arterial plaque is not the same as dental plaque.) An *atheroma* is a deteriorated, thickened area on the inner lining of a large or medium-sized artery. *Sclerosis* refers to loss of elasticity, or hardening of these arteries. Atherosclerosis is one form of *arteriosclerosis* (hardening of the arteries).

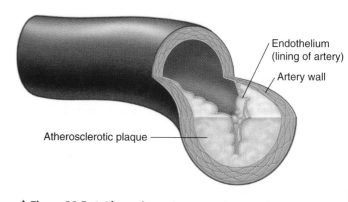

▲Figure 12-5 **A Plaque in an Artery.** A plaque is formed by a buildup of fatty material on an artery wall. This illustration shows the interior of an affected artery that has been narrowed by plaque.

Atherosclerosis occurs most often in the aorta, and in the coronary, femoral, iliac, internal carotid, and cerebral arteries. Most of these vessels are labeled on Figure 12-3. As you can see, these arteries supply blood to the heart, torso, legs, and head. The cerebral arteries, not shown in the diagram, branch from the carotid arteries and other vessels to supply large portions of the brain with blood. Atherosclerosis is most serious when it develops in the vessels that supply the heart, which can lead to heart attacks, and in the vessels that supply the brain, which can result in strokes.

Any blockage of vessels other than those to the heart is often referred to as **peripheral vascular disease.** This disease affects the organs and tissues that blocked vessels serve. One result of peripheral vascular disease, for example, can be erectile dysfunction (impotence) in men (see Chapter 6).

Coronary Artery Disease

In CAD, coronary vessels may become partially or completely blocked by one or more of the following: fatty deposits, which narrow blood vessels (see "Atherosclerosis"), a blood clot that develops at the site of fatty deposits, or a floating blood clot that lodges in a vessel. A stationary blood clot, called a **thrombus,** can block a vessel already narrowed by fatty deposits. Blood clots frequently form in vessels in which blood flow is slowed by fatty deposits. The development of a thrombus that blocks a coronary artery is called **coronary thrombosis.**

A thrombus may dislodge from the place in which it forms and become a floating blood clot, or **embolus.** An embolus can block a coronary artery downstream from where it was formed, producing a **coronary embolism.** In the early stages of CAD, coronary arteries may also become narrowed by muscle spasms of these vessels, frequently triggered by exposure to cold, physical exertion, or anxiety. Usually such muscle spasms are short-lived and do not damage the heart muscle.

Angina Pectoris Spasms, partial blockage, or complete blockage of one or more of the coronary vessels can cause insufficient blood to reach part of the heart, which is called **ischemia.** When this happens, the heart does not receive sufficient oxygen and a person experiences **angina pectoris,** or chest pain. Angina is felt beneath the breastbone and extends to the left shoulder and down the left arm. (Pain in the arm may help you distinguish between angina and heartburn or other gastric distress.) Angina pain may also be felt in the jaw and neck and, infrequently, in the back. The pain is described as aching, squeezing, burning, heaviness, or pressure. Some people experience *silent* (painless) *angina,* which consists of strange feelings at angina sites without pain. Silent angina can be diagnosed by exercise testing or by wearing a portable device that monitors the electrical activity of the heart during a 24-hour period.

Angina attacks may come and go, brought on by physical exertion or by mental or emotional stress, but they are signs of serious coronary artery disease. Angina should not be ignored; a person experiencing angina attacks should seek medical attention immediately. Rest and drugs that dilate, or widen, the blood vessels (such as nitroglycerin) relieve attacks of angina. Other drugs used to treat angina include those to reduce blood pressure or those that slow the heart rate. Both types of drugs reduce the workload of the heart and its need for oxygen.

In cases of angina, a physician may suggest assessing the degree and location of vessel blockage to determine whether further treatment is necessary to reduce symptoms and avoid a heart attack. One common technique to visualize the coronary blood vessels is *coronary angiography.*

An *angiogram* is an x-ray image of blood vessels after they have been injected with a fluid called a *contrast medium.* The contrast medium used in angiography is composed primarily of iodine because it absorbs x rays, making visible the interiors of blood vessels. To perform coronary angiography, physicians first thread a thin plastic tube called a *catheter* through an artery in the arm or the groin until it reaches the coronary arteries. After injecting the contrast medium into the catheter, they take high-speed x-ray movies of blood flowing through the arteries. ▮ **Figure 12-6** shows frames of such a movie and indicates where physicians are able to detect irregularities and narrowing of the coronary arteries.

Other tests such as magnetic resonance imaging (MRI) are also performed at many medical centers to create images of the heart and its vessels for various diagnostic purposes. MRI uses magnetic fields and radio waves to visualize structures.

If a patient has atherosclerosis in many coronary vessels, a physician may recommend coronary artery bypass graft surgery. If only one of a patient's coronary arteries is narrowed significantly, a physician may recommend widening the interior of the artery with a type of **angioplasty,** the reconstruction of damaged blood vessels. In balloon angioplasty, the physician threads a catheter through an artery in the arm or the groin until it reaches the coronary arteries, as done when performing an angiogram. However, instead of injecting dye into the catheter, the physician threads a second,

peripheral vascular disease any blockage of vessels other than those to the heart.

thrombus (THROM-bus) a stationary blood clot.

coronary thrombosis (throm-BOW-sis) the development of a stationary blood clot that blocks blood flow in an artery that brings blood to the heart muscle.

embolus (EM-bow-lus) a floating blood clot.

coronary embolism (EM-bow-lizm) a floating blood clot that lodges in an artery that brings blood to the heart muscle, blocking blood flow.

ischemia (is-KI-me-ah) insufficient blood in part of the heart.

angina pectoris (an-JEYE-nah PECK-tor-iss) chest pain due to insufficient oxygen in a portion of the heart.

angioplasty (AN-jee-oh-PLAS-tee) the reconstruction of damaged blood vessels.

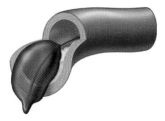

▲ **Figure 12-7 Balloon Angioplasty.** In balloon angioplasty, a thin tube containing a balloon is threaded through an artery until it reaches the area of plaque that is narrowing the vessel. The balloon is inflated, compressing the plaque against the artery wall and stretching the artery.

balloon-tipped catheter through the first. When the second catheter reaches the area of blockage, the balloon is inflated, breaking up the plaque while compressing it against the arterial wall (■ **Figure 12-7).** This balloon technique also stretches the artery somewhat. Two newer techniques are atherectomy and stenting.

Atherectomy refers to methods that remove plaque from the interior of an artery. The procedure is performed like balloon angioplasty, but the second catheter contains a cutting and collecting tip instead of a balloon tip. A variety of styles are presently in use.

Stenting is similar to balloon angioplasty in that a catheter device first compresses plaque against the artery wall. A springlike mesh device, the stent, (■ **Figure 12-8)** is then implanted within the artery, covering the compressed plaque, supporting the artery, and smoothing the artery wall. There are many styles of stents. After a time, tissue may grow around a stent, however, increasing the risk of the artery reclogging. One type of stent has been invented recently that continues to expand inside the blood vessel in which it is placed. As it expands, it continues to widen the blood vessel, reducing the risk of reclogging (Roguin et al., 1999).

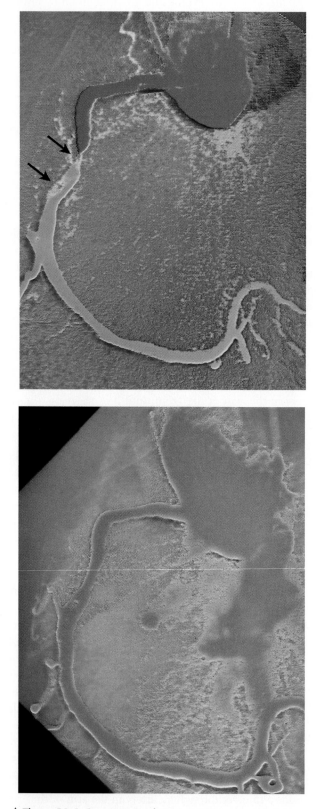

▲ **Figure 12-6 Coronary Angiogram.** The arrows on the top angiogram point out some of the irregularities and areas of narrowing of this coronary artery. This same vessel is shown in the bottom image, taken minutes after balloon angioplasty.

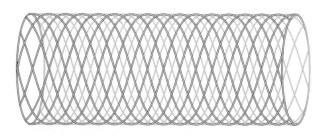

▲ **Figure 12-8 An Arterial Stent.** This springlike mesh device is implanted in an artery after balloon angioplasty to cover the compressed plaque, smooth the artery wall, and support the vessel.

▲Figure 12-9 **Heart failure ended the professional and personal partnership of Sergei Grinkov and Katerina Gordeeva.** The couple had won gold medals for Russia in pairs figure skating in both the 1988 and 1994 Olympics. Grinkov died suddenly during a practice session in November 1995—he was just 28 years old and in the prime of his life.

Heart Attack Victims of coronary artery disease are often unaware that the arteries supplying their heart with blood have become blocked. They may have no signs or symptoms of CAD or may not notice any. For this reason, one-third to one-half of persons with CAD are stricken suddenly and unexpectedly with a **heart attack**, which healthcare practitioners call a *myocardial infarction (MI)*. Myocardial simply means heart *(cardium)* muscle *(myo-)*. An infarction is an area of heart muscle that dies because it does not receive enough oxygen due to insufficient blood. As heart muscle dies, it may trigger abnormal electrical activity that causes the ventricles to beat irregularly. Abnormal heart beats are called **arrhythmias.** Heart failure, cardiac arrest, and death may occur during ventricular arrhythmia.

Heart failure is sometimes called *congestive* heart failure because the veins bringing blood to the heart become congested, or overfilled, with blood when the heart cannot pump effectively. Heart failure (ineffective pumping) may be the result of all forms of cardiac disease, including CAD, structural heart defects, and rheumatic heart disease, and may also be a chronic condition, resulting in shortness of breath, retention of fluid, congestion of the lungs, and fa-

tigue. A person experiencing severe cardiac failure may be a candidate for a heart transplant or the implantation of a left ventricular assist device (which has replaced the artificial heart) while waiting for a donor heart. The pump is implanted in the abdomen and is connected to the main pumping chamber of the heart, the left ventricle. The power source for the pump is located outside of the patient's body on a rolling cart, or is a portable battery that hangs by a strap from the shoulder.

Sudden cardiac death (cardiac arrest) may also occur as a result of a heart attack. During cardiac arrest, the heart suddenly stops beating. Getting immediate medical care is crucial in such a situation because the heart must be *defibrillated* (given electric shock) within a few minutes of its stopping to cause it to begin beating again and avoid heart, lung, kidney, and brain damage, and to avoid death. Sudden cardiac death is the result of an unresuscitated cardiac arrest.

About 250,000 persons in the United States die each year from sudden cardiac death (AHA, 1999c). The average age for sudden cardiac death in the United States is 60 years. Eighty percent of the time the underlying cause of cardiac arrest is coronary artery disease. The other 20% of cases are due to a variety of other conditions such as an inflammation of the heart caused by infection, rheumatic fever, or medications; heart muscle disorders having unknown causes; congenital heart defects; and drug abuse. (Rheumatic fever is a disorder that sometimes occurs as a result of strep throat. It affects the heart.) One of these conditions is often the reason a young, physically fit person such as an athlete dies suddenly on the basketball court, track, or skating rink (▌ **Figure 12-9).**

Learn the warning signs of a heart attack and what to do if you or someone you are with experiences them (see the "Managing Your Health" feature on page 282). You can distinguish a heart attack from angina by the severity of the pain: Heart attack pain is much more severe and lasts longer than that of angina. The pain of a heart attack is usually described as pressure (heaviness), burning, aching, and tightness, which is felt in the same locations as angina pain. The person suffering a heart attack may also experience shortness of breath, profuse sweating, weakness, anxiety, or nausea.

If you experience some or all of these signs and symptoms or are with someone who does, obtain emergency medical care *immediately*. Many

atherectomy (ATH-er-EK-toe-me) the removal of plaque from the interior of an artery.

stenting the implantation of a springlike mesh device within an artery to cover compressed plaque, support the artery, and smooth the artery wall.

heart attack myocardial infarction (MI); an area of heart muscle that dies because it does not receive enough oxygen due to insufficient blood.

arrhythmias (uh-RITH-me-uhs) Abnormal heart beats.

heart failure ineffective pumping of the heart, which results in the overfilling of the veins that bring blood to the heart.

sudden cardiac death (cardiac arrest) cessation of the heart beat.

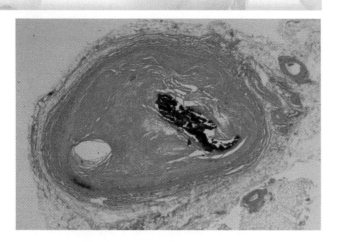

▲**Figure 12-10 An Occluded (Blocked) Vessel.** This coronary artery is totally blocked with plaque and a blood clot (dark area).

heart attack victims die because they do not seek medical attention quickly, denying that they are having a heart attack. Today, 35% of people who suffer an MI die before they reach the emergency room. However, if you call for help quickly, an emergency response team trained to provide prompt medical care can keep a heart attack victim alive and help reduce damage to the heart while transporting him or her to the hospital.

Most heart attacks are results of coronary artery thrombosis. Blood clots often form suddenly when the plaque in an artery breaks apart and blood platelets clump at that site (⬛ **Figure 12-10**). Therefore, in the emergency room, heart attack patients are quickly given clot-dissolving drugs intravenously.

Most patients who survive a heart attack do not experience complications after the attack if they receive appropriate medical treatment. Some may not even have detectable heart abnormalities if their MI involved only a

Heart Attack Symptoms: What to Do in an Emergency

IF YOU THINK YOU ARE HAVING A HEART ATTACK, CALL YOUR EMERGENCY MEDICAL SYSTEM IMMEDIATELY.

The American Heart Association says the body likely will send one or more of the following warning signals of a heart attack.

Common or "classic" signs of heart attack

- Uncomfortable pressure, fullness, squeezing, or pain in the center of the chest that lasts more than a few minutes, or goes away and comes back
- Pain that spreads to the shoulders, neck, or arms
- Chest discomfort with light-headedness, fainting, sweating, nausea, or shortness of breath

Less common warning signs of heart attack

- Atypical chest pain, stomach, or abdominal pain
- Nausea or dizziness (without chest pain)

- Shortness of breath and difficulty breathing (without chest pain)
- Unexplained anxiety, weakness, or fatigue
- Palpitations, cold sweat, or paleness

   Not all of these signs occur in every heart attack. Sometimes they go away and return. If some occur, get help fast. IF YOU NOTICE ONE OR MORE OF THESE SIGNS IN ANOTHER PERSON (OR YOU HAVE THEM YOURSELF), DON'T WAIT. CALL 911 or YOUR EMERGENCY MEDICAL SERVICES AND GET TO A HOSPITAL RIGHT AWAY!

Be Prepared

- Keep a list of emergency rescue service numbers next to the telephone and in your pocket, wallet, or purse.
- Find out which area hospitals have 24-hour emergency cardiovascular care.
- Know (in advance) which hospital or medical facility is nearest your home or office.

Take Action

- If you have heart attack symptoms that last more than a few minutes, don't delay! Immediately call 911 or the EMS number so an ambulance (ideally with advanced life support) can quickly be sent for you.
- If ambulance service isn't available in your area, immediately have someone drive you to the nearest hospital emergency room (or another facility offering 24-hour life support).
- If you're with someone who may be having heart attack symptoms, immediately call 911 or the EMS. Expect the person to protest—denial is common. Don't take "no" for an answer. Insist on taking prompt action.
- Give CPR (mouth-to-mouth breathing and chest compression) if it's needed and you're properly trained.

Source: American Heart Association

small portion of the heart muscle. Unfortunately, some patients do experience life-threatening complications. If a substantial portion of the heart was involved, the MI victim may develop cardiogenic shock, in which the left ventricle of the heart does not pump sufficient blood to sustain the body. Although physicians can treat this condition with angioplasty or surgery, cardiogenic shock is fatal 50% to 80% of the time (Hollenberg et al., 1999).

After an MI, the physician evaluates the health of the patient's heart. Using measurements of enzymes released from the heart and techniques to visualize the heart and blood vessels, such as an angiogram or MRI, the physician assesses cell damage and ventricular function (the ability of the heart to pump blood to the body) to select a patient's post-MI therapy. Such therapy may include surgical procedures, medications, and lifestyle changes.

Stroke

A **stroke** occurs when arteries that supply the brain with blood become blocked, preventing blood flow. The primary cause of stroke is the same as that for heart attacks or angina pectoris: atherosclerosis—the buildup of plaque or a blood clot that blocks arteries bringing blood to the organ. Blood clots are a common cause of a stroke. If the stroke is due to a stationary clot, the condition is called a **cerebral thrombosis.** If the blood clot was formed elsewhere and becomes lodged in a cerebral artery, blocking flow, it is called a **cerebral embolism.**

A stroke may also occur if an artery supplying the brain bursts. This situation is called a **cerebral hemorrhage** and may occur when atherosclerosis and high blood pressure are present. Cerebral hemorrhage may also occur from a head injury or from a burst **aneurysm** (a swollen, weakened blood vessel).

During a stroke, the brain cells normally supplied by the blocked or burst vessel do not receive oxygen. Brain cells, like heart cells, die when they do not receive the oxygen they need. A cerebral hemorrhage affects the brain in an additional way: Pressure builds in the brain due to blood that has leaked out of the burst vessel. When this blood clots, it can damage brain tissue, causing physical disability.

The signs and symptoms of a stroke vary (▌ **Table 12-1**), depending on the location of the damage. In most cases, one side of the body becomes weak, numb, or paralyzed.

One group at highest risk for a stroke is people with **atrial fibrillation.** Atrial fibrillation is a type of arrhythmia. During atrial fibrillation, the upper chambers of the heart contract with no set pattern, which upsets the normal rhythm of the heartbeat. This arrhythmia can result in the formation of floating blood clots (emboli) that can travel to the brain, block a blood vessel, and result in a stroke.

More than 1 million Americans have atrial fibrillation. Its incidence increases with age because the incidences of its primary underlying causes, hypertension and coronary artery disease, also increase with age.

Table 12-1	Signs of Stroke
Some or all of these signs accompany a stroke:	
Weakness, numbness, or paralysis on one side of the body	
Loss or dimming of vision, particularly in one eye	
Loss of speech, or difficulty speaking or understanding speech	
Sudden, severe headache	
Sudden dizziness, unsteadiness, or episodes of falling	

Another group at high risk for strokes is persons with *stenosis* (narrowing) of one or both of the carotid arteries. The right and left carotid arteries branch off major vessels leaving the heart and bring blood up the neck to the brain (see Figure 12-3). Physicians diagnose carotid artery stenosis by using ultrasound (a technique that uses sound waves to visualize soft tissues of the body; see Chapter 6) or angiography.

Physicians often recommend *carotid endarterectomy* to reduce significantly the risk of stroke in patients with carotid artery stenosis. In this procedure, surgeons remove the inner lining of the partially blocked carotid artery along with the plaque. Also, physicians may prescribe long-term aspirin therapy or anticoagulant drugs for treatment of either carotid artery stenosis or atrial fibrillation.

In the hospital, physicians usually perform computed tomography (CT) scans (detailed x rays of cross-sectional slices of body structures) or MRI scans on the brain of the stroke victim to confirm the diagnosis and determine the location and extent of injury (▌ **Figure 12-11**). Until recently, no good treatment for stroke existed. The first drug that has shown promising results is a clot-dissolving drug called tissue plasminogen activator (tPA). If given within 3 hours of a stroke's onset, it raises the chances that no permanent brain damage will occur. Dozens of other drugs, each aimed at a specific event in the complex set of events that causes brain damage during a stroke, are in or near clinical trials (Benavente & Hart, 1999). Poststroke therapy

stroke a brain injury that occurs when arteries that supply the brain become blocked and prevent blood flow, or become damaged and leak blood onto or into the brain.

cerebral thrombosis a stroke due to a stationary blood clot.

cerebral embolism a stroke due to a floating blood clot that becomes lodged in a cerebral artery, blocking blood flow.

cerebral hemorrhage (HEM-ah-rij) a stroke due to a burst artery that supplies the brain.

aneurysm (AN-you-rizm) a swollen, weakened blood vessel.

atrial fibrillation (fih-brih-LAY-shun) a type of arrhythmia in which the upper chambers of the heart contract with no set pattern.

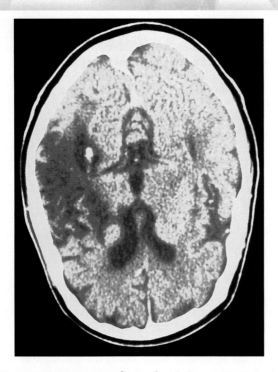

▲Figure 12-11 CT Scan of a Stroke Victim. The darkened area on the left side of the brain scan reveals dead tissue due to a lack of oxygen during a stroke.

focuses on helping patients redevelop motor skills that may have been lost due to damage to part of the brain.

Just as heart attacks may be preceded by smaller angina attacks, major strokes may be preceded by minor strokes called **transient ischemic attacks (TIAs).** Ischemic attacks are similar to strokes, usually cause no permanent damage, and have signs that last only a short time. A TIA is a serious warning that a stroke may occur within weeks or months. Persons experiencing a TIA should see their health-care practitioners immediately. Often, blood-thinning drugs such as aspirin are prescribed to lessen the possibility of a stroke.

Healthy
LIVING PRACTICES

- Any person who experiences chest pain, especially pain beneath the breastbone that extends to the neck, shoulders, and/or arms, should seek medical attention immediately.
- Any person experiencing weakness, numbness, or paralysis on one side of the body; loss or dimming of vision; loss of speech, or difficulty speaking or understanding speech; a sudden, severe headache; or sudden dizziness or unsteadiness should seek medical attention immediately.

www.jbpub.com/healthyliving

Risk Factors for Cardiovascular Disease

Medical researchers have identified several risk factors for cardiovascular disease, traits that have been shown to be associated with the incidence of CVD. In general, people with more than one of these traits, which are listed in ▌ Table 12-2, have a greater probability of developing atherosclerosis and suffering a heart attack or stroke than people with one or none of these risk factors.

The major risk factors for the development of CVD are male gender (the average man with CAD has his first heart attack in his mid 50s; the average woman with CAD in her mid 60s), increasing age (the incidence of coronary artery disease rises in both men and women with each decade from age 40 to age 79), family history of cardiovascular disease, cigarette smoking, obesity, hypertension, elevated blood cholesterol levels, and lack of physical activity. All these risk factors are important in the development of CAD. However, hypertension is the most important risk factor for stroke; high blood cholesterol levels play only a small role in the development of this disease.

Table 12-2	Risk Factors for Cardiovascular Disease
Cigarette smoking
Diabetes mellitus
Blood cholesterol above 200 mg/dl
A ratio of total cholesterol to high-density (HDL) cholesterol above 5:1 (Optimum ratio is 3½:1)
High levels of low-density lipoprotein (LDL) cholesterol
Physical inactivity
Family history of cardiovascular disease
Obesity
Uncontrolled, persistent high blood pressure
Heavy alcohol use
Gender (women are at lower risk of heart attack until menopause)
Age (risk increases with age)
Anxiety disorders (increased risk of fatal heart attack in men)

Family History

A family history of atherosclerosis, stroke, or coronary artery disease indicates a genetic predisposition to these conditions or reflects similar diets, stresses, and lifestyles among family members. A person with a family history of premature CAD is twice as likely to suffer a heart attack as a person with no family history. A history of premature atherosclerosis (MI or sudden death before 55 years of age in the father or other male first-degree relative, or before 65 years of age in the mother or other female first-degree relative) is more meaningful than having relatives who developed atherosclerosis in the elderly years. The genetic effect decreases at older ages. Unfortunately, you cannot change your family history, but you can monitor other factors to reduce your risk in other ways.

Elevated Blood Cholesterol

Another major risk factor in the development of atherosclerosis, coronary artery disease, and stroke is elevated blood cholesterol levels (also called serum cholesterol). The American Heart Association states that the desirable range of total blood cholesterol is less than 200 milligrams per deciliter (200 mg/dl). Only 48% of American adults have total blood cholesterol levels within this range. The borderline-to-high range is 200 to 239 mg/dl, a category encompassing 32% of American adults. The high range is 240 mg/dl and higher, a category that includes 20% of adult Americans (AHA, 1998).

What is cholesterol? This substance is a *steroid,* a type of lipid. The most abundant steroid in the human body, cholesterol is used to make the sex hormones and composes part of the membranes of the body's cells. We take in cholesterol in most animal foods, such as egg yolks, fatty meats, and butter, but our bodies also make this chemical.

The blood levels of lipid-carrying molecules called lipoproteins are also critical to cardiovascular health. The major lipoproteins are **high-density lipoproteins (HDL)** and **low-density lipoproteins (LDL).** HDL carries cholesterol from the cells and to the

transient ischemic attacks (TIAs) (is-KI-mik) minor strokes that usually cause no permanent damage and have signs that last for only a short time.

high-density lipoproteins (HDL) (LIP-oh-PRO-tea-in) "good" cholesterol that carries cholesterol from the cells and to the liver for removal from the body.

low-density lipoproteins (LDL) "bad" cholesterol that carries cholesterol to the cells, including the cells that line the blood vessel walls.

DIVERSITY in Health

The Italian Gene: A Hope for Reversing Atherosclerosis?

The University of Milan's Dr. Cesare Sirtori could hardly believe it: Thirty-eight members of one Italian family had no atherosclerosis. If that was not surprising enough, many of them smoked cigarettes and ate high amounts of fat in their diets. What was protecting them from developing plaques in their blood vessels? The answer to that question is what some are calling a "miracle mutation" in the gene that directs the production of a cholesterol-lowering protein.

We all have this cholesterol-lowering protein in our bodies: apolipoprotein A-I (apoA-I). ApoA-I is a primary component of high-density lipoprotein (HDL), so-called good cholesterol. HDL helps bring excess cholesterol to the liver for transport out of the body. (Researchers do not fully understand the exact mechanism of this action.) In women, estrogen increases the body's production of apoA-I, and is thought to be one reason that pre-menopausal women have a greater protection than men of the same age from the development of atherosclerosis and heart attacks.

Apolipoprotein A-IMilano (apoA-IM) is a mutant apoA-I protein produced by the mutated Italian gene. The change in the molecular structure of apoA-IM from the nonmutant form makes this HDL molecule more stable and alters its properties so that it works even better than its normal counterpart. Those who carry the apoA-IM gene—the members of the Italian family that Sirtori studied—are protected against vascular disease.

Currently, medical researchers are conducting experiments on mice that have been altered genetically to include the apoA-IM gene in their genetic makeup. These mice will be used to study the mutation and its effects in a controlled laboratory setting. Additionally, researchers have been able to make apoA-IM in the laboratory. They are using this synthetic molecule on animal models to study its potential as a treatment to reverse atherosclerosis and cardiovascular disease. If successful, scientists and generations of one Italian family will have made a medical breakthrough in slowing the death rate from the United States' number one killer.

Sources Chiesa, G., Stoltzfus, L. J., Michelagnoli, S., Bielicki, J. K., Santi, M., Forte, T. M., Sirtori, C. R., Franceschini, G., & Rubin, E. M. (1998). Elevated triglycerides and low HDL cholesterol in transgenic mice expressing human apolipoprotein A-I(Milano). *Atherosclerosis, 136:*139-146.
Sirtori, C. R., Calabresi, L., & Franceschini, G. (1999). Recombinant apolipoproteins for the treatment of vascular diseases. *Atherosclerosis, 142:*29-40.
Soma, M. R., Donetti, E., Parolini, C., Sirtori, C. R., Fumagalli, R., & Franceschini, G. (1995). Recombinant apolipoprotein A-IMilano dimer inhibits carotid intimal thickening induced by perivascular manipulation in rabbits. *Circulation Research, 76:*405-411.

Table 12-3 Classifications of HDL and LDL Cholesterol Levels

Serum Levels	Classification
HDL Cholesterol	
Less than 35 mg/dl	Low
More than 35 mg/dl	Desirable
LDL Cholesterol	
Less than 130 mg/dl	Desirable
130–159 mg/dl	Borderline to high
160 mg/dl or higher	High

Source: American Heart Association.

liver for removal from the body. LDL carries cholesterol to the cells, including the cells that line the blood vessel walls. You may have heard these molecules referred to as "good" cholesterol and "bad" cholesterol, respectively.

It is firmly established that the level of bad cholesterol, or LDL, is of major importance in the development of atherosclerosis and coronary artery disease. As the level of LDL rises, the risk of coronary artery disease and atherosclerosis rises because LDL is related to the formation and growth of plaques.

The level of good cholesterol, or HDL, is very important too. As the level of HDL rises, the risk of coronary artery disease and atherosclerosis falls. (■ **Table 12-3** lists the classification levels for HDL and LDL.) High HDL levels are the key to why premenopausal women, in general, do not experience heart attacks at as young an age as men; the female sex hormone estrogen raises women's HDL levels by about 20%. As noted in Table 12-3, desirable levels of HDL cholesterol are above 35mg/dl. ■ **Figure 12-12** shows the estimated percentage of Americans age 20 and older with HDL cholesterol of 35 mg/dl or lower by race and sex.

The protective mechanism of HDL is not fully understood at this time. The "Diversity in Health" essay on page 285 describes a primary component of HDL called apolipoprotein A-I (apoA-I) and how a mutant form of this cholesterol-lowering protein found in a certain Italian family protects them against vascular disease.

Cigarette Smoking

Smoking cigarettes significantly increases the risk of heart attack and stroke. Cigarette smokers are more than five times as likely to develop cardiovascular disease than are nonsmokers. In addition, smoking interacts with other risk factors, multiplying its negative health effects. Smoking is directly responsible for as many as 30% of deaths from heart disease (Ockene & Miller, 1997) and 15% of strokes. Even more alarming is that cigarette smoking is directly responsible for 40% of heart disease deaths in women under the age of 55. These figures show that premenopausal women, who are generally protected from heart attacks by estrogen, raise their risk of heart disease significantly when they smoke.

Research results show that cigarette smokers tend to have reduced HDL levels, increased LDL levels, and increased levels of blood clotting factors (Robbins et al., 1994). In addition, evidence suggests that compounds in cigarette smoke enter the bloodstream and may damage blood vessel linings directly, leading to the formation of plaques (Gidding et al., 1994). Chewing tobacco is a significant CVD risk factor also, but cigar and pipe smoking appear to be less important because cigar and pipe smokers are less likely than cigarette smokers to inhale the smoke (AHA, 1999b).

The AHA believes that more study is needed to determine the specific effects of passive smoking on CVD risk in nonsmokers. However, it estimates that approximately 40,000 people die each year from heart and blood vessel disease caused by breathing in other people's smoke, or second-hand smoke (AHA, 1999b).

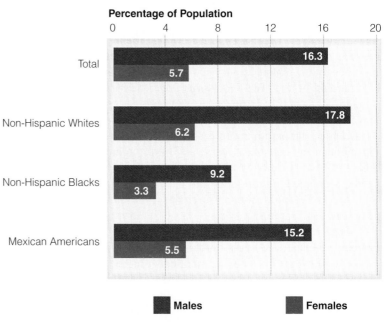

▲ **Figure 12-12 Estimated Percentage of Americans 20 and Older with HDL Cholesterol of 35 mg/dl or Lower by Race and Sex.**

Source: National Center for Health Statistics. (1997). *National Health and Nutrition Examination Survey III* (1988–1994).

High Blood Pressure

Blood pressure becomes elevated during periods of excitement or exertion; however, in healthy individuals it returns to normal levels when the activity stops. **Hypertension**, persistently high arterial blood pressure, is a major risk factor for heart attack and the most important risk factor for stroke.

The cause of most cases of high blood pressure is unknown. It has been shown, however, that hypertension may have a genetic link; it runs in families. There are also racial genetic links in hypertension. African Americans and Latinos are more likely to have hypertension than Whites and, as a result, suffer strokes at an earlier age and with greater severity. Nongenetic factors that contribute to hypertension are obesity, cigarette smoking, stress, and eating excessive amounts of salt.

You may know your blood pressure reading, such as 120/75 mmHg (millimeters of mercury). The first (higher) number is the **systolic pressure**, which is the pressure exerted by the blood on the artery walls when the left ventricle contracts. The second (lower) number is the **diastolic pressure**, which is the pressure exerted by the blood on the artery walls when the left ventricle relaxes. The units, mmHg, refer to the force needed to push a column of mercury to a particular height, such as 120 mm or 75 mm. The normal blood pressure level for people over 18 ranges from approximately 110/75 mmHg in their 20s to about 150/82 mmHg in their 80s. A blood pressure level of 160/90 mmHg is considered significant hypertension, while a reading of 240/115 is considered severe.

Research results are mixed regarding the importance of the systolic blood pressure as a predictor of cardiovascular risk (Kannel, 1996; Lenfant, 1996). Some results suggest that it is more important than the diastolic blood pressure in predicting risk. Other reports place equal importance on systolic and diastolic pressures. Medical researchers currently agree, however, that health-care practitioners have erroneously emphasized the diastolic component of the blood pressure over the systolic component in assessing cardiovascular risk and evaluating treatment.

Persistently high arterial blood pressure contributes to the development of atherosclerosis in two ways. First, high blood pressure may injure the lining of artery walls, triggering plaque formation. In addition, the increased pressure enhances the amount of lipid added to plaques, especially if serum LDL cholesterol levels are elevated.

Physical Inactivity

Within the past decade, physical inactivity has been shown to be a major risk factor for developing cardiovascular disease. Physically inactive people are almost twice as likely as active people to develop coronary artery disease. As a group, Americans are relatively sedentary; less than 10% of Americans report that they are physically active for at least 30 minutes every day, either exercising, walking, gardening, or engaging in other physical activities. Only about 15% engage in regular vigorous physical activity three times a week for at least 20 minutes (AHA, 1998). Routine exercise helps alleviate stress, reduce body weight, and control diabetes—other CVD risk factors. (Chapter 11 discusses the importance of a physically active lifestyle to health.)

Obesity

Most medical researchers agree that obesity increases the risk of cardiovascular disease. (An obese person weighs at least 20% more than his or her desirable weight.) If you are obese, you nearly double your risk of CAD. Being mildly overweight also increases your risk. Studies show a strong positive association between weight and heart disease in both men and women. The most recent (1995) weight guidelines issued by the U.S. Department of Health and Human Services are shown in Table 10-1. Are you within the desirable weight range for your age and height? Do you have a body-mass index (BMI) of 25 or less? (See Chapter 10 for an explanation of BMI and for BMI tables.)

Diabetes Mellitus

Diabetes mellitus is a group of diseases in which glucose is not metabolized properly. Affected individuals are at a higher risk of developing cardiovascular disease because of their elevated blood glucose levels, which damage heart muscle, small coronary vessels, and major arteries. Therefore, atherosclerosis occurs more frequently and at an earlier age in diabetic patients, particularly women. Unfortunately, people with diabetes mellitus are about five times as likely to develop cardiovascular disease as are persons without this disease.

Anxiety

As mentioned previously, stress can result in spasms of the coronary arteries, which can contribute to angina attacks. In addition, recent studies link anxiety disorders (such as phobias and panic disorders; see Chapter 2) to an increased risk of fatal CAD and particularly to sudden, fatal heart attacks in men (Jiang et al., 1996; Kawachi et al., 1994). Persons with anxiety disorders are from two to six times as likely to die from a heart attack as persons without anxiety disorders. Current studies are investigating the impact of stress on cardiovascular health in women.

hypertension persistently high arterial blood pressure.

systolic pressure (sis-TOL-ik) the higher number in the blood pressure reading, which is the pressure exerted by the blood on the artery walls when the left ventricle contracts.

diastolic pressure (DIE-as-TOL-ik) the lower number in the blood pressure reading, which is the pressure exerted by the blood on the artery walls when the left ventricle relaxes.

Healthy LIVING PRACTICES

- If any of your male first-degree relatives had a heart attack before age 55, or female first-degree relatives before age 65, you may be genetically predisposed to heart disease. See your health-care practitioner for an evaluation and advice.
- If you are a healthy adult, you should have your serum cholesterol level and HDL level measured once every 5 years.

www.jbpub.com/healthyliving

Maintaining Cardiovascular Health

Table 12-4 presents a summary of recommendations to help you maintain cardiovascular health and lower your risk of cardiovascular disease. As you can see, there are many factors to consider. You cannot control heredity, gender, and age. However, you can stop smoking, exercise regularly, lose weight, eat less fat, learn to relax, and reduce your salt intake especially if you are older than 45 years. Results of a recent large-scale study, which included more than 350,000 participants, reconfirm that making these lifestyle changes enhances cardiovascular health and the life span. In the study, persons with favorable levels of cholesterol and blood pressure who did not smoke and did not have diabetes or heart abnormalities lived from 5.8 to 9.5 years longer than those who had elevated cholesterol or blood pressure levels, or smoked (Stampfer et al., 1999).

Emotional stress contributes to hypertension and the incidence of angina attacks (Carels et al., 1999). Chapter 3, "Stress and Its Management," describes stress management skills and coping strategies that may help you lower your risk of stress-related hypertension and angina.

If you have diabetes mellitus, work with your health-care practitioner to develop a diabetes management plan that is specific for you; diabetics who conscientiously manage their disease and their blood sugar level lower their risk of cardiovascular disease.

Getting regular medical checkups (the frequency of which should be determined by your health-care practitioner) can help you assess your CVD risk factors. Your health-care practitioner may recommend other steps to lower CVD risks. The following sections describe actions that health-care practitioners often recommend for reducing CVD risk and maintaining cardiovascular health.

Table 12-4	How to Reduce Your Risk of Cardiovascular Disease
Get regular medical checkups.	
Do not smoke cigarettes.	
Manage diabetes mellitus properly.	
Exercise regularly.	
Maintain an intake of dietary cholesterol of less than 300 mg per day.	
Maintain an intake of dietary fat of less than 30% of daily calories.	
Maintain an intake of saturated fats of less than 10% of daily calories.	
Eat foods rich in soluble fiber, such as fruits, beans, and oats.	
Maintain an appropriate weight for your height.	
Limit alcohol consumption to 1 oz. of ethanol per day.	
Maintain salt intake at less than one-half teaspoon per day if older than 45 years.	
Reduce your stress level.	
Take estrogen replacement after menopause if advisable.	

Smoking Cessation

If you smoke, stop now. If you do not smoke, avoid breathing in second-hand (other people's) smoke. Approximately 115,000 cardiovascular deaths could be avoided each year if people did not smoke cigarettes. Studies suggest that the smoker who quits cuts his or her elevated risk of CAD in half only 1 to 2 years after quitting (Kawachi et al., 1994). The risk of stroke reverts to that of nonsmokers 2 to 5 years after quitting (National Stroke Association, 1999). Studies vary, however, regarding the time it takes for the elevated risk of a former smoker to decline to the level of a non-smoker. Some studies show that this level is nearly achieved 5 to 9 years after quitting, while others show that the former smoker must wait from 10 to 15 years to achieve this goal (Kawachi et al., 1994). The more cigarettes a person smokes and the earlier a person started to smoke are factors that lengthen this recovery time. In addition, the risk of cardiovascular disease increases as the number of cigarettes smoked increases. Therefore, smoke fewer cigarettes if you cannot quit. Smoking "low-yield" (low tar and nicotine) cigarettes does not appear to reduce CVD risk.

Weight Control

If you are above a body-mass index (BMI) of 25 (see Chapter 10) or above the healthy weight range for your height, losing weight will reduce your risk of cardiovascular disease. Chapter 10, "Body Weight and Its Management," presents background and suggestions for weight management. In general, a regular exercise program coupled with a low-calorie diet will reduce body fat. Weight reduction lowers total blood cholesterol levels, raises HDL levels, and lowers LDL levels. It also helps maintain proper blood glucose levels.

Exercise

In the late 1980s, a review of 43 studies about the relationship between physical activity and the risk of CAD and atherosclerosis was conducted (Powell et al., 1987). Two-thirds of these studies documented a substantial inverse relationship between physical activity and risk for these two related

Con$umer Health | Vitamin Pills for a Healthier Heart?

Vitamins A, C, E, B_6, B_{12}, folate and the non-nutrient beta-carotene . . . what do they have to do with cardiovascular health? Should you be rushing to the store for vitamin supplements to keep your blood vessels healthy?

Vitamins play many roles in cardiovascular health. For example, our bodies use vitamins B_6, B_{12}, and folate in the metabolism of amino acids, including the essential amino acid methionine. In the process of metabolizing methionine, cells produce another amino acid, homocysteine (ho-mo-sis-TEA-in). High blood levels of this amino acid can damage artery walls and encourage the formation of blood clots and plaques. However, if the cells have enough folate, B_6, and B_{12}, then methionine is metabolized normally and the blood level of homocysteine does not rise.

Methionine intake also affects homocysteine levels. In general, the more methionine people eat, the higher their blood levels of homocysteine. Diets rich in animal protein contain high amounts of methionine and may elevate blood homocysteine levels. Conversely, diets rich in plant protein may lower homocysteine levels, because plant foods are relatively low in methionine yet rich in folate and vitamin B_6.

Other factors also influence homocysteine blood levels. Smoking cigarettes, drinking coffee, and a sedentary lifestyle are all associated with decreased B_6 activity, and therefore higher homocysteine levels. The use of oral contraceptives and hormone replacement therapy lower homocysteine blood levels in women. Homocysteine levels also depend on age, gender, kidney function, genetics, and general health.

So do you need to take vitamin pills to lower your blood homocysteine levels? The answer is not simple, and only your health-care practitioner can tell you for sure. If you show evidence of B_6 or B_{12} deficiency (more likely in elderly than in younger populations) or evidence of folate deficiency (more likely in younger than in elderly populations), your health-care practitioner may suggest testing. Also, if you are experiencing kidney failure, are on a special metabolic diet, have cancer, or have a strong family history of heart attack, stroke, or abnormal blood clotting, your physician may recommend that your homocysteine levels be checked. The determination of homocysteine levels is complex and interpretation of the finding is not simple.

So what about vitamins A, C, E, and beta-carotene? (Beta-carotene is a yellow pigment in plants that the body converts to vitamin A.) As discussed on Chapter 9, vitamins E and C, and beta-carotene are antioxidants, substances that can protect cells by preventing or reducing the formation of free radicals. Studies have consistently shown that the more antioxidants a population consumes in its food, the lower the rate of cardiovascular disease. But what about vitamin supplements? Randomized controlled trials of antioxidant supplementation show mixed results. In fact, supplementation with beta-carotene was found to increase lung cancer and coronary artery disease in smokers.

So . . . should you take vitamin pills to reduce your risk of CVD? Only your physician can advise you properly, since the answer depends on the status of various facets of your health, family history, and lifestyle. The best advice at this time is to get your vitamins in the food you eat—be sure to have at least 5 servings of fruits and vegetables every day, including dark, leafy greens and members of the cabbage family. Consult your health-care practitioner to determine if you might also need to take vitamin pills to have a healthier heart and blood vessels.

Sources: Havranek, E. P. (1999) Primary prevention of CHD: Nine ways to reduce risk. *American Family Physician*, 59:1455-1463.
Kiningham, R. (1999). The value of antioxidant vitamin supplements. *American Family Physician*, 60:742-743.
Langman, L. J., & Cole, D. (1999). Homocysteine: Cholesterol of the 90s? *Clinica Chimica Acta*, 286:63-80.

diseases: As the level of physical activity rose, the risk of CAD and atherosclerosis declined and vice versa. These findings have been upheld by more recent studies (U.S. Dept. of Health and Human Services, 1996). Results of recent studies also show that exercise is associated with a decreased risk of stroke in men (Lee et al., 1999).

Exercise has been shown to lower blood pressure and boost HDL levels. Many health-care professionals recommend 30 minutes of physical activity, such as jogging, walking, gardening, or swimming, at least 5 days per week. The American College of Sports Medicine recommends 20 to 60 minutes of vigorous aerobic exercise 3 to 5 days per week. Aerobic exercises are those that raise the heart rate for a sustained period of time. Examples of aerobic exercise are jogging, stair-stepping, and fast walking.

Lowering Blood Pressure

One of every four American adults has hypertension. In 90% to 95% of cases, hypertension can be controlled. Doing so reduces the risk of both stroke and heart attack. The American Heart Association recommends having your blood pressure checked every 2 years if it is lower than 130/85 mmHg. If your blood pressure is higher, they suggest having it checked yearly, or more often if your health-care practitioner recommends it.

To lower blood pressure, the AHA suggests decreasing sodium intake to a maximum of 3 grams (3000 mg) per day. Three grams of sodium per day amounts to only 1 to 1 1/2 teaspoons of salt. Nutritionists suggest checking the amount of sodium that you consume in prepackaged, processed foods and not salting your food. The sodium in salt causes the body to retain fluids and may contribute to hypertension in some people. Recent research results suggest that dietary sodium restriction is effective in lowering blood pressure only in individuals aged 45 years and older (Midgley et al., 1996) and in overweight persons (He et al., 1999).

The blood pressure of overweight individuals often drops when they lose weight. If you are overweight and have high blood pressure, weight reduction is the most important action you can take to lower your blood pressure and risk of CVD. Regular aerobic exercise will lower blood pressure in hypertensive people and will also help control weight. Reducing the intake of dietary saturated fat and cholesterol will promote overall cardiovascular health and will also help reduce caloric intake, which is important for weight control.

The heavy consumption of alcoholic beverages has also been shown to lead to high blood pressure, increasing the risk of heart attack, stroke, and death from CAD. Limiting consumption to 1 oz. of alcohol (ethanol) per day (two drinks or fewer) may help lower blood pressure and may reduce your risk of cardiovascular disease. One ounce of ethanol is equivalent to 2 oz. of 100-proof whiskey, 8 to 10 oz. of wine (the alcohol content in wines varies), or two 12-oz. cans of beer.

If none of these lifestyle changes lowers the blood pressure sufficiently, hypertension can be treated with a wide array of antihypertensive drugs. These drugs are not suitable or appropriate for all hypertensive individuals, but may be essential therapy for people with severe hypertension (blood pressure above 210/120 mmHg).

Reducing Blood Cholesterol

Pioneering experiments were conducted in the 1950s and 1960s regarding the effect of diet on serum cholesterol levels. These early experiments pointed out that, in general, animal fats raised the blood cholesterol level and vegetable oils (with the exception of the tropical oils) lowered them. Therefore, dietary recommendations included eating less animal fat and eating more vegetable oils. Since that time, further experimentation has revealed that the cholesterol-lowering effects of vegetable oils were overestimated. In addition, eating certain types of margarine to reduce your intake of animal fat, cholesterol, and saturated fats from butter is not a good idea. Margarines contain trans fatty acids, compounds that may be associated with a risk of heart attack (Ascherio et al., 1999). Trans fatty acids are formed as hydrogen atoms are added to the unsaturated fats in vegetable oil to harden it. Stick margarines contain more trans fatty acids than tub or liquid margarines.

In general, today's guidelines recommend diets low in total fat, saturated fat, and cholesterol to reduce the blood cholesterol level, raise the "good" cholesterol (HDL) level, and lower the "bad" cholesterol (LDL) level. Additionally, omega-3 fatty acids, which are found in certain fish such as salmon, tuna, cod, and sole, appear to lower the risk of CAD and stroke. The American Heart Association suggests that the overall fat intake should be less than 30% of the daily intake of calories, and that the saturated fat intake (primarily animal fats and tropical oils) should be less than 10%. (Chapter 9 describes the types of fats in foods. Table 9-5 lists a variety of foods and their percentages of saturated fatty acids.) Refer to Chapter 9 to help you understand how to calculate the percentage of fat in foods.

To achieve a diet low in cholesterol, restrict your cholesterol intake to 300 mg per day. (One large egg, for example, has slightly over 200 mg, and a quarter-pound cheeseburger has slightly over 100 mg. Table 9-6 lists a variety of foods and their cholesterol content.) Studies show that, on average, people can achieve a 10% reduction in cholesterol levels by following these dietary guidelines. Each 1% reduction in the blood cholesterol level reduces the risk of CAD by 2% to 3%, so a 10% reduction reduces your risk of CAD by 20% to 30%. However, medical experts are uncertain at this time whether reducing the blood cholesterol level reduces the risk of stroke.

◄Figure 12-13 Foods High in Soluble Fiber. Soluble fiber helps lower the cholesterol level by binding to cholesterol-containing compounds in the digestive system and carrying them out of the body. The foods shown here include barley, oatmeal, whole-grain breads, rye crackers, carrots, broccoli, potatoes, dried beans and other legumes, oranges, bananas, and dried apricots.

As was mentioned in Chapter 9, eating whole-grains (Liu et al., 1999) and foods rich in soluble fiber (such as fruits, beans, oats, and barley) can help reduce your blood cholesterol level (▪ Figure 12-13). Soluble fiber helps reduce blood cholesterol because it binds to cholesterol-containing compounds in the digestive system, carrying them out of the body. Research data indicate, however, that eating more than 35 g of dietary fiber a day may be unwise since fiber may bind to minerals in the diet also, removing them from the body. (Thirty-five grams of fiber is the equivalent 14 apples, or 14 raw whole carrots, or nearly 2 cups of uncooked oats.)

If eating a heart-healthy diet and exercising regularly do not significantly reduce elevated blood cholesterol levels, cholesterol-lowering medications called "statins" are available by prescription. Some studies show that, on average, 20% reductions in the cholesterol level are achieved with drug therapy. Recent research results have shown that statins are safe, reduce CAD deaths, and appear to reduce the risk of stroke (Ansell et al., 1999; Steinberg & Gotto, 1999).

Aspirin Therapy

A treatment to reduce the risk of cardiovascular disease that has gained attention in recent years is long-term use of low-dose aspirin. The use of long-term aspirin therapy in the treatment and prevention of cardiovascular diseases in healthy men and women is still being studied (Hennekens, 1999), as are the effects of this therapy on the reduction of the incidence of colon cancer. Since aspirin can have damaging effects on the gastrointestinal system and reduces the blood's ability to clot, long-term aspirin therapy should be undertaken only on the advice of a physician.

Estrogen Replacement Therapy

The conclusions from more than 30 studies show that women who take estrogen after menopause reduce their risk of heart attack by about 44% (Peterson, 1998; Stampfer et al., 1991). Estrogen therapy, however, is not associated with a reduction in the risk of stroke. Estrogen is beneficial because this hormone reduces total cholesterol and LDL levels and often increases HDL levels. It also helps prevent osteoporosis, a decrease in bone density that has major health effects, especially in elderly women (see Chapter 9). New evidence suggests that estrogen replacement therapy may also lower the risk of colon cancer. However, there are risks from taking postmenopausal estrogen, such as an increased risk of endometrial cancer, gallbladder disease, and breast cancer. Therefore, before any woman chooses estrogen replacement therapy, she should weigh the risks and benefits in her particular situation and consult her physician.

Healthy LIVING PRACTICES

- One of the most important things you can do to lower your risk of coronary artery disease and stroke is to reduce your modifiable risk factors.
- If you smoke cigarettes, quitting will significantly reduce your risk of cardiovascular disease.

- Researchers estimate that you will reduce your risk of heart attack from 35% to 55% if you maintain a healthy body weight.
- You can lower your risk of heart attack 35% to 55% by maintaining an active lifestyle that includes regular aerobic exercise.
- To lower your blood pressure, engage in regular aerobic exercise, lose weight if you are overweight, limit your alcohol consumption to 1 oz. of ethanol per day, and limit your daily sodium intake to 3 g if you are older than 45 years.
- To reduce your total cholesterol level, raise your HDL level, and lower your LDL level, eat no more than 30% of your daily intake of calories from fat and no more than 10% from saturated fat. Also, eat foods rich in soluble fiber, such as fruits, beans, and oats.

across the lifespan

Cardiovascular Health

Approximately 32,000 babies are born each year with a variety of heart and blood vessel structural abnormalities—about 35 types are recognized. Many congenital defects (those present at birth) can now be diagnosed before birth with the use of echocardiography, or ultrasound of the heart. Sound waves are directed through the heart of the fetus; as they pass through different types of tissues (such as heart muscle and blood), they are reflected, or echoed, producing an image of the movements of the heart structures. This technique can also be used with infants, children, and adults. Such early diagnostic techniques have helped surgeons correct infants' cardiovascular defects within the first few weeks of life. This approach helps avoid complications from cardiovascular defects in older children and adults. Presently 950,000 American adults have congenital heart defects.

Cardiovascular disease due to atherosclerosis is a process that has been shown to begin in childhood. Habits of diet and lifestyle develop at an early age and often continue into adulthood, affecting this disease process. Data from the Bogalusa Heart Study (Nicklas, 1995), a long-term study of CVD in the community of Bogalusa, Louisiana, show that the average diet of children and adolescents consists of 13% of energy from protein, 49% from carbohydrate, and 38% from fat. Such diets do not meet the recommendations of the American Heart Association and can lead to the development of atherosclerosis and obesity, both risk factors for coronary artery disease and stroke. It is estimated that more than one-third of American youths aged 19 and younger have blood cholesterol levels of 170 mg/dl or higher, which corresponds to 200 mg/dl in adults.

In the Bogalusa study, school breakfasts and lunches had a major impact on the diets of children, providing approximately half of the day's total intake of energy and about 49% of daily total fat intake—too high a proportion. Many school lunch programs have reduced their percentages of total fat, saturated fat, and sodium. In addition, several innovative "heart-healthy" school lunch programs such as Healthy Edge, Lunch Power, and Heart Smart have been developed in schools across the nation.

Nearly one-third of people in the United States over the age of 75 have cholesterol blood levels higher than 240 mg/dl. Until recently, medical experts used medication to treat elderly patients with high blood cholesterol levels. Data from current studies suggest that high cholesterol levels in the elderly do not place them at higher risk for heart attack or stroke. Therefore, medical researchers recommend that cholesterol-lowering therapies should be discontinued in elderly patients older than 75 years, thus removing risk of side effects of medications (such as kidney damage) or disruption to their lifestyles from cholesterol-lowering diets. Researchers still recommend that adults younger than 75 years with high blood cholesterol levels be treated to lower these levels.

Nontreatment of the elderly does not extend to high blood pressure, however. The results of recent studies show that high blood pressure *should* be treated in all elderly patients because lower blood pressure in old age, as in middle age, is associated with better rates of survival (Glynn et al., 1995).

ANALYZING *Health-Related Information*

This article focuses on minority populations and their cardiovascular risks. Explain why you think this article is a reliable or an unreliable source of information. Use the model for analyzing health information to guide your thinking; the main points of the model are noted below. The model is fully explained on pages 12–13.

1. Which statements are verifiable facts, and which are unverified statements or value claims?
2. What are the credentials of the authors? Does their background and education qualify them as experts in this area?
3. What might be the motives and biases of the authors? State reasons for your answers.
4. Which information is relevant to the issue or main points of the article? Which information is irrelevant?
5. Is the source reliable? Does it have a reputation for publishing misinformation?
6. Does the ad or article attack the credibility of conventional scientists or medical authorities?

Racial and Ethnic Minorities: A Disease Profile

AFRICAN AMERICANS constitute 12.1% of the U.S. population. Hispanic Americans make up 9% of the population (Mexican Americans, 62.3%; Puerto Ricans, 11.1%; Cuban Americans 4.9%; South Central Americans, 13.8%; and other Hispanic Americans, 7.6%). Asian Americans and Pacific Islanders constitute 2.9% and include Chinese, Japanese, Koreans, Filipinos, Asian Indians, Hawaiian Natives, and Vietnamese and other Southeast Asians. Native Americans are 0.8% of the U.S. population and include American Indians and Alaska Natives (Eskimo and Aleut). Hawaiian Natives and Samoans, as aboriginal peoples, are also Native Americans, although the U.S. Census Bureau classifies them as Asian and Pacific Islanders.

African Americans In 1990 the poverty rate for blacks was 31.9%, almost twice that of the total U.S. rate. The percentage of blacks older than 25 who had not completed high school was at least 50% higher than the percentage of the total population. And about half as many blacks had completed college as had members of the general population.

On average, black men die seven years and black women five years earlier than other U.S. residents. In 1989, approximately 36% of total deaths in blacks were due to heart disease and stroke. Major risk factors include hypertension, smoking (for black men), overweight (for black women), high blood cholesterol levels, and diabetes.

Hispanic Americans From 1980 to 1990, the U.S. Hispanic population grew by 53%, compared with 10% for the general population. In 1990, the poverty rate for Hispanics was more than twice the U.S. average. More than twice as many Hispanics as non-Hispanics over the age 25 had not completed high school, and fewer than half as many had completed college.

Life expectancy in Hispanic men and women is only slightly lower than in other groups. Heart disease is the leading cause of death, accounting for approximately 25% of deaths. Stroke is responsible for another 5%. Risk factors among Hispanics include hypertension, overweight, smoking, and high serum cholesterol levels. Diabetes prevalence in Mexican Americans and Puerto Ricans is about double that in non-Hispanic Whites.

Asians and Pacific Islanders This group had a growth rate of 108% between 1980 and 1990. In 1990 the overall poverty rate for Asians and Pacific Islanders was slightly lower than that of the general population. Asian American and Pacific Islander adults completed high school at a rate similar to the total population, but their college completion rate was considerably higher.

Heart disease and stroke accounted for 36% of total deaths. Major risk factors include smoking, hypertension, and high blood cholesterol. The prevalence of overweight is especially high in Native Hawaiian men (66%) and women (63%).

Native Americans Native Americans are also a rapidly growing population, with a 1980-1990 growth rate nearly four times that of the total population. The poverty rate is nearly double that of the total U.S. rate, and more than twice as many adults have not completed high school. Roughly one-third as many have completed college.

In 1988, 28% of deaths were due to heart disease and stroke. Major cardiovascular risk factors include smoking (most prevalent in American Indian men), diabetes, and obesity, which is prevalent in both men and women.

Sources: Reprinted from Francis, C. K., Oberman, A., and Saunders, E. (1994). Who's at risk and why. *Patient Care*, 6/15/94. p. 29.

Prepared by Joy Noel Travalino, Contributing Editor. Article Consultants:

Charles K. Francis, M.D., professor of clinical medicine, Columbia University College of Physicians and Surgeons; and director, department of medicine, Harlem Hospital Center, New York City.

Albert Oberman, M.D., professor and director, division of preventive medicine, department of medicine, University of Alabama School of Medicine, Birmingham.

Elijah Saunders, M.D., associate professor of medicine and head, hypertension division, University of Maryland School of Medicine, Baltimore.

Chapter Review
Summary

The leading cause of death in the United States is a non-infectious disease: coronary artery disease (CAD). In CAD, the arteries that supply blood to the heart become blocked, restricting blood flow. CAD is only one disease of the cardiovascular system; hypertension, stroke, and rheumatic heart disease are three other prominent cardiovascular diseases. Atherosclerosis is an important cardiovascular disease process that is an underlying cause of CAD and stroke.

The cardiovascular system includes the heart and blood vessels. The heart, a muscular, fist-sized organ, pumps blood to the body. The blood performs many functions such as bringing nutrients and oxygen to the tissues and removing wastes, including the waste gas carbon dioxide. Blood vessels called arteries bring blood away from the heart; veins return blood to the heart. Microscopic vessels called capillaries join the two and allow the exchange of nutrients, gases, and wastes at the tissues.

Fatty deposits develop in arteries as part of a disease called atherosclerosis. Atherosclerosis occurs most frequently in the arteries supplying blood to the heart, brain, and legs. In coronary artery disease, the coronary arteries, which supply the heart muscle with blood, become blocked by fatty deposits, a blood clot, or both. When the heart is deprived of the blood (and therefore the oxygen) that it needs, chest pain (angina pectoris) or a heart attack results. A physician usually performs diagnostic tests to assess the degree and location of blockage. Medication can help widen blood vessels and reduce symptoms.

During a heart attack, part of the heart muscle dies. As the muscle dies, it may trigger electrical activity that causes the ventricles to stop beating properly, possibly resulting in heart failure and death. A heart attack victim needs immediate medical care.

A stroke occurs when arteries that supply blood to the brain become blocked by fatty deposits or by a blood clot. A stroke may cause a loss or dimming of vision, difficulty in speaking or understanding speech, headache, dizziness, unsteadiness, and even death.

The major risk factors for developing cardiovascular disease are family history, elevated blood cholesterol, cigarette smoking, high blood pressure, physical inactivity, obesity, diabetes mellitus, and stress. Behaviors that may lower the risk of cardiovascular disease are stopping smoking, controlling weight, exercising, lowering the blood pressure, reducing the blood cholesterol level, managing diabetes mellitus to stabilize the blood glucose level, coping effectively with stress, and using estrogen replacement therapy (for postmenopausal women) when advised by a physician.

Infants may be born with a wide variety of heart and blood vessel structural abnormalities. Many of these congenital defects can now be diagnosed before birth and treated during the first few weeks of life.

Cardiovascular disease due to atherosclerosis may begin in childhood. American children are still consuming diets that promote cardiovascular disease. Healthy school meal programs can help change this fact, and education can promote healthy lifestyles.

Nearly one-third of people in the United States who are over the age of 75 have cholesterol blood levels higher than 240 mg/dl, but recent data suggest that physicians should not treat these high blood cholesterol levels. Conversely, other data show that high blood pressure should always be treated, regardless of the person's age.

Applying What You Have Learned

1. If a family member experienced a transient ischemic attack, how would you recognize it? What would you do? What long-term action might this family member take to avoid the onset of a stroke? *(Analysis)*

2. Analyze your lifestyle to determine which modifiable risk factors are raising your probability of developing cardiovascular disease. List these risk factors. *(Analysis)*

3. Using the list you developed by answering question 2, describe how you could modify your behavior to lower your risk of developing cardiovascular disease. *(Synthesis)*

4. List all of your risk factors for developing cardiovascular disease, both those you can change and those you cannot. Using the information from answer 3, evaluate your course of action. Which changes do you realistically expect to make and which do you expect not to make? Give rationales for your answers. If you follow this plan, do you think that you will substantially reduce your risk of developing CVD? Why or why not? *(Evaluation)*

KEY

Analysis: Breaking down information into component parts.

Synthesis: Putting together information from different sources.

Evaluation: Making informed decisions.

Reflecting On Your Health

1. If you are a parent or plan to be a parent some day, what are you doing (or will you do) to encourage your child's "heart healthy" lifestyle?

2. If you are a cigarette smoker, do you think your risk for cardiovascular disease is affected by your habit? After learning about the effects of smoking on cardiovascular health, are you willing to quit? If not, discuss the reasons behind your answer and explain why you are willing to risk your health to continue smoking. If you are a nonsmoker, list the situations in which you regularly breathe second-hand smoke. Reflect on what you believe to be your increased risk of cardiovascular disease because of your exposure. What can you do to lessen your exposure?

3. Do you feel confident that you would be able to recognize when another person is having a stroke, TIA, or heart attack and help them? Why or why not? If not, what do you think you need to do to be prepared better to handle such an emergency?

4. Rate your lifestyle on a scale of 1 to 10, with 1 being an extremely heart-unhealthy lifestyle and 10 being an extremely heart-healthy lifestyle. Why did you rate your lifestyle as you did? Based on what you read in this chapter, what changes can you make to move closer to a "10" if you're not already there?

5. Do you think medical researchers are able to assess accurately the factors that are detrimental or helpful to cardiovascular health? Why do you feel this way? How do you think your attitudes concerning medical research affect your behavior? Have your attitudes about medical research and cardiovascular health changed since reading this chapter? Why or why not?

References

American Heart Association (AHA). (1998). *1999 Heart and Stroke Statistical Update*. Dallas, TX: American Heart Association.

American Heart Association (AHA). (December, 1999a). *Cardiovascular Disease Statistics*. http://www.americanheart.org/Heart_and_Stroke_A_Z_Guide/cvds.html

American Heart Association (AHA). (December, 1999b). *Cigarette Smoking and Cardiovascular Disease: AHA Scientific Position*. http://www.americanheart.org/Heart_and_Stroke_A_Z_Guide/cigcvd.html

American Heart Association (AHA). (December, 1999c). *Sudden Cardiac Death*. http://www.americanheart.org/Heart_and_Stroke_A_Z_Guide/sudden.html

Ansell, B. J., Watson, K. E., & Fogelman, A. M. (1999). An evidence-based assessment of the NCEP adult treatment panel II guidelines. *Journal of the American Medical Association, 282:*2051-2057.

Ascherio, A., Katan, M. B., Zock, P. L., Stampher, M. J., & Willett, W. C. (1999). Trans fatty acids and coronary heart disease. *New England Journal of Medicine, 340:*1994–1998.

Benavente, O., & Hart, R. G. (1999). Stroke: part 2. Management of acute ischemic stroke. *American Family Physician, 59:*2828-2834.

Berenson, G. S., Srinivasan, S. R., Bao, W., Newman, W. P. 3rd, Tracy, R. E., & Wattigney, W. A. (1998). Association between multiple cardiovascular risk factors and atherosclerosis in children and young adults: The Bogalusa Heart Study. *New England Journal of Medicine, 338:*1650-1656.

Carels, R. A., Sherwood, A., Babyak, M., Gullette, E. C., Colemen, R. E., Waugh, R., Jiang, W., & Blumenthal, J. A. (1999). Emotional responsivity and transient myocardial ischemia. *Journal of Consulting and Clinical Psychology, 67:*605-610.

Galli, M., Zerboni, S., Politi, A., Llambro, M., Bonatti, R., Molteni, S., & Ferrari, G. (1999). Percutaneous transmyocardial revascularization with holmium laser in patients with refractory angina: A pilot feasibility study. *Giornale Italiano di Cardiologia, 29,:*1020-1026.

Gidding, S. S., Morgan, W. M., Perry, C., Isabel-Jones, J, & Bricker, T. (1994) Active and passive tobacco exposure: A serious pediatric health problem. *A Statement from the Committee on Atherosclerosis and Hypertension in Children, Council on Cardiovascular Disease in the Young, American Heart Association.* http://www.americanheart.org/Scientific/statements/1994/119401.html

Glynn, R. J., Field, T. S., Rosner, B., Hebert, P. R., Taylor, J. O., & Hennekens, C. H. (1995). Evidence for a positive linear relation between blood pressure and mortality in elderly people, *The Lancet, 345:*825-829.

He, J., Ogden, L. G., Vuppaturi, S., Bazzano, L. A., Loria, C., & Whelton, P. K. (1999). Dietary sodium intake and subsequent risk of cardiovascular disease in overweight adults. *Journal of the American Medical Association, 282:*2027-2034.

Hennekens, C.H. (1999). Update on aspirin in the treatment and prevention of cardiovascular disease. *American Heart Journal, 137*(4 Pt. 2):S9-S13.

Hollenberg, S. M., Kavinsky, C. J., & Parillo, J. E. (1999). Cardiogenic shock. *Annals of Internal Medicine, 131:*47-59.

Jiang, W., Babyak, M., Krantz, D. S., Waugh, R. A., Coleman, R. E., Hanson, M. M., Frid, D. J., McNulty, S., Morris, J. J., O'Connor, C. M., & Blumenthal, J. A. (1996). Mental stress-induced myocardial ischemia and cardiac events. *Journal of the American Medical Association, 275:*1651-1656.

Kannel, W. B. (1996). Blood pressure as a cardiovascular risk factor: Prevention and treatment. *Journal of the American Medical Association, 275:*1571-1576.

Kawachi, I., Graham, A., Stampfer, M., Willett, W., Manson, J., Rosner, B., Speizer, F., & Hennekens, C. (1994). Smoking cessation and time course of decreased risks of coronary heart disease in middle-aged women. *Archives of Internal Medicine, 154:*169-175.

Kawachi, I., Sparrow, D., Vokonas, P., & Weiss, S. (1994). Symptoms of anxiety and risk of coronary heart disease: The Normative Aging Study. *Circulation, 90*(5):2225-2229.

Korkola, S., Lachapelle, K., Chiu, R. C. (1999). Exploring the scientific basis of surgery: Transmyocardial revascularization. *Journal of the Formosan Medical Association, 98:*301-308.

Lee, I. M., Hennekens, C. H., Berger, K., Buring, J. E., & Manson, J. E. (1999). Exercise and risk of stroke in male physicians. *Stroke, 30:*1-6.

Lenfant, C. (1996). High blood pressure: Some answers, new questions, continuing challenges. *Journal of the American Medical Association, 275:*1604-1606.

Liu, S., Stampfer, M. J., Hu, F. B., Giovannucci, E., Rimm, E., Manson, J. E., Hennekens, C. H., & Eillett, W. C. (1999). Whole-grain consumption and risk of coronary heart disease: Results from the Nurses' Health Study. *American Journal of Clinical Nutrition, 70:*412-419.

McGill, H. C. Jr., & McMahan, C. A. (1998). Determinants of atherosclerosis in the young: Pathobiological determinants of aterosclerosis in Youth (PDAY) research group. [Review]. *American Journal of Cardiology, 82*(10B):30T-36T.

Midgley, J. P., Matthew, A. G., Greenwood, C. M., & Logan, A. G. (1996). Effect of reduced dietary sodium on blood pressure: A meta-analysis of randomized controlled trials. *Journal of the American Medical Association, 275:*1590-1597.

McDaniel, D. H., Ash, K., Lord, J., Newman, J., Adrian, R. M., & Sukowski, M. (1999). Laser therapy of spider leg veins: clinical evaluation of a new long pulsed alexandrite laser. *Dermatologic Surgery, 25:*52-8.

National Center for Health Statistics. (1999). Deaths: Final data for 1997. *National Vital Statistics Reports, 47*(19).

National Stroke Association. (1999). Prevention of a first stroke: A review of guidelines and a multidisciplinary consensus statement from the National Stroke Association. *Journal of the American Medical Association, 281:*1112-1120.

Nicklas, T. A. (1995). Dietary studies of children: The Bogalusa Heart Study experience. *Journal of the American Dietetic Association, 95:*1127-1133.

Oalmann, M. C., Strong, J. P., Tracy, R. E., & Malcom, G. T. (1997). Atherosclerosis in youth: Are hypertension and other coronary heart disease risk factors already at work? *Pediatric Nephrology, 11:*99-107.

Ochene, I. S., & Miller, N. H. (1997). Cigarette smoking, cardiovascular disease, and stroke. *Circulation, 96:*3243-3247.

Peterson, L. R. (1998). Estrogen replacement therapy and coronary artery disease. *Current Opinion in Cardiology, 13:*223-231.

Powell, K., Thomposon, P., Caspersoen, C., & Kendrick, J. (1987). Physical activity and the incidence of coronary heart disease. *Annual Review of Public Health, 8:*253-287.

Robbins, A., Manson, J., Lee, I., Satterfield, S., & Hennekens, C. (1994). Cigarette smoking and stroke in a cohort of U.S. male physicians. *Annals of Internal Medicine, 120*:458-462.

Roguin, A., Grenadier, E., Linn, S., Markiewicz, W., & Beyar, R. (1999). Continued expansion of the nitinol self-expanding coronary stent: Angiographic analysis and 1-year clinical follow-up. *American Heart Journal, 138*(2 Pt. 1):326-333.

Stampfer, J., Stamler, R., Meaton, J. D., Wentworth, D., Daviglus, M. L., Garside, D., Dyer, A. R., Liu, K., Greenland, P. (1999). Low risk-factor profile and long-term cardiovascular and noncardiovascular mortality and life expectancy. *Journal of the American Medical Association, 282*:2012-2018.

Stampfer, M., Colditz, G., Willett, W., Manson, J., Rosner, B., Speizer, F., & Hennekens, C. (1991). Postmenopausal estrogen therapy and cardiovascular disease: Ten-year follow-up from the Nurses' Health Study. *New England Journal of Medicine, 325*:756-761.

Steinberg, D., & Gotto, A. M. Jr. (1999). Preventing coronary artery disease by lowering cholesterol levels: Fifty years from bench to bedside. *Journal of the American Medical Association, 282*:2043-2050.

U.S. Department of Health and Human Services. (1996). *Physical Activity and Health: A Report of the Surgeon General.* Atlanta, GA: U.S. Departments of Health and Human Services, Centers for Disease Control and Prevention, National Center for Chronic Disease Prevention and Health Promotion.

Van den Oever, R., Hepp, B., Debbaut, B., & Simon, I. (1998). Socioeconomic impact of chronic venous insufficiency: An underestimated public health problem. *International Angiology, 17*:161-167.

Cancer

"Many cancers can be cured, especially those detected early."

"**B**y winning the Tour, you stick in the minds and hearts of the cycling public. You can win every classic and the world championship, but the Tour is everything. It's a global event."

These words were uttered to newspaper reporters by Lance Armstrong, only the second American ever to win the Tour de France. On that clear sunny day in July of 1999, he won more than this most rigorous and prestigious three-week cycling race, however. He showed the world that he had truly won his battle with testicular cancer—a battle that had nearly cost him not only his career but also his life. The photo shows the champion nearing the end of the grueling course, which took competitors over the Alps and Pyrenees Mountains and into five countries bordering France. Armstrong is wearing a yellow jersey, the race's symbol of overall leadership. The jersey shows who is ahead over the various days and stages of the Tour. Armstrong wore the jersey throughout most of the three weeks. Although it is still the nation's second biggest killer (cardiovascular disease is the first), cancer is not an automatic death sentence. Armstrong and other cancer survivors are living testimony to that fact. Many cancers can be cured, especially those detected early. Even cancers in advanced stages, as was Armstrong's, may respond to therapies available today.

Cancer researchers are making discoveries daily that help win the war against cancer. For example, Canadian researchers Anil Srivastava and Nancy Kreiger recently discovered (2000) that teenage boys who exercise regularly and men who have physically demanding jobs in their 20s may be more likely to develop testicular cancer than less active teenage boys and young men. Although the mechanism for this increased risk is unknown, Srivastava and Kreiger speculate that exercise affects the levels of male hormones, which may somehow increase risk of the cancer. Although more research is needed to formulate recommendations regarding exercise and testicular cancer risk in these age groups, a tremendous body of research is already available that provides guidelines to help people avoid cancer. However, avoiding cancer is a primary health goal, and there are many actions people can take to lessen their risk of developing certain cancers. We discuss such preventive measures throughout this chapter.

What Is Cancer?

People often talk about cancer as if it were a single disease. However, cancer is many diseases. Lung cancer, for example, is a very different disease from leukemia (cancer of the blood) or skin cancer. Although different, all cancers have common characteristics: Their cells exhibit abnormal growth, division, and differentiation. Differentiation is the process by which cells develop into certain types, such as liver cells or muscle cells. In addition, cancer cells have the potential to **metastasize**, or spread from where they develop to another part of the body.

Cells are the building blocks of all organisms; they are the smallest unit of living material. In any multicelled organism such as humans, cells divide and differentiate as an individual grows and develops, and when its tissues need repair. The timing and events of cell division, growth, and differentiation are highly controlled by regulatory proteins. Cells make regulatory proteins in response to the instructions of the hereditary material, or genes. Normal cells are programmed to grow and divide, and to stop growing and dividing at appropriate times.

metastasize (meh-TAS-tah-size) the ability of cancer cells to spread from where they develop to another part of the body.

malignant tumors (mah-LIG-nant) masses of cancer cells that invade body tissues and interfere with the normal functioning of tissues and organs.

mutations (myou-TAY-shunz) changes in genes or chromosomes; damaged genes.

oncogenes (ONG-ko-geenz) tumor genes that manufacture altered proteins that speed cell growth and decrease the level of cell differentiation.

tumor-suppressor genes pieces of hereditary material that slow cell growth; anti-oncogenes.

carcinogens (kar-SIN-oh-jenz) cancer-causing substances.

benign tumors (be-NINE) encapsulated masses of abnormal cells that remain in one location and do not invade surrounding tissues.

carcinomas (KAR-si-NO-mahz) cancers that arise from epithelial tissues.

Unlike normal cells, cancer cells do not stop growing and dividing at appropriate times. Additionally, cancer cells do not differentiate normally and tend to spread. These cells may form masses called **malignant tumors** that invade body tissues and interfere with the normal functioning of tissues and organs. Tumors often cause pain as they invade nerves or press on nerves. Why do cancer cells behave differently from noncancer cells? The answer lies in the genetic material in the cell.

How Cancers Develop and Spread

Cancer develops only in cells that have **mutations**, that is, damaged genes. Mutations can be inherited or can occur from exposure to low-dose radiation, drugs, or toxic chemicals. Infection with certain viruses can also cause changes in genes. Excluding inheritance, then, cancer is determined largely by environmental factors, including components of lifestyle. Lifestyle factors play a major role in cancer prevention.

Genes and Cancer Development

Oncogenes are "on" switches that speed cell growth. Successive mutations to the hereditary material of particular body cells produce oncogenes. **Tumor-suppressor genes** are "off" switches that slow cell growth. If tumor-suppressor genes mutate or are lost from the hereditary makeup of a cell, they will no longer restrict cell growth.

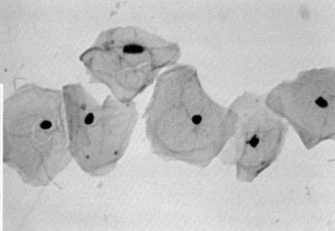

(b)

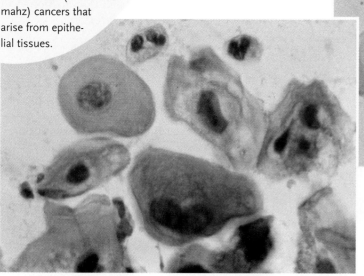

(a)

Figure 13-1 A Comparison of Dysplastic and Normal Cells.
◀(a) Dysplastic cells. These cells (stained differently from those in b) are irregular in size and the appearance of their nuclei.
▲(b) Normal cells. These cells are all approximately the same size and have nuclei that look similar.

The activation of oncogenes and deactivation of tumor-suppressor genes (and, therefore, the development of cancer) is a multistage process. In other words, successive genetic changes must take place for a normal cell to change into a cancer cell. These changes take place over time as various environmental factors affect cells and cause mutations. Therefore, the chances of developing cancer generally increase with increasing age and with exposure to cancer-causing substances, or **carcinogens.** Of course, many factors determine an individual's risk for developing cancers. These factors, which we will discuss throughout this chapter, modify this generalization.

Cells that begin to grow abnormally, although not yet cancer cells, may form growths called **benign tumors.** Surrounded by a fibrous capsule, benign tumors remain in one location; they do not invade surrounding tissues. Usually these growths are not life threatening unless their presence interferes with a vital function. For example, a benign brain tumor may be life threatening if it compresses blood vessels serving a vital center in the brain. In most cases benign tumors can be removed completely by surgery.

Some benign tumor cells exhibit traits that are characteristic of the development of cancer cells. These cells are said to exhibit dysplasia. Notice that the dysplastic cells in Figure 13-1a vary in size, shape, and the appearance of their nuclei. They are not differentiating properly into a spe-cific type of cell. The normal cells, however, are somewhat regular in these same characteristics (Figure 13-1b). Dysplastic cells have the potential to develop into cancer cells.

Metastasis

One of the characteristics of cancer cells is their ability to spread, or metastasize, from where they initially developed to other places in the body. Cells with the ability to metastasize are *malignant*. As a cancer develops, metastasis does not take place immediately. As cancer cells grow and divide, they often form a malignant tumor. At this stage the cancer is in situ (in place), because it has not invaded other tissues. However, these localized cancer cells begin to secrete chemicals that destroy the substances that hold the surrounding tissues together. When this occurs, cancer cells enter blood and lymph vessels and travel to other parts of the body. Cancerous cells can move out of the blood vessels at a distant location, enter the tissues there, and divide to form new masses of malignant cells. Figure 13-2 shows this process of cancer cell division

▼**Figure 13-2 How Cancer Cells Multiply and Spread.**
Cancer cells secrete chemicals that destroy the substances holding tissues together. As these tissues break down, cancer cells move from their original site, enter the blood and lymph, and travel to other parts of the body.

Tumor in bronchial epithelium.

Connective tissue

Capillary

(a)

Cells break through base of epithelium to invade capillary.

(b)

Cells travel through bloodstream and may eventually adhere to the capillary wall in the liver or other organ.* The cells then move out of the capillary.

Cells multiply to form metastasis of the liver.

*Less than 1 in 1000 survive to form metastases.

(c)

(d)

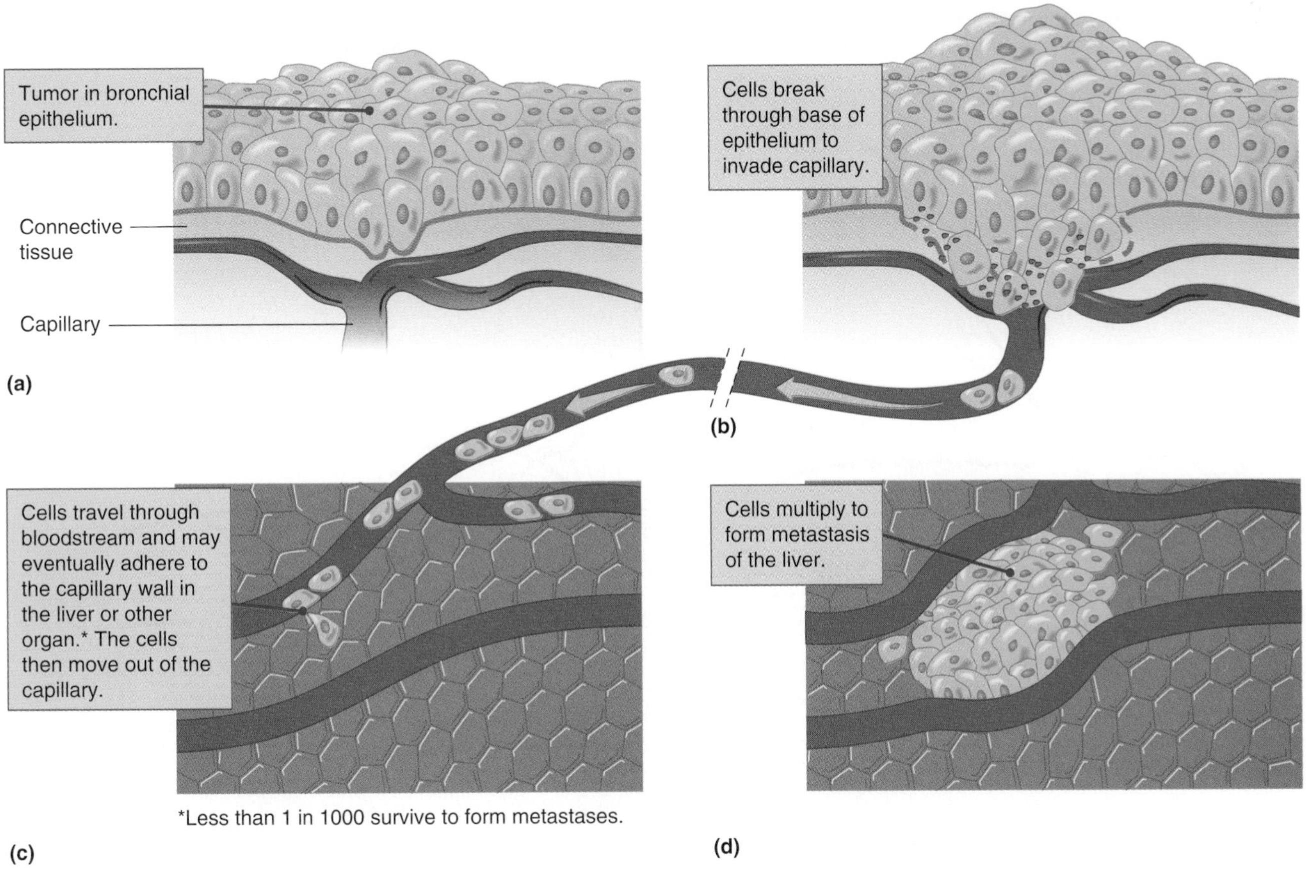

and metastasis. Once metastasis occurs, the cancer becomes much more difficult to control.

Cancers are named according to the type of tissue from which they develop. **Carcinomas** (which comprise most adult cancers) arise from epithelial tissue, which lines and covers internal and external body surfaces. Lung, oral, stomach, skin, breast, colon, and ovarian cancers are carcinomas. **Sarcomas** are cancers that arise from connective or muscle tissue. **Leukemias** are cancers of the blood and related cells. **Lymphomas** are cancers of the lymphatic system, the network of vessels and nodes that transports and filters tissue fluid. Cancers of the nervous system have a variety of names. ■ **Figure 13-3** shows death rates (the number of persons dying per year per 100,000 people) of various cancers in the United States. Most of these cancers are carcinomas.

sarcomas (sar-KO-mahz) cancers that arise from connective or muscle tissue.

leukemias (lew-KEY-me-ahz) cancers of the blood and related cells.

lymphomas (lim-FOE-mahz) cancers of the lymphatic system.

cancer screening an examination to detect malignancies in a person who has no symptoms.

Cancer Detection

Cancer screening is an examination to detect malignancies in a person who has no symptoms. The American Cancer Society (ACS) recommends the screening procedures listed in the "Managing Your Health" box on p. 303. Some screening procedures are expensive, invasive (that is, they require entering a body cavity or interrupting normal body functions), or both. Most such procedures are not performed unless a person is in a high-risk category for a particular cancer, or if symptoms indicate that a particular cancer may be present.

Cancer screening or detection methods vary depending on the location of the possible cancer. Superficial cancers, such as cancers of the skin and oral cavity, can be detected by visual examination. Some cancers in internal areas can be detected by collecting cells for microscopic examination. This process is possible, for example, for detecting cancer of the cervix and of the esophagus. Some cancers, such as colon cancer and stomach cancer, can be detected by fiberoptic examination. To see these internal areas of the body, the physician inserts a flexible tube called a fiberscope in the area to be examined. The fiberscope contains bundles

▼**Figure 13-3 Cancer death rates, 1930-1995.** (a) male, and (b) female. Source: American Cancer Society, 1999.

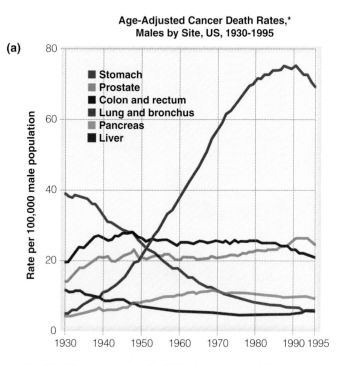

*Per 100,000, age-adjusted to the 1970 US standard population.
Note: Due to changes in ICD coding, numerator information has changed over time. Rates for cancers of the liver, lung and bronchus, and colon and rectum are affected by these coding changes. American Cancer Society, Surveillance Research, 1999.
Data source: Vital Statistics of the United States, 1998.

*Per 100,000, age-adjusted to the 1970 US standard population.
†Uterus cancer death rates are for uterine cervix and uterine corpus combined.
Note: Due to changes in ICD coding, numerator information has changed over time. Rates for cancers of the uterus, ovary, lung and bronchus, and colon and rectum are affected by these coding changes. American Cancer Society, Surveillance Research, 1999.
Data source: Vital Statistics of the United States, 1998.

of specially coated glass or plastic fibers that transmit an image from the lighted end of the scope to an eyepiece.

Other cancers that grow embedded in tissues, such as breast cancer and lung cancer, can be detected by x rays. CT scans and MRI can also be used to detect deeply embedded cancers, such as brain cancer. CT scans, or computed tomography, are x rays of thin sections of the body that the computer constructs into three-dimensional images (**Figure 13-4**). MRI, or magnetic resonance imaging, uses magnetic fields and radio waves instead of x rays. As in CT scans, a computer constructs three-dimensional images of internal tissues. Ultrasound, an imaging technique that

Summary of American Cancer Society Recommendations for the Early Detection of Cancer in Asymptomatic People

Test or Procedure	Sex	Age	Frequency
Sigmoidoscopy, preferably flexible with digital rectal exam OR	M&F	50 and older	Every 5 years
Colonoscopy with digital rectal exam OR	M&F	50 and older	Every 10 years
Double contrast barium enema with digital rectal exam	M&F	50 and older	Every 5 to 10 years
Fecal occult blood test	M&F	50 and older	Every year
Prostate exam*	M	50 and older	Every year
Pap test and pelvic examination	F		All women who are, or who have been, sexually active, or have reached age 18, should have an annual Pap test and pelvic examination. After a woman has had three or more consecutive satisfactory normal annual examinations, the Pap test may be performed less frequently at the discretion of her physician.
Endometrial tissue sample	F	At menopause if at high risk†	At menopause and thereafter at the discretion of the physician
Breast self-examination	F	20 and older	Every month
Breast clinical examination	F	20 to 39 40 and older	Every 3 years Every year
Mammography	F	40 and older‖	Every year
Health counseling and cancer checkup§	M&F M&F	Over 20 Over 40	Every 3 years Every year

*Annual digital rectal examination and prostate-specific antigen should be performed on men 50 years and older. If either is abnormal, further evaluation should be considered. Men in high risk groups (i.e., two or more affected first-degree relatives) or African Americans may begin at 45 years.
†History of infertility, obesity, failure to ovulate, abnormal uterine bleeding, or unopposed estrogen or tamoxifen therapy.
§To include examination for cancers of the thyroid, testicles, ovaries, lymph nodes, oral region, and skin.
‖The National Institutes of Health (NIH) held a consensus development conference on breast cancer screening for women aged 40 to 49 on January 21–23, 1997, in Bethesda, Maryland. This federal panel decided that the evidence was still not strong enough to recommend breast cancer screening tests for this age group. The American Cancer Society disagrees on this point and recommends screening for women aged 40 to 49.
Source: American Cancer Society.

uses sound waves, is used occasionally to detect cancerous growths. (See p. 114 for a more thorough description of ultrasound.)

The 5-year survival rate is the percentage of persons who are alive 5 years after their cancer is diagnosed, whether they are disease-free, under treatment, or in remission (having a partial or complete disappearance of the signs and symptoms of the cancer). ▌ **Table 13-1** shows the 5-year survival rate for cancers discussed in this chapter.

Table 13-1	Five-Year Relative Survival Rates* by Stage at Diagnosis, 1989–1994			
Site	**All Stages %**	**Local %**	**Regional %**	**Distant %**
Breast (female)	85	97	77	22
Uterine cervix	70	91	48	11
Colon & rectum	62	91	66	9
Uterine corpus	84	96	66	27
Esophagus	12	24	12	2
Kidney	61	89	62	10
Larynx	66	83	54	44
Liver	5	15	5	2
Lung & bronchus	14	50	20	2
Melanoma	88	96	59	12
Oral cavity	53	82	42	20
Ovary	50	95	79	28
Pancreas	4	17	6	1
Prostate	93	100	99	33
Stomach	21	60	21	2
Testis	95	99	98	73
Thyroid	95	100	94	44
Urinary bladder	82	95	50	6

*Rates are adjusted for normal life expectancy and are based on cases diagnosed from 1989–1994, followed through 1995. **Local:** An invasive malignant cancer confined entirely to the organ of origin. **Regional:** A malignant cancer that 1) has extended beyond the limits of the organ of origin directly into surrounding organs or tissues; 2) involves regional lymph nodes by way of lymphatic system; or 3) has both regional extension and involvement of regional lymph nodes. **Distant:** A malignant cancer that has spread to parts of the body remote from the primary tumor either by direct extension or by discontinuous metastasis to distant organs, tissues, or via the lymphatic system to distant lymph nodes.
Source: NCI, Surveillance, Epidemiology, and End Results Program, 1998.

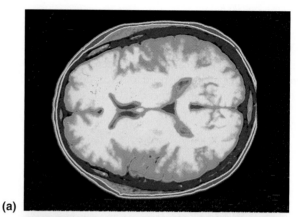

(a)

(b)

▲**Figure 13-4 (a) CT and (b) MRI Scans of the Brain.** Both have color added to visualize structures better. The outer skull, underlying fat, and brain tissues can be seen clearly in both. The MRI shows the convolutions of the brain.

www.jbpub.com/healthyliving

Cancer Treatment

The principal forms of cancer treatment are surgery, radiation, and chemotherapy. A newer mode of treatment is biomodulation (formerly known as immunotherapy). In the past, physicians referred to a cancer as "cured" if the patient survived for 5 years with no sign of the cancer returning. This is no longer the case, however, because some cancers grow after extended periods and others recur after they seem to have been eliminated. Today, the term *cure* means that all traces of a nonmetastasized (localized) tumor have been removed from the body and the former cancer patient has the same life expectancy as a person who never had cancer.

Surgery

Most cancer cures are accomplished by surgery. During surgery, physicians remove a localized cancer by cutting it away from noncancerous tissue. Microscopic extensions of cancerous tissue may not be easy to detect during surgical procedures, so a physician usually removes tissue beyond the obvious cancer to increase the probability that all the cancerous tissue is removed. Although surgery is often a life-saving treatment, one drawback is that removal of healthy tissue with unhealthy tissue may impair the body's functioning or cause disfigurement.

Radiation

Radiation is also used to treat localized cancers, either alone or in conjunction with surgery. Radiation is energy or particles emitted from the nucleus of an atom. The energy of any high-dose radiation interferes with the molecular structures of cells, killing them. Healthy cells recover more quickly and easily from radiation treatment than do cancer cells, so the healthy tissue surrounding a cancer usually survives while the cancer dies. For this reason, a physician may recommend radiation over surgery in particular instances. Preserving healthy tissue surrounding a cancer is extremely important, especially with cancers such as laryngeal cancer (cancer of the voice box), in which it may mean the difference between a patient's retaining or losing the ability to speak. Physicians also choose radiation over surgery for treatment of cancers that respond well to radiation therapy, such as cervical cancer, prostate cancer, and Hodgkin's disease. Additionally, physicians often use radiation treatment with elderly patients because their chances of recovering from it may be higher than that of recovering from surgery.

High-dose x-ray and gamma-ray irradiation are widely used today. Patients may undergo one of two methods of radiation treatment. One method is to focus a beam of radiation on the cancerous tissue from an outside source. The machine delivering the beam of radiation rotates around the patient while continually targeting the tumor, so that various areas of healthy tissue receive minimal doses of radiation but the tumor receives high doses. Another method is to implant tiny radioactive "beads" in the cancerous tissue for a specific time and then remove them. With either approach, cancer patients usually undergo numerous treatments over a 5- to 8-week period.

▎**Figure 13-5** shows a new, highly effective treatment against cancer called *proton therapy.* In this treatment, a patient's cancer is bombarded with a stream of positively charged, subatomic particles called protons. The machine used to deliver the treatment is called a particle accelerator, which has two parts: one that increases the speed of the protons to a high velocity and one that delivers the accelerated protons to the patient. All you see in the photograph is the part of the machine that delivers the protons.

At high doses, proton irradiation kills cells, as does any type of high-dose radiation. Proton radiation, however, can be focused more precisely on the cancer than can other forms of radiation (Archambeau et al., 1994). Therefore, a

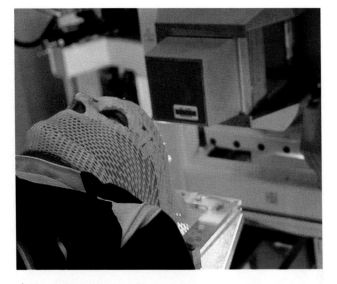

▲**Figure 13-5 Proton Therapy.** This patient at the Proton Treatment Center at Loma Linda University is ready to receive proton therapy to treat cancer of the eye. The mask immobilizes the head to assure that the beam will hit its target.

higher dose of radiation can be used with less radiation affecting surrounding cells. However, proton therapy is still not in widespread use because it is about three times as costly as traditional radiation therapies. Additionally, a few treatment facilities in the United States offer proton irradiation (Suit & Urie, 1992).

Chemotherapy

Chemotherapy is the use of anticancer drugs to inhibit cancer cell reproduction or destroy cancer cells. Chemotherapy is used most often when cancer has spread to various regions of the body. As with radiation therapy, chemotherapy may be used in conjunction with surgery. In certain cases, physicians combine all three approaches to cancer treatment.

Radiation and chemotherapy treatments also kill and damage healthy cells and may cause serious side effects such as severe nausea and hair loss. In addition, these treatments do not always destroy cancers completely because their doses are not high enough to do so. Doses sufficiently high to kill all cancer cells often cause too much damage to normal tissue. Also, certain tumors are drug resistant or develop drug resistance during therapy.

Biomodulation

Recently, a new breed of cancer treatment emerged in the war against cancer: the manipulation of the body's own immune system to rid the body of its cancer (Boon, 1993). (The immune system is discussed in Chapter 14.) The umbrella term for these new and generally experi-

Alternative Cancer Therapies

In the spring of 1991, a physician told 54-year-old actor Michael Landon (photo at right) that he had a cancerous tumor of the pancreas. By the time it was detected, the cancer had spread to his liver. Physicians specializing in the treatment of cancer recommended that he undergo chemotherapy, but they told the actor that his prognosis was grim. At first, Landon agreed to try chemotherapy, but soon decided to discontinue the medication and use unproven approaches to cancer treatment. Convinced that he needed to strengthen his immune system, the actor followed a vegetarian diet with plenty of fruits and vegetables. Several times a day he drank a homemade concoction of blended organic apples, carrots, and beet tops. He took vitamins and enzymes, submitted to acupuncture treatment, and endured a daily coffee enema. Despite determined efforts to overcome cancer, Michael Landon died on July 1, 1991.

Modern medicine has its limitations; not every condition can be prevented, managed, or cured. It is not surprising, therefore, that some individuals such as Michael Landon who are diagnosed with incurable conditions seek help from anyone who offers a cure. Cancer patients who seek alternative therapies also hope to find a "softer" treatment with fewer side effects. Many want to use a holistic approach or "take charge" of their health when conventional medicine offers no more options. When faced with a potentially life-threatening illness such as cancer, most people feel the need to do "everything possible" to survive.

Most users of alternative cancer therapies expect their treatments to boost their immune system or slow the progression of or cure their cancer. However, the effectiveness of most alternative therapies in cancer treatment has not been established in scientific studies. Additionally, cancer patients erroneously perceive alternative therapies as safe because they are "natural," but therapies such as herbal and vitamin supplements may interact in dangerous ways with drugs or therapies being used in conventional cancer treatment. Many have serious side effects of their own. And if cancer patients delay conventional treatment in favor of unconventional treatment, they may diminish their chances of survival, spend money needlessly, and lower their quality of life.

Herbal therapies, plant extracts, and therapeutic vitamins are the most common alternative therapies in cancer treatment today, and up to 45% of cancer patients use some form of alternative treatment. A few of the more popular of these therapies are discussed on the next page. The greatest danger with the use of substances not controlled by the Food and Drug Administration (FDA) in cancer treatment is the risk of contamination, misidentification, or substitution with a harmful substance because of lack of quality control.

If you or someone you know is thinking about using alternative therapies for cancer treatment, remember that it is important to evaluate all evidence about these methods carefully and make decisions with a qualified health-care provider. At the least, informing the health-care provider about other therapies being used can help avoid adverse drug interactions. Also, in evaluating therapies, remember that any remedy used by a large number of people will, by chance, be used by a long-term survivor. In many cases, the patient used conventional treatments as well as alternative ones. However, the alternative method often gets the credit even though there is no evidence to show that it played a role in the patient's long-term survival.

Sources: Fernandez, C.V., Stutzer, C.A., MacWilliam, L, & Fryer, C. (1998). Alternative and complementary therapy use in pediatric oncology patients in British Columbia: Prevalence and reasons for use and nonuse. *Journal of Clinical Oncology*, 16:1270–1286.
Kaegi, E. on behalf of the Task Force on Alternative Therapies of the Canadian Cancer Research Initiative. (1998). Unconventional therapies for cancer 1: Essiac. *Canadian Medical Association Journal*, 158:897–902.
Kaegi, E. on behalf of the Task Force on Alternative Therapies of the Canadian Cancer Research Initiative. (1998). Unconventional therapies for cancer 2: Green tea. *Canadian Medical Association Journal*, 158:1033–1035.
Kaegi, E. on behalf of the Task Force on Alternative Therapies of the Canadian Cancer Research Initiative. (1998). Unconventional therapies for cancer 5: Vitamins A, C, and E. *Canadian Medical Association Journal*, 158:1483–1488.
Spaulding-Albright, N. (1997). A review of some herbal and related products commonly used in cancer patients. *Journal of the American Dietetic Association*, 97, S2:S208–S215.
Verhoef, M. J, Hagen, N., Pelletier, G., & Forsyth, P. (1999) Alternative therapy use in neurologic disease: Use in brain tumor patients. *Neurology*, 52:617–622.

Alternative Therapy	What is it?	Claims and Research Studies	Possible Side Effects
Huang ch'i	Extract from the plant *Astragalus membranaceus*	*Claims:* Stimulation of the immune system. *Studies:* Results of a U. of Texas study show that it may boost immune system function. It may also reduce the side effects of chemotherapy.	Can trigger low blood pressure. May induce dizziness and fatigue. Too much may suppress the immune system.
Essiac	Herbal tea. Mixture of 4 herbs: burdock root, Indian rhubarb, sheep sorrel, & slippery elm	*Claims:* strengthens immune system, improves appetite, relieves pain, may reduce tumor size. *Studies:* There are no reports of controlled studies demonstrating positive outcomes in cancer patients. Tests at Memorial Sloan-Kettering and the National Cancer Institute show no activity in reducing the size of animal tumors.	Nausea, vomiting, diarrhea
Green tea	Tea made from the steamed and then dried leaves and leaf buds of the shrub *Camellia sinensis.* (Black tea is prepared from the fermented leaves of this plant.)	*Claims:* Results of a variety of studies suggest that regular consumption moderately decreases the risk of cancer, especially cancers of the upper digestive tract. Therefore, use as a treatment is being studied. *Studies:* There are no data from human studies and limited data from animal studies. Results are contradictory. Some researchers think green tea may play a role in delaying metastasis.	High caffeine content may cause nervousness, insomnia, and irregularities in heart rate. Moderate consumption appears safe.
Vitamins A (or beta-carotene), C, & E	Vitamin "cocktail" taken in megadoses	*Claims:* Combination of these vitamins improves general well-being, strengthens immune system, and may delay the development and progression of serious disease. *Studies:* Some animal studies have shown the ability of vitamin A and beta-carotene to enhance the immune response, to retard tumor growth, and to decrease the size of established tumors. In laboratory experiments, vitamin C has been shown to inhibit tumor growth. Results of some studies also suggest that vitamin C may kill tumor cells and may enhance the effects of some cancer drugs. Very little research has been conducted on the role of vitamin E in cancer treatment. At this time, there is not enough evidence for physicians to recommend that cancer patients take vitamin supplements.	Vitamin A: Headache, irritability, drowsiness, dizziness, itchiness. Megadoses may cause liver damage. Taking beta-carotene, which is transformed into vitamin A in the body, is safer than taking vitamin A. Vitamin C: Generally well tolerated. Megadoses may cause stomach irritation, heartburn, nausea, vomiting, drowsiness, headaches, rash, and abnormalities in iron metabolism. Vitamin E: Toxicity in adults appears to be low. High levels can adversely affect the absorption of vitamins A and K. Long-term megadoses may cause nausea, diarrhea, and blurred vision.

mental methods is biomodulation (biological response modification).

Formerly called immunotherapy, **biomodulation** is the manipulation of the body's own immune system to enhance the body's response to its cancer. It includes the use of gene therapy techniques (Culver & Blaese, 1994). Gene therapy is the introduction of hereditary material into cells to treat a specific disorder or condition. A key factor in the body's capability to mount its defense is its ability to recognize an intruder as foreign. Like other foreign substances, cancer cells are marked as intruders because they contain proteins called antigens that are not normally found in the body. However, tumor cells appear to contain antigens that evoke only a weak response from the immune system. As a result, the immune system has difficulty detecting and identifying malignant tumors, so it does a poor job destroying these abnormal cells.

What kinds of things do biomodulators do to help the body ward off cancer? Injecting tumor antigens into the patient's bloodstream can increase the numbers of tumor-fighting immune system cells in the body (Linehan et al., 1999). This procedure is similar to the way in which a vaccine works to boost the body's immune response against an infectious disease. For this reason, such cancer-fighting products are called *cancer vaccines*. However, cancer vaccines are given to patients who already have cancers to help rid them of their diseases. They are not given to cancer-free persons to prevent cancer. At this time, cancer vaccines, which are experimental, are being developed for prostate, colorectal, lung, and breast cancers, and for malignant melanoma (de Gruijl & Curiel, 1999; Houghton, 1995).

Examples of other biomodulators are drugs that decrease the suppressor mechanisms of the immune system, thus increasing the host's immune response. Another approach

biomodulation manipulation of the body's immune system to rid itself of cancer.

is to augment the patient's immune system by bone marrow transplants (tissue that produces immune system cells) or transfusions of particular immune system cells. Other biomodulators are chemicals that act on tumor cells by making them more recognizable by the body or more susceptible to dying as a result of immune system processes.

These experimental therapies may be only the beginning of what the future holds for cancer therapy. Health-care practitioners and researchers hope that treatments such as these and new radiation therapies such as proton therapy will change the mortality rates from all types of cancers dramatically. However, even as scientists discover new ways to treat the nation's number two killer, prevention and early detection are still the best ways to live a healthy, long, cancer-free life.

www.jbpub.com/healthyliving

Prevalent Cancers in the United States

Over decades of research, scientists have learned what causes certain cancers. In many cases, scientists are unsure of the cause but know which factors are related to cancer development. These factors, which, when present, increase the chances that a person will develop a particular cancer, are called risk factors.

This chapter organizes the discussion of cancers according to factors that appear to be significant in the development of particular cancers, most of which are prevalent in the United States. Advanced age is a significant risk factor for most cancers except certain childhood cancers, testicular cancer, cervical cancer, and, in part, breast cancer. In some cases, heredity is a significant factor in cancer development.

Before reading this section, fill out the Cancer Prevention Behavior Scale in the student workbook to determine if your behaviors are healthy with respect to cancer prevention.

Cancers Caused by or Related to Tobacco

In 1989, U.S. Surgeon General C. Everett Koop issued a report on smoking and health that listed tobacco smoking as a cause of various airway cancers. ▌ Table 13-2 lists these cancers, as well as cancers in which tobacco use plays a contributory role and cancers in which tobacco use is simply associated with the cancer. This section explores the first seven cancers on this list because they are all caused primarily by or strongly associated with this preventable risk. Stomach cancer and cancer of the cervix are discussed in other sections of this chapter because their primary causes relate to factors other than tobacco use.

Lung Cancer Looking at ▌ Table 13-3, you can see that lung cancer is the leading cause of cancer deaths in both men and women in the United States. Death rates due to lung cancer have risen dramatically in men since the

Table 13-2	Cancers to Which Smoking Is Related
Causal role of tobacco	Lung and bronchus
	Larynx
	Oral cavity (mouth and throat)
	Esophagus
Contributory role of tobacco	Bladder
	Kidney
	Pancreas
Association with tobacco	Stomach
	Cervix (invasive)

Source: United States Department of Health and Human Services. (1989). *Reducing the health consequences of smoking: 25 years of progress. A report of the Surgeon General.* (DHHS Publication No. [CDC] 89-8411).

Table 13-3	Leading Sites of New Cancer Cases and Death*

Cancer Cases by Site and Sex		Cancer Deaths by Site and Sex	
Male	Female	Male	Female
Prostate 179,300	Breast 175,000	Lung & bronchus 90,900	Lung & bronchus 68,000
Lung & bronchus 94,000	Lung & bronchus 77,600	Prostate 37,000	Breast 43,300
Colon & rectum 62,400	Colon & rectum 67,000	Colon & rectum 27,800	Colon & rectum 28,800
Urinary bladder 39,100	Uterine corpus 37,400	Pancreas 13,900	Pancreas 14,700
Non-Hodgkin's lymphoma 32,600	Ovary 25,200	Non-Hodgkin's lymphoma 13,400	Ovary 14,500
Melanoma of the skin 25,800	Non-Hodgkin's lymphoma 24,200	Leukemia 12,400	Non-Hodgkin's lymphoma 12,300
Oral cavity 20,000	Melanoma of the skin 18,400	Esophagus 9,400	Leukemia 9,700
Kidney 17,800	Urinary bladder 15,100	Liver 8,400	Uterine corpus 6,400
Leukemia 16,800	Pancreas 14,600	Urinary bladder 8,100	Brain 5,900
Pancreas 14,000	Thyroid 13,500	Stomach 7,900	Stomach 5,600
All Sites 623,800	All Sites 598,000	All Sites 291,100	All Sites 272,000

*Excluding basal and squamous cell skin cancer and carcinomas in situ except urinary bladder. American Cancer Society, Surveillance Research, 1999.

1940s and in women since the 1960s. These increases are due primarily to increases in the percentage of the population who smoked tobacco in the decades prior to the 1960s. Lung cancer, like most cancers, takes years to develop, so a rise in lung cancer death rates occurs decades after a rise in the percentage of the population who smoke. We know today that tobacco smoking is the cause of 87% of lung cancers (American Cancer Society [ACS], 1999).

Evidence suggests that women are more susceptible than men to developing lung cancer caused by tobacco use. Results of recent research show that a gene called GRPR, which is linked to the abnormal growth of lung cells, is much more active in women than in men. Located on the X chromosome, a piece of hereditary material that determines gender, the GRPR gene is turned on more frequently in women nonsmokers than in men nonsmokers, and is activated earlier in women than in men in response to cigarette smoke. The presence of two copies of the GRPR gene in women, one on each of their two X chromosomes, may be a factor in their increased susceptibility to tobacco-induced lung cancer (Shriver et al., 2000). Men have only one X chromosome, along with a Y chromosome.

Incidence rates of lung cancer in both sexes have begun to stabilize, and to drop slightly in males (see Figure 13-3). This stabilization reflects the beginning of a predicted decline in incidence rates due to the steady decline in cigarette smoking in the U.S. population since 1964. In that year, U.S. Surgeon General Luther Terry issued a report that linked cigarette smoking with the development of lung cancer and other diseases (U.S. Public Health Service,

1964). In 1999 the American Cancer Society set goals for 2015 of a 25% reduction in cancer incidence and a 50% reduction in cancer mortality rates (Byers et al., 1999).

Signs and Symptoms In the early stages of disease, the signs and symptoms of lung cancer may be hard to detect. Cigarette smokers often have chronic cough, chronic bronchitis, or excess sputum (saliva and mucus) production (see Chapter 8). Tumors growing in the bronchioles (small airways in the lungs) also cause a cough and sputum production; they may also cause blood to appear in the sputum as they disrupt airway tissues. A lung cancer victim may also wheeze when breathing if the airways become substantially narrowed by tumor growth. In addition, the air sacs in that part of the lung may collapse and cease to function; infection may develop. The patient may experience pain in the chest, shoulder, and arm if the cancer spreads to the chest wall and affects certain nerves there.

Physicians use chest x rays, analyses of the types of cells in the sputum, and fiberoptic examination of the bronchial passageways to assist in their diagnoses.

Risk Factors and Prevention Malignant growths develop in the lungs and airways in many persons as they inhale cancer-causing substances such as tobacco smoke over long periods of time.

Table 13-4 Documented Occupational Lung Carcinogens

Substance	Occupational Exposures
Arsenic	Smelters, pesticide manufacturers
Asbestos	Miners, millers, insulators, railroad and shipyard workers
Beryllium	Workers in electronic industries and for aerospace and nuclear reactor parts manufacturers
Chloromethyl ethers	Ion-exchange resin manufacturers
Chromium	Chromate and pigment manufacturers
Hydrocarbons	Coal gas workers, roofers
Mustard gas	Poison gas manufacturers
Nickel	Refiners
Radiation (radon)	Miners of uranium and other ores

Source: Frank, A. L. (1989). Epidemiology of lung cancer. In Roth, J., Ructersall, J., & Weisenburger, T. (Eds.). *Thoracic surgery*. Philadelphia: W. B. Saunders Co., p. 6. Reprinted with permission.

The incidence of lung cancer rises proportionately with the number of cigarettes (or cigars or pipes) a person smokes per day, the number of years a person smokes, and how deeply he or she inhales. Persons who smoke low-tar cigarettes have a lower risk of lung cancer than those who smoke high-tar cigarettes. (Smoking "low-yield" cigarettes does not lower cardiovascular disease risk; see Chapter 12.) Likewise, those who smoke filter-tipped cigarettes have a lower risk of lung cancer than those who smoke unfiltered cigarettes. However, cigarette smokers, on average, are 10 times more likely to develop lung cancer than are nonsmokers (Hecht, 1994). Additionally, results of recent research show that people who smoke filter-tipped or "low-yield" cigarettes are at increased risk for developing deep lung tumors because, when smoking, they inhale more deeply and forcefully than people who smoke non-filter-tipped or "regular-yield" cigarettes (U.S. Dept. of Health and Human Services [USDHHS], 1999b). If you are a smoker (of any age), giving up cigarette smoking will slowly lower your risk of developing lung cancer, several other cancers, and cardiovascular disease as well. Your risk of developing lung cancer will return to that of a nonsmoker in about 10 years. (However, your risk of developing cardiovascular disease will lower considerably in only 1 year, and return to that of a nonsmoker in 3 to 15 years, depending on how much and how long you smoked.)

Scientists have been unable to show that lung cancer is inherited. However, correlational studies show that relatives of lung cancer patients have a higher risk of developing lung cancer if they smoke than do smokers with no relatives who have lung cancer. Scientists speculate that relatives of lung cancer patients may inherit a defect in their cells' ability to resist genetic damage by the carcinogens in cigarette smoke (Sellers et al., 1992).

In the early 1970s medical researchers began investigating the effects of **passive smoking** on the development of lung cancer. Passive smoking is the inhalation by nonsmokers of environmental tobacco smoke (ETS) present in the air from others who smoke. Environmental tobacco smoke is associated with a 35% to 50% increase in lung cancer risk. That is, nonsmokers exposed to ETS on a regular basis are 0.35 to 0.5 times more likely to develop lung cancer than nonsmokers not exposed to ETS. Additionally, children exposed to ETS have higher blood levels of certain tobacco-related carcinogens than unexposed children (Hecht, 1994).

Substances other than those in tobacco smoke have also been linked to lung cancer and are listed in ▌ **Table 13-4.** Only people in certain occupations encounter most of these substances. Two substances significantly associated with the development of lung cancer and often encountered in the environment are asbestos and radon.

Asbestos is a fiberlike mineral found in rocks that resists damage by fire or other natural processes. Because of these properties, asbestos has been used in the manufac-

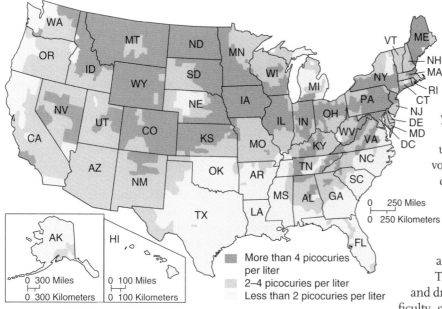

More than 4 picocuries per liter
2–4 picocuries per liter
Less than 2 picocuries per liter

risk of developing cancer of the larynx, oral cavity, and esophagus.

Cancers of the larynx, or voicebox, are usually detected early if they involve the vocal cords because the voice quickly becomes hoarse. However, cancers of the larynx that do not involve the vocal cords are more difficult to discover early. Their symptoms may include a sore throat, difficulty in swallowing, or a visible lump in the neck.

The esophagus is the tube that carries food and drink from the mouth to the stomach. Difficulty swallowing is also a symptom of esophageal cancer. In addition, people who have recurrent heartburn or a burning sensation while swallowing should be checked for possible esophageal carcinoma.

In oral cancer, malignant or benign growths are often visible (▌ Figure 13-7). Malignancies may appear as sores that bleed easily and do not heal, red or white patches that do not go away, or thickened areas of tissue. Oral cancer metastasizes relatively quickly; approximately 50% of cases are diagnosed in advanced stages. To detect oral cancer early, persons over the age of 50 should have complete oral examinations as part of their annual physical checkups. Dentists should routinely screen all of their patients for oral cancer.

passive smoking the inhalation, by non-smokers, of tobacco smoke in the air.

asbestos (as-BES-tose) a fiberlike mineral found in rocks that, when inhaled, can cause lung cancer or other lung conditions.

radon gas a colorless, odorless, radioactive gas present in the rocks and soils in many areas in the United States that, when inhaled, can cause mutations in cells.

ture of a variety of products and is used in the construction, shipbuilding, and railroad industries. People in these industries as well as those who mine asbestos are at risk of developing lung cancer if they inhale asbestos particles. Additionally, the effects of inhaling asbestos particles multiplies the effects of smoking tobacco and therefore greatly increases risk. Chapter 16 discusses asbestos in greater detail.

Exposure to **radon gas** also appears to multiply the carcinogenic effect of tobacco smoke (USDHHS, 1999a). Radon gas is colorless and odorless, and is produced as the radioactive element uranium decays, emitting subatomic particles and energy. When inhaled, radon can cause mutations in cells because it is radioactive also. Radon is present in the rocks and soils in many areas in the United States (▌ Figure 13-6). People who live in these regions may be exposed to radon gas if it leaks through cracks in basement walls and collects in their homes. Home radon detectors can ascertain the presence of this gas. If radon is present, specialists in radon abatement can advise a homeowner on procedures to prevent this gas from leaking into and accumulating in the house.

Treatment Physicians treat lung cancer with surgery, radiation, and chemotherapy. Surgeons often remove the lobe of the cancerous lung. They may combine therapies if the cancer has spread, using radiation or chemotherapy with surgery.

Cancers of the Larynx, Oral Cavity, and Esophagus Although these cancers are not as prevalent as others, they have preventable causes: tobacco use, which includes the use of cigarettes, cigars, pipes, and smokeless (chewing) tobacco of all types; and excessive alcohol consumption. Heavy consumption of alcohol is often a causal factor in cancers of the esophagus and liver, but if a heavy drinker is also a smoker, the effects of both substances multiply the

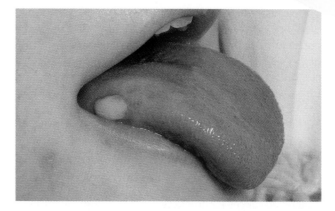

▲Figure 13-7 **Tongue Cancer.** This close-up of a cancer patient's mouth shows a malignant tumor on the edge of the tongue. This type of cancer spreads rapidly. The survival rate is low.

Cancers of the Kidney and Bladder The kidneys and bladder are organs of the urinary system, yet tobacco smoking is correlated with the incidence of cancers of these organs. These organs come in contact with inhaled carcinogens in tobacco smoke (or other inhaled carcinogens) after they enter the bloodstream at the lungs. The kidneys filter the carcinogens into the urine, exposing the bladder to these substances before urination.

Most signs and symptoms of kidney and bladder cancer are the same as those of several other conditions, so experiencing any of them is not a sure sign of cancer. One such sign of both cancers is blood in the urine. Frequent, urgent, or difficult urination are also signs of bladder cancer. Additional signs and symptoms of kidney cancer include a fever of unknown origin, weight loss, and anemia (a decrease in the hemoglobin in the blood).

Most people who get bladder or kidney cancer are men over 50 years of age who are heavy smokers. Cigarette smokers have 2 to 10 times the risk of developing bladder or kidney cancer as do nonsmokers. Carcinogens in cigarette smoke enter the bloodstream at the lungs and then are filtered by the kidneys into the urine. Therefore, these substances can affect both kidney and bladder cells. As with lung cancer, the risk increases with the number of cigarettes smoked per day and the number of years a person has been a smoker. People lessen their risk when they decrease the number of cigarettes they smoke or stop smoking.

Cancer of the Pancreas A long, slender gland, the pancreas lies near the stomach. As an accessory organ of the digestive system, the pancreas secretes digestive enzymes that enter the small intestine by means of a duct. As an endocrine gland, the pancreas secretes the hormones insulin and glucagon, which help regulate blood levels of glucose.

Pancreatic cancer is a particularly deadly form of cancer, striking men and women fairly equally. The fourth most common cause of cancer death (see Table 13-3), pancreatic cancer is often called a silent cancer because the early symptoms, which include nausea, vomiting, and weakness, are vague and nonspecific. The more specific signs and symptoms of pancreatic cancer—jaundice (yellowing of the eyeballs and skin), pain, and weight loss—do not occur until the disease is advanced and then may be confused with many other diseases, such as gallbladder or liver disease.

The risk of pancreatic cancer increases after age 50; most cases occur in persons aged 65 to 79 years. Although medical researchers do not know what causes pancreatic cancer, results of studies show an association between tobacco smoking and pancreatic cancer; the incidence of pancreatic cancer for smokers is twice as high as for nonsmokers. Other persons at risk for developing pancreatic cancer are chemists and those in occupations that involve close exposure to gasoline and dry cleaning agents. Inhaled carcinogens appear to reach the pancreas via the bloodstream.

Only 3% of people who have pancreatic cancer survive beyond 5 years, and only 1% of people with pancreatic cancer are cured. Late detection and metastasis reduce survival. For the rare patients who discover their cancer in its early stages, surgery is a primary treatment that may lead to a cure and long-term relief of symptoms. Occasionally, radiation therapy and anticancer drugs are used.

Cancers Related to Diet

Scientists who study cancer think that diet accounts for as much as 35% of human cancers (ACS, 1999). The results of numerous research studies suggest that diet has both a positive and a negative effect on the development of cancer. There are dietary components that raise the risk of certain cancers and others that lower the risk of certain cancers. One cancer strongly related to diet is stomach cancer. The other cancer related to diet—colorectal cancer—can be affected significantly by one's heredity. Other cancers such as breast cancer may have risk factors related to diet, but the evidence is unclear at this time.

Cancer of the Stomach The incidence of and mortality from stomach cancer has declined dramatically over the past 60 to 70 years in the United States. In the early part of this century, stomach cancer, not lung cancer, was the number one cancer killer of Americans. (See the "Diversity in Health" essay on page 314 for an explanation of this decline.)

Stomach cancer is another of the silent cancers because no signs and symptoms appear early in its course. As the disease progresses, a person may experience mild stomach discomfort with gas pains or vague sensations of fullness. Suspecting minor digestive problems, a person with these symptoms may take antacid tablets and the symptoms disappear. As the cancer continues to grow, the malignancy causes more severe pain that is less responsive to antacids. The stomach cancer victim may then experience a decreased appetite, a feeling of fullness after just beginning to eat, pain on eating, nausea and vomiting, weight loss, excessive burping, and weakness.

The risk of stomach cancer increases with age and doubles each decade over the age of 55. However, the primary risk factors for cancer of the stomach are dietary factors. Diets high in salt-cured, nitrate-cured, or smoked food increase the risk of stomach cancer. Cigarette smoking and consuming large quantities of alcoholic beverages are also risk factors. The "Diversity in Health" essay discusses the risk factors for stomach cancer in greater detail.

Stomach cancer is easily diagnosed with barium studies. During this procedure, the patient swallows a milky fluid called barium sulfate. As this material reaches the stomach, a series of x rays are taken that show the movement of this fluid through the stomach, while visualizing obstructions and other growths. Additionally, physicians often obtain stomach cells by the use of a fiberoptic tube, which can be fitted with instruments for such procedures. If a tumor is found, a **biopsy**, or small piece of tissue, is taken of the growth so that the cells can be studied and the diagnosis confirmed.

In the United States, stomach cancer is no longer a major killer; therefore, routine screening is not performed as it is in high-risk populations such as Japan. Thus, most stomach cancers are not diagnosed early in the United States. If found early, however, stomach cancers are treated with surgery to remove the tumor. Chemotherapy is also used to treat stomach cancer; many stomach cancers respond well to this treatment.

Cancer of the Colon and Rectum The **colon**, or large intestine, is an organ of the digestive system that reabsorbs water and certain chemicals from waste materials (feces). Bacteria in the colon decompose materials that the human body cannot digest. The **rectum** is the lower part of the large intestine; it terminates at the anus.

Cancer of the colon and rectum, jointly referred to as *colorectal cancer,* is the third most deadly cancer killer in the United States (see Table 13-3). The signs and symptoms of colorectal cancer depend on the location of the tumor. A person may have no symptoms or few symptoms at first. Some persons first experience vague or crampy abdominal pain that may be mistaken for an ulcer. Other indications may be a change in bowel habits, such as constipation alternating with diarrhea. Blood may be visible in the stool (feces) or, on screening, a person may have a positive occult (hidden) blood test. Blood loss is an early sign of colorectal cancer. As the cancer worsens, a person with colorectal cancer may have a complete obstruction of the colon that requires emergency surgery.

The primary risk factors for developing colorectal cancer are advanced age, heredity, and diet. Other risk factors are low levels of physical activity and occupational exposure to various materials such as asbestos and certain chemical compounds. At increased risk are workers in glass foundries and automobile manufacturing plants, and those who work with formaldehyde.

Beginning at age 40, both men and women are at increased risk for developing colorectal cancer; this risk doubles with each decade after age 50 and peaks at about age 70. People who have hereditary conditions in which they tend to grow numerous (sometimes hundreds) small growths called *polyps* in their gastrointestinal tracts have very high incidences of colorectal malignancies. In addition, people who have a first-degree relative (parent or sibling) with colon cancer are 3 to 5 times more likely to develop colorectal cancer than are people with no such family history of this disease.

Scientists have also discovered that persons with diets high in fat and low in fiber are at increased risk for developing colorectal cancer. In areas of the world in which low-fat, high-fiber diets prevail, such as Africa and Asia, the incidence of colorectal cancer is low. Scientists are unsure why this is so, but think that high-fat diets cause an increased concentration of certain chemicals in the stool, such as components of bile and digestive by-products of cholesterol. They hypothesize that these substances are converted by fecal bacteria into carcinogens. In addition, a high-fat diet results in changes in the types of bacteria in the colon, favoring those that are likely to play a role in these carcinogenic changes.

Scientists have found that supplementing the diets of laboratory animals with either pectin (a type of fiber in apples and citrus fruits) or wheat bran (found in certain grains) produces a protective effect in animals exposed to carcinogens that induce colon cancers. This effect occurs in humans also. Pectin and wheat bran are two types of **dietary fiber**, which is plant material that humans cannot digest. Dietary fiber aids defecation because it adds bulk to the fecal material, providing substance against which the muscular colon wall can push as it moves wastes along.

Researchers are unsure how dietary fiber protects the colon from cancer, but suggest a variety of mechanisms. Dietary fiber in the feces decreases the amount of time they take to pass through the colon; scientists hypothesize that this results in decreased exposure of the colon wall to carcinogens. Sufficient dietary fiber in the feces also results in the growth of colon bacteria that do not convert food waste into carcinogens as do high-fat bacteria.

Results of recent studies (Alberts et al., 2000; Schatzkin et al., 2000) show that a high-fiber low-fat diet does not prevent the recurrence of precancerous growths in the colon and rectum. These results call into question the long-held ideas presented here about the relationship between diet and colorectal cancer. More research is needed to clarify this relationship.

Recently, aspirin has been found to have a protective effect in both men and women against colorectal cancer, reducing the risk by about 40% to 50% (Giovannucci, 1999). However, chronic aspirin use can cause stomach irritation and bleeding, so this preventative therapy should be undertaken only on the advice of one's physician.

As with all cancers, early detection of colorectal cancer usually results in a high chance of survival. Although colorectal cancer may have no easily recognizable early symptoms, tests are available to screen for this cancer. Common tests are the fecal occult blood test, digital rectal examination, sigmoidoscopy, and colonoscopy.

The **fecal occult blood test** detects hidden blood in the stool. The patient performs the simple test at home by

biopsy (BI-op-see) a small piece of tissue that is taken from a growth so that the cells can be studied and a diagnosis confirmed.

colon the large intestine.

rectum the lower part of the large intestine.

dietary fiber plant material that humans cannot digest, that aids defecation, and that helps protect the colon from cancer.

fecal occult blood test (FEE-kle ok-KULT) home test that detects hidden blood in the stool.

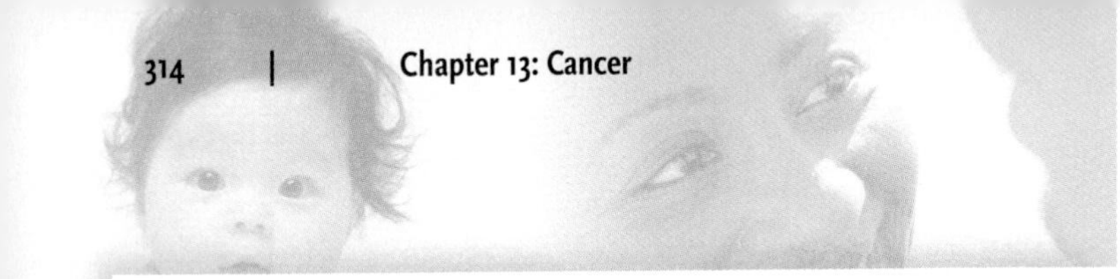

smearing stool onto a piece of paper that has been sensitized to detect occult blood. Often, the test papers can be mailed to a laboratory or to the physician for interpretation. This test will not detect all colorectal cancers, however, because not all colorectal cancers bleed. Also, positive tests may indicate conditions other than colorectal cancer.

To perform the **digital rectal exam,** a physician uses a gloved finger to feel the rectum for abnormal growths. This test, however, detects only 10% of colorectal cancers. **Sigmoidoscopy** can detect up to 50% of colorectal cancers. It is a procedure in which the physician views the lower portion of the colon (the sigmoid [S-shaped] colon) with a flex-

DIVERSITY in Health

Stomach Cancer: Variation in Mortality among Countries

More Americans died of stomach cancer in 1930 than of any other type of cancer. In the United States, the death rate due to this cancer has fallen dramatically since then (see Figure 13-3). However, stomach cancer is still the number two cancer killer worldwide. Why has the death rate from this cancer fallen in the United States? Why is this cancer so prevalent in other parts of the world?

As scientists studied worldwide patterns of mortality from stomach cancer, they noticed high mortality rates in Central and South American countries such as Brazil, Chile, Colombia, Costa Rica, and Venezuela. They also noticed large differences in death rates from stomach cancer in some of these countries. In Colombia, for example, death rates from this disease differ dramatically in populations living in the mountains compared with populations living along the coast. A similar situation exists in Central and Eastern European countries. There are high mortality rates from stomach cancer in these countries; however, the death rates between countries and within countries in this part of the world vary. As you can see in Figure 13-A, Japan and the former Soviet Union (the Russian Federation) also have high mortality rates from stomach cancer. Why are some countries' rates of death due to stomach cancer dramatically higher than others?

Scientists have determined that these differences are related to diet and environment rather than to race or country of origin. Likewise, the reduction in stomach cancer deaths in the United States is due primarily to these factors.

Regarding diet, methods of food processing and preservation affect the incidence of stomach cancer. In the early 1900s in the United States, methods of food processing and preservation changed dramatically. By mid-century, refrigeration and freezing replaced salting, pickling, and smoking as the primary methods of food preservation. Scientists have since discovered that the regular consumption of highly salted foods (including pickled foods) increases the risk of developing stomach cancer. Foods that are smoke-cured, charbroiled, or grilled contain high quantities of polycyclic aromatic hydrocarbons (PAHs), which are carcinogenic and mutagenic. These compounds are also found in cigarette smoke and air pollution, since they are the products of the incomplete combustion of fossil fuels such as charcoal and gasoline. Although many Americans enjoy eating grilled foods, their consumption of smoked, salted, and pickled foods has decreased since the early 1900s, reducing Americans' risk of developing and dying from stomach cancer. However, peoples of various cultures still use salting and smoking to preserve meats and pickling to preserve vegetables, thereby increasing their risk of stomach cancer.

Another dietary factor with an environmental link plays a role in the development of this disease. Ingesting nitrosamines, which are found in nitrite-cured foods (such as bacon, cold cuts, and some hot dogs) and in water supplies in some parts of the world (such as Colombia and South America), appears to increase the risk of stomach cancer.

Nitrosamines are also found in cigarette smoke. Additionally, chemical reactions that occur in the stomach produce nitrosamines from other compounds. For example, substances in certain fish consumed in Japan and in fava beans consumed in Colombia are converted in the stomach to nitrosamines.

Eating fruits and vegetables appears to inhibit the reactions in the stomach that form nitrosamines. In addition, they appear to protect the stomach from the effects of carcinogens. Populations who consume large quantities of fruit and vegetables generally have a low risk of stomach cancer. Scientists are unsure how these foods reduce this risk. At this time, researchers think that fruits and vegetables containing antioxidants—vitamin E, vitamin C, and beta-carotene (a substance from which the body makes vitamin A)—may play important roles in protecting against stomach cancer and possibly other cancers. (See Chapter 9 for a discussion of foods rich in the antioxidant vitamins and their mechanism of action.) However, research data are inconsistent at this time. Some scientists suggest that the protective effect of fruits and vegetables may be due to other, as yet undetermined, substances in these foods. Recent studies have confirmed that taking high-dose beta-carotene pills does not lower the risk of any cancer and appears to raise the risk of lung cancer in smokers.

▶ **Figure 13-A Death Rates from Stomach Cancer around the World 1994–1997.**
Data: World Health Organization, 1999; Mortality Database, 1994–1997

ible fiberoptic tube. Persons at high risk for colorectal cancer are often screened with a similar procedure called a **colonoscopy,** during which the fiberoptic tube is threaded through the length of the colon. The sigmoidoscope or colonoscope can also be used to remove or biopsy polyps or other growths. See the "Managing Your Health" box on p. 303 for the American Cancer Society's screening guidelines for early detection of colorectal cancer.

When colorectal cancer is detected early, surgery is the primary treatment. Physicians often use chemotherapy and radiation therapy after surgery to kill any metastasized cancer that was not detected or removed by surgery. If surgery is not possible, a physician may treat the cancer with radiation therapy alone. Biomodulation techniques are often used to treat colorectal cancer.

Cancers Related to Hormone Function

Breast Cancer From the late 1940s until 1985 in the United States, breast cancer was the number one cancer killer of women. Lung cancer recently usurped the top position, but only because its death rate rose. The mortality rate from breast cancer in women has remained stable for decades, but its incidence increased about 4% per year in the 1980s and then leveled off in the 1990s to about 110 cases per 100,000 (ACS, 1999). The rise may reflect more wide-spread use of screening techniques such as mammography, which will be discussed shortly. Breast cancer is unusual in men, but it does occur.

Signs and Symptoms The signs and symptoms of breast cancer involve changes in the breast tissue, including lumps in the breast; dimpling, thickening, discoloration, irritation, or scaling of the breast skin; tenderness of the nipple or nipple discharge; and swelling or distortion of the breast. Pain is not usually a sign of breast cancer; most breast cancers are painless in their early development. Breast pain is usually due to cyclic hormonal changes and related breast swelling.

Risk Factors and Prevention Approximately 5% of breast cancers are due to heredity. Women with first-degree relatives (mothers, sisters, daughters) who have breast cancer are at increased risk for developing the disease. In 1994 an American team of researchers identified the exact location of one gene thought to be responsible: a tumor-suppressor gene called BRCA1 (Jenks, 1994). Inheriting a defective copy of this gene puts a woman at high risk for developing breast cancer and may also influence her risk for ovarian cancer. The BRCA1 gene is thought to account for about half the inherited cases of breast cancer.

digital rectal exam a test in which a physician uses a gloved finger to feel the rectum or the prostate for abnormal growths.

sigmoidoscopy (SIG-moid-OS-ko-pee) a procedure in which a physician views the lower portion of the colon via a flexible fiberoptic tube.

colonoscopy (KO-lon-OS-ko-pee) a procedure in which a physician views the entire length of the colon using a flexible fiberoptic tube.

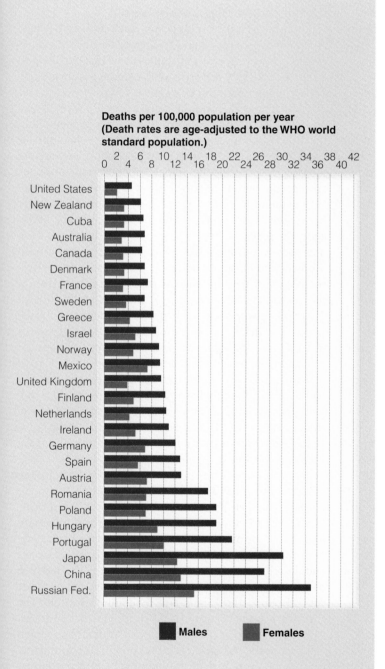

Deaths per 100,000 population per year (Death rates are age-adjusted to the WHO world standard population.)

Males · Females

The following year, a British team identified the approximate location of a second breast cancer gene, BRCA2, which is responsible for male breast cancers as well as most of the rest of inherited female breast cancers (Wooster et al., 1995). This gene does not appear to influence ovarian cancer risk, unlike the BRCA1 gene. Scientists suspect that another, as yet undiscovered, gene also confers risk for breast cancer.

Genetic testing is now available for people whose family history suggests that they carry the BRCA1 or other harmful genes. The "Analyzing Health-Related Information" activity on page 318 includes the article "Do You Have a Cancer Gene?" Read this article and determine if it is a reliable source of information. If so, it may help you decide whether you should consider being genetically tested for cancer.

Another major risk factor for the development of breast cancer in women is age. Breast cancer is rare in women younger than 20, but its incidence increases from age 20 to about 45 or 50 years. In fact, breast cancer is a major cause of death of women between the ages of 35 and 45. After the age of 50, risk still increases with age, but not as dramatically as in previous years.

In addition to age and heredity, a third major group of breast cancer risk factors appears to be those that increase a woman's cumulative exposure to ovarian hormones, particularly estrogen. Evidence suggests that having a high number of menstrual cycles is a breast cancer risk factor. For example, early menarche (age 12 or younger) and late menopause (age 55 or older) are risk factors for breast cancer. Also, women who have not borne children (therefore did not have their cycles interrupted) are at a higher risk than those who have (ACS, 1999).

A recent analysis of the results of more than 50 studies on the relationship between the use of estrogen replacement therapy (ERT) and breast cancer risk shows that there is about a 2% increased risk for each year of use, which levels off after stopping use (Tavani & LaVecchia, 1999). This is considered a slight, though significant, increase. A new class of drugs has been developed, however, that prevent bone loss and reduce blood cholesterol in postmenopausal women but do not raise their risk of breast cancer. These drugs are called selective estrogen receptor modulators, or SERMs. An example of a SERM that is now available in the United States is raloxifene (Genazzani & Gambacciani, 1999). A recent reanalysis of worldwide data regarding the relationship between breast cancer risk and use of combination oral contraceptives shows that breast cancer risk is slightly elevated in women currently taking oral contraceptives and remains slightly elevated until about 10 years after they discontinue oral contraceptive use (Westhoff, 1999).

A high-fat diet and obesity may also influence circulating levels of estrogen. A high-fat diet stimulates estrogen production and contributes to early menarche. To be certain of this link, however, more research must be conducted on the relationship of dietary factors to the development of breast cancer. At this time, the evidence is conflicting (Rose, 1997; Wynder et al., 1997). Obesity that appears after the teenage years is associated with a higher risk of postmenopausal breast cancer (Stoll, 1999). Fat tissue produces estrogen, so obese women have higher circulating levels of estrogen than nonobese women.

Some breast cancer risk factors such as heredity, age, and exposure to estrogen are impossible or difficult to control. However, results of studies show that engaging in 4 hours of physical activity a week reduces a woman's risk of developing breast cancer by about 5% for women under 40 (Bernstein et al., 1994; Latikka et al., 1998). Women who exercise less cut their risk less. Medical researchers think that one reason for the risk reduction may be that exercise modifies a woman's menstrual cycle, possibly lengthening the cycle and altering the production of ovarian hormones such as estrogen (Hoffman-Goetz et al., 1998).

In addition to exercising regularly, a woman can lower her risk of breast cancer by not drinking alcoholic beverages. The intake of three or more alcoholic drinks per week increases a woman's risk of developing breast cancer. Women who drink alcohol while taking estrogen replacement therapy may as much as triple their blood levels of the hormone (Ginsburg, 1999; Ginsburg et al., 1997). Therefore, a woman should consult her physician for advice on balancing the benefit of drinking a few glasses of wine per week to reduce her risk of cardiovascular disease against the increased risk of breast cancer.

Women who live in Western countries (North America and Northern Europe) have 5 to 6 times the risk of developing breast cancer as women who live in Asia and Africa. Evidence suggests that this association is not genetic but is connected to lifestyle or environmental factors that have yet to be discovered. Approximately 75% of women diagnosed with breast cancer have no identifiable risk factors other than that they are from a Western culture.

Early Detection Three methods are generally used to detect breast cancer as early as possible: the breast self-examination, the breast clinical examination, and mammography. The "Managing Your Health" box on page 321 shows and describes how to do a breast self-exam. The purpose of this exam is to detect any of the breast changes that were listed in the "Signs and Symptoms" section. The American Cancer Society (ACS) recommends that breast self-examination be performed every month by women aged 20 years and older. The breast clinical examination follows the procedure of the breast self-exam but is performed by a health-care professional. The ACS recommends that a clinical examination be performed every 3 years for women from ages 20 to 39, and every year thereafter (see "Managing Your Health," p. 303).

Mammography is the process of taking x rays of breast tissue to detect benign and malignant growths. As you can see in ▌ **Figure 13-8,** each breast is placed over a plate containing x-ray film and the tissue is compressed. The ACS recommends that women aged 40 and older have a mammogram every year. Women at high risk for breast cancer, such as those with a strong family history of the disease, should consult their physicians regarding the need for mammograms on a different schedule (e.g., at an earlier age, or more often).

If screening reveals a suspicious mass in the breast tissue, a physician usually performs a biopsy. To perform this procedure, a physician inserts a fine needle into the mass and withdraws cells. An individual trained to detect cancer studies the cells to determine if the growth is malignant. Fine-needle biopsy is relatively painless and is about 90% accurate.

Treatment Data suggest that a **lumpectomy,** surgical removal of the tumor, followed by breast irradiation is appropriate therapy for women with a breast tumor measuring 4 cm (about 1½ in.) or less in diameter. The surgeon also removes a layer of normal tissue surrounding the tumor so that it is less likely that cancer tissue is left in the breast. The physician also removes some lymph nodes under the nearby armpit to determine if the cancer has spread. Following this procedure, the physician may recommend radiation therapy. Data show that lumpectomy is as effective as **total mastectomy** (removal of the entire breast and involved lymph nodes) in patients with tumors of this size (Fisher et al., 1995).

Women with breast malignancies larger than 4 cm may need more aggressive surgery. In a **radical mastectomy,** the surgeon removes the entire breast and underlying muscle as well as the underarm lymph nodes and fat. In a **modi-fied radical mastectomy,** underlying muscle is not removed. However, these procedures are performed much less often than in the past because lumpectomy followed by radiation therapy has been so successful in curing breast cancers.

Today hormonal therapy is often used to treat advanced breast cancer. The primary drug used is tamoxifen (Kotwall, 1999), an antiestrogen. It counteracts the effects of estrogen on breast cancers that depend on estrogen for their growth. It has few serious side effects compared to other anticancer drugs and positively affects approximately one-third of patients for whom it is prescribed.

Chemotherapy is also used to treat breast cancer (sometimes in conjunction with tamoxifen), but many anticancer drugs have serious side effects and breast cancer is only moderately sensitive to such agents. However, in recent years new compounds have been discovered that have demonstrated good antitumor activity in breast cancer treatment. These drugs are called taxanes. The drug taxol was the first of this group to be discovered. (Taxol is found in the bark of the Pacific yew tree [*Taxus brevifolia*].) Taxane drugs play a significant role in breast cancer therapy (Hudis, 1999).

Endometrial Cancer The endometrium is the lining of the uterus, the organ in which a fetus develops until birth (see Chapter 6). Endometrial cancer most often occurs in postmenopausal women; only 15% to 25% of endometrial cancers occur in premenopausal women. The primary symptom of this cancer is abnormal uterine bleeding. Premenopausal women usually experience symptoms of irregular, heavy, or prolonged uterine bleeding during menstrual periods or bleeding between periods. Postmenopausal women experience uterine bleeding although they no longer have menstrual periods.

For early detection of endometrial cancer, women aged 40 and older should have annual pelvic examinations by a health-care provider. Unfortunately, the Pap test for cervical cancer does not detect cancer in the body of the uterus. (This test will be discussed shortly.) However, if the physician suspects that a patient has endometrial cancer, he or she usually performs an endometrial biopsy, in which a sample of tissue is removed from the endometrium and examined microscopically.

Although the cause of endometrial cancer is unknown, it is associated with prolonged exposure to estrogen. Therefore, the risk factors for endometrial cancer are similar to those for breast cancer: early menarche, late menopause, not bearing children, and delaying pregnancy. However,

lumpectomy (lum-PECK-toe-me) surgical removal of a breast tumor, including a layer of surrounding tissue.

total mastectomy (mas-TEK-toe-me) surgical removal of a breast and involved lymph nodes for the treatment of breast cancer.

radical mastectomy surgical removal of a breast, underlying muscle, and underarm fat and lymph nodes as a treatment for breast cancer.

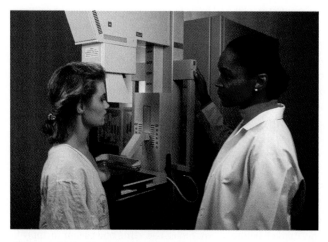

▲**Figure 13-8 Mammography.** Each breast is placed on a platform and the tissue is compressed while the x ray is taken.

text continues on p. 321

ANALYZING Health-Related Information

Do You Have a Cancer Gene?

by Rita Rubin

Divining whether a person will be long-lived has become a lot more scientific than palm reading or crystal ball gazing. Once the stuff of science fiction, the ability to peer into people's DNA and predict whether they're likely to develop common scourges such as cancer has now arrived in the marketplace.

Today any doctor can ship a patient's blood to a commercial laboratory to be analyzed for genetic changes that might signal danger ahead. Since last year, OncorMed of Gaithersburg, Md., has been promoting tests for mutations that may raise the risk of breast, colon, and thyroid cancers and melanoma, a lethal skin malignancy. In March 1996, Athena Neurosciences of South San Francisco introduced a test that probes for a genetic variation researchers have linked to Alzheimer's disease. And Myriad Genetics of Salt Lake City expects such a large demand for its tests—starting with one aimed at breast and ovarian cancers due later this year—that it's building a 48,500-square-foot laboratory. All this action prompted a flurry of scientific seminars on genetic testing last month; as one moderator aptly put it: "The future is now."

It's easy to grasp why genetic testing for common killers is so appealing. Imagine the boon to public health if people forewarned about potential medical disasters could derail fate by taking appropriate medication and monitoring vigilantly for signs of the disease at its earliest, most curable stage. It worked for Melody Jenkins: Because she found out she was almost certain to get colon cancer, she now almost certainly won't.

The 32-year-old Falls Church, Va., resident saw her father die of colon cancer, her

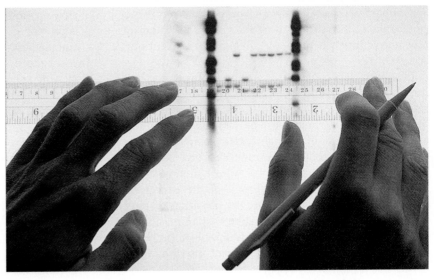

sister from surgery for a precancerous condition. But she put off having a colonoscopy—which can detect precancerous cells—because she dreaded the discomfort. Two years ago, though, genetic testing at Johns Hopkins University revealed that of her father's eight surviving children, Jenkins alone had inherited the mutation linked to his cancer. That information propelled her to her first colonoscopy, which uncovered hundreds of the trademark polyps of her father's disease. She had her colon removed before the polyps became malignant, as they likely would. Meanwhile, her siblings—and their kids—can skip annual colonoscopies.

Too Soon?

But medical and legal experts worry that the new tests have hit the market before we've had the chance to learn to use them well. Certainly, many questions must be answered before genetic testing becomes routine. One big one: What do the test re-

sults really mean? Classic genetic disorders, such as Huntington's disease, involve a mutation in a single gene, whose presence virtually assures a diagnosis. But common killers such as cancer and Alzheimer's disease are thought to arise from the interplay of changes in multiple genes and environmental factors. So inheriting a mutation in any single gene linked to one of these ailments isn't always enough to make people sick. Likewise, not inheriting a mutation doesn't guarantee good health; favorable test results could provide a false sense of security.

Overall, the genetic alterations linked to cancer so far do appear to increase a carrier's risk dramatically. People who inherit their family's mutation in any of a handful of genes associated with colon cancer have upwards of a 90% chance of getting it, for example. The same odds seem to apply to people with mutations in a gene linked to hereditary thyroid cancer. And women who inherit an alteration in BRCA1 or BRCA2, the so-called breast cancer genes, are thought to have roughly an 85% chance of developing the disease by age 85. The risk in the general population is only about 10%. BRCA1 mutations also seem to inflate the lifetime risk of ovarian cancer to nearly 50%, compared with the usual 1%.

Uncertainty about the value of the new tests' predictions makes long-debated concerns about genetic testing especially urgent. Should people be tested to see if they might develop a disorder that cannot be prevented or successfully treated? Could a positive result lead to the loss of insurance or a job? A number of scientists and consumer groups argue that it's premature to test people outside research centers, where they can be fully informed about what they're getting into and assured that the results will be kept private.

Everyone is a potential candidate for genetic testing—though the tests cost hundreds of dollars and are not yet covered by most insurers. And everyone is a potential victim of genetic discrimination. "We all have four or five really fouled-up genes," says Francis Collins, director of the National Center for Human Genome Research. Only 5% to 10% of all cancers are thought to be inherited, but that translates into several million Americans with genetic alterations that dramatically increase their risk of developing malignancies, says Richard Klausner, director of the National Cancer Institute. Countless others may be genetically prone to heart disease, diabetes, osteoporosis, allergies, and asthma, for which genetic tests are expected in coming years.

Importance of History

For now, genetics experts generally agree that no one should be tested just because of fear of an illness; doctors should offer testing only to people whose family history suggests that they carry a harmful form of the target gene. The uncertainties about test results are even more pronounced in people without such a background. "Have I screened my own BRCA1 gene? No," says Mary-Claire King, the University of Washington scientist whose research led to the discovery of that first breast cancer gene. Breast cancer doesn't run in King's family. "I truly don't think it's meaningful for people like me," she says of testing. "I think the real issue here is what about women who

are in high-risk families. Is it time yet for those women to consider testing? For some women, the answer is yes." Because ovarian cancer is so difficult to detect, for example, women with a strong family history might want to be tested for BRCA1 mutations. The results could help the women decide whether they should have their ovaries removed as a preventive.

But family history doesn't always indicate hereditary disease, or the lack of it. Sporadic—or noninherited—breast and colon tumors are common enough to give the illusion of inheritance in some families. On the other hand, some people who inherit a mutation that does raise their risk of disease appear to have no family history of it.

Even in families with striking medical history, testing usually is informative only if at least one relative with the disease is still alive and willing to be tested. The reason: Some of the genes associated with inherited diseases are large, giving rise to a variety of mutations. So far, for example, more than 100 alterations have been discovered in BRCA1, but few appear to increase a woman's risk. Finding one in a family member already diagnosed with breast cancer is considered significant—if a healthy woman carries the same mutation, she also is assumed to be at risk for breast and/or ovarian cancer. If not, her risk is thought to be no greater than that of the general population. But not finding a mutation in a relative with the disease could simply mean today's tests overlooked it.

Finding out that a disorder is inherited affects an entire extended family, not just one patient. "This has raised a whole new way of looking at family relationships and responsibilities," notes Karen Rothenberg, director of the Law and Health Care Program at the University of Maryland Law School in Baltimore. One sister might want to know if her mother's and aunt's breast cancers were inherited, for example, while another would prefer not to know.

The implications of the one genetic test available for Alzheimer's disease are so unclear that the medical community agrees it should not be used to screen healthy people. The test assesses a gene called apolipoprotein E—APOE for short—which had been thought only to help transport cholesterol. In 1993, Duke University researchers reported that one of the

three common variations of APOE was associated with an increased risk of Alzheimer's disease. Because not everyone with this form of APOE develops the disease—and many people with Alzheimer's do not carry this variation—genetic testing is useful only in deciding whether people with dementia really have Alzheimer's.

Even if the test were highly accurate at predicting a healthy person's risk, with Alzheimer's—as with Huntington's disease and many cancers—knowledge isn't always power. "It does very little good to tell someone they have an 85% chance of getting a particular cancer at some point in their lives if we can't also tell them what they can do about it," says Klausner. Some people with a family history of a deadly disease would rather not know their genetic status, says Barbara Biesecker, co-director of the genetic counseling program at the National Center for Human Genome Research. "They remain more hopeful and feel more in control," Biesecker explains.

Sadly, little is known about how to prevent cancer. And while identifying people at high risk may allow doctors to catch tumors early, no screening method is foolproof. Conventional x-ray mammography, for instance, isn't all that useful in screening women under 40—the age group in which breast cancers are more likely to be inherited—because their dense breasts often obscure tiny tumors. Screening tools to detect early ovarian cancer, such as ultrasound, are just about as effective. In desperation, some women with a strong family history of breast and/or ovarian cancer have decided to have these organs removed before they are hit with a diagnosis. But even that drastic step doesn't erase the chance of developing one of those cancers.

Genetic testing wasn't available when Liz Karnes of Omaha was diagnosed with ovarian cancer in 1991, so her sisters, who had completed their families, decided to have their ovaries removed as a precaution. Prophylactic mastectomies are more controversial—especially considering the trend away from performing such disfiguring surgery in women already diagnosed with breast cancer.

Because colon cancer is almost inevitable in people who carry the relevant mutations, some doctors now recommend that they have their colons removed—even though

ANALYZING *Health-Related Information*

detecting tumors in that organ is easier than in the breasts or ovaries. "Their destiny is pretty well determined," says Henry Lynch, a physician at Creighton University in Omaha who in the 1960s first recognized the main hereditary colorectal cancer syndrome. People reluctant to take such a radical step can opt for early and yearly colonoscopies to screen for tumors. The same advice applies for a type of inherited thyroid cancer: There are screening methods, but it appears that the best way to save the lives of susceptible people is to remove the thyroid.

Debate about the proper medical use of genetic testing could be moot unless legal protections against its misuse are put in place. In the worst case, testing could foster a genetic underclass, subject to discrimination on a variety of fronts. "This could be the new civil rights issue in this country," says GOP Rep. Cliff Stearns of Florida, co-sponsor with Rep. Joseph Kennedy, a Massachusetts Democrat, of a bill that could ban disclosure of genetic information unless authorized in writing by the patient. The bill also would prohibit employers or health insurers from discriminating against people on the basis of genetic information.

Jacob's Story

Already, healthy people have reported being denied health insurance just on the basis of their family medical history; not surprisingly, such individuals are reluctant to be tested for fear that the results could mean a lost job or lost insurance. It happened to young Jacob Turner. After Jacob's mother died suddenly, testing revealed that he inherited the same heartbeat irregularity that killed her. Once diagnosed, the disorder can be controlled with medication. But when Jacob's father started his own business and switched to an individual health plan, his son was denied coverage, says the boy's grandmother, Doris Goldman of Irvine, Calif. "Something is terribly wrong when a healthy little boy is denied insurance because of his genetic makeup," Goldman says. After some wrangling, Jacob, who is now 5, obtained coverage last month.

A dozen states now have passed laws barring health insurers and/or employers from discriminating on the basis of genetic test results, or, in some cases, any kind of genetic information, such as family history. However, the state laws do not protect people who work for self-insured companies—which represent more than half of all employers—from being slapped with higher premiums or denied coverage altogether. The Americans with Disabilities Act prohibits companies from rejecting job applicants on the basis of genetic information, according to an as-yet untested interpretation last year by the Equal Employment Opportunity Commission. The American Council of Life Insurance argues that its members depend on information such as genetic test results to set appropriate rates for each customer. Indeed, Rothenberg says it's unlikely that life insurance companies will be blocked from using genetic information.

With so much at stake, a patient's first step—deciding whether to be tested—is critical. Yet most doctors don't know enough to counsel people considering being tested. ("I didn't become a doc to have to function as an insurance agent, or, God help me, a lawyer!" one cancer specialist told Rothenberg.) Test manufacturers are developing educational materials for doctors and patients, but their financial benefit in having the tests accepted creates an apparent conflict of interest. The National Center for Human Genome Research is helping medical and nursing groups develop training programs. And the National Cancer Institute is setting up a network of experienced doctors and institutions to which individuals can be referred for genetic testing trials and follow-up. Unless genetic testing is handled wisely, consumers will certainly shy away. This promising technology could fail in the marketplace and land in the history books.

Reprinted from: *U.S. News and World Report.* May 13, 1996, pp. 67–77.

The article "Do You Have a Cancer Gene?" focuses on new tests for cancer and determining if people like you should have such tests. Explain why you think this article is a reliable or an unreliable source of information. Use the model for analyzing health information to guide your thinking; the main points of the model are noted below. The model is explained fully on pages 12 to 13.

1. Which statements are verifiable facts, and which are unverified statements or value claims?

2. What are the credentials of the author? If this information is available, does her background and education qualify her as an expert in this area?

3. What might be the motives and biases of the author? State the reasons for your answers.

4. Which information is relevant to the issue or main points of the article? Which information is irrelevant?

5. Is the source reliable? Does it have a reputation for publishing misinformation?

6. Does the article attack the credibility of conventional scientists or medical authorities?

7. Based on this analysis, do you think this article is a reliable source of health-related information? Explain why or why not.

Breast Self-Examination

There are many good reasons for doing a breast self-exam (BSE) each month. One is that breast cancer is most easily treated and cured when it is found early. Another is that the more you do it, the better you will get at it. When you get to know how your breasts normally feel, you will quickly be able to feel any change. Another reason: it is easy to do.

The best time to do breast self-exam is after your period, when breasts are not tender or swollen. If you do not have regular periods or sometimes skip a month, do it on the same day every month.

1. Lie down and put a pillow under your right shoulder. Place your right arm behind your head.
2. Use the finger pads of your three middle fingers on your left hand to feel for lumps or thickening. Your finger pads are the top third of each finger.
3. Press firmly enough to know how your breast feels. If you're not sure how hard to press, ask your health-care provider. Or try to copy the way your health-care provider uses the finger pads during a breast exam. Learn what your breast feels like most of the time. A firm ridge in the lower curve of each breast is normal.

4. Move around the breast in a set way. You can choose either the circle (a), the up-and-down line (b), or the wedge (c). Do it the same way every time. It will help you to make sure that you've gone over the entire breast area, and to remember how your breast feels each month.
5. Now examine your left breast using the right-hand finger pads.
6. If you find any changes, see your doctor right away.

You might want to check your breasts while standing in front of a mirror right after you do your breast self-exam each month. See if there are changes in the way your breasts look: dimpling of the skin, changes in the nipple, redness, or swelling.

You might also want to do an extra breast self-exam while you're in the shower. Your soapy hands will glide over the wet skin, making it easy to check how your breasts feel.

Remember: A breast self-exam could save your breast—and your life. Most breast lumps are found by women themselves, but in fact most lumps in the breasts are not cancer. Be safe; be sure.

Source: American Cancer Society.

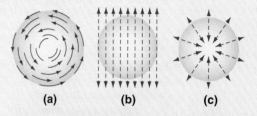

(a)   (b)   (c)

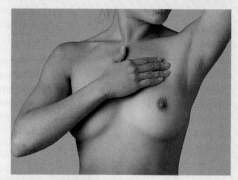

research results suggest that estrogen replacement therapy without the accompanying ovarian hormone progesterone (unopposed ERT) is a risk factor for the development of endometrial cancer. Using oral contraceptives that combine estrogen and progesterone appears to decrease the risk of endometrial cancer. Additionally, women who are more than 50 pounds overweight, especially postmenopausal women, have a tenfold greater risk for developing endometrial cancer than women who are not overweight. Diabetes mellitus and hypertension are also associated with endometrial cancer.

Most women diagnosed with endometrial cancer undergo total hysterectomy: removal of the uterus, fallopian tubes, and ovaries. Additionally, certain types of radiation

therapy are sometimes used after surgery. The outlook for survival after treatment for endometrial cancer is good: About 90% of patients with endometrial cancer survive their disease.

Cancers Related to Viral Infection: Cervical Cancer

Certain viruses are implicated in the development of a variety of cancers; ▌ **Table 13-5** lists these viruses and the cancers to which they are related. However, viruses alone do not appear to cause cancer. Scientists think that interactions between these viruses and other agents, or co-carcinogens, result in the development of cancer. For example, the high incidence of liver cancer in certain regions of Africa and Asia appears to be caused by interactions between the hepatitis B virus and aflatoxins. Aflatoxins are a group of carcinogens produced by a mold that grows on improperly stored peanuts and grains. Many people in these regions eat these moldy foods.

The virally related cancer most prevalent in the United States is cervical cancer. Since 1960 the incidence of cervical cancer has declined by 63%, primarily because of the widespread routine use of the **Papanicolaou test (Pap test)** to screen women for cervical cancer. To perform the Pap test, a physician or other specially trained health-care professional uses a small wooden spatula to remove cells from the cervical canal. These cells are smeared on a glass slide for microscopic examination.

Most women who are diagnosed with cervical cancer have no symptoms; their cancers are discovered at an early stage during their annual gynecologic examination and Pap test. If undiagnosed, the cancer may cause symptoms of abnormal vaginal bleeding (the most common symptom), pelvic pressure or pain, and/or a foul-smelling vaginal discharge.

Cervical cancer most often develops in young women, generally between the ages of 20 and 40 years, peaking at approximately age 30. If untreated, cervical cancer can invade sur-

Papanicolaou test (Pap test) (PAP-eh-nik-eh-LOUW) a screening procedure for cervical cancer in which cells from the cervical canal are removed and then smeared on a glass slide for microscopic examination.

basal cell carcinoma (BAY-sl) the most common cancer of the skin, which frequently develops on portions of the skin exposed to the sun.

rounding tissues and metastasize. Having regular screening tests can reduce the risk of developing invasive cancer of the cervix.

A causal association exists between human papilloma virus (HPV) and cervical cancer. HPV is transmitted by infected men to their female partners during sexual intercourse, and vice versa (see Chapter 14). Therefore, the greater the number of male sexual partners a woman has over time, the greater are her chances of becoming infected with HPV. If a woman is monogamous but her male sex partner is not, her risk rises because he is more likely to become infected than if he were monogamous. Also, women who had their first sexual intercourse before age 17 are at increased risk because they are more likely to have a greater number of sexual partners over time than those women who became sexually active at an older age.

At low risk for cervical cancer are women who are celibate, such as Roman Catholic nuns, or who are monogamous with a monogamous partner over many years. Sexually active women with multiple partners or with non-monogamous partners can lower their risk by using male or female condoms to protect themselves against infection with HPV.

Scientists are studying possible HPV co-carcinogens. The most documented co-carcinogen is tobacco smoke. Women who are infected with HPV and who smoke cigarettes are more likely to develop cervical cancer; the carcinogens of tobacco smoke affect the cervix by passing out of the blood and into the cervical mucus. Additionally, oral contraceptives have been shown to confer an increased risk for cervical cancer in HPV-infected women. Conflicting data exist regarding herpes simplex virus type II (HSV-II) as a co-carcinogen. (See Chapter 14 for more information concerning HPV and herpes viruses.)

The American Cancer Society recommends that all women who are or have been sexually active and who have reached the age of 18 should have annual Pap tests and pelvic examinations. The ACS suggests that after three consecutive normal Pap tests, a woman may have this test performed every 3 years.

If the Pap test shows that cervical cancer may be present, a physician usually performs a *colposcopy*. Using a specially designed microscope, the physician examines the cervix. If the physician observes abnormal cervical tissue during this procedure, he or she usually performs a biopsy to confirm the diagnosis.

Physicians treat most dysplasia or cervical cancers in situ with carbon dioxide (CO_2) laser surgery. Laser energy destroys the tissue. Cryotherapy, the use of extreme cold to destroy cells, is another treatment. Usually solid carbon dioxide or liquid nitrogen is applied briefly to the abnormal tissue with a sterile cotton-tipped applicator. A blister forms and the tissue dies.

Table 13-5 — Viruses and Cancers to Which They Are Related

Virus	Cancer Type
Hepatitis B virus (HBV)	Primary liver cancer
Human T-cell lymphotropic/leukemia virus (HTLV)	Adult T-cell lymphoma/leukemia
Cytomegalovirus (CMV)	Kaposi's sarcoma
Human papillomavirus (HPV)	Cervical cancer, penile cancer
Epstein-Barr virus (EBV)	Burkitt's lymphoma, nasopharyngeal cancer

Depending on the extent of the cancer, surgeons may perform a simple hysterectomy (removal of just the uterus) or a total hysterectomy (removal of the uterus and ovaries). With certain cervical cancers, radiation is the treatment of choice. Detected early, cervical cancer is highly survivable.

Cancers Related to Ultraviolet Radiation: Skin Cancers

Lying on the beach or on a tanning bed to develop a tanned "healthy" look is anything but healthy! When skin tans it is a sign of skin damage. Certain skin cells produce a pigment called *melanin* to protect the skin from the damaging rays of the sun. Melanin is a built-in sun protector for dark-skinned people and is produced in response to sun damage in light-skinned people. In addition to causing the skin to wrinkle and age prematurely, the ultraviolet (UV) radiation in sunlight can result in the development of skin cancer. In fact, UV light exposure is the most important factor (other than heredity and age) that influences the development of skin cancer.

There are three types of ultraviolet radiation: UVA, UVB, and UVC. All three types are harmful and have the potential to cause skin cancer. Claims by tanning parlors that using only UVB rays will protect you from the effects of UV radiation are false. This type of ultraviolet radiation is associated with sunburn and skin cancer formation, as is UVA radiation. UVA radiation is also strongly associated with premature aging effects. Artificial UV sources, such as sun lamps and tanning beds, may also generate UVC rays. UVC radiation is a highly potent cancer-causing radiation. Although a danger from artificial sources, these rays are filtered out by the Earth's atmosphere and pose little danger from environmental sources.

There are three main types of skin cancer: basal cell carcinoma, squamous cell carcinoma, and malignant melanoma. Approximately 60% of skin cancers are basal cell carcinomas and approximately 30% are squamous cell carcinomas. Although malignant melanoma makes up less than 10% of skin cancers, this fast-growing, metastasizing cancer results in the most deaths. Malignant melanoma spreads quickly via the blood and lymph. Death is usually due to either respiratory failure or to brain or spinal cord complications.

Since 1970 the incidence of malignant melanoma has risen about 4% per year (ACS, 1999). This rise is attributed to the increase in ultraviolet radiation reaching the Earth due to the partial loss of the protective layer of ozone (O_3) in the upper atmosphere. Ozone shields the Earth against the sun's powerful ultraviolet rays. Although the UV light increase due to ozone loss is more pronounced the closer one gets to the poles, the risk for developing malignant melanoma and other skin cancers is still higher the closer a person lives to the equator because of the increasing intensity of UV rays. Additionally, fair-skinned people are at greater risk than those who have darker skin. Incidence rates are more than 10 times higher in Whites than in African Americans (ACS, 1999). At highest risk are persons with light blue eyes, very light hair, and skin that burns easily and freckles rather than tans.

Basal cell carcinoma is the most common cancer of the skin, often affecting persons older than 40 years of age. A slow-growing cancer that rarely metastasizes, basal cell carcinoma frequently develops on portions of the skin exposed to the sun: the face, head, neck, and arms. Lesions may look like moles or chronic pimples with pearl-like borders. They often become crusty and scaly and may ulcerate and bleed (■ **Figure 13-9a).** Basal cell carcinoma tumors are usually removed by surgery and cryotherapy, freezing with liquid nitrogen. The cure rate for basal cell carcinoma is high.

Squamous cell carcinoma is the second most common skin cancer in light-skinned persons; it develops in the same sun-exposed areas as does basal cell carcinoma. However, dark-skinned people *can* develop this type of cancer, not from sunlight exposure, but from exposure to noxious chemicals and high levels of x rays, as well as from trauma (burns and chronic ulcers). The skin lesions of squamous cell carcinoma look flat, red, scaling, and may be slightly elevated (■ **Figure 13-9b).** These tumors are removed by the same methods as basal cell carcinoma.

Both basal and squamous cell carcinomas develop from prolonged, repeated exposures to the sun. At risk are persons who are outdoors much of the time, such as construction workers, farmers, and people who regularly sunbathe.

Malignant melanoma is a deadly skin cancer. It is the most frequent cancer in women aged 25 to 29 and is the second most frequent cancer in women aged 30 to 34. (Breast cancer is the most frequent cancer of this age group.) Half of all melanoma victims are younger than 50.

Malignant melanoma has slightly different risk factors from basal cell and squamous cell cancers. Malignant melanoma develops more often in persons who are exposed to the sun in short intense sessions, such as persons who work indoors and then vacation in a sunny climate. Severe sunburn and extensive sun exposure in childhood also increase the risk for developing malignant melanoma in adulthood. Additionally, first-degree relatives of people with melanoma have a two- to eightfold increase in their risk of developing this cancer. Individuals who have two or

squamous cell carcinoma (SKWAY-muss) a common form of skin cancer that develops from exposure to noxious chemicals and high levels of x rays, as well as from trauma.

malignant melanoma (MEL-ah-NO-mah) a deadly form of skin cancer that develops most often in persons who have been exposed to the sun in short, intense sessions, have had severe sunburn and extensive sun exposure in childhood, or have first-degree relatives who had the disease.

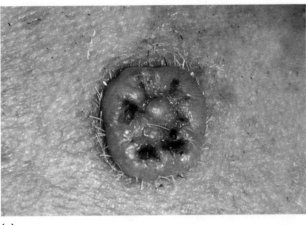

(a)

Figure 13-9 Skin Cancers.
▲(a) This basal cell carcinoma is on the cheek of a man. It is a raised lesion with central depressions that bleed and crust over.
▶(b) Squamous cell carcinoma looks like a red rounded mass or a flat sore as shown in the photo. ▼(c) Lesions of malignant melanoma are characterized by irregular borders with red, white, blue, or blue-black spots. Some portions may be raised.

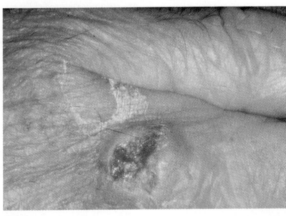

(b)

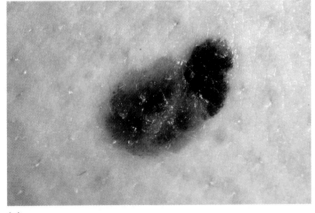

(c)

more relatives with a history of melanoma may be at substantially higher risk.

Malignant melanoma can develop on any skin surface as well as in the eye and on mucous membranes. In men, the trunk is the most common site; in women, the legs are a common site. If you are in a high-risk group for skin cancer, especially melanoma, examine your skin regularly. Early detection is key to curing this disease. Typically, melanoma tumors are asymmetrical, have irregular borders, multiple colors (such as blue, black, red, or gray), and

have a diameter greater than a pencil eraser (Figure 13-9c). An easy way to remember these signs is ABCD: asymmetry, border, color, and diameter.

To reduce your risk of developing malignant melanoma and other skin cancers, do not use tanning beds and avoid exposure to the sun (particularly sunbathing), especially at midday when ultraviolet radiation is at its highest levels (from 10 A.M. to 3 P.M.). When outdoors, use sunscreens regularly that have a sun protection factor (SPF) of 15 or higher. Additionally, wear sunglasses that block out at least 99% of UVA and UVB radiation because these rays stimulate the formation of cancer as well as cataracts—a clouding of the lens of the eye. Larger glasses protect the eyes better than do smaller glasses; wraparounds are the best protection.

A *Healthy People 2000* goal is to increase to at least 60% the proportion of persons of all ages who limit sun exposure, use sunscreens and protective clothing when exposed to sunlight, and avoid artificial sources of UV light. Data from the 1992 National Health Interview Survey show, however, that this goal was far from being realized at that time. Only 31% of U.S. adults reported that they limited their exposure to the sun, 28% said that they used sunscreen routinely, and 28% noted that they wore protective clothing (USPHS, 1995).

Cancers with Unknown Causes

Prostate Cancer The prostate is a walnut-sized accessory sex organ in men. It lies beneath the bladder, surrounding the urethra, and secretes part of the seminal fluid. (See Chapter 6 for more information on this gland.)

Prostate cancer is the most prevalent cancer in men, and the second most prevalent cause of cancer deaths in men (see Table 13-3). (Lung cancer is the most prevalent cause of cancer death in men.) The signs and symptoms of prostate cancer mimic those of benign prostatic hypertrophy (BPH) and other noncancerous conditions of the prostate (see p. 135). Therefore, experiencing symptoms that include uneven flow of urine while urinating, incomplete emptying of the bladder, reduced urine flow, and urinating more frequently at night does not necessarily mean a man has prostate cancer. However, serious signs and symptoms that are more likely to be related to prostate cancer are pain in the floor of the pelvis, sudden development of impotence, and presence of blood in the urine.

Men living in Western countries are more likely to develop prostate cancer. Scientists suspect that a high-fat diet, which is characteristic of the Western world, may contribute to the development of prostate cancer (Rose, 1997). Race also plays a role in one's risk of this disease. African Americans have about a 30% higher risk than that of Caucasians, while Native American men and Asians living in the United States have the lowest incidence. Men with certain occupations also have higher rates of prostate cancer: loggers, chemists, farmers, textile workers, painters, and rubber tire workers. However, researchers are unsure which factors related to working in these environments influence the development of this disease.

Advanced age and heredity are also strong risk factors for prostate cancer. This disease is rare in men younger than 45 years, but its incidence rises as men age further. More than 75% of prostate cancers are diagnosed in men 65 years or older (ACS, 1999). Also, if a man's father or brother had prostate cancer, he may have as much as an 11-fold increase in risk and may be stricken before age 50.

Scientists have been unsuccessful in determining the cause of or other risk factors for prostate cancer. Diet is a controversial factor. The results of studies strongly suggest that vitamin A may lessen the risk of developing prostate cancer. The body converts beta-carotenes found in such foods as leafy green vegetables, yellow fruits and vegetables, milk, and cheese into vitamin A. Also, a particular pigment in tomatoes called lycopene appears to have a protective effect.

For early detection of prostate cancer, the American Cancer Society and the American Urological Association recommend that all men older than 50 have an annual digital rectal exam and annual prostate specific antigen (PSA) test. During the digital rectal exam, a physician inserts a gloved finger into the rectum to feel the prostate gland (see p. 135). The PSA is a blood test that detects a protein secreted by the prostate. If the protein concentration in the blood is elevated, it indicates that the prostate may be abnormal but not necessarily cancerous, and should be checked further. Chapter 6 describes methods of screening the prostate.

Physicians may treat localized prostate cancer by surgically removing the prostate. However, this treatment can result in impotence, incontinence, and other complications. New surgical techniques with fewer side effects have been developed, leading to a resurgence of prostate surgery as a treatment. Advanced prostate cancer is sometimes treated with drug/ hormone therapy or by removal of the testicles to reduce male sex hormone levels, which may influence the progression of this cancer. Medical researchers are currently experimenting with implanting tiny radioactive particles in the prostate to destroy the cancer, and with using cryotherapy to destroy the gland.

Prostate cancer is, in many cases, a slow-growing cancer. Data show that about 95% of prostate cancer patients ultimately die with prostate cancer rather than of it. Therefore, studies are being conducted to determine if treating prostate cancers makes a difference in patient survival rates. Because the side effects of prostate cancer treatment can be quite serious, physicians carefully consider "watchful waiting" as the treatment of choice for this cancer (Henkel, 1994; Randal, 1994).

Testicular Cancer The testicles, or testes, are the organs in which sperm develop and are located in the scrotal sac beneath the penis. Cancer of the testicles is a rare and highly curable cancer. Only 1% of cancers in men occur in the testicles.

The signs and symptoms of testicular cancer are a painless, swollen testis and a sensation of heaviness or aching in the testis. Men who perform testicular self-examination might feel a small lump in one testis.

Youth is a risk factor with testicular cancer. Additionally, results of a recent study show that teenage boys who exercise regularly and those with physically demanding jobs in their 20s may be more likely to develop testicular cancer than less active boys and young men (Srivastava & Kreiger, 2000). This cancer strikes primarily teenagers and men between the ages of 15 and 35. Its incidence declines steadily after age 40. Another risk factor for testicular cancer is the failure of one or both of the testicles to descend into the scrotum by age 6 years. As with breast and prostate cancer, testicular cancer occurs most frequently in Western countries. Its incidence is lowest in Asia and Africa. Caucasian males are at highest risk, Latino males are at less risk, and African American men are at least risk.

To detect testicular cancer early, the American Cancer Society recommends that men perform a **testicular self-examination (TSE)** once a month after a warm bath or shower (see the "Managing Your Health" box on the next page). The heat relaxes the scrotal skin, making tumors easier to detect. If detected and treated early, testicular cancer is one of the most curable cancers. Chemotherapy is most often used; radiation and surgery are also used in some cases.

Ovarian Cancer The ovaries are female organs in which eggs mature and are ovulated each month. Ovaries also produce the female sex hormones estrogen and progesterone. Cancer of the ovaries is difficult to detect, especially in its early stages when most women have no symptoms. However, as the cancer progresses and the ovarian tumor enlarges, many women develop symptoms such as frequent urination or bloating and pressure in the abdomen. Thus, advanced ovarian cancer is confused frequently with other urinary and gastrointestinal tract disorders. Additionally, postmenopausal women may experience vaginal bleeding, while premenopausal women may have irregular or heavy menses.

Eighty-five to 90% of ovarian cancers develop in postmenopausal women; only 10% to 15% are diagnosed in premenopausal patients. The median age for developing ovarian cancer is 60 to 65 years. Other than advanced age, the risk factors for ovarian cancer are similar to those of

testicular self-exam (TSE) (tes-TIK-you-lar) a self-screening test that males can perform to detect cancer of the testicles.

Testicular Self-Examination

A simple procedure called testicular self-exam (TSE) can increase the chances of finding a tumor early. Men should perform TSE once a month—after a warm bath or shower. The heat causes the scrotal skin to relax, making it easier to find anything unusual. TSE is simple and only takes a few minutes.

- Examine each testicle gently with both hands. The index and middle fingers should be placed underneath the testicle while the thumbs are placed on the top. Roll the testicle gently between the thumbs and fingers. One testicle may be larger than the other. This is normal.

- The epididymis is a cordlike structure on the top and back of the testicle that stores and transports the sperm. Do not confuse the epididymis with an abnormal lump.
- Feel for any abnormal lumps—about the size of a pea—on the front or the side of the testicle. These lumps are usually painless.

If you do find a lump, contact your doctor right away. The lump may be due to an infection, and a doctor can decide the proper treatment. If the lump is not an infection, it is likely to be cancer. Remember that testicular cancer is highly curable, especially when detected and treated early. Testicular cancer almost always occurs in only one testicle, and the other testicle is all that is needed for full sexual function.

Routine testicular self-exams are important, but they cannot substitute for a doctor's examination. Your doctor should examine your testicles when you have a physical exam. You also can ask your doctor to check the way you do TSE.

Source: National Cancer Institute (NIH Publication No. 93-2636).

---

breast and endometrial cancer: early menarche, late menopause, and not bearing children. The links between these risk factors and ovarian cancer, however, are not as well-defined as they are in breast and endometrial cancer. Additional risk factors are being Caucasian, living in a Western country, and eating a high-fat diet (Risch et al., 1994).

Research shows that the use of oral contraceptives containing both estrogen and progesterone lower a woman's risk of developing ovarian cancer. Most studies show that for each year a woman uses oral contraceptives, her risk of ovarian cancer decreases by 40% to 50% (LaVecchia & Franceschi, 1999). Additionally, estrogen replacement therapy does not raise a woman's risk of this cancer.

The cause of ovarian cancer is unknown. Hereditary factors seem to play a role in only 3% to 4% of ovarian malignancies. Even though the risk factors mentioned previously have been defined, almost all cases of ovarian cancer seem to arise in patients for whom there is no apparent risk factor or genetic predisposition.

A reliable means of detecting ovarian cancer in its early stages has not yet been developed. There is a blood test for ovarian cancer, but it detects only 50% of ovarian cancers. During a woman's annual pelvic examination, a physician feels a woman's ovaries in an attempt to detect abnormal growths. Almost three-fourths of patients have advanced disease by the time it is diagnosed.

If a physician suspects that a woman has ovarian cancer, a reliable diagnosis may be possible only through surgery.

Ultrasound techniques (see p. 114) are also used occasionally to confirm the diagnosis of ovarian cancer. Treatment for ovarian cancer involves removal of the cancerous ovary and chemotherapy. Radiation is occasionally used.

Healthy LIVING PRACTICES

- To lower your risk of developing lung cancer, do not smoke cigarettes, avoid inhaling airborne asbestos fibers, and avoid exposure to radon gas.
- If you are exposed to lung carcinogens at your place of work, explore ways to avoid future exposure.
- To prevent the development of larynx, mouth, and esophagus cancers, avoid smoking and chewing tobacco, and excessive drinking of alcoholic beverages.
- Have a complete oral examination annually for early cancer detection.
- To lower your risk of developing cancer of the bladder and kidney, avoid smoking cigarettes.
- To lower your risk of pancreatic cancer, avoid smoking cigarettes and inhaling chemical fumes.
- To lower your risk of developing stomach cancer, avoid eating salt-cured, nitrate-cured, or smoked foods. Also avoid smoking cigarettes and drinking excessive amounts of alcoholic beverages.
- To reduce your risk of developing colorectal cancer, eat a diet high in fiber and low in fat. Follow the

American Cancer Society's screening test guidelines to detect this cancer early.

- If you are female, you can reduce your risk of breast cancer by exercising at least 4 hours per week and avoiding alcoholic beverages.
- To detect breast cancer in its early stages, conduct a breast self-examination every month and follow the ACS guidelines for breast clinical examination and mammography.
- If you are female, you can reduce your risk of developing endometrial cancer by losing weight if you are overweight, and by controlling diabetes mellitus if you have this disease.
- Discuss the impact of estrogen replacement therapy on the development of endometrial cancer with your health-care provider, if you are considering or are taking this medication.
- If you are female and older than 40 years, have annual pelvic examinations for early detection of endometrial cancer.
- If you are a sexually active woman with multiple partners or with nonmonogamous partners, you can lower your risk of cervical cancer by using male or female condoms to protect yourself against HPV.
- All women can lower their risk of cervical cancer by avoiding cigarette smoking.
- If you have been sexually active and are age 18 or older, the American Cancer Society recommends that you have annual Pap tests and pelvic examinations to screen for cervical cancer.
- To protect against skin cancer, stay out of the sun and wear sunscreen when outdoors.
- Detect melanoma early by checking your skin for growths that exhibit these warning signs: asymmetry, irregular border, multiple colors, and large diameter.
- If you are male and older than 50, talk to your health-care provider about annual digital rectal exams and PSA tests for the early detection of prostate cancer.
- If you are male, perform a testicular self-examination once every month to detect this cancer early.
- If you are a woman past menopause, consider annual pelvic examinations to check for ovarian cancer.

Managing Your Health

Reducing Your Risk for Cancer

DO'S

- Eat a diet low in fat and high in fiber, such as found in apples, citrus fruits, and grains.
- Eat a variety of fruits and vegetables daily.
- Follow the American Cancer Society's recommendations for screening tests to detect cancer in its early stages.
- Women should perform monthly breast self-examinations.
- Men should perform monthly testicular self-examinations.
- Know the warning signs of cancer and see your health-care provider immediately if you detect any of them.
- Sexually active women with multiple partners or with nonmonogamous partners should use male or female condoms during sexual intercourse to protect themselves against infection with human papillomavirus.
- Women should consult their health-care providers regarding the use of oral contraceptives and estrogen replacement therapy with respect to cancer prevention and risk.
- Premenopausal women should exercise at least 4 hours per week to reduce the risk of breast cancer.

DON'TS

- Don't smoke cigarettes. If you can't quit, cut down.
- Avoid breathing environmental tobacco smoke.
- Don't chew tobacco products.
- Don't drink excessive amounts of alcoholic beverages.
- Women should avoid drinking alcoholic beverages altogether to reduce the risk of breast cancer.
- Avoid unnecessary exposure to ionizing radiation, such as x rays and ultraviolet light.
- Don't lie in the sun or in tanning beds.
- Avoid exposure to toxic chemicals, such as certain occupational carcinogens.
- Avoid inhaling chemical fumes, such as gasoline fumes.
- Avoid breathing asbestos dust and radon gas.
- Avoid eating salt-cured, nitrate-cured, or smoked foods.
- Women should avoid obesity to reduce the risk of endometrial cancer.

www.jbpub.com/healthyliving

Cancer's Seven Warning Signs

You can remember the following signs easily by knowing that they are a CAUTION—these signs do not necessarily mean you have cancer but that you should see your health-care provider to evaluate the sign.

Change in bowel or bladder habits
A sore that does not heal
Unusual bleeding or discharge
Thickening or lump in breast or elsewhere
Indigestion or difficulty in swallowing
Obvious change in a wart or mole
Nagging cough or hoarseness

Reducing Your Risk for Cancer

You cannot change some of your cancer risk factors: heredity, age, ethnicity, lifelong exposure to naturally produced estrogen (in women), and the nondescent of testes (in male children). However, you can avoid many risk factors, thereby reducing your risk of developing one or more cancers. The "Managing Your Health" box entitled "Reducing Your Risk for Cancer" on the previous page lists modifiable cancer risks and actions you can take to lower your risk.

A summary of the American Cancer Society's recommendations for the early detection of cancer is listed in the "Managing Your Health" box on p. 303. Finally, the "Managing Your Health" box above on cancer's seven warning signs. In addition to being aware of these signs, you can learn the more detailed early warning signs for the various cancers described in this chapter. If you have concerns about your risk of developing cancer, discuss them with your health-care provider. Early detection and treatment are critical to winning the war against cancer.

Cancer

Most cancers arise in people older than 50 years, and the risk continues to rise as people grow older. The only cancers described in this chapter that are prevalent in young adults are malignant melanoma, testicular cancer, cervical cancer, and breast cancer. Additionally, only 1% of cancers occur in children. However, cancer is the most frequent cause of death from disease in American children older than 1 year of age. The most prevalent cancers of children up to 5 years old are listed in ▌Table 13-6.

Adult cancers rarely occur in children. These cancers are largely related to the effects of cancer-causing agents acting on cells over a lifetime, while children's cancers seem more often related to genetic factors.

Although pediatric cancers usually grow more rapidly than adult cancers, they are, in general, more responsive to anticancer drugs than are adult cancers. For this reason chemotherapy is the treatment of choice for most childhood cancers, while surgery and radiation are the primary treatments for adult cancers. Effective cancer chemotherapy has produced a remarkable decline in childhood deaths due to cancer over the past 25 years.

Table 13-6	The Most Prevalent Cancers of Children up to Age 5

Leukemia (cancer of the blood)

Central nervous system cancers

Lymphomas (cancer of the lymph nodes)

Nervous system tumors (often in adrenal glands)

Wilms' tumor (cancer of the kidney)

Bone cancer

Retinoblastoma (cancer of the eye)

Liver cancer

Chapter Review

Summary

Cancer is a variety of diseases that have common characteristics: Their cells exhibit abnormal growth, division, and differentiation and have the potential to spread from where they develop. These cells form masses called malignant tumors that interfere with normal body processes.

Cancer develops in cells that have damaged or mutated genes. Mutations can be inherited or can occur from exposure to low-dose radiation, drugs, toxic chemicals, or certain viruses. Successive genetic changes must take place for a normal cell to change into a cancer cell. Therefore, the probability of developing cancer generally increases with increasing age and with exposure to cancer-causing substances.

This chapter organizes the discussion of cancers according to factors that appear to be most significant in their development. Advanced age is a risk factor for most cancers; heredity is a significant risk factor in some cancers.

Cancers caused by or related to tobacco use are lung, larynx, oral cavity, esophageal, kidney, bladder, pancreatic, stomach, and cervical cancer. To lower the risk of developing any of these cancers, avoid smoking and chewing tobacco products. Additionally, avoid drinking excessive amounts of alcoholic beverages to lower the risk of developing larynx, oral, and esophageal cancer. Have a complete oral examination annually for early cancer detection in this area.

Diet accounts for a significant number of cancers, and has both a positive and a negative effect on the development of cancer. A primary risk factor in the development of stomach cancer is eating salt-cured, nitrate-cured, or smoked foods. To lower the risk of developing this cancer, avoid eating these foods. The incidence of colorectal cancer is also related to diet. To reduce the risk of developing this cancer, eat a high-fiber, low-fat diet. People older than 50 years of age should have a fecal occult blood test and a sigmoidoscopy annually. People older than 40 years should have a digital rectal examination annually.

The cancers related to hormone function are breast cancer and endometrial cancer. These cancers are associated significantly with prolonged exposure to estrogen. Risk factors associated with these cancers are early menarche, late menopause, not bearing children, and delaying pregnancy. Obesity, diabetes mellitus, and unopposed estrogen replacement therapy are also risk factors in endometrial cancer. Exercising at least 4 hours per week helps reduce breast cancer risk in premenopausal women. Avoiding alcoholic beverages also reduces the risk. For early cancer detection, women older than 20 years should do breast self-examination every month. Additionally, women aged 20 to 39 years should have a breast clinical examination every 3 years, and every year age 40 and after. Women aged 40 and older should have a mammography every year. For early detection of endometrial cancer, women older than 40 should have annual pelvic examinations.

Certain viruses are implicated in the development of a variety of cancers. The virally related cancer most prevalent in the United States is cervical cancer. The virus implicated in this disease, human papilloma virus (HPV), is transmitted by infected men to their female partners during sexual intercourse, and vice versa. Sexually active women with multiple partners or with nonmonogamous partners can lower their risk of cervical cancer by using male or female condoms to protect themselves against HPV. Women can also lower their risk by avoiding cigarette smoking.

The ultraviolet radiation in sunlight is the most important factor that influences the development of cancer of the skin. There are three main types of skin cancer: basal cell carcinoma, squamous cell carcinoma, and malignant melanoma. Malignant melanoma results in the most deaths of these cancers because it is a fast-growing metastatic cancer. Light-skinned, fair-haired Caucasians are a high-risk group for developing skin cancer. To protect against skin cancer, stay out of the sun and wear sunscreen when outdoors. Detect melanoma early by checking your skin for growths exhibiting these warning signs: asymmetry, irregular border, multiple colors, and large diameter.

Cancers with unknown causes include prostate cancer, testicular cancer, and ovarian cancer. The risk factors for prostate cancer are age and heredity. For early detection of this cancer, men older than 50 should have annual digital rectal exams and prostate-specific antigen blood tests. Men between the ages of 15 and 35 are at the highest risk for testicular cancer. For early detection of this disease, all males older than 15 should perform monthly testicular self-examinations. Ovarian cancer is primarily a disease of postmenopausal women. Women should have annual pelvic examinations to check for this cancer.

Childhood cancers, although rare, are the most frequent cause of death from disease in American children older than 1 year. Children develop cancers due to hereditary or developmental reasons. Occasionally environmental agents are the cause. Treatment for childhood cancers is highly effective.

Applying What You Have Learned

1. Imagine that you or a female friend had an annual Pap test. The report from the lab stated that cells exhibiting dysplasia were seen in the smear. What does this statement mean? How would these cells look different from normal cells? What would be your or your friend's next course of action? *(Application)*

2. List three cancer risk factors over which a person has no control. Suppose that at least one of them was a risk factor for you. List this hypothetical (or real) factor and the cancer(s) related to this risk. What might you do regarding cancer prevention if you are aware of this (these) factor(s)? *(Application)*

3. Your good friend is a heavy drinker, eats lots of spicy food, and experiences heartburn regularly. He takes antacids, but recently they have not helped. He also tells you that he seems to have some difficulty swallowing but he's not quite sure. He thinks it's "all in his head." What would you advise your friend to do? Might cancer be causing his problems? If so, which type? Which symptoms lead you to this conclusion? *(Application)*

4. List two dietary factors related to the development of cancer and two dietary factors related to lowering the risk of cancer. Name the cancers to which these dietary factors relate. Now list, as best you can remember, the foods you ate for the past two days. What is your intake of the types of foods related to cancer development and prevention? Based on this analysis, should you make changes in your diet to lower your risk of certain cancers? *(Evaluation)*

5. With respect to the cancers discussed in this chapter, which cancer(s) are you at least risk for developing? Why? Which cancers are you at highest risk for developing? Why? *(Synthesis)*

6. Referring to your answer to question 5, what can you do to lower your risk of developing the cancers for which you are at high risk? State rationales for each suggestion. Why will these lifestyle changes lower your risk? *(Evaluation)*

....

KEY

Application: Using information in a new situation.
Synthesis: Putting together information from different sources.
Evaluation: Making informed decisions.

Reflecting On Your Health

1. In what ways have your attitudes about cancer changed since reading this chapter?

2. The "Analyzing Health-Related Information" activity on pages 318–320 includes an article about genetic testing for cancer. Would you want to be tested for genetic factors that might signal high cancer risk? Why or why not? If you found that you were genetically "at risk" for a particular cancer, would you be more, or less, concerned about controlling your lifestyle risk factors for cancer? Why?

3. Were you aware of all the ACS recommendations for the early detection of cancer prior to reading this chapter? If you were not, which recommendations were new to you? Will you follow these recommendations? Why or why not? If you were aware of all the ACS recommendations, do you follow those recommendations for your gender and age group? Why or why not?

4. Do you know anyone who has or has had cancer, or have you read stories written by cancer patients about their disease? What did you learn about cancer from them that affected your life?

5. The highest score one could attain on the Torabi Cancer Prevention Behavior Scale (see the self-assessments in the student workbook) is 150. Take the assessment and compare your score to 150. The closer your score is to 150, the healthier your behavior is regarding cancer prevention. Does your score match your self-perception of your behavior? Did the self-assessment identify behaviors you should change? If so, discuss what you might do to change those behaviors.

References

Alberts, D. S., Martínez, M. E., Roe, D. J., Guillén-Rodríguez, J. M., Marshall, J. R., Van Leeuwen, J. B., Reid, M. E., Ritenbaugh, C., Vargas, P. A., Bhattacharyya, A. B., Earnest, D. L., Sampliner, R. E., and the Phoenix Colon Cancer Prevention Physicians' Network (2000). Lack of effect of a high-fiber cereal supplement on the recurrence of colorectal cancer. *The New England Journal of Medicine, 342*:1156–1162.

American Cancer Society (ACS). (1999). *1999 Facts and Figures.* Atlanta: American Cancer Society.

Archambeau, J. O., Slater, J. M., Coutrakon, G. B., Miller, D. W., Preston, W., Slater, J. D., DiCello, J. F., Robertson, J. B., & Slater, J. W. (1994). Proton-beam irradiation for the cancer patient: An approach to optimal therapy and normal-tissue sparing. In K. I. Altman & John T. Lett, eds. *Advances in Radiation Biology:* Vol. 18 (pp. 53–89). London: Academic Press.

Bernstein, L., Henderson, B. E., Hanisch, R., Sullivan-Halley, J., & Ross, R. (1994). Physical exercise and reduced risk of breast cancer in young women. *Journal of the National Cancer Institute, 86*:1403–1408.

Boon, T. (1993). Teaching the immune system to fight cancer. *Scientific American, 268*(3):82–89.

Byers, R., Mouchawa, J., & Marks, J. (1999). The American Cancer Society challenge goals: How far can cancer rates decline in the U.S. by the year 2015? *Cancer, 86*:715–727.

Culver, K. W., & Blaese, R. M. (1994). Gene therapy for cancer. *Trends in Genetics, 10*:174–178.

de Gruijl, T. D., & Curiel, D. T. (1999). Cancer vaccine strategies get bigger and better. *Nature Medicine, 5*:1124–1125.

Fisher, B., Anderson, S., Redmond, C. K., Wormark, N., Wickerham, D. L., & Cronin, W. M. (1995). Reanalysis and results after 12 years of follow-up in a randomized clinical trial comparing total mastectomy with lumpectomy with or without irradiation in the treatment of breast cancer. *The New England Journal of Medicine, 333*:1456–1461.

Genazzani, A. R., & Gambacciani, M. (1999). Hormone replacement therapy: The perspectives for the 21st century. *Maturitas, 32*:11–17.

Ginsburg, E. S. (1999). Estrogen, alcohol, and breast cancer risk. *Journal of Steroid Biochemistry & Molecular Biology, 69*: 299–306.

Ginsburg, E. S., Mello, N. K., Mendelson, J. H., Barbieri, R. L., Teoh, S. K., Rothman, M., Gao, X., & Sholar, J. W. (1997). Effects of alcohol ingestion on estrogens in postmenopausal women. *Journal of the American Medical Association, 276*(21):1747–1752.

Giovannucci, E. (1999). The prevention of colorectal cancer by aspirin use. *Biomedicine & Pharmacotherapy, 53*:303–308.

Hecht, S. S. (1994). Environmental tobacco smoke and lung cancer: The emerging role of carcinogen biomarkers and molecular epidemiology. *Journal of the National Cancer Institute, 86*: 1369–1370.

Henkel, J. (1994). Prostate cancer: New tests create treatment dilemmas. *FDA Consumer, 28*(10):5–9.

Hoffman-Goetz, L., Apter, D., Demark-Wahnefried, W., Goran, M. I., McTiernan, A., & Reichman, M. E. (1998). Possible mechanisms mediating an association between physical activity and breast cancer. *Cancer, 83*(3 Suppl.):621–628.

Houghton, A. N. (1995). On course for a cancer vaccine. *The Lancet, 345*:1384–1385.

Hudis, C. A. (1999). The current state of adjuvent therapy for breast cancer: Focus on paclitaxel. *Seminars in Oncology, 26* (1 Suppl. 2):1–5.

Jenks, S. (1994). Breast cancer gene found. *Journal of the National Cancer Institute, 86*:1444–1445.

Kotwall, C. A. (1999). Breast cancer treatment and chemoprevention. *Canadian Family Physician, 45*:1917–1924.

Latikka, P., Pukkala, E., & Vihko, V. (1998). Relationship between the risk of breast cancer and physical activity: An epidemiological perspective. *Sports Medicine, 26*:133–43.

LaVecchia, C., & Franceschi, S. (1999). Oral contraceptives and ovarian cancer. *European Journal of Cancer Prevention, 8*:297–304.

Linehan, D. C., Bowne, W. B., & Lewis, J. J. (1999). Immunotherapeutic approaches to sarcoma. *Seminars in Surgical Oncology, 17*:72–77.

Randal, J. (1994). Early-stage prostate cancer study compares therapy to watchful waiting. *Journal of the National Cancer Institute, 86*:1376–1377.

Risch, H. A., Jain, M., Marrett, L. D., & Howe, G. R. (1994). Dietary fat intake and risk of epithelial ovarian cancer. *Journal of the National Cancer Institute, 86*:1409–1415.

Rose, D. P. (1997). Dietary fatty acids and cancer. *American Journal of Clinical Nutrition, 66*(4 Suppl.):998S–1003S.

Schatzkin, A., Lanza, E., Corle, D., Lance, P., Iber, F., Caan, B., Shike, M., Weissfeld, J., Burt, R., Cooper, M. R., Kikendall, J. W., Cahill, J., and the Polyp Prevention Trial Study Group (2000). Lack of effect of a low-fat, high-fiber diet on the recurrence of colorectal adenomas. *The New England Journal of Medicine, 342*: 1149–1155.

Sellers, T. A., Potter, J. D., Bailey-Wilson, J. E., Rich, S. S., Rothschild, H., & Elston, R. C. (1992). Lung cancer detection and prevention: Evidence for an interaction between smoking and genetic predisposition. *Cancer research, 52*(9 Suppl.):2694s–2697s.

Shriver, S. P., Boordeau, H. A., Gubish, C. T., Tirpak, D. L., Gaither Davis, A. L., Luketich, J. D., & Siegfried, J. M. (2000). Sex-specific expression of gastrin-releasing peptide receptor: Relationship to smoking history and risk of lung cancer. *Journal of the National Cancer Institute, 92*:24–33.

Srivastava, A., & Krieger, N. (2000). Relation of physical activity to risk of testicular cancer. *American Journal of Epidemiology, 15*:78–87.

Stoll, B. A. (1999). Perimenopausal weight gain and progression of breast cancer precursors. *Cancer Detection & Prevention, 23*:31–36.

Suit, H., & Urie, M. (1992). Proton beams in radiation therapy. *Journal of the National Cancer Institute, 84*:155–163.

Tavani, A., & LaVecchia, C. (1999). The adverse effects of hormone replacement therapy. *Drugs & Aging, 14*:347–357.

U.S. Department of Health and Human Services (USDHHS). (1999a). Radon testing in households with a residential smoker—United States, 1993–1994. *Morbidity and Mortality Weekly Report, 48*:683–686.

U.S. Department of Health and Human Services (USDHHS). (1999b). Tobacco use—United States, 1900–1999. *Morbidity and Mortality Weekly Report, 48*:986–993.

U.S. Public Health Service. (1964). *Smoking and Health: Report of the Advisory Committee to the Surgeon General of the Public Health Service*. Atlanta, GA: U.S. Department of Health, Education, and Welfare, Public Health Service, CDC. (PHS Publication no. 1103).

U.S. Public Health Service. (1995). *Healthy people 2000: National health promotion and disease prevention objectives—midcourse review and 1995 revisions*. Washington, DC: US Department of Health and Human Services, Public Health Service.

Westoff, C. L. (1999). Breast cancer risk: Perception versus reality. *Contraception, 59*(1 suppl.):25S–28S.

Wooster, R., Bignell, G., Sancaster, J., Swift, S., Seal, S., Mangion, J., Collins, N., Gregory, S., Gumbs, C., & Micklem, G. (1995). Identification of the breast cancer susceptibility gene BRCA2. *Nature, 378*(6559):789–792.

Wynder, E. L., Cohen, L. A., Muscat, J. E., Winters, B., Dwyer, J. T., & Blackburn, G. (1997). Breast cancer: Weighing the evidence for a promoting role of dietary fat. *Journal of the National Cancer Institute, 89*:766–75.

Infection, Immunity, and Noninfectious Disease

Jackie Joyner-Kersee: Olympian gold, silver, and bronze medalist. Some consider Joyner-Kersee the greatest woman athlete ever. *Sports Illustrated for Women* named Joyner-Kersee the "Female Athlete of the Century" in their Winter, 1999, issue. Capturing the gold in consecutive Olympics from 1984 through 1992 and the bronze in 1996, Joyner-Kersee is one of the most decorated U.S. woman athletes in Olympic history.

Exercise-induced asthma has not deterred this outstanding athlete from making her indelible mark in the world of sports, nor has it deterred other athletes. Sixty-seven of the Olympians who participated in the 1984 games with Joyner-Kersee suffer from this ailment, as did many Olympians in the 1996 competition.

Exercise-induced asthma is a condition in which the airways narrow after sustained exertion, making it more difficult than usual for a person to breathe. What triggers this problem is the cooling and reheating of the airways as a person exercises. As exercise begins, a person begins to breathe deeply and rapidly. During this deep and rapid inhalation, more air is

"Exercise-induced asthma has not deterred this outstanding athlete from making her indelible mark in the world of sports . . ."

moistened and warmed in the respiratory passageways than before exercise began, which draws moisture and heat from the airways. After a person is warmed up, the breathing rate falls, and the airways return to their normal temperature. Health scientists do not know how airway cooling and reheating triggers asthma attacks.

Asthma is one of a variety of noninfectious diseases. **Diseases** are processes that affect the proper functioning of the body and are usually accompanied by characteristic signs and symptoms. **Infectious diseases,** such as colds or the flu, are caused by **pathogens,** which are agents of infection: bacteria, rickettsias, viruses, fungi, protozoans, and parasitic worms. (Infectious diseases are discussed later in this chapter.) **Noninfectious diseases** are caused by abnormalities in the hereditary material (genetic diseases), interactions between heredity and environmental factors (especially those related to lifestyle such as asthma), or environmental factors alone, as in repetitive-use injuries or lead poisoning (see Chapter 16, "Environmental Health").

What You'll Learn

www.jbpub.com/healthyliving

The web site for this book offers many useful tools and supplementary health information for both students and instructors. Visit the site at www.jbpub.com/healthyliving for information on these topics:

Noninfectious Diseases
Trends in Infectious Disease
Protection Against Infectious Diseases
Sexually Transmitted Infections Caused by Viruses
Protecting Yourself Against STIs

Chapter Overview

Causes of noninfectious diseases.
Symptoms of and treatments for noninfectious diseases.
Trends in infectious diseases since 1900.
How the chain of infection works.
How nonspecific and specific immunity work.
How to protect yourself against infectious disease.
Symptoms of sexually transmitted infections.
Treatments and prevention methods for sexually transmitted infections.

DIVERSITY *in Health* Sickle-Cell Anemia

Con$umer *Health* Over-the-Counter Cold Medications

Managing Your Health Eliminating or Reducing Your Risk of HIV Infection and Other STIs

across the lifespan Infectious and Noninfectious Diseases

Applying Concepts for Healthy Living A Workbook

Student Workbook

Self Assessment: STI Attitude Scale
Changing Health Habits: Reducing Your Risk of Contracting an STI.

Do You Know?

- How to protect yourself from sexually transmitted infections?
- If over-the-counter cold remedies really work?
- Which types of diseases you can catch and which you cannot?

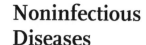

Noninfectious Diseases

Genetic Diseases

There are two types of genetic diseases: inherited diseases and diseases caused by errors when gametes (sex cells) are formed. **Inherited diseases** are transmitted solely by gene transfer from parents to offspring. They occur more frequently among close relatives than in the general population and show patterns in their transmission. For example, an inherited disease may strike only males, or there may be no male-to-male transmission of the disease.

Inherited diseases are caused by disorders of the hereditary material, or genes. Genes carry information about every aspect of an organism and may carry normal instructions in one person and defective instructions in another. A defective gene in the sex cells of an individual can be passed on to a child unless it results in death before the person reaches reproductive age.

Defective genes arise through mutation. A **mutation** is a change in a gene or a chromosome. Mutations in eggs and sperm can occur for no apparent reason or from exposure to a variety of environmental sources. One source is ionizing radiation such as x rays, which is the reason the dentist places a protective lead shield over your pelvic area when taking x rays of your teeth. Another source of damage to genes is drugs such as lysergic acid diethylamide (lysergide, LSD) or marijuana (*Cannabis sativa*). Chapter 7 describes these drugs and their effects on the body in more detail. Toxic chemicals are a third source of genetic damage. (Poisoning, another effect of toxic chemicals, is discussed in Chapter 16.) People often come into contact with toxic chemicals in the workplace and do not realize the danger because they feel no ill effects.

Three hereditary diseases that are common in the United States are sickle-cell anemia, cystic fibrosis, and Duchenne muscular dystrophy.

The "Diversity in Health" essay, "Sickle-Cell Anemia: Why Does This Deleterious Gene Persist?" discusses this hereditary disease, which is common among African Americans.

Cystic fibrosis (CF) is the most common, lethal genetic disease in the Caucasian population. (It seldom affects African Americans, Asians, or Jews.) Cystic fibrosis affects the glands that secrete mucus and sweat. In CF patients, the sweat glands produce an abnormally salty secretion and the mucous glands produce an exceptionally thick and sticky secretion that builds up and plugs the ducts of glands and other passageways. Although the pancreas (an organ that secretes digestive juices) is often seriously affected, lung disease accounts for most of the illness and nearly all deaths from CF. Multiple disorders of the lungs arise when mucus blocks the airways. Infections result and breathing becomes impaired. Today a person with CF can expect to live only about 24 years.

Duchenne muscular dystrophy (DMD) is the most common type of muscular dystrophy (*dys* means "abnormal"; *trophy* means "growth"). DMD is a disease in which the muscles gradually weaken and degenerate. It occurs in about 1 in 3500 to 4000 newborn males and kills an average of 2 boys per day, usually striking before the age of 6 years. These children are usually slow to walk and talk. Their thigh and pelvic muscles gradually deteriorate, resulting in unsteadiness in standing, walking, climbing stairs, and getting up from a seated position. As the muscles of the shoulder, trunk, and back weaken, the child's spine begins to curve and the posture becomes swayback. This abnormal body posture interferes with the functioning of internal organs, especially the lungs. Although heart problems sometimes cause sudden death in DMD patients, these children and young adults usually die in their teens or 20s of respiratory infections or respiratory failure when the diaphragm (a sheetlike muscle that forms the floor of the chest cavity and that is essential to breathing) becomes affected.

As mentioned previously, the second category of genetic diseases or disorders is caused by errors in cell division that can occur when gametes, or sex cells, are produced in the ovaries or testes. Sometimes eggs or sperm are made that have too many or too few chromosomes; some gametes may be formed in which parts of chromosomes have been lost, gained, or moved to new positions. If conception takes place with a gamete that has a severe defect, the usual result is a spontaneous abortion. However, some genetic defects result in a fertilized egg that is capable of developing into a full-term baby. The child may be born with structural or functional problems, or both.

Down syndrome, which affects approximately 1 in 700 to 800 newborns, is a common genetic disorder caused by improper cell division in gametes. Cell division problems occur more often in eggs than in sperm because men produce new sperm throughout their lives, while women are born with all the potential eggs they will ever have. Therefore, a woman's eggs age as she ages. Each month, a

---

disease
a process that affects the proper functioning of the body and is usually accompanied by characteristic signs and symptoms.

infectious disease (in-FEK-shus) a disease caused by bacteria, rickettsias, viruses, fungi, protozoans, or parasitic worms.

pathogen (PATH-oh-jen) a disease-causing agent of infection; the first link in the chain of infection.

noninfectious disease (NON-in-FEK-shus) illness caused by genetic abnormalities, by interactions between hereditary and environmental factors, or solely by environmental factors.

inherited disease a genetic disease transmitted solely by gene transfer from parents to offspring.

mutation (mew-TAY-shun) in reference to human biology, a change in a gene or a chromosome.

cystic fibrosis (SIS-tik fie-BROH-sis) a common, lethal, inherited disease that affects the glands that secrete mucus and sweat, resulting in multiple disorders of the lungs and pancreas.

Duchenne muscular dystrophy (do-SHEN MUSS-ku-lar DIS-tro-fee) an inherited disease in which the muscles gradually weaken and degenerate. It usually strikes boys before the age of 6 years.

Down syndrome a genetic disease usually caused by the presence of three (rather than two) number 21 chromosomes; the child is usually mentally retarded with a short body and a broad, flat face.

Sickle-Cell Anemia: Why Does This Deleterious Gene Persist?

Sickle-cell anemia is one of the most common genetic disorders among African Americans, having arisen in their African ancestors. It has also been observed in people whose ancestors came from the Mediterranean basin, the Indian subcontinent, the Caribbean, and parts of Central and South America (particularly Brazil). The sickle-cell gene has persisted in these populations—even though the disease eventually kills its victims—because of a curious interaction between this disease and another prevalent in these regions. Today, an estimated 50,000 Americans of African American and Hispanic origins have the disease, and approximately 2.5 million carry the trait (Rausch & Pollard, 1998).

Sickle-cell anemia gets its name from the curved (sickle) shape of the red blood cells of individuals with this disease (■ Figure 14-A). Anemia, or a low number of red blood cells, results from the short life of these abnormal cells. An error in the gene that codes for hemoglobin, the oxygen-carrying molecule in red blood cells, is responsible for the signs and symptoms of sickle-cell disease.

These sickle-shaped cells cause pain when they become trapped in the small blood vessels of the body. This condition results in oxygen depletion to the tissues surrounding the blocked vessels, which damages tissues and causes infections. Most sickle-cell patients die in their 40s or 50s from conditions such as stroke, infection, kidney failure, or congestive heart failure.

To have sickle-cell anemia, a person must inherit two defective hemoglobin genes—one from each parent. A person who inherits a single defective gene is a carrier and is said to have *sickle-cell trait*. This gene is quite prevalent in the populations mentioned previously. For example, 1 in 400 African American newborns has sickle-cell disease and 1 in 12 has sickle-cell trait. People with sickle-cell trait do not have sickle-cell anemia, but they do have something in common with sufferers of sickle-cell anemia—resistance to malaria.

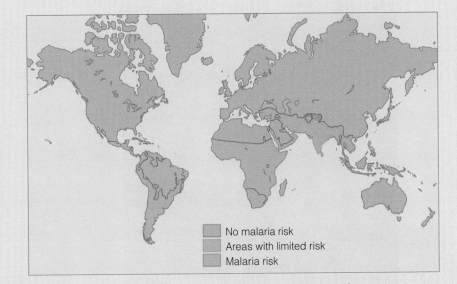

▲Figure 14-B **Areas of the World in Which Malaria Is Prevalent.** Malaria is a serious infectious desease in the tropical and subtropical regions of the world. Sickle-cell anemia is prevalent in these regions as well.

Those with the sickle-cell gene have a survival advantage in regions of the world in which malaria is prevalent. The map in ■ Figure 14-B shows where malaria is widespread; notice from the listing of affected populations in the first paragraph that sickle-cell anemia is prevalent in these areas as well. Although many of these peoples have since migrated from these areas, this ancestral gene persists in their populations.

How does a defective hemoglobin gene protect against malaria? In sickle-cell trait, red blood cells sickle under a variety of conditions, such as when the oxygen tension is low (at high altitudes, for example) and if these cells become acidic. Results of research show that infection of the red blood cells by malaria parasites causes the infected cells to become acidic due to the metabolism of the parasite. This change induces the red blood cells to sickle, which interrupts multiplication of the parasite. The spleen, an organ that destroys worn-out red blood cells, traps the sickled cells. Under these conditions, the parasites die and malaria does not develop. For populations who live in regions where malaria is prevalent, the sickle-cell gene persists because people harboring the gene are more likely to live to reproductive age than those who do not have the gene and die from malaria. Therefore, this "deleterious" gene is beneficial to those with sickle-cell trait living in malaria-infested areas and is passed from generation to generation. Unfortunately, some offspring inherit sickle-cell disease and not simply sickle-cell trait.

Health-care providers alleviate symptoms by administering painkillers and blood transfusions. Penicillin is given to children aged 1 to 5 years to ward off infection. But a recent breakthrough in treatment may increase the quality and duration of life for sickle-cell sufferers. In February 1995, the National Heart, Blood, and Lung Institute released the results of an extensive study showing that the drug hydroxyurea reduces the frequency of pain, hospital admissions, and life-threatening complications by about 50% (Marwick, 1995).

Until 1998 there was no cure for sickle-cell anemia. Then, in December 1998 a 13-year-old boy underwent an experimental blood cell transfusion with stem cells from the umbilical cord of an infant unrelated to him. (Stem cells are undifferentiated cells that give rise to all types of blood cells.) After one year, the cord blood cells were making all healthy blood cells in the boy, and he was declared "cured" of sickle-cell anemia (Associated Press, 1999).

Couples can be screened to detect if they are carriers of the trait to help them in their family-planning decisions. Eventually, medical experts may discover a way to weed out this life-threatening gene in populations no longer living in malaria-prone areas, but that genetic shift in the population may take millions of years.

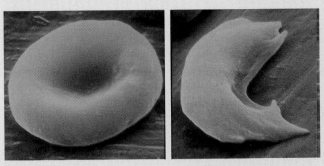

▲Figure 14-A **Normal and Sickled Red Blood Cells.** The red blood cells to the left have a normal, rounded shape. Those to the right have the curved shape of sickle-cell anemia, which results in their becoming trapped in the small blood vessels of the body.

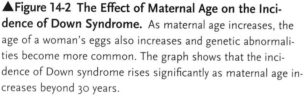

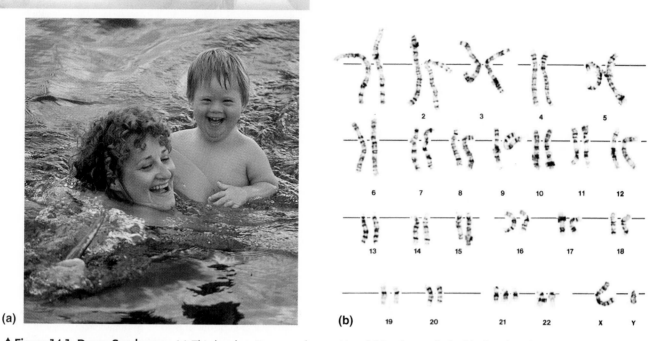

(a)

(b)   2   3   4   5   6   7   8   9   10   11   12   13   14   15   16   17   18   19   20   21   22   X   Y

▲Figure 14-1 Down Syndrome. (a) This boy has Down syndrome. He exhibits the stocky build, short hands, and flattened facial features characteristic of this genetic condition. (b) Down syndrome is called *trisomy 21* because it is caused by the presence of an extra 21st chromosome as shown in the karyotype, the array of chromosomes in a cell.

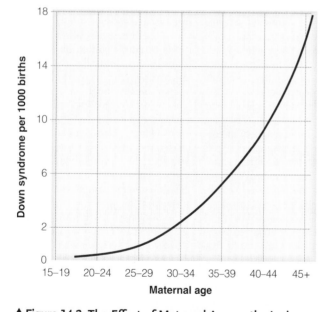

▲Figure 14-2 The Effect of Maternal Age on the Incidence of Down Syndrome. As maternal age increases, the age of a woman's eggs also increases and genetic abnormalities become more common. The graph shows that the incidence of Down syndrome rises significantly as maternal age increases beyond 30 years.

single egg reaches maturity, during which time a division of the potential egg takes place. The division may result in an error in the number of chromosomes in the mature egg. The majority of Down syndrome children have three number 21 chromosomes instead of the usual pair (█ Figure 14-1). For this reason Down syndrome is also called *trisomy 21*. As the graph in █ Figure 14-2 shows, the risk of bearing a child with Down syndrome or another chromosomal abnormality rises dramatically after the maternal age of 30. Therefore, various screening methods have been developed to detect whether a fetus is affected with trisomy 21 or other chromosomal problems. Prenatal diagnosis is discussed in Chapter 6 on pages 114 to 115.

Diseases Caused by an Interaction of Genes and the Environment

During the development of certain noninfectious diseases, there is often an interplay between genetic and environmental factors. Environmental factors may include substances to which an individual is exposed, such as air pollution, or may relate to a person's lifestyle, such as maintaining a high-fat diet or exercising very little or not at all. Genetic factors can predispose a person to a disease; that is, a person may contract a particular disease more readily or easily than other people in the general population exposed to the same environmental factors. For example, persons with asthma may have genetic factors that influence the functioning of their airways. They may also live in environments in which cigarette smoke and air pollution are present. These factors may lead to a chronic inflammatory state in their airways and result in asthma. However, other people with no genetic link to the disease may remain disease-free while living in the same environments.

Asthma, ulcers, diabetes mellitus, migraine headaches, cardiovascular disease, and cancer are common diseases that have both genetic and environmental causes. Ulcers are sores in the lining of the esophagus, stomach, or duodenum. They are discussed on pages 51 to 52 of Chapter 3. Diabetes mellitus is a group of diseases in which a person does not metabolize carbohydrates properly. Diabetes is discussed in Chapter 9 on pages 203 to 204. Migraine headaches are thought to be an inherited disorder that can be triggered by a variety of environmental factors. Migraines are discussed on pages 52 to 53 of Chapter 3. The nation's number one killers—cardiovascular disease and cancer—are discussed in separate chapters (Chapters 12 and 13, respectively) because they affect the nation's health so significantly.

Asthma, the most common chronic illness in childhood, is a disease of the airways. The bronchioles of asthmatics narrow in response to certain stimuli much more easily than do the bronchioles of nonasthmatics. (*Bronchioles* are air passageways, about the diameter of a pencil lead, that lead to the air sacs of the lungs [❚ **Figure 14-3**]). When these airways become narrowed, air flow to and from the lungs is blocked. As a result, asthmatic people have trouble breathing and begin to wheeze, which people refer to as having an *asthma attack*.

Environmental factors such as air pollution, respiratory infections, tobacco smoke, and allergens such as dust mites often trigger asthma attacks. (Dust mites are microscopic organisms that live in carpets, mattresses, pillows, and curtains.) As mentioned in the opening paragraphs of this chapter, exercise may also stimulate asthma attacks.

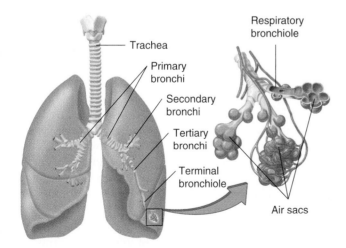

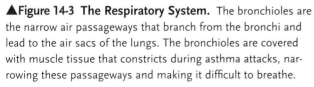

▲**Figure 14-3 The Respiratory System.** The bronchioles are the narrow air passageways that branch from the bronchi and lead to the air sacs of the lungs. The bronchioles are covered with muscle tissue that constricts during asthma attacks, narrowing these passageways and making it difficult to breathe.

Breathing warm, moist air is best for the athlete with exercise-induced asthma. For example, swimming in a warm pool will usually cause fewer problems than snow skiing. Also, warming up before exercise reduces the likelihood of an exercise-induced asthma attack. With other types of asthma, the key to management is discovering what stimulates attacks and avoiding these factors. For example, if a trigger is house dust mites, exposure can be reduced by not using carpeting or draperies, and washing bedding often in hot water. Medication is another important tool for asthma management.

Noninfectious Conditions with Environmental or Unknown Causes

Many conditions are caused by exposure to various substances in the environment. In general, environmental factors that are the sole cause of disease are toxic chemicals (see Chapter 16, "Environmental Health"). Not only are toxic chemicals present in the home, workplace, and environment, they are used and abused in ways that seriously affect health. The adverse effects of drug and alcohol abuse are described in Chapters 7 and 8, respectively. The toxic chemicals found in tobacco products are discussed in Chapter 8.

A few noninfectious conditions are caused by the ways in which people use their bodies. Temporomandibular disorder, characterized by pain in the jaw and chewing muscles that often results from grinding or clenching the teeth, is discussed in Chapter 3 on page 56. **Carpal tunnel syndrome**, a painful condition of the hands and fingers, results from improper positioning of the wrist while engaging in repetitive activities that use the hands, wrists, and arms. Ten percent of the population experiences occasional symptoms of this syndrome.

Carpal tunnel syndrome is usually the result of repetitive use. Activities such as using power tools frequently, typing for a long time, and playing piano or guitar often result in such injuries because people hold the wrist in a bent position rather than holding it straight. The injury causes inflammation and a buildup of fluid in a tunnel that runs through the bones of the wrist, or carpals. The fluid presses on the nerve and blood vessels in the tunnel. Other conditions such as arthritis, diabetes, and pregnancy may also contribute to pressure in the carpal tunnel (Crouch & Madden, 1992). To help avoid injury when typing for a long time, place your computer keyboard at elbow height

asthma
(AZ-mah) a common, chronic, childhood illness characterized by sensitive airways.

carpal tunnel syndrome
numbness, pain, or pins-and-needles sensations in either of the hands that extends down the fingers, resulting from improper alignment of the wrist while engaging in repetitive-use activities.

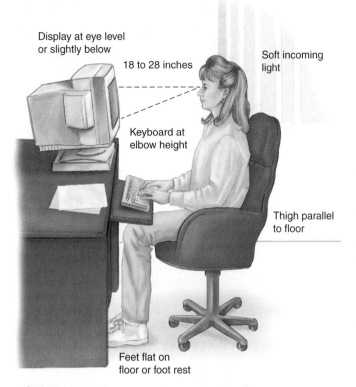

▲Figure 14-4 The Proper Sitting Position for Typing at the Computer. The screen should be at eye level or slightly lower. The keyboard should be at elbow height, the forearms parallel to the floor, the back supported, the thighs parallel to the floor, and the feet flat on the floor or foot rest.

Display at eye level or slightly below

18 to 28 inches

Soft incoming light

Keyboard at elbow height

Thigh parallel to floor

Feet flat on floor or foot rest

and keep your wrists unbent as shown in ▌Figure 14-4. Use wrist rests and arm rests only when you are resting, not when you are typing.

Healthy LIVING PRACTICES

- The risk of chromosomal abnormalities in a woman's eggs increases significantly after her thirtieth birthday. Therefore, if you and your partner are considering a pregnancy at or beyond this age, consult your health-care provider for advice regarding options to increase your chances of having a healthy infant.
- If you have asthma, learn your asthma triggers and avoid them. If you have exercise-induced asthma, consider restricting your activity on cold days or when the pollen count or air pollution levels are high.
- Abusing drugs, or living and working under toxic conditions, can damage the hereditary material of your cells, particularly the sex cells. Therefore, to protect your health and possibly that of your offspring, avoid exposure to toxic substances.

- Carpal tunnel syndrome often results from bending the wrists while engaging in a repetitive activity such as typing, using hand tools, or engaging in various household chores. To help prevent repetitive-use injury, always keep your wrists unbent while engaging in such activities.

Trends in Infectious Disease

www.jbpub.com/healthyliving

In 1900 the three leading causes of death were infectious diseases: pneumonia, tuberculosis, and enteritis (inflammation of the intestine, causing severe diarrhea) (Centers for Disease Control and Prevention [CDC], 1999a). Since that time, the United States (and other industrialized countries) have made achievements in public health that have changed this picture dramatically. Early in the twentieth century, United States' departments of public health were established, whose activities provided for clean drinking water, uncontaminated food, and proper sewage disposal and treatment. These actions have reduced the transmission of pathogens tremendously. *Antibiotics,* which are medications that kill bacteria, and *vaccines,* which are preparations that boost the immune system to help it ward off infection from specific pathogens, combat infection as well. Additionally, new treatments for certain viral illnesses such as influenza have been developed recently (Winquist et al., 1999). As a result, after nearly a century, the three leading causes of death in 1998 were no longer infectious diseases, but were noninfectious diseases: heart disease, cancer, and stroke. The only infectious diseases in the "top ten" were pneumonia and influenza, together ranked as the sixth leading cause of death (CDC, 1999b).

Although infectious diseases are not significant contributors to death in the United States at this time, the worldwide picture is much different. On World Health Day in 1997, Secretary-General of the United Nations Kofi-Anan noted in a press release that infectious diseases are the leading cause of death in the world. He continued to say that at least 30 new diseases have emerged in the past two decades, including HIV infection, Ebola viral hemorrhagic fever, and a new strain of hepatitis—hepatitis C (WHO, 1997). Additionally, many bacterial diseases once easily cured with antibiotics are appearing as incurable diseases, resistant to the variety of antibiotics available at this time. "Old" diseases that once seemed under control, such as diphtheria and tuberculosis, are making a comeback as well.

We are living in an age when international travel is commonplace, making transmission of infection a worldwide concern, not just a concern in our own country, state, or city. The resistance of many strains of bacteria to antibiotics and the reemergence of serious diseases once thought conquered makes complacency to infection a dangerous attitude. In this time of increasing illness and death from infectious disease in the global community, it is important to understand how infectious diseases are transmitted and how pathogens interact with the body. This knowledge is key to avoiding infection and staying healthy.

The Chain of Infection

Infection results from the interaction between a pathogen (also called an agent of infection) and a **host**, the organism that supports the growth of the pathogen. The pathogen is considered the first link in the chain of infection. The host is the third and last link. Joining these two links is **transmission**, the route by which the pathogen gets to the host. ▌**Figure 14-5** depicts the **chain of infection**, the relationship among the factors important in the development of infectious diseases.

The First Link: Pathogens

The severity of an infectious disease depends on a variety of factors:

- the type of pathogen (such as a bacterium or virus),
- its *virulence* (how easily it causes disease),
- its ability to multiply and spread within the body,
- its ability to combat the defense mechanisms of the body, and
- the body's reaction to this invader.

This chapter describes pathogens that cause infectious diseases next. A later section focuses on the host's defense mechanisms.

Bacteria and Rickettsias Bacteria produce infections such as strep throat, bacterial pneumonia, food poisoning, and infected cuts. These organisms are unicellular and microscopic, with a simple cell structure.

When bacteria enter the body, they adhere to the surfaces of host cells and grow and multiply there. Some bacteria penetrate deeply into the tissues (moving between body cells). Many pathogenic bacteria produce one or more chemicals that aid their invasion. A few types of bacteria produce toxins, or poisons, that cause diseases such as certain types of food poisoning.

Rickettsias are bacterialike organisms that live *within* host cells. These organisms cause diseases such as typhus, which is transmitted by lice, and Rocky Mountain Spotted Fever, which is transmitted by ticks.

Viruses Viruses cause many diseases with which you are familiar: the common cold, influenza (the flu), mumps, measles (▌**Figure 14-6**), chicken pox, hepatitis, and **acquired immunodeficiency syndrome (AIDS)**. Viruses are very different from bacteria, and, in fact, are very different from *any* organism: They do not have a cellular structure. Since the basis of life is the cell, viruses are not considered living organisms. They are simply hereditary material surrounded by a coat of protein.

Like bacteria, viruses cause disease by adhering to host cells, but unlike bacteria, viruses enter the cells of the body and use those cells to make more virus particles. The new virus particles break open the infected cell, killing

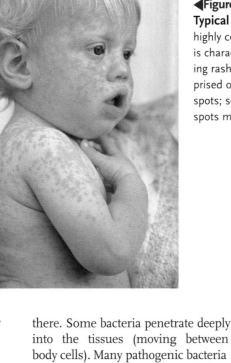

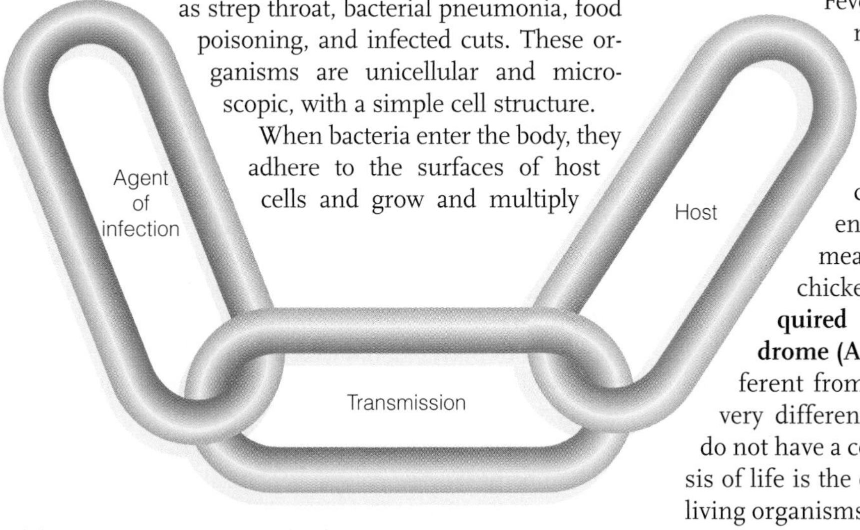

◀**Figure 14-6 Child with the Typical Rash of Measles.** This highly contagious, viral disease is characterized by a spreading rash. The rash is comprised of small, red spots; some of the spots may be raised.

host in reference to disease, an organism that supports the growth of a pathogen; the third, and last, link in the chain of infection.

transmission in reference to disease, the means by which a pathogen gets to a host; the second link in the chain of infection.

chain of infection the relationship among the factors important in the development of infectious diseases: the pathogen, transmission, and the host.

bacteria unicellular, microscopic organisms with a simple cell structure; some are pathogenic to humans and produce infections such as strep throat, bacterial pneumonia, food poisoning, and infected cuts.

virus hereditary material surrounded by a coat of protein; some viruses are pathogenic to humans and produce infections such as the common cold, influenza, mumps, measles, chicken pox, hepatitis, and AIDS.

acquired immunodeficiency syndrome (AIDS) a set of certain diseases and conditions that results from infection by the human immunodeficiency virus (HIV).

Agent of infection

Host

Transmission

◀**Figure 14-5 The Chain of Infection.** Infection is the invasion of the body by disease-causing organisms, or pathogens. Infection results when the pathogen (the first link in the chain) is transmitted (the second link) to a host (the third link). The host is the organism that supports the growth of the pathogen.

it, and are then ready to infect additional body cells. The death of body cells causes many of the signs and symptoms of viral disease.

Certain types of viruses invade cells but enter a *latent state* during which time infective virus particles are not produced. Although no signs or symptoms of the viral infection are apparent, latency may cause changes in a cell that lead to cancer (see Chapter 13). In many instances, the latent viral hereditary material can become reactivated and replicate once again, causing disease.

Some infections are characterized by a cycling of latent and actively replicating periods, such as the sexually transmitted infection (STI) genital herpes. During the usual course of this disease (see pages 358–359), a person suffers active episodes when he or she can transmit this disease to others. The infection then subsides (latency) only to reappear at another time, often triggered by stress or other factors.

Fungi You have probably heard of, or may have experienced, yeast infections or athlete's foot (■ Figure 14-7), which is a type of ringworm (a fungal infection of the skin, hair, or nails). These diseases are caused by **fungi**, more commonly known as molds and yeasts. Fungi cannot make their own food and, therefore, grow on a wide range of organisms that they use as food sources, such as rotting logs, spoiling fruit, and the human body. Most human fungal infections, with the exception of yeast infections, are caused by molds.

Medical researchers know less about how fungi cause disease in humans than they know about the other agents of infection. However, fungi appear to invade humans in much the same way as do bacteria. Humans have a high degree of resistance to fungi, which may explain why humans become infected with fungi less often than with

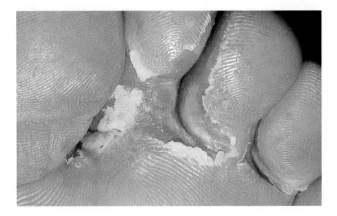

▲Figure 14-7 Athlete's Foot. Athlete's foot, or tinea pedis, is a fungal infection that usually arises between the toes or on the soles of the feet. This condition often develops when a person wears enclosed footwear without socks or stockings, and the feet become moist for long periods. To help avoid athlete's foot, dry the feet between the toes after bathing or showering and use powder to help keep the feet dry.

bacteria or viruses. Fungi are considered *opportunistic* organisms; that is, they invade the human body when the host has another disease or condition that diminishes its ability to combat fungal infection. People with diabetes or AIDS, for example, are more likely to contract fungal infections than people with no underlying illness.

Other Types of Pathogens Two additional groups of organisms cause infections in humans: *protozoans* and *worms*. Protozoans cause diseases such as malaria (a tropical disease transmitted by mosquitoes) and trichomonas urogenital infections, or "trich" infections. All protozoans that cause infectious diseases in humans are single-celled organisms, but they differ from one another in the ways they cause disease.

The other group of infectious organisms are the parasitic worms: certain types of roundworms, flatworms (tapeworms), and flukes. Tapeworms are contracted by eating infected pork or beef; these worms live in the intestines, producing digestive disturbances. Adult roundworms also inhabit the intestinal tract and cause digestive disorders; they enter the body in various ways depending on the species of worm. Flukes differ in that they can inhabit the intestine, the liver, the lungs, or the veins depending on the species; they are contracted from water infected with human feces and are not prevalent in the United States.

One other group of organisms important to mention is the *arthropods*. Certain species of this group live on or in the skin of humans, a condition usually referred to as *infestation* rather than infection. Arthropods are organisms such as lice, fleas, mites, and ticks. Some STIs are caused by certain lice and mites (see pages 363–364). Ticks only occasionally infest humans but may transmit other pathogens to humans, as can mosquitoes, lice, and flies.

The Second Link: Transmission

Some infectious diseases are passed from person to person and others are not. Those that are spread from person to person, such as colds, flu, strep throat, and STIs, are **communicable** diseases. Diseases that are *not* transmitted from person to person, including both infectious and noninfectious diseases are **noncommunicable.**

Noncommunicable Infectious Diseases Noncommunicable infectious diseases can be caused in various ways: by the growth of bacteria that normally inhabit the body, the ingestion of poisons produced by some bacteria, or infection with pathogens from environmental or animal sources.

Many species of bacteria normally reside on and in the human body. However, these beneficial bacteria can cause occasional problems. For example, *Staphylococcus* bacteria normally present on the skin can multiply and cause skin infections, especially in persons with chronic diseases such as diabetes.

Noncommunicable infections can also be caused by the ingestion of *toxins,* or poisons, produced by some bacteria.

Staphylococcal food poisoning (formerly called ptomaine poisoning), for example, is caused by taking in a toxin that certain staphylococcal bacteria produce when they grow on foods. Dairy products and poultry are the foods most commonly contaminated with staphylococcal bacteria from their animal sources or from infected food handlers. The staphylococcal bacteria grow well in high-protein, high-carbohydrate foods. Most often, staphylococcal food poisoning occurs when people eat foods such as potato salad, chicken salad, custard, or cream pies that have not been refrigerated properly after preparation. Picnics are a common time of infection because such foods are left out under warm conditions for long periods of time, which allows the bacteria to grow and produce toxin. Because the bacteria grow on the food and not in the body, this type of noncommunicable infection is more properly called *intoxication* (poisoning) rather than infection. Staphylococcal food poisoning should not be confused with *Salmonella* food infection, in which the bacteria are taken in with food and multiply in the small intestine.

Botulism is another type of food poisoning, caused by a powerful toxin produced by the bacterium *Clostridium botulinum*. This organism most often grows in improperly home-canned, low-acid foods such as green beans and green peppers. Boiling home-canned foods for 10–15 minutes inactivates the toxin. (Infants can contract botulism from raw honey [see Chapter 9, page 203].)

A third type of noncommunicable infection is caused by pathogens that infect people via environmental or animal sources. Legionnaire's disease, caused by the bacterium *Legionella pneumophila,* is an infectious disease contracted from an environmental source. Under favorable conditions, this pathogen can grow in and be dispersed by any apparatus that provides a water aerosol or mist, such as air conditioners, whirlpool spas, humidifiers, decorative fountains, showerheads, and water faucets. When this water mist is inhaled, these microbes lodge in the lungs and multiply, producing a pneumonialike disease that includes high fever, cough, chest pain, and diarrhea. This disease is quite serious; 5% to 30% of its victims die. To reduce the growth of this organism and protect yourself against infection, periodically clean and thoroughly disinfect mist-creating items, such as those mentioned previously, and maintain an appropriate concentration of chlorine in home spas.

Lyme disease is an example of a noncommunicable infection contracted from an animal source. Named for the small community of Lyme, Connecticut, where the disease was first recognized in 1975, this bacterial disease is transmitted by ticks that infest animals such as white-footed mice and white-tailed deer. The ticks ingest the bacterial pathogen that causes Lyme disease from infected animals. When a tick harboring this bacterium bites a human, it injects the bacterium into the bloodstream. Usually a painless but large rash (often looking like a "bulls-eye") appears

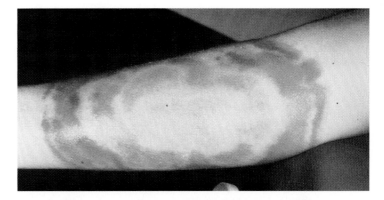

▲Figure 14-8 **The Typical Rash That Develops at the Site of a Tick Bite in Lyme Disease.** Not everyone who contracts Lyme disease will develop this type of rash.

at the site of the bite from a few days to one month after being bitten (■ **Figure 14-8).** This rash is generally accompanied by severe headaches, fatigue, chills, and fever. If the disease is not treated with antibiotics at this early stage, it may develop into severe inflammation of the heart muscle or nervous system weeks to months later. Within two years, if untreated, arthritic attacks develop (inflammation of the joints) that can become chronic.

In the United States, Lyme disease is found primarily in the northeast, the mid-Atlantic (Virginia and North Carolina area), and the upper midwest. It has also been reported in several areas in northwestern California. Deer ticks favor a moist, shaded environment, particularly areas of woods, brush, or tall grass. If you are walking, gardening, or engaging in other activities in the areas described above and in which deer and mice live (and therefore deer ticks), wear long pants and a long-sleeved shirt. Tuck your pant legs into your socks or boots. Spray insect repellent containing at least 30% DEET on your clothing and exposed skin. (Do not spray it on your face. Spray it on your hands and pat that on your face.) Check yourself carefully for ticks, removing any you find with tweezers. Another way to protect yourself is by immunization. A Lyme disease vaccine was introduced in 1999, but it is not completely protective (CDC, 1999c).

Communicable Infectious Diseases Communicable diseases are transmitted from person to person by direct or indirect contact, by means of a common vehicle, through the air, and by means of vectors such as mosquitoes.

fungi (FUN-jeye) cellular organisms that cannot make their own food; some are pathogenic to humans and produce infections such as athlete's foot, ringworm, and yeast infections. *Fungus* is the singular term.

communicable (ka-MYOO-ni-kah-bl) transmissible from person to person.

noncommunicable not transmissible from person to person.

Some infectious diseases, such as STIs, are passed from person to person by close, physical (direct) contact. In the case of STIs, of course, the close contact is usually sexual intercourse but may involve genital contact without intercourse. Other diseases such as colds and the flu are often transmitted by direct contact also, such as shaking hands. These diseases can also be transmitted indirectly by means of an object, such as a shared drinking glass, or through close contact with droplets sneezed or coughed by a person. Strep throat and measles are spread in this way.

Frequently, a source contaminated with pathogens from humans may transmit an infectious disease to many people. Examples of common sources of infection are a blood supply contaminated with human immunodeficiency virus, food contaminated with the hepatitis virus by an infected food handler, and water contaminated by the feces of a person infected with typhoid fever. A variety of infectious diseases are transmitted via food or water.

Some communicable diseases can be transmitted from infected persons to noninfected persons through the air on microscopic water droplets or on dust particles. Certain disease-causing organisms of the respiratory tract, such as the bacterium that causes tuberculosis, for example, can be transmitted in this way, propelled into the air when an infected person coughs or sneezes.

Other communicable diseases are spread indirectly by means of vectors. A *vector* is an organism (other than a human) that transmits a pathogen from one person to another. Usually a part of the life cycle of the pathogen takes place in or on the vector. For example, the malaria organism is a protozoan that carries out part of its life cycle in humans and another part in the gut of *Anopheles* mosquitoes. When a mosquito bites an infected person, it ingests blood that contains the protozoan. After the organism undergoes sexual reproduction in the mosquito, its progeny can infect new hosts when the mosquito bites them.

The Third Link: The Host

Why do you remain healthy sometimes, yet get sick at other times? How did you avoid getting the cold that everyone else seems to have? Why didn't your husband come down with the flu like the rest of the family? So far we've seen that some of the answers to these questions have to do with the pathogen and certain of its characteristics, such as its virulence. Transmission may also mean the difference between infection and health. Persons exposed fre-

quently to pathogens are likely to become infected more often than those exposed less frequently. The other answers to these questions have to do with your body's resistance to the invading microbe.

As described in Chapter 3, stress can be one factor that reduces your resistance to infection. High-intensity or exhaustive exercise, such as running more than 60 miles per week or for 3 or more hours per session, also suppresses the immune system. Moderate exercise, however, such as running fewer than 20 miles per week or walking for 45 minutes per day for 5 days per week, stimulates the immune system. Exercising when you are sick lowers the body's defenses.

Race and age affect an individual's resistance or susceptibility to certain diseases. Africans or people with African ancestry, for example, have a higher resistance to tropical diseases such as malaria and yellow fever than do non-Africans. Asians are more resistant to the sexually transmitted infection syphilis than are non-Asians. Children are more likely to contract certain "childhood" infectious diseases such as measles and chicken pox, while the elderly are more susceptible to pneumonia and influenza. And, as mentioned earlier, people with other diseases, such as AIDS, diabetes, and cancer, have weakened defense mechanisms.

Your body has two main types of defense against infectious agents: mechanisms of nonspecific resistance, which are a variety of defenses that combat any foreign invader, and the immune system, which is a specific defense system that combats the particular invading pathogen. The following sections describe these two major defense mechanisms.

Healthy
■■■LIVING PRACTICES■■■

- Refrigerate cold starchy and protein-rich foods and cold foods made with dairy products or poultry immediately after preparation. At picnics, keep these foods chilled until it is time to eat.
- Boil all low-acid home-canned foods before eating or avoid eating home-canned foods.
- Periodically clean and thoroughly disinfect mist-creating items such as humidifiers and maintain an appropriate concentration of chlorine in home spas.
- Avoid close contact with people who have communicable diseases.
- Do not share drinking glasses and eating utensils with others.
- Do not share hypodermic needles with others because they may be contaminated with pathogens such as the hepatitis B virus or the AIDS virus.
- Use a condom when engaging in sex unless you are in a long-term, mutually monogamous relationship

immunity
(im-MYOU-nih-tea) resistance to disease.

nonspecific immunity a variety of defense mechanisms that combat any type of damage to the body, including the invasion of infectious agents.

specific immunity defense mechanism carried out by the immune system.

immune system a collection of cells and organs of the body that recognizes and combats pathogens and other foreign substances with cells and proteins that are specific for particular invaders. The immune system has two branches: antibody-mediated immunity and cell-mediated immunity.

with an uninfected partner. Infectious bodily secretions can be passed from one partner to another during sexual activity.

- Use insect repellents formulated to repel ticks and flying insects that may be carriers of disease-producing organisms.
- Do not drink the water when traveling in developing countries. Also avoid raw fruits, vegetables, and salads because they may have been washed with contaminated water.
- Avoid the following hazardous foods when traveling in developing countries: uncooked or poorly cooked beef, pork, fish, and seafood; and unpasteurized milk and other local dairy products.
- Avoid stress; high levels of stress reduce your resistance to infection.
- Avoid high-intensity or exhaustive exercise because it reduces your resistance to infection.
- Engage in moderate exercise to boost the immune system.

Immunity

Immunity is protection from disease, particularly infectious disease. You have two types of immunity: nonspecific and specific. **Nonspecific immunity** comprises a variety of defense mechanisms that combat any type of damage to the body, including the invasion of infectious agents. **Specific immunity** is carried out by the immune system. The **immune system** recognizes and combats pathogens and other foreign cells (such as cancer cells or tissue transplants) with cells and proteins that are specific for particular invaders. The immune system is discussed later in this chapter.

Nonspecific Immunity

Pathogens can enter the body at sites called **portals of entry** (■ **Figure 14-9**). The mucous membranes lining the respiratory, digestive, urinary, and reproductive systems are all portals of entry. Whether due to a cut, insect bite, burn, or injection, broken skin is a portal of entry. The placenta may be a portal of entry for a fetus, which may become infected with pathogens (mostly viruses) from an infected mother. Unbroken skin is a portal of entry only for some fungi and the larvae of certain parasitic worms.

The Skin and Mucous Membranes The skin provides a *mechanical barrier* to pathogens. The hardened cells at the surface of the skin provide a waterproof barrier that most infective agents cannot penetrate. In addition, acidic skin oils and sweat help make the skin an inhospitable environment for most organisms.

Body openings, such as the eyes, and tubes that open to the outside, such as the digestive and respiratory tracts, are lined with tissue called *mucous membranes*. Most mucous membranes have a thin layer of cells that produces a sticky,

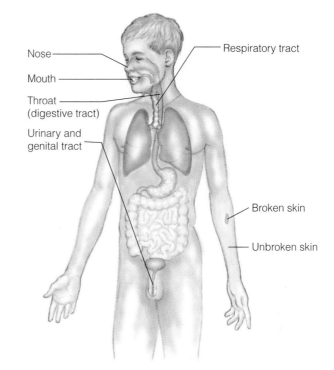

▲ **Figure 14-9 Portals of Entry of the Human Body.** Portals of entry are areas of the body where pathogens can intrude: the skin and mucous membranes lining the respiratory, digestive, urinary, and reproductive systems; the placenta; broken skin; and unbroken skin (only for some fungi and the larvae of certain parasitic worms).

viscous secretion called mucus. Mucus keeps the membrane moist and traps foreign particles and organisms.

Another defense mechanism that works with the mucous membranes is *cilia*. These short, hairlike structures project from the surfaces of the cells lining the upper respiratory tract. As they beat in wavelike fashion, they move mucus that contains trapped foreign material such as dust and bacteria up toward the back of the mouth where it can be swallowed, keeping it away from lower respiratory structures, especially the lungs.

Other tissues have a *chemical defense* mechanism. The lacrimal glands (located above the upper, outer corners of the eyes) produce tears that wash away foreign material on the eyes and also contain a chemical called *lysozyme* that kills certain bacteria. Lysozyme is also found in saliva. Another structure that provides a nonspecific chemical defense is the stomach. Stomach acid kills most of the microorganisms ingested with food.

White Blood Cells and Phagocytosis Another nonspecific line of defense is the action of certain white blood cells, or **leukocytes,** that ingest foreign cells and debris, such as the dirt or dead cells in a cut. This process is **phagocytosis**

portal of entry
site on or in the body at which pathogens enter.

leukocytes (LEWK-oh-sites) white blood cells; active in both specific and nonspecific defenses of the body.

phagocytosis (FAG-oh-site-OH-sis) the process of white blood cells ingesting foreign cells and debris, such as the dirt or dead cells in a cut.

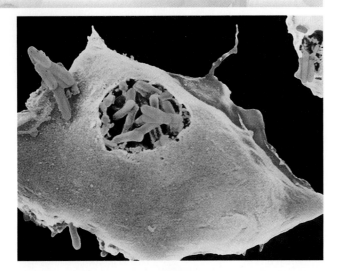

▲Figure 14-10 **White Blood Cell Ingesting Bacteria.** This is a highly magnified, colorized photo of a white blood cell called a macrophage (yellow/orange). Macrophages are the scavengers of the body, and protect it by "eating" bacteria and other foreign material. The bacteria (green) it is ingesting cause tuberculosis in humans.

(literally, *phago,* "eating" and *cyto,* "cell") and is shown in ▌ **Figure 14-10.** Two types of leukocytes—the neutrophils and the macrophages—are important phagocytes in the human body. Other white blood cells called *lymphocytes* help protect the body against infection and are part of the immune system.

The Lymphatic System The lymphatic system, another key player in nonspecific immunity, is composed of vessels and nodes through which tissue fluid, or **lymph,** flows. Pictured in ▌ **Figure 14-11,** the lymphatic system also consists of lymphocytes and three lymphatic organs: the tonsils, the spleen, and the thymus (which is only active until puberty). The lymphatic system removes microorganisms and other foreign substances from the tissue fluid, the fluid surrounding the cells that is derived from the blood.

Lymph nodes are located at many points along the lymphatic vessels. Lymphatic vessels enter and exit each lymph node, which is a mesh of tissue containing lymphocytes and macrophages. The nodes cleanse tissue fluid by trapping microorganisms and other foreign substances in their weblike structures; macrophages in the nodes phagocytize this material.

The tonsils are large groups of lymph nodes located at the back of the oral cavity; they rid the nose and mouth area of bacteria and other debris. The spleen, located in the upper left corner of the abdominal cavity (see Figure 14-11), not only performs the function of a lymph node but also destroys worn-out red blood cells and stores red blood cells to provide an emergency supply in the case of severe loss. The thymus, located just above the heart at the midline of the chest, is the place where the lymphocytes destined to be T cells mature during fetal life and early childhood (see the section "Specific Immunity"). (These T cells then reside in the lymphatic tissue and will produce new T cells when the thymus is no longer active.)

Inflammation Can you remember the last time you got a splinter or a cut? If so, you can probably remember (quite well!) your body's response. The inflammatory response is a series of events that takes place when the body is harmed by occurrences such as bacterial or viral invasion (infection), cuts, chemical damage, and burns. This response

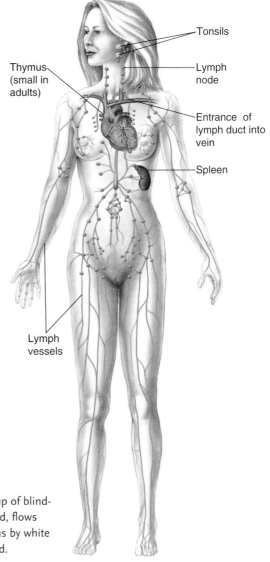

Tonsils

Thymus (small in adults)

Lymph node

Entrance of lymph duct into vein

Spleen

Lymph vessels

▶Figure 14-11 **The Lymphatic System.** The lymphatic system is made up of blind-ended vessels, nodes, and a few organs. Tissue fluid, derived from the blood, flows through the lymphatic vessels and is cleansed of debris and microorganisms by white blood cells that reside in the nodes. The fluid eventually returns to the blood.

can be *local,* as in the case of getting a splinter in your finger, or *systemic* (affecting the whole body), as in the case of contracting a cold. Inflammation involves a variety of defense mechanisms that isolate and destroy the pathogens or other injurious agents and then remove the foreign materials and damaged cells so the body can repair itself.

The presence of infectious agents or damage to the body triggers the inflammatory response. As a result, many chemicals are released. Some of these chemicals, such as histamine, cause an increase of blood flow to the affected area, which brings phagocytes and other white blood cells to ingest microorganisms and debris—pieces of a splinter, for example. In addition, other chemicals stimulate phagocytes to move to the affected area, where they leave the blood and enter the damaged tissues. Yet other chemicals allow the surrounding blood vessel walls to leak, permitting phagocytes, certain blood-clotting factors, and other chemicals that enhance the inflammatory response to enter the tissues. The blood-clotting factors wall off the infected area, which prevents the spread of the infection. ▌ **Figure 14-12** illustrates the inflammatory process.

The signs of local inflammation are redness, heat, swelling, pain, and a loss of function. The redness, heat, and swelling are results of increased blood flow to the affected area, including movement of fluids into surrounding tissues. Pain results as nerves are stimulated by the swelling and the chemicals released during inflammation. The pain, tissue damage, and swelling may contribute to a temporary loss of function of the affected body part.

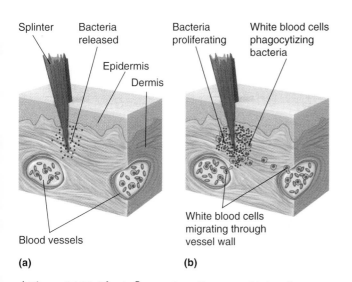

(a) **(b)**

▲**Figure 14-12 The Inflammatory Process.** (a) A splinter damages the skin, thrusting bacteria deep into the wound. Injured cells release chemicals such as histamine that cause the blood vessels to widen, bringing more blood to the area. (b) White blood cells squeeze through vessel walls and migrate to the bacteria, where they phagocytize them. Blood clots and connective tissue wall off the area.

Systemic inflammation occurs when you have a widespread infection such as a cold, the flu, strep throat, or pneumonia. Systemic inflammation has the same signs as local inflammation, but additional processes occur that result in more significant signs. The red bone marrow, located in the ends of certain bones, produces and releases large numbers of white blood cells. In addition, invading microorganisms and white blood cells release chemicals that affect the body's temperature-regulating system in the brain, resulting in a fever.

A *fever* is a rise in the internal body temperature from the average of about 98.6°F. A fever lower than 104°F helps the body fight infection by enhancing phagocytosis and inhibiting the growth of certain microorganisms. However, a prolonged fever of 104°F, or a fever higher than 104°F, is dangerous because it can destroy proteins in the body. Other signs of systemic inflammation are fatigue, aches, and weakness.

The inflammatory process continues until the pathogens are killed or inactivated, or other injurious agents are walled off from the rest of the body and no longer pose a threat. Phagocytes ingest cellular debris and other organic material as the tissues recover from the infection.

lymph (limf) tissue fluid.

interferons (IN-ter-FEAR-onz) proteins produced by the body during a viral infection that protect uninfected cells from viral invasion.

Natural Killer Cells Natural killer cells are specialized white blood cells that attack cancer cells and body cells invaded by viruses. Natural killer cells secrete a chemical that pokes holes in the membranes of these two types of cells, destroying them. The response of natural killer cells to viral infections or developing cancer cells is quick, providing the body with protection until the immune system takes over (see "Specific Immunity").

Interferons Released from virally infected cells, **interferons** are proteins that protect uninfected cells from viral invasion. Interferons stimulate these cells to produce a protein that breaks down the hereditary material of the virus. When the damaged viruses enter cells they are unable to replicate and the viral infection is eventually halted. Interferons enhance the activity of the phagocytes as well as the action of other, more specific, immune system responses. In this role, interferons enhance the body's ability to fight invasions from most disease-causing agents, not just viruses.

Specific Immunity

Specific immunity is a function of the immune system. The immune system is made up of cells residing in tissues scattered throughout the body. These cells are able to react to specific pathogens and foreign molecules.

The immune system has two branches: *antibody-mediated immunity* and *cell-mediated immunity,* which will be discussed shortly. Each branch works slightly differently to attack foreign invaders and stop an infection. The immune system also has a memory: cells that react quickly to subsequent attacks by an invader.

Antigens: The Triggers of Specific Immunity Antigens are usually foreign, or "non-self" proteins. Sometimes, entire infectious agents act as antigens. In other instances, parts of pathogens or the poisons they may secrete act as antigens. Noninfectious agents such as plant pollens, blood transfusions, or tissue transplants are antigenic, although the response to these antigens may differ from person to person. Unfortunately, the body sometimes perceives its own cells as foreign, attacking them and causing localized and systemic reactions, as in the case of **autoimmune diseases** such as *rheumatoid arthritis*. In this disease, the reactions include inflammation and deformity of the joints. The following sections describe how the immune system reacts to antigens that enter the body.

Antibody-Mediated Immunity The antibody-mediated portion of the immune system reacts to *extracellular* antigens, that is, antigens that reside outside of body cells, such as most bacteria and any toxins they produce. **Antibodies** are proteins that interact in a lock-and-key fashion with antigens. When they bind with an antigen, antibodies interfere with the normal functioning of the antigen. Antigen–antibody binding also stimulates the inflammatory response and promotes phagocytosis of the antigen.

The workhorses of antibody-mediated immunity (the cells that produce antibodies) are specialized white blood cells called **B lymphocytes**, or **B cells**. Each B cell has receptors on its membrane that bind to a specific antigen. When a foreign antigen enters the body, B cells bind to it. After stimulation by lymphocytes called helper T cells, the B cells reproduce in large numbers and become plasma cells, which produce antibodies. ▌ **Figure 14-13** illustrates the antibody-mediated immune response.

Some of the stimulated B cells do not differentiate into plasma cells. These cells circulate as *memory B cells*, which respond more rapidly and forcefully whenever the antigen is encountered in the future. Memory cells confer immunity (resistance) to a disease. Many infections stimulate lifelong immunity (measles and chicken pox, for example); others, such as diphtheria, confer immunity for only a few years. Unfortunately, not all infectious agents stimulate the formation of memory cells, so no immunity is produced as a result of their infection. Examples of such infections are strep throat and gonorrhea (an STI).

anti-gens (AN-tih-jenz) proteins that are foreign or recognized as "non-self" by the body.

autoimmune diseases diseases in which the body perceives its own cells as foreign, attacking them and causing localized and systemic (whole body) reactions.

antibodies proteins that interact in a lock-and-key fashion with antigens, interfering with the normal functioning of the antigen.

B cells specialized white blood cells (lymphocytes) that function in antibody-mediated immunity and produce antibodies.

T cells specialized white blood cells (lymphocytes) that function in cell-mediated immunity; there are four types of T cells.

Cell-Mediated Immunity The cell-mediated portion of the immune system reacts to *intracellular* antigens; that is, antigens that reside inside our body cells, such as viruses, fungi, a few types of bacteria, and parasites. It also acts against foreign tissues such as organ transplants and controls the growth of tumor cells.

Lymphocytes called **T cells** function in cell-mediated immunity. T cells reside in lymphoid tissues and in the bloodstream with the B cells. The body contains thousands of different T cells. Upon binding to antigens, T cells reproduce and differentiate into four types: cytotoxic T cells, helper T cells, suppressor T cells, and memory T cells.

Cytotoxic T cells destroy invading intracellular pathogens (primarily viruses) by secreting chemicals that break apart infected host cells. By destroying host cells, the cytotoxic T cells take away what a virus or any other intracellular infective agent needs to reproduce or replicate. Cytotoxic

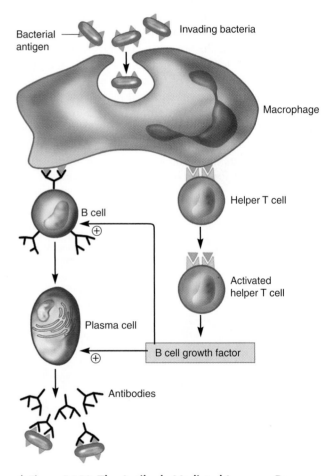

▲**Figure 14-13 The Antibody-Mediated Immune Response.** White blood cells called macrophages ingest invading microbes and display their antigenic parts. Helper T cells and B cells specific to the antigens attach to them, which activates both types of cell. The helper T cells produce a chemical that stimulates the growth of the B cells. These B cells, now called plasma cells, secrete proteins called antibodies. Antibodies attach to and promote the death of the invading microbes.

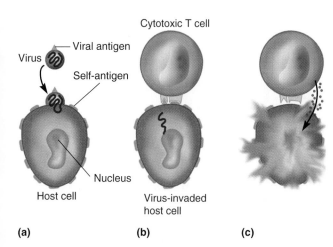

Cytotoxic T cell

Viral antigen

Virus

Self-antigen

Nucleus

Host cell

Virus-invaded
host cell

(a)   (b)   (c)

▲**Figure 14-14 The Cell-Mediated Immune Response.**
Cytotoxic T cells are key to the cell-mediated immune response.
Here, whole T cells, not just antibodies, attach to cells infected
with viruses, to cancer cells, or to tissue transplants. The T cell
then secretes chemicals that destroy the host cell before the
virus can enter the nucleus and begin to replicate.

T cells destroy non-self tissue transplants or tumorous
growths in much the same way (**Figure 14-14**).

Helper T cells and *suppressor T cells* regulate the activities
of both branches of the immune system. Helper T cells secrete various chemicals that enhance the activity of cytotoxic T cells and suppressor T cells and attract phagocytes
to the area. Some helper T cells secrete chemicals that enhance the development and reproduction of B cells.

When the infection has subsided, suppressor T cells
shut down the immune system. Although these cells inhibit the activity of various immune system cells, they increase in number more slowly than do other T cells. Therefore, suppressor T cells shut down the immune response
only after it has successfully done its job.

A group of stimulated T cells circulates as *memory T cells.*
Like memory B cells, memory T cells respond rapidly and
forcefully during subsequent encounters with antigens, resulting in immunity to a disease.

Interactions between Specific and Nonspecific Immunity

The mechanisms of nonspecific and specific defense work
together to prevent infection or combat infection once it occurs. For example, the intact skin, mucous membranes,
and chemicals in body fluids are effective barriers against
viral invasion. However, if viruses gain entry to the body,
macrophages phagocytize them before they can enter body
cells. Activated helper T cells secrete chemicals that stimulate the B cells to become antibody-producing cells.

If some of the virus particles enter body cells in spite of
these defenses, the infected cells produce interferons,
which protect uninfected cells. Natural killer cells poke

holes in the infected cells, killing them, thus destroying
the virus's host. After binding to infected cells, cytotoxic
T cells reproduce, developing large populations specific for
this viral infection. As armies of cytotoxic T cells break
apart infected cells, the freed viruses are phagocytized by
macrophages and inactivated by antibodies. Usually this
complex process stops the viral infection. The memory
B cells and T cells continue to circulate, and recognize this
same virus quickly if it re-enters the body. Most likely, the
virus will never again cause infection, for it will have been
stopped before it could gain a foothold in the cells.

www.jbpub.com/healthyliving

Protection Against Infectious Diseases

A variety of factors determine whether a person develops
an infectious disease. In general, to prevent infectious disease, you must break the chain of infection. This chapter
offers many tips on breaking the chain of infection and
preventing disease. However, one of the best ways to protect yourself against infection is to increase your resistance.

Specific immunity is either inborn or acquired. *Inborn immunity* is inherited, such as immunity to infectious diseases that attack other organisms (your cat or dog, for
example) but not humans. **Acquired immunity** is
not inherited; it develops during a person's
lifetime. Acquired immunity develops in a
variety of ways: either actively or passively, and by natural or artificial means.

Active acquired immunity is an immune system response developed as a
result of contact with a pathogen,
which includes development of memory B cells or T cells. Contact with the
pathogen can occur naturally, during
day-to-day life. It can also occur artificially, by being given a **vaccine** prepared
from a killed or weakened pathogen or its
antigenic parts. Depending on how the vaccine is
prepared, it may have long- or short-term effects. That
is why people need booster vaccinations every few years
against some infectious diseases.

Children develop active acquired immunity to many serious childhood diseases by being vaccinated according to
a schedule recommended by the American Academy of
Pediatrics and the American Academy of Family Physicians. The Web site of this textbook contains a link to the
current childhood immunization schedule. Prior to travel
to foreign countries, immunization of adults and children
leads to active acquired immunity to diseases not generally
found in the United States. If you are traveling outside the
United States, consult your physician 4 to 6 weeks prior to
your trip for the required and recommended immuniza-
tions. A link provided on the Web site to this textbook gives

**acquired immu-
nity** specific resis-
tance to infection that is
not inherited but develops
during a person's lifetime.

vaccine a preparation of a
killed or weakened pathogen
or its antigenic parts to be
administered to a person
to induce immunity and
thereby prevent in-
fectious disease.

Con$umer Health | Over-the-Counter Cold Medications: Do They Help?

Every year Americans spend millions of dollars on over-the-counter (nonprescription) cold and cough remedies. Thousands of products on the market purport to relieve your aches, fever, coughs, and congestion. But do these medications help?

Dr. Nancy Hutton of the Johns Hopkins School of Medicine in Baltimore answers no when it comes to cold remedies helping children. Dr. Hutton conducted a study with 96 5-year-olds suffering from colds. She divided the children into three groups. One group received an antihistamine-decongestant product, a second group received a placebo (pill with no active ingredients), and the third group received nothing. Two days later, half the children in each group reported feeling better—those taking "cold remedies" did as well as those taking the placebo or nothing (Hutton et al., 1991).

What about the use of these remedies with adults? Decongestants may make you feel less stuffed up, but you may feel worse when you stop taking the medicine due to rebound congestion—the blood vessels may swell beyond their original swollen state when the medication wears off. You may choose to treat your dripping nose and sneezing with an antihistamine, but these products may be effective only against allergy, not cold, symptoms. Cough suppressants may help you cough less, but you need to expel the buildup of thick mucus to keep your airways clear. Expectorants can help thin the mucus and facilitate its removal from the airways as you cough. Drinking lots of water gives the same result. Cough drops may help keep a dry throat lubricated but

may upset your stomach. Sucking on hard candy may be just as lubricating. You can spray your sore throat with an anesthetic, but gargling with warm salty water several times a day can also relieve the soreness.

Sorting out the pros and cons of taking cold remedies can be made easier by becoming more informed. Physicians generally recommend that you simply drink plenty of fluids (without alcohol or caffeine), get lots of rest, and take one of the medications listed below for fever and aches.

The following information lists each cold symptom along with its over-the-counter (OTC) remedies approved by the federal Food and Drug Administration (FDA). Precautions for the drugs are also noted. Don't let the sometimes long and difficult-to-pronounce names bother you; just match the names to those on the list of active ingredients of particular products. As with all OTC medications, follow the directions for taking the product and the recommended dosage on the packaging. (The Consumer Health feature on page 157 explains OTC package labels.) If you suffer an unexpected or severe side effect, discontinue taking the medication and contact your physician. Do not drink alcoholic beverages while you are taking medications. Ask your pharmacist or physician which medications can be taken together—drugs can interact with one another.

Note: The authors are not promoting the use of OTC remedies but are presenting information for educational purposes only. Consult your physician for advice on taking medication.

Minor Aches, Pains, and Fever

Pain and fever relievers (also called analgesics) are products such as aspirin, acetaminophen, ibuprophen, and naproxen sodium. Each works just about as well as the others.

Precautions: Don't give children aspirin when they have a cold or other viral infection. Except under a doctor's instruction, none of these drugs should be taken for more than 10 days by adults or more than 5 days by children to relieve pain, and not more than 3 days to relieve fever. Overdoses of acetaminophen can cause severe liver damage and even death. Aspirin can irritate the gastric lining and cause gastrointestinal bleeding. In addition, aspirin interferes with blood clotting and can cause allergic reactions.

Sore Throat

Anesthetics in spray or lozenge (cough drop) form will inhibit all sensations from the throat, including temperature and pressure sensations as well as pain sensations. However, using analgesics (mentioned above) may help with the pain without affecting the other sensations. Benzocaine, benzyl alcohol, dyclonine hydrochloride, hexylresorcinol, phenol preparations, and phenolate sodium are FDA-approved medications found in anesthetic sprays and lozenges.

Precautions: Never give children younger than age 2 throat lozenges because they can choke on them. Many of these drugs have restrictions regarding their use with children; read directions carefully.

Dry Coughs

Cough suppressors (also called antitussives) inhibit coughing with dry coughs that produce no mucuslike discharge. Drugs that affect the cough center in the brain are codeine and dextromethorphan. In some states, the purchaser of a codeine cough product must sign a special register. In other states, these products can be obtained only with a doctor's prescription. Other types of cough suppressors act on the throat and bronchial tubes to lessen pain, relax the involuntary muscles involved in coughing, and/or thin out the mucus in the throat. Two common cough suppressors of this type are camphor and peppermint oil (menthol). Both are found in topical ointments to rub on the neck and chest or in liquids to put in vaporizers; these active ingredients are breathed in as they vaporize with body heat or in a steam vaporizer. Menthol and dextromethorphan are the only active ingredients found in throat lozenges (cough drops) that appear to be effective.

Precautions: Codeine is a narcotic and is addictive in large quantities; the potential for abuse exists. The effectiveness of camphor and menthol in rubs and inhalants is still under question by the FDA. Do not take cough suppressants for more than one week; see your physician if the cough lasts beyond this time. People with chronic lung disorders such as emphysema, who need to clear their airways, should not take cough suppressants.

Wet (Secretion-Laden) Coughs

Expectorants thin the secretions, allowing them to be coughed up and removed from the airways. A variety of expectorant products have been on the market for decades with conditional FDA approval. Recent studies suggest, however, that only one expectorant, guaifenesin (glycerol guiacolate), is safe and effective, so the others have been (or will be) taken off the market.

Precautions: Do not give this drug to children younger than 2 years unless instructed by your physician.

Congestion

Nasal decongestants narrow, or constrict, the blood vessels of the nasal lining that become swollen during a cold. As these vessels swell, the nasal passageways become narrowed, impeding air flow.

The FDA-approved active ingredients in inhalants (from inhalers or steam vaporizers) are desoxyephedrine-L and propylhexedrine. Camphor and menthol are conditionally approved; their effectiveness is in question.

The FDA-approved active ingredients in medications applied directly to the nasal mucosa, such as nasal drops, sprays, and jellies, are ephedrine preparations, naphazoline hydrochloride, oxymetazoline hydrochloride, phenylephrine hydrochloride, and xylometazoline. Bornyl acetate, cedar-leaf oil, menthol, and phenylpropranolamine preparations are conditionally approved.

The FDA-approved active ingredients in oral (pill) medications are phenylephrine hydrochloride and pseudoephedrine preparations. Ephedrine preparations and phenylpropanolamine preparations are conditionally approved.

Precautions: Decongestants can cause rebound congestion. Medications placed directly in the nasal area are more likely to have this effect than oral medications. However, oral medications affect the entire body, whereas nasal preparations do not. To reduce the possibility of rebound congestion, take the lowest dose of the decongestant for no more than 3 days. The topical medication naphazoline hydrochloride should not be used by children younger than 12 and can be habit-forming. Phenylephrine hydrochloride (topical or oral) and pseudoephedrine preparations should not be used by people who take drugs prescribed for severe depression or high blood pressure containing monoamine oxidase (MAO) inhibitors because the decongestants may interact with these drugs, seriously affecting the heart.

Runny Nose

Antihistamines are supposed to dry up cold secretions, but their usefulness with colds is questionable. Antihistamines are allergy medications and work by counteracting the effects of histamines. Histamines promote the manufacture of fluids by tissues, but histamines are not released during a cold. Because antihistamines cause drowsiness, a cold-sufferer may want to take them at night as a sleep aid. (Sleep aids are antihistamines.) Of the many antihistamines, most formerly prescription medications, the following are currently approved by the FDA: brompheniramine maleate, chlorcyclizine hydrochloride, chlorpheniramine maleate, dexbrompheniramine maleate, diphenhydramine hydrochloride, doxylamine succinate, phenidramine tartrate, pheniramine maleate, pyrilamine maleate, thonzylamine hydrochloride, and triprolidine hydrochloride. The one conditionally approved antihistamine is phenyltoloxamine dihydrogen citrate.

Precautions: Pregnant or nursing women should not take doxylamine succinate because of its questionable link to birth defects and adverse effects on infants.

the most recent health information for travel to various areas of the world and a list of vaccinations necessary for those areas.

Passive acquired immunity is conferred when a person is given antibodies. Passive immunity can be acquired naturally when antibodies from a mother cross the placenta and enter the bloodstream of a developing fetus. After birth, a breast-fed infant passively acquires antibodies from its mother's milk. These antibodies help a newborn resist disease for the first month of life until its own immune system becomes functional. Passive immunity can also be acquired artificially, when a person receives an injection of antibodies after exposure to a serious infection (such as hepatitis A or rabies) or a lethal poison (such as certain snake venoms).

- Protect yourself against infection by having the appropriate vaccinations before traveling.
- Protect children from infection by having them immunized according to the most recent childhood immunization schedule.

Drugs That Combat Infection

Once a person has an infection like the common cold, what can he or she do to combat it? Most often, getting rest and drinking sufficient fluids helps the body as it mounts its defense. (Sometimes over-the-counter cold medications can help relieve symptoms. See "Over-the-Counter Cold Medications: Do They Help?") For other infections, the individual can obtain specific recommendations from health-care professionals who are trained to diagnose and treat the illness. These medical practitioners often prescribe medicines to inhibit the growth of or inactivate the infectious agent.

Antibiotics are a group of chemicals that kill bacteria or inhibit their growth. Antibiotics work by attacking parts of bacterial cells or bacterial processes that differ from human cells. When taking an antibiotic, it is important to finish the medication your physician prescribed, even though your symptoms may be gone prior to that time. All the bacteria may not have been killed, and the infection could return.

Antibiotics do nothing to combat viral infections and may kill some of the body's normal bacterial inhabitants. These bacteria control the growth of troublesome microorganisms; when they are gone, it is easier for unwanted disease-causing bacteria to multiply and cause a secondary bacterial infection. Therefore, taking antibiotics when they

antibiotics (AN-tie-by-OT-iks) a group of chemicals that kill bacteria or inhibit their growth.

sexually transmitted infection (STI) infection spread from person to person by intimate sexual contact, primarily sexual intercourse.

hepatitis B a serious infectious disease of the liver transmitted via blood or blood products.

are unnecessary can be harmful. Furthermore, the unnecessary use of antibiotics provides additional opportunities for antibiotic-resistant strains of bacteria to develop.

Various topical antibiotics (those applied to the skin, such as bacitracin) are available without prescription to treat or prevent minor skin infections. Over-the-counter topical antifungal drugs are also available to treat fungal infections of the skin, such as athlete's foot and ringworm, and vaginal yeast infections. Antifungal drugs that must be taken orally for more serious fungal infections require a prescription.

Progress in the production of effective antiviral drugs has been slow because viruses reside inside the body's cells. Therefore, a drug must inactivate the virus without harming its host. A few antiviral drugs treat infections caused by the herpes virus (such as genital herpes, cold sores, and chicken pox) and others treat diseases associated with AIDS. Antiviral medications have been developed recently to control influenza (flu) infection (Sintchenko & Dwyer, 1999).

Specific medications have also been developed to treat protozoal diseases such as malaria, amoebic dysentery, and trichomoniasis. Likewise, prescription medicines are available to treat infestations of worms such as tapeworms and pinworms.

- If you contract an infection, consult a health-care professional for specific recommendations on treating it.
- If you contract a systemic infection such as a cold or the flu, rest and drink sufficient fluids to help your body mount its defense.
- If a health care professional prescribes medication for you to combat an infection, follow all instructions and take the prescribed amount of medication.

Sexually Transmitted Infections

Sexually transmitted infections (STIs) are spread from person to person by the intimate contact that occurs during sexual activity, primarily sexual intercourse. In general, the pathogens that cause STIs are passed from the sores, secretions, or tissues of an infected individual's reproductive system to the mucous membranes or broken skin of the reproductive system and surrounding tissue of another. (The reproductive system is described in Chapter 6. As you read the rest of this chapter please refer to Figure 6-1, which shows the male reproductive organs, and Figure 6-3, which shows the female reproductive organs.)

Contracting a sexually transmitted infection is more likely when other STI infections are present. For example, infection with the herpes simplex virus (HSV) or with syphilis has been shown to increase the risk of human immunodeficiency virus (HIV) transmission by as much as 10- to 100-fold for a single act of intercourse. Both HSV and syphilis cause sores on the genitals, which apparently facilitate the transfer of the human immunodeficiency virus.

Most pathogens that cause STIs cannot survive long (or at all) outside the human body. Therefore, most STIs cannot be contracted by genital contact with contaminated toilet seats or bed linens. Most STIs are passed directly from one person to another.

Some sexually transmitted infections are caused by yeasts, protozoans, mites (organisms closely related to spiders), and lice (organisms closely related to fleas). Most STIs are caused by bacteria and viruses.

Before you read more of this chapter, complete the STI Attitude Scale Self-Assessment in the student workbook. A high score on this assessment indicates a predisposition toward high-risk STI behavior. A low score indicates a predisposition toward low-risk STI behavior. This chapter will help you develop low-risk behaviors.

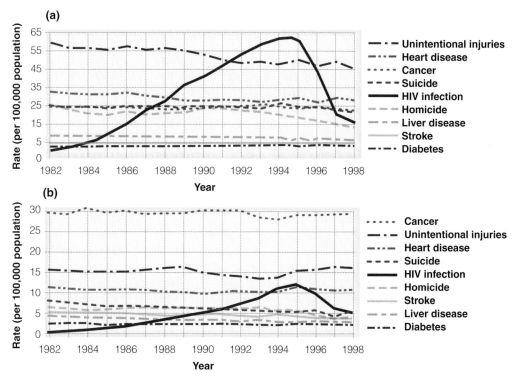

▲ Figure 14-15 **Leading Causes of Death for Men (a) and Women (b) Aged 25 through 44, United States, 1982–1998.** When the data for males and females are combined, they show that AIDS was the leading cause of death in this age group in 1995. By 1996, this was no longer the case. Source: National Center for Health Statistics, National Vital Statistics System. U.S. Department of Health and Human Services.

Healthy
LIVING PRACTICES

To protect yourself and others against the transmission of sexually transmitted infections, use latex condoms during sexual intercourse.

www.jbpub.com/healthyliving

Sexually Transmitted Infections Caused by Viruses

Sexually transmitted infections caused by viruses are extremely serious because they cannot be cured. Certain medications ease the discomfort of viral STI symptoms, but virus particles remain in the tissues and can cause recurrent symptoms. Also, the virus can be passed continually from chronically infected individuals to others during sexual activity.

In addition to causing STIs, three sexually transmitted viruses have been implicated in the development of particular cancers: HIV, human papillomavirus (HPV), and **hepatitis B virus (HBV).** Therefore, contracting any one of these viruses not only results in an incurable infectious disease but also increases the risk of developing particular types of cancer. HPV is discussed on pages 359 to 360. HBV causes a serious inflammation of the liver and can result in liver cancer. Although hepatitis is caused by a variety of hepatitis viruses (such as A, B, C, and D), hepatitis B virus is the one most commonly transmitted by sexual contact. Although hepatitis B is a serious and long-term disease, people can recover from it.

Human immunodeficiency virus is the most serious viral sexually transmitted infection. HIV not only raises the risk of developing the cancer Kaposi's sarcoma, it also attacks the immune system, disabling the body's defenses. Eventually the immune system of an HIV-infected individual becomes so weakened that he or she succumbs to an array of illnesses (the syndrome known as AIDS) that lead to death.

Human Immunodeficiency Virus

As of January 1995, AIDS became the leading cause of death among all Americans aged 25 to 44. By 1996 death rates from AIDS began to decline, and by 1998 AIDS had dropped to the fifth leading cause of death in this age group. However, as ▌ **Figure 14-15** shows, the death rate from AIDS is much higher for men than it is for women.

Since AIDS was first recognized in the early 1980s, the number of known deaths in all age groups in the United States increased annually, until the decline in 1996 (■ **Figure 14-16).** The number of cases reported increased steadily until its dramatic increase in 1993. Much of the 1993 increase is due to a change in the definition of AIDS, which broadened the list of conditions reportable as AIDS and included measures of immune system function. Since 1993 the number of AIDS cases reported has declined steadily. This decrease reflects, in part, the waning effect of the 1993 definition change.

Globally, HIV infection has become a widespread epidemic disease, and will soon enter the top five causes of death worldwide. Ninety percent of people infected with HIV live in developing countries, where death rates from AIDS have not fallen as they have in industrialized countries. In industrialized countries such as the United States, costly treatment regimens have allowed HIV-infected people to manage their disease better and live longer (Nicoll & Gill, 1999; Temesgen, 1999).

The Progression of the Disease: HIV Infection and AIDS
Although medical researchers realized in 1981 that AIDS was a new disease, its cause (infection with human immunodeficiency virus) was not discovered until 1983. AIDS is a *syndrome,* a set of signs and symptoms occurring together. Being infected with HIV does not mean that a person has AIDS; infection *leads* to AIDS. Current data suggest that all infected individuals will develop AIDS eventually because HIV infection results in a continuous, prolonged, and ongoing disease process that still cannot be cured.

Approximately 1 to 3 weeks after becoming infected with HIV, most people (about 90%) experience a brief flu-like illness. This illness lasts for 1 to 2 weeks and includes such symptoms as fever, sore throat, headache, rash, and general weakness and discomfort. During this stage of infection, people usually do not know that they are infected with HIV and think that they have a particularly bad case of the flu. After learning of their infection, many people remember this flu-like illness and realize that it marks the time shortly after their infection.

When this initial illness subsides, the HIV-infected person seems to be healthy, but is in the *asymptomatic phase* of HIV disease, which usually lasts about 8 to 10 years (Bartlett & Moore, 1998). (*Asymptomatic* means that no disease symptoms are apparent.) This time varies widely among individuals; it can be as short as a few months or longer than 12 years. During this time, many HIV-infected individuals do not realize that they are infected and may pass the virus on to others.

Although people with asymptomatic HIV infection may feel well, the virus is actively killing helper T cells in their bodies. Gradually, the number of helper T cells declines.

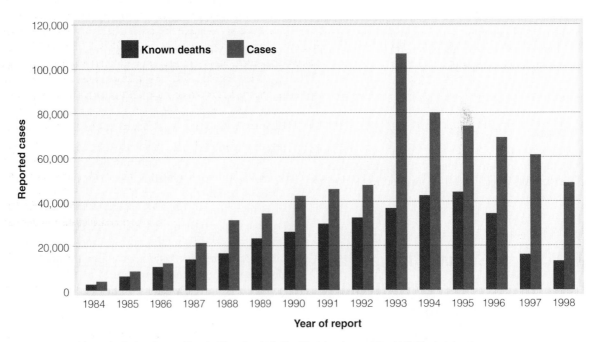

Notes: Includes Guam, Puerto Rico, the U.S. Pacific Islands, and the U.S. Virgin Islands.
1998 data are preliminary.

▲**Figure 14-16 Reported Cases and Known Deaths from AIDS, United States, 1981–1998.** The extreme rise in reported cases in 1993 is due to a change in the definition of AIDS, which broadened the list of conditions reportable as AIDS and included measures of immune-system function. Source: National Center for Health Statistics, National Vital Statistics System U.S. Dept. of Health and Human Services, Centers for Disease Control and Prevention.

Although various laboratory tests can detect abnormalities in infected asymptomatic patients, these persons remain relatively symptom-free until they enter the *symptomatic phase* of HIV disease. The symptomatic phase usually begins when helper T cells have declined to about 500 cells (or fewer) per cubic millimeter of blood (500 cells/mm³). The normal level is 800 to 1200 helper T cells/mm³. When the T cell count drops to 500/mm³, the body begins to have trouble warding off infections that a normal, healthy body resists. These infections are called *opportunistic infections* because they are caused by organisms that normally cannot produce infections except in people with lowered resistance.

During this phase of disease, the HIV-infected individual experiences a tremendous array of signs and symptoms. Some of these are nonspecific; that is, they are not in response to any opportunistic infection. These nonspecific signs and symptoms include fever, night sweats, headache, and fatigue. Chronic diarrhea usually occurs as opportunistic organisms infect the digestive system. Also, the HIV-infected individual often contracts minor oral infections such as thrush, caused by the yeast *Candida albicans* (KAN-de-dah AL-bih-kanz) (▮ **Figure 14-17**). These symptoms and infections of the symptomatic phase are not usually life-threatening, but the infected individual has trouble maintaining the normal pace of his or her lifestyle.

As the helper T cell count declines further to about 200/mm³, the rate of contracting serious opportunistic dis-

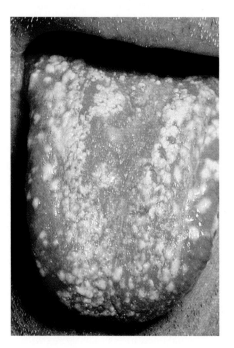

▲**Figure 14-17 Thrush, or Oral Candidiasis.** This oral infection is caused by the yeast *Candida albicans* and is a common infection of the symptomatic stage of HIV infection. It can also occur in persons taking broad-spectrum drugs or medications that suppress the immune system. Infants can acquire the disease during birth from mothers with vaginal candidiasis.

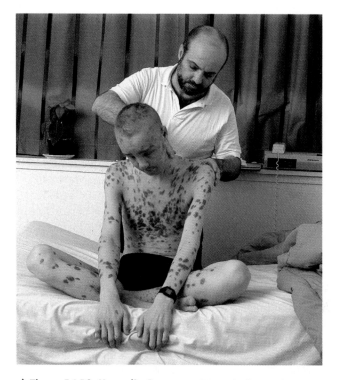

▲**Figure 14-18 Kaposi's Sarcoma.** Named after an Austrian dermatologist, this cancer is a serious opportunistic disease of the HIV-infected person. It begins in the skin and metastasizes to the lymph nodes and body organs.

eases increases. Common infections at this stage include *Pneumocystis carinii* pneumonia (a fungal infection of the lungs), *Cryptococcus* meningitis (a fungal infection of the coverings that surround the brain), toxoplasmosis (a protozoal infection of the brain, heart, and/or lungs), Kaposi's sarcoma (a type of cancer; ▮ **Figure 14-18**), and cytomegalovirus retinitis (a viral infection of the retina). A condition called *wasting syndrome* can also occur at this stage, which includes a marked loss of weight and a decrease in physical stamina, appetite, and mental activity. A person with HIV infection is usually diagnosed as having AIDS when the helper T cell count falls below 200/mm³ and one of these conditions (or another condition typical of this stage) is present.

On average, people diagnosed with AIDS live for about 2 years (Bartlett & Moore, 1998). Again, the amount of time varies tremendously from individual to individual. But as the T cell count falls below 50/mm³, the risk of death increases dramatically.

How HIV Is Transmitted Human immunodeficiency virus is transmitted in three ways: sexual contact with an infected person; exposure to infected blood or blood products; and placental transfer during fetal development, during labor and delivery, and during breast-feeding. These transmission routes are related in that, with the exception of breast-feeding, they all require the blood of the uninfected person to come into direct contact (or close contact, as in the case of placental transfer) with the blood, semen, or vaginal secretions of an infected person.

In 1998, 57% of the men in the United States with AIDS were homosexuals. However, heterosexual men and women become infected with HIV also. Nearly 40% of the women in the United States with AIDS contracted the disease through heterosexual sex (CDC, 1999d). Sexual behaviors that carry risk of HIV infection are unprotected anal intercourse between men, and unprotected anal or vaginal intercourse between a man and a woman. However, any sexual behavior that results in the contact of infected blood, semen, or vaginal secretions with the blood of an uninfected individual is risky because it may result in HIV transmission. Since minor abrasions or tears in the skin and mucous membranes of the genitals often occur during sex without partners being aware of it, such contact may take place much more readily than might be thought. Another primary route of HIV transmission is the sharing of contaminated needles and syringes among injecting drug abusers. (Chapter 7 describes drug abuse in detail.)

Some children and adults with AIDS acquired the disease by receiving contaminated blood during blood transfusions. These incidents occurred before blood banks instituted HIV antibody testing. In addition, the staff at U.S. blood banks use new, sterile needles and syringes with each person who donates blood, so that donating blood never has been a risk and is not a risk now.

Most children with AIDs contracted it before or at birth from their infected mothers. However, not all infants of HIV-infected mothers are born with HIV disease. Various maternal factors influence whether the fetus becomes infected, such as the mother's stage of HIV infection. Recent studies suggest that pregnant women who take zidovudine (AZT) during pregnancy decrease the chances of HIV being transmitted to their fetuses (Cooper et al., 1996). Evidence also suggests that transmission is possible through breast milk, so HIV-infected mothers should not breast-feed their babies.

How HIV Is Not Transmitted There is no need to worry about contracting HIV disease if you work, go to school, and come into casual contact with a person who is infected with HIV. People in certain professions, such as health professionals and police officers, are at some risk of HIV infection because they may come into contact with HIV-infected blood. The results of numerous studies show that HIV is not transmitted by sharing such things as telephones or drinking fountains. Likewise, living with an HIV-infected person and sharing personal items such as combs, towels, eating utensils, and dishes do not transmit the virus.

Although HIV has been detected in saliva, it does not appear to be transmitted by kissing. A protein in the saliva attaches to the surfaces of certain white blood cells and prevents their infection with HIV. The oral cavity is rarely a site of HIV transmission (Shugars, 1999). However, evidence suggests that HIV transmission can take place through oral sex, from penis to mouth and vagina to mouth. Transmission from mouth to penis is less likely (Edwards & Carne, 1998).

Certain insects are known to transmit pathogens from human to human. Thus, some persons worry about contracting HIV disease from insect bites. Research data indicate that transmission of the virus by mosquitoes or other insects does not occur (Friedland, 1990).

Protecting Yourself against HIV Infection The primary means of protecting yourself against becoming infected with HIV is not to engage in any behavior that puts your blood in contact with the blood, semen, or vaginal secretions of an infected person. Abstaining from sex with infected individuals will eliminate that particular risk of HIV infection. Engaging in sex in a mutually monogamous relationship in which neither partner is infected also eliminates that risk. HIV testing before engaging in sex will assure both of you that there is no risk of contracting the disease. Of course, both of you must *remain* monogamous throughout your relationship.

Unfortunately, you may not know if a potential sexual partner is infected; also, the partner may be unaware of his or her own infection. Therefore, to reduce your risk of HIV infection, reduce your number of sexual partners. Table 14-1 lists the characteristics of high-risk partners. Avoid casual sexual encounters (having sex with people you do not know well) so that you have time to evaluate whether potential partners have any of these characteristics.

Always use a latex condom or a polyurethane vaginal pouch (female condom) during each act of sexual intercourse. Both types of condoms provide a barrier between

Table 14-1 — People at High Risk for HIV Infection (United States)

Injecting drug users

People who have had sex with injecting drug users

Homosexual or bisexual men

Women who have had sex with bisexual men

People who received blood transfusions between 1978 and 1985

People with hemophilia

People who have another STI, particularly syphilis or herpes

Women from countries where heterosexual transmission is common (Latin America, the Caribbean, and Africa)

you and the body fluids of another. Never use a male condom and a female condom at the same time. The two materials may tear as they rub against one another and the condoms may not stay in place. The ingredients in some spermicides, such as nonoxynol-9, have been shown to inactivate HIV and other sexually transmitted pathogens. Results of studies indicate that nonoxynol-9 alone and condoms with or without nonoxynol-9 are extremely effective in preventing transmission of HIV (Wittkowski et al., 1998). (See pages 128–129 for more detailed information on the use of condoms.)

Another risk factor for HIV infection is drug abuse of both injecting and non-injecting drugs. Eliminate this risk by abstaining from using drugs. Injecting drug abusers are primarily at risk because HIV-contaminated needles transmit the virus to anyone who shares the contaminated needles. Non-injecting drug abusers are also at an increased risk of contracting HIV because drug abusers engage in risky sexual behaviors while under the influence of drugs.

If you use drugs, you can reduce your risk of HIV infection by never sharing needles or syringes. If you do share needles and syringes, cleaning this equipment with bleach and then rinsing it with water will reduce your risk of infection. Do not have sex while under the influence of drugs.

In summary, medical researchers have discovered the ways in which HIV is transmitted and the ways in which it is not. This information was used to develop the lists shown in the "Managing Your Health" box "Eliminating or Reducing Your Risk of HIV Infection and Other STIs" below. One list summarizes the behaviors that virtually eliminate your risk of HIV infection and the other summarizes the behaviors that reduce your risk.

Treatment of HIV Infection There is no cure for HIV infection and AIDS. Progress in the development of a vaccine has been difficult because the virus mutates (changes) quite readily. Some of the most promising animal vaccine trials have led to the conclusion that the vaccines being tested were not safe. A vaccine that is both safe and effective is unlikely to be developed in the near future (Ezzell, 1999).

Researchers are continually working on ways to treat HIV infection by boosting the immune system, inactivating the virus, or protecting immune system cells from infection. All approved anti-HIV drugs interfere with viral replication (copying). However, the virus becomes immune to the drugs quite quickly as it mutates. Therefore, combinations of drugs appear to work best to retard HIV.

At this time, AIDS researchers consider a drug regimen referred to as HAART (highly active antiretroviral therapy) to be the most effective. However, these drugs have some unpleasant side effects, which make it difficult for an AIDS patient to take the medications on the prescribed schedule. When doses are missed, drug-resistant strains of HIV often emerge, making the medication much less effective or not effective at all. Therefore, physicians are

Eliminating or Reducing Your Risk of HIV Infection and Other STIs

How to Eliminate Your Risk of Becoming Infected with HIV or Other STIs

Abstain from sex. If that is not an option:

- Do not have sex with HIV-infected individuals or those infected with any STI.
- Engage in sex only in a monogamous relationship in which it is certain that neither partner is infected.
- Abstain from using drugs.

Note: People in certain professions, such as health-care workers and police officers, have additional risks of infection due to the nature of their work. Such risks are not eliminated by these practices. These people can become infected with hepatitis B virus or HIV if their blood mixes with the blood or bodily secretions of an infected person.

How to Reduce Your Risk of Becoming Infected with HIV or Other STIs

- Reduce your number of sexual partners.
- Avoid having sex with high-risk partners.
- Avoid having sex with people you do not know well.
- Avoid having sex while under the influence of drugs, including alcohol.
- Use a new latex condom during each act of sexual intercourse.
- Never share needles or syringes.

suggesting that patients not take these drug cocktails until absolutely necessary, since an AIDS patient must take the drugs on a regular basis for the rest of his or her life (Bartlett & Moore, 1998; Leutwyler, 1998; Moyle & Gazzard, 1999).

The newest class of anti-HIV drugs under study are *fusion inhibitors*. As their name suggests, these drugs are designed to prevent HIV from fusing with host cells so that the virus cannot inject these cells with its genetic material. AIDS researchers are hopeful that these drugs may help those AIDS patients for whom HAART regimens do not work (Stephenson, 1999). Another promising area of research in the treatment of AIDS is *gene therapy*. In this approach, the HIV-infected cells of an AIDS patient are replaced with cells engineered to resist virus replication. The results of clinical trials suggest that this approach may be useful, but many obstacles remain (Amado et al., 1999).

Genital Herpes

Genital herpes is another STI that many people fear contracting because it is painful and incurable. When asked, "Do you worry about contracting an STI?" one health student responded:

> I am really worried about getting herpes. Once you have it, you can't get rid of it. That's scary!

The herpes "scare" began in the United States in the 1970s, and the incidence of this disease has been on the rise since then as the graph shows. Since genital herpes is not a disease that must be reported to the CDC, epidemiologists (medical researchers who study such topics as the spread of disease) can only estimate its prevalence. (Reportable STIs are AIDS, gonorrhea, hepatitis B, lymphogranuloma venereum, syphilis, chlamydia, and chancroid, a disease that is rare in most parts of the United States and is not discussed in this chapter.) The CDC estimates that at least 500,000 people are diagnosed with genital herpes each year in the United States, and that approximately 20 million Americans are infected with the virus at this time.

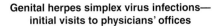

Genital herpes simplex virus infections— initial visits to physicians' offices

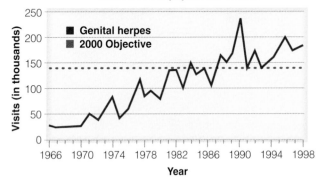

Like all STIs, genital herpes is contracted through sexual intercourse with an infected individual. However, herpes infections are caused by two herpesviruses, a fact that increases the ways in which this disease is transmitted. Herpes infections are caused by *herpes simplex virus type 1 (HSV-1)*, which causes sores primarily on the mouth and lips (cold sores), and *herpes simplex virus type 2 (HSV-2)*, which usually causes sores in the genital and anal areas. Each viral type, however, is capable of infecting *both* oral and genital areas. Therefore, a person who has cold sores can infect his or her partner's genital area during oral sex. Likewise, a person who has genital herpes can infect a partner's oral area during oral sex.

The virus first infects the skin cells in the immediate area of contact and spreads to surrounding cells. During an incubation period (the time between exposure to the pathogen and the onset of symptoms) that lasts about a week, the virus begins to replicate and destroy skin cells. The patient may experience irritation at these sites of infection prior to the eruption of skin lesions. These first lesions appear as groups of tiny, raised, solid bumps that turn clear or yellowish and become filled with fluid. These blisters eventually break open, oozing fluid containing viruses, and then develop into painful sores. The sores turn gray, crust over, and heal usually in 5 to 10 days. With this initial infection, the patient often experiences a headache, fever, weakness, and muscle pain.

Herpes simplex virus usually infects the labia, vagina, and cervix in women and the penis in males, but it can also infect tissues in the genital/anal area that are not protected by a condom. Therefore, the use of latex condoms can only *reduce* the risk of herpes transmission; it does not eliminate the risk for neighboring tissues. Follow the practices outlined in the section "Protecting Yourself against STIs" (pages 365–366).

Transmission of the herpesvirus occurs when the infected tissues of a person who is shedding virus come in contact with the mucous membranes or with small cracks in the skin in the genital or anal areas of another. A person sheds virus when the virus is present in the skin cells, usually just prior to the appearance of sores and when they first appear. Often, a person shedding virus is unaware of this danger; he or she may have no symptoms of disease at the time. The sexual partners of a person shedding virus may not see sores or other indications that their partner is infected.

When the sores heal, the herpes infection is not cured— the virus is establishing itself in the nervous system for life. The virus particles enter the nerve endings in the area of infection and move up these nerves until they are close to the base of the spinal cord. There, the virus particles lie dormant. During the dormant phase, the infected person shows no signs or symptoms of herpes, and is not shedding the virus.

From time to time, the virus becomes reactivated. Researchers are unsure about the exact mechanisms of how and why reactivation occurs, but infected individuals appear to have triggers that initiate a recurrence of infection. Common triggers are stress, lack of sleep, and menstruation. During a recurrence, the virus descends along the nerves close to the areas of original infection. No symptoms may be present, but the person sheds virus and can infect others during this time. Often, skin lesions appear, but these sores are not usually as painful nor do they last as long as during the initial infection. Most individuals experience five to eight recurrences per year. However, treatment with the drug acyclovir reduces the recurrence rate dramatically. Some persons have no recurrences for as long as 2 years.

Herpesvirus can also infect newborns as they pass through the cervical opening and vagina of a mother with an active infection. Infected newborns may die or suffer damage to their nervous systems. In cases of active maternal infection, cesarean section (delivering the baby surgically, by cutting through the abdominal wall and the uterus) is often recommended.

Genital Warts

Genital warts *(Condylomata acuminata)* are not painful, unlike the sores of herpes infection, but some of the viruses that cause this STI are associated with the development of cervical cancer. This association with cancer and the possible transmission of this disease to the respiratory tract of infants during birth are the gravest concerns of this disease.

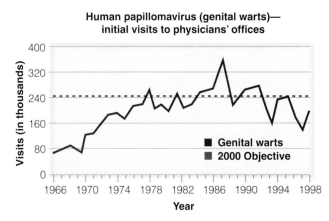

Human papillomavirus (genital warts)— initial visits to physicians' offices

Warts are noncancerous skin tumors, masses of cells that result from uncontrolled cell growth. All warts are called *papillomas* and are caused by the *human papillomavirus* (PAP-ih-LOW-mah-vigh-rus) *(HPV)*. However, there are over 60 types of papillomaviruses (named HPV-1, HPV-2, and so on); each affects only certain areas of the body.

More than 20 types of HPV can infect the genital tract, but visible genital warts are usually caused by HPV-6 and HPV-11. These viruses cause warts particularly in the cervical, vaginal, and vulvar areas in women and various parts of the penis in men. They can also infect the urethra and anal areas in both sexes (■ **Figure 14-19**). The HPV types

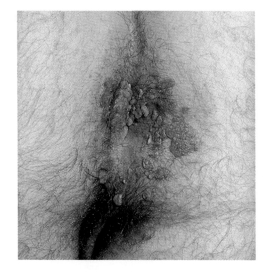

▲**Figure 14-19 Condylomata acuminata (Genital Warts).** These warts are growing around the anus of a man, nearly obscuring that opening.

that infect the genital area but do not result in the growth of warts result in tissue changes that a health-care provider usually can see by using special techniques. Some of these viruses, particularly HPV-16 and HPV-18, are associated with cancer of the cervix and less often with cancer of the vulva and penis. The American Cancer Society recommends that women have regular Papanicolaou tests (Pap smears) to detect atypical, precancerous, or cancerous cells within the cervix and that men consider having any abnormal tissue growth in the genital area microscopically examined for the presence of cancer.

Health-care professionals are not required to report cases of genital warts to the CDC, so only estimates of prevalence are available as shown in the graph. Although more Americans have genital warts than herpes because of the much higher prevalence of warts in past decades, the incidence of warts is falling while the incidence of herpes is rising. In 1998 the number of initial visits to physicians' offices for these two STIs was approximately equal.

To avoid infection with this cancer-causing virus, follow the precautions in "Protecting Yourself against STIs." Remember, however, that HPV, like genital herpes, can infect genital and anal tissue that is not protected by a condom. Additionally, because skin-to-skin contact can transmit HPV, infection can occur even if anal or vaginal intercourse does not take place. Transmission is also possible during oral sex, so that a person with genital HPV could infect the lips, tongue, or palate of an uninfected sexual partner. Adults as well as infants can develop warts on the larynx, or voice box, if the virus is breathed in. Furthermore,

genital herpes an STI caused by the herpes simplex virus that results in sores in the genital and anal areas.

genital warts an STI caused by the human papillomavirus that results in noncancerous skin tumors of the genital area.

infants may acquire such infections from an infected mother during the birth process.

Although genital warts may go away on their own, the virus particles remain in the tissue, so they can infect others. These warts may also persist, grow larger, and spread. The removal of genital warts involves applying medications to the skin that break down the wart tissue, freezing them with liquid nitrogen, cauterizing (burning) them, or treating them with carbon dioxide lasers. Treatment for hard-to-remove warts involves the injection of the antiviral agent alpha-interferon directly into the tumorous growths.

If you contract genital warts, you may want to discuss the benefits and drawbacks of various treatments with your health-care provider. Many treatments are far more painful than the warts, interferon treatments can be costly, and medical researchers are unsure whether treatment to remove warts reduces the risk of transmission. Efforts to develop a vaccine to protect against HPV infection or to use in its treatment have proved fruitless, primarily because the virus is extremely difficult to culture in the laboratory.

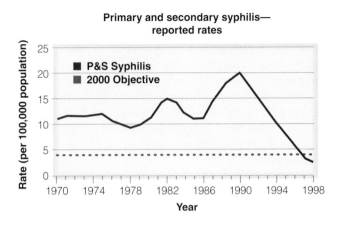

Primary and secondary syphilis— reported rates

An individual can contract syphilis by having sex with a person who has skin lesions (sores) caused by *T. pallidum*. These bacteria enter the body through a break in the skin of an uninfected person. Some syphilis bacteria remain in the skin at the site of entry, where a dime-sized sore called a chancre forms. Some of these bacteria move to the lymph nodes.

The incubation period for syphilis is about 3 weeks. The first sign of the disease is a chancre, which is characteristic of the first stage of syphilis, *primary syphilis*. Most often this sore appears in the genital or anal areas, but it can occur on the lips, tongue, breast, or fingers. The chancre first appears as a dull, red, flat spot, but becomes raised and then ulcerates. **Figure 14-20** is a photograph of a chancre on the penis. Although it looks as though it would be extremely painful, a chancre does not hurt. If untreated, a chancre usually heals in 3 to 6 weeks. During that time, however, *T. pallidum* is multiplying in the body; the disease is not gone.

After the chancre heals, the signs and symptoms of *secondary syphilis* appear. These symptoms are systemic be-

Healthy
LIVING PRACTICES

- To virtually eliminate your risk of contracting HIV infection, do not have sex with infected persons or share needles and syringes.
- To reduce your risk of contracting HIV, use a new latex condom with each act of sexual intercourse.

Sexually Transmitted Infections Caused by Bacteria

In contrast to viral STIs, bacterial STIs can be cured. Nevertheless, bacterial infections can be quite serious. If not treated, or not treated promptly and properly, bacterial STIs can damage the reproductive system, possibly resulting in infertility. Some diseases such as syphilis can cause even more devastating health effects. Therefore, it is crucial to seek medical attention immediately if you suspect that you are infected and to refrain from sex to avoid transmitting the disease to others.

Syphilis

For centuries, **syphilis,** a serious STI caused by the bacterium *Treponema pallidum* (TREP-oh-NEE-mah PAL-ih-dum), has been a dreaded disease. Historically, the infection rate of syphilis reached a peak in the United States at the end of World War II. Physicians were soon able to demonstrate the effectiveness of the antibiotic penicillin against the syphilis bacterium. Although syphilis is not as prevalent as it once was, its incidence increased in the late 1980s, but has since declined as the graph shows. Despite the overall decline, syphilis remains an important problem

in the South, particularly among the African American population (CDC, 1999e).

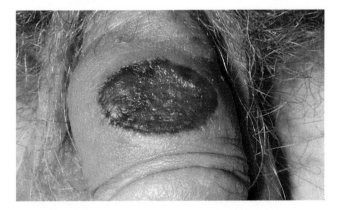

▲**Figure 14-20 A Syphilitic Chancre of the Penis.** These painless sores can occur on the genital or anal areas, lips, tongue, breast or fingers. They are characteristic of the first stage of syphilis.

cause the bloodstream has distributed the bacteria to most of the tissues. Common symptoms of secondary syphilis are sore throat, weakness, headache, weight loss, fever, and muscle pain. In some patients, wartlike growths develop in moist areas of the body such as the genital region and under the arms. Most persons develop a rash that covers the body—even the soles of the feet. Although the appearance of this rash varies from person to person, it is often scaly.

When the symptoms of secondary syphilis subside, the infected person is said to be in *latent syphilis*. He or she has no outward signs of disease but is still infected. This stage may last a lifetime, or the infected individual may enter *tertiary syphilis*. During the tertiary stage of infection, tissue-destroying lesions called *gummas* develop. Gummas not only affect the skin but can destroy any type of tissue in the body—even bones. This stage of syphilis is, therefore, often disfiguring. If the tissues of the heart, major blood vessels, or brain are destroyed, paralysis and death can result.

Since the introduction of antibiotics, few people with syphilis in the United States reach this stage of the disease. Most people are given antibiotics for various infectious diseases over a period of years; even if they are not treated specifically for syphilis, the administration of penicillin for any reason will kill *T. pallidum*. Nevertheless, approximately 100 people each year die in the United States as a result of untreated tertiary syphilis.

Unfortunately, the syphilis bacterium can cross the placenta during pregnancy, infecting the fetus. Infants infected with *T. pallidum* are born with a wide variety of serious conditions, such as bone deformities, low birth weight, lung damage, brain damage, deafness, and blindness. In addition, the infant can be infected during birth or after birth by coming into contact with the mother's lesions.

Gonorrhea

Despite the fact that the incidence of gonorrhea has declined dramatically since 1975, it still has not reached the level set by the *Healthy People 2000* report, as shown in the graph. The age group with the highest prevalence of gonorrhea infection is young adults aged 15 to 24 years (CDC, 1999e). This is worrisome to health officials because gonorrhea can cause irreversible damage to the reproductive tract.

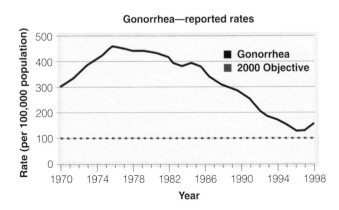

Gonorrhea—reported rates

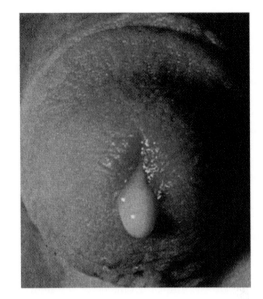

▲ **Figure 14-21 Pus-Containing Discharge from the Penis as a Result of Gonorrhea.**

Gonorrhea is caused by tiny, spherical bacteria called *Neisseria gonorrhoeae* (neye-SEE-ree-ah GON-ah-REE-ah) that enter the body via the mucous membranes. The bacteria infect primarily the urethra in men and the cervix in women. Therefore, condoms are an excellent measure to prevent gonorrhea because they protect these areas well.

The incubation period of gonorrhea is from 2 to 8 days. In men, infection with gonorrhea bacteria usually causes urethritis, an inflammation of the urethra, the tube through which urine exits the body. Urethritis is also commonly known as a urinary tract infection (UTI). A UTI caused by the gonorrhea bacterium results in a pus-containing discharge from the urethra (▐ **Figure 14-21**). (Pus is a thick fluid made up of tissue fluid, white blood cells, dead microorganisms, and dead body cells.) The infected male then experiences painful urination and an urgency to urinate. Most men seek attention quickly because of these symptoms, but if untreated, within several weeks to several months their body's natural defenses will suppress the infection. Until an infection is suppressed, however, a man can spread it to his sexual partners.

Gonorrhea infection in females may cause urethritis, but it more commonly causes inflammation of the cervix and uterus, resulting in a pus-containing vaginal discharge, uterine bleeding, and abnormally long and heavy menstrual periods. A woman also experiences the symptoms of urethritis if the urethra is infected.

syphilis (SIF-ih-lis) an STI that can progress from skin sores to more generalized symptoms (e.g., weight loss and muscle pain) to life-threatening, tissue-destroying skin abnormalities.

gonorrhea (GON-ah-REE-ah) an STI characterized by infection of the urethra in men and the cervix in women, usually resulting in a thick discharge from the penis or vagina.

The bacteria can infect the prostate, epididymis, and seminal vesicles in males. Although infection of these male reproductive structures is rare, it does occur and can result in sterility. Women are more prone to widespread infection of the reproductive tract than are men. Infection of the uterine (fallopian) tubes or other female reproductive organs is called *pelvic inflammatory disease (PID)*.

Gonorrhea is the most common cause of PID, which develops in approximately 10% to 20% of women infected with gonorrhea. PID is a serious, painful condition. Its symptoms are lower abdominal pain, pain during sexual intercourse, abnormal menstrual periods, bleeding between periods, and sometimes fever. Often, the uterine tubes become constricted from infection, resulting in sterility or in ectopic pregnancy. An *ectopic pregnancy* occurs when a fertilized egg implants outside of the uterus, most often in a uterine tube (see Figure 6-7, page 118). Ectopic pregnancies are extremely serious situations. Abscesses (collections of pus) on the pelvic organs are also complications of PID and may require a hysterectomy, an operation to remove some or all of a woman's reproductive organs.

Another complication of gonorrhea is that the eyes of newborns can become infected with *N. gonorrhoeae* during birth if the mother is infected. If untreated, blindness may occur. For this reason, the eyes of all newborns in the United States are treated with antibiotic ointment or silver nitrate immediately after birth.

Gonorrhea can be treated with a variety of antibiotics. In recent years, many antibiotic-resistant strains of bacteria have emerged, sometimes making treatment difficult. However, laboratory testing of the particular strain can determine the most effective antibiotic to administer. Although gonorrhea is curable, reinfections are possible.

Chlamydial Infections

Chlamydia trachomatis (klah-MID-dee-ah trah-ko-MA-tiss) causes **chlamydial infections,** which are similar to gonorrhea. The bacteria that cause both STIs infect mucous membranes in the genital area, primarily infecting the urethra in males and the urethra and cervix in females. The symptoms of both infections are similar, and both organisms can travel throughout the reproductive tract to spread infection. Both can cause PID in women. One difference is that the incubation period for gonorrhea is from 2 to 8 days, and that of chlamydial infections is from 2 to 3 weeks.

chlamydial infection (klah-MID-dee-ahl) an STI that results in gonorrhealike symptoms.

T. vaginalis **infection** an STI caused by a protozoan, resulting in infection of the urethra in men and of the urethra and walls of the vagina in women.

yeast infection a condition in which the fungus *Candida albicans* grows in the vagina or on the penis; also known as candidiasis or moniliasis.

pubic louse a close relative of fleas that causes sexually transmitted infestation; also called crabs.

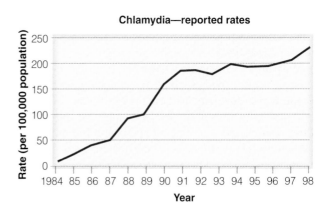

Chlamydia—reported rates

Rate (per 100,000 population) / Year
1984 85 86 87 88 89 90 91 92 93 94 95 96 97 98

Chlamydia is the most prevalent STI in the United States and its rate is increasing, as the graph shows. One reason for its prevalence is that infection with the organism causes only mild symptoms in most infected men and no symptoms in approximately 70% of infected women. Therefore, many infected people transmit the disease unknowingly to their sexual partners. Complicating the situation, until recently, was the lack of a suitable laboratory test to detect this bacterium. So diagnosing chlamydial infections in persons with very mild, or no, symptoms has been extremely difficult. This disease is important to diagnose, however, because women with silent chlamydial infections are at a high risk for developing more serious illness such as PID, and they can transmit the infection to their children during birth. Men rarely develop serious disease from *C. trachomatis* infection, but men with undiagnosed infection continue to transmit the organism to women.

The symptoms of chlamydial infection in men are painful urination and a whitish or clear discharge from the urethra. The amount of discharge and the level of pain are usually much milder than with gonorrheal infections, so men tend to wait longer to seek treatment than with gonorrheal infections. Occasionally, *C. trachomatis* travels to other parts of the male reproductive tract and causes epididymitis, an inflammation of the epididymides, tubules located on the back of the testes in which sperm mature. This bacterium also infects the rectum in people who engage in anal sex.

From 15% to 25% of women develop urethritis when they are infected with *C. trachomatis*. Most often, the main site of female infection is the cervix, and a vaginal discharge may occur.

One of the most serious consequences of infection with chlamydia is pelvic inflammatory disease; it causes approximately one-third of all cases of PID. No matter which organism causes it, PID has similar symptoms and can result in sterility or ectopic pregnancy, even though chlamydia causes less painful infection than other organisms such as *N. gonorrhoeae*.

Babies born to mothers with chlamydial infections not only can develop serious eye infections but their lungs can become infected as well. Chlamydial pneumonia in a newborn can cause long-term damage to the lungs, which affects lung function throughout childhood.

Chlamydia trachomatis infections are treated with various antibiotics. The CDC suggests using latex condoms to reduce the risk of contracting chlamydial infections and following suggestions such as those in the section entitled "Protecting Yourself against STIs."

Other Sexually Transmitted Infections

Organisms other than bacteria and viruses also cause sexually transmitted infections. The itch mite (a close relative of spiders) and the pubic louse (a close relative of fleas) cause sexually transmitted *infestations,* conditions in which these organisms live on the skin in the genital area. A yeast, *Candida albicans,* causes an infection of the genital tract, primarily in women, that can be acquired sexually or in nonsexual ways. *Trichomonas vaginalis,* a protozoan (a single-celled organism much more complex than a bacterium), causes an infection of the lower genital tract of both men and women.

Trichomonas vaginalis Infections

As the name of this organism implies, **T. vaginalis infections** (trichomoniasis) are more of a problem for women than for men. Women are 20 times more likely to contract trichomoniasis than are men. The reason for higher infection rates in women is that *T. vaginalis* lives on the surface tissues of the reproductive tract, such as the walls of the vagina, and uses glucose (a sugar) as a principal nutrient. This nutrient is more abundant in the reproductive tract of women than men. However, *Trichomonas* does not grow well in acidic conditions, which is the normal environment of the vagina (and of the male urethra). If the acid environment of the vagina changes, such as when a woman has another genital infection, is taking antibiotics, or when she is pregnant, the organism will grow easily if she becomes infected.

An estimated 12% to 15% of women in the United States are infected with *Trichomonas.* These infections are almost always contracted by having sexual intercourse with an infected partner. (Men do become infected, but usually the infection goes away quickly without treatment.) It is possible to contract a *Trichomonas* infection from contaminated objects such as toilet seats, but such transmission is rare.

The symptoms of this STI in men are that of a mild infection of the urethra: mildly painful urination and urgency to urinate. The symptoms in women are more extensive and serious: an abnormal, bad-smelling vaginal discharge, which may be thin and foamy, along with itching, burning, swelling, redness, and tenderness of the vulva. These symptoms vary in their severity among patients. *Trichomonas* infections are treated with a specific drug that kills the organism.

Yeast Infections

Yeast infections (candidiasis) are common among women; medical researchers estimate that 75% of women experience at least one yeast infection during their childbearing years. Yeast infections are acquired in a variety of ways, including sexual intercourse.

Candida albicans is the organism most commonly responsible (85% to 95% of the time) for causing yeast infections. (These infections are *not* caused by the yeasts used to make certain baked products or beer.) These organisms are thought to be always present in the genital-anal area (as are a variety of bacteria) because they are present in fecal material. The bacteria that normally inhabit the vagina in high numbers keep yeast and other bacteria from growing because they produce acids and outcompete other organisms for nutrients and space. However, under certain conditions, yeast may grow in the vagina.

Yeast may begin to grow and produce a vaginal infection during antibiotic use or pregnancy. Women who have poorly controlled diabetes or other STIs are also prone to yeast infections. Yeast grow best under warm and moist conditions, so clothing that is tight and poorly ventilated in the crotch may also contribute to the development of yeast infections. All these factors change the vaginal environment, allowing the yeast to grow.

The most common symptom of yeast infections in women is itching in the genital area. Other symptoms are soreness, burning, irritation, swelling, and a vaginal discharge that is white and looks somewhat like cottage cheese. Although numerous over-the-counter preparations are available to treat yeast infections, women should report symptoms to their health-care providers before self-treatment.

Women infected with *Candida* can pass the infection to their male partners during sexual intercourse. Typically, the penis becomes infected; parts of this organ, the scrotum, and the groin may become irritated and swollen, and may develop a rash, white patches, or both. Infected men may also experience the symptoms of a mild urethritis.

Pubic Lice

Phthirus pubis (THIR-us PEW-bis) is a **pubic louse,** often called a crab louse because it has crablike claws (█ **Figure 14-22).** Therefore, infestation with pubic lice is often referred to as "having crabs." Pubic lice are closely related to head lice, but are not found in the scalp or on head hair. Crab lice can also attach to underarm hair and eyelashes, and occasionally infest these body areas.

▲**Figure 14-22 The Pubic Louse.** This color-enhanced scanning electron microscope image shows two pubic lice, one adult and one juvenile, magnified about 40 times. They are hanging from pubic hair by their massive, crablike claws.

Sexual partners must also be treated at the same time, as with all STIs, so that reinfestation (or reinfection) does not occur.

Scabies

Scabies *(Sarcoptes scabiei)* (sar-COP-tees SKAY-bee-ee) produce infestations of the pubic area similar to those of the pubic louse. These spiderlike organisms (often called *itch mites*) burrow into the skin and lay eggs there. Therefore, one sign of infestation with scabies is thin, red lines or bumps in the skin, which result from burrowing and egg laying. In addition to the pubic region, these organisms infest other areas of the body (▊ **Figure 14-23**).

Itch mites are transmitted by prolonged, close, personal contact, including sexual intercourse. However, if one member of a family becomes infested, the infestation can spread to other family members via infected bed linens, towels, or other household items. Outbreaks also occur in institutional settings such as hospitals and nursing homes. Scabies is treated with prescription medications that are applied to the skin and sometimes with accompanying oral medications.

Pubic lice are transmitted primarily by sexual contact and are rarely spread via contaminated toilet seats and bed linens, although these routes of infestation are possible. They move from the pubic hairs of an infected individual to a partner when the genital areas touch. The lice then anchor themselves by grasping pubic hairs. For nourishment, pubic lice pierce the host's skin with their mouthparts and suck the blood of their host. When a person contracts pubic lice, he or she may notice tiny droplets of blood on the underwear before the symptoms of itching, swelling, redness, and irritation begin.

Pubic lice also reproduce in the pubic area. Female lice lay their eggs and then glue them to pubic hairs, where they eventually hatch and mature. Unless the infestation is treated, the lice will continue to reproduce and infest their host.

Both nonprescription and prescription medications are available to treat infestations of pubic lice, but a health-care provider should be consulted to confirm the diagnosis. Bed linens and clothing should be washed in hot water and dried to kill any eggs or lice.

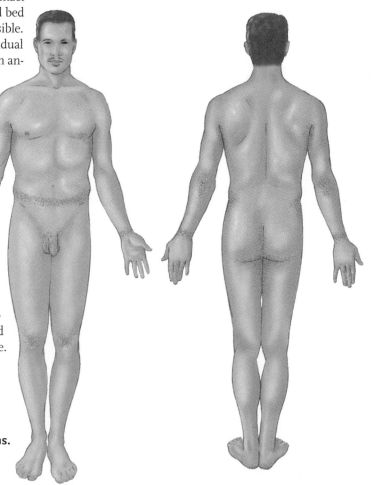

▶**Figure 14-23 The Distribution of Scabies Skin Lesions.** The red dotted areas are where infestation usually occurs. The areas without dots are rarely affected.

www.jbpub.com/healthyliving

Protecting Yourself Against STIs

The first step in protecting yourself against sexually transmitted infections is to realize that STIs can strike anyone who is sexually active. Regardless of your age, gender, ethnicity, or socioeconomic status, if you are sexually active you can contract an STI.

The "Managing Your Health" box on page 357 lists behaviors that will help protect you from infection with HIV and other STIs. Of course, you may choose to abstain from sexual activity and drug use, which virtually eliminates your risk of contracting a sexually transmitted infection. If you choose not to abstain from sex, having sex with non-infected individuals also eliminates your risk. How do you know if your partner is infected?

The best way to know if you are having sex with an uninfected partner is to be in a *long-term,* monogamous relationship in which you and your partner have been tested for STIs. A monogamous relationship is one in which a person has only one mate or partner at any one time. Unfortunately, monogamy is not foolproof. You must be absolutely certain that your partner is not having sex with anyone else. Consider the comment by a health student when asked, "Do you know someone who has a sexually transmitted infection? What was their reaction when they found out?":

> A married friend of mine went to the doctor right away after she suspected she had a sexually transmitted infection. The doctor said she had herpes. She was so upset with her husband; she . . . later divorced him.

Apparently, this "monogamous" relationship was one-sided. It obviously did not eliminate this woman's risk of contracting an STI. Also, don't equate *serial monogamy* with elimination of risk. Having sex with only one person for a short period and then having sex only with a new partner, and so on, does not eliminate your risk of contracting a sexually transmitted infection.

Because it is difficult to eliminate your risk of contracting an STI (or to be certain that you have no risk), it is prudent to adhere to behaviors that reduce your chances of becoming infected.

Limiting your number of sexual partners statistically reduces your chances of contracting any STI. With regard to the partners you have, you will lower your risk if you delay having sex with people until you know them well enough to assess their risk as sexual partners. Although you may question your partner about his or her previous sexual experiences, history of STIs, and drug use habits, be aware that people often conceal this information. Avoid having sex with individuals who consistently have sex with multiple partners. Also avoid having sex with individuals who

are in the high-risk categories listed in Table 14-1. If you choose to have sex with a person in one or more of these categories, avoid penetrating activities: anal, vaginal, and oral sex.

If you use drugs, you are putting yourself in jeopardy of contracting an STI. To avoid contracting STIs, never share needles and syringes if you are an injecting drug user, and never have sex while under the influence of drugs or alcohol. While under the influence, you are more likely to engage in sexually risky and dangerous behaviors.

The most effective strategy to prevent HIV and other STIs is to refrain from sexual intercourse with infected partners. The second most effective strategy is to use latex condoms during sexual activity. According to the CDC, condom use substantially reduces the risk for contracting the following STIs: gonorrhea, HSV infection, syphilis, HIV infection, hepatitis B, and chlamydial infection. By reducing the risk of gonorrheal and chlamydial infections in women, condoms also reduce their risk of contracting pelvic inflammatory disease.

Although the use of synthetic condoms will reduce your risk of becoming infected, they do not provide a guarantee against transmission because they may tear or slip (although with proper use, this is unlikely) and they do not cover the entire genital area. Condoms made of natural membranes such as sheep intestine are not effective barriers. HIV and other sexually transmitted viruses can penetrate this type of condom, so use latex ones. When using latex condoms, however, do not use oil-based lubricants such as petroleum jelly, mineral oil, vegetable oils, massage oils, and body lotions, which can weaken the latex. Apply only water-based lubricants such as K-Y Jelly.

scabies
(SKAY-beez) an infestation of the pubic area in which a flealike organism burrows into the skin and lays eggs there.

Another practice to avoid is storing condoms in hot cars or wallets for extended periods of time; keep them in a cool, dry place and out of direct sunlight. Do not use them after the expiration date, or if the packaging or condom shows signs of damage or deterioration, such as brittleness, stickiness, or discoloration.

It is important to use condoms consistently (a new one for each act of intercourse) and properly for them to be effective in reducing your risk against STIs. As you use a condom, handle it carefully, being sure not to damage it with your fingernails, teeth, or other sharp objects. Figure 6-18 and the accompanying text show and describe the correct procedure for putting on a male condom.

Female polyurethane condoms are also available. Laboratory tests show that viruses such as HIV cannot pass through the polyurethane. However, there have been few studies conducted regarding STI transmission during use, and no clinical trials to compare the differences in disease transmission between male and female condoms (Bounds, 1997; Fontanet et al., 1998; Gibson et al., 1999).

The female condom is a plastic sheath that covers the cervix much like a diaphragm, lines the vagina, and covers the labia. The same precautions and care regarding the use of male condoms should be followed when using female condoms. Figure 6-19 and the accompanying text show and describe the correct procedure for a female condom.

Healthy LIVING PRACTICES

- If you are sexually active, you are at risk for contracting sexually transmitted infections. You can virtually eliminate your risk by abstaining from sex, or by engaging in sex only within a mutually monogamous relationship in which you and your partner are free of disease.
- You can reduce your risk by limiting your number of sexual partners, never sharing needles and syringes during drug use, and not engaging in sex while under the influence of alcohol or drugs.
- Another way to reduce your STI risk is by using synthetic condoms for each act of sexual intercourse. If you choose not to use condoms, you can reduce STI risk by having both yourself and your partner screened for STIs before engaging in sex.

Infectious and Noninfectious Diseases

Noninfectious diseases and conditions that are present at birth are termed *birth defects*. Some birth defects are caused by environmental influences such as fetal exposure to *teratogens*—drugs, alcohol, viruses, or other substances that directly damage the tissues of the embryo (during weeks 3 to 8 of pregnancy) or fetus (during week 9 of pregnancy through birth). Table 6-1 lists some teratogens known to cause birth defects. Chapter 7 describes problems that can occur during prenatal development when a pregnant woman takes drugs. Chapter 8 discusses fetal alcohol syndrome. Dietary deficiencies during pregnancy can also cause birth defects.

Metabolic diseases are also types of birth defects. An infant born with a metabolic disease lacks an enzyme necessary for normal metabolism. Such problems are genetic and result in an infant's cells being unable to make a necessary body compound. Sometimes abnormal substances are made that build up in the blood and urine; these substances can damage tissues in the body such as the liver, brain, and kidney.

Most metabolic diseases are rare; two of the more well-known are Tay-Sachs disease and phenylketonuria. In Tay-Sachs disease, which occurs predominantly among Ashkenazi Jews (the descendants of Jews who settled in Eastern and Central Europe), certain fatlike molecules accumulate in the brain and other tissues, retarding development and causing death by the age of 3 to 4 years. In phenylketonuria (PKU), cells are unable to convert the amino acid phenylalanine to other needed compounds. Phenylalanine and related chemicals build up in the blood and damage tissues, causing mental retardation. Because the ill effects of this disease can be avoided by restricting the amount of phenylalanine in the diet, most newborn infants are tested for this disorder.

Although many genetic diseases claim the lives of infants and children, genetic disorders persist in those children who survive to become adolescents or young adults. Down syndrome, cystic fibrosis, and Duchenne muscular dystrophy are all noninfectious diseases, mentioned on pages 336 and 338, that affect children. The hope for curing these and other genetic diseases is *gene therapy*, in which corrected copies of defective genes are inserted into the hereditary material of infected individuals. A preventive measure is *genetic counseling*, in which prospective parents seek advice regarding the probability that they will have a child with particular genetic disorders. Couples can use this information to make family planning decisions (see the "Managing Your Health" essay "Genetic Counseling and Prenatal Diagnosis" in Chapter 6).

Most genetic diseases strike early in life. However, one disease, Huntington's chorea (also called Huntington's disease), does not become evident until approximately age 40. By this time, victims may have already passed on the genes for this disease to their children. In Huntington's chorea, the patient makes involuntary, purposeless, rapid motions such as flexing and extending the fingers or raising and lowering the shoulders. (*Chorea* refers to involuntary muscle twitching.) The mental faculties of the person also deteriorate. Fifteen years or so after the onset of the disease, the patient dies. Although there is no cure or effective treatment for this disease, certain medications can relieve or lessen some of the symptoms. Genetic testing is available so that young adults who have affected parents can learn whether they carry the lethal gene. The gene is dominant, which means that if you inherit one gene from either parent, you will develop this disease. This information allows people at risk for this disease to make informed reproductive choices.

Other than heart disease, cancer, and stroke, which are discussed in Chapters 12 and 13, one of the most well-known noninfectious diseases of the elderly is Alzheimer's disease. This disease has a strong genetic link and is discussed on pages 382 to 383 in Chapter 15.

Infectious diseases also have a variety of effects across the life span. As life begins, infection can do harm. Viral infections can be dangerous to a pregnant woman because many viruses can cross the placenta, the organ through which the fetus absorbs nutrients and excretes wastes. Certain viruses, such as the German measles virus, can cause birth defects, including deafness, heart defects, and mental retardation. Other viruses, such as the human immunodeficiency virus (HIV), can infect the fetus, resulting in an infected newborn. Most bacteria cannot cross the placenta, but if bacteria infect the birth canal at the time of delivery, the baby can become infected as it passes through, as in the case of gonorrhea (see page 362).

In the past, certain bacterial diseases (e.g., diphtheria and whooping cough) and viral diseases (e.g., measles, mumps, and German measles) were common childhood infectious diseases in the United States. However, vaccines for these diseases have been developed, and children are immunized routinely in the United States according to a schedule. Occasionally, outbreaks of these diseases occur in people who are not immunized, but such events are rare. However, these childhood diseases are still prevalent in developing countries.

Other than contracting common infections such as colds and the flu, sexually active adolescents are at highest risk for contracting STIs because they frequently have unprotected intercourse and are biologically more susceptible to infection. The rates of many STIs are highest among adolescents. For example, the rate of gonorrhea is highest among females aged 15 to 19 years. Chlamydial infections and human papillomavirus (HPV) infections are also highest among adolescents (CDC, 1998).

The one nonsexually transmitted infectious disease prevalent in adolescents and young adults is infectious mononucleosis. "Mono" primarily strikes young adults ranging in age from 15 to 25 years (although some suggest this age range extends from 10 to 35).

Infectious mononucleosis has been nicknamed the "kissing disease" because it is spread via infectious saliva. However, it is also contracted by inhaling infectious droplets sneezed or coughed into the air by an infected person or by drinking from an infected person's glass. This disease is usually not serious, but the Epstein-Barr (EB) virus (a herpesvirus), which causes mononucleosis, has been associated with the subsequent development of two forms of cancer: Burkitt lymphoma in certain African populations and nasopharyngeal (nose and throat) carcinoma in Asian populations. Furthermore, infection with EB virus can cause a prolonged period of exhaustion, lasting up to 2 to 3 months. Rest is the primary treatment.

The most common symptoms of infectious mononucleosis are a sore throat; low-grade, long-term fever; swollen lymph nodes and spleen (which may result in pain in the upper left side of the abdomen); fatigue; and weakness. However, the symptoms can vary and may include a rash, headache, or nausea. Previously difficult to diagnose in some cases, health-care practitioners can now test for mono in their offices.

Infections are a major cause of illness and death among the elderly; respiratory infections are the fourth and fifth leading causes of death in this group. Bacterial pneumonia and influenza, for example, together have approximately 20 times the fatality rate for persons over 65 than for those between the ages of 45 and 64 years and approximately 100 times the fatality rate than for those between the ages of 25 and 44 (Hoyert, 1999).

The elderly are more susceptible to infections and have a more difficult time recovering from them than younger persons for a variety of reasons. The cell-mediated component of the immune system functions less well as people age. Also, the respiratory tract changes during the aging process, resulting in decreased elasticity of the lungs and a diminished cough reflex, making elderly people more susceptible to respiratory infections. Other organ systems may also experience structural and degenerative changes that predispose elderly persons to infection. Many elderly people have chronic diseases too, which lower their organs' functional reserves and contribute to their decreased resistance to infection. However, older adults and the elderly are in a low-risk category for contracting STIs because they usually have fewer sexual partners than younger people.

ANALYZING Health-Related Information

The following article was written for high school students to inform them about the dangers of body piercing and tattooing. Explain why you think this article is a reliable or an unreliable source of information. Use the model for analyzing health information to guide your thinking; the main points of the model are noted after the article. The model is fully explained on pages 12 to 13.

1. Which statements are verifiable facts, and which are unverified statements or value claims?
2. What are the credentials of the person who wrote the article? Does her background and education qualify here as an expert in the topic area? Is it difficult to tell if the author has specific health expertise?
3. What might be the motives and biases of the author? State the reasons for your answer.
4. What is the main point of the article? Which information is relevant to the issue or main point? Which information is irrelevant?
5. Is the source reliable, or does it have a reputation for publishing misinformation? Does the article present both the pros and cons of body piercing and tattooing?
6. Does the article attack the credibility of conventional scientists or medical authorities?

Based on the above analysis, do you think that this article is a reliable source of health-related information? Summarize your reasons for coming to this conclusion.

Getting the FACTS about Body Piercing

by Katie Sharp

Jackie, Carmen, and Lisa sat at their usual table in the cafeteria. Carmen and Lisa mentioned they were going shopping on Saturday for new earrings.

"I wish I had pierced ears," Jackie said.

"You're probably the only girl at school who doesn't," Lisa teased.

"Even most of the boys have theirs pierced," laughed Carmen.

Jackie laughed, but she really was envious. She had asked her parents time and time again, but they just didn't like the idea of pierced ears. They did, however, agree to consider it for her 16th birthday, which was only two months away.

That night she decided to bring it up again.

"Mom, Dad, do you remember saying that you would think about letting me get my ears pierced for my 16th birthday? Well, can I?"

Jackie's mom spoke first. "Have you looked into what it means to have pierced ears? You know, what's involved and what the risks are?"

Jackie thought for a moment before answering. "Not really."

"I'll tell you

what," Jackie's dad said, "you do some research on the risks of piercing your ears and report back to us what you find. If, based on what you learn, you still want to go ahead with it, you may get them pierced."

Here's what Jackie learned.

Today, it is not uncommon to see people of all ages with pierced ears, as well as other body parts. And decorating the body goes beyond piercing. Body tattoos are showing up on more people—in more places. But just because tattooing and body piercing are trendy, that doesn't necessarily mean they are safe. Knowledge about these processes is very important before jumping onto the body-piercing bandwagon.

Body-Piercing Precautions

Piercing any part of the body can be risky, especially if precautions are not taken. The biggest danger is that of transmitting diseases, such as hepatitis. Another complication is infection of the earlobe.

If you plan to have your ears pierced, it's best to leave the job to health professionals. This helps to ensure sterile conditions and correct placement of the holes. Piercing can be done with a sterile needle or with a device that punctures the earlobe while inserting the post of a sterilized earring. Using other objects or piercing the cartilage of the ear is not recommended, as this can lead to infection.

Once the ears are pierced, caring for them is very important. The newly inserted stud must be rotated or moved frequently to keep it from sticking. Many physicians recommend the ears be swabbed on a regular basis with alcohol or an antibiotic ointment. This keeps the ears clean and bacteria-free. It usually takes four to eight weeks for the ears to heal. Once healed, it's best to wear earrings with posts or wires made of gold, silver, platinum, or stainless steel. Earrings made of other materials may cause severe reactions, which include pain, swelling, and infection. Alcohol treatment should be continued to keep ear lobes clean, and earrings should be removed each evening before going to bed.

If you're not careful and don't keep up with the care routine, problems can arise. Elongated holes may result from earrings that are too heavy, and lobe injuries may occur when hoop earrings or longer earrings get caught on other objects. To help minimize these complications, avoid these types of earrings, or wear them for only limited amounts of time.

Skin Paintings can be Dangerous

Jackie found out a lot about tattooing, too. And while she had no desire to get a tattoo herself, she knew some people who had one—and she was curious.

Tattooing, a technique of marking the skin with colors, is not new. Some people view tattoos as works of art. Others see them as identifying with a group or as being different.

Permanent tattoos are applied with a machine that pierces the skin with needles. Tattooing is illegal in seven (U.S.) states and heavily regulated in others, mostly because in the past many tattoo parlors were known to operate without concern for the health and safety of their customers. Today a major health concern of tattooing is the spread of hepatitis B and HIV, the virus that causes AIDS. While there are no documented cases of someone contracting HIV as a result of getting a tattoo, the threat is still there.

To help prevent the spread of disease, professional organizations for tattoo artists now recommend certain procedures that they say all professional tattooists should follow. Some of these organizations even hold classes for tattooists to teach them cleanliness and sterilization techniques. They say that anyone considering a tattoo should ask the tattooist whether he or she has taken the class and ask to see the certificate of completion.

Getting a tattoo can be a painful experience. A small tattoo can take up to an hour to complete. Once a tattoo is finished, proper care is essential until the area has healed. Some complications include adverse reactions to the dyes used, which is rare, and infection. Infection typically can be avoided with proper care.

Although tattoos are meant to be permanent, there are methods for removing them but they are costly and can be painful.

Jackie reported her findings to her parents. They discussed what would be expected of her in the care of her ears. Jackie made an appointment with her physician—and guess what she got for her birthday?

Chapter Review

Summary

Noninfectious diseases are processes that affect the proper functioning of the body, are usually accompanied by characteristic signs and symptoms, and are not caused by pathogens. Rather, abnormalities in the hereditary material, factors in the environment, or an interaction of the two cause noninfectious diseases.

Genetic factors are the sole cause of some noninfectious diseases; such genetic diseases are inherited or are caused by mistakes during cell division when gametes are formed. Inherited diseases are caused by disorders of the hereditary material, or genes. Two inherited diseases that are prevalent in the United States are cystic fibrosis and Duchenne muscular dystrophy. Down syndrome is a genetic disease caused by errors during gamete formation.

Some diseases are caused by an interaction of genetic and environmental factors. Genetic factors can predispose a person to a disease. Diseases having both genetic and environmental causes include asthma, ulcers, diabetes mellitus, and migraine headaches.

Some noninfectious conditions have environmental or unknown causes. Many of these conditions are discussed in Chapter 16, "Environmental Health." A few noninfectious conditions are caused by improperly performing certain activities. Carpal tunnel syndrome, for example, is a painful condition of the hands and fingers that results from improper positioning of the wrist while engaging in repetitive activities that use the hands, wrists, and arms.

Birth defects are noninfectious conditions present at birth that affect either the body's structures or how it functions. Anatomical defects can be caused by genetic or environmental factors or a combination of both. Metabolic defects are genetic and affect a person throughout life. Alzheimer's disease, which is discussed in Chapter 15, is a prominent noninfectious disease of the elderly.

Infectious diseases affect the proper functioning of the body, are usually accompanied by characteristic signs and symptoms, and are caused by disease-producing (pathogenic) bacteria, viruses, fungi, protozoans, or worms. Some infectious diseases are communicable; that is, they are spread from person to person either directly or by means of an intermediary organism called a vector. Other infectious disease are noncommunicable; they are caused by organisms such as bacteria that normally (and usually harmlessly) reside on a person's body, by the ingestion of toxins produced by pathogens, or by pathogens from environmental or animal sources.

The severity of a disease's symptoms depends on a variety of factors: the type of organism; its virulence; the manner in which it enters, multiplies, and spreads in or on the body; the chemicals it produces, if any; its ability to combat the defense mechanisms of the body; and the body's reaction to the invading microbe.

Two primary causes of infectious diseases are bacteria and viruses. Bacteria, microscopic organisms that have a simple cell structure, cause disease by first adhering to the surfaces of cells. Some penetrate more deeply into tissues, and many bacteria produce chemicals that break down the connections between cells, aiding their invasion. Viruses are noncellular, nonliving, protein-coated pieces of hereditary material. They cause infection by adhering to cells also, but then enter cells and use them to make more viruses, killing the cells in the process.

The human body has two main types of immunity, or defense against disease: nonspecific and specific immunity. Nonspecific immunity combats any foreign invader. Mechanisms of nonspecific immunity include the skin and mucous membranes, white blood cells and their phagocytic properties, the lymphatic system, the inflammatory response, natural killer cells, and interferons.

Specific immunity combats each specific invading pathogen and is carried out by the immune system. The immune system has two branches: antibody-mediated immunity and cell-mediated immunity. Antibody-mediated immunity reacts to antigens (foreign proteins) that reside outside of the body cells, such as most bacteria and the toxic products they produce. Cell-mediated immunity reacts to antigens that reside inside body cells, such as viruses, fungi, a few types of bacteria, and parasites. It also acts against foreign (non-self) tissues such as transplanted organs and controls the growth of tumor cells.

Immunity is either inborn or acquired. Inborn immunity is inherited, such as immunity to infectious diseases that attack other organisms but not humans. Acquired immunity develops during a person's lifetime. Immunity is acquired either actively or passively, and by natural or artificial means.

Many drugs have been developed to combat infection. Antibiotics kill or inhibit the growth of bacteria and are in wide use. Antiviral drugs are limited in availability and scope. Specific medications have been developed to treat protozoal diseases and infections caused by worms.

Sexually transmitted infections (STIs) are infectious diseases spread from one person to another during sexual activity, primarily sexual intercourse. Most pathogens that cause STIs can survive for only a short time outside of the body; therefore transmission of these diseases from objects, such as toilet seats, is either impossible or rare, depending on the STI. Sexually transmitted infections are caused primarily by viruses and bacteria, but some infections and infestations are caused by yeasts, protozoans, mites, and lice. The transmission of STIs is often facilitated in persons infected with other STIs.

Sexually transmitted infections caused by viruses are incurable. In addition to causing STIs, three sexually transmitted viruses have been implicated in the development of particular cancers: human immunodeficiency virus (HIV), human papillomavirus (HPV), and hepatitis B virus (HBV).

The most serious viral sexually transmitted infection is HIV infection because it not only raises the risk of developing a particular type of cancer, the virus attacks the immune system, disabling the body's defenses. Eventually the immune system of an HIV-infected individual becomes so weakened that he or she succumbs to an array of illnesses that lead to death. This stage in HIV infection is called acquired immunodeficiency syndrome (AIDS). The best ways to protect yourself against contracting this deadly disease or any STI are to refrain from having sex with infected individuals, to reduce your number of sexual partners, to avoid sex with high-risk partners, and to use a latex condom with each act of sexual intercourse.

Sexually transmitted infections caused by bacteria are curable with antibiotics. Three prevalent bacterial STIs are syphilis, gonorrhea, and chlamydial infections.

One protozoan, *Trichomonas vaginalis,* causes a sexually transmitted infection primarily in women. The yeast *Candida albicans* may cause troublesome, itchy infections in women that can be transmitted sexually. The crab louse, *Phthirus pubis,* and itch mite, *Sarcoptes scabiei,* both can cause sexually transmitted infestations of the genital area.

Adolescents and young adults are in the highest risk age category for contracting sexually transmitted infections. Infants are at risk of infection from infected mothers. Middle-aged and older people are less likely to contract sexually transmitted infections because they are less likely to have multiple sex partners. However, anyone practicing high-risk behaviors or having sex with an infected person can contract a sexually transmitted infection.

Applying What You Have Learned

1. Based on the information in this chapter, describe two ways (other than picking your relatives!) in which you can lower your or your unborn children's risk of contracting noninfectious diseases. (Analysis)
2. The human immunodeficiency virus (HIV) attacks helper T cells. Why is this attack so devastating to the body's ability to resist disease? (Application)
3. Think about the last infectious disease you contracted. Outline what you think might have been the chain of infection for this disease. Could you have done anything to break the chain of infection and avoid becoming infected? (Analysis)
4. Analyze your behaviors regarding your risk for contracting STIs. What can you do to lower your risk of contracting a sexually transmitted infection? (Analysis)
5. A man develops a sore on his genitals but is too busy to go to his health-care provider. The sore heals, so he decides that he "got better" on his own. State two reasons why his reasoning is faulty and dangerous. With which STI(s) might this man be infected? Support your answer with evidence. (Synthesis)
6. State a behavior or behaviors that you could adopt or change to help you become more resistant to infection in general. How would this behavioral change increase your resistance to infection? (Evaluation)

KEY

Application: Using information in a new situation.
Analysis: Breaking down information into component parts.
Synthesis: Putting together information from different sources.
Evaluation: Making informed decisions.

Reflecting On Your Health

1. Think back to a time when you dated a person you'd only recently met. What did you do to be sure that you would not catch an STI from this person? What did you do to reduce your risk of infection? After reading this chapter, would you behave any differently now to protect yourself? Why or why not? If so, what would you do differently?
2. When you have a common communicable infectious disease like a cold or the flu, do you do anything to protect others, like members of your family, from catching your illness? If so, what? Would you do anything differently after reading this chapter? If so, what?
3. Have you ever traveled outside the United States? If so, to what countries did you travel? Think back to your trip and describe what you did before departing to protect yourself from infection. What did you do to protect yourself while you were there? Has reading this chapter alerted you to additional steps you should take to protect yourself from infection? If so, what? If you have never traveled outside of the country, pick a country to which you would like to travel and explain what steps you would take before you left to protect yourself from infection. What steps would you take while you were there?
4. Do any hereditary diseases run in your family? If you are not sure, ask your family members, including parents, grandparents, uncles, aunts, and cousins if possible. What steps can you take to protect your future children from a hereditary disease? Include specifics about diseases that run in your family, if any.
5. Many strains of bacteria are becoming resistant to the antibiotics used to treat them. One reason for this is that people pressure their health-care providers for antibiotics when they do not have bacterial illnesses. Also, some people stop taking antibiotics before their physician says they should. Both these situations provide an opportunity for resistant strains of bacteria to develop and replicate. Do you practice either of these behaviors? If so, why? What have you learned in this chapter that may cause you to change those behaviors?

References

Amado, R. G., Mitsuyasu, R. T., & Zack, J. A. (1999). Gene therapy for the treatment of AIDS: animal models and human clinical experience. *Frontiers in Bioscience, 4*:D468-475.

Associated Press. (December 15, 1999). Boy cured of sickle cell anemia. *San Diego Union-Tribune, A-9.*

Bartlett, J. G., & Moore, R. D. (1998). Improving HIV Therapy. *Scientific American, 279*(1):84-89.

Bounds, W. (1997). Female condoms. *European Journal of Contraception & Reproductive Health Care, 2*:113-116.

Centers for Disease Control and Prevention (CDC). (1998). 1998 Guidelines for Treatment of Sexually Transmitted Diseases. *Morbidity and Mortality Weekly Report, 47*(RR-1):1-118.

Centers for Disease Control and Prevention (CDC). (1999a). Achievements in Public Health, 1900–1999. Control of Infectious Diseases. *Morbidity and Mortality Weekly Report, 48*:621-629.

Centers for Disease Control and Prevention (CDC). (1999b). Mortality Patterns U.S., 1997. *Morbidity and Mortality Weekly Report, 48*:664-668.

Centers for Disease Control and Prevention (CDC). (1999c). Recommendations for the use of Lyme disease vaccine. *Morbidity and Mortality Weekly Report, 48*(RR-7):1-37.

Centers for Disease Control and Prevention. (1999d). U.S. HIV and AIDS cases reported through December 1998. *HIV/AIDS Surveillance Report, 10*(2):1-43.

Centers for Disease Control and Prevention: Division of STD Prevention. (1999e). *Sexually Transmitted Disease Surveillance, 1998.* U.S. Department of Health and Human Services, Public Health Service. Atlanta: Centers for Disease Control and Prevention.

Cooper, E. R., Nugent, R. P., Diaz, J. P., Hanson, C., Kalish, L. A., Mendez, H., Zorrilla, C., Hershow, R., Moye, J., Smeriglio, V., & Fowler, M. G. (1996). After AIDS clinical trial 076: The changing pattern of zidovudine use during pregnancy, and the subsequent reduction in the vertical transmission of human immunodeficiency virus in a cohort of infected women and their infants. *Journal of Infectious Diseases, 174,*:1207-1211.

Crouch, T., & Madden, M. (1992). Carpal tunnel syndrome and overuse injuries. Berkeley, CA: North Atlantic Books.

Edwards, S., & Crane, C. (1998). Oral sex and transmission of viral STIs. *Sexually Transmitted Infections, 74*(1):6-10.

Ezzell, C. (1999). Death of a vaccine? *Scientific American, 281*(1):27.

Fontanet A. L., Saba, J., Chandelying, V., Sakondhavat, C., Bhiraleus, P., Rugpao, S., Chongsomchai, C., Kiriwat, O., Tovanabutra, S., Dally, L., Lange, J. M. & Rojanapithayakorn, W. (1998). Protection against sexually transmitted diseases by granting sex workers in Thailand the choice of using the male or female condom: results from a randomized controlled trial. *AIDS, 12*:1851-1859.

Friedland, G. (1990). Risk of transmission of HIV to home care and health care workers. *Journal of the American Academy of Dermatology, 22*(6 pt. 2):1171-1174.

Gibson, S., McFarland, W., Wohlfeiler, D., Scheer, K., & Katz, M. H. (1999). Experiences of 100 men who have sex with men using the Reality condom for anal sex. *AIDS Education & Prevention, 11*:65-71.

Hoyert, D. L., Kochanek, K. D., & Murphy, S. L. (1999). Deaths: Final Data for 1997. *National Vital Statistics Reports, 47*(19):1-105.

Hutton, N., Wilson, M. H., Mellits, E. D., Baumgardner, R., Wissow, L.S., Bonuccelli, C., Holtzman, N. A., DeAngelis, C. (1991). Effectiveness of an antihistamine-decongestant combination for young children with the common cold: a randomized, controlled clinical trial. *Journal of Pediatrics. 118*:125-130.

Leutwyler, K. (1998). Treating HIV. *Scientific American,* July 6. Available: http://www.sciam.com/exhibit/070698aids/index.html

Marwick, C. (1995). Trial halted as sickle cell treatment proves itself. *Journal of the American Medical Association, 273*:611.

Moyle, G. J., & Gazzard, B. G. (1999). A risk-benefit assessment of HIV protease inhibitors. *Drug Safety, 20*:299-321.

Nicoll, A., & Gill, O. N. (1999). The global impact of HIV infection and disease. *Communicable Disease & Public Health, 2*:85-95.

Rausch, M., & Pollard, D. (1998). Management of the patient with sickle cell disease. *Journal of Intravenous Nursing, 21*:27-40.

Shugars, D. C. (1999). Endogenous mucosal antiviral factors of the oral cavity. *Journal of Infectious Diseases, 179*(Suppl 3):S431-435.

Sintchenko, V., & Dwyer, D. E. (1999). The diagnosis and management of influenza: an update. *Australian Family Physician, 28*:313-317.

Stephenson, J. (1999). New class of anti-HIV drugs. *Journal of the American Medical Association, 282*:1994.

Temesgen, Z. (1999). Overview of HIV infection. *Annals of Allergy, Asthma, & Immunology, 83*:1-5.

Winquist, A. G., Fukuda, K., Bridges, C. B., & Cox, N. J. (1999). Neuraminidase inhibitors for treatment of influenza A and B infections. *Morbidity and Mortality Weekly Report, 48*(RR14):1-9.

Wittkowski, K. M., Susser, E., & Dietz, K. (1998). The protective effect of condoms and nonoxynol-9 against HIV infection. *American Journal of Public Health, 88*:590-596.

World Health Organization (WHO). (1997). Secretary-general calls for international solidarity to face risks posed by spread of infectious diseases. Retrieved December 19, 1999, from the World Wide Web: http://www.un.org/News/Press/docs/1977/

Aging, Dying, and Death

Ask a woman her age, and you're likely to get no response and a frown. Ask Catherine Wanslow, and you'll not only get her age, but also her birthdate and a big smile. Born in Boston, Massachusetts, on April 1, 1899, Catherine is one of more than 50,000 centenarians who live in the United States. Although her mind is very sharp, she resides in a nursing home because she is too frail to care for herself. She loves to chat with visitors, but don't try to visit her on Wednesday mornings—that's "bingo time." She won't miss bingo.

When asked if she did anything special to live such a long life, Catherine chuckled and responded, "I don't think I led a very exciting life—I never thought about how long I'd live!"

Catherine has lived longer than her grandparents and parents, so inheritance does not seem to explain her longevity. Information about her lifestyle offers some clues.

"I drank wine on social occasions, and I only smoked 1 cigarette—never liked the smell of cigarettes."

"I was never fat . . . bowling and dancing were my favorite activities. Waltzes, the one-step," Catherine blushes. "But I really liked

> *"I never thought about how long I'd live!"*

to square dance. Even now, whenever I hear dancing music, my toes start tapping!"

In the past, Catherine had gallbladder surgery and some problems with her thyroid gland, but she says, "I was pretty healthy—got regular checkups."

A graduate of a two-year business school, Navy veteran of World War I, mother of three children, grandmother, and great-grandmother, Catherine has endured several hardships. When she was 7 years old, her mother died; her first child died before it was a month old, and her marriage ended in divorce. She credits her sense of humor and strong religious faith with helping her cope with the sad and distressing times in her life. She maintains her upbeat psychological attitude by attending the Catholic mass that is held every day at the nursing home.

When asked what she thought were the most important inventions of the twentieth century, Catherine sat back and pondered the question.

"Airplanes and television," she replied. "Cars were important too, but I didn't learn to drive until I was 32. When I was 72, I flew to Europe.

www.jbpub.com/healthyliving

The web site for this book offers many useful tools and supplementary health information for both students and instructors. Visit the site at www.jbpub.com/healthyliving for information on these topics:

Aging
Dying
Death
Diversity in Health: Hunting for Supercentenarians

Chapter Overview

The status of aging Americans.
Why we age.
The effects of aging on health and well-being.
The spiritual and emotional aspects of dying.
The options for terminal care.
The definition of death.
How to prepare for death.

DIVERSITY **in Health** Hunting for Supercentenarians

Con$umer **Health** Choosing a Nursing Home

Managing Your Health After the Death of a Loved One

across the Lifespan Dying and Death

Student Workbook

Applying Concepts for Healthy Living A Workbook

Self Assessment: Preparing for Aging and Death
Changing Health Habits: Can Changing a Habit Extend Your Life?

Do You Know?

- Who was the oldest person to ever live?
- What happens to your body as you age?
- How to increase your chances of living a long and healthy life?

I went to Gallway County, Ireland, to visit my mother's birthplace." Clearly, Catherine has made the most out of what life has to offer.

Gerontologists, scientists who study aging, are learning more about the factors that influence longevity. Scientists have observed that some families have many members who live to be 90 and older; therefore, heredity appears to play a role in determining how long people can live (Perls, 1999). Nevertheless, an important key to *enjoying* a long and healthy life is taking actions now to improve your health and well-being.

For humans, growing old is a natural and universal process. The prospect of aging and dying, however, has troubled people for centuries. Instead of dreading this time of life, many elderly Americans are busy pursuing a variety of enjoyable and rewarding activities. Healthy people do not let the aging process interfere with their active lifestyles.

The "Across the Lifespan" sections of each chapter of this textbook highlight specific health concerns of elderly persons. This particular chapter provides more detailed information concerning the aging process, including ways to enjoy good health and a positive sense of well-being while growing old. Additionally, this chapter examines dying and death as well as ways of coping with loss and grief. To determine if you are prepared for aging and death, answer the questions in the Assessment activity for this chapter that is in the student wookbook.

gerontologist
(JER-on-TOL-oh-jist) a scientist who studies aging.

aging the sum of all changes that occur in an organism during its life.

▲ Figure 15-1 Jeanne Calment.

www.jbpub.com/healthyliving

Aging

We can define **aging** as the sum of all changes that occur in an organism during its life. The **life span** is the maximum number of years that members of a species can live when conditions are optimal. The life span of a mayfly is a few days; the life span of a human is 122 years. In 1997 Jeanne Calment of Marseilles, France, died at the age of 122. According to official records, Ms. Calment lived longer than any other person (■ **Figure 15-1**). However, very few people live longer than 105 years. Contrary to popular belief, there are no regions of the world where populations usually live more than 100 years (see the "Diversity in Health" feature "Hunting for Centenarians" on page 377).

Medical experts customarily divide the human life span into stages or periods (See Chapter 1, Table 1-4). Most people reach physical maturity or adulthood by the time they are 25 years old, but adulthood usually refers to the period spanning 21 through 65 years of age. Older adulthood or **senescence** is the stage of life that begins at 65 years of age and ends with death. In this chapter, the terms *growing old, aging,* and *elderly* are interchangeable with senescence. The ages that define these life stages are arbitrary; there are no obvious physical signs that indicate the precise ages when one passes from young adulthood into middle age or from middle age into senescence.

Life Expectancy

Life expectancy is the average number of years that an individual who was born in a particular year can expect to live. In the United States, life expectancies vary according to age, sex, and socioeconomic status. Overall, American females outlive American males by about 6.3 years (Martin et al., 1999). As a result, the elderly population consists of about one-third more women than men. White Americans outlive African Americans by about 6 years. The reasons for these differences are unclear, but hormonal, genetic, and socioeconomic factors are thought to influence life expectancy.

As mentioned in Chapter 1, life expectancies increased dramatically during the twentieth century, especially for people who live in developed countries. In the United States, for example, individuals born in 1900 could expect to live 47 years; individuals born in 1998 can expect to live 76.7 years. An increase in life expectancy generally occurs when fewer people die during the earlier stages of life rather than in the later ones.

In the first part of the twentieth century, people lived past 65 years of age, but so many younger individuals died from serious injuries, infections, and in childbirth that these statistics lowered overall life expectancy. By the

1950s advances in scientific and medical technology significantly reduced the number of deaths from these conditions. Today, a greater proportion of the American population lives beyond age 65 than in the past, and the number of Americans who are in this age group is expected to increase over the next 50 years. ▌**Figure 15-2** shows estimates of the number of Americans who are or will be 65 to 84 years of age and 85 and more years of age in 2000, 2010, 2020, and 2030.

Scientists are learning more about the causes of aging and are seeking ways to extend life expectancy. Their efforts have led to the development and testing of new therapies for today's major killers: cancer and cardiovascular disease. Advances in genetic engineering offer ways to prevent and treat inherited disorders that can lead to disability and premature death. Additionally, organ transplantation gives thousands of dying individuals the opportunity to survive by replacing their failing organs with healthy ones. Living longer, however, does not necessarily mean living better.

Preserving the quality of life becomes increasingly important as people grow older. By the time Americans reach 65 years of age, chronic illnesses and disabilities often reduce their quality of life. A measurement called "years of healthy life" estimates the negative impact that quality of life can have on life expectancy. A broad goal of *Healthy People 2000* (USDHHS, 1991) was to increase years of healthy life from 64 years to at least 65 years. Presently, Americans can still expect to live in good health for about 64 years.

life span the maximum number of years that members of a species can expect to live when conditions are optimal.

senescence (seh-NES-ens) the stage of life that begins at age 65 and ends with death.

life expectancy the average number of years that an individual who was born in a particular year can expect to live.

DIVERSITY in Health Hunting for Supercentenarians

Despite the high standard of living and excellent quality of medical care in the United States, few Americans live to be 100 years old. According to verifiable records, no one in the United States has lived longer than 120 years. Yet in certain isolated parts of the world, hundreds of people claim to be more than 120 years old (supercentenarians). Do people who live in these places actually live longer than Americans or the rest of the world's population?

In the first half of this century, reports emerged concerning the extreme longevity of people living in the Hunza area of Northern Pakistan, in the village of Vilcabamba in Ecuador, and in the Caucasus region in the Eastern European country of Georgia. Scientists visited these regions to question the very old people and determine factors that were associated with their extreme longevity. After interviewing the oldest people in these regions, some experts concluded that living in an isolated and unpolluted rural environment, eating a simple nutritious diet, avoiding the use of alcohol and tobacco, and maintaining an active daily schedule were the keys to superlongevity.

By the 1970s, however, the real story began to unfold concerning the existence of the so-called supercentenarians. As some investigators returned to locate and interview the same old people that they had met previously, their elderly subjects gave ages that did not match. For example, if 5 years had lapsed since the first interview, instead of being 5 years older, the old person reported being 7 or 10 years older. It did not take researchers long to realize that these elderly people typically inflated their ages. How could so many people have been fooled into believing that supercentenarians existed?

It is difficult to verify the ages of very old individuals who live in rural, underdeveloped places. During the 1800s birth records that could document the ages of very elderly persons were not kept, or they were destroyed. In some cases, investigators initially believed the authenticity of an extremely old individual's birth record, but later rejected it after determining that the person shared the name of a long-dead ancestor who was the rightful owner of the document. Even if individuals claiming to be extremely old have their birth records, the documents' value is questionable because birth dates can be altered.

Why would elderly people add years to their actual ages? In many isolated and impoverished places, conditions are not ideal for enjoying a lengthy life. Aged members of these populations know that the longer they live, the more fame, respect, and status they can expect to receive from younger members of the population. Government officials often do little to refute citizens' astounding superlongevity claims because the notoriety attracts a steady stream of curious international visitors whose money supports the local economy.

Scientists who study individuals who claim to be supercentenarians think that their subjects are old, but not that old. They may be over 80 years of age, but few are over age 90. Thus, no convincing evidence exists that supports the amazing longevity claims of supercentenarians. Many people, however, persistently believe stories that there are concentrations of extremely old people living in certain regions of the world.

Although communities of supercentenarians do not exist, a few people do live longer than 100 years. At present, researchers are conducting studies that may determine why they outlive the rest of the population.

www.jbpub.com/healthyliving

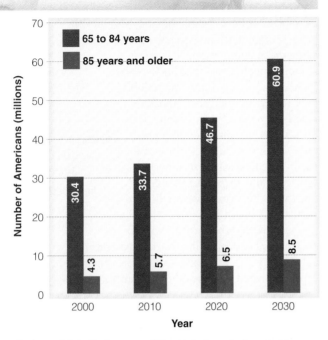

▲Figure 15-2 **Estimates of the U.S. Population 65 Years of Age and Older in 2000, 2010, 2020, and 2030.** The number of people living in the United States is expected to increase significantly in the next 30 years. Source: National Center for Health Statistics. *Health, United States, 1999.* Hyattsville, MD: US Department of Health and Human Services.

The Characteristics of Aged Americans

About 13% of the U.S. population is 65 years of age and older (Kamimoto et al., 1999). These older Americans comprise the fastest growing segment of the population. Much of this growth reflects the aging of the baby-boom generation. Between the mid-1940s and the mid-1960s, the birthrate was unusually high in the United States. As a result, experts estimate that 22% of the U.S. population will be 65 years and older by the year 2030.

The majority of Americans over 65 years of age own their homes or live with family members, and they can handle their financial matters and manage various daily living activities such as bathing, dressing, and cooking. Many older adults with mild physical disabilities live independently by making some adaptations to their homes. For example, installing elevated toilets, grab-bars, and shower seats makes it easier for people with physical conditions such as arthritis to take care of their personal hygiene (■ Figure 15-3). In 1997 about 4% of Americans 65 years of age and older lived in nursing homes, but almost 20% of people older than 85 years lived in these facilities (National Center for Health Statistics [NCHS], 1999).

In 1999 about 1 million Americans were 90 years of age or older; this population is increasing so rapidly, experts think 10 million will be in this age group by 2050 (Glass et al., 1999). People who are 85 years of age and older, the

"oldest of the old," are more likely to be severely disabled and impoverished than the "young old" who are 65 to 74 years of age.

A significant number of the elderly are independent and financially secure, often because they planned for their retirement needs when they were young. Today, fewer older Americans live in poverty than in the late 1960s, thanks largely to federal programs such as Social Security, Medicaid, and Medicare. Nevertheless, many elderly people must live on lower incomes than when they were younger. In 1997 10% of older adults lived in families with incomes that were less than the federal government's poverty line (NCHS, 1999). Elderly members of minority groups, particularly African Americans and Latinos, are more likely to have lower retirement incomes and live in poverty than elderly White people.

While some of their expenses are less because they are no longer working, health-care costs of retirees are generally higher than those of younger individuals. People who are 65 years of age and older comprise only 13% of the population but they account for 35% of personal health-care expenditures in the United States (Desai & Zhang, 1999). *Medicare,* a federal health insurance program that provides benefits for people over 65 years of age, does not pay for every medical expense. Thus, elderly people must often buy additional health insurance. The cost of

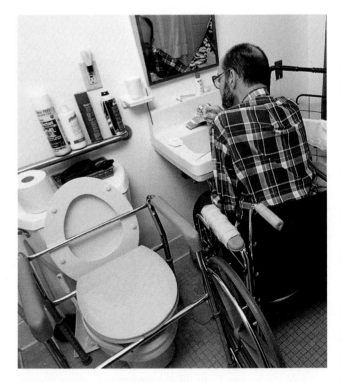

▲Figure 15-3 **Independent Living.** By adding certain features to their homes, older adults with physical disabilities are able to live independently.

health care is not a barrier to health care for most elderly Americans. However, people with low incomes and less education are more likely to report difficulty paying for medical expenses not covered by insurance (Kamimoto et al., 1999). Without adequate insurance, serious chronic health conditions can drain the financial resources of older adults and their families.

Why Do We Age?

Scientists have proposed several theories to explain why people grow old. According to some aging theories, preset biological clocks control the timing of aging which explains why some people look younger or older than their chronological ages. Although no specific clocklike structures have been identified in the body, various internal factors seem to determine when certain physiological events or developmental processes occur. For example, in young persons, several hormones control the timing of puberty; in women, menopause results when the production of certain hormones declines at a predictable age.

Numerous cellular events also occur in an expected manner. For example, body cells can divide a specific number of times. After dividing its maximum number of times, a cell dies. Most tissues produce a surplus of cells, so they can afford the death of some cells. As people age, however, the rate of new cell production in tissues normally slows and the number of living cells declines as existing cells die.

People age at different rates. A person's *chronological age,* as measured in years, may not match his or her *physiological age,* as measured in functional ability. For example, some people begin to experience the physical changes of aging earlier than average; they look, act, and feel older than others who are the same chronological age. Inheritance probably accounts for some of this variation, but external factors such as environment and lifestyle also influence the aging process.

Exposure to certain environmental conditions can damage genes, the hereditary material that is found in most cells. Genes are chemical instructions that control the production of vital proteins in cells. Damaged genes make mistakes in copying and transferring information concerning protein production. Young cells can correct many of these errors, but aging cells are less efficient at correcting such mistakes. When the parts of cells that manufacture proteins receive faulty instructions from the genes, they are unable to produce these compounds. Without an adequate supply of proteins, the affected cells eventually die.

An organ fails if it does not contain enough functioning cells. The systems of the body are interrelated, so when the organs of one system fail, the organs of the other systems soon lose their functional capacities. For example, when a heart that has been weakened by disease cannot pump blood efficiently, the lungs and kidneys are not be able to function properly. As a result, other organs fail to perform their jobs, and death occurs.

Radiation, pollution, and some drugs and viruses may damage genes, thereby accelerating the rate of aging and shortening life expectancy. By limiting contact or exposure to these agents, you may be able to lengthen your life expectancy. Furthermore, adopting lifestyles that include regular exercise and that avoid smoking can reduce your risk of heart disease and cancer. Eating more fruits and vegetables may lower your risk of cancer also. The "Changing Health Habits" feature of this and the other chapters can help you identify and change unhealthy practices (see student workbook).

The Effects of Aging on Physical Health

People begin to experience a gradual and irreversible decline in the functioning of their bodies when they are about 30 years old. Even healthy people experience this progressive decline as they grow older. Some common signs of aging such as menopause, delayed sexual responsiveness, graying and thinning hair, loss of height, and *presbyopia,* the inability to see close objects clearly, reflect normal changes associated with growing old. ▌ **Table 15-1** describes some significant physical changes that are associated with normal senescence. As you can see, growing old affects every system of the body.

Aging is an individual process. There is no timetable that specifies at what age people can expect a particular physical change to occur. The rate at which these alterations occur, however, accelerates after 65 years of age. As a result of these normal changes, the aging body is less able to adapt to stress, repair itself, and resist or fight infection. Infections and accidents that were minor health problems when a person was young can become disabling or deadly experiences when a person is old. Additionally, people over 65 years of age are more likely than younger people to have at least one serious health problem, such as cardiovascular disease, hypertension, osteoporosis, or cancer. These disorders are associated with lifestyles and are preventable to some extent. Previous chapters discuss cardiovascular disease, hypertension, osteoporosis, and cancer in depth.

Although certain chronic health problems such as cataracts, glaucoma, arthritis, and urinary incontinence commonly affect elderly people, they are not normal aspects of aging. These ailments may not be life-threatening, but they frequently reduce the quality of life. ▌ **Table 15-2** lists some chronic disorders that are prevalent among the aged population and the percentages of men and women affected by them in 1995.

Cataracts Although the reasons for their occurrence are unclear, **cataracts** are common in people over 50 years of age. A cararact forms when the normally transparent

cataracts a chronic condition in which the lens of the eye becomes cloudy and opaque, impairing vision.

lens of the eye becomes cloudy and opaque with aging. Clouded lenses scatter light as it enters the eyes, making it difficult to see images clearly. Symptoms of cataracts include blurry and double vision, sensitivity to bright light, and seeing halos around objects. Without surgery to remove damaged lenses, cataracts can lead to blindness. In many cases, surgeons can replace natural lenses with artificial ones; in others, they remove the damaged lenses and prescribe eyeglasses or contact lenses.

Some medical experts think that exposure to ultraviolet light can cause cataracts. You may be able to prevent cataracts by wearing sunglasses to shield your eyes.

glaucoma
(glaw-KO-mah) a chronic ailment that occurs when fluid pressure increases in the eye.

arthritis a group of diseases characterized by inflammation of the joints.

Glaucoma **Glaucoma** is another ailment that frequently affects the vision of aged people. In this condition, an abnormal amount of fluid accumulates in the eyeball. Over time, the high fluid pressure causes vision loss by permanently damaging the optic nerve, the nerve that transmits visual information to the brain. Eye pain, headache, and loss of peripheral vision are symptoms of glaucoma. Risk factors for developing glaucoma include family history, African ancestry, diabetes, and cardiovascular disease. In most cases, placing medicinal drops into the eyes can control the condition.

Glaucoma may not produce noticeable symptoms; therefore, early detection is the best way to control the effects of the disorder. A simple, painless screening test is available that can identify the disease before serious damage to the optic nerve occurs. Thus, you can prevent the irreversible

Table 15-1 Biological Effects of Normal Aging

System	Normal Changes
Cardiovascular	Heart function remains normal, but the heart muscle thickens; arterial walls thicken; pulse rate declines
Skeletal	Bone loss occurs, which can be abnormal if excessive (osteoporosis)
Nervous	Brain weight decreases, especially in the cerebral cortex; neurotransmitter levels decline, nervous message transmission and muscular responses slow; short-term memory becomes less efficient; visual and hearing ability decreases; the ability to taste bitter and salty foods declines; sleep disturbances, such as taking longer to fall asleep and frequent awakening during the night, often occur
Immune	Immune response against pathogens or developing cancer cells declines
Endocrine	Many hormone levels decline, including insulin (regulates carbohydrate metabolism), aldosterone (regulates sodium metabolism), and thyroid, estrogen, and growth hormones
Digestive	Tooth loss becomes more likely as gums recede; levels of stomach acid drop; intestinal absorption of calcium is less efficient; constipation can occur, often the result of medications or poor diet
Muscular	Muscle mass declines, resulting in less strength; stamina reduction occurs
Reproductive	Menopause occurs in women, resulting in thinning of vaginal lining, less vaginal lubrication, and shrinkage of reproductive organs; breast tissue shrinks; prostate glands enlarge in men; sexual responsiveness slows so that it takes longer for erections to occur; orgasms are shorter and less intense
Urinary	Kidneys become less efficient at filtering wastes from the blood
Skin (integument)	Skin becomes drier and less elastic, resulting in wrinkles; scalp hair growth slows, and its loss increases; hair growth in the nose and ears increases; fingernails often become yellow, develop ridges, and split

Table 15-2	Chronic Conditions Associated with Aging by Age and Sex: 1995			
Condition	Males (%) 65 to 74 years	Males (%) 75 and older	Females (%) 65 to 74 years	Females (%) 75 and older
Arthritis	38.6	43.7	49.8	61.6
Hypertension	35.2	34.5	42.4	46.5
Hearing impairment	33.3	42.4	15.9	30.7
Heart conditions	31.6	43.9	22.9	31.8
Cataracts	7.2	21.4	13.2	24.7
Diabetes	13.1	10.1	13.4	12.1

Source: U.S. Bureau of the Census (1998). *Statistical abstract of the United States: 1998* (118th ed.). Washington, DC: U.S. Government Printing Office.

effects of glaucoma by having a physician or optometrist perform periodic screenings.

Arthritis Arthritis is a broad group of chronic joint diseases characterized by inflammation, pain, swelling, and loss of mobility ("stiffness") of affected joints. Half of all older adults have some form of arthritis (Hwang et al., 1999). In *osteoarthritis,* the cartilage that protects the ends of bones and keeps them from rubbing together at joints wears away and breaks down. As a result, tiny bits of cartilage or bone float in the fluid that fills the joint and the joint becomes misshapen (■ **Figure 15-4).** People often confuse osteoarthritis with *osteoporosis,* a different condition that affects older adults. Information about osteoporosis is in Chapter 9.

Aging is the strongest risk factor for osteoarthritis (Mankin & Brandt, 1997). Joints simply wear out as a person ages. Other contributing factors include heredity, overuse, injury, and obesity. Overuse and injury of joints can occur when performing sports or jobs that place stress on joints. Obese older adults have a high risk of developing osteoarthritis, because carrying around extra weight stresses joints, especially the knees.

The symptoms of osteoarthritis tend to come and go. Treatment includes medications to relieve inflammation and pain, and exercises to strengthen muscles and improve or maintain joint mobility. Losing weight reduces stress on weight-bearing joints in obese people. In some cases, surgery is necessary to replace damaged joints with artificial implants.

Urinary Incontinence **Urinary incontinence,** the inability to control the flow of urine from the bladder, is an embarrassing and costly problem for an estimated 7.5 million Americans (Wagner & Hu, 1998). As people age, the muscles that control bladder emptying weaken, making it easier for urine to leak out when they move, sneeze, cough, or

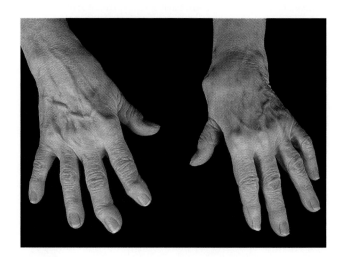

▲**Figure 15-4 Effects of Arthritis on the Hands.** Arthritis damages joint tissue, resulting in deformities and the loss of flexibility.

lift heavy things. Additionally, many older adults experience involuntary contractions of their bladders that cause some urine to be eliminated unexpectedly. Medications, infections, strokes, tumors, history of childbirth in women, and enlargement of the prostate gland in men can contribute to urinary incontinence.

The fear of leaking urine accidentally while in public makes many incontinent people avoid social situations. In severe cases, family members cannot manage the incontinent elderly relative, and they find it necessary to place him or her in a nursing home.

urinary incontinence the inability to control the flow of urine from the bladder.

The majority of individuals who experience urinary incontinence can benefit from treatment, such as behavioral techniques that enable them to be more aware of the bladder's state of fullness. By learning to empty the bladder more frequently, a person may be able to avoid the leakage. Furthermore, people can learn and practice a series of exercises that strengthen the pelvic muscles that control urination. These exercises, the *Kegel exercises,* involve imitating the muscular movements that individuals make when they voluntarily stop urinating. Incontinent people can also wear absorbent pads and undergarments designed to prevent embarrassing incidents of urine leakage. Medication and surgery may alleviate incontinence. Embarrassment or concerns about surgery, however, keep many incontinent people from discussing this common problem with health-care practitioners.

Alzheimer's Disease You cannot find your keys; you forget an appointment; you sometimes call your child by your cat's name. Do you ever have the feeling that you are losing your mind? It may be reassuring to know that everyone has these and other similar annoying experiences from time to time, but many middle-aged Americans worry that instances of forgetfulness are early symptoms of Alzheimer's disease.

About 4 million Americans, mostly elderly, have Alzheimer's disease, a severe degenerative disorder that affects the brain (Howarth et al., 1999). By the year 2030, experts predict that 9 million Americans will suffer from this dreaded disorder. Alzheimer's disease is the most common form of *age-related dementia;* strokes and Parkinson's disease are also major causes of age-related dementia. Memory loss, mental confusion, and loss of control over behavior and body functions are characteristics of Alzheimer's disease.

The incidence of Alzheimer's disease increases with advancing age. An estimated 5% to 7% of people over 65 years of age have the condition; this percentage increases to 40% of people over 85 years old (Howarth et al., 1999). Although the disease is common among the elderly, it is not a normal feature of growing old. What are signs of Alzheimer's disease? Is it preventable?

In the early stages of Alzheimer's, affected people may notice lapses in their memories and intellectual abilities. These symptoms usually begin between the ages of 40 and 60. Over time, people with the disease become increasingly forgetful, confused, restless, and moody. Communicating becomes difficult as their speech deteriorates; depression is common. These changes are distressing to patients with Alzheimer's disease, their family members, and their associates. One woman recalls her affected mother-in-law's gradual loss of cognitive functioning:

> Looking back to the days before the diagnosis, I see a pattern of behaviors that held no significance—just mild irritation. Often she would ask me to make a decision for her: what blouse to buy, where to stop for lunch, or what to order from the menu. Forgetfulness is the most noticeable symptom, but confusion seemed the most troublesome to

her. Early on she would cover her forgetfulness by pretending to tease me when I corrected her. She could not tease away the confusion. As her ability to remember details decreased, her confusion and inability to make decisions increased. Much like grieving, she moved past teasing to denial then anger, mostly at herself for being a bother.

As Alzheimer's disease progresses, its victims neglect their personal hygiene, and they exhibit inappropriate and unpredictable behaviors such as undressing in public and attacking caretakers. In the terminal stages, individuals with this devastating illness are bedridden, unable to talk and eat. Alzheimer's patients require constant care. Nothing can be done to stop the relentless progression of the disease. After diagnosis, the affected person can expect to survive about 8 to 12 years. Death often results from pneumonia and starvation as the degenerating brain is unable to control vital functions such as breathing, swallowing, and digestion. In 1998 more than 22,500 Americans over the age of 65 died of Alzheimer's disease, making it the ninth leading cause of death for people in this age group (Martin et al., 1999).

The factors that cause Alzheimer's disease are unclear, and many health experts think that the condition cannot be prevented. At least two forms of the disorder are inherited. Although genetic testing is available to determine whether relatives of patients with Alzheimer's have the genes associated with the disease, many people who test positive do not develop the disease. Other forms of Alzheimer's disease may be the result of slow-acting brain viruses, brain injury, or exposure to pollutants. At one time, scientists thought that aluminum poisoning caused the disease because they found higher than normal amounts of this metal in the brains of patients who died of Alzheimer's. Many people are concerned about the safety of using aluminum cookware and the natural presence of this element in drinking water. Most experts think that the unusual concentration of aluminum in the brains of people with Alzheimer's disease is a result of the disorder and not its cause.

Physicians often diagnose Alzheimer's disease when patients cannot answer questions like those listed in ▌ Table 15-3. However, the only way to confirm the diagnosis is by examining the patient's brain after death. In advanced cases, the cerebral cortex, the thinking part of the brain, has shrunk considerably. Upon microscopic examination, the affected regions of the brain usually contain abnormal protein deposits called *senile plaques* and nerve cells with tangled masses of useless material.

Although Alzheimer's disease is incurable, medications can control some of the behavior of patients with the disease and improve their mood. Researchers are testing the usefulness of other treatments, such as anti-inflammatory agents, vitamin E, and an extract of the leaves of the ginkgo tree, to determine if these substances can prevent the disease or slow or stop its progression.

Table 15-3	Simple Memory Test for Identifying Dementia

Ask the person

1. his or her age
2. his or her date of birth
3. the time to the nearest hour
4. his or her address
5. the current year
6. where he or she is
7. the names of two people who are pictured in family photos
8. the years of World War II
9. the name of the current president of the United States
10. to count backwards from 20 to 1

Source: Adapted from Wattis, J. (1996). What an old age psychiatrist does. *British Medical Journal, 313*:101-104.

Women often experience memory loss around menopause, the time when levels of the female hormone estrogen decline dramatically. Thus, scientists suspect estrogen protects brain cells. Estrogen replacement therapy may delay the onset and reduce the risk of Alzheimer's disease (Davis, 1999). Additional research is needed to determine if estrogen therapy is safe and effective for people at risk for Alzheimer's disease.

Patients with Alzheimer's can live at home until they reach the terminal stage and require the skilled care provided in nursing homes. Living with an affected loved one is emotionally stressful and physically demanding. While caring for a patient with this disease, family members must try to maintain their own health and well-being. To provide assistance, many communities have nursing homes or special centers where persons with Alzheimer's disease can spend a few hours during the day before returning to their homes. Not every community or nursing home offers this service, so if you need help caring for someone with Alzheimer's disease, check with your local mental health association or Alzheimer's Association for information about adult day care centers in your area. The "Analyzing Health-Related Information" feature on pages 384 to 385 involves evaluating excerpts of an article about Alzheimer's disease.

The Effects of Aging on Psychological Health

As they approach the end of middle age, most employed people face retirement, and many aging parents have grown children with families who have moved away. If older adults equate retirement from jobs and separation from their families with being old and useless, they may experience serious psychological distress. Additionally, the dramatic reduction of financial resources that often accompanies retirement can mean a serious loss of economic stability.

Many older adults began planning for their future financial security while they were young. Therefore, not every older adult dreads the prospect of retiring from job and family responsibilities. Many people approach retirement with a positive outlook and look forward to this time of life. Retired individuals often find pleasure from traveling, volunteering in their communities, caring for their grandchildren, and exploring new interests. Other retirement-age adults choose to continue working, especially if they enjoy what they do and their work is intellectually stimulating and personally fulfilling. The elderly often have a wealth of knowledge and experience that they can share with younger members of society.

Elderly people, especially those over 85 years of age, frequently experience deteriorating health, difficult social circumstances, and poor economic conditions. Deaths of spouses and friends, separations from family, and reductions in financial resources create emotional stress. As a result, the elderly often suffer depression. Like younger people, depressed or isolated aged individuals can benefit from participation in social and physical activities. In addition, antidepressant medications or psychotherapy may be necessary to help them regain their emotional balance.

The Effects of Aging on Social Health

Although a large segment of the U.S. population is over 65 years old, our society is highly youth-oriented. Not surprisingly, middle-age Americans often worry that aging will mean losing their jobs to younger people, being forced into early retirement, becoming widowed, and suffering from debilitating illnesses. Growing old in America can have serious social impacts on the elderly; they may be ignored, neglected, and abused by younger members of the population.

ageism a bias against elderly people.

Some people in our society have negative attitudes toward the elderly. For example, they stereotype elderly people as poor, sick, useless, and dependent. Additionally, some young adults believe that the elderly demand too much from the rest of society. **Ageism** is a bias against the elderly. Ageism creates conflict between the generations because the old do not trust the young and vice versa. To combat ageism, people need to recognize that growing old does not always mean having poor health, living in an institution, depending on public support, and being useless.

Elderly Americans represent a valuable social asset that is not well used. Aging parents and grandparents often have experience and wisdom that they can share with

ANALYZING *Health-Related Information*

The following article is an abbreviated version of "Alzheimer's: Few Clues on the Mysteries of Memory" that appeared in *FDA Consumer* magazine. Read the article and evaluate it using the model for analyzing health-related information. The main points of the model are noted below; the model is fully explained on pages 12 to 13.

Alzheimer's
Few Clues on the Mysteries of Memory

by Audrey T. Hingley

It happened some years ago but the memory is still firmly implanted in my mind. One sunny afternoon I heard the sound of a car pulling into our driveway, peered out of my living room window, and saw one of my father's friends, Sam (not his real name), then in his early 80s. Sam got out of his car and walked just a few steps. I watched as he stood for a few moments, gazing at our house with an expressionless face. Then he silently returned to his car, got in, and drove away, without ever knocking on our door or communicating with us in any way.

I thought the incident puzzling, but it wasn't until months later that I learned the reason for it. Sam had Alzheimer's, a progressive disease in which nerve cells in the brain degenerate and brain substance shrinks.

A widower living alone, Sam clearly was in a dangerous position. Once he was followed home by a police officer, who told his grown children he had found Sam stopped by the side of the road, not able to remember how to get home by himself.

Sam's story is being played out in the lives of up to 4 million Americans who suffer from Alzheimer's disease. The disease plays no favorites, attacking rich and poor, famous and ordinary. Among its most famous sufferers: former President Ronald Reagan.

With an average lifetime cost of care per patient of $174,000, it is the third most expensive disease in America, following only heart disease and cancer. But perhaps even more staggering than the monetary costs are the emo-tional and psychological costs borne by both patients and their families.

"People are very frightened of the possibilities because they know it represents a loss of one's self," says Steven T. DeKosky, M.D., director of the Alzheimer's Disease Research Center at the University of Pittsburgh and a practicing neurologist. "It's a very frightening prospect to see a loved one who looks the same but doesn't talk or act the same."

"I Have Lost Myself"

Alzheimer's disease, a progressive, degenerative disease attacking the brain and resulting in impaired thinking, behavior and memory, was first described by Alois Alzheimer, M.D., in 1906. German researchers recently found an important set of notes from Alzheimer's journal of the world's first documented case of the disease. The patient exhibited many of the symptoms seen in Alzheimer's patients today. But perhaps most poignant of all is the patient's own description of the disease: "I have lost myself."

In Alzheimer's, nerve cells in the part of the brain responsible for memory and other thought processes degenerate for still-unknown reasons. Some of the most severely affected cells normally use acetylcholine, a brain chemical, to communicate. Tacrine (brand name Cognex, also called THA), the first drug approved by the Food and Drug Administration specifically to treat Alzheimer's disease, works by slowing the breakdown of acetylcholine. This results in relieving some memory impairment.

Tacrine does not cure Alzheimer's or slow the disease's progression. It has only been studied in those with mild to moderate Alzheimer's disease who were otherwise in generally good health. Because tacrine can increase the blood levels of a liver enzyme that can indicate liver damage, regular monitoring is necessary. Other side effects include nausea, vomiting, diarrhea, abdominal pain, skin rash, and indigestion.

Aricept (generic name donepezil hydrochloride, also called E2020), approved by the FDA in 1996, is by far the most used drug for Alzheimer's treatment. Like tacrine, Aricept inhibits the breakdown of acetylcholine but does not cause the kind of increase in liver enzymes that tacrine does. It can also cause diarrhea, vomiting, nausea, fatigue, insomnia, and anorexia, but in most cases, such side effects are mild and decline with continued use of the drug. Again, the drug helps only those patients with mild to moderate symptoms of Alzheimer's and does not stop or slow the disease's progression.

Forgetfulness or Alzheimer's?

While most people understand at least some of the horrifying aspects of Alzheimer's disease, DeKosky says a big challenge is educating people regarding the widely held assumption that people are supposed to have memory impairment as they age.

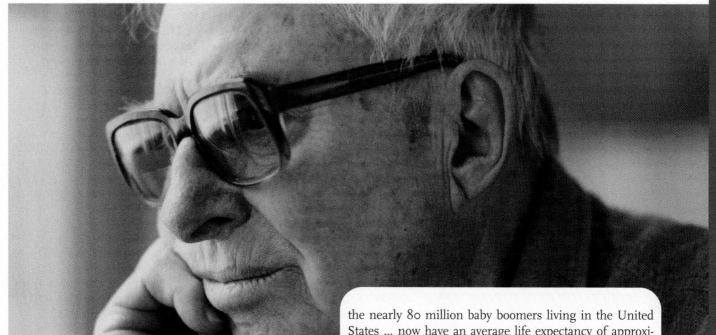

"There's this huge prejudice where we think people should have severe mental impairment as they get older," he says. Memory loss, disorientation, and confusion are not part of the normal aging process, he explains. They are symptoms of dementia, and the most common form of dementia is Alzheimer's.

"You need to look at the functional consequences of what someone cannot remember," DeKosky says. "If mom forgets where she put her car in the parking lot at the mall, that's not abnormal. But if she walks home from the mall because she forgot she took her car, that's not normal. Memory is the first and worst change, but you will also see social withdrawal and less willingness to interact with others."

The Need for Answers

Although no cure for Alzheimer's is available now, planning and medical/social management can help ease the burden on both patient and family members. Physical exercise, good nutrition, and social activities are important. A calm, structured environment may also help the person to continue functioning.

At some point, however, people with Alzheimer's require 24-hour care. The financing of such care, including diagnosis costs, treatment, and paid care, is estimated to be $100 billion annually, according to the Alzheimer's Association. The federal government covers $4.4 billion and the states another $4.1 billion, with much of the remaining costs borne by patients and their families.

"It's a national imperative to find effective means to diagnose, treat and prevent this disease," says David Banks, R.Ph., a public health specialist in the FDA's Office of Special Health Issues. "When you look at it demographically, the nearly 80 million baby boomers living in the United States ... now have an average life expectancy of approximately 78 years.

One in five Americans could be age 65 or older by 2030, and tens of millions of baby boomers will live into their 80s. The Alzheimer's Association projects that as many as 14 million Americans could have Alzheimer's disease in 2050. When viewed in the context of accelerating Social Security and Medicare costs ... , the future monetary costs of Alzheimer's disease may be unsustainable. The human costs could be even greater."

Note: Audrey T. Hingley is a freelance writer in Mechanicsville, Virginia.

1. Which statements are verifiable facts, and which are unverified statements or value claims?
2. What are the credentials of the woman who wrote the article? If this information is available, does her background and education qualify her as an expert in the topic area?
3. What might be the motives and biases of the woman who wrote the article? State reasons for your answer.
4. Which information in the article is relevant to the topic? Which information is irrelevant?
5. Is the source reliable? Does it have a reputation for publishing misinformation?
6. Does the article attack the credibility of conventional scientists or medical authorities?

Based on the above analysis, do you think that this article is a reliable source of health-related information? Explain why you think it is or is not. Summarize your reasons for coming to this conclusion.

younger family members. Additionally, many retirees have a variety of talents and special organizational skills that enable them to serve as consultants, managers, or advisors in business, governmental, or educational settings. Both young and old benefit when each accepts, values, and trusts the other.

Successful Aging

Many people would like to believe that it is possible to prevent aging or delay the process. The modern search for a "fountain of youth" has resulted in the promotion of pills, potions, diets, or treatments that are touted as having "anti-aging" or "life-extending" capabilities. Contrary to the claims of advertisers, none of these substances or regimens prevents or slows aging.

Instead of searching for magic formulas to extend your life, you can take various actions while you are young to increase your chances of aging *successfully*. People who age successfully are in good health, and the final stage of their lives is productive, enjoyable, and satisfying.

To increase your chances of aging successfully, evaluate your health status and lifestyle, identify specific unhealthy or risky behaviors, and then work at changing those behaviors. Although modifying all unhealthy behaviors is commendable, certain practices are associated more closely with lengthening one's life span than others.

Scientists who conduct aging research on animals have consistently found that restricting the animals' caloric intakes without creating nutritional deficiencies slows their rate of aging (Lee et al., 1999). In humans, excess body fat is associated with the increased risk of premature death (Calle et al., 1999). Thus, it is extremely important for you to eat a nutritious, low-fat diet and maintain a weight that is appropriate for your height and body build.

Physically active people live longer than people who are sedentary or become sedentary as they age (Bijnen et al., 1999; Sherman et al., 1999). Engaging in regular exercise throughout your life will help you control your body weight as well as improve your circulation, strengthen your heart, and maintain your muscle and bone mass. People over 65 years of age who perform regular exercise improve their physical strength and flexibility, features that can enhance their quality of living (Mazzeo et al., 1998). Aerobic exercise can even improve some cognitive abilities of aging adults, such as memory, but more research is needed to further support these findings (Kramer et al., 1999).

After studying more than 2700 older adults, Thomas Glass and colleagues (1999) report that aging people can derive significant health benefits from engaging in social and productive activities such as attending religious services and participating in group shopping trips. According to the results of Glass's study, aging adults live longer and better when they are involved in social and meaningful activities.

Table 15-4	Tips for Successful Aging

Taking the following actions now, while you are still young, may help you enjoy a healthier, longer life:

- Maintain a healthy weight and eat a nutritious, low-fat diet that includes plenty of fruits and vegetables.
- Be physically active; exercise daily.
- Do not smoke, drink too much alcohol, or abuse other drugs.
- Manage stress; take time to relax daily.
- Have regular physical examinations.
- Adopt safer sex practices.
- Do not drive while under the influence of alcohol or other drugs; always wear a seat belt in vehicles.
- Protect your skin and eyes from sunlight.
- Obtain enough sleep.
- Be concerned about your safety at home, work, or play.
- Maintain social networks with your family and friends.
- Be flexible; expect changes.
- Develop a positive attitude; have a sense of humor.
- Find opportunities to learn new skills or information.
- Get involved with living while accepting your mortality.

Sources: Adapted from Kerschner, H., & Pegues, J. A. (1998). Productive aging: A quality of life agenda. *Journal of the American Dietetic Association, 98*:1445-1448; and Turner, L. W., Sizer, F. S., Whitney, E. N., & Wilks, B. B. (1992). *Life choices: Health concepts and strategies.* Minneapolis: West Publishing Co.

▌ **Table 15-4** lists some basic recommendations for enhancing your health and quality of life as you age, such as managing stress, maintaining relationships, and developing a positive attitude. The other chapters of this textbook provide more detailed information about these recommendations. It is worth remembering the words of Eubie Blake, a jazz musician who died in 1983 at the age of 100, "If I had known that I was going to live this long, I would have taken better care of myself."

Healthy LIVING PRACTICES

- Planning for your future financial needs while you are still young can help you enjoy your retirement years.
- To age successfully, evaluate your present health and lifestyle, identify risky behaviors, and then consider changing those behaviors.

 www.jbpub.com/healthyliving # Dying

Many Americans, including health professionals, fear dying and death, especially the possibility that dying will be premature and painful. Fearing death makes it difficult to be around someone who is dying. One reason many Americans fear dying and death is that few have had contact with dying persons or dead bodies. Usually an ambulance rushes the critically injured or terminally ill person to a hospital, where he or she is connected to a variety of life-support machines and placed in an intensive care unit (█ Figure 15-5). Most hospitals permit family members to visit the seriously ill patient for only a few minutes each hour. In other instances, elderly or incurably ill patients die in nursing homes with few or no family members present. In the United States, dying often becomes a mechanized, isolated, and depersonalized process.

Dying was very different a hundred years ago. In that era, nearly everyone died at home, surrounded by family and friends. Shortly after death, the body often remained in the home for the funeral ceremony. It was even customary for people to have photographs taken of their deceased loved ones to remember them (█ Figure 15-6). These practices helped survivors accept dying and death as a part of life.

The Spiritual Aspects of Dying

Some people who have been revived after being unresponsive describe "near-death" experiences and relate them as spiritually uplifting events. They report that they were aware of what was happening before they recovered consciousness. They often recall feeling temporarily disengaged from their bodies and having unusual but peaceful sensations. Accounts of near-death experiences often include some features of the person's spiritual or religious

▲ Figure 15-6 Remembrance Photo, Circa 1895. A hundred years ago, nearly everyone died at home, surrounded by their families and friends. It was customary for people to have photographs taken of their deceased loved ones to remember them.

beliefs. People who have been in these situations are often profoundly affected by their experiences, but scientists have no ways of verifying their stories.

People who believe in an afterlife may have less fear of dying and death. Many people believe that a soul exists, which leaves the body after death and goes to heaven or hell. Others believe in *reincarnation,* coming back to life as another person or organism after death. Some individuals are not concerned with what happens to them after death. In many instances, cultural and religious backgrounds provide the foundation for a person's feelings about life after death.

The Emotional Aspects of Dying

Although coping with the death of a beloved person is one of life's most difficult experiences, knowing that your own death is near is especially difficult. In the late 1960s Elisabeth Kübler-Ross, a psychiatrist at the University of Chicago Billings Hospital, pioneered efforts to understand the psychological processes of dying and death (Kübler-Ross, 1969). After interviewing more than 200 terminally ill patients, she formulated a five-stage model to describe the emotional responses that people often experience as they face their deaths (█ Table 15-5).

The first stage of this coping process is *denial.* People in denial may act shocked after receiving news of their terminal condition. Frequently, they do not believe their physician's prognosis. While in denial, dying individuals may ignore their troublesome symptoms or seek more optimistic outlooks from other health-care practitioners. Some dying patients completely lose faith in the value of conventional

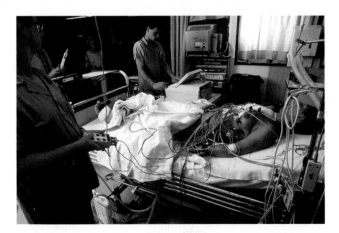

▲ Figure 15-5 Intensive Care. Treatment of a critically injured or terminally ill person may include being connected to a variety of life-support machines in a hospital's intensive care unit.

medical care; some maintain hope of "beating this thing" by using untested alternative treatments.

As the dying begin to accept their situation, they may enter the second stage, *anger.* In this stage, dying people are provoked easily; they may lash out at loved ones, medical staff, and anything or anybody. They often demand to know "Why me? Why not someone else?" It is important for people who care for or visit dying individuals to expect this reaction and not take such anger personally.

The third emotional stage of dying is *bargaining.* Incurably ill individuals may make deals with medical staff or God, promising to exchange exceptionally good behavior for a few more years of life or a painless death. In the fourth stage, *depression,* dying people become increasingly aware that their conditions will not improve. Terminally ill individuals mourn for themselves after realizing that they will not live long enough to enjoy experiences such as watching their children mature or playing with their grandchildren.

The final emotional stage of dying is *acceptance.* Although terminally ill people continue to hope for cures, they accept the possibility that nothing can be done to save them. Friends, family members, and caretakers can help maintain the self-esteem and dignity of the dying by visiting and touching them, as well as by listening to their concerns.

Critics of Kübler-Ross's research charge that she focused on people who were dying prematurely of chronic illnesses and had time to experience each stage. Therefore, her findings may have been different if she had studied people who were dying of acute illnesses or very sick elderly persons. Some people, particularly the elderly, may not experience all five stages of dying. Additionally, aged people who are terminally ill may accept their impending deaths more readily than people who face the prospect of dying while they are still young. The Kübler-Ross model, however, is useful for understanding the complex emotions of dying people.

Dying people are usually under extreme emotional distress. They often feel helpless and hopeless, and they have difficulty relaxing. Treatments such as surgery, chemotherapy, or radiation add to their discomfort. Some terminally ill people fight the prospect of dying; others accept what is happening to them and choose to make the most out of the time they have remaining. In modern societies, death can be the final stage of personal fulfillment if dying people have opportunities to satisfy their social and emotional needs. Thus, some terminally ill people choose to spend more time with their friends and families; others travel far from home.

As the end of life nears, terminally ill people may become more detached from others and the environment. They tend to sleep more often and may lapse in and out of consciousness. When awake or conscious, dying persons may not want to talk as much as they did before reaching this stage. According to Kübler-Ross, dying individuals are almost without feelings; most die without fear. Although the biological mechanisms are not known, some terminally ill people seem to be able to control the timing of their deaths (Phillips & Smith, 1990).

When you know that a beloved person is dying, you may experience a variety of intense emotions. You may be afraid of enduring the emotional pain of watching a close friend or relative die. You may be angry at the dying person, physicians, or God because you feel they are responsible for the impending death, or they are unable or unwilling to prevent it. You may feel guilty about your feelings toward the dying individual. Recognizing that someone is terminally ill forces us to face the reality that we will someday die.

Family and friends of a dying person typically feel helpless and intensely sad. As a result, they may avoid the person because such feelings are difficult to hide and uncomfortable to bear. This reaction does little to boost the dying person's dignity and sense of well-being. Being avoided makes the dying person feel isolated and rejected at a time when he or she usually has a high need for the compassionate support and comfort of others.

Physicians and family members have become increasingly aware that positive thinking, including hopefulness, can improve the well-being of the dying. Meeting the emotional and spiritual needs of terminally ill persons can help them live better while dying. Many physicians ac-

Table 15-5	Kübler-Ross's Stages of Emotional Responses to Dying
Stage	**Typical Responses**
Denial	Feels emotionally numb, avoids thinking about his or her condition, ignores the reality of his or her condition
Anger	Lashes out at health-care practitioners and loved ones
Bargaining	Makes deals with health-care practitioners, loved ones, or God to live long enough to do special things or experience certain events
Depression	Mourns his or her own impending death, withdraws socially
Acceptance	Realizes that his or her condition is terminal, gives away cherished items, makes funeral plans

Source: Compiled with information from Kübler-Ross, E. (1969). *On death and dying.* New York: MacMillan Co.

tively seek the participation of their seriously ill patients and their families in decisions concerning treatment. Health-care practitioners can enhance the dignity and self-worth of dying patients by discussing the serious nature of their conditions with them, listening carefully to their concerns, and allowing them to make decisions regarding their medical care.

Terminal Care: The Options

The majority of Americans die in hospitals or nursing homes. The goal of hospital-based health care is to provide technologically sophisticated medical care that enables sick people to become well. Since hospital care is costly, elderly patients who are too ill or frail to return home often move into nursing homes. Nursing homes offer less comprehensive medical care than hospitals, but they are designed and equipped to manage the long-term care of people recovering from surgery or illness. Not every condition is curable; many chronically ill patients die while residing in these facilities.

Choosing to place an aged parent or relative into a nursing home is often an emotionally difficult decision. Family members may have to select an available facility quickly and without researching their options. The "Consumer Health" feature "Choosing a Nursing Home" below lists some important questions to answer when selecting a nursing home.

When patients have only a few months to live, their personal physicians may refer them to **hospice.** Hospice is health care specifically designed to give emotional support and pain relief to terminally ill people in the final stage of life. This care may be provided in the patient's home or in a hospice center. The primary goal of hospice care is not to save dying patients with aggressive treatments but to relieve their discomfort. Hospice physicians often prescribe powerful medications to keep terminally ill patients as free from pain as possible. Freedom from extreme pain permits the dying person to manage his or her activities more effectively and die with dignity.

Hospice staff receive specialized training to work closely with and to provide emotional and spiritual support to dying patients and their families. Staff encourage patients and their relatives to participate in decision making regarding care. Most terminally ill people and their families can obtain hospice services in their homes from a team of medical professionals. Family members are taught simple medical procedures such as care of surgical wounds or maintenance of feeding tubes. Hospice nurses make home visits to check patients' conditions and are available to answer questions concerning their care. Dying at home allows patients to remain in a comfortable and familiar environment where they can participate in holiday and other family-oriented events.

Some dying patients receive hospice care in clinical settings that have rooms designed to look more like patients'

hospice
(HOS-piss) health care specifically designed to give emotional support and pain relief to terminally ill people in the final stage of life.

Con$umer Health | Choosing a Nursing Home

The most important feature to consider when choosing a nursing home is the quality of care that it provides. Before making this decision for a loved one, visit a few facilities, observe the condition of the buildings, its rooms, and residents, and answer the following questions:

1. Is the facility licensed by the state?
2. Is the facility clean, well maintained, and free of objectionable odors?
3. Are staff members friendly, helpful, and respectful to visitors and residents?
4. Are the rooms clean, comfortably furnished, well lit, and cheerful?
5. Do the residents appear to be appropriately dressed, clean, and well groomed?
6. Are there enough staff members to take care of the number of residents?
7. Are there handrails along the hallways and grab-bars in the bathrooms?
8. Does the facility have rehabilitation and exercise areas, a quiet place with reading material, and a chapel?
9. Does the facility have an activities director and scheduled social events that are appropriate for elderly people?
10. Are the dining room and kitchen areas clean?
11. Are menus nutritious? Do menus indicate that a variety of foods are offered? Can you sample a meal? How are the special dietary needs of patients handled?
12. If you have an opportunity, ask some residents (privately) what they like and dislike about the nursing home.
13. What are the monthly fees? Can you afford this nursing home?

Before making a final decision, visit the nursing home at least one additional time to make another set of observations.

Source: Adapted from Goldsmith, S. B. (1990). *Choosing a nursing home.* New York: Prentice-Hall Press.

homes than hospitals. The staff encourage patients to decorate their rooms with favorite possessions to foster a homelike environment. Visiting family and friends provide additional social, emotional, and spiritual support and often participate in caring for their ill loved ones. Regardless of whether the terminally ill person dies at home or in a hospice center, hospice staff provide grief counseling services for survivors.

As the popularity of hospice care in the United States grows, many nursing homes and hospitals are offering hospice services that are covered by health insurance plans. To find such resources in your community, contact local hospitals or check the Yellow Pages under Hospice. Social workers in these facilities can provide information about local support groups for the terminally ill and their families. The National Hospice Organization can also provide information about hospice programs in your area; this group's toll-free phone number is 800-658-8898.

www.jbpub.com/healthyliving

Death

Many people have a difficult time thinking about and discussing death. For example, they may avoid using the term *died*, preferring to use euphemisms such as *passed away*. Whether people believe in an afterlife or not, most are reluctant to handle matters concerning their own dying and death, such as preparing a will or signing an organ donor card.

What Is Death?

Death, the cessation of life, occurs when the heart or lungs stop functioning. When this happens, no oxygen is available for metabolism, and brain cells begin to die. Within 4 to 5 minutes, the dying person loses consciousness. As remaining body cells die, other signs of death become obvious.

When a person dies, the muscles that control voluntary and involuntary movements no longer function. As a result, the body eliminates the contents of the bladder and rectum, and reflexes are absent. *Reflexes* are neuromuscular responses that do not require thinking, such as eye blinking. Gradually, skeletal muscles become rigid, and body temperature cools until it matches that of the environment. Unless the body is treated with embalming chemicals, it decomposes. Decomposition occurs because the immune system no longer prevents bacteria and other microorganisms from breaking down the organic material of the body.

The physician who attended the dying patient is usually responsible for certifying that the patient has died. Then

death the cessation of life, which occurs soon after a person's heart or lungs stop functioning.

autopsy various medical examinations and tests that usually can determine the cause of death.

the medical staff informs family members. In most cases, they deliver the body to a funeral home or medical school, according to the deceased person's wishes. If there are any questions or suspicions about the cause of death, the family, physicians, or coroner can request an **autopsy.** During an autopsy, medical experts conduct various medical examinations and tests that usually determine the cause of death.

In 1968 a team of experts at the Harvard Medical School (Ad Hoc Committee, 1968) defined death according to four irreversible physical criteria:

- The absence of electrical activity in the brain
- No spontaneous muscular movements, including breathing
- No reflexes
- No responses to the environment

These criteria define what is commonly referred to as *brain death*. The majority of state laws recognize these criteria as the basis for defining death. A legal definition of death is important for criminal cases that involve murder. Defining death is especially important for physicians who need to establish that patients are dead before removing any tissues or organs for transplantation.

Since the 1980s advances in medical technology have made it necessary for medical experts to reconsider the traditional definition of death. By using cardiopulmonary resuscitation (CPR), respirators (devices that assist breathing), and feeding machines, health-care practitioners can often save the lives of certain seriously ill persons, and in some instances, may sustain patients who have virtually no chance of recovering.

Cerebral Death The *cerebral cortex* of the brain controls thoughts, interprets sensory information, and integrates voluntary muscular activities. Individuals who experience severe damage to the cerebral cortex are *comatose*, that is, unresponsive to their environments. If the damage is irreversible, it is unlikely that the person will regain consciousness. In some comatose patients, the areas of the brain that control and regulate vital activities, including digestion and breathing, continue to function. Although their conditions do not meet the standard criteria for brain death, such individuals have experienced *cerebral death*. With specialized care, a person with a nonfunctioning cerebral cortex can exist in an irreversible coma, a *persistent vegetative state,* for years.

The level of care required to maintain patients in persistent vegetative states is stressful for their families, as well as expensive. Under what circumstances can physicians remove life-sustaining care from a patient in an irreversible coma? The U.S. Supreme Court decision in the Quinlan case provides an answer.

In 1975 Karen Ann Quinlan, a 21-year-old New Jersey woman, was hospitalized in an unconscious state after al-

▶**Figure 15-7 Karen Ann Quinlan.** In 1975, Karen Ann Quinlan was hospitalized in an unconscious state after allegedly consuming a combination of alcohol and tranquilizers. When Karen's physicians refused to remove her life-support system at the request of her parents, the ensuing court battles focused national attention on the right-to-die issue.

legedly consuming a combination of alcohol and tranquilizers (▌ **Figure 15-7**). After realizing that she would not recover, Ms. Quinlan's parents requested that the medical staff and hospital administrators allow their daughter to die by disconnecting her respirator. However, the administrators and attending physicians denied the parents' request, noting that the young woman was not dead according to established criteria.

After lower state courts supported the hospital's position, the Quinlans took their daughter's case to the New Jersey Supreme Court. In 1976 this court ruled that since Karen had previously told her mother and some friends that she would not want to live in a persistent vegetative state, her parents had the right to ask physicians to remove her respirator. After being removed gradually from the ventilation device, Karen was able to breathe without the machine's assistance, but she continued to be fed through tubes. The Quinlans moved their comatose daughter to a nursing home, where she died 10 years later.

Since the Quinlan case, several states have passed laws that establish steps for withholding or removing life-sustaining care in similar cases involving the terminally ill. A later section of this chapter describes how you can inform other people in advance about your wishes concerning such medical care.

Euthanasia and the Right to Die

Euthanasia is the practice of allowing permanently comatose or incurably ill persons to die. In cases of *active* euthanasia, physicians hasten the deaths of dying people by giving them large doses of pain-relieving medications that can completely suppress breathing. *Passive* euthanasia involves cases in which terminally ill people die because health-care practitioners do not provide life-sustaining treatments, or they withdraw such care.

Since the Quinlan case, the courts have decided several right-to-die cases, particularly those involving people who were seriously ill but not dying. Some chronically ill individuals decide that life is not worth living, or that they are tired of living in pain. To hasten death, these people may refuse life-prolonging medical treatment, demand that it be withdrawn, or remove it themselves. In recent years, the courts often have made or upheld decisions that give such seriously ill people the right to die. After physicians discontinued their life support, many of these patients died naturally within a couple of weeks.

In some instances, the seriously ill person is too physically or mentally incapacitated to actively end his or her life. Concerned relatives, friends, or caregivers risk criminal prosecution by helping people commit suicide. Although most physicians strive to preserve life, some assist in the suicides of dying patients by prescribing overdoses of certain drugs. In the 1990s retired Michigan physician Jack Kevorkian focused national attention on the controversial practice of physician-assisted suicide by helping more than 100 people end their lives. In 1999 a Michigan judge sentenced Kevorkian to prison for injecting a deadly dose of drugs into a man who was suffering from an incurable deadly disease.

euthanasia (YOU-thah-NAY-zhe-ah) the practice of allowing a permanently comatose or an incurably ill person to die.

Oregon is the only state that allows physicians to prescribe lethal doses of drugs to terminally ill patients so they can end their lives. In 1999 the U. S. Congress considered the Pain Relief Promotion Act of 1999, which would make such physician-assisted suicides a federal crime. If this bill becomes law, the state of Oregon may challenge it in court.

Preparing for Death

Young adults may see the need to plan for a comfortable retirement, but planning for a *good death* seems too morbid to consider. A dying person has a good death if he or she maintains a high degree of dignity and experiences little physical and emotional pain during the dying process. Additionally, a good death causes minimal amounts of emotional trauma for the person's survivors. ▌ **Figure 15-8** shows the Dying Person's Bill of Rights, which, when honored, help a person die with dignity.

Not everyone has time to prepare for a good death; death can be premature and unexpected, such as in cases of homicides or fatal accidents. Healthy people, however, can make various legal, financial, emotional, and spiritual preparations for their deaths. Such planning can reduce their survivors' confusion and anxiety.

Advance Directives The Patient Self-Determination Act gives people the right to prepare *advance directives* that indicate their wishes concerning treatment if they become incapacitated. The act also allows physicians and administrators of certain medical facilities to withhold or remove life-support care from comatose patients who have no hope

The Dying Person's Bill of Rights

I have the right

- to be treated as a living human being until I die.
- to maintain a sense of hopefulness, however changing its focus may be.
- to be cared for by those who can maintain a sense of hopefulness, however challenging this might be.
- to express my feelings and emotions about my approaching death in my own way.
- to participate in decisions concerning my care.
- to expect continuing medical and nursing attention even when the "cure" goals must be changed to "comfort" goals.
- to not die alone.
- to be free from pain.
- to have my questions answered honestly.
- not to be deceived.
- to have help from and for my family in accepting my death.
- to die in peace and dignity.
- to retain my individuality and not be judged for my decisions, which may be contrary to the beliefs of others.
- to discuss and enlarge my religious or spiritual experiences, whatever these may mean to others.
- to expect that the sanctity of the human body will be respected after death.
- to be cared for by caring, sensitive, and knowledgeable people who will attempt to understand my needs and will be able to gain some satisfaction in helping me face my death.

▲**Figure 15-8 The Dying Person's Bill of Rights.** By honoring the Dying Person's Bill of Rights, people who care for the terminally ill can help them die with dignity. Source: Donovan, M. I., & Girton, S. E. (1984). *Cancer Care Nursing.* East Norwalk, CT: Appleton-Century-Crofts Publishing Company.

of regaining consciousness and who would not want to be kept alive in such condition.

A living will or a durable power of attorney document can specify your wishes concerning your medical care in the event that you become permanently incapacitated. **Figure 15-9** shows a sample *living will.* Not every state honors such documents. For example, your state may exclude the right to have artificial feeding and hydration (water) tubes removed, regardless of your wishes.

Although some states do not sanction living wills, they allow other advance directives such as a *durable power of attorney.* In this document, you identify a mentally competent individual to serve as a health-care surrogate or proxy. A health-care proxy will make decisions concerning your care if you become unable to do so. Additionally, you may indicate which life-prolonging medical actions are acceptable or necessary under certain circumstances. The results

of surveys indicate that most Americans would want limited care if they became incapacitated. Few Americans, however, have prepared living wills or other advance directives.

Before preparing an advance directive, it is a good idea to discuss your wishes with family and address their concerns. Your physician can probably answer questions that you or your family may have about life-support care. Family members or the person who agrees to serve as your health-care surrogate and your health-care practitioner will need copies of these documents. It is a good idea to store your copy along with your other important documents in a safety deposit box.

Estate Management In addition to an advance directive, it is important to have a *will,* a legal document that specifies how you want your property to be distributed after your death. To prepare a formal will, it is a good idea to consult an attorney, preferably one who specializes in estate administration. For the will to be valid, you must be of "sound mind" (aware of your actions) when you write and sign your will, and the document must be signed and witnessed by at least two people.

Most Americans die without having a will. When this happens, probate courts follow state laws concerning the division and distribution of the deceased person's estate. An estate includes the individual's sources of money, such as checking and savings accounts, life insurance policies, and retirement plans. In addition, possessions that can be sold, such as jewelry, real estate, furniture, and collectibles, are part of one's estate. A carefully constructed will can ensure that these assets go to whomever you want, and not to whom the courts choose. Furthermore, a will can eliminate much unhappiness, stress, and confusion among your survivors. If family members feel that provisions stated in your will unfairly distribute the estate, they can contest it in court.

In addition to making a will, it is a good idea to appoint an executor to manage your estate after your death. The executor uses income from the estate to pay your debts and funeral costs. If you have young children, it is important to identify and ask a person who will act as their legal guardian in case they become orphans. Most people choose a guardian who is a close relative or friend to whom they can entrust the care of their children.

In addition to having a will and an executor, you can protect your survivors' assets by having enough health and life insurance to cover your final medical and funeral expenses. The best time to buy life and health insurance is while you are young and healthy.

Organ Donation In dying, people can make a priceless contribution to the living by donating their tissues or organs. Soon after death, a donor's kidneys, skin, heart, and the corneas can be removed and transplanted into people whose organs or tissues are failing. Many seriously ill patients who would have died without receiving donated or-

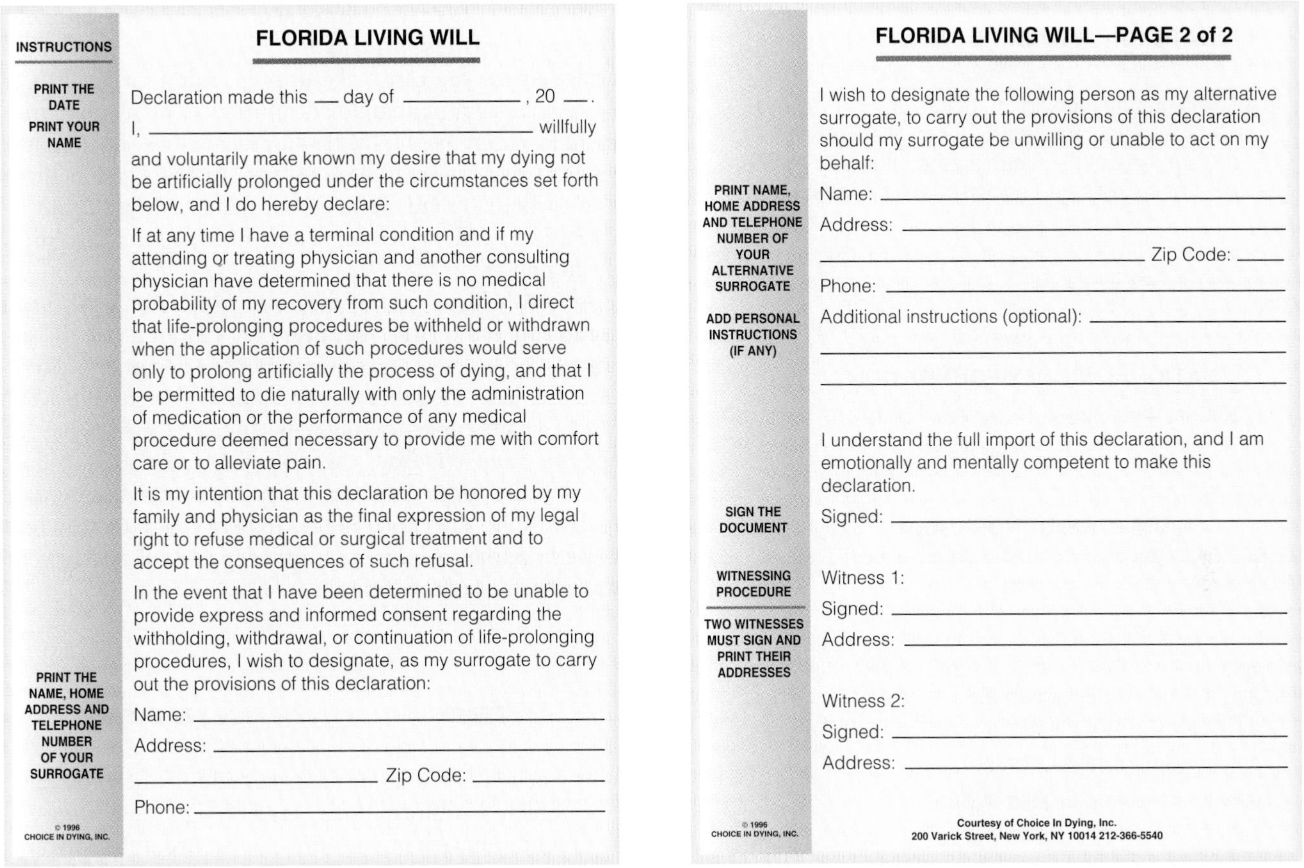

INSTRUCTIONS

FLORIDA LIVING WILL

PRINT THE DATE — Declaration made this ___ day of __________, 20 ___.

PRINT YOUR NAME — I, ______________________________ willfully

and voluntarily make known my desire that my dying not be artificially prolonged under the circumstances set forth below, and I do hereby declare:

If at any time I have a terminal condition and if my attending or treating physician and another consulting physician have determined that there is no medical probability of my recovery from such condition, I direct that life-prolonging procedures be withheld or withdrawn when the application of such procedures would serve only to prolong artificially the process of dying, and that I be permitted to die naturally with only the administration of medication or the performance of any medical procedure deemed necessary to provide me with comfort care or to alleviate pain.

It is my intention that this declaration be honored by my family and physician as the final expression of my legal right to refuse medical or surgical treatment and to accept the consequences of such refusal.

In the event that I have been determined to be unable to provide express and informed consent regarding the withholding, withdrawal, or continuation of life-prolonging procedures, I wish to designate, as my surrogate to carry out the provisions of this declaration:

PRINT THE NAME, HOME ADDRESS AND TELEPHONE NUMBER OF YOUR SURROGATE

Name: ______________________________

Address: ______________________________

______________________________ Zip Code: __________

Phone: ______________________________

FLORIDA LIVING WILL—PAGE 2 of 2

I wish to designate the following person as my alternative surrogate, to carry out the provisions of this declaration should my surrogate be unwilling or unable to act on my behalf:

PRINT NAME, HOME ADDRESS AND TELEPHONE NUMBER OF YOUR ALTERNATIVE SURROGATE

Name: ______________________________

Address: ______________________________

______________________________ Zip Code: __________

Phone: ______________________________

ADD PERSONAL INSTRUCTIONS (IF ANY)

Additional instructions (optional): ______________________________

____

____

I understand the full import of this declaration, and I am emotionally and mentally competent to make this declaration.

SIGN THE DOCUMENT

Signed: ______________________________

WITNESSING PROCEDURE

TWO WITNESSES MUST SIGN AND PRINT THEIR ADDRESSES

Witness 1:

Signed: ______________________________

Address: ______________________________

Witness 2:

Signed: ______________________________

Address: ______________________________

Courtesy of Choice In Dying, Inc.
200 Varick Street, New York, NY 10014 212-366-5540

▲**Figure 15-9 A Living Will.** While still able, a person can sign a living will to specify wishes concerning medical care in the event that he or she becomes permanently incapacitated. Source: Reprinted by permission of Choice in Dying, New York.

gans are able to live nearly normal lives after having the procedures.

More than 67,000 people in the United States are on waiting lists to receive organ transplants (United Network for Organ Sharing, 1999). The Organ Procurement and Transplantation Network, a private system created by the U.S. government in 1984, oversees the distribution of scarce donor organs. However, the demand for organs is greater than the supply. Each year about 4000 Americans die while waiting for matching organs to become available for transplantation (Davis, 1999). Although people may express an interest in having their organs donated if they die, they often do not make their wishes known or document them formally. For example, potential donors may fail to inform family members of their decision or sign organ donor cards. In most states, family members can override the deceased person's wishes concerning organ donation.

People can help those who need healthy tissues and organs by completing and signing uniform donor cards like the one shown in **Figure 15-10.** This card should be kept in a person's wallet. Additionally, people can fill in and sign the organ donor declaration on the back of their drivers' licenses. Individuals who would like to become organ donors when they die should inform their relatives of their wishes. Although there are no guarantees that surgeons will be able to transplant a person's tissues after death, it may be reassuring for some people to know that, even after death, they might be able to help others.

Some Final Thoughts on Death

Funeral and memorial services can help friends and family members deal with the loss of a loved one. You can ease some of the emotional and financial burdens of your survivors by planning your funeral arrangements. A funeral can be very costly, and it is often a difficult emotional task for families to make such arrangements when a loved one dies.

Many mortuaries offer prearranged funerals that enable you to specify the kind of funeral you want and the most affordable services. For example, you could choose to have a simple memorial service, your body cremated (burned), and your ashes placed in a container and given to your survivors. You can contact mortuaries in your area for more information about making funeral and burial prearrangements.

NATIONAL KIDNEY FOUNDATION
Please detach and give this portion of the card to your family.

This is to inform you that, should the occasion ever arise, I would like to be an organ and tissue donor. Please see that my wishes are carried out by informing the attending medical personnel that I have indicated my wishes to become a donor. Thank you.

_____   _____
Signature   *Date*

For further information write or call:

NATIONAL KIDNEY FOUNDATION
30 East 33rd Street, New York, NY 10016

(800) 622-9010

- -

UNIFORM DONOR CARD

Of _____
          (print or type name of donor)

In the hope that I may help others, I hereby make this anatomical gift, if medically acceptable, to take effect upon my death. The words and marks below indicate my wishes.

I give: ☐ any needed organs or parts

☐ only the following organs or parts

_____

(specify the organ[s], tissue[s], or part[s])

for the purposes of transplantation, therapy, medical research or education:

☐ my body for anatomical study if needed.

Limitations or special wishes, if any: _____

- -

Signed by the donor and the following two witnesses in the presence of each other:

_____   _____
Signature of Donor   *Date of Birth of Donor*

_____   _____
Date Signed   *City and State*

_____   _____
Witness   *Witness*

This is a legal document under the Anatomical Gift Act or similar laws.

☐ Yes, I have discussed my wishes with my family. For further information consult your physician or

National Kidney Foundation
30 East 33rd Street, New York, NY 10016

▲**Figure 15-10 A Uniform Donor Card.** By completing and signing a donor card like this one, people can help others who need healthy tissues and organs. Source: The National Kidney Foundation, Inc. Copyright ©1996. Reprinted with permission.

In addition to making funeral and burial arrangements, you can prepare spiritually for your death. One spiritual arrangement you can make in preparation for death is to write your own obituary or death notice. Many obituaries include a brief biography. If you prepare these documents, you can give copies of them to your survivors and let them know where to send them. Newspapers, college alumni associations, and professional organizations usually print death notices.

After a beloved person dies, survivors often experience confusion and distress because they cannot locate the deceased person's will and other important documents. To reduce the likelihood that this situation will occur after your death, share copies of these personal papers with your spouse, adult children, the executor, and the individual who has the power of attorney. A safety deposit box is a safe place to store such documents. To help your survivors find these important papers, you can keep a small card in your wallet that lists their location.

LIVING PRACTICES

- If you would like to be an organ donor when you die, complete a uniform donor card or sign the declaration on the back of your driver's license. Inform your relatives of this decision.
- Preparing a will can help your survivors manage your estate.
- To convey your wishes concerning treatment in case you become severely disabled and cannot communicate, consider preparing an advance directive.

Grief

Grief is the emotional state that nearly everyone experiences when they lose something special or someone with whom they enjoyed a close relationship. Losing someone you love is one of the most significant emotional events that can occur during your life. Some of life's losses are predictable, such as the death of beloved grandparents, parents, and spouses. Unexpected or premature losses, such as the death of a child or the sudden death of a spouse, can be emotionally devastating to the surviving parents, spouse, and other family members. Regardless of the circumstances surrounding a death, resolving the grief that follows the loss of a loved one *(bereavement)* involves regaining emotional balance and stability. Mourning, the culturally defined way in which survivors observe bereavement, can be a difficult and lengthy process.

The emotional and physical reactions to the death of a beloved person vary; some people have a more difficult time coping with the loss than others. People's emotional reactions are usually more severe after unexpected deaths than anticipated deaths. Typically, the initial responses of survivors are psychological shock, disbelief, and denial. They next enter the acute mourning stage, which is characterized by crying, withdrawal, and other symptoms of depression. In many societies, people in mourning are expected to display their grief, for example, by crying and by wearing somber clothing. After mourning, survivors are often able to accept the death of their loved one, recognize that they have grieved, and regain a sense of emotional balance.

The most intense period of grieving normally lasts about 4 to 6 weeks after the death. It is not uncommon for people to continue mourning for a year or longer after the loss. Some people experience psychological and physical distress if they are unable to resolve their feelings of grief.

Much of the research that examines the impact of grieving on health involves people whose spouses have recently died. Most widowed people experience some signs and symptoms of depression, such as sadness, withdrawal,

Managing Your Health | After the Death of a Loved One

The "Managing Grief" sections of this box provide some suggestions that may help you cope with the death of a beloved individual. The "Managing Legal, Social, and Financial Concerns" sections provide some actions that you can take to manage various concerns that often arise after the death of a spouse or other beloved person.

Immediate Actions and Concerns

Managing grief

- Resolve to survive the first few days of the sorrowful event.
- Accept the support and company of clergy, friends, and family.
- Permit yourself to vent your feelings: to cry or to feel anger.

Managing legal, social, and financial concerns

- Notify your attorney; obtain the deceased person's will and make several photocopies of it.
- Order many (12) copies of the death certificate; the funeral director may do this for you.

Within the First Four Weeks

Managing grief

- Acknowledge those who sent food or flowers or who made memorial donations. Consider responding to those who visited or sent cards. This is an emotionally difficult task, but the process may be beneficial in itself.

- Anticipate feelings of grief: the tears, anger, guilt, and blame. Delayed or prolonged absence of grief may lead to negative physical and psychological consequences.
- If troubled by sleeplessness, nightmares, agitation, headaches, and even skin rashes, consult your physician for help to alleviate these conditions.

Managing legal, social, and financial concerns

- Notify relevant government agencies and other organizations of the death, such as the Social Security Administration, Veterans' Administration, and insurance companies.
- Submit insurance claims and apply for refunds and benefits where applicable. Keep records of all response letters from agencies and organizations.
- Notify your banks, credit card accounts, mutual funds, annuities, and accountant of the death.

Within Six Months

Managing grief

- Join a grief support group. For information concerning support groups in your area, contact social workers at a local hospital or hospice or your local United Way.
- Adapt to lifestyle changes. You may need to learn how to do unfamiliar chores such as maintaining the house, tracking investments, cooking meals, or paying bills.

- Continue previous activities such as participating in hobbies or clubs if they are satisfying.
- Participate in healthful physical activities such as walking, swimming, or golfing. Join a health spa or similar organization.

Managing legal, social, and financial concerns

- Note changes in your appetite; keep your pantry well-stocked with nutritious foods. Share meals with friends and accept the invitations of others to dine out with them.
- Update your will: change beneficiaries, trustees, or executors if necessary.
- Consult your accountant; your tax situation may have changed.

Long-Term

Managing grief

- Establish your own identity to function independently. Your degree of dependence and attachment to the deceased may determine the time needed for adjustment.
- Establish new relationships; continue existing relationships.
- Consider participating in activities or organizations that help others.

Managing legal, social, and financial concerns

- Plan for the future. Do not rush into making major changes or decisions.

and sleep disorders. With the support of family and friends, however, grieving individuals can often regain their emotional balance within a few months. Survivors may become saddened again over the loss of a spouse, especially on anniversaries, on holidays, and during family reunions. An estimated 10% to 20% of widowed people suffer severe depression that lasts a year or more after their spouses die. The "Managing Your Health" feature "After the Death of a Loved One" on page 395 contains some suggestions that can help people endure the first year after the death of a spouse or other beloved individual.

In addition to affecting emotional health, bereavement often influences the physical health of survivors. Most grieving people are emotionally distressed, and such stress often has a negative impact on their immune systems. Individuals who have weakened immune systems are at risk of developing frequent infections and chronic health problems such as cardiovascular disease. Additionally, grieving people may not take good care of themselves; for example, they may not eat nutritious foods or exercise, and some may abuse drugs, including alcohol.

People who undergo an abnormal grieving process may have had a poor relationship with the deceased person. According to Kübler-Ross, grief includes some degree of anger that is directed toward the dead individual. Survivors may hide their anger; others may express it by lashing out at someone else or by grieving for an unusually long period. ▌ **Table 15-6** lists the signs of abnormal grieving. People with these signs may need professional counseling.

Table 15-6 — Grieving Danger Signs

Professional counseling to handle grief may be necessary if the grieving person

- doubts that his or her grieving is normal.
- experiences frequent outbursts of anger.
- finds little or no pleasure in life and has persistent suicidal thoughts.
- is preoccupied with thinking about the deceased loved one, or has hostile or guilty feelings that persist for more than a couple of years.
- experiences significant weight loss, weight gain, or persistent insomnia.
- begins engaging in risky behaviors such as abusing drugs or practicing unsafe sex.
- loses interest in taking care of personal hygiene for more than two weeks.

Source: Adapted from Kouri, M. K. (1991). *Keys to dealing with the loss of a loved one.* Hauppauge, NY: Barrons Educational Series, Inc.

Healthy
LIVING PRACTICES

Consider seeking professional counseling if your grief is severe or does not subside after the death of a loved one.

across the lifespan

Dying and Death

In the United States, parents often find it difficult to discuss death with their children until someone or something, such as a pet, is dying or has died. Young children have difficulty grasping the concepts of dying and death. For example, if a 4-year-old child attends a funeral and views a loved one's body, the youngster may think this person is asleep.

Children as young as 2 years old miss a familiar person who has died, especially if the deceased was a parent. Preschool-aged children, however, do not express grief as older children or adults do. At this age, children typically grieve differently than adults; they may act unconcerned about the death and become intensely involved in play activities or misbehave.

School-age children are able to understand that dead things do not come back to life, and they respond to the loss much like adults: crying, withdrawing, or being angry. Older children often associate death with being old, particularly if they have experienced the death of a grandparent. Thus, they may have a great deal of difficulty coping when a peer dies.

Adults need to be honest and straightforward when discussing terminal illness and death with children. They should consider the child's ability to understand the meaning of death. Frequently, children begin to understand and accept death when caring people share what is happening with them. Adults need to allow grieving children to express their concerns and feelings about dying and death. Professional counseling may be necessary if the child's responses are excessive, if the young person becomes preoccupied with death, or if the child becomes depressed.

Healthy
LIVING PRACTICES

If your child becomes preoccupied with death or depressed after someone or something has died, professional counseling can help your child deal with the loss.

Chapter Review
Summary

Aging is the sum of all changes that occur in an organism over its life span. The human life span is divided into stages. The final stage, senescence, generally refers to the stage of life that begins at 65 years of age.

The overall life expectancy of Americans has increased since 1900. In the United States, a person born in 1998 can expect to live for more than 76 years. Life expectancies, however, vary according to age, sex, and socioeconomic status. For example, American females outlive American males by about 6 years.

As of 1999, about 13% of the U.S. population is 65 years of age and older. By the year 2050, nearly 20% of Americans will be in this age group. The segment of the American population that includes people who are 85 years of age and older is growing at the fastest rate. People in this age group are more likely to be severely disabled and impoverished than younger people.

Aged people must often live on incomes that are lower than when they were younger. In the United States, elderly members of certain minority groups are more likely to have lower retirement incomes and live in poverty than are White aged persons. With appropriate financial planning, Americans who have adequate incomes when they are young may be able to maintain adequate incomes during their retirement years.

A gradual and irreversible decline in the functioning of the human body begins to occur around 30 years of age. People, however, age at different rates. Genetic, environmental, and lifestyle factors influence the rate of aging.

Some of the physical changes associated with the aging process, such as gray hair, presbyopia, and menopause, are normal and inevitable. Other age-related physical changes such as heart disease, cancer, and osteoporosis are not normal and are signs of disease processes. People who modify their lifestyles while they are young may be able to prevent or delay such conditions.

According to Kübler-Ross, the typical emotional responses to dying include denial, anger, bargaining, depression, and acceptance. However, death can be the final stage of personal fulfillment if dying people have opportunities to satisfy their social and emotional needs. Family, friends, and health-care practitioners can help terminally ill individuals live better while dying by taking steps to enhance their dignity and self-worth.

Death occurs when the heart or lungs cease functioning and cells in the brain do not receive oxygen. The criteria for brain death include no brain waves, no spontaneous muscular movements, no reflexes, and no responses to the environment. A brain-dead person can exist in a persistent coma for years as long as the heart is functioning, nutritional needs are met, and the supply of oxygen to the heart is maintained by the use of a respirator. Euthanasia is the practice of allowing a permanently comatose or an incurably ill person to die.

The Patient Self-Determination Act gives people the right to prepare advance directives, documents that indicate a person's wishes concerning life-support measures if the individual becomes incapable of making such decisions.

Nearly everyone experiences grief with the loss of something special or someone with whom he or she enjoyed a close relationship. Although it is normal to grieve after such a loss, grief can have a negative impact on health. To resolve grief, a person accepts the death of a loved one, recognizes that he or she has grieved for this person, and regains a sense of emotional balance. An individual who grieves for a prolonged period may require professional counseling.

Preschool children do not understand the concept of death, yet they still experience distress over the missing loved one. At this age, children may mourn by acting disinterested about the death or by misbehaving. Older children often grieve like adults by crying, withdrawing, and being angry. Grieving youngsters need to express their concerns and feelings about death. Like adults, children may need professional counseling if their emotional responses to death are severe or prolonged.

Applying What You Have Learned

1. Develop a will that reflects your wishes concerning the distribution of your assets after death. *(Application)*
2. Analyze how your present lifestyle may affect your life span. *(Analysis)*
3. Propose a special program that would prevent ageism by promoting understanding and cooperation between young and old members of your community. *(Synthesis)*
4. Choose a position concerning the issue of euthanasia. How would you defend your position? *(Evaluation)*

KEY

Application: Using information in a new situation.
Analysis: Breaking down information into component parts.
Synthesis: Putting together information from different sources.
Evaluation: Making informed decisions.

Reflecting On Your Health

1. How do you feel about growing old? Are you undergoing the age-related changes that Table 15-1 describes? Which age-related changes trouble you the most? Are you making any lifestyle changes that will increase your chances of living a long and healthy life? If you answered yes to the previous question, what changes are you making, and how do you think they will affect your longevity?
2. If you suffered severe brain damage in an accident, would you want to be maintained in a persistent vegetative state? Why or why not? If so, for how long would you want to be kept alive? Why?
3. Do you intend to donate your organs if you die in an accident? Why or why not? Have you signed an organ donor card or the back of your license, enabling survivors to donate your organs when you die?
4. Have you ever known someone who knew he or she was dying? If so, describe any stages of Kübler-Ross's emotional responses to dying that you observed in that person.
5. If someone you loved has died, how did the grieving process affect your health, including your psychological, social, and spiritual health?

References

Ad Hoc Committee of the Harvard Medical School to Examine Brain Death. (1968). A defintion of irreversible coma. *Journal of the American Medical Association, 205*:337-340.

Bijnen, F. C., Feskens, E. J., Caspersen, C. J., Nagelkerke, N., Mosterd, W. L., & Kromhout, D. (1999). Baseline and previous physical activity in relation to mortality in elderly men: The Zutphen elderly study. *American Journal of Epidemiology, 150*(12):1289-1296.

Calle, E. E., Thun, M. J., Petrelli, J. M., Rodriguez, C., & Heath, C. W. (1999). Body-mass index and mortality in a prospective cohort of U.S. adults. *The New England Journal of Medicine, 341:* 1097-1105.

Davis, K. L. (1999). Alzheimer's disease: Seeking new ways to preserve brain function. *Geriatrics, 54*(2):42-47.

Desai, M. M., & Zhang, P. (1999). Surveillance for morbidity and mortality among older adults—United States, 1995–1996. *Morbidity and Mortality Weekly Report, 48*(SS-8):7-25.

Glass, T. A., Mendes de Leon, C., Marottoli, R. A., & Berkman, L. F. (1999). Population-based study of social and productive activities as predictors of survival among elderly Americans. *British Medical Journal, 319*:478-483.

Howarth, D. F., Heath, J. M., & Snope, F. C. (1999). Beyond the Folstein: Dementia in primary care. *Primary Care, 26*(2):299-314.

Hwang, M. Y., Glass, R. M., & Molter, J. (1999). Living with arthritis. *Journal of the American Medical Association, 282*(20):1982.

Kamimoto, L. A., Easton, A. N., Maurice, E., Husten, C. G., & Macera, C. A. (1999). Surveillance for five health risks among older adults—United States, 1993–1997. *Morbidity and Mortality Weekly Report, 48*(SS-8):89-124.

Kramer, A. F., Hahn, S., Cohen, N. J., Banich, M. T., McAuley, E., Harrison, C. R., Chason, J., Vakil, E., Bardell, L., Boileau, R. A., & Colcombe, A. (1999). Aging, fitness, and neurocognitive function. *Nature, 400*(7643):418-419.

Kübler-Ross, E. (1969). *On death and dying.* New York: Macmillan Co.

Lee, C. K., Klopp, R. G., Weindruch, R., & Prolla, T. A. (1999). Gene expression profile of aging and its retardation by caloric restriction. *Science, 285*(5432):1390-1393.

Mankin, H. J., & Brandt, K. D. (1997). Pathogenesis of osteoarthritis. In W. N. Kelley, E. D. Harris, S. Ruddy, & C. B. Sledge. *Textbook of rheumatology (5th ed.).* (pp. 1369–1382). Philadelphia: W. B. Saunders Co.

Martin, J. A., Smith, B. L., Mathews, M. S., & Ventura, S. J. (1999). Births and deaths: Preliminary data for 1998. *National Vital Statistics Reports, 47*(25):1-25.

Mazzeo, R., S., Cavanagh, P., Evans, W., J., Fiatarone, M., Hagberg, J., McAuley, E., & Startzell, J. (1998). ACSM position stand on exercise and physical activity in older adults. *Medicine & Science in Sports & Exercise, 30*(6):992-1008.

National Center for Health Statistics (NCHS). (1999). Health, United States, 1999. Hyattsville, Maryland: U.S. Department of Health and Human Services.

Perls, T. T. (1999). *Who are centenarians?* www.med.harvard.edu/program/necs/centenarians.html

Phillips, D. P., & Smith, D. G. (1990). Postponement of death until symbolically meaningful occasions. *Journal of the American Medical Association, 263*(14):1947-1951.

Sherman, S. E., D'Agostino, R. B., Silbershatz, H., & Kannel, W. B.(1999). Comparison of past versus recent physical activity in the prevention of premature death and coronary artery disease. *American Heart Journal, 138*(5):900-907.

United Network for Organ Sharing, Richmond, Virginia, www.unos.org. Accessed December 25, 1999.

U.S. Department of Health and Human Services (DHHS). (1991). *Healthy people 2000: National health promotion and disease prevention objectives.* U.S. Public Health Service, Washington DC: U.S. Government Printing Office.

U.S. Department of Health and Human Services (USDHHS), Public Health Service. (1991). *Healthy People 2000: National health promotion and disease prevention objectives.* Washington, DC: Government Printing Office.

Wagner, T. H., & Hu, T. W. (1998). Economic costs of urinary incontinence in 1995. *Urology, 51*(3):355-361.

Environmental Health

Azarcon, greta, and pay-loo-ah . . . if you have Hispanic or Asian ancestry, the names of one or more of these traditional ethnic remedies may be familiar to you. Greta and azarcon are Mexican remedies for empacho, a colicky digestive disorder. Pay-loo-ah is a Southeast Asian tonic for rash or fever. All three are fine powders and may be given as a tea, or a pinch may be added to a baby's bottle. They also can be mixed with milk or sugar and administered by teaspoon. Family members who rely on folk medicine give these remedies regularly to children.

Many folk remedies contain substances that are useful in medical practice. In fact, pharmaceutical companies often start looking for new drugs by chemically analyzing the herbs and other plants used in many traditional folk remedies that have been part of a culture for generations. However, some remedies, like those mentioned above, can cause harm.

> *". . . children are poisoned by lead . . . by eating lead-based paint chips . . ."*

Azarcon, greta, and pay-loo-ah all contain high levels of lead (Centers for Disease Control and Prevention [CDC], 1993). This metal is only one of the many substances in our environment that can cause serious illness, especially among children. Other ways in which children are poisoned by lead are by eating lead-based paint chips and by inhaling lead particles in contaminated dust or soil.

The study of the effects of environmental factors on humans and the effects of humans on their environments is called **environmental health**. People often affect the environment in ways that later influence their health. For example, people emitted chlorofluorocarbons (CFCs) into the atmosphere when they used certain spray can propellants prior to their being banned in 1979. CFCs contribute to the depletion of the ozone layer in the upper atmosphere. These depleted areas are commonly referred to as **ozone holes**. The upper atmospheric ozone layer protects people from some of the sun's harmful ultraviolet (UV) radiation, which can cause skin cancer. (Chapter 13 discusses the relationship between the depletion of the ozone layer and skin cancer.) Many automobile air conditioners still contain chemicals harmful to the ozone layer.

What You'll Learn

www.jbpub.com/healthyliving

The web site for this book offers many useful tools and supplementary health information for both students and instructors. Visit the site at www.jbpub.com/healthyliving for information on these topics:

Environmental Health in and around the Home
Environmental Health in the Workplace
Environmental Health in the Outdoor Environment
Diversity in Health: Hunger, the Environment, and the World's Population

Chapter Overview

Which types of poisoning are prevalent in the United States.
How to avoid poisoning in the home.
Which toxic chemicals are prevalent in the workplace.
What factors contribute to indoor air pollution.
How water supplies become contaminated.
Why air pollution is a threat to health.
How noise pollution affects hearing.

DIVERSITY in Health   Hunger, the Environment, and the World's Population

Con$umer Health   Carbon Monoxide Detectors: Are They Reliable?

Managing Your Health   Tips on Rededucing the Incidence of Poisoning in the Home | Avoiding ELF Radiation | Reducing Pesticide Levels in the Food You Eat

across the lifespan   Environmental Health

Student Workbook

Self Assessments: Poison Lookout Checklist | Checklist for the Prevention of Carbon Monoxide Poisoning
Changing Health Habits: Can You Reduce Environmental Threats to Your Health?

Do You Know?

- If you work or go to school in a "sick" building?
- If you are in danger of pesticide poisoning?
- If your house or apartment is painted with lead-based products?

environmental health the effects of environmental factors on humans and the effects of humans on their environments.

ozone holes depleted areas of the ozone (O_3) layer in the upper atmosphere.

municipal solid waste nonhazardous refuse generally collected from homes and offices.

toxic chemicals poisonous substances present in the home, workplace, or outdoor environments that affect human health.

toxicity (tok-SIH-si-tea) poisonous quality.

In another example, people in industrialized countries such as the United States produce millions of tons of **municipal solid waste** per year—all of those items that trash collectors pick up from homes and offices each week. This waste is usually placed in landfills. Along with running out of space for this trash, a problem with landfills is that chemicals may seep into the ground from these massive waste sites and pollute water supplies. We discuss water pollution from various sources later in this chapter.

Many **toxic chemicals** present in the home, workplace, or outdoor environments affect human health. They may be in the form of dusts, fumes, particles, or liquids and are found in a wide variety of substances, such as household products, plants, products manufactured or used in the workplace, and prescription and illegal drugs. (The adverse effects of drug abuse are described in Chapter 7, and of alcohol abuse in Chapter 8. The hazardous substances in tobacco products are also discussed in Chapter 8.) Additionally, toxic chemicals are present in the air we breathe and the water we drink.

Toxic chemicals result in poisoning, or **toxicity**, which damages body tissues and affects bodily functioning in various ways. Toxins may affect chemical reactions of the body. They may also hinder the normal functioning of body cells. Additionally, toxins may cause cells in the body to release chemicals that may have an adverse effect on certain body structures. The consequences of these effects are a variety of conditions such as dermatitis (inflammation of the skin), asthma, lung disease, and immune system disorders.

www.jbpub.com/healthyliving

Environmental Health in and Around the Home

Poisoning

A research project conducted by the National Center for Health Statistics (Fingerhut & Cox, 1998) studied trends in poisoning deaths from 1985 to 1995. Results of this study show that the number of poisoning deaths in 1995 were higher than in any year since 1979. Poisoning was the underlying cause of death for 18,549 people in the United States in 1995, and drug overdoses were the cause of 77% of those deaths. Poisoning was the leading cause of injury death for people aged 35 to 44 years in 1995 and was the third leading cause of injury death for all age groups com-

bined. From 1985 to 1995, poisoning death rates for males aged 35 to 54 years nearly tripled.

Another research study, conducted by the Maryland Poison Center (Shepard & Klein-Schwartz, 1998), studied poisoning deaths in American adolescents from 1979 to 1994. The results of this study reveal that during this time period there were slightly more than 4,000 suicides of persons aged 10 to 19 years and slightly less than 4,000 unintentional deaths due to poisoning in the same age group. Although poisoning was more often the method of suicide used by adolescent girls than boys, the poisoning victims in this age group were predominantly white males.

Most poisonings, however, are not fatal. Nonfatal poisonings are most often caused by the ingestion of household products and over-the-counter or prescription drugs. They occur in children under the age of 6 approximately 53% of the time (Litovitz, 1998). ▌ **Table 16-1** lists the substances most frequently involved in the poisoning of children under 6 years. ▌ **Table 16-2** lists substances that are usually not toxic. See the self-assessment "Poison Lookout Checklist" in the student workbook to determine whether your home is free of situations that can lead to poisoning.

Unless a child or adult is observed ingesting a toxic substance, it may be difficult to determine if he or she is poisoned. Poisoning does not always start the moment exposure occurs. Also, symptoms vary depending on the substance and how it entered the body, which can occur by ingestion, inhalation, or skin contact (▌ **Figure 16-1**).

Suspect poisoning in a person who becomes suddenly ill with symptoms that affect many systems of the body, appears drowsy and indifferent, or exhibits bizarre behavior. Also, consider poisoning as a possibility in children or young adults with chest pain; they may have ingested poison or an overdose of drugs. If poisoning may have occurred, call the local poison control center immediately. If the suspected poisoning victim is experiencing severe symptoms such as unconsciousness, seizures, intense chest pain, or repeated vomiting, he or she should be rushed to the emergency room of the closest hospital. Follow the tips in the "Managing Your Health" box on page 405 entitled "Tips on Reducing the Incidence of Poisoning in the Home" to lessen the chances of being accidentally poisoned.

Toxic Plants Toxic (poisonous) plants can be the source of poisoning emergencies, especially in children. Each year, more than 100,000 exposures to toxic plants are reported to poison control centers around the United States (Furbee & Wermuth, 1997). Ingesting toxic plants is the fourth most common cause of poisoning, and 86% of plant poisonings involve small children (Krenzelok et al., 1996).

A wide variety of plants have parts that are poisonous and parts that are not. For example, tomatoes are not poisonous, but the stems and leaves of tomato plants are. Some common plant parts that are poisonous include holly berries, morning-glory seeds, narcissus and daffodil bulbs, rhubarb leaves, and sweet pea seeds. The entire hemlock, jimson weed, dieffenbachia, philodendron, and mountain laurel plants are poisonous. Some plants are so poisonous that drinking the water from a vase in which their cut flowers were kept can result in poisoning.

Table 16-1	Substances Most Frequently Involved in the Poisoning of Children under 6 Years Old		
Substance		**Number**	**%***
Cosmetics and personal care products		157,551	13.3
Cleaning substances		129,441	11.0
Analgesics		89,985	7.6
Plants		84,185	7.1
Foreign bodies		73,983	6.3
Cough and cold preparations		64,781	5.5
Topicals		63,623	5.4
Insecticides/pesticides (including rodenticides)		46,447	3.9
Vitamins		39,396	3.3
Antimicrobials		36,597	3.1
Gastrointestinal preparations		35,391	3.0
Arts/crafts/office supplies		29,898	2.5
Hydrocarbons		26,018	2.2
Antihistamines		22,854	1.9
Hormones and hormone antagonists		22,655	1.9

Note: Despite a high frequency of involvement, these substances are not necessarily the most toxic, but rather may be only the most accessible.
*Percentages are based on the total number of exposures in children under six years, rather than the total number of substances.
Source: 1998 Annual Report of the American Association of Poison Control Centers Toxic Exposure Surveillance System. p. 441.
Reference: Litovitz, T. L., Klein-Schwartz, W., Caravati, E. M., Youniss, J., Crouch, B., & Lee, S. (1999). 1998 Annual Report of the American Association of Poison Control Centers Toxic Exposure Surveillance System. *The American Journal of Emergency Medicine, 17*:435-487.

Although many plants are not poisonous—including the poinsettia, which for years has been inaccurately reported to be toxic—house plants and cut flowers should be kept out of reach of children under 5 years old, and all children should be instructed that eating house and yard plants can make them sick. Many plants such as the poinsettia may be highly irritating when ingested, even if they are not poisonous. If a child ingests a plant, call the local poison control center and describe the plant, where it was growing, and what part of the plant the child ate. If possible, take a leaf from the plant for identification when seeking emergency medical treatment. Only plant experts should rely on their knowledge of whether the plant is poisonous.

In addition to plants, approximately 1% to 2% of mushroom species are poisonous. (Mushrooms are not plants, but fungi.) One type of mushroom is so poisonous that eating one-third of its cap can be lethal.

Symptoms of mushroom poisoning may occur immediately after ingestion and may include increased salivation, tearing, increased urination, diarrhea, difficulty breathing, and an abnormal heartbeat. Other mushroom species have toxins that produce symptoms 12 to 24 hours after ingestion that include headache, jaundice

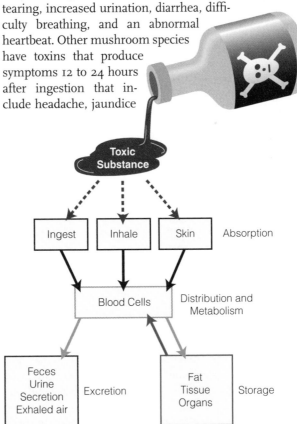

▲Figure 16-1 The Path of Toxic Substances Through the Body. The body absorbs toxic substances via the digestive system if they are ingested, or via the respiratory system if they are inhaled. Some toxic substances can also be absorbed through the skin. Once in the body, toxic substances reach the blood and lymph, which brings them to all the cells. Body cells (principally the liver) metabolize toxins; the products of metabolism are stored or excreted.

Table 16-2 Frequently Ingested Products That Are Usually Nontoxic[a]

Abrasives	Deodorizers (spray and refrigerator)	Pencil (lead-graphite, coloring)
Antacids	Etch-A-Sketch	Perfumes
Antibiotics	Fabric softeners	Petroleum jelly
Ballpoint pen inks	Fertilizer	Play-Doh
Bathtub floating toys	(if no insecticides or herbicides	Polaroid picture coating fluid
Bath oil (castor oil and perfume)	added and no caution label)	Porous tip ink marking pens
Body conditioners	Fish bowl additives	Putty (less than 2 oz)
Bubble bath soaps	Glues and pastes	Rubber cement[b]
Calamine lotion	Golfball (child may choke on core)	Sachets (essential oils, powder)
Candles (beeswax or paraffin)	Greases	Shampoos (regular, not treated)
Caps (toy pistol)	Hair products (dyes, sprays, tonics)	Shaving creams and lotions
(potassium chlorate)	Hand lotions and creams	Soap and soap products
Chalk (calcium carbonate)	Hydrogen peroxide (medicinal, 3%)	(hand soaps)
Cigarettes or cigars	Incense	Spackling compound
(small amounts of nicotine)	Indelible markers	Suntan preparations
Clay (modeling)	Laxatives (small amounts)	Sweetening agents
Contraceptives	Lipstick	(Saccharin, aspartame)
Cosmetics	Lubricant	Teething rings (water sterilized)
Crayons	Lubricating oils	Toilet water
(marked A.P., C.P., C.S. 130–46)	Matches	Toothpaste (with or without fluoride)
Dehumidifying packets	Mineral oil	Vitamins (without fluoride or iron)
(silica or charcoal)	Motor oil	Water colors
Detergents (phosphate type, anionic)	Newspaper	Zinc oxide
Deodorants	Paint (indoor or latex)	Zirconium oxide

[a]In the event that large quantities of any of these substances are ingested, consult a poison control center.
[b]May cause acute poisoning if inhaled in a closed area.
Source: Mofenson, H. C., Greensher, J., & Caraccio, T. R. (1984). Ingestions considered nontoxic. *Clinics in Laboratory Medicine, 4*:587-602.

(a yellowish cast to the skin), confusion, convulsions, and possible coma. Because poisonous mushrooms can be lethal or cause severe poisoning, do not eat any mushrooms that you find growing wild. Only a person trained in mushroom identification should attempt to distinguish between mushrooms that are safe to eat and those that are not.

Ingestion of Household Cleaning Aids, Medications, and Vitamins Children under the age of 5 years are those most in danger of being poisoned from household cleaning aids and from over-the-counter and prescription drugs and vitamins. The Federal Hazardous Substances Act, passed into law by the Consumer Product Safety Commission in 1966, has been helpful in lowering the incidence of poisoning in children by controlling the concentration of toxic chemicals in household products. The Poison Prevention Packaging Act of 1972 established standards for the packaging of potentially harmful household products and medications by requiring child-resistant caps and packaging on products that present a serious danger to children. The intent of this packaging is to make it difficult for children to open toxic substances so that adults will discover their attempts before they are successful. The use of blister packs

in which pills are individually encased is another approach to lessen a child's ability to remove pills from packaging.

Although warning stickers such as Mr. Yuk (▮ **Figure 16-2**) are available for placing on hazardous sub-

▲**Figure 16-2 Poison Prevention Symbols.** The skull and crossbones is the traditional warning of poison. Mr. Yuk is a warning label designed for children, but using such labels is an unreliable deterrent. Lock all toxic substances in cabinets, away from children. Source: Gossel, T. A. & Bricker, J. D. (1990). *Principles of clinical toxicology, 2nd ed.* Philadelphia, PA: Lippincott-Raven Publishers, pp. 13–14.

Tips on Reducing the Incidence of Poisoning in the Home

If there are children in the home:

- Store all medications and household cleaning aids in locked cabinets and away from food.
- Replace child-resistant caps securely after use.
- Replace medications and household cleaning items in their locked cabinets immediately after use. If the phone or doorbell rings when you are using a toxic chemical or medication, take it with you.
- Never refer to medicines as candy when administering drugs to children.
- Never take medicines in front of small children or make light of taking medicine to them.
- Keep plants away from children or others likely to ingest them. Many plants are poisonous.
- Educate children about the dangers of poisons in the home.

- Use adhesive stickers showing Mr. Yuk, or similar characters, to help children identify dangerous substances.

In all homes:

- Store all medications and household chemicals separately from each other and away from food.
- Periodically check and discard medications and household cleaning aids you no longer use. Flush the product down the toilet and then rinse the containers before discarding them.
- Work with household chemicals only in well-ventilated areas.
- Do not mix chemicals (e.g., bleach and toilet bowl cleaner) unless specifically directed to do so. They can react, emitting dangerous fumes.
- Keep all medications and toxic substances in their original containers. Never store such items in soda bottles, food containers, or any other unmarked containers.

- In houses built prior to 1978, check for peeling paint or loose plaster, both of which can be a significant source of lead poisoning.
- Never operate fuel-consuming engines, kerosene heaters, or charcoal fires in poorly ventilated areas.
- Develop a plan of action in case a poisoning should occur. Right now, look up important phone numbers (local poison center, doctor, pharmacist, emergency rescue squad, etc.) and record these by the phone.
- Stock emergency antidotes (activated charcoal and syrup of ipecac). Call the local poison control center for guidance as to when to administer these substances because they can cause serious problems when administered under inappropriate conditions.

Source: Adapted from Gossel, T. A., & Bricker, J. D. (1990). *Principles of clinical toxicology* (2nd ed.). New York: Raven Press, pp. 13–14.

stances, the results of research suggest that their use has not lowered the incidence of poisoning in children (Fergusson et al., 1982; Vernberg et al., 1984). Therefore, since child-resistant packaging *can* be opened by children (although with difficulty) and since warning stickers do not appear to deter children from investigating package contents, all dangerous household substances, including medications and cleaning aids, should be locked in cabinets. Special child-proof locks are available that enable an adult to open a cabinet easily but bar the child from doing so. Placing items on high shelves is not a good substitute and is not safe; children easily stack items and climb on them to reach these substances.

Never suggest to a child that any medication or vitamin pill is candy because the child will seek out the pills at another time. Additionally, never take medication or vitamins in front of a young child who may think that it is candy or food and try to do the same.

Children become poisoned by vitamins and mineral supplements due to accidental overdose, but adults become poisoned by intentional overdose. Megadosing with vita-

mins (taking much greater amounts than that recommended per day) has become a popular practice but may cause health problems. Vitamin overdosing in adults most often occurs with vitamins A and D, two fat-soluble vitamins that are readily stored in the body. Daily overdoses of most fat-soluble vitamins build up, resulting in chronic intoxication. Daily doses of 3 to 10 times the recommended amount of vitamin A over a few months to a few years produce toxic symptoms. Accutane, a form of vitamin A taken to treat skin conditions, can cause vitamin A toxicity when taken by mouth. Daily doses of 10 times the recommended amount of vitamin D over 6 months to a year produce toxic symptoms as well. Minerals that most commonly cause poisoning are iron, selenium, and zinc. Chapter 9 discusses vitamins and minerals and their roles in the body in more detail. Table 9-7 (p. 210) lists vitamin toxicity symptoms and Table 9-9 (p. 212) lists mineral toxicity symptoms.

Lead Poisoning Lead poisoning is still a health problem in children in the United States even though many sources of lead poisoning

lead poisoning

a toxic condition that affects the central nervous system, caused by the ingestion or inhalation of the metallic element lead.

have been eliminated in this country: leaded gasoline, leaded solder in food and soft drink cans, and leaded paint. (Solder is a metal that is heated and then used, when soft, to join other metals. It hardens on cooling and makes the joint solid.)

Even though many sources of lead have been removed from the environment, leaded dangers still exist. Ceramicware that is poorly made can have very high levels of leaching lead (that is, lead that dissolves out of the dishes and passes into food). Car batteries contain lead and should be brought to collection centers for proper disposal or recycling. Some pipes that bring water to homes contain lead-based solder. Additionally, the soil surrounding roads and highways often contains lead from years-past auto emissions.

carbon monoxide poisoning a toxic condition that affects red blood cells' ability to carry oxygen, caused by the inhalation of the gas carbon monoxide.

Houses and apartments built before 1978 were often painted with lead-based paint (Office of Pollution Protection and Toxics [OPPT], 1994). Although layers of non-leaded paint may cover leaded paint, the top coats of paint can chip. The exposed leaded paint creates leaded dust that may be inhaled, or the leaded paint may chip and children may eat it. Leaded paint used on the exterior of homes and apartments often contaminates the surrounding soil in which children may play.

Many cases of lead poisoning occur when older homes are remodeled without attention to the containment of leaded dust and paint chips. When doing such work, use a high-efficiency particulate air filter–equipped vacuum cleaner, properly fitted respirators, wet sanding equipment, and protective clothing (Figure 16-3). Seal off work areas with heavy-duty polyethylene plastic sheeting, and keep all nonworkers away from the area (OPPT, 1994).

Lead poisoning is serious because it affects the central nervous system and can cause coma, convulsions, and even death. Today, few deaths result from lead poisoning; nonetheless, many children are severely affected by this toxin. While adults absorb about 11% of lead reaching the digestive tract, children absorb from 30% to 75%. When lead is inhaled, up to 50% is absorbed (Farley, 1998).

Low levels of lead in the blood (10 micrograms per deciliter [μg/dl]) are associated with decreased intelligence, learning disabilities, impaired development of the nervous system, and delayed or stunted growth. Behavioral disorders also have been linked to lead poisoning. At slightly higher levels of lead poisoning, the body does not metabolize certain vitamins properly or manufacture red blood cells correctly.

A child with high blood levels of lead (70 μg/dl) will show some of the following symptoms: decreased appetite, vomiting, abdominal pain, constipation, drowsiness, and indifference. Children who have even higher blood levels will exhibit some of the signs and symptoms of degenerative brain disease: coma, seizures, bizarre behavior, impaired muscular coordination, and vomiting. Either situation is a medical emergency and the child should be hospitalized. Tests should be performed to determine the child's lead blood level and medications will be administered to reduce that level. However, the most important therapy is removing sources of lead from the child's environment. Call the National Lead Information Center at 800-LEAD-FYI or 800-424-LEAD for more information on how to avoid lead poisoning.

Carbon Monoxide Poisoning Carbon monoxide (CO) is a colorless, odorless, tasteless gas that can kill. In fact, unintentional CO poisoning causes approximately 2100 deaths in the United States per year (Yoon et al., 1998). Carbon monoxide is produced by the incomplete combustion of carbon-containing fuels such as oil, coal, wood, natural gas, charcoal, and gasoline. Fires are a major source of **carbon monoxide poisoning**; persons caught in a fire often die

▶Figure 16-3 **Lead Paint Removal.** These experts are removing lead paint from an old home in Nashua, New Hampshire. They are using a specialized vacuum cleaner and are wearing protective clothing and respirators.

from inhaling carbon monoxide and other toxic gases rather than from the fire. Firefighters also are at risk for carbon monoxide poisoning. Other primary sources of carbon monoxide poisoning are automobile exhaust, malfunctioning furnaces, charcoal fires, gasoline-powered tools, wood stoves, fireplaces, unvented kerosene and gas space heaters, gas cooking stoves and ovens, and tobacco smoking. See the self-assessment "Checklist for the Prevention of Carbon Monoxide (CO) Poisoning" in the student workbook to determine if your home, auto, cabin, or camper are as safe as they can be.

The proper maintenance and use of tools and appliances that burn fuel cuts down on the amount of CO they produce; these levels are usually not hazardous. Improper maintenance and incorrect use often result in dangerous levels of CO. To protect against these dangers, be certain that home heating stoves or furnaces are vented properly and are inspected regularly for carbon monoxide leakage. Use charcoal grills and gas-powered tools only in well-ventilated areas. (Don't use your charcoal grill in your garage or in a tent while camping.) Additionally, do not leave a car running in an attached garage where fumes can leak into the house. Run the car engine outdoors only. Carbon monoxide can also leak into a car if the exhaust system is faulty.

Carbon monoxide sensors are available for home use. These products are designed to sound an alarm when indoor air contains dangerously high levels of this toxin. Results of a recent study show that the use of carbon monoxide detectors could reduce by half the number of unintentional deaths by CO poisoning in the home (Yoon et al.,

1998). (See the "Consumer Health" box below "Carbon Monoxide Detectors: Are They Reliable?")

Carbon monoxide kills because it binds to the oxygen-carrying molecule hemoglobin. When CO is bound to hemoglobin, oxygen cannot bind and the person dies of suffocation. Before carbon monoxide poisoning kills, however, it produces signs and symptoms that become more severe as blood levels of this gas increase. At first, a person may have a slight headache that worsens as blood levels rise. (This level of poisoning can even occur if you jog near rush-hour traffic.) Fatigue sets in and the poison victim may become dizzy. As the poisoning continues, nausea, vomiting, a cherry-red skin color, and blurry vision result. Eventually the person collapses, may have convulsions, and dies.

Carbon monoxide poisoning is an emergency; immediately get the victim to fresh air and seek medical help. Health-care practitioners treat CO poisoning victims with oxygen and test them for other medical problems that may have occurred at the time of the poisoning (such as a blow to the head in a fall). In some circumstances, the poisoning victim is placed in a hyperbaric (pressure) chamber and administered oxygen.

Inhalation of Asbestos Fibers

Asbestos is a fiberlike mineral that resists damage by fire and other natural processes. Because of these qualities, asbestos has been used in the manufacture of products exposed to fire, such as stoves, furnaces, and appliances; insulation in walls and ceilings; insulation surrounding pipes; patching compounds and textured paints (as a

Con$umer Health — Carbon Monoxide Detectors: Are They Reliable?

Carbon monoxide (CO) detectors should be thought of only as a back-up to proper use and maintenance of fuel-burning appliances. The technology of these detectors is still developing, and a variety of types are currently available for home use. However, none is considered to be as reliable as home smoke detectors.

The U.S. Environmental Protection Agency reports that CO detectors have been laboratory tested with varying results. Some performed well, others failed to alarm at high CO levels, and still others alarmed at low levels that do

not pose any immediate health risk. Because CO is invisible and odorless, it is hard to tell if an alarm is false or a real emergency.

When purchasing a CO detector, research the features of various models and brands and use this knowledge, not the price, as your basis for selection. Carefully follow the manufacturer's instructions for its placement, use, and maintenance. If your CO detector goes off:

- Make certain it is the CO detector alarm and not the smoke detector alarm.

- Seek medical help for anyone experiencing CO poisoning symptoms.
- Ventilate the home with fresh air and turn off all potential sources of CO.
- Have a qualified technician inspect all fuel-burning appliances and chimneys to make sure they are operating correctly and that there is nothing blocking fumes from being vented.

Source: U.S. Environmental Protection Agency, Indoor Environments Division, Office of Air and Radiation (1996, October). *Protect your family and yourself from carbon monoxide poisoning.* EPA-402-F-96-005.

binding compound and texturizer); roofing and siding materials; and vinyl flooring (as a strengthener).

Asbestos-containing products came into use beginning in the 1920s, but by the early 1970s scientists discovered that long-term inhalation of microscopic asbestos fibers can result in **asbestosis** as well as cancer of the lungs and stomach. During asbestosis, scar tissue forms in the lungs as a response to irritation by asbestos fibers. The patient experiences shortness of breath, which progresses to a fatal lack of oxygen or heart failure. Because of the danger that asbestos exposure poses to humans, the U.S. Environmental Protection Agency (EPA) banned the use of various asbestos-containing products during the 1970s and 1980s. In 1989 the EPA announced a ban on all asbestos products by 1996 (U.S. Consumer Product Safety Commission [CPSC], 1989).

asbestosis

(AS-bes-TOE-sis) a condition in which scar tissue forms in the lungs as a response to irritation by asbestos.

Aside from the danger to those who mine asbestos, those in primary danger of asbestos exposure are people who live in homes built between 1920 and 1978. Various asbestos products were developed at different times during those years and were used in home construction. Asbestos was also widely used in schools built between 1950 and 1973. Intact asbestos products do not pose a hazard. Danger exists when asbestos fibers are released from the products of which they were a part and become airborne. Asbestos fibers are released from products that are deteriorating; banged, rubbed, or handled frequently; or disturbed during home remodeling. Asbestos fibers are also released when asbestos-containing flooring is sanded or seriously damaged.

To protect against the inhalation of asbestos fibers, avoid disturbing this material. Do not vacuum particles that may be asbestos-laden; vacuuming them releases microscopic asbestos fibers that are inhaled. If possible, contact the contractor who built the home to determine if asbestos was used. If this is not possible, contact a certified professional trained in asbestos removal and repair to determine if the home contains asbestos. Sometimes materials must be sent to a laboratory to assess their content. If so, use a laboratory accredited to perform asbestos analysis. If removal, repair, or sealing of the material is necessary, hire only trained, certified personnel who can do this job safely and properly.

Electromagnetic Radiation

Are computer screens, television sets, electric blankets, or electric appliances health hazards? Are people putting their health at risk if they live near high-tension electric power lines or electrical distribution substations? A variety of studies have been conducted regarding the effects of extremely low frequency (ELF) radiation on the body, and so far most scientists see no reason to recommend extreme caution. Research of the past decade does not demonstrate clear links between ELF radiation and cancer or other health problems, but calls for more study of ELF radiation and its effects on humans (Horn, 1995; Kirsner & Federman, 1998; Salvatore & Weitberg, 1989). However, taking reasonable preventive measures against undue exposure may be prudent.

Extremely low frequency radiation is a type of *electromagnetic radiation*—electric and magnetic fields of energy that travel at the speed of light through the atmosphere. Sunlight, for example, is electromagnetic energy. Other forms of electromagnetic radiation include x rays, ultraviolet light, infrared light, and radio waves.

Extremely low frequency radiation is emitted by the sources mentioned previously: electric power lines, electrical distribution substations, video display terminals, television sets, electric blankets, and electrical appliances. The electric fields generated by these sources are not as potentially problematic as the magnetic fields. Although the strength of both the electric and magnetic fields decreases dramatically and quickly as a person moves away from the source, magnetic fields penetrate the walls of buildings that electric fields cannot.

Laboratory studies of animals show that ELF radiation *may* increase the incidence of a variety of cancers. It may also cause changes in the ability of certain minerals to move through cell membranes, the behavior of certain cells of the immune system, and the firing pattern of nerve cells (Smith, 1996). Studies on humans exposed to ELF radiation sources, however, are inconclusive and show little or no risk from exposure. Nevertheless, both animal and human studies do show that exposure to ELF electromagnetic fields results in a decrease in the amount of melatonin that is secreted by the brain. This hormone regulates the sleep–wake cycle (Reiter, 1994).

Many studies have been conducted on computer monitors (video display terminals [VDTs]) because they are so prevalent in the home and workplace. Studies suggest that some people experience minor health problems as the result of using VDTs. Video display terminals produce radiation that spans the electromagnetic spectrum from x rays to radio waves. However, these terminals are manufactured with protective shielding to prevent most of the radiation from escaping. The small amount that does escape results in electric and magnetic fields in the atmosphere surrounding the VDT user, but this level of radiation is well below occupational and exposure limits recommended by governmental and industrial safety standards. Additionally, the levels of electromagnetic radiation emitted by newer models of VDTs are generally lower than older models, reducing the health hazard further.

One minor health effect that has been documented is the association of the use of VDTs with dry eyes. This situation occurs because VDT users tend to blink less frequently than when reading a book, for example, and hold their eyes

Avoiding ELF Radiation

- Do not sleep or sit for a long time near electric devices, particularly those with motors.
- Sit a minimum of 18 inches (at arm's length) from your computer screen.
- Turn off your computer monitor when it is not being used.

- Sit several feet away from the back or sides of a computer monitor or television. Follow this rule even if the TV or monitor is in another room; magnetic fields travel through walls.
- Adults and especially children should sit several feet away from a television screen.

- Turn on your waterbed heater or electric blanket before going to bed. Unplug them when you get into bed.

Source: Adapted from Lamarine, R. J., & Narad, R. A. (1992). Health risks associated with residential exposure to extremely low frequency electromagnetic radiation. *Journal of Community Health*, 17:291–301.

open more widely in order to see the screen. This effect can be reduced by lowering the height of the VDT and tilting the screen slightly upward. Additionally, persons with dry eyes can use over-the-counter eye-lubricating products to moisten the eyes (Tsubota & Nakamori, 1993).

Although the data are unclear regarding the risk to humans of exposure to ELF radiation, medical researchers have adopted the position of "prudent avoidance" until research data indicate that another course of action should be taken (Lamarine & Narad, 1992). What can people do to avoid or reduce their exposure to ELF radiation? The "Managing Your Health" box above entitled "Avoiding ELF Radiation" gives some tips.

Irradiation of Food: The Debate

Many types of organisms contaminate the food supply. *E. coli* (a common intestinal bacterium) can be found in such foods as hamburger and unpasteurized apple juice. A particularly deadly strain of *E. coli* (0157:H7) has caused illness and death. Salmonella bacteria are common contaminants of poultry. Certain insects and their larvae contaminate wheat and wheat flour. A wide range of organisms cause not only foodborne illness but the spoilage of food.

In 1996 President Clinton upgraded the rules for inspecting meat and poultry in the United States. For 90 years prior, inspection of these food products had been by touch, sight, and smell, as called for in the Meat Inspection Act of 1906. However, inspection is only one way to ensure the safety of the food we eat. Proper storage and handling is another. Killing bacteria and pathogens is a third.

One method of killing organisms in food is irradiation; that is, treating food with radiation. Radiation is the emission of energy by the unstable nuclei of certain atoms in the form of rays or waves. Food is irradiated in its packaging by either exposing it to gamma (γ) rays (a form of electromagnetic radiation similar to x rays) or to high-energy electron beams produced by electron accelerators. Radiation is harmful to living tissue, so it kills living organisms

in the food as the energy passes through it, much like microwaves pass through food in a microwave oven. And just as a dentist's x ray does not make your teeth radioactive, irradiation does not make food radioactive—food is not transformed into a radioactive substance.

Food irradiation is a process that was patented in the United States in 1921, but was not approved for use on the first food products (wheat, wheat flour, and white potatoes) by the Food and Drug Administration (FDA) until the early 1960s. Since then, whether or not to irradiate food in the United States has been a contentious issue. Approximately 40 years after its approval, irradiation remains in limited use, although the FDA has since approved the use of irradiation on fresh produce, herbs, spices, pork, poultry, and red meat.

So what is the debate about? Numerous national and international organizations (such as the American Medical Association and the World Health Organization) as well as many university-based research institutes endorse the irradiation of food. Supporters point out that irradiation has been shown to be the only way to rid ground beef of *E. coli* 0157:H7 before cooking. (Cooking ground beef thoroughly also kills this pathogen.) Irradiation also kills other bacteria, as well as insects and fungi that can make people sick or spoil food. Additionally, irradiating food can inhibit the sprouting of vegetables and delay the ripening of fruits. Food irradiation proponents hold, therefore, that using this process would make the food supply safer, would provide a better quality of food, and would extend the "shelf life" of food.

The opposition to food irradiation comes primarily from consumers and consumer groups. They point out that irradiation induces chemical changes in the nutrients that compose food (lipids, proteins, carbohydrates, water, and vitamins). Therefore, opponents argue, these changes can affect the color, odor, and texture of food, and could result in unidentified toxins remaining in food that might be harmful to humans and might even cause cancer. Additionally, opponents charge that irradiation lowers the nutritional value of food; some vitamins, for example, are affected by radiation. Some persons simply oppose technologies that involve radiation, citing problems such as nuclear waste.

The "Analyzing Health-Related Information" activity on pages 412 to 413 contains a newspaper article on this topic that discusses the process of food irradiation and the debate surrounding this issue.

Healthy
LIVING PRACTICES

- Teach children not to ingest house or yard plants because they may be poisonous. In homes with young children, substitute safe plants for poisonous ones.
- Eat only mushrooms that you are certain are nonpoisonous.
- In homes with small children, store all dangerous household substances, including medications and cleaning aids, in locked cabinets.
- Never suggest to a child that medications or vitamin pills are candy.
- Do not take large doses of fat-soluble vitamins except under the direction of a physician.
- If you live in a house or apartment built before 1978, be certain that children do not ingest peeling paint. Consult a professional to test for lead, and, if lead is present, to minimize its release into the home.
- To avoid carbon monoxide poisoning, maintain and use fuel-burning tools and appliances properly, be certain that heating stoves and furnaces are correctly vented, and warm up the car outside rather than in the garage.
- Seek medical assistance immediately for anyone who exhibits symptoms of carbon monoxide poisoning.
- Do not disturb asbestos that is deteriorating.
- Seek professional help for asbestos cleanup.

www.jbpub.com/healthyliving

Environmental Health in the Workplace

Exposures to some toxins can occur both at home and at work, depending on one's occupation. Accidental carbon monoxide poisoning, for example, is certainly a hazard for automobile mechanics if car exhaust is not properly vented, but carbon monoxide poisoning more frequently occurs in the home. Pesticides are another group of toxic substances that persons may accidentally ingest at home if these chemicals are placed in unlabeled containers. However, pesticide poisoning more frequently occurs on the job in people

pesticides
chemicals that kill plant and animal pests and that can cause poisoning when ingested.

who manufacture or apply pesticides. Poisoning by exposure to certain solvents, metals, plastics, and adhesives generally occurs only during their manufacture.

Pesticide Poisoning

Pesticides are chemicals that kill plant and animal pests; they are used on farms and in homes and businesses to control insects, rodents, and weeds. People rarely become poisoned from spraying pesticides in their homes or yards; however, they should be cautious, spray downwind, and protect their skin and eyes. Occasionally, people accidentally drink or eat pesticides (or other toxic chemicals) stored in unmarked food containers in storage areas. For this reason, pesticides always should be kept in clearly marked containers. A person who has ingested pesticides should receive immediate medical attention.

People also contact pesticides in the food they eat. These pesticides are not simply what is sprayed on fruits and vegetables but are found in fish, seafood, and meat. Animals often ingest foods sprayed with pesticides. Marine and freshwater organisms also eat food contaminated with pesticides when rain washes chemicals from the land into the water. Animals store certain pesticides they eat (and other toxic chemicals such as heavy metals) in their tissues, especially in fat.

Although many harmful pesticides, such as DDT, have been banned in the United States, these toxic chemicals, as well as pesticides being manufactured today, persist in the food chain. In addition, certain harmful pesticides such as DDT are still used in other countries on crops that are imported to the United States. However, pesticide levels in humans from eating supermarket produce are not considered toxic. The FDA, EPA, and Food Safety and Inspection Service of the U.S. Department of Agriculture together ensure that the levels of pesticides in food are not hazardous to the health of consumers. Data collected by the FDA over a seven-year period shows that pesticide residues on infant foods and adult foods that infants and children eat are almost always *well below* the highest levels legally allowed by the EPA (and that includes testing foods such as bananas without washing and peeling them) (Foulke, 1993). See the "Managing Your Health" feature for tips on reducing the level of pesticides in your food.

Most often, pesticide poisoning occurs in workers who manufacture or apply pesticides (■ **Figure 16-4).** These people inhale or have their skin exposed to toxic chemicals over a period of time if their skin and respiratory passageways are not properly protected. The signs and symptoms of poisoning in such cases may be vague and nonspecific at first: headache, intermittent dizziness, and general discomfort. As the poisoning worsens, the symptoms progress to include insomnia, nausea, increased sweating, involuntary eye movements, double or blurred vision, ringing in the ears, and involuntary body movements. If exposure contin-

Reducing Pesticide Levels in the Food You Eat

- Scrub all fruits and vegetables with water.
- Remove and discard the outer leaves of leafy vegetables.

- Trim the fat from red meats.
- Remove the skin and underlying fat from fish and poultry.

- Discard pan drippings and broths from animal products.

ues, the poisoning victim may have convulsions. Treatment of chronic pesticide poisoning requires careful medical evaluation and is individualized for each patient.

Exposure to and Inhalation of Other Toxic Chemicals

A *solvent* is a liquid in which another substance is dissolved. Solvents are varied and perform a broad range of tasks in business and industry, such as removing unwanted substances (e.g., dry-cleaning solvents remove stains from clothing), or helping add coatings such as paints and sealers to surfaces. (In the latter case, the coating is dissolved in the solvent, which then evaporates upon drying.)

Exposure to most solvents slows nerve transmission in the brain and spinal cord, resulting in slowed movements and thought processes. Continued solvent exposure can lead to unconsciousness. Some solvents are irritants that can cause fluid to collect in the lungs or cause the skin to redden. Chronic exposure to solvents can also cause cracking or scaling of the skin.

Metals (such as aluminum, tin, copper, and iron) are elements that are usually shiny, are good conductors of heat and electricity, and can be melted, fused, hammered into thin sheets, or drawn into wires. Metals are extracted from ores by various processes. During these processes, ores are crushed, melted, and poured, which results in the production of metal dusts and vapors (■ Figure 16-5). Processing metal ores sometimes uses toxic and caustic chemicals such as sulfuric acid or cyanide, and often produces other toxic gases such as carbon monoxide and sulfur dioxide (see page 415–416). Various industries use metals in the manufacture of products such as bearings, solder, batteries, cutting tools, plumbing, cookware, and roofing materials.

Exposure to heavy metals results in a variety of signs and symptoms depending on the metal and how it enters the body. Inhaling metal dusts or fumes, for example, can cause a variety of lung disorders such as lung scarring, fluid in the lungs, and emphysema (a lung disease in which the air sacs break apart and breathing is difficult). Inhaling fumes of heavy metals can also irritate the eyes

▲Figure 16-4 Protection against Pesticides. This worker is properly protecting his skin and respiratory passageways from the pesticide spray.

▲Figure 16-5 Processing Steel. This woman is working at a blast furnace in a steel mill. She is wearing an asbestos suit for protection as she opens the furnace with a long tool to release the molten steel. In the process, she is exposed to metal vapor.

ANALYZING *Health-Related Information*

The following newspaper article discusses food irradiation and various points of view regarding this process. Read the article and evaluate it using the model for analyzing health-related information. The main points of the model are noted below; the model is fully explained on page 12–13.

1. Which statements are verifiable facts, and which are unverified statements or value claims?
2. What are the credentials of the person who wrote the article? If this information is available, does the author's background and education qualify him or her as an expert in the topic area?
3. What might be the motives and biases of the person who wrote article? State reasons for your answer.
4. Which information in the article is relevant to the topic? Which information is irrelevant?
5. Does the article attack the credibility of conventional scientists or medical authorities?

Based on the above analysis, do you think that this article is a reliable source of health-related information? Summarize your reasons for coming to this conclusion.

A bug-zapper for food

Many health experts say irradiation is not only safe but needed

Jill Burcum; Staff Writer

Salmonella. Listeria. *E. coli.* Campylobacter.

If there were a most-wanted list of culprits causing gastric distress and worse, these bacteria, or "bugs," would top it. Each year, they sicken millions and kill thousands of people, according to the Centers for Disease Control and Prevention. And during this decade, they've been responsible for some of the biggest and deadliest outbreaks of foodborne illness in U.S. history.

But if these bugs are the supercriminals of food safety, many experts believe there's a supercop available—irradiation—to stop these and other perpetrators. Approved by the federal government for use in a variety of foods, irradiation is a process in which food is zapped briefly with low levels of radiation to kill virtually all pathogens it may contain.

Nevertheless, the role irradiation will play in protecting the food supply is not yet clear. Although the most prestigious well-known health organizations favor irradiation, irradiated foods aren't yet sold on a widespread basis. In addition, a small but vocal group of activists who say the process is dangerous have added to consumer concerns.

What is clear, according to those on both sides of the issue, is the need for public education. "The best thing consumers can do is find out more information about it to help make the right decision for themselves," said Donald Derr, a Maryland-based food safety consultant.

Straightforward method

Irradiation may sound like a complex, futuristic innovation, but neither the concept nor the technology is new.

Scientists long have known that irradiation can sterilize and help preserve food, according to the International Food Information Council, in Washington, D.C. Its development began in the early part of the century and gained momentum in the 1950s as scientists sought peaceful applications of nuclear research.

In the early 1960s, the Food and Drug Administration approved the use of irradiation for white flour and potatoes. Two decades passed before the FDA approved irradiation of pork in 1985 and spices and fresh produce in 1986. In the meantime, use of irradiation grew to disinfect medical supplies, cosmetics, contact lens solution and baby pacifiers. In the 1990s, the FDA added poultry to the list of approved foods and in November 1997, red meat. Internationally, irradiated food is sold in more than 40 countries.

Both food and nonfood items undergo essentially the same process during irradiation, according to Dennis Olson, professor of animal science at Iowa State University (ISU), in Ames, and head of its irradiation center, which is the only such facility in the Upper Midwest.

In both its design and the way it works, the ISU facility is typical of many commercial operations, Olson said. It has three parts—a receiving room for the goods to be irradiated, a chamber in which they are exposed to radiation and then an area in which the products are picked up and transported away.

The foods are put in carts on a conveyor belt and moved automatically through the building.

Radiation is generated by a machine that accelerates electrons to 99 percent of the speed of light, according to Olson. Food passes through the electron beam thus produced. Other radiation sources approved for food use at other facilities include gamma rays, which are produced by the radioisotopes cobalt-60 or cesium-137, and machine-generated X rays.

'Nuked,' not radioactive

No matter what the source of radiation, pathogens in food are killed in the same way, according to Craig Hedberg, an epidemiologist with the Minnesota Department of Health.

Pathogens—which include bacteria, viruses and fungi—are both alive and replicating themselves, he said. Radiation exposure causes the pathogens' DNA, the double helix-shaped structure containing a cell's genetic material, to break, disabling the pathogens' ability to reproduce, so their populations rapidly wane.

Other types of contaminants, such as insect larvae, are eliminated the same way. So are the molds and fungi that play a role in ripening and spoilage in fruits and vegetables-one reason why irradiation can prolong the shelf life of many foods.

Irradiated food does not become radioactive, according to Olson and other experts. The reasons are that food is simply exposed to radiation, and approved doses don't cause changes at the atomic level that would result in radioactivity.

It's no more cosmic than a trip to the dentist, said Derr. "After you have an X ray, you don't think that you're radioactive, do you?"

Opposing views

Opponents of food irradiation point out that some molecular changes do occur after irradiation. Chemical bonds are broken during the process and new compounds, called radiolytic compounds, are produced.

Food and Water, a Vermont-based activist group, says some of these compounds never have been seen before, much less studied. Michael Colby, the group's executive director, said the safety of these compounds and other effects of irradiation, therefore, is not known.

The Internet has dozens of antifood-irradiation sites. Another group, the Center for Science in the Public Interest, doesn't oppose irradiation, but it worries that food handlers will rely on irradiation to sterilize food processed under filthy conditions.

Most-studied option

More traditional health organizations have endorsed the use of food irradiation, including the World Health Organization, the American Medical Association, the American Dietetic Association and the American Gastroenterological Association. The head of the FDA also has stated he is satisfied that the process doesn't change the nutritional content of food, its flavor or aroma.

Many proponents feel the safety issue is moot from a scientific point of view. "All questions about the safety of irradiated foods have been answered," said Derr.

Former Minnesota epidemiologist Michael Osterholm agreed, noting that studies on irradiation safety have been conducted for decades.

"It is the most extensively studied food safety technology in our history," said Osterholm, who has long advocated food irradiation. "There's more data on this than freezing, drying and canning combined."

Osterholm said radiolytic compounds do occur in irradiated food, but said the same ones occur in foods that are cooked, canned or exposed to sunlight.

Osterholm said irradiation complements other measures to ensure food safety, and it is more effective than any of them in preventing pathogens in food. Delaying its use, he said, costs lives.

"We are not going to get to the next level of food safety without irradiation," he said.

Will it sell?

The question is: Will consumers buy irradiated products? Because regulations require irradiated food to be labeled with a readily recognized symbol, consumers will know if the product they're buying has been irradiated by a symbol of circle with a plant inside. But most consumers thus far have not had a choice.

Even though food irradiation has been approved for years, few supermarkets—none in Minnesota, according to the state's Department of Health—carry irradiated produce.

That may be changing. While polls in the 1980s showed that a majority of consumers would not buy irradiated products, recent studies by advocates suggest that consumers may be more likely to buy them if they are told about irradiation's benefits.

Nationally, trade organizations for supermarkets, restaurants and meat producers greeted with enthusiasm the FDA's approval of red meat in November 1997. In Minnesota, Cargill has said it hopes to have a meat irradiation facility in a year. SuperValu, the Eden Prairie-based food wholesaler and retailer, and the Minnesota Department of Health also are working together to introduce irradiated ground beef. However, experts say that a shortage of irradiation facilities in this region may prevent treated products from reaching shelves soon.

Despite the controversy over food irradiation, many experts predict that it eventually will become as widespread and accepted as milk pasteurization, a heating process that kills pathogens but was itself controversial when first begun.

"Twenty years from now, we're going to look back and say `What was the discussion about?' " Osterholm said.

and mouth, damage the kidneys, and damage the brain and spinal cord, especially with exposure to lead, mercury, or manganese. Skin contact with fumes can cause burns, rashes, reddening, swelling, and itching. Exposure to many heavy metals also causes cancer.

Adhesives are used to join substances during assembly operations. In order to join parts, other processes may also be used, such as etching, roughening, or solvent cleaning. Each of these processes may introduce its own specific hazards.

In most cases, the U.S. Occupational Safety and Health Administration (OSHA) of the U.S. Department of Labor regulates procedures in industries to protect the health of workers. However, many small companies, such as auto repair shops, are not regulated by OSHA.

Indoor Air Pollution

As people became concerned about the excessive use of energy in the 1970s and started creating "tighter" buildings to conserve energy in heating and cooling, they also became concerned about the quality of indoor air. Numerous studies have been conducted during the past two decades to address this concern and determine the cause of "sick building syndrome."

sick building syndrome a variety of vague health-related problems reported by many occupants of large buildings.

formaldehyde (form-AL-de-hide) a chemical used in the manufacture of certain building materials and furnishings; may cause health problems when released into indoor air.

radon gas a substance present in the rocks and soils in many areas in the United States; may seep through cracks in basements and cause health problems.

Sick building syndrome refers to a variety of symptoms reported by occupants of large buildings. Buildings are identified as problems when a large proportion (sometimes as many as 30%) of their occupants complain about the same vague health-related problems, such as headaches; unusual fatigue; eye, nose, and throat irritation; and shortness of breath (Jaakkola & Miettinen, 1995).

The results of studies of sick buildings show the predominant problem to be inadequate ventilation (Jaakkola & Miettinen, 1995). A less frequent cause of health problems is chemical contamination from a variety of sources such as building materials, carpets, and plastic panels used as office dividers (Jaakkola & Seppanen, 1994). Other individual sources of contamination of indoor air are asbestos and combustion-generated pollutants (discussed earlier in this chapter), radon, and formaldehyde.

Formaldehyde is a chemical used in the manufacture of many building materials and furnishings, which then release formaldehyde into the air. Specific products that are most frequently responsible for high levels of formaldehyde in indoor air are pressed wood products such as fiberboard, particleboard, and hardwood plywood paneling; and urea-formaldehyde foam, which is usually used to insulate walls.

Formaldehyde irritates the eyes, nose, and sinuses; people who inhale formaldehyde may have difficulty breathing, experience chest pain, and begin to wheeze. Some people experience headaches, fatigue, nausea, and have difficulty sleeping, while others exhibit gastrointestinal disturbances such as vomiting and diarrhea. Formaldehyde's role in the development of asthma and cancer is controversial.

If formaldehyde contamination occurs in a home or public building (as noted by occupants' symptoms), the source must be determined and removed, or other measures must be taken to reduce the level of this gas in the indoor air. This process may be difficult and expensive. Removing urea-formaldehyde foam insulation from walls is costly and damages the walls. (However, urea-formaldehyde foam insulation installed 5 to 10 years ago is unlikely to still release formaldehyde.) Paneling may need to be removed or furniture discarded. Alternatives are to install an air ventilation system designed to remove toxic substances such as formaldehyde from the air, bring large amounts of fresh air into the building, or seal the surfaces of the formaldehyde-containing products (U.S. CPSC, 1997).

Radon gas may also contaminate indoor air. Radon is present in the rocks and soils in many areas in the United States. People who live in these regions may be exposed to radon gas if it leaks through cracks in basement walls and collects in their homes. Chapter 13 contains a discussion of this colorless and odorless gas and its relationship to lung cancer.

■ LIVING PRACTICES ■

- Always keep pesticides and other chemicals away from children and stored in sealed, marked containers.
- When working with pesticides, wear clothing that protects your skin, eyes, nose, and mouth.
- If you work with toxic chemicals, take measures to protect yourself from damage to skin and eyes, assess the danger from toxic fumes that may be created as a result of your work, and contact OSHA for more information.

www.jbpub.com/healthyliving

Environmental Health in the Outdoors

Water Pollution

People get the water they drink from underground reservoirs called *aquifers* and from above-ground sources: lakes, rivers, and man-made reservoirs. Both sources of water can become contaminated with toxic chemicals. Surface water, however, can also become contaminated with pathogens, plant fertilizers, sediments (soil), radioactivity, and heat.

In developed countries, waterborne pathogens are infrequently a cause of disease because sewage plants treat wastewater so it will not contaminate water supplies. Additionally, public drinking water is chlorinated to kill pathogens. However, infection can occur when water purification and supply systems break down. Waterborne infectious disease is a widespread problem in developing countries, which have no water purification systems.

Plant fertilizers, sediments, and heat, which often contaminate surface waters, do not generally harm humans. The radioactivity emitted by nuclear power plants that enters the water supply is thought to be so low as to be harmless to humans. However, chemical contaminants such as toxic chemical compounds (including pesticides), heavy metals (such as mercury and lead), and acids (from acid precipitation; see "Air Pollution" below) can cause noninfectious diseases and poisoning.

Chemical contaminants pollute both groundwater (aquifers) and surface water. Such pollutants enter surface water when industries spill waste chemicals into waterways, mining wastes flow into rivers, pesticides wash into rivers and lakes during a rain, and salt used to de-ice roads washes into rivers and streams during spring rains.

Heavy metals can also contaminate surface water. Metals enter the water when they are dumped into rivers and streams from industrial sources. However, the Clean Water Act of 1972 and the Federal Water Pollution Control Act of 1972 and their amendments have all been instrumental in prohibiting industry from discharging such toxic chemicals into surface water. Metals also get into drinking water on its way to homes by leaching from lead solder in water pipes. (Leaching is the removal of the dissolvable parts of a substance as water moves through or over it.) The Safe Drinking Water Act and its 1986 amendments authorize the EPA to monitor the safety of drinking water and requires the use of lead-free solder in plumbing pipes.

Groundwater becomes polluted from deteriorating underground petroleum storage tanks at gasoline stations, chemicals from road salting, or agricultural chemicals that leach into the ground. However, **hazardous waste** (toxic chemical waste) is the primary source of groundwater pollution as toxic chemicals leach into aquifers.

In 1980 Congress passed a toxic waste clean-up bill and allocated funds to clean up hazardous substances. Known as the Superfund, it provides money to find the parties guilty of dumping toxic waste at specific sites and force them to pay clean-up costs. If the government cannot find the guilty parties, it pays to have the sites cleaned up. Superfund has not worked because of massive legal problems (McKinney & Schoch, 1998). Two decades after this bill was passed by Congress, more sites have been created than have been cleaned up. Today, 1 in 4 Americans lives near a toxic waste site.

To ensure the safety of drinking water, purification methods in the United States often involve chlorination to kill unwanted pathogens. In fact, 75% of the nation's drinking water is treated with chlorine (Morris et al., 1992). In 1974, however, scientists realized that this chemical interacts with other chemicals in drinking water to form new compounds such as chloroform. Since this discovery, scientists have been studying whether these compounds are associated with the incidence of cancer. Although there is controversy in the scientific community regarding the conclusions that can be drawn from the data that has been collected, there does appear to be an association between the long-term consumption of chlorinated water and rectal, colon, and bladder cancers, as well as miscarriages, and birth defects (Cantor, 1994; Mills et al., 1998; Morris et al., 1992).

Becoming aware of the potential for water pollution is only the first step in protecting against the short-term and long-term health effects of drinking contaminated water. Tap water can be tested to be sure that it does not contain toxic or other unwanted chemicals. If it does, it can be treated using various methods such as carbon filtration. Carbon filters remove many carbon-containing compounds and chlorine from the water, improving its taste, odor, and color. The filters are not useful for all water-treatment needs. Some persons choose to use only bottled water for cooking and drinking. However, bottled water is not necessarily better than tap water. To judge its purity, have your bottled water tested for the presence of toxic chemicals, or write to the International Bottled Water Association (IBWA), 113 N. Henry St., Alexandria, VA 22314 for information regarding a specific bottler.

Air Pollution

Air pollution is also a threat to health. The primary substances in the air that harm humans are sulfur dioxide (SO_2), nitrogen dioxide (NO_2), carbon monoxide (CO), ozone (O_3), and particulates. These substances are formed when fossil fuels are burned. Fossil fuels are carbon-containing substances formed over time and under pressure from once-living organisms (both plants and animals). Gasoline, coal, natural gas, and oil are all fossil fuels.

The two main contributors to air pollution are automobiles and coal-fired power plants. The use of small gasoline-powered machines such as leaf blowers, chain saws, weed cutters, and snow blowers also contributes to air pollution.

Coal-fired power plants generate particulates and sulfur dioxide as their primary pollutants. People who live downwind of such power plants experience the greatest impact from these pollutants. Sulfur dioxide combines with water in the atmosphere to produce sulfuric acid, the major component of **acid precipitation**. Acid precipitation (rain, snow, and fog)

hazardous waste toxic chemical refuse.

acid precipitation rain, snow, or fog combined with sulfur dioxide from fossil fuel emissions.

damages both living and nonliving things, and acidifies surface water. Acid water in reservoirs leaches metals from pipes carrying the water into the drinking water supplies. The regions of the United States affected most heavily by acid precipitation are the Great Lakes area and New England. Southern Canada also experiences the effects of American power plant emissions.

Sulfur oxides and particulates also combine with atmospheric moisture to form a haze called **smog** (smoke plus fog). Cities with sulfur oxide smog are called *gray-air cities*. They are usually located in cold, moist climates and rely on coal and oil for electricity and home heating. Nashville, New York, Philadelphia, St. Louis, and Pittsburgh are among the gray-air cities of the United States (█ **Figure 16-6a**).

Of the sulfur oxides and particulates in smog, particulates do the most damage to the lungs. *Particulates* are small particles that are dispersed in the air. Although nasal hairs and mucus in the nose and throat trap large particles, particulates reach the lungs and accumulate over time. Eventually, this material irritates the lungs and blocks their microscopic air sacs, making breathing more difficult. Particulates in the air passageways and lungs can also be a factor in the development of respiratory diseases such as bronchitis, emphysema, and asthma. They also make existing respiratory illness worse.

Sulfur dioxide in the air irritates the mucous lining of the eyes and lungs. Like particulates, sulfur dioxide worsens

smog
(smoke and fog) a haze in the atmosphere formed by various pollutants.

Pollutant Standards Index (PSI) a guide to air quality that uses levels of various pollutants to determine its values.

respiratory illness. Together, particulates and sulfur dioxide have a greater effect on respiratory problems than if only one of these pollutants were present. At highest risk are the elderly and people with chronic lung and/or heart disease.

Carbon monoxide (see pages 406–407), nitrogen dioxide, and ozone are produced primarily as a result of emissions from vehicles. Nitrogen dioxide is formed when nitrogen gas in the air chemically combines with oxygen during the combustion of fuel. This compound irritates the eyes, lungs, and other mucous membranes. It also reacts with hydrocarbons (the hydrogen and carbon in fuel) in the presence of sunlight to produce a secondary pollutant—ozone. In the upper atmosphere, ozone protects us from the sun's damaging ultraviolet rays. But when it is in the air we breathe, ozone is irritating to the lungs.

Cities polluted primarily by the emissions of automobiles, or photochemical smog, are called *brown-air cities* (Figure 16-6b). They are located primarily in the western United States and include Denver, Los Angeles, and Albuquerque.

The **Pollutant Standards Index (PSI)** is a means by which the public is informed of air quality (█ **Table 16-3**). Levels of each of six pollutants (CO, NO_2, O_3, SO_2, particulates, and lead) contribute to the value shown for each level of air quality. The descriptor for air quality (good, moderate, unhealthful, and so forth) is determined by the concentration of the pollutants in the air. When the air is unhealthful or worse, the PSI cautionary statements should be heeded; many elderly persons and those with chronic lung or heart conditions can die during times of unhealthful and hazardous air quality. Since strict amendments to the Clean Air Act were passed in 1970 and even tougher standards were set with the passage of amendments in 1990, the quality of the air in the United States has improved greatly, but many cities and areas of the country still have high levels of pollution.

Noise Pollution

Noise pollution can have a negative effect on health, but it is unlike any of the environmental dusts, fumes, vapors, gases, and liquids discussed previously. Noise is composed of sound waves. If sound waves were visible, they would look much like ripples on water—areas of compressed air molecules followed by areas in which the molecules are more spread out. These waves in the air are the result of the vibration of an object disturbing the air around it.

The human ear detects these sound vibrations in the air as they hit the eardrum, causing it to vibrate. The vibrating eardrum moves the tiny bones of the

(a)

Figure 16-6 Gray-Air and Brown-Air Cities.
▲(a) New York City.
▶(b) Los Angeles, California.

(b)

Table 16-3	The Pollutant Standards Index			
psi Value	**Description**	**General Health Effects**	**psi Episode Level**	**Cautionary Statements**
0–50	Good	None		
51–100	Moderate	None		
101–199	Unhealthful	Mild aggravation of symptoms in susceptible persons, with irritation symptoms in the healthy population		Persons with existing heart or respiratory ailments should reduce physical exertion and outdoor activity
200–299	Very unhealthful	Significant aggravation of symptoms and decreased exercise tolerance in persons with heart or lung disease, with widespread symptoms in the healthy population	Stage 1 Health advisory alert	Elderly and persons with existing heart or lung disease should stay indoors and reduce physical activity
300–399	Hazardous	Premature onset of certain diseases in addition to significant aggravation of symptoms and decreased exercise tolerance in healthy persons	Stage 2 Health advisory warning	Elderly and persons with existing heart or lung disease should stay indoors and avoid physical exertion. General population should avoid outdoor activity
400–500	Hazardous	Premature death of ill and elderly. Healthy people will experience adverse symptoms that affect their normal activity	Stage 3 Emergency	All persons should remain indoors, keeping windows and doors closed. All persons should minimize physical exertion and avoid traffic

Source: U.S. Environmental Protection Agency.

middle ear, which, in turn, cause the fluid of the inner ear to move across delicate hairs. The hairs of the inner ear are connected to nerves that send messages to the brain. These messages are interpreted as sound. The fragile hairs, however, can be permanently injured by sound waves that are too loud.

How loud are everyday sounds? ▌ **Table 16-4** lists some everyday sounds and their loudness. Sound intensity, or loudness, is expressed in *decibels* (dB). The faintest sound a human can hear is considered zero (0) dB. As the intensity of sound increases on the decibel scale, each 10-dB increase means a tenfold increase in the intensity of the sound. Therefore, a 50-dB sound is 10 times louder than a 40-dB sound.

Sounds that are considered quiet or soft are 50 dB or less. The Environmental Protection Agency considers sounds at 55 dB or below to be safe (Shapiro, 1993). When sounds get as loud as 80 dB, they begin to be annoying. At 85 dB, hearing is at risk of permanent damage. Pain sets in at 120 dB.

The EPA estimates that 40% of the U.S. population is exposed to enough noise to cause permanent hearing loss (Angus, 1994). The average person can damage his or her hearing if he or she:

- Uses a power lawn mower (90 dB) for 8 hours
- Is at a loud party (90 dB) for 6 to 8 hours
- Uses a chain saw (100 dB) for 2 hours
- Uses a gasoline-powered leaf blower (110 dB) for 30 minutes
- Is at a dance club or rock concert (115 dB) for 15 minutes

Although you may not be at one party for 8 hours, damage to hearing from loud sounds is cumulative. That is, the effects add up. These effects can be devastating; the National Institutes of Health have determined that permanent hearing loss *will* result from years of exposure, 8 hours per day, to 85-dB and louder sounds (Shapiro, 1993). Permanent deafness may result from such continual exposure and can also result from a

DIVERSITY in Health

Hunger, the Environment, and the World's Populations

Nearly 1 out of 6 people in the world suffers from acute or chronic hunger. Hunger is more than appetite, the psychological desire for food, or feeling hungry after not eating for a few hours. Acute hunger, or starvation, is a condition in which a person has not eaten for a prolonged period and will eventually die from lack of food. Chronic hunger refers to a long-term condition in which food intake is inadequate. Persons experiencing chronic hunger are undernourished (see Chapter 9) and do not have the nutrients they need for proper growth, development, and body function.

Although many of the factors that lead to hunger are political, social, and economic, environmental conditions play a role in the many perceived causes of world hunger. Overpopulation, environmental limits to food production, and land use problems are factors that scientists debate with regard to their roles in hunger. In fact, many scientists assert that there is no global hunger problem. Instead, they assert, regional hunger problems exist, each with diverse causes.

The world population is approximately 6 billion people, increasing at a rate of approximately 100 million per year. Various experts in the United Nations predict that the world population will level off, reaching its carrying capacity between 12.4 billion and 14 billion people. The carrying capacity is the maximum number of individuals that can be supported by the available resources. However, scientists disagree as to whether the global food output can support that many individuals. Many scientists calculate that even with the use of the best agricultural technologies, the carrying capacity of the earth will be limited to 7.5 billion people.

Scientists disagree as to whether the increase in food production during the 1980s kept up with the need for food worldwide. They also disagree as to whether technological advances in various areas of agriculture, such as changes in machinery, seed varieties, fertilizers, pesticides, and management practices, as well as the genetic engineering of plants to resist certain crop pests, will allow the world's farmers to produce greater and greater crop yields. Many scientists assert that to increase sufficiently the amount of food produced around the world, farmers must increase the amount of land they cultivate. However, using marginal land (land not well-suited for cultivation) may increase the danger of erosion, landslides, and floods. Marginal land is also likely to produce lower crop yields than land already in cultivation. Additionally, the limited availability of water in many regions may constrain agricultural expansion.

Many parts of the earth cannot support the population that now exists on their lands. A country is overpopulated when its natural resources cannot sustain its people. An example of such overpopulation is Africa, the continent with the fastest population growth in the world. More than 50% of the African population is under the age of 15. Therefore, the size of this population will increase in the next decade and beyond because a large proportion of the population will be in its reproductive years. Much of the land in Africa has a low natural carrying capacity. Additionally, its climate is highly changeable and therefore unreliable for growing crops.

The problem of world or regional hunger is serious. Environmental issues such as overpopulation, methods of food production, and approaches to land use interact with political, cultural, social, and economic issues to create situations that can affect the health of many peoples throughout the world.

Source: Barbour, S., & Dudley, W. (Eds.). (1995). *Hunger.* San Diego: Greenhaven Press, Inc.

www.jbpub.com/healthyliving

single exposure, such as being close to an explosion of 140 dB.

How do people know if they are losing their hearing? First, a person may lose the ability to hear high-frequency sounds. He or she may be unable to hear occasional words in conversation or have difficulty hearing on the telephone. Additionally, people with partial hearing loss often experience ringing or roaring in their ears, called *tinnitus*. Tinnitus makes hearing even more difficult. Hearing aids may be helpful to the person with partial hearing loss but cannot totally compensate for the problem.

Total or partial hearing loss is only one of the effects of listening to sounds that are too loud. Parts of the body other than the ear react to noise. Researchers have shown that exposure to 70-dB noise results in an increase in the heart rate and a rise in blood pressure; muscles tighten and breathing patterns change. Exposure to noise also increases the rate at which stress-related hormones are secreted into the bloodstream. Even moderate daytime noise levels have been shown to increase anxiety and hostile behavior in some persons. In a variety of studies, environmental noise exposure has also been linked to

Table 16-4	Loudness of Some Everyday Sounds	
Sound Loudness		**(dB)**
Rustling leaves		10
Nornal conversation		50
Suburban neighborhood noise		52
Vacuum cleaner		70
City noise; busy traffic		80
Inside a passenger jet (takeoff)		78–83
Heavy trucks at 50 feet		76–88
Home shop tools		65–110
Subway noise		80–114
Nearby jet airplane		150
Shooting a gun		150–170

impaired learning ability and performance in school (Staples, 1996).

Paying attention to the noise in your environment will help save your hearing. For example, many health clubs blast loud music as an aerobics instructor yells commands. Often, these sounds top 110 dB. Request that the volume be turned down. If you wear ear protection, use only materials and items manufactured to reduce sound; placing cotton or tissue in your ears does not do an adequate job of protecting your ears.

If you attend loud concerts, check your hearing when you leave. Set your car or home radio to a level at which you can barely hear the words. Then, as soon after the concert as possible, turn on the radio. Can you hear the words? If not, you have sustained short-term hearing loss from the loudness of the music. Frequently listening to such loud music could result in a permanent hearing problem.

Healthy LIVING PRACTICES

- To avoid hearing loss and the other effects of noise pollution, avoid situations in which the sound is over 80 dB. Pay attention to noise levels and complain if they are too high.
- If you must work or be temporarily in an environment with noise over 80 dB, wear ear protection.

Environmental Health

Environmental health hazards are a risk for all segments of the population. However, young children are most at risk for unintentional poisoning by ingestion of toxic substances because they lack understanding that these materials are harmful and they put most things in their mouths; this is a normal exploratory behavior for small children. Additionally, carbon monoxide and lead are particularly injurious to fetuses and young children because their brains and nervous systems are still developing. Also extremely susceptible to carbon monoxide poisoning or air pollutants are the elderly and persons with chronic lung or heart disease, whose lung function may be impaired.

Chapter Review

Summary

In general, environmental factors that are the sole cause of disease are toxic chemicals. Such substances damage body tissues and affect bodily functioning; they are present in the home, workplace, and environment. Toxic chemicals are found in a wide variety of substances, such as household products, plants, products used in the workplace, and prescription and illegal drugs.

Toxic (poisonous) plants can be the source of poisoning emergencies, especially in children. Ingesting toxic plants is the fourth most common cause of poisoning, and 86% of plant poisonings involve small children. Although many plants are not poisonous, house plants and cut flowers should be kept out of reach of children under 5 years old. In addition to plants, approximately 1% to 2% of mushroom species are poisonous.

Children under the age of 5 years are those most in danger of being poisoned from household cleaning aids and from over-the-counter and prescription drugs and vitamins. Special packaging that makes it difficult for young children to open hazardous products has lowered the incidence of poisoning in this age group. Nevertheless, such substances should be locked in cabinets in homes in which young children reside or visit often.

Lead poisoning is still a health problem in children in the United States even though many sources of lead poisoning have been eliminated in this country. Lead poisoning is serious because it affects the central nervous system and can cause coma, convulsions, and death. Children can exhibit a wide range of symptoms of lead poisoning, depending on the level of lead in the blood. It is extremely important to remove sources of lead, such as lead-based paint, from a child's environment.

Carbon monoxide poisoning can occur when levels of this gas build up in an enclosed environment. Major sources of carbon monoxide poisoning are fires, automobile exhaust, malfunctioning furnaces, charcoal fires, gasoline-powered tools, woodstoves, fireplaces, unvented kerosene and gas space heaters, gas cooking stoves and ovens, and tobacco smoke. To avoid this hazard, properly maintain and use tools and appliances that burn fuel, avoid running the car in the garage, vent home heating stoves and furnaces properly, and use charcoal grills and gas-powered tools only in well-ventilated areas.

The data are unclear regarding the risk to humans of exposure to the extremely low frequency (ELF) radiation emitted by computer screens, television sets, electric blankets, electric appliances, high-tension electric power lines, and electrical distribution substations. Medical researchers suggest, however, that people avoid being unnecessarily close to products and power lines that emit ELF radiation.

Many types of environmental hazards exist in the workplace. Common workplace hazards include exposure to pesticides while manufacturing or applying them, and exposure to toxins in the industrial manufacture and use of certain solvents, metals, plastics, and adhesives. People who work with toxic chemicals should protect themselves from damage to their skin and eyes and should assess the danger from toxic fumes that may be created as a result of their work.

Indoor air may be contaminated with pollutants such as formaldehyde, asbestos, and combustion-generated products. Some buildings have poor ventilation systems, which are the primary cause of vague health-related symptoms in building occupants.

The air we breathe and the water we drink are also contaminated with toxins to a greater or lesser degree in various parts of the United States. Contaminated drinking water can result in both short-term and long-term health effects. The air is contaminated with emissions from coal-fired power plants and vehicles. When the air is unhealthful, the elderly and those with respiratory illness are most at risk for further damage to their health.

Noise pollution can have a negative effect on health. Sounds at 55 dB and below are considered safe. To avoid hearing loss and other negative health effects of noise pollution, persons should avoid situations in which the sound is over 80 dB or should wear specially designed ear protection in such situations.

Applying What You Have Learned

1. Your 4-year-old cousin is coming to visit for the summer. What steps would you take to make your house or apartment safe for your cousin? *(Application)*

2. List and then analyze your interactions with the environment in the last 24 hours. Develop a list of environmental threats to your health from these interactions. *(Analysis)*

3. You have just moved to a part of the country that is new to you. Develop a plan to assess whether you are being exposed to hazardous chemicals and toxins and to evaluate which health hazards might be present, if any. *(Synthesis)*

4. Develop a fictitious set of at least three outcomes based on question 3. What will be your course of action to diminish or eliminate these threats to your health? *(Evaluation)*

KEY
Application: Using information in a new situation.
Analysis: Breaking down information into component parts.
Synthesis: Putting together information from different sources.
Evaluation: Making informed decisions.

Reflecting On Your Health

1. Do you take steps to protect your hearing? If so, what do you do? Do you think about possible hearing loss when you are in noisy environments? Describe three situations in which you regularly are exposed to harmful noise levels and discuss what you can do to avoid hearing loss in these situations.

2. Go through your house or apartment and identify environmental health risks. What can you do to reduce these risks to health?

3. Do you ever put yourself or others at risk for carbon monoxide poisoning? If so, describe your risky behaviors and what you can do to eliminate the risk. If not, identify behaviors in others that you have observed that put people at risk for carbon monoxide poisoning. How might you help others avoid such risks?

4. Find out about environmental risks in your area. For example, is your tap water chlorinated to levels that are worrisome? Do you live in a region of the country in which water comes to your home in lead pipes? What might you do in either of these situations to reduce or eliminate your health risks from water? Investigate air pollution in your area. Do you live in a gray-air city or in a brown-air city or neither? How can you protect your respiratory health in the region in which you live? Describe any environmental health risks that affect your community and suggest what you might do to reduce health risks to yourself and your family.

5. Do you ever discard toxic waste improperly, such as putting old batteries (especially car batteries), solvents, or paints in the trash? If so, describe the proper disposal methods for these substances in your city or town.

References

Angus, R. (1994). Sounds. Raising a ruckus about noise: It threatens your hearing and your health. *Omni, 16*(5):18.

Cantor, K. P. (1994). Water chlorination, mutagenicity, and cancer epidemiology. *American Journal of Public Health, 84*:1211–1213.

Centers for Disease Control and Prevention (CDC). (1993). Lead poisoning associated with use of traditional ethnic remedies—California, 1991–1992. *Morbidity and Mortality Weekly Report, 42*:521–524.

Farley, D. (1998). Dangers of lead still linger. *FDA Consumer, 32*(1):16-21.

Fergusson, D. M., Horwood, L. J., Beautrais, A. L., & Shannon, F. T. (1982). A controlled field trial of a poisoning prevention method. *Pediatrics, 69*:515–520.

Fingerhut, L. A., & Cox. C. S. (1998). Poisoning mortality, 1985–1995. *Public Health Reports, 113*:218–233.

Foulke, J. E. (1993). FDA reports on pesticides in foods. *FDA Consumer, 27*(5):29–32.

Furbee, B., & Wermuth, M. (1997). Life-threatening plant poisoning. *Critical Care Clinics, 13*:849–888.

Horn, Y. (1995). The potential carcinogenic hazards of electromagnetic radiation: A review. *Cancer Detection & Prevention, 19*:244–249.

Jaakkola, J. J. K., & Miettinen, P. (1995). Type of ventilation system in office buildings and sick building syndrome. *American Journal of Epidemiology, 141*:755–765.

Jaakkola, J. J. K., & Seppanen, P. T. O. (1994). Textile wall materials and sick building syndrome. *Archives of Environmental Health, 49*:175–180.

Kirsner, R. S., & Federman, D. G. (1998). Video display terminals: Risk of electromagnetic radiation. *Southern Medical Journal, 91*:12–16.

Krenzelok, E. P., Jacobsen, T. D., & Aronis, J. M. (1996). Plant exposures: A state profile of the most common species. *Veterinary & Human Toxicology, 38*:289–298.

Lamarine, R. J., & Narad, R. A. (1992). Health risks associated with residential exposure to extremely low frequency electromagnetic radiation. *Journal of Community Health, 17*:291–301.

Litovitz, T. (1998). The Toxic Exposure Surveillance System (TESS) database. Use in product safety assessment. *Drug Safety, 18*(1):9–19.

McKinney, M. L., & Schoch, R. M. (1998). *Environmental Science: Systems and Solutions.* Sudbury MA: Jones & Bartlett Publishers.

Mills, C. J., Bull, R. J., Cantor, K. P., Reif, J., Hrudey, S. E., & Huston, P. (1998). Workshop report. Health risks of drinking water chlorination by-products: Report of an expert working group. *Chronic Diseases in Canada, 19*:91–102.

Morris, R. D., Audet, A., Angelillo, I. F., Chalmers, T. C., & Mosteller, F. (1992). Chlorination, chlorination by-products, and cancer: A meta-analysis. *American Journal of Public Health, 82*: 955–963.

Office of Pollution Prevention and Toxics (OPPT). (1994). *Reducing lead hazards when remodeling your home.* Washington, DC: United States Environmental Protection Agency.

Reiter, R. J. (1994). Melatonin suppression by static and extremely low frequency electromagnetic fields: Relationship to the reported increased incidence of cancer. *Reviews on Environmental Health, 10*:171–186.

Salvatore, J. R., & Weitberg, A. B. (1989). Non-ionizing electromagnetic radiation and cancer—is there a relationship? *Rhode Island Medical Journal, 72*:15–21.

Shapiro, S. A. (1993, Spring). Rejoining the battle against noise pollution. *Issues in Science and Technology, 9*:73–79.

Shepard, G., & Klein-Schwartz, W. (1998). Accidental and suicidal adolescent poisoning deaths in the United States, 1979–1994. *Archives of Pediatrics & Adolescent Medicine, 152*:1181–1185.

Smith, I. (1996). Electromagnetic radiation and health risks. *Journal of Environmental Health, 59*:19–21.

Staples, S. L. (1996). Human response to environmental noise. *American Psychologist, 51*:143–150.

Tsubota, K., & Nakamori, K. (1993). Dry eyes and video display terminals. *The New England Journal of Medicine, 328*:584.

U.S. Consumer Product Safety Commission (CPSC). (1989). Asbestos in the home. Washington, DC: U.S. Environmental Protection Agency.

U.S. Consumer Product Safety Commission (CPSC). (1997). *An Update on Formaldehyde. 1997 Revision.* Washington, DC: U.S. Environmental Protection Agency.

Venberg, K., Culver-Dickinson, P., & Spyker, D.A. (1984). The deterrent effect of poison-warning stickers. *American Journal of Diseases of Children, 138*:1018–1020.

Yoon, S. S., Macdonald, S. C., & Parrish, R. G. (1998). Deaths from unintentional carbon monoxide poisoning and potential for prevention with carbon monoxide detectors. *Journal of the American Medical Association, 279*:685–687.

Injury Prevention and Emergency Care

Injury Prevention

During the next hour, at least 11 people will die in the United States from unintentional injuries. The causes will be diverse, including automobile crashes, drownings, poisonings (see Chapter 16), and fires. Some of those who die this hour will probably be children, because unintentional, preventable injury is the number one killer of children (through young adulthood, from 1 through 21 years old) in the United States. In fact, unintentional injuries kill more children than all childhood diseases combined.

Until recently, the number of fatal unintentional injuries had been steadily declining, reaching a 68-year low of approximately 89,000 in 1994. However, that number has been rising annually since then. In 1997, slightly more than 92,000 people died from unintentional injuries. This appendix will alert you to the most prevalent types of unintentional injuries and deaths in the United States today, and discusses their causes, prevention, and emergency treatment.

Automobile Safety

Motor-vehicle crashes are the greatest cause of preventable death due to injuries and have been increasing since 1992. In 1997, approximately 43,500 people died on America's roads and highways. Nearly half of them were driving while intoxicated or were killed by drunk drivers. In addition to deaths, motor-vehicle accidents are the leading cause of unintentional injury in the United States. To keep yourself and others safe while riding in automobiles, heed the following recommendations. For general vehicle safety:

- Never drink and drive or take other drugs that impair your ability to drive.
- Always wear your seat belt; this practice reduces by half your chance of injury or death in a motor-vehicle crash.
- Slow down and prepare to stop as you approach yellow lights. Many people cause automobile crashes because they try to "beat" the light.
- Yield the right of way at intersections.
- Don't tailgate; allow at least one car length for each 10 mph (e.g., stay four car lengths behind the car ahead if you are traveling at 40 mph).
- Know the traffic laws of the state in which you are driving and obey these laws.
- Read and heed traffic signs, especially railroad warning signals and gates. Always proceed cautiously across railroad tracks. Not all railroad crossings have gates or sound warnings to signal oncoming trains.
- Obey the speed limit.

Children and Automobile Safety To protect children while they are passengers in automobiles, follow these safety recommendations:

- Place infants in properly secured rear-facing safety seats until they are one year of age and weigh at least 20 lb.
- Always put rear-facing child safety seats in the back seat. Deploying passenger-side air bags in the front seat can injure or kill infants in rear-facing seats.
- Properly restrain all children in safety seats, lap belts, or lap and shoulder belts. Children should be restrained in car seats until they weigh 40 lb. and then should be in booster seats until they are about 8 years old and weigh 80 lb.
- An infant's or child's car seat needs to be secured so tightly that it will not move more than one inch from side to side. Locate a certified Child Passenger Safety Seat Technician in your area to check the installation of your child's safety seat.
- It is best to have children of any age ride in the back seat to avoid injury from a deploying air bag. If a child must ride in the front, push the seat back as far as possible to create distance between the child and the bag.
- Never leave a child alone in the car.

Pedestrian Safety

Pedestrians account for 14% of preventable deaths involving motor vehicles in the United States and approximately 3% of motor-vehicle-related injuries. Not only are drunk drivers often a cause of these injuries and deaths, but intoxicated pedestrians put themselves at increased risk. Other high-risk groups for sustaining unintentional pedestrian-automobile injuries and deaths are the elderly and young children. Children are most frequently hit when they dart into traffic from between parked cars. Children younger than 10 years old do not have fully developed cognitive, developmental, behavioral, physical, and sensory abilities to be safe pedestrians on their own. To help prevent pedestrian injuries, practice these safety steps:

- Help children develop injury-prevention skills by modeling proper safety behaviors such as those listed here.
- Be sure that children younger than 10 years of age are accompanied by an older person when they cross the street.
- Cross at marked crosswalks and at corners whenever possible. Do not assume that drivers will stop because you are in a crosswalk.

- Stop, look both ways, and listen before deciding that it is safe to cross. Continue to look and listen as you cross.
- Cross only on a green light or a "walk" signal.
- Never cross between parked cars.
- Never run into the street.
- Walk on sidewalks whenever possible. If you must walk in the street, walk to the left facing traffic.
- When walking at dusk or at night, wear light colors and some type of reflective device. Walk with someone, not alone.
- Do not allow children to play in driveways, in adjacent unfenced yards, in streets, or in parking lots.

Water Safety

In 1997, slightly more than 4,000 people died from drowning. Drowning is the second leading cause of injury-related death for children aged 1 through 14 years, the highest rates being for children aged 1 through 4 years. (Fatalities involving automobiles is the leading cause of injury-related death for children.) Most drownings of children happen in pools, hot tubs, or spas owned by their parents, relatives, or friends, and they happen within five minutes of the child's being missing from sight. Children usually drown silently, so don't think that splashing or screaming will alert you to the danger.

Safety for Small Children To protect small children from drowning in residential pools or other accessible bodies of water, follow these safety practices:

- Provide barriers to water, such as fences and walls. If the house is part of the barrier, install door alarms so you know when the child has gone outside, and install a power-safety cover over the pool, hot tub, or spa.
- Fence gates should be self-closing and self-latching. The latch should be out of a child's reach.
- Never prop open the fence gate.
- Instruct babysitters about pool hazards for young children.
- If a young child is missing, check the pool first.
- Do not assume that children will not drown because they know how to swim.
- Never leave a child unsupervised near a pool, and while at the pool, watch small children continuously; do not become preoccupied with something else.
- Children can drown in the bathtub, in a bucket of water, or in the toilet. Never leave children alone, even for a minute, when they are in or near any type of water.

Safety for Swimmers Even good swimmers have accidents in the water and drown. For safety in the water, follow these guidelines:

- Never swim alone.
- Don't push or jump on others.
- Check water depth before you dive or jump into the water.
- Never swim in unsupervised areas such as quarries, canals, or ponds.
- Don't swim or use a hot tub or spa while drinking alcoholic beverages or taking other drugs that could impair your judgment, impair your ability to swim, or make you drowsy. (Alcohol is involved in 25% to 50% of adolescent and adult deaths associated with water recreation.)

Bicycle Safety

In the United States, approximately 700 people die annually in traffic-related bicycle crashes. Seventy-five percent of these deaths are due to head injuries. Supporters of wearing bicycle helmets contend that 40% to 75% of head-injury deaths could be prevented if riders wore helmets. Opponents suggest that these statistics are unreliable and that most bicycle fatalities involve a crash with an automobile, a situation in which a helmet cannot protect the bicyclist. Those who take a middle stance suggest that it is prudent to wear helmets because they protect the head in many types of falls and make bicyclists more visible to automobile drivers.

By early 1999, 15 states and more than 65 local governments had enacted legislation about bicycle helmets. Most of these laws pertain to children and adolescents. Also in 1999, the U.S. Consumer Product Safety Commission issued a new safety standard for bike helmets.

Bicycle helmets are designed to absorb much of the impact when the head hits another object like a car or the road. Oftentimes, a cyclist hits a car and then the road, so the helmet needs a strap to ensure that it stays on during multiple hits. Also, it should not be covered with any material that can catch on something during a fall and twist the cyclist's head. When purchasing a helmet, make sure that it is level on the head, covers the top of the forehead, touches all around, and is comfortably snug. Many sellers and manufacturers of helmets offer instructions about the proper fit of helmets.

Bicycle injuries are a leading cause of preventable death in children, exceeding the death rate from poisonings, falls, and firearm injuries combined. Most bicycle-related deaths occur from head trauma and are not caused by colliding with cars. Rather, children fall from their bikes or lose control of their bikes and collide with objects such as curbs and trees. Therefore, all children benefit from wearing helmets while bicycling. They should also wear helmets while being carried as passengers on adults' bikes. Have a pediatrician check a toddler's helmet, however, because the neck muscles of toddlers are weak and may be unable to properly support a helmeted head.

Bicycle Safety Rules For bicycling safety, follow these simple rules:

- Make yourself or your children visible with light-colored clothing and reflective tape.
- Be certain that your bicycle horn or bell is working properly.
- Drive on the right-hand side of the road in single file, obeying all traffic signs and signals. Small children should ride their bikes on the sidewalk.
- When cycling in the road, leave a distance of about three feet between you and parked cars. You will be more noticeable to drivers and will not be knocked off your bike by the opening doors of parked cars.
- Walk your bike at busy street corners in pedestrian crosswalks.
- Never carry a passenger on your bicycle unless you have a tandem bike or are carrying a child in a properly mounted child seat.
- When exiting a driveway into a lane of traffic, stop, look both ways, and listen to determine that it is safe to enter.
- Before turning, use hand signals and look in all directions.
- Don't ride your bike on rainy nights. Your chances of being involved in a crash are 30 times greater than on a dry night because roads are slippery, wet bicycle brakes do not work well, and automobile drivers cannot see bicyclists well in the rain.
- If you are falling off your bike, tuck and roll rather than extending an arm to break your fall.
- Children should not ride in the street until they are 10 years old, demonstrate good riding skills, and are able to observe the basic rules of the road.

Fire Prevention

Although the number of residential fires has declined about 30 percent since 1980, every year there are still over 400,000 residential fires (one every 70 seconds) in which more than 3,000 people die. Most fires are started by home cooking equipment. However, residential fires caused by lit cigarettes, cigarette lighters, or matches are the leading cause of fire-related death. A fewer number of fires are ignited by faulty electrical wiring or supplemental home heating devices such as wood stoves, kerosene heaters, gas-fired space heaters, and portable electric heaters.

The number of supplemental home heaters has decreased in recent years, as has the number of fires associated with them. However, supplemental heaters still cause about 22% of residential fires. Additionally, thousands of people are burned each year by coming into contact with the hot surfaces of these devices, and hundreds are poisoned by their carbon monoxide emissions (see Chapter 16).

Home Heaters Some safety recommendations for the use of supplemental home heaters include:

- Be certain that any supplemental heater is properly installed and meets building codes.

- Inspect wood stoves according to the manufacturer's directions (usually twice monthly) and have chimneys inspected and cleaned by a professional chimney sweep.
- Use a floor protector designed for use under the type of supplemental heater you have. It should extend 18 inches beyond the heater on all sides.
- Follow directions regarding how far the heater must be from combustible walls and other materials such as draperies.
- Never burn trash in a wood-burning stove because this practice could cause overheating.
- Never use gasoline to start a wood fire.
- Use only the fuel(s) the manufacturer has designated as safe in the heater.
- If using a liquid fuel, be certain that its container is well marked and is out of the reach of children.
- Place kerosene heaters out of the path of traffic and where they cannot be knocked over.
- Always fill a kerosene heater outdoors and when the heater is not operating.
- Kerosene heaters are not usually vented; therefore, keep a window ajar for ventilation.
- Use unvented gas heaters only in large, open areas that are well ventilated; do not operate vented styles unvented.
- Do not use supplemental heating devices while you are sleeping or not at home; many fires and deaths occur at these times from the unsupervised use of supplemental heaters.
- With electric heaters, follow the manufacturer's recommendations regarding the type of power cord to use. Avoid using extension cords, but if you do, be certain that it is marked with a power rating at least as high as that of the heater itself. Keep the cord stretched out and do not place anything on top of the cord.

General Fire Prevention Many residential fires could have been prevented with little trouble. To decrease your risk of fire, take the following precautions:

- Keep matches and cigarette lighters away from children.
- Do not store food items such as candy or other items attractive to children above the stove.
- Always check ashtrays to be certain that cigarettes are out. After a party or other gathering, check under and between the cushions of upholstered furniture to make sure that no smoldering ashes are present.
- Never place ashtrays on the arms of furniture, especially upholstered furniture that is likely to ignite from lit cigarettes or their ashes.
- Avoid placing lit candles near draperies or other flammable materials. Be certain that they do not tip easily and are not positioned where they can be easily knocked over.

- Consider purchasing clothes made out of fabrics that are difficult to ignite and tend to self-extinguish, such as 100% polyester, nylon, wool, and silk. Cotton, cotton/polyester blends, rayon, and acrylic ignite easily and burn rapidly.
- Store flammable liquids, such as gasoline and paint thinners, outside the house. They produce invisible explosive vapors.
- Install at least one smoke detector on each floor of your home and near the bedrooms. Replace the batteries annually or when they make a chirping sound.
- Plan an escape route from each room in the house. Have each family member rehearse the plan often. Designate a safe place to meet if you have to escape a fire in your home. This helps firefighters determine if there are people in a burning building.

Source of statistics for injury prevention: Centers for Disease Control and Prevention, National Center for Injury Prevention and Control.

Emergency Care

When to Call for Help

Know the emergency number in your area; in most areas that number is 9-1-1. Calling for help in a medical emergency is important and may save a person's life. When a serious situation occurs, call for emergency medical help *first*. Do not call your doctor, the hospital, a friend, relatives, or neighbors. Calling anyone else first only wastes time.

Call for emergency help in the following situations:

- severe bleeding
- drowning
- electrocution
- possible heart attack
- breathing difficulty or no breathing
- choking
- altered mental status (e.g., as confused, disoriented as to time and place, cannot speak clearly or make sense)
- poisoning
- attempted suicide
- some seizure cases (most do not require emergency assistance)
- critical burns
- paralysis
- spine injury
- imminent childbirth

When in doubt, CALL.

Good Samaritan Laws

States have enacted laws to protect physicians and other medical personnel from legal actions that may arise from emergency treatment they give while not on duty. Although Good Samaritan laws cover medical personnel primarily, several states have expanded them to include laypersons who, in good faith, help others in emergency situations. Unless a person acts in a reckless or wantonly negligent manner when trying to voluntarily assist another, he or she is usually immune from conviction in a legal action. These laws vary from state to state; find out about your state's Good Samaritan laws by contacting a legal professional or checking with your local library.

Heart Attack

For information on recognizing the signs of a possible heart attack and on how to respond, see Chapter 12, especially page 282.

Poisoning

For information on preventing poisonings and how to treat a person who has been poisoned, see Chapter 16, especially pages 402 to 407.

Bleeding

If a person is bleeding heavily from a wound, it is important to stop the bleeding as quickly as possible. First, take the following action, then call for help or take the person to an emergency room.

- Expose the wound by removing or cutting the clothing to see where the blood is coming from.
- Place a sterile gauze pad or a clean cloth (such as a washcloth or towel) over the entire wound and apply direct pressure with your fingers or the palm of your hand.
- If the bleeding is from an arm or leg, while still applying pressure, elevate the injured area above heart level to reduce blood flow.
- When the bleeding stops, wrap a roller gauze bandage tightly over the dressing to hold it in place and prevent further bleeding.

Breathing Emergencies

Signs of inadequate breathing include a rate of breathing significantly less than 12 times per minute (for adults), skin that is pale or bluish and cool, and nasal flaring, especially in children. Ask someone to call for emergency help, and then if the person is *not* breathing:

- Tilt the head back and lift the chin to open the airway.
- Pinch the victim's nose shut, take a deep breath, and make a tight seal around the victim's mouth with your mouth.
- Slowly blow air into the victim's mouth until you see the chest rise.
- Remove your mouth to allow the air to come out, and turn your head away as you take another breath.
- Repeat one more breath.

- Check to see if the victim has a pulse. If the victim is not breathing and has a pulse:
- Give one breath about every 5 seconds for an adult.
- Recheck for pulse and breathing about every minute.
- Continue this process as long as the person has a pulse but is not breathing, until help arrives.

If the first breath does not go in, retilt the victim's head and try a second breath. If the second breath does not go in, use the procedure to aid a choking victim.

Choking

You can tell if a person is choking if he or she is unable to speak, breathe, or cough; or breathes with a high-pitched wheezing. A choking victim may instinctively reach up and clutch his or her neck. To help, first tell someone to call for emergency care. Then,

- stand behind the choking person.
- wrap your arms around the victim's waist. (Do not allow your forearms to touch the ribs.)
- make a fist with one hand and place the thumb side just above the victim's navel.
- grasp your fist with your other hand.
- press your fist into the victim's abdomen with 5 quick upward thrusts. (This procedure is called the Heimlich maneuver or abdominal thrusts.)

Each thrust should be a separate and distinct effort to dislodge the object. After every 5 abdominal thrusts, check the victim and the positioning of your hands.

Burns

If a person is burned by fire and his or her clothing is on fire, have the victim roll on the ground using the "stop, drop, and roll" method. You can also smother the flames with a blanket or douse the victim with water. Ask someone to call for emergency help. Then,

- remove jewelry and hot or burned clothing immediately, but *do not* remove clothing stuck to the skin.
- cool the burn. Use large amounts of cool water, not ice. Immerse the burn in cool water if possible.
- Cover the burn with dry, sterile dressings or clean cloths.
- Wait for help or transport the person to the emergency room of the local hospital.

Heat-Related Emergencies

Everyone is susceptible to heat illness if environmental conditions overwhelm the body's temperature-regulating mechanisms. Such illnesses are progressive conditions, and could become life threatening. Therefore, it is important to recognize heat-related illness early and treat it immediately.

Heat cramps are painful muscular spasms that happen suddenly, usually in the legs and abdomen. If someone has heat cramps, have him or her

- rest in a cool place,
- drink lightly salted cool water (1/4 tsp. salt per quart of water) or a commercial sports drink diluted to half strength, and
- lightly stretch and gently massage the cramped muscle.

Heat exhaustion is another heat-related emergency. It is characterized by heavy perspiration with normal or slightly above normal body temperatures and is caused by water or salt depletion or both. To help a person with heat exhaustion, have him or her

- rest in a cool place,
- drink lightly salted cool water (1/4 tsp. salt per quart of water) or a commercial sports drink diluted to half strength,
- remove excess clothing, and
- lie down and raise the legs 8 to 12 inches, while keeping them straight.

Sponge the victim with cool water and fan him or her. If no improvement is seen within 30 minutes, seek medical attention.

In its advanced stages, heat exhaustion is called heat stroke and can cause death. It must be treated rapidly. Heat stroke is characterized by red, hot, dry skin and an altered mental state ranging from slight confusion and disorientation to coma. To treat heat stroke, send someone for emergency care and

- have the person rest in a cool place,
- remove clothing down to the victim's underwear,
- keep the victim's head and shoulders slightly elevated,
- cool the person by placing ice bags wrapped in wet towels on the wrists, ankles, groin, and neck, and in the armpits, and
- fan the person.

Source of emergency care information: National Safety Council. (1999). *First Aid and CPR.* Sudbury, MA: Jones & Bartlett Publishers.

Appendix B

Food and Nutrition Board, National Academy of Sciences—National Research Council Recommended Dietary Allowances,[a] Revised 1989 (Abridged)

Designed for the maintenance of good nutrition of practically all healthy people in the United States

Category	Age (years) or Condition	Weight[b] (kg)	Weight[b] (lb)	Height[b] (cm)	Height[b] (in)	Protein (g)	Vitamin A (µg RE)[c]	Vitamin E (mg α-TE)[d]	Vitamin K (µg)	Vitamin C (mg)	Iron (mg)	Zinc (mg)	Iodine (µg)	Selenium (µg)
Infants	0.0–0.5	6	13	60	24	13	375	3	5	30	6	5	40	10
	0.5–1.0	9	20	71	28	14	375	4	10	35	10	5	50	15
Children	1–3	13	29	90	35	16	400	6	15	40	10	10	70	20
	4–6	20	44	112	44	24	500	7	20	45	10	10	90	20
	7–10	28	62	132	52	28	700	7	30	45	10	10	120	30
Males	11–14	45	99	157	62	45	1,000	10	45	50	12	15	150	40
	15–18	66	145	176	69	59	1,000	10	65	60	12	15	150	50
	19–24	72	160	177	70	58	1,000	10	70	60	10	15	150	70
	25–50	79	174	176	70	63	1,000	10	80	60	10	15	150	70
	51+	77	170	173	68	63	1,000	10	80	60	10	15	150	70
Females	11–14	46	101	157	62	46	800	8	45	50	15	12	150	45
	15–18	55	120	163	64	44	800	8	55	60	15	12	150	50
	19–24	58	128	164	65	46	800	8	60	60	15	12	150	55
	25–50	63	138	163	64	50	800	8	65	60	15	12	150	55
	51+	65	143	160	63	50	800	8	65	60	10	12	150	55
Pregnant						60	800	10	65	70	30	15	175	65
Lactating	1st 6 months					65	1,300	12	65	95	15	19	200	75
	2nd 6 months					62	1,200	11	65	90	15	16	200	75

NOTE: This table does not include nutrients for which Dietary Reference Intakes have recently been established (see Dietary Reference Intakes for Calcium, Phosphorus, Magnesium, Vitamin D, and Fluoride [1997] and Dietary Reference Intakes for Thiamin, Riboflavin, Niacin, Vitamin B₆, Folate, Vitamin B₁₂, Pantothenic Acid, Biotin, and Choline [1998]).

[a] The allowances, expressed as average daily intakes over time, are intended to provide for individual variations among most normal persons as they live in the United States under usual environmental stresses. Diets should be based on a variety of common foods in order to provide other nutrients for which human requirements have been less well defined.

[b] Weights and heights of Reference Adults are actual medians for the U.S. population of the designated age, as reported by NHANES II. The median weights and heights of those under 19 years of age were taken from Hamill et al. (1979). The use of these figures does not imply that the height-to-weight ratios are ideal.

[c] Retinol equivalents. 1 retinol equivalent = 1 µg retinol or 6 µg β-carotene.

[d] α-Tocopherol equivalents. 1 mg d-α tocopherol = 1 α-TE.

Appendix B

Food and Nutrition Board, Institute of Medicine—National Academy of Sciences
Dietary Reference Intakes: Recommended Intakes for Individuals

Life-Stage Group	Calcium (mg/d)	Phosphorus (mg/d)	Magnesium (mg/d)	Vitamin D (μg/d)[a,b]	Fluoride (mg/d)	Thiamin (mg/d)	Riboflavin (mg/d)	Niacin (mg/d)[c]	Vitamin B6 (mg/d)	Folate (μg/d)[d]	Vitamin B12 (μg/d)	Pantothenic Acid (mg/d)	Biotin (μg/d)	Choline (mg/d)[e]
Infants														
0–6 mo	210*	100*	30*	5*	0.01*	0.2*	0.3*	2*	0.1*	65*	0.4*	1.7*	5*	125*
7–12 mo	270*	275*	75*	5*	0.5*	0.3*	0.4*	4*	0.3*	80*	0.5*	1.8*	6*	150*
Children														
1–3 yr	500*	460	80	5*	0.7*	0.5	0.5	6	0.5	150	0.9	2*	8*	200*
4–8 yr	800*	500	130	5*	1*	0.6	0.6	8	0.6	200	1.2	3*	12*	250*
Males														
9–13 yr	1,300*	1,250*	240	5*	2*	0.9	0.9	12	1.0	300	1.8	4*	20*	375*
14–18 yr	1,300*	1,250*	410	5*	3*	1.2	1.3	16	1.3	400	2.4	5*	25*	550*
19–30 yr	1,000*	700	400	5*	4*	1.2	1.3	16	1.3	400	2.4	5*	30*	550*
31–50 yr	1,000*	700	420	5*	4*	1.2	1.3	16	1.3	400	2.4	5*	30*	550*
51–70 yr	1,200*	700	420	10*	4*	1.2	1.3	16	1.7	400	2.4[f]	5*	30*	550*
>70 yr	1,200*	700	420	15*	4*	1.2	1.3	16	1.7	400	2.4[f]	5*	30*	550*
Females														
9–13 yr	1,300*	1,250*	240	5*	2*	0.9	0.9	12	1.0	300	1.8	4*	20*	375*
14–18 yr	1,300*	1,250*	360	5*	3*	1.0	1.0	14	1.2	400[g]	2.4	5*	25*	400*
19–30 yr	1,000*	700	310	5*	3*	1.1	1.1	14	1.3	400[g]	2.4	5*	30*	425*
31–50 yr	1,000*	700	320	5*	3*	1.1	1.1	14	1.3	400[g]	2.4	5*	30*	425*
51–70 yr	1,200*	700	320	10*	3*	1.1	1.1	14	1.5	400	2.4[f]	5*	30*	425*
>70 yr	1,200*	700	320	15*	3*	1.1	1.1	14	1.5	400	2.4[f]	5*	30*	425*
Pregnancy														
≤18 yr	1,300*	1,250*	400	5*	3*	1.4	1.4	18	1.9	600[h]	2.6	6*	30*	450*
19–30 yr	1,000*	700	350	5*	3*	1.4	1.4	18	1.9	600[h]	2.6	6*	30*	450*
31–50 yr	1,000*	700	360	5*	3*	1.4	1.4	18	1.9	600[h]	2.6	6*	30*	450*
Lactation														
≤18 yr	1,300*	1,250*	360	5*	3*	1.5	1.6	17	2.0	500	2.8	7*	35*	550*
19–30 yr	1,000*	700	310	5*	3*	1.5	1.6	17	2.0	500	2.8	7*	35*	550*
31–50 yr	1,000*	700	320	5*	3*	1.5	1.6	17	2.0	500	2.8	7*	35*	550*

NOTE: This table presents Recommended Dietary Allowances (RDAs) in bold type and Adequate Intakes (AIs) in ordinary type followed by an asterisk (*). RDAs and AIs may both be used as goals for individual intake. RDAs are set to meet the needs of almost all (97 to 98 percent) individuals in a group. For healthy breastfed infants, the AI is the mean intake. The AI for other life-stage and gender groups is believed to cover needs of all individuals in the group, but lack of data or uncertainty in the data prevent being able to specify with confidence the percentage of individuals covered by this intake.

[a] As cholecalciferol. 1 μg cholecalciferol = 40 IU vitamin D.
[b] In the absence of adequate exposure to sunlight.
[c] As niacin equivalents (NE). 1 mg of niacin = 60 mg of tryptophan; 0–6 months = preformed niacin (not NE).
[d] As dietary folate equivalents (DFE). 1 DFE = 1 μg food folate = 0.6 μg of folic acid (from fortified food or supplement) consumed with food = 0.5 μg of synthetic (supplemental) folic acid taken on an empty stomach.
[e] Although AIs have been set for choline, there are few data to assess whether a dietary supply of choline is needed at all stages of the life cycle, and it may be that the choline requirement can be met by endogenous synthesis at some of these stages.
[f] Because 10 to 30 percent of older people may malabsorb food-bound B12, it is advisable for those older than 50 years to meet their RDA mainly by consuming foods fortified with B12 or a supplement containing B12.
[g] In view of evidence linking folate intake with neural tube defects in the fetus, it is recommended that all women capable of becoming pregnant consume 400 μg of synthetic folic acid from fortified foods and/or supplements in addition to intake of food folate from a varied diet.
[h] It is assumed that women will continue consuming 400 μg of folic acid until their pregnancy is confirmed and they enter prenatal care, which ordinarily occurs after the end of the periconceptional period—the critical time for formation of the neural tube.

Appendix C

Nutritional Composition of Selected Fast Foods

Food Description	Measure (servings)	Calories	Pro (g)	Carb (g)	Fiber (g)	Fat (g)	Chol (mg)	Calcium (mg)	Iron (mg)	Sodium (mg)	Vit C (mg)
McDonald's®											
Hamburger	1	270	13	35	2	9	30	200	2.70	600	2.4
Cheeseburger	1	320	16	35	2	13	40	250	2.70	830	2.4
Quarter Pounder®	1	430	23	37	2	21	70	200	4.50	840	2.4
Filet-O-Fish®	1	470	15	45	1	26	50	200	1.80	890	—
French Fries (med)	1	450	6	57	5	22	0	20	1.08	290	18.0
Chicken McNuggets®	4 pieces	190	10	13	1	11	35	—	0.72	360	—
Egg McMuffin®	1	290	17	27	1	12	235	200	2.70	790	1.2
Sausage Biscuit	1	470	11	35	1	31	35	80	2.70	1080	—
Breakfast Burrito	1	320	13	21	1	20	195	150	1.80	660	9.0
Vanilla Shake (small)	1	360	11	59	0	9	40	350	0.36	250	1.2
Kentucky Fried Chicken®											
Original Recipe® Chicken											
Whole wing	1	140	9	5	0	10	55	—	0.36	414	—
Breast	1	400	29	16	1	24	135	40	1.08	1116	—
Drumstick	1	140	13	4	0	9	75	—	0.72	422	—
Thigh	1	250	16	6	1	18	95	20	0.72	747	—
Hot & Spicey											
Wing	1.9 oz	210	10	9	<1	15	55	20	0.72	350	—
Breast	6.5 oz	505	38	23	1	29	162	60	1.08	1170	—
Thigh	3.8 oz	355	19	9	<1	26	126	20	0.72	630	—
Drumstick	2.3 oz	175	13	13	1	10	77	—	0.72	360	—
Extra Crispy™ Chicken											
Whole wing	1.9 oz	220	10	10	<1	15	55	—	0.36	415	—
Breast	5.9 oz	470	39	17	<1	28	160	20	1.08	874	—
Drumstick	2.4 oz	195	15	7	<1	12	77	—	0.72	375	—
Thigh	4.2 oz	380	21	14	<2	27	118	20	1.08	625	—
Pizza Hut®											
Pan Pizza											
Supreme	1 med. slice	385	14	45	4	17	18	140	3.24	757	6.0
Cheese	1 med slice	361	13	44	3	15	11	200	2.52	678	2.4
Pepperoni	1 med slice	353	12	44	3	14	14	130	2.52	697	2.4
Thin 'N Crispy Cheese	1 med slice	243	13	44	3	10	11	200	1.10	627	2.4
Hand-Tossed Cheese	1 slice	309	14	43	3	9	11	190	1.26	848	2.4
Stuffed Crust											
Meat Lover's®	1 med slice	543	26	46	3	29	48	390	2.70	1427	0.6
Veggie Lover's®	1 med slice	421	20	48	3	17	19	290	2.70	1029	9.6
Taco Bell®											
Soft Taco	1	210	11	20	3	10	30	80	1.08	570	0
Taco Supreme®	1	210	9	14	3	14	40	100	1.08	350	3.6
Bean Burrito	1	370	13	54	12	12	10	150	2.70	1080	0
Burrito Supreme®	1	430	17	50	9	18	40	150	2.70	1210	4.8
Chalupa Supreme Beef™	1	380	14	29	3	23	40	150	1.80	580	4.8
Gordita Supreme Beef™	1	300	17	27	3	14	35	150	1.80	550	3.6
Nachos	1	320	5	34	3	18	<5	100	0.72	560	0
Long John Silver's®											
Fish sandwich	1	430	16	46	n/a	20	35	n/a	n/a	1150	n/a
Popcorn shrimp	4 oz	320	15	33	n/a	15	85	n/a	n/a	1440	n/a
Batter-dipped fish	3.25 oz	230	12	16	n/a	13	30	n/a	n/a	700	n/a
Breaded clams	1 order	250	9	26	n/a	14	35	n/a	n/a	560	n/a
Lemon-crumb fish meal	1 meal	730	31	89	n/a	29	60	n/a	n/a	1720	n/a

Source: Nutritional information provided with permission from Kentucky Fried Chicken®, McDonald's® Corporation, Long John Silver's® Inc., Pizza Hut®, and Taco Bell® Corporation.
n/a = information not available
— = none or negligible amount

Nutrition Recommendations for Canadians

- *The Canadian diet should provide energy consistent with the maintenance of body weight within the recommended range.* Physical activity should be appropriate to circumstances and capabilities.[1] Both longevity and the incidence of a number of chronic diseases are associated adversely with body weights above or below the recommended range. There is, thus, a health benefit to controlling weight, but a possible downside to control by energy intake alone. Physical activity should also play a role. While the importance of maintaining some activity throughout life can be stressed, it is not possible to specify a level of physical activity appropriate for the whole population. As a general guideline it is desirable that adults, for as long as possible, maintain an activity level that permits an energy intake of at least 1800 kcal or 7.6 MJ/day while keeping weight within the recommended range.

- *The Canadian diet should include essential nutrients in amounts recommended.*[2] One of the reasons for including physical activity as a desirable element in weight control is the increasing difficulty in meeting the recommended nutrient intake (RNI)[3] as energy intake falls below 1800 kcal or 7.6 MJ/day. While it is important that the diet provide the recommended amounts of nutrients, it should be understood that no evidence was found that intakes in excess of the RNIs confer any health benefit. There is no general need for supplements except for vitamin D for infants and folic acid during pregnancy. Vitamin D supplementation might be required for elderly persons not exposed to the sun, and iron for pregnant women with low iron stores. It should be noted that while the habitual intake of certain nutrients, for example, protein and vitamin C, greatly exceeds the RNI, there is no reason to suggest that present intakes can be reduced.

- *The Canadian diet should include no more than 30% of energy as fat (33 g/1000 kcal or 39 g/5000 kJ) and no more than 10% as saturated fat (11 g/1000 kcal or 13 g/5000 kJ).* Diets high in fat have been associated with a high incidence of heart disease and certain types of cancer and a reduction in total fat intake is an important way to reduce the intake of saturated fat. The evidence linking saturated fat intake with elevated blood cholesterol and the risk of heart disease is among the most persuasive of all diet/disease relationships and was an important factor in establishing the recommended dietary pattern. Dietary cholesterol, though not as influential in affecting levels of blood cholesterol, is not without importance. A reduction in cholesterol intake normally will accompany a reduction in total fat and saturated fat. The recommendation to reduce total fat intake does not apply to children under the age of two years.

- *The Canadian diet should provide 55% of energy as carbohydrate (138 g/1000 kcal or 165 g/5000 kJ) from a variety of sources.* Sources selected should provide complex carbohydrates, a variety of dietary fibre and β-carotene. Carbohydrate is the preferred replacement for fat as a source of energy since protein intake already exceeds requirements. There are a number of reasons why the increased carbohydrate calories should be in the form of complex carbohydrates. Diets high in complex carbohydrates have been associated with a lower incidence of heart disease and cancer, and are sources of dietary fibre and of β-carotene.

- *The sodium content of the Canadian diet should be reduced.* The present food supply provides sodium in an amount greatly exceeding requirements. While there is insufficient evidence to support a quantitative recommendation, potential benefit would be expected from a reduction in current sodium intake. Consumers are encouraged to reduce the use of salt (sodium chloride) in cooking and at the table, but individual efforts will be relatively ineffective unless the food industry makes a determined effort to reduce the sodium content of processed and prepared food. A diet rich in fruits and vegetables will ensure an adequate intake of potassium.

- *The Canadian diet should include no more than 5% of total energy as alcohol, or two drinks daily, whichever is less.* There are many reasons to limit the use of alcohol. From the nutritional point of view, alcohol dilutes the nutrient density of the diet and can undermine the consumption of RNIs. The deleterious influence of alcohol on blood pressure provides more urgent reason for moderation. During pregnancy it is prudent to abstain from alcoholic beverages because a safe intake is not known with certainty.

- *The Canadian diet should contain no more caffeine than the equivalent of four regular cups of coffee per day.* This is a prudent measure in view of the increased risk for cardiovascular disease associated with high intakes of caffeine.

- *Community water supplies containing less than 1 mg/litre should be fluoridated to that level.* Fluoridation of community water supplies has proven to be a safe, effective and economical method of improving dental health.

---

[1] For more information see "Canada's Physical Activity Guide to Healthy Active Living" at: http://www.paguide.com

[2] See "Canada's Food Guide to Healthy Eating" on the next two pages for general dietary guidelines.

[3] Visit the website of the Dietitians of Canada at: http://www.dietitians.ca/english/profile/nut_index.html, to compare your food choices for one day to the "Recommended Nutrient Intakes for Canadians."

From: Nutrition Recommendations . . . A Call for Action Summary Report of the Scientific Review Committee and the Communications/Implementation Committee, 1992, 1989.

Appendix D

© Minister of Public Works and Government Services Canada, 1997.

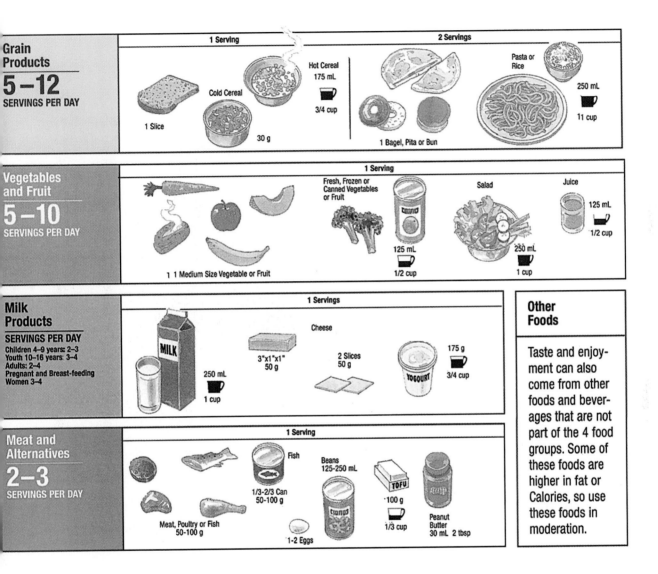

Grain Products
5–12
SERVINGS PER DAY

1 Serving

1 Slice

Cold Cereal
30 g

Hot Cereal
175 mL
3/4 cup

2 Servings

1 Bagel, Pita or Bun

Pasta or Rice
250 mL
11 cup

Vegetables and Fruit
5–10
SERVINGS PER DAY

1 Serving

1 1 Medium Size Vegetable or Fruit

Fresh, Frozen or Canned Vegetables or Fruit
125 mL
1/2 cup

Salad
250 mL
1 cup

Juice
125 mL
1/2 cup

Milk Products
SERVINGS PER DAY
Children 4–9 years: 2–3
Youth 10–16 years: 3–4
Adults: 2–4
Pregnant and Breast-feeding Women 3–4

1 Servings

MILK
250 mL
1 cup

Cheese
3"x1"x1"
50 g

2 Slices
50 g

175 g
3/4 cup
YOGOURT

Other Foods

Taste and enjoyment can also come from other foods and beverages that are not part of the 4 food groups. Some of these foods are higher in fat or Calories, so use these foods in moderation.

Meat and Alternatives
2–3
SERVINGS PER DAY

1 Serving

Meat, Poultry or Fish
50-100 g

1-2 Eggs

Fish
1/3-2/3 Can
50-100 g

Beans
125-250 mL
1/3 cup

TOFU
100 g

Peanut Butter
30 mL 2 tbsp

Index

Index

Index

Index

Index

Images on chapter opening banners © PhotoDisc; p. m2, © PhotoDisc; p. m4, © PhotoDisc; p. m5, *Healthy People 2010* web site screenshot courtesy of DHHS; p. xiv, © David Young-Wolff/PhotoEdit;p. 2, © AP Photo/Mark Holm; p. 3, © AP Photo/Gary Kazanjian; p. 7, © Spencer Grant/Stock Boston; p. 15, © Rachel Epstein/PhotoEdit; p. 17 l, © Jennie Woodcock: Reflections Photolibrary/CORBIS; p. 17 r, © Randall Hyman/ Stock Boston; p. 20, © Hank Morgan/Rainbow, p. 23, © David Young-Wolff/PhotoEdit; p. 29, © AP Photo/Eyal Warshavsky; p. 32, © Owen Franken/Stock Boston; p. 33, © AP Photo/The Kansas City Star, Kelley Chin; p. 36, © Jack Hollingsworth/PhotoDisc; p. 39, © Dennis MacDonald/PhotoEdit; p. 44, © David Young-Wolff/ PhotoEdit; p. 48, © AP Photo/David Guttenfelder; p. 49, © PhotoDisc; p. 55, © Frank Siteman/Stock Boston; p. 59, © Don Smetzer/Stone; p. 62, © Eric Fowke/ PhotoEdit; p. 64, © Jonathan Nourok/PhotoEdit; p. 66, © AFP/CORBIS; p. 70, © Craig Jackson/In the Dark Photography, p. 73, © Spencer Grant/PhotoEdit; p. 76, © Janis Christie/PhotoDisc; p. 80, © Joel Gordon; p. 84, © Hubertus Kanus/Photo Researchers, Inc.; p. 92, © Jon Riley/Stone; p. 95, © Joel Gordon; p. 97, © Donna Day/Stone; p. 98, © Courtesy of Anne and Johan Santesson; p. 98, © Courtesy of Anne and Johan Santesson; p. 102, © Lennart Nilson, Albert Bonniers Publishing Company, Behold Man; p. 107, © Professor P.M. Motta, G. Macciarelli, S.A Nottola/SPL/Photo Researchers; p. 114, © Michael Newman/PhotoEdit; p. 118 l, © Neil Harding/Stone; p. 118 r, © Lennart Nilson, Albert Bonniers Publishing Company, A Child is Born; p. 119 l, © Neil Bromhall/Science Photo Library/Photo Researchers, Inc.; p. 119 r, © Petite Format/Nestle/Science Source/Photo Researchers; p. 122 l & r, © Joel Gordon; p. 127, © Joel Gordon; p. 127, © Joel Gordon; p. 131, © M. Siluk/The Image Works; p. 136, CDC web site screen shot courtesy of CDC; p. 140, © Michael Newman/PhotoEdit; p. 146, © Einhorn/Gamma/Liaison; p. 149, © AP Photo/HO, NBC, Mary Ellen Matthews; p. 152, © Nigel Cattlin/Holt Studios International/Photo Researchers, Inc.; p. 154, © R. Konig/Jacana/Photo Researchers, Inc.; p. 156, © L. West/Photo Researchers, Inc.; p. 166, © Courtesy of Health Canada; p. 168 l, © A. Ramey/PhotoEdit; p. 168 r, © AP Photo/Elaine Thompson; p. 173, © PhotoEdit; p. 174 t, © PhotoDisc; p. 175 b, © PhotoDisc; p. 185, © SIU/Photo Researchers, Inc.; p. 187 l & r, © America Academy of Otolaryngology— Head and Neck Surgery, Inc.; p. 187b, © Science Photo Library/Photo Researchers, Inc.; p. 193, © David H. Wells/CORBIS; p. 198, © Nathan Benn/Stock Boston; p. 213, © Bill Aron/PhotoEdit; p. 214, © Mitch Hrdlicka/ PhotoDisc; p. 221, © David M. Grossman/Photo Researchers, Inc.; p. 224, © Ursula Ruhl; p. 230, © David Young-Wolff/PhotoEdit; p. 232 l, © SPL/Custom Medical Stock Photo; p. 232 r, © SPL/Custom Medical Stock Photo; p. 237, © John Bolivar/Custom Medical Stock Photo; p. 242, © David Young-Wolff/PhotoEdit; p. 246, © Bob Torrez/Stone; p. 253, © A. Ramey/PhotoEdit; p. 254, © Dick Spahr/The Gamma Liaison Network; p. 269 t, © Michael Newman/PhotoEdit; p. 269 b, © Timothy Healy/Design Conceptions/Joel Gordon; p. 270, © James D. Wilson/The Gamma Liaison Network; p. 274, © SIU, School of Medicine/Peter Arnold, Inc.; p. 278, © Robin L. Sachs/PhotoEdit; p. 280 t, © Simon Fraser/Science Photo Library/Photo Researchers, Inc.; p. 280 b, © Simon Fraser/Science Photo Library/Photo Researchers, Inc.; p. 281, © AP/Wide World Photos; p. 282, © W. Ober/Visuals Unlimited; p. 284, © Mehau Kulyk/Science Photo Library/Photo Researchers, Inc.; p. 291, © Ursula Ruhl; p. 293, © PhotoDisc; p. 298, © AP Photo/Laurent Rebours; p. 300 l & r, © Cabisco/Visuals Unlimited; p. 304 t, © Custom Medical Stock Photo; p. 304 b, © Scott Camazine/Photo Researchers; p. 305, © Courtesy, Proton Treatment Center, Loma Linda University; p. 306, © AP Photo/Julie Markes; p. 311, © John Radcliffe Hospital/SPL/Photo Researchers; p. 317, © ATC Productions/Custom Medical Stock; p. 318, © Peter Menzel/ Stock, Boston; p. 321, © Joel Gordon; p. 321, © Joel Gordon; p. 324 t, © Dianora Niccolini/Medical Images, Inc.; p. 324 ctr, © Biophoto Associates/Photo Researchers, Inc.; p. 324 b, © Ken Greer/Visuals Unlimited; p. 334, © Robin Jerstad/CORBIS; p. 337, © Stan Flegler/Visuals Unlimited; p. 338 l, © J. Cancalosi/DRK Photo; p. 338 r, © The Children's Hospital, Denver, Cytogenics Laboratory; p. 341, © Lowell Georgia/Science Source/Photo Researchers, Inc.; p. 342, © Science Photo Library/Photo Researchers, Inc.; p. 343, © Visuals Unlimited; p. 346, © Prof. S.H.E. Kaufman & Dr. J.R. Golecki/SPL/Photo Researchers, Inc.; p. 355 l, © Biophoto Associates/Photo Researchers, Inc.; p. 355 r, © A. Ramey/PhotoEdit; p. 359, © Biophoto Associates/Science Source/ Photo Researchers, Inc.; p. 360, © Biophoto Associates/Photo Researchers, Inc.; p. 361, © Visuals Unlimited; p. 364, © Oliver Meckes, Science Source/Photo Researchers, Inc.; p. 368, © Photodisc; p. 374, © Ursula Ruhl; p. 376, © Ficaro Magazine/The Gamma Liaison Network; p. 378, © Joel Gordon; p. 381, © Susan Lerner/Design Conceptions/ Joel Gordon; p. 385, © PhotoDisc; p. 387 t, © The Burns Collection, Ltd; p. 387 b, © K. Opgenhaffen/The Gamma Liaison Network; p. 391, © AP/Wide World Photos; p. 400, © Tony Freeman/PhotoEdit; p. 406, © Seth Resnick/Stock Boston; p. 411 l, © Jose Carrillo/PhotoEdit; p. 411 r, © Cary Wolinsky/Stock Boston; p. 412, © PhotoDisc; p. 413, © PhotoDisc; p. 416 l, © Frank S. Balthis; p. 416 r, © Bruno J. Zehnder/Peter Arnold, Inc.; p. 432, © Minister of Public Works and Government Services Canada, 1997

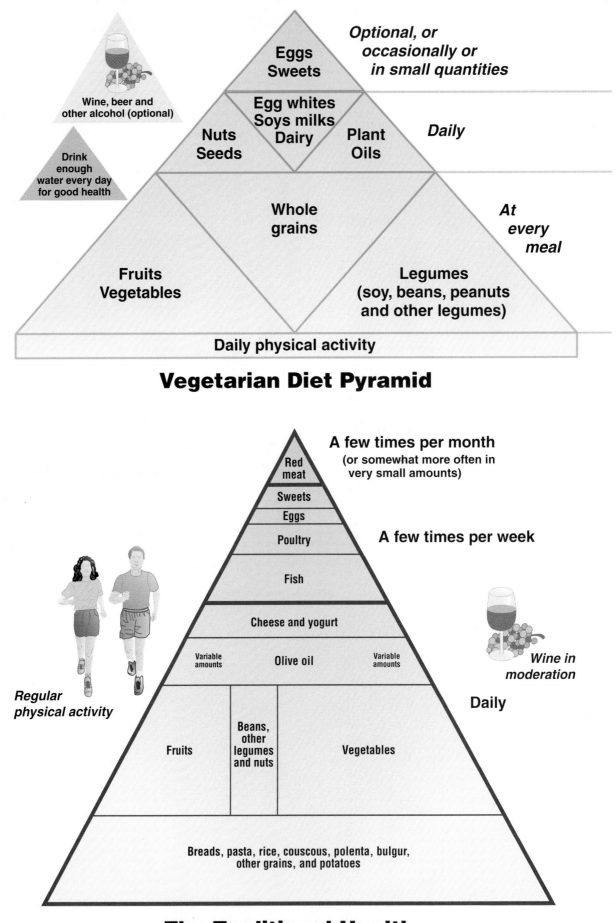

Vegetarian Diet Pyramid

Optional, or occasionally or in small quantities

Eggs
Sweets

Daily

Egg whites
Soys milks
Dairy

Nuts
Seeds

Plant
Oils

Wine, beer and other alcohol (optional)

Drink enough water every day for good health

Whole grains

At every meal

Fruits
Vegetables

Legumes
(soy, beans, peanuts and other legumes)

Daily physical activity

The Traditional Healthy Mediterranean Diet Pyramid

A few times per month
(or somewhat more often in very small amounts)

Red meat

Sweets

Eggs

Poultry

A few times per week

Fish

Cheese and yogurt

Variable amounts

Olive oil

Variable amounts

Wine in moderation

Regular physical activity

Fruits

Beans, other legumes and nuts

Vegetables

Daily

Breads, pasta, rice, couscous, polenta, bulgur, other grains, and potatoes